THE
TEXAS
DOG LOVER'S
COMPANION

By Larry D. Hodge

Foghorn
Press
BOOKS BUILDING COMMUNITY™

1-57354-045-5

9 781573 540452

52095

Foghorn Outdoors' guidebooks are available wherever books are sold. To find a retailer near you or to order, call 1-800-FOGHORN (364-4676) or (707) 521-3300 or visit the Foghorn Press Web site at www.foghorn.com. Foghorn Press titles are available to the book trade through Publishers Group West (800-788-3123) as well as through wholesalers.

Library of Congress ISSN Data:
July 1998
The Texas Dog Lover's Companion:
The Inside Scoop on Where to Take Your Dog
First Edition
ISSN: 1098-8270

THE
TEXAS
DOG LOVER'S
COMPANION

By Larry D. Hodge

BOOKS BUILDING COMMUNITY

NOTE TO ALL DOG LOVERS:

While our information is as current as possible, changes to fees, regulations, parks, roads, and trails sometimes are made after we go to press. Businesses can close, change ownership, or adopt new policies. Fires, rainstorms, and other natural phenomena can radically alter the condition of parks, campgrounds, and hiking trails. Before you and your dog begin your travels, please be certain to call the phone numbers for each listing for current information.

ATTENTION DOGS OF TEXAS:

If we've missed your favorite park, campground, restaurant, hotel, or dog-friendly activity, please let us know. You'll be helping countless other dogs get more enjoyment out of life in the Lone Star State. We always welcome your comments and suggestions about *The Texas Dog Lover's Companion*. Please write us at Foghorn Press, 340 Bodega Avenue, Petaluma, CA 94952.

*For Bobby, Sonny, and Bullet, who wait on the
other side for the little boy they loved,*

*and for Taylor Rebecca, who has
yet to know the joy of dogs.*

The Texas Dog Lover's Companion

The Inside Scoop on Where to Take Your Dog

CONTENTS

TEXAS CHAPTER REFERENCE MAP

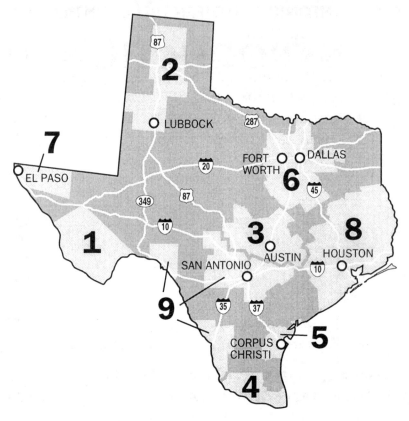

INTRODUCTION

GRRRRR

When wooded hills with crimson light
      Are bright
      We'll stroll where trees and vines are growing,
And see birds warp their southern flight
      At sundown, when the Day King's throwing
Sly kisses to the Queen of Night.

When shadows fall in life's fair dell,
      And knell
      Of death comes with the autumn's ev'n
To separate us, who can tell
      But that, within the realm of heaven,
We both together there will dwell?

           —From *To My Setter, Scout,* by Frank H. Seldon

Traveling with a dog can be an eternal journey. For sure it seems so when you've got a long way to go, a short time to get there, and a dog with a pea-sized bladder in the backseat. Still, for many people there are two things they won't leave home without, and one of them has a cold, wet nose.

Traveling dogs are a common sight in Texas, so much so that when the editors at Foghorn Press approached me about writing this book, my first reaction was, "What's the big deal? In Texas we just tell the dog to get in the back of the truck with the kids." However, I knew it wasn't that simple. Not everyone in Texas has a pickup truck.

Yet.

Not long after beginning work on the book, I realized that Sport Dog, Samantha Dog, and I were pioneers. "You want to bring a what in here?" people would ask. "How big is it? Will it bite?" The answers, of course, were dog, huge, and only if you ask for it. But the repetition of this experience time and again throughout Texas made me realize that there is not a well-entrenched tradition of traveling with dogs in the largest state in the Lower 48.

Yet.

It behooves traveling dogs and their people, therefore, to remember that they will be, in many cases, trailblazers and ambassadors for those who we hope will be allowed to come later. Just as many times as a motel or restaurant owner exclaimed, "Oh, we love dogs!" there was a long pause followed by a story about the dog who ate the curtains or scarfed a steak off a stranger's plate. How your dog behaves as you travel Texas together will influence the attitude of people about whether dogs should be allowed or banned. (How you behave will have a lot to do with it, too.)

Like most dogs, Sport and Samantha don't seem to care where they go, just as long as they go. The moment I step out the door and head for the car, they adopt that pleading look that says, "Utter those two little words I'm longing to hear: Kennel up!" Then the battle for the coveted front passenger seat is on. Possession changes mile by mile until finally it's time for a nap. Every gas stop requires scrubbing nose and paw marks off the inside of the windshield to restore visibility.

Samantha came to live with us first. She's half Australian blue heeler and half "wedunno," but she's all appetite. We raised her from a tiny puppy, and apparently something about being the only dog at the trough during her formative years set her appestat permanently on "glutton." If there is anything she will not eat, we have not found it. This includes plastic shower curtains. The grounds around our house look like an artillery duel was fought here because of her avid pursuit of gophers. We tried putting her on a diet once; shortly thereafter we began to find (to put it delicately) digestively processed bird parts in the yard. Solving the mystery was alimentary. Samantha was stalking, flushing, catching, and eating meadowlarks. All that time spent chasing tennis balls served her well. She gained weight until we took her off the diet.

Sport is as sweet and well mannered as Samantha is hyperactive and insecure. She moved in while I was on an extended trip to the Big Bend. During one of my periodic calls home to get the sugar report, Sally mentioned there was something we needed to talk about. I don't know about you, but when I'm 500 miles from home and having a good time, I don't ask a lot of questions about statements like that. Nothing more was said, and I forgot about it until I was driving down the lane to our house. There bounding toward me was a huge black hound that, I swore, could put both front feet on a giraffe's chest and lick it in the mouth. Close behind her sped Sally, assuring me before I even got out of the car that Sport was there just on a trial basis.

You don't need me to tell you how that turned out.

Sport is half Rhodesian Ridgeback and half handsome stranger. While she stands thigh-high to an elephant, she is also the calmest, nicest dog I've ever been around. How nice is she? So nice that her head is not swelling even as she reads this. She is the ideal dog to have played the role of First Professional Traveling Dog of Texas. Other than one unauthorized encounter with a loaf of fresh-baked gingerbread, I don't think Sport has ever been guilty of a single crime. Well, there is that one large stain on our best rug, but its authorship is questionable, and Sally and I do sleep rather soundly sometimes.

Raccoons are Sport's passion, a fact that you will be reminded of many times as you read this book. Samantha lives to eat; Sport lives to chase raccoons up trees and bark at them all night. When we visit parks together, Samantha heads straight for the garbage cans, and Sport heads straight for any trees, brush, or water. In between holding on to both leashes is me, feeling like a medieval miscreant being racked.

Most Texas dogs probably fall somewhere between Sport and Samantha, too. You'll probably recognize your own pooch in some of the adventures my dogs and I shared while researching this book. But if your dog has never charmed a class of third-graders on a field trip, rolled on a dead fish on the beach, or publicly humiliated you by depositing a steaming pile of used dog food on a downtown sidewalk, just wait. Your time will come.

Carefree traveling with a dog in Texas requires either luck, careful planning, or a copy of this book. Only about 3 percent of the land in Texas is publicly owned, severely limiting the opportunities for outdoor recreation with a four-footed companion. And while many hotels and motels welcome dogs, the concept of people eating out in the company of a dog seems barely to have penetrated most of the state. That's where this book can be invaluable to you. I've included hundreds of dog-friendly parks, motels, restaurants, festivals, and tourist attractions throughout the state. Never again should you and your pooch have to spend a weekend at home memorizing wallpaper patterns. You can climb mountains, ride trains and surreys, get married in the middle of a public road, or gaze at the outer limits of the universe. The sky is no longer the limit.

Texas is going to the dogs. And it's about time.

THE PAWS SCALE

One of the mysteries of life on this earth is how dogs and people ever got together in the first place. To quote Maria Goodavage, who wrote *The California Dog Lover's Companion,* "We like eating oranges and smelling lilacs and covering our bodies with soft clothes. They like eating roadkill and smelling each other's unmentionables and covering their bodies with horse manure." Dogs also like exploring dumpsters, jumping in mud puddles, and chasing cats, squirrels, and other furry critters. (Especially raccoons, Sport says.)

Keep these differences in mind when you visit the parks, beaches, and recreation areas listed in this book. All were rated from a dog's point of view. While I didn't always get down on hands and knees and look around, I did pay close attention to what Sport and Samantha found appealing. They couldn't care less about a wonderful view unless it includes the rear end of a retreating cat. Beautiful lakes are of no interest unless swimming is allowed. Open grassy spaces in a park mean little unless running off leash is permit-

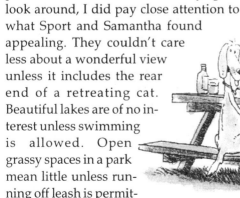

ted. A great people park is not necessarily a great dog park. Therefore, since this book is for dogs (you're just along as interpreter and guide until your dog learns to read and drive), the ratings are based on what a dog would find pleasing.

The lowest rating for a park is the fire hydrant symbol (🔥). That means the park is just "worth a squat." Visit one of these spots only if your pooch's crossed legs and pleading whimpers tell you she just can't hold it any longer.

The next highest rating is one paw (🐾), and so on up to four paws (🐾 🐾 🐾 🐾). A one-paw park isn't a great place, but it'll do until something better comes along. One-paw parks range from tiny neighborhood parks taken up mostly by playgrounds to athletic field complexes to national parks where dogs are allowed only in campgrounds and on vehicle roads. However, one-paw parks can be very important to maintaining a hound's sense of self-respect (and the wholesome atmosphere inside your car), so I included many such spots, especially those easily accessed from major thoroughfares.

Texas, alas, has almost no four-paw parks. A four-paw park has to have it all: trees, shade, swimming places, lots of room for hiking, and no rule forbidding dogs to run off leash. Leash laws are practically universal in Texas, although I did find a number of leash-free areas. The most significant of these are on Lower Colorado River Authority land northwest of Austin, several parks in Austin itself, and the approximately 700,000 acres of national forests and state wildlife management areas, most of which are located in Southeast Texas. Even when you see the leash-free symbol, read the park description carefully for any restrictions; you don't always have total freedom.

The paws scale does have half-paw increments (such as 🐾 🐾 🐾 ½), and a number of excellent state parks achieved this near-perfect rating. Naturally, Sport, Samantha, and I disagreed on a rating from time to time, and the reasons are detailed in the park descriptions. I spared you the snarling and grumbling indulged in by the losers of these arguments.

Now and again you'll notice a foot symbol (👣). The foot means that there's something special in the park for people. You have to do all the driving, get up in the middle of the night to walk the dog and save the hotel's carpet, and pick up the check for all the meals, so you deserve a little reward once in a while. Follow the footprints and drag your dog with you. There's always the chance you'll find a dead raccoon in the road.

This book does not include all the parks in Texas. (Get real!) It does include what I consider to be the biggest, best, and most convenient. Some parts of the state are blessed with more parks than others. Space prevented me from listing all the great parks in some areas, while a dearth of parks in others led me to include some that wouldn't have made it otherwise. Sport said I did the right thing. As she wisely pointed out, a great park does a dog no good when it's 300 miles away, while a lousy park in the right place at the right time can cause a water-logged dog to shout "howlelujah!"

I've given specific driving directions to major parks and to parks located near highways. Others are listed by their cross streets. The maps in this book will get you close, but I highly recommend picking up detailed street maps when venturing to unfamiliar cities. If you can't drive and read the directions at the same time, just give the book to your hound and have him bark once to turn right and twice to turn left.

AT LEASH READ THIS

As noted earlier, leash laws are nearly universal in Texas, and public land is in short supply. Therefore, you won't often be faced with the question of whether to let your dog run off leash or not. In most places it's just plain illegal. Of course, the leash law is probably the most-ignored regulation in Texas, after the signs that say "right lane must turn right." In many of the parks you visit where we state that dogs are required to be on leash, you'll see happy hounds running free. Their owners choose to ignore the law, and it's the dogs who may suffer the consequences. Suffice it to say that if some dog owners continue to ignore the law and create problems, all dogs and dog lovers may suffer from even stricter regulations. Dogs are already walking a pretty thin line in many Texas communities; my advice is not to risk making it worse. Besides, having a criminal record could jeopardize your dog's career, unless she's thinking of going into politics.

Use common sense even where letting your dog run off leash is permitted. You can easily spot these places throughout the book by looking for the running dog symbol ( ). Dogs unaccustomed to running free in a large space may overdo it and get into trouble. One of the most heart-wrenching visits Sport and I made was to a national forest in East Texas that is a popular off-leash spot for city dogs from Houston. Sign after sign stapled to trees held the same message: Please help me find my lost dog. At some recreation areas, a dog would bound up eagerly when we arrived, hoping no doubt that a missing person had returned. If you don't trust your dog to respond to voice control when a deer bursts across the trail, keep her leashed. Otherwise, take her picture before you go. That may be all you come home with.

Dogs are required to be on a leash no longer than six feet in all state parks. Period. No exceptions. Because some people persist in ignoring this rule and fail to clean up after their dogs, some park superintendents I talked to expressed a desire to someday ban dogs from state parks. It would be a black day for dogs in Texas if this ever came to pass, as the state parks system has the best hiking and camping areas for them. Don't let your dog aggravate this problem.

RIVERS RUN THROUGH IT

Even if—imagine—your pooch cannot walk on water, Texas rivers offer some great rest stops for traveling hounds. Many Texas streams—but not all—are classified by law as navigable. The river channel and the water in it are public property. What this means to you and your pooch is that you are free to play in the water of these streams and on the riverbank itself as long as you stay within the streambed. Once you leave the river channel, you will be trespassing on private property unless you are in a public park. The trick in Texas is finding access to the river channel where no parks exist to provide it. This access generally occurs where road rights-of-way cross streams, and fortunately, the Texas Parks and Wildlife Department has built public boat ramps at many of these places. Anytime you see a brown and white sign identifying a public boat ramp—usually under a highway bridge—you can barge right in with your pooch. I've listed some other areas commonly used as recreation spots by people and dogs.

HOT DOGGEDY DOO

Dogs have no modesty, and their digestive tracts border on hyperactive. Therefore, you will often find yourself in a public place wielding plastic bag, newspaper, or pooper-scooper to retrieve the remnants of what your dog ate for dinner the night before. Naturally, there are lots of other ways you'd rather spend that time. You'd also rather not have to lug your disgusting burden—warm, squishy, and fragrant—until you find a place to dispose of it.

However, unscooped poop is one of the chief reasons communities have for banning dogs from parks. It's politically incorrect for a city council member to tell the mother of a two-year-old who ate some doggy doo in the park that nothing can be done about it. Something can be done about it: They can pass a law forbidding dogs in the park. I found only one community in Texas where dogs are banned from all city parks—Rosenburg—but that could change. Several parks directors told me a ban on dogs was being considered because of the actions—or inaction—of a few irresponsible dog owners.

The best way to keep the parks open for all dogs is to clean up after your dog. Keep a supply of plastic bags in your pockets, purse, backpack, or car. The plastic bags newspapers come in make good doggy doo picker-uppers. Just insert your hand all the way into the bag, grab the yucky stuff, and with the free hand, pull the top of the bag down your arm and around the contents of your hand. As the bag turns inside out, it traps the offending matter inside. Plastic food storage bags with press-together closures can be used the same way and may be more leak-proof. Listen to me. I speak from experience.

I found some communities that require dog walkers to have a pooper-scooper visibly in their possession while walking their dog; these are noted in the park descriptions. Pet supply stores have a number of models ranging from el cheapo cardboard to long-handled metal tools you could shovel a sidewalk with. The disposables have the advantage of not needing to be cleaned, but then there's the added impact to the environment: Your dog would rather have living trees he can hike a leg on.

As has often been said, it's a dirty job, but somebody's got to do it. In this case, it's no joke.

MANNERS AND MUTTLEY

Dogs learn what is and is not acceptable behavior the same way children do (or should): through example and constant correction. It's a real pain in the hindquarters to be constantly watching and instructing your dog as he grows, but the reward—a well-behaved dog whom everyone goes gaga over—is worth every minute spent. Training a dog is a lot of trouble, but you'll enjoy a great deal more quality time together as a result.

All traveling dogs need to know and obey the following rules. No biting. No jumping on people. No barking until you drive everyone nuts. Come when you're called. Stay when you're told. Lift not thy leg against thy neighbor's leg, purse, backpack, or other personal possession.

That's a lot for a dog to remember, and they will need reminding from time to time. Just remember: You are the alpha dog, the leader of the pack. What you say goes. When rule violations occur, don't tell the dog they'll be punished when Daddy or Mommy gets home. Make your displeasure known immediately, do whatever you can to repair any damage (pay for the shredded slacks), and try to see it doesn't happen again. Even the most bone-headed dog doesn't like getting fussed at and will, eventually, shape up. This is one area in which dogs are definitely superior to children.

SAFE SEX

Actually, there's nothing in this section about sex, but I got your attention, didn't I? While you're here, keep on reading. The following information could save your dog's life. Sex and otherwise.

• *Heat:* An early visitor to Texas commented that it was heaven for men and dogs but hell on women. He was too kind. Texas summers can be hell on everybody. In any part of the state south of Waco, summer lasts most of the year, and some winter days would be a Chicago dweller's idea of paradise. Another of those early visitors to Texas said if he owned both Hell and Texas, he would live in Hell and rent out Texas. In short, it can get hot here any time of year.

I'm only going to say this once: Never, ever, leave a dog in a car with the windows rolled up. Not even in winter. Not even if you leave the windows cracked at the top. Roast rottweiler à la sedan is not a dish you want on your menu. Depending on your dog, where you are, and how desperately you need to go somewhere your dog can't, you might consider tying your dog to your car's bumper, so she can lie in the shade. If you're going to be gone more than a few minutes and it's hot, leave the dog a bowl of water, too. Be sure not to tie her where she can be hit by a passing car. When doing this in a busy parking lot, it's best to park far away from any other cars.

Dogs in moving cars can get hot, too, if exposed to the sun through slanting glass in rear doors or windows. If you are using the air conditioner, be sure enough cool air is reaching the backseat. You may be freezing in front while Rover is roasting in the rear, but it's the right thing to do. Several kinds of window shades for cars are available and would make a great birthday gift for a deserving dog.

• *Water:* Hot or not, dogs drink a lot of water. Sally and I always travel with a couple of two-liter pop bottles of water and a plastic margarine dish for each dog. Watering a dog in a moving car is a bad idea for several reasons. Take a water break now and again. We usually water and dewater at the same time. What goes down, keeps on going down.

• *Potty stops:* No matter how big a hurry you're in, stop and dewater your dog according to her needs. Most dogs will let you know when they need to stop. Restlessness, pacing back and forth, frequent changes of position, nose nudges, and pitiful whines are all signs your dog needs to make a pit stop. Most dogs (and people) benefit from a stop every couple of hours. Texas highways have plentiful picnic areas and rest stops along them; some include special dog areas with fireplugs. (Texas had the very first roadside park in the nation.) Get a free highway map from any Texas Travel Information Bureau or local office of the Texas Department of Transportation. Most chambers of commerce and convention and visitors bureaus have them, too. Picnic areas and rest stops are shown on these maps by blue dots. When covering cities in this book, I've made a special effort to include parks close to freeways and major arterial streets.

Just remember the following ditty:

In Texas, land of fun and sun,
We always stop for Number One.
And when you think your pooch is through,
Remember after One comes Two.

• *To restrain, or not to restrain:* That is the question. Dog seat belts are available. Some dogs will sit still for being strapped in; others won't. How much protection the seat belts offer is debatable. Similarly, some experts recommend keeping a dog in a pet carrier while traveling. We've seen cars outfitted with wire partitions between front and back seats. The idea is that it's safer for the dog to be restrained if there's an accident, and it's safer for the driver not to have a dog bounding about. As far as I am aware, no studies have been done on air bags and dogs, but since air bags were designed to protect adults sitting upright, it's doubtful they'd be effective on dogs lying down.

Sport and Samantha roam freely in all our vehicles, endlessly migrating from one seat to another until they finally go to sleep. We've found that a good feeding just before departing helps bring on a long nap and the peace that goes with it. Of course, you also have to be alert to the need for a potty stop, usually immediately after the dog wakes up.

Dogs love to ride in the back of pickup trucks or with their head sticking out the window. I've seen dogs riding on top of tool boxes and even on top of truck cabs. My feeling is that these dogs are accidents waiting to happen. Any dog riding in the back of a truck should be tied on a leash short enough so that the dog cannot jump or fall over the side of the truck and be strangled. A dog riding with her head out the window can be in danger, too. Especially in spring and summer, there are lots of bugs in the air, and taking a grasshopper in the eye at 70 miles per hour can result in serious damage. You don't want to even think about rocks thrown up by other cars. Look at the damage they can do to a windshield.

There are two possible ways to keep your pooch happy and safe. One is to roll the window down just enough so your dog can stick the end of her snout out the window, but not her whole head. She can still sniff the air. Sport has another method. She stands with her front feet on the console between the bucket seats. Since she is a large dog, this puts her nose about a foot from the top vent of the air conditioner. She can see out the windshield and savor the aromas at the same time, and she'll stand this way for many miles.

• *When dogs fly:* In my opinion, dogs ought to start flying right after pigs do. If the Big Dog had meant canines to fly, airplanes would come with water bowls in the seat backs, little patches of grass in the lavatories, and copies of *American Coon Hunter* in the magazine rack. (And, in a perfect world, the female flight attendants would wear poodle skirts.) Most airlines will accept dogs in carriers, but I'd as soon send a dog to that little room with no windows in the pound as I would put one in a cargo hold. Sure, it's supposed to be pressurized, but heat and cold can still be a problem, and the experience has to be terrifying to a dog who has no idea what's happening.

Small dogs are sometimes allowed to fly in the passenger section, but if the size of your dog or the airline's policy make this impossible, it would be better to drive or find a dog sitter.

If you must fly your dog, well-meaning friends may suggest having him tranquilized. Maybe it worked for their dog, but drugs may not be right for yours. Consult your veterinarian on the pros and cons, and in any case, have your dog's health evaluated to make sure he is fit to fly.

The American Kennel Club offers a free travel kit with tips on how to make travel less stressful for your dog. Order by contacting them at 5580 Centerview Drive, Raleigh, NC 27606; (919) 233-9767. For $1.50, you can get the booklet "Traveling with Your Companion" from the Humane Society of the United States. Send your money and a stamped, self-addressed business-size envelope to the Humane Society of the United States, Travel Department, 2100 L Street NW, Washington, D.C. 20037. Hunters may want to make note of the fact that the latter organization is strongly anti-hunting; you may want to get your information elsewhere.

THE WELL-PACKED POOCH

When you're about to walk out the door at the beginning of a trip, you may do what I do: mentally review all you've packed to be sure you haven't forgotten anything. First I mentally dress myself from the bare hide out, making sure I packed everything worth mentioning as well as unmentionables. Then I go through the rest of the list. Camera? Check. Computer? Check. Sleeping bag? Check. Pillows? Uh-oh. Wait a minute while I run upstairs.

Dogs have to rely on you to pack their bags. Depending on the duration of the journey, you'll need food, water, snacks, and chew toys. Samantha ("Jaws") Dog can go through a large rawhide chew between San Antonio and Corpus Christi.

Other necessities include food and water bowls, a sheet or blanket, plastic bags and pooper-scooper, towel, brush, any medicines, toys, and a doggy first-aid kit (tweezers for pulling thorns or ticks, antiseptic for cuts, bandage material and tape, and baking soda for insect stings at a minimum). And, unless you want to wander around lost and have a miserable time, take a copy of this book.

No Texas dog should leave home without his or her rabies tag and written proof of current rabies vaccination from your veterinarian. Due to a rabies epizootic in Texas in recent years, these items are required of dogs crossing a county line. I haven't seen anyone checking to see that this law is being obeyed, but there's no point in taking a chance. Plus, some state parks now require you to show proof of rabies vaccination before they will allow your dog to enter.

It's also a good idea to have your dog wear identification tags showing his name along with your name, address, and telephone number. Even better is to get one of the little containers for her collar into which you can put information for contacting you while you are on vacation. Cellular phone and pager numbers are one way to go. Another is to put your veterinarian's name and number inside and leave your vacation itinerary with the vet's office. You don't necessarily want some stranger getting this information. A person who finds your dog can call your vet, who can call you.

It's especially important to have your veterinarian's name and number on a dog who is taking medication, as well as a request that anyone finding the dog contact the vet for instructions. If your dog becomes lost and is impounded, the animal control officer can get the information needed to continue the medication until you retrieve your pooch.

NOSH! NOSH, YOU HUSKIES!

Time was when dogs served a vital function at meals. While the lord of the manor and his knights and ladies feasted, dogs lay under tables and policed the area for scraps and bones. A dog's status was determined by whether he sat below or above the salt, not by which other members of the pack he could whip in a dirty fight. Ancient memories of those times lurk in modern dogs' genes, and they think they should still be allowed at table with their people. (If truth be known and if my experience with Samantha and Sport is any guide, the chief reason dogs allowed themselves to be domesticated was because of better groceries.)

Dogs in Europe still sit at the table in restaurants, but Paris, Texas, is not Paris, France. The Texas health regulation regarding dogs in restaurants is specific. Dogs are not allowed in food preparation areas or in areas immediately adjacent to food preparation areas. The state health department inspectors I talked to interpret this to mean that, except for service dogs, you cannot take a dog into an inside dining area of a restaurant. Nor can you pass through the inside of a restaurant on your way to an outside seating area. The state regulations do permit dogs in outside seating areas with outside access, such as patios, decks, and sidewalk tables. However—and this is a big however—the management of the restaurant has the say over whether they will allow dogs in such areas or not. I found that many restaurant managers are vague on what the law says, and once it is explained to them, they welcome dogs. It amazed me how many people said, "Nobody has ever asked that question before," and then went on to say they saw no problem with bringing a dog onto their patio. There's a lesson here: Ask, and maybe you will receive. As I noted earlier, this book is breaking new ground in Texas, and nowhere was this more evident than in the area of dining out with a dog. If you find a restaurant not in this book that welcomes dogs, please let the publisher know (see the address in the front of the book) so I can include it in future editions.

If you are traveling to Houston, be aware that this was the only city in Texas I found where health regulations forbid taking a dog into the outside seating area of restaurants. In fact, the health inspector I spoke with said that he interprets the law as forbidding dogs from even being in the parking lots of restaurants. Sadly, many Houston restaurants would welcome dogs if the law allowed them to. Perhaps a little lobbying is in order.

Several things besides the law limit dining-out opportunities for dogs in Texas. One is the climate. Amarillo lies 800 miles north of the Rio Grande Valley. In winter it's too cold to eat outside in much of the state; in summer it's too hot. During milder seasons you may find temporary outside seating at restaurants just about anywhere in the state, but daily weather conditions may determine whether those areas are being used. (Tables have been known to blow off the sidewalk in the Panhandle.) It's always best to call ahead if you can.

Another limiting factor is the attitude of the community. I found that in general, the more tourist oriented the city, the more likely you are to find restaurants that welcome dogs. Small towns often not only do not have any restaurants with outside seating (with the possible exception of a drive-in burger place), but residents regard anyone who would want to eat with a dog as a little "teched" in the head.

The third and most important factor affecting whether you will eat at a table or in your car is whether the restaurant owner or manager likes dogs or not. In most cases, this person has the ultimate authority to say yes or no. I found many restaurants in Texas, in towns both large and small, where dogs are at least as welcome as people. However, I found many, many more where the mere mention of bringing a dog onto the premises got the opposite reaction. In several cases I had the phone slammed down in my ear.

The managers of the restaurants in this book gave me permission to list their businesses as dog-friendly eateries. In no case did I attempt to talk anyone into being listed. Special conditions imposed for allowing dogs on the premises have been noted in the descriptions. Complying with these and making sure your pooch is well behaved will help to ensure not only that you will be welcomed back but also that other dogs to follow will be allowed to eat there, too.

And how should your dog behave at a restaurant? Emily Post's rules for people do well for dogs, too. Be quiet. Be clean. Be polite. Don't beg food off other diners. Keep your feet on the floor. And never, ever, conduct private business in public places.

Here's one final tip about eating out with your dog in Texas. Since many restaurants have had so few canine customers in the past, they are unaware of the niceties that dining dogs require and appreciate. While a few will volunteer to bring a bowl of water for your pooch, most are simply unaware that it's torture for a dog to watch people slurping and munching without so much as a sip of water of their own. In most cases, if you politely ask for a bowl of water for your dog, they'll be happy to oblige.

Oh. And here's a final, final tip. It's about tipping. When you find a waitperson who takes good care of your dog, remember that hounds often conveniently leave their money at home so you'll have to pick up the check and leave the tip. One explanation of the origin of the word tip is that it stood for the phrase "to insure promptness." From a dog's point of view, it could as well stand for "to invite pooches." Don't expect a waitperson you shorted on the tip to tell the manager how well behaved and cute your dog was. Do your pooch a favor and leave a tip from her, too, perhaps with a little thank-you note. Your waitperson will be pawsitively delighted, and next time your dog won't have to ask for a bowl of water.

ROOMING WITH ROVER

Lots of hotel operators told me they'd rather host dogs than children or grumpy adults. Good dogs don't tear up and down hallways shouting. They don't use up all the room towels at the pool and then call housekeeping for more. They don't burn holes in bedspreads or throw noisy parties.

However, the question of dogs in hotel rooms raised lots of hackles, too. The litany of complaints ranged from incessant barking to furniture gnawing to piddling on the carpet. None of these things are the fault of the dogs who do them. Most serious problems with dogs in hotels stem from the same cause, leaving a dog alone in the room. Fear, boredom, or a desperate need to dewater can lead dogs to eat chair cushions, gouge huge scratches in the door, or dig holes entirely through mattresses. They would do none of these things if you were with them. Don't leave your dog alone in a hotel room unless you put her in a carrier. Just don't do it.

While most hotels do not require you to bring something for your dog to sleep on, they will appreciate your doing so. Some offer to provide a sheet to cover the bed or carpet with, but your dog will feel more at home if you bring along a favorite "binkie" or his bed.

Common sense dictates that you would never take a dog to a hotel unless she is housebroken. However, many hotels specifically require that dogs be well behaved, trained, or housebroken—there are a lot of ways to say "doesn't do his business on the rug," but they all mean the same thing. If a hotel specifically mentioned this as a requirement for admitting dogs, I noted that in the description. While a wet spot on the carpet will draw the ire of the manager (and perhaps the assessment of a fee for damages) at any inn, woe be to the dog who piddles at a place where it is strictly forbidden. Walk your dog regularly (and clean up after her) to avoid this problem.

As with restaurants, I did not try to talk any hotels into accepting dogs. If a place of lodging is listed in this book, it is because their policy is to accept dogs (or at least it was when I checked—ownership, management, and dog policies do change). It's always best to call ahead and let the hotel know you will be traveling with a dog. In some hotels dogs are allowed only in what they call "regular" rooms, which means smoking rooms. Inquire about this policy when making reservations; if you must have a nonsmoking room, that could affect your choice of hotels.

Fortunately, in most larger towns and cities, you will have a choice of accommodations. All Motel 6s and most La Quinta Inns accept dogs, although rules about size vary. Many hotels say they accept only small dogs, but if you show up with a sweet, cute, not-so-small dog and you look fairly normal, the size of the dog won't really matter. Sometimes it helps if you offer to pay for any damages, or sign a waiver, or promise not to leave the dog in the room alone. The one thing you should not do is sneak a dog into a room. That creates ill will toward all dogs and may get you thrown out of the hotel if your dog starts barking. With this book, you should be able to plan your travels so that you are always able to spend the night in a dog-friendly inn.

The rates quoted in this book are for double rooms. Specific fees, deposits, size limits, and other regulations regarding dogs are stated as the hotels gave them to me. Where no restrictions or fees are listed, none were in force at the time this book was being researched, but it's a good idea to ask anyway.

TENTING ON THE OLD CAMPGROUND

Camping with Samantha and Sport is an interesting experience in opposites. Samantha apparently has some chicken blood: she goes down with the sun and is, for all practical purposes, dead until dawn. One of Sport's ancestors must have been a Transylvanian vampire dog, because she comes alive at dusk and spends most of the night looking for nocturnal creatures to pursue, hoping to suck their blood.

Texas campgrounds are great places to take a dog, but it's not a good idea to leave them outside your tent or vehicle at night. At many state parks, in fact, rangers interpret the rule against leaving dogs unattended as meaning they cannot be left outside at night. I've noted many such rules in the descriptions, as well as the existence of hazards such as javelinas, feral hogs, coyotes, and mountain lions in the area. Dogs like Sport are also more prone to bark if left outside at night. Sally and I solve this problem by bedding down with our hounds in the back of our Suburban. It's a little crowded, but once everyone gets used to the rule that turning over is done by all in unison, it's not too bad. And in cold weather it feels good to have a hot dog on either side of you.

HITTING THE TRAIL

One of the reasons state parks are such good places for dogs is that most of them have trails you can walk with your leashed pooch. The
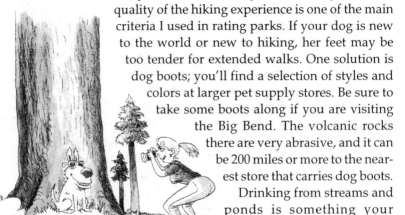
quality of the hiking experience is one of the main criteria I used in rating parks. If your dog is new to the world or new to hiking, her feet may be too tender for extended walks. One solution is dog boots; you'll find a selection of styles and colors at larger pet supply stores. Be sure to take some boots along if you are visiting the Big Bend. The volcanic rocks there are very abrasive, and it can be 200 miles or more to the nearest store that carries dog boots. Drinking from streams and ponds is something your pooch is going to do sometimes

even when it's not a good idea, particularly when he's running off leash. Several parks I visited did not make it into this book because of signs around ponds warning against coming in contact with the water. While the water in a river, creek, or pond may be safe to drink, you can never be sure. I especially don't like to let a dog drink from a creek or pond in an urban area. Such waters can easily be loaded with bacteria, pesticides, and herbicides. The safest thing is to carry enough water for you and your dog when hiking.

Doggy backpacks are available that let you share the burden with your hound. Most dogs should be able to carry their own food and bowls; big dogs, of course, can carry heavier items such as water, although they may not like it. If you will be hiking in areas where your dog can run off leash and visibility is limited, you might want to consider a backpack in blaze orange. Hunting dogs like orange vests for safety. Boating dogs will be relieved to know that doggy life preservers are available. Large pet supply stores such as PetsMart and Petco, as well as many smaller specialty shops, carry a selection of gear for the outdoor dog.

BOO-BOOS AND OWIES

Nobody expects trouble when they take their dog out for a romp, but as the bumper stickers warn, the opposite of magic happens. Your veterinarian can supply you with literature detailing basic first aid for your buddy.

Ticks are abundant in Texas, especially when a mild winter is followed by a wet spring. Most will be the large gray "dog ticks" or the flat, round bloodsuckers with the white spot on their back. These are easily removed with tweezers if you get to them before they have a chance to get dug in good. Inspect yourself and your dog at least once a day; more often if you begin finding ticks on either of you. There have been a few cases of Rocky Mountain spotted fever and Lyme disease in Texas, so watch for any sign of illness in your dog and yourself after an outing.

Some parts of Texas have what I called "spear grass" when I was growing up. Also called foxtail, this grass's seeds take the form of tiny barbed darts that can impale themselves in your clothes, you, or your dog. Check your dog's eyes, ears, nose, and mouth and remove them promptly; they can continue to work their way in and cause serious problems.

Far more common in Texas are sandburrs (also called grass burrs) and the many varieties of cactus. Both can deal dogs much misery. Sport and Samantha are skilled at removing sandburrs from their feet, but they need help with cactus thorns. I've noted in park descriptions where you are likely to meet with these hazards, as well as with poison ivy and poison oak. With the latter two, the threat is not so much to the dog as it is to you. As the dog runs through the plants, secretions that can cause serious skin rashes rub off on her fur, and you pick them up when you pet the dog. If your dog gets into either of these plants, she'll need a good bath administered while wearing rubber gloves.

I thought skunks were the worst thing Sport would ever run into until the wee hours one morning when her nonstop barking finally dragged me out of bed. We'd been under a steady siege of skunks for weeks, and Sport had cornered and I'd shot half a dozen or more. As I stumbled toward the back door this time, she suddenly stopped barking. When I shined my flashlight into the backyard, there was Sport rolling on the ground pawing at her face. I figured she'd gotten too close to the skunk and been sprayed. But as I got closer, I saw white things sticking out all over her face. Sport had met her first (and I hope last) porcupine. By the time I returned with a pair of pliers, she'd broken every one of the quills in two. I have read that cutting the quills allows them to deflate and makes them easier to pull out, so this was, as Martha Stewart would say, a good thing. I got Sport between my legs and started pulling quills, and that sweet dog stood there and let me pull all 25 or so without so much as a whimper or growl, and she never tried to pull away. I've never been more proud of her than I was at that moment. I wasn't happy about being in the backyard pulling porcupine quills at 5 A.M., but it would have been a lot worse if she hadn't cooperated.

Ah, the sweet aroma of perfume. The best perfume, as you may know, uses an extract of skunk spray as its base because the odor lasts, and lasts, and lasts. Until some smart scientist figures a way to alter skunk's genes so their spray smells like Chanel No. 5, though, we'll have to keep deodorizing dogs. Our experience with skunks and Sport indicates that bathing a large, black dog in tomato juice leaves one with a large, reddish black dog who smells like a Bloody Mary-drinking skunk. A new formula published recently claims to attack the chemicals in skunk spray that make it smell bad. We have not, thank goodness, had the opportunity to put it to the test, but you might. Here's the recipe.

Mix together one quart of 3 percent hydrogen peroxide (available at any pharmacy or the drug section in your supermarket), a quarter cup of baking soda, and a teaspoon of liquid detergent. Work it into your dog's fur and let it stand for about 15 minutes. Rinse well.

A DOG IN NEED

I could name many heartfelt reasons for the dogless (the canine challenged) among you to visit your nearest animal pound and adopt a homeless dog. Thousands of dogs are euthanized every day in this country; the one you save could become your best friend, traveling companion, bed warmer, lifeguard, and food critic. Some insurance companies now offer better rates to pet owners, knowing they tend to be healthier and live longer. However, in the spirit of this book, I'll simply offer the following quotations and leave your conscience to be your guide.

> "If you pick up a starving dog and make him prosperous, he will not bite you; that is the principal difference between a dog and a man."
> —*Mark Twain*

> "Man is a dog's idea of what God should be."
> —*Holbrook Jackson*

> "A dog is the only thing on earth that loves you more than he loves himself."
> —*Josh Billings*

> "No one appreciates the very special genius of your conversation as the dog does."
> —*Christopher Morley*

> "To his dog, every man is Napoleon; hence the constant popularity of dogs."
> —*Aldous Huxley*

STEPPING OUT BIG-TIME

Texas is a big place and the best in the world to live, but there may be times when you are tempted, forced, or otherwise induced to visit other, less fortunate parts of the world. If so, you'll be happy to know that Foghorn Press publishes Dog Lover's books for California, the San Francisco Bay Area, Seattle, Boston, Atlanta, Florida, and Washington, D.C. Call (800) FOGHORN (364-4676) to order, or contact your bookseller. Beware of cheap imitations: Only Foghorn Press books describe and rate parks, give complete dog rules and rates for hotels, and identify dog-friendly restaurants. All dogs and all guides for traveling with dogs are not equal. Foghorn Press is top dog in its field.

ONE LAST WAG OF THE TALE . . .

Linda Walker, a resident of the Big Bend hamlet of Lajitas, told me why the Big Bend is such a special place for dogs and people. She might well have been talking about the rest of the state, too: "It's the land that brings out what's inside us. Here the wide-open spaces distill out the very best in people. There's no fluff. There's a beauty and clarity I believe you find only in open spaces."

And, I might add, in the eyes of a dog.

Get out there. Texas is waiting.

1
ALPINE/ THE BIG BEND COUNTRY

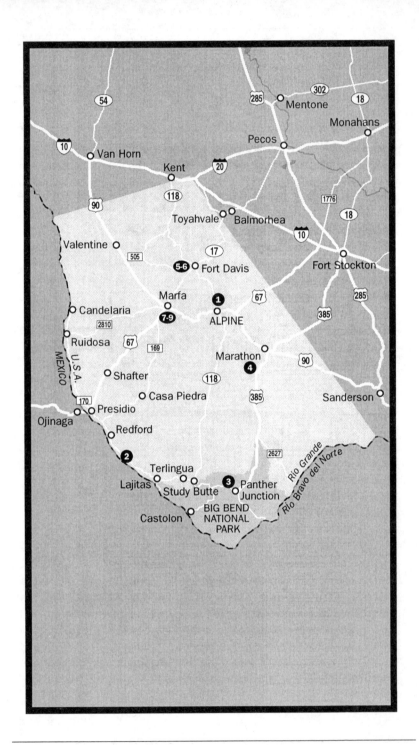

ALPINE/THE BIG BEND COUNTRY

An oft-used quote attributed to an anonymous cowboy describes the Big Bend as a place "where rainbows wait for rain, and the river is kept in a big stone box, and the mountains hang in the sky, except at night, when they go away to play with other mountains." Dogs couldn't care less about this poetic description. Dogs love the Big Bend because it is like a big old bloody hunk of deer liver—raw, untamed, wild, real, something you can get your teeth into. It's a place where dogs can do as humans there do: be themselves without apology. Arooooooo!

The Big Bend is my favorite part of Texas. Sport and Samantha like it, too, but for different reasons. I love its rugged mountains, 91 of them over a mile high, separated by wide valleys so you can admire them standing in silent majesty. I love the smell of the creosote bushes in the desert after a rain. (Dogs like that, too, as well as all the other smells.) I love the open plains and the big sky, the fiery sunsets and darkest nighttime skies in Texas, with stars hanging low overhead like ripe fruit waiting to be plucked. I love drifting through Santa Elena Canyon in a rubber raft during a storm, when thunder tries to free itself by shaking down the chasm walls, raindrops raise miniature geysers from the Rio Grande, and thousands of waterfalls fling themselves into the river in a watery lover's leap. I love sitting in the ghost town of Terlingua watching a full moon rise over the Chisos Mountains, whose name means ghost. This country has lots of ghosts. I number some of them among my best friends.

The Big Bend country is a good place to spend time alone, but it's an even better place to share a campfire and a skillet of supper with a good old dog. Life in the Big Bend gets back to the elemental, the important stuff, like what do we eat next and where will we sleep tonight and why don't we just sit by the Rio Grande all day and listen to the water roll by on its way to the sea. That's what dogs like about the Big Bend. It's a place where their humans are freed from the distractions of "normal" life, so their minds go quiet enough to rediscover that living is what's really important in life, to realize that there is a place where they belong, and this is it. Dogs know these things from the time they first love a person; humans sometimes forget them along the way. A human makes a better companion for a dog when they are both cognizant of these facts.

Three things define the Big Bend: distance, desolation, and diversity. Its remoteness protects it from most of the people who have no business coming here in the first place, the kind of people who talk about "doing" Big Bend National Park in a day and a half before rushing off to the next roadside attraction. You know these people. They are the same ones who give their leashed dogs whiplash every time the poor creatures spend more than five seconds trying to decipher a delicious cacophony of smells. Distance is the only protection any of us have from such people. In the Big Bend you can put a lot of it between yourself and them.

The desolation of the Big Bend puts off some people. It makes them ask, "What good is it?" as if value is derived only from having some economic purpose. Dogs know that the worth of things is measured in more than dollars. Desolation does this: It concentrates our attention on what remains. It makes us appreciate what we have. It reminds us that so many of the trappings of "civilization" we hold dear are simply the obverse of desolation.

Diversity is a deceptive thing in the Big Bend. It's easy to dismiss this huge area as just one big homogeneous desert. Nothing could be more wrong. There are places in the Big Bend where you can drive 10 miles and the climate changes from tropical to alpine. To discover the diversity of the Big Bend—its plants, its animals, its hidden springs and valleys— you have to do as a dog does and put your nose to the ground. Follow the trail where it leads. Around the next rock—or under it—may be a hidden treasure well worth discovering. Quite likely, it will be a part of yourself you never knew.

Three counties comprise the heart of the Big Bend, which takes its name from the huge crook in the Rio Grande at its southern edge. There are no cities here, or even large towns. Except for two huge parks—one national and one state—and two large wildlife management areas, virtually all the land is private and off-limits to you and your dog. But—and it's a Saint Bernard–sized but—this is country where most people own dogs, love dogs, and welcome visitors with dogs. In fact, as many of them will plainly tell you, they think a lot more of the dogs who visit here than they do of some of the people. The Big Bend is a place where dogs belong, and they know it.

ALPINE

A mix of western ranching heritage, education and culture, and spectacular scenery defines Alpine. Cattle graze the Texas-size ranches surrounding the town, Sul Ross State University enriches culture and life, and the community's name derives from its mountainous setting.

Alpine grew from Old West roots of cattle ranching and hard-rock mining, but today it seeks to build a New West based on tourism and fine arts. Its stress-free lifestyle won it a place in the book *The 100 Best*

Small Art Towns in America, and the region's natural beauty makes it popular with Hollywood movie producers. In early 1995, large parts of the made-for-TV movie *Streets of Laredo* were filmed near Alpine. Frank Dobbs, producer of this film version of the Larry McMurtry novel, says the varied scenery of the Alpine area makes it the best in the country for filming. (*Giant* and *The Good Old Boys* also showcased the Big Bend's scenic assets.) "You can take a silver dollar and drop it on the average size Texas map, centered below Alpine, Fort Davis, and Marfa, and in the area it covers you could shoot a movie that crosses the continent," Dobbs says. "All it lacks is beaches."

Art and scenery aren't the only attractions in Alpine. A steady stream of visitors drops in at the Apache Trading Post west of town. They come to see Sasha, a Maltese dog who is the gift emporium's official greeter. She loves visitors, whether they have two legs or four, and has a nationwide fan club.

You'll see local dogs roaming all over town, even though there is a leash law. A warning we picked up from locals was never to try petting a dog in the back of a pickup parked on the street. Many of these dogs guard their owners' property with bared teeth.

PARKS, BEACHES, AND RECREATION AREAS

• **Kokernot Park** 🐾½ *See* ❶ *on page 34.*

When I last visited, this park of about 60 acres was alive with dogs— none of them on the required leash. However, they were all closely supervised and well behaved. The park offers plenty of open grassy spaces for a pooch to roam, and for West Texas it has an abundance of trees for shade and leg-hiking. There are also picnic tables with barbecue grills and a half-mile paved track where three athletic dogs and their people were burning up the pavement. The children's playground includes something unusual that seems right at home here—a covered wagon. Dogs will enjoy crossing the big open field east of the track and sniffing along the margins of the dry creekbed on the other side.

From Highway 118 north, go three blocks east on Jeff Davis Street to the park. Hours are from 6 A.M. until midnight. (915) 837-3301.

RESTAURANTS

Corner House Bed-and-Breakfast and Cafe: Dogs can eat outside on the porch at one of three tables. Breakfast only is served. You'll choose from four combination breakfasts ranging from continental to eggs and bacon. The homemade bread, scones, marmalade, and potato cakes, as well as egg-in-the-hole (sometimes called the one-eyed Mulligan), reflect owner Jim Glendinning's Scottish heritage. 801 East Avenue E; (915) 837-7161.

La Casita: The Mexican food here was voted best in the Big Bend in 1996 by readers of a regional publication, but Sport and I would like to reserve judgment until we've tried every place a few more times. If you're going to do research, be thorough, we always say. However, the version of nachos (called *campechanas* here) Sport and I shared at a picnic table on the covered porch in front did rate highly—three nudges of the snout from an under-the-table dog asking for more. 1104 East Avenue H; (915) 837-2842.

Reata: The next time the movie *Giant* comes on late-night television, pop an extra-big bowl of popcorn and curl up with your kernel-crunching canine while James Dean, Rock Hudson, and Elizabeth Taylor act out lives of mythical West Texans living on a ranch called Reata (Spanish for rope). Much of the movie was filmed outside nearby Marfa (see page 65), and a mural on one wall of the restaurant's patio pays tribute to the movie. Take a table on the patio, and while you gaze at James Dean in the mural gazing at the West Texas countryside, your pooch will be gazing at your dinner, so don't get carried away, or your steak might. The Reata serves Hereford beef from the local CF Ranch, and the mesquite-grilled rib eyes and T-bones are big favorites here. (Hint: If your hound likes bones, order the T-bone. The rib eye is boneless.) However, you can also have fettuccine with crushed tamales and smoked chile cream, pan-fried trout with wild rice and jicama, or angel-hair pasta with mesquite-grilled shrimp. Save room for a Texas-sized slice of pecan pie, chocolate torte with blackberry sauce, or sweet potato custard. On summer weekends you may find some pickin' and grinnin' happening on the patio as well. Some of the local musicians are quite good, and you never know when a well-known personality from Austin will show up and put on a free gig. 203 North Fifth Street (Highway 118); (915) 837-9232.

Sunday House Restaurant: This cafe next to the motel of the same name serves chicken-fried steak, seafood, chicken, and Mexican food. You can order to go and eat at the picnic tables under the trees beside the motel. On U.S. 90 East across from Sul Ross State University; (915) 837-3363.

The White House Inn Bistro: This bed-and-breakfast does not accept dogs as overnight guests, but it does serve meals and has a patio out back where, in clement weather, pooches may join their people at table. The menu changes seasonally, with heavier foods in the winter and lighter offerings in the summer. A year-round favorite, though, is owner Anita Bradney's creation called the White House Salad. It's a variety of baby greens with a five-nut mix and a house dressing. The soup of the day is whatever strikes Anita's fancy, and there may be quiche, chicken salad, or pasta. Another standard menu item is the Mountain Quesadillas, toasted flour tortillas stuffed with spinach, cream cheese, onions, mushrooms, jack cheese, and peppers. For dessert there's homemade pies, bread pudding, cheesecake, or whatever Anita feels like making that day. 2003 Fort Davis Highway; (915) 837-1401.

PLACES TO STAY

Antelope Lodge: This collection of white cottages with red tile roofs ought to be called Dog Town, judging by the number of canine residents Sport and I met on our last visit. It seemed that half the cabins had a dog in residence. Small and medium-sized dogs stay for free; the management may charge a deposit if they don't like the looks of your dog. There's lots of grass and trees for dogs to do their things under and on. Rooms are $34 to $45. 2310 Highway 90 West, Alpine, TX 79830; (915) 837-2451.

Best Western: "No 200-pound dogs, please," the desk clerk joked. Then he went on to say that just about any dog will be allowed to stay here "if you are nice and cool about it." This new hotel is just east of Sul Ross State University. Rooms are $59, and there's a $20 deposit for dogs. 2401 Highway 90 East, Alpine, TX 79830; (915) 837-1530.

Corner House Bed-and-Breakfast and Cafe: Scottish breed dogs will feel right at home here: owner Jim Glendinning, a native of Lockerbie, Scotland, claims to fly the only Scottish flag in West Texas. (The couch in the parlor also boasts the only plaid stuffed dog I've seen.) Glendinning welcomes any size wee beastie—Scottish breed or no—and he charges no fee or deposit. The five rooms (four with private baths) are all decorated slightly differently (when I last stayed, mine featured maps from around the world and a great reading shelf, although there were no books for or about dogs). Rates range from $60 to $65, which includes your choice of four breakfasts.

Located between Sul Ross State University and downtown, the inn has only a small yard where you can walk your dog, but the nearby university campus is spacious, and from the mountain to its east (which is public land and therefore open for walking) you can get a panoramic view of the town that will make your dog say "Wowza!" A bonus is that Glendinning authored an excellent travel guide to the Big Bend region, so he'll be able to point you to all the area attractions. For a price, of course. Just kidding, Jim. I am kidding, right? Jim?

The garden area out back, which has hammocks, chairs, tables, and an unusual fountain resembling a group of inebriated mushrooms, is available not only for lounging but also for weddings and parties. If your pooch wants to entertain her friends while she's visiting in Alpine, this is the place to do it. They can all sit around munching barbecued pigs' ears, commenting on the latest fashions in collars or bandannas, and speculating on who's wormy now. 801 East Avenue E, Alpine, TX 79830; (915) 837-7161 or (800) 585-7795.

Danny Boy RV Park: Dogs under 15 inches tall and under 25 pounds may stay here. They must be leashed and may not be left outside unattended. You must clean up after them and keep them quiet. There are small trees and grassy areas about and a security gate out front. The fee is $14 per night. 2305 Highway 90 East, Alpine, TX 79830; (915) 837-7135.

Days Inn: This modern motel near Sul Ross State University takes any size dog with no fee or deposit required. Rooms are $42 to $44. There's a pool for you and a very large paved parking lot for your pooch to explore. 2000 Highway 90 East, Alpine, TX 79830; (915) 837-3417.

Pecan Grove RV Park: This campground has something most don't: a windmill out front with a whirling fan to bark at and four legs to hike a leg on. Dogs are welcome, but they must be leashed and cleaned up after. You may not leave them unattended or tied to trees. There's a dog walk along the city street out back. Most of the sites are shaded by (surprise!) pecan trees. Sites with full hookups are $16; pickups and vans are $11; tent sites are $9. 1902 Highway 90 West, Alpine, TX 79830; (915) 837-7175 or (800) 644-7175.

Ramada Limited: Rooms at this modern motel on the western edge of town are $55 to $75, which includes a continental breakfast. All dogs are welcome. There is a $25 deposit, which you'll get back if your room is damage-free at check-out. There should be no accidents, as there's ample room to walk your dog behind and beside the motel. 2800 Highway 90 West, Alpine, TX 79831; (915) 837-1100 or (800) 272-6232.

Sunday House Motor Inn: Mister the Poodle runs this motel for his owners, Sanford and Maurine DeVoll, and according to the desk clerk, he does so with an iron paw. Small and medium-sized dogs may stay for no fee or deposit. Rooms are $47. On U.S. 90 East across from Sul Ross State University. P.O. Box 578, Alpine, TX 79830; (915) 837-3363 or (800) 510-3363.

Woodward Ranch: For a real outdoor experience the way cowboys and cowdogs did it back in the olden days, spend a night in the primitive campground on the banks of a mountain creek. Large oak trees shade fire rings just a few yards from the water. The shallow creek is a good place for both of you to wade while enjoying the views of the mountains on one side and the sheer bluff on the other. A pool below a small dam is deep and wide enough to get in a quick dog paddle or two. Dogs may run free as long as they remain in sight and under your control. This is a working ranch, and chasing cows is not permitted. There are no facilities. Camping is $6 per night.

RV camping with full hookups is available at the ranch headquarters and rock shop. There is a rest room with showers there; sites are $10.

The ranch is 16 miles south of Alpine off Highway 118. Turn west at the Woodward Ranch sign and follow the dirt road 1.7 miles to the headquarters. HC 65, Box 40, Alpine, TX 79830; (915) 364-2271.

DIVERSIONS

Arf for art: Leashed dogs may bone up on their fine art while shopping with you in Kiowa Gallery, a center for regional artists. Items for sale range from paintings to pottery to Indian crafts to handmade furniture. Dogs who read this book will know to go to the office in the back and beg a snack from Katie Elms, who owns the gallery with daughter Keri Null. 105 East Holland Avenue; (915) 837-3067.

Climb a mountain: Now, pay attention here. Do not go climb A Mountain. That's the one on the southwest edge of Alpine with a giant letter A outlined in rocks on its side; it's private property. The mountain you want to climb is Hancock Mountain, immediately east of Sul Ross State University. It's public land, and you'll get a great view of the town and the surrounding valleys and mountains. Since the mountain is in the city, the only leash law in Brewster County applies; but just say "Mush" frequently and let your husky haul you up the hillside. You can park anywhere on the traffic circle in front of the college administration building, or in the large parking lot to its south. There are no reserved parking places; not even the university president has an assigned space. All dogs are equal here. The university is located along U.S. 90 on the east side of town.

Hound a rock: The Woodward Ranch is known worldwide for its red plume and pom-pom agates. When cut, these rocks reveal intricate treelike formations inside crystals. Rock hounds and their hounds pay a $5 entrance fee to hunt rocks on the 2,400-acre ranch and 50 cents a pound for any they want to keep. Ranch personnel will show you where to hunt and help you determine what you've found. There's also a rock shop where you can buy cut and polished specimens of the local agate as well as nifty rocks from around the world. Take your pooch here and confirm what she's always suspected—that you have rocks in your head. Dogs may sniff out rocks with you off leash as long as you keep them in sight and under control. This is a working ranch with cows, deer, and snakes.

The ranch is 16 miles south of Alpine off Highway 118. Turn west at the Woodward Ranch sign and follow the dirt road 1.7 miles to the ranch headquarters and rock shop. (915) 364-2271.

Sashay by Sasha: The Apache Trading Post offers the Big Bend's best

---

selection of maps, books, and gift items, but that's not the reason people flock here. People come to see Sasha the Wonder Dog, a Maltese who entertains visitors (and is entertained by them) by playing dress-up. Shop owner and Sasha mom Charlotte Allen keeps a bag of poodle-sized clothes behind the counter, and while parents shop, bored kids (of all ages) dress and undress Sasha and pose for pictures with her. (Good children receive a "pawtographed" photo of Sasha.) She has a cowboy outfit, a Native American headdress, biker leathers—you name it. She also has a nationwide fan club and a scrapbook to prove it. When I last visited, Sasha was proudly showing off her latest garb, a set of angel wings and halo given to her by a customer. (This may be the only store in Texas whose customers often give it more than they buy.) Sasha is getting a little long in the tooth and now has an understudy, Heidi-Snowflake, another Maltese. Out in the parking lot, a grizzled Siberian husky named Cassie rules, and nearby is Jack-Assic Park, which is inhabited by a growing collection of donkeys. Your pooch will fit right in here, whether he's an angel or a jackass. Some days dogs are both.

The store is at 2701 Highway 90 West, about four miles west of Alpine. (915) 837-5506.

Take a history hike: Snap a leash on your hound and pick up a copy of a historic walking and windshield tour from the Chamber of Commerce office at 106 North Third Street. You'll meet some of Alpine's old buildings as well as some of the free-ranging local dogs, most of whom appear to pay no attention whatsoever to the leash law. (915) 837-2326.

BREWSTER COUNTY

Brewster County is the largest in Texas. So what? Well, for one thing, its 6,193 square miles make it almost as big as Connecticut and Rhode Island combined. (Or, looked at another way, it's equal to 5.1097359736 Rhode Islands.) For another thing, Brewster County has no leash law, and only one town in the county does. Unfortunately, this is not as wonderful as it sounds, since most of the land is privately owned, and Big Bend National Park, the only large piece of public land in the county, does not extend a warm welcome to pooches. However, dogs abound and flourish here. You'll probably see more tails wagging over the sides of pickup trucks and more wet, black noses sticking out of car windows here than you will anywhere else in Texas. There's a leash-free park with—howlelujah!—a swimming hole. Plus, down along the Rio Grande is a 25,000-acre resort where dogs pretty much have the run of the place. Brewster County just may be the best place for dogs west of the Pecos.

STATE WILDLIFE MANAGEMENT AREAS

See the National and State Forests/State Wildlife Management Areas chapter starting on page 621 for important information and safety tips on visiting these areas with your dog.

• **Black Gap Wildlife Management Area** 🐾🐾🐾 🐕
See page 625 for a description of the Black Gap Wildlife Management Area.

LAJITAS

Lajitas may be the best town for dogs in the Big Bend. What dog wouldn't like a town with a beer-drinking goat for a mayor? Mayor Clay Henry Jr. is confined to a pen, but dogs roam freely here everywhere except on the boardwalk in what passes for downtown. There, even a leashed dog may have the opportunity to mooch a tidbit off a gullible refugee from Dallas or Houston. Dogs may roam off leash on the 25,000 or so surrounding acres, which are owned by the same company that owns the town. The Rio Grande runs (or, as during the drought of the middle 1990s, stumbles) at the edge of town, and some of the surrounding ravines may hold trickles and pools of water. You are welcome to hike all of them with your hound, or go mountain biking or horseback riding. You can get all the equipment locally, as well as guides for rock hunting, botany, or birding expeditions. Inquire at the front (and only) desk of the Badlands Hotel, on the boardwalk, or follow your sniffer until you find what you're looking for. Warning: Using the latter method sometimes results in discovering something you didn't even know you wanted.

PARKS, BEACHES, AND RECREATION AREAS

• **Big Bend Ranch State Natural Area** 🐾1/2 *See* ❷ *on page 34.*
Let's cut right to the chase: This is Texas's biggest and most scenic state park, and dogs are banned from all but a tiny sliver of it. The park's more than 265,000 acres of Chihuahuan Desert wilderness extend along the Rio Grande from southeast of Presidio to near Lajitas. It contains two mountain ranges, extinct volcanoes, canyons, waterfalls, and diverse animal and plant species. Your pooch will feel like Moses viewing the Promised Land when he visits here: he can look, but he can't go in.

Leashed dogs are allowed only in that part of the park south of Highway 170. You may drive this public highway free of charge if you are just passing through. The 50 miles between Presidio and Lajitas have been called one of the most scenic drives in North America. If you wish to get out of your car and walk or camp, you must pay a $3 per person entrance fee plus a $3 activity fee each day. The highway parallels the Rio Grande, and you are allowed to walk along the river with your leashed pooch. Dogs are not allowed on float or canoe trips on the river.

You are permitted to camp with your dog in primitive campgrounds at Grassy Banks, 9.2 miles west of Lajitas, and Madera Canyon, 11.4 miles west. Camping is included in your $3 day-use fee, and reservations are not accepted. These campgrounds offer little in the way of either scenery or comfort, with a composting toilet as the only facility. Campsites are not designated; just pick a spot. The most pleasant places are on the riverbank, but be aware that the river can rise suddenly. There is little or no shade in these campgrounds, which also serve as access points for commercial float trips down the river, making for little privacy as well. However, you can take your dog for a walk along the river and even let her wade or swim as long as she remains on a six-foot leash. Dogs may not be left unattended, and you must pick up after them. Mountain lions are a known hazard in the park, and they do visit the Rio Grande to drink. According to park rangers, they love the taste of dog.

The park has two official entry points where you can pay your fees and get information. The Barton Warnock Environmental Education Center is one mile east of Lajitas on Highway 170. The Fort Leaton State Historical Site acts as the western entrance; it is four miles east of Presidio on Highway 170. (915) 229-3416.

RESTAURANTS

Frontier Drug Company: You can get a sandwich, sundae, or ice-cream cone and share it with your dog at one of the benches on the boardwalk. On the Lajitas Boardwalk; (915) 424-3252.

Lajitas Bakery: Have your morning sweet roll or "dognut" and coffee at one of the benches on the boardwalk. The bakery is at the southern end of the main "street" in Lajitas; no phone.

Lajitas Trading Post: Capture the true flavor of the border by purchasing the ingredients for a Lajitas lunch—cheese, crackers, and bologna—at the trading post and eating at one of the covered picnic tables out front beside the goat pen holding Lajitas mayor Clay Henry Jr. and friends. Your pooch can rub noses with resident dog Fluffy and her buddy, a brindle cat named Fatty Two (successor to the original Fatty). Beware of any horses or burros "parked" outside, however—they may kick. To reach the trading post, turn at the sign just west of the Lajitas Boardwalk and go down the hill and to the right. (915) 424-3234.

PLACES TO STAY

Big Bend Ranch State Natural Area: See Big Bend Ranch State Natural Area on page 43 for camping information.

Lajitas on the Rio Grande: This resort development offers a variety of accommodations ranging from rooms in the Old West–style Badlands Hotel to modern motel rooms. Assistant Manager Terry Lavelett's black Lab, Sombra, thinks she owns the place, and why not—people feed her T-bone steaks from the restaurant. Dogs must be leashed while on the street in front of the hotel but not on the 25,000 acres surrounding it. Inside, they are allowed only if kept in a cage. Rates vary from $55 to $75, and there is a 48-hour cancellation policy. There is no deposit or fee for dogs. All rooms must be booked at the Badlands Hotel, on the board-walk in Lajitas. HC 70, Box 400, Terlingua, TX 79852; (915) 424-3471 or (800) 944-9907 (reservations only).

Lajitas RV Park: The 80 RV sites all have full hookups and cable tele-vision; they rent for $15. There are small trees at many of them, but don't expect much shade—this is the desert. Tent sites are $9 and have water, showers, and rest rooms nearby. One dog per campsite is allowed. Dogs must be leashed and cleaned up after. They may not be left unattended. The park is "under the hill"; turn off Highway 170 at the sign just past the main street in Lajitas and go down the hill and to the left. HC 70, Box 435, Terlingua, TX 79852; (915) 424-3471.

DIVERSIONS

Make your pooch the hubcap of your universe: An artist with the syn-chronistic name of Collie Ryan will paint a portrait of your pooch (or anything else you want) on a discarded hubcap, or you can buy one of her creations featuring the local landscape. Sally and I furnished Collie with snapshots of Sport and Samantha and a brief description of their love of the outdoors (and their lack of hunting skills), and she painted the two busily sniffing the bushes on one side of the scene while the object of their search, a rabbit, sits placidly on the other side. She cap-tured them quite well. All of Collie's paintings have a Southwestern fla-vor and bear two names, one in English and the other in Spanish. She will immortalize your hound on a hubcap for $125 plus $5 shipping. Send her two or three clear photos of your dog from different angles plus a description of him or her. "Tell me whether it's sober, serious, or a flap-doodle fool, whatever details would add to the character of the portrait," Collie says. She has no phone; write her at Box 263, Terlingua, TX 79852. When you are in Lajitas, you can see samples of her work at the Frontier Drug Company.

Go buy the fork in the road: Right behind the Lajitas Trading Post you'll find Larry Harris' shop, Arrowhead Sotol. Larry makes walking sticks and other items from stalks of a local desert plant, the sotol. He also makes wind chimes, bud vases, bracelets, and earrings from sterling silver hollowware. Sally, Sport and Samantha's mom, has earrings made from a baby spoon and fork and a bracelet made from two forks with the tines spread, elongated, and interlocked to form a spring to hold the bracelet in place. Browse Larry's shop with your dog and you're sure to find something one of you will like. Turn at the sign for the Lajitas Trading Post on Highway 170 and follow the road down the hill and to the right to the trading post. Arrowhead Sotol is on the west side, around the corner from the trading post entrance; there's no phone.

DEH-zert your dog: The Lajitas Resort includes about 25,000 acres of land along both sides of Highway 170 east of Lajitas. You and your dog are free to explore this land on foot; no leash is required. For one good walk, follow Highway 170 east past the airstrip at the edge of town. Turn north at the stone entrance marked "Mesa Vista/Spear Point." Follow the dirt road north for 0.3 miles, turn right, and go another 0.4 miles to the end. You'll be at the base of Lajitas Mesa, in an area with colorful rock formations, volcanic ash deposits, and a red bentonite arch over a dry gulch. Another good hike is to park alongside the road at the dry wash half a mile east of the Barton Warnock Environmental Education Center on Highway 170 and walk south along the dry streambed. You can explore the other gullies that enter it or follow the main branch all the way to the Rio Grande a mile away.

Deh-ZERT your dog: Four of the main activities here are river rafting, horseback riding, mountain biking, and hiking in Big Bend National Park and Big Bend Ranch State Natural Area. Unfortunately, dogs are banned from most areas of the parks and the river, and the folks who conduct guided horseback and mountain bike trips will not take dogs along, because most are simply not rugged enough to survive the desert conditions. If you want to go on one of these excursions and can stand to be away from your pooch for a few hours or overnight, leave her with a friend and go for it. You'll come back with lots of great stories to tell your dog.

The following businesses in Lajitas and nearby Terlingua will take you on guided trips in the Big Bend area.

- **Big Bend River Tours:** Float trips from half a day to 21 days on the Rio Grande. (915) 424-3219 or (800) 545-4240.
- **Big Bend Stables:** Horse, mule, and burro rides in the Study Butte area. (915) 371-2212 or (800) 887-4331.
- **Big Bend Touring Society:** Guided trips on private land. Dogs may go along on some trips. (915) 371-2548.
- **Desert Sports:** Mountain bike trips. Some rides take place on private land where dogs can go along if properly equipped with boots, or they can ride in the support vehicle. (915) 371-2727.
- **Far Flung Adventures:** Float trips on the Rio Grande. (915) 371-2489 or (800) 359-4138.

- *Lajitas Stables:* Horseback rides and overnight camping trips as well as horseback excursions into Mexico. (915) 424-3238.

MARATHON

PARKS, BEACHES, AND RECREATION AREAS

- **Big Bend National Park** 🐾🐾🐾 *See* ❸ *on page 34.*

At over 700,000 acres, this is the largest park in Texas. Unfortunately, dogs are required to be on leash at all times and are also barred from all trails within the park. However, this is not as bad as it sounds. Your pooch can camp with you, and dogs are allowed on all roads within the park that are open to vehicles. There are well over 200 miles of such roads, ranging from paved to primitive. You'll be able to see most of the natural wonders of the park with a cold, wet nose nuzzling your hand, even if some must be viewed from a distance.

New regulations regarding dogs in the park were issued in early 1997. Briefly, the rules state that dogs must be kept on a six-foot leash at all times while in the park. They may not go on any trails, but they are allowed in improved campgrounds, within designated backcountry campsites, in established picnic areas, in the Castolon Historic Compound, in paved parking areas, and on any road open to vehicles. Basically this means that if you can drive to get there, your dog can go with you. The Park Service spokesperson was very specific, however, that dogs are not allowed off the road surface. For example, while you and your pooch can drive or walk the River Road, you cannot take your pooch onto the land between the road and the river.

People seeing Big Bend National Park for the first time may find it hard to believe they are in Texas. One Big Bend creation myth holds that it was the dumping ground for all the materials left over from the creation of the Earth. Indeed, there is a little bit of everything here: desert, mountains, valleys, springs, a river, huge pine trees, and tiny cactus. Deer, lions, and bears (oh my) all inhabit the park, along with more than 400 kinds of birds. The climate can range, on the same day, from torrid along the Rio Grande to frigid in the Chisos Mountains only 20 miles away (as the crow flies, not as the dog walks).

Your first stop in the park should be at the Panther Junction Visitor Center. For one thing, some of the best water to be had in the Big Bend spurts from a faucet in the parking lot, where you are welcome to fill your canteen, cooler, or dog dish. You'll have to leave your hound in your car or tied outside for the few minutes it takes you to go inside and buy two booklets you will come to treasure. One is the *Road Guide to Paved and Improved Dirt Roads*; the other is the *Road Guide to Back Country*

Dirt Roads. These inexpensive booklets (about $2 each) will help you plan where to go, tell you how to get there, and explain what you'll see once you arrive. Best of all, there is a road log for each route that tells you how far it is between points, so you can decide whether to drive or walk each particular section. Walking, of course, is by far the best way to appreciate the sights, smells, and sounds of the desert, and during most times of the year you and your dog will be the only traffic.

You and your dog will discover your own favorite places in the park, and that's part of the fun. However, Samantha and Sport would like to put their two bark's worth in for the following drives: (1) From the Panther Junction Visitor Center, drive three miles west to the paved road following Green Gulch into the Chisos Basin. During this journey of less than seven miles, you will pass from the Chihuahuan Desert, where rainfall is about four inches annually, into the Chisos Mountains, where the amount is nearer to 25 inches. Vegetation will change from cactus and creosote bush to pine trees of a respectable size, and as you ascend, you can stick an arm or nose out the car window and feel the temperature dropping with each turn of the tires. This is a great drive for a dog who likes to ride with her head out the window. There are a few turnouts along the way where you can park, but walking along this narrow, well-traveled road is not a good idea. It's not just the traffic. This area is where most of the park's black bear sightings have taken place. Once you are in the Chisos Basin, your dog can walk the paved roads with you from the ranger station to the campground; the views of the mountains towering several thousand feet above you on all sides are awesome. (2) The eight-mile unpaved road to Grapevine Hills passes by Government Spring (a favored watering hole for wildlife), threads its way by huge rock formations, and fetches up at a primitive camping area with a spring and large trees. Walking should be no problem anywhere along this lightly traveled road. (3) The unpaved Old Maverick Road runs 14 miles from Santa Elena Canyon to the park's western entrance. It crosses several draws that may, when conditions are right, support dense growths of the tall Big Bend bluebonnet in January and February. Traffic is scarce on this road, but it's one you should ask about before attempting. Rains can make some of the draws difficult to cross without four-wheel drive. Inquire about road conditions at the visitor center or ranger stations. (4) The paved, 32-mile-long Ross Maxwell Scenic Drive takes you within view of most of the outstanding geologic formations in the park. There are nearly two dozen interpretive stations along the way to inform you about the sights. This is one of the most heavily traveled roads in the park, but the scenery makes it worth taking.

Camping in Big Bend National Park can be one of the best outdoor experiences you'll have with your hound in Texas. Your choices range from RV sites with full hookups to primitive backcountry sites consisting of a bare spot beside a dirt road. But no matter where you camp, the scenery will be spectacular and there will be a world of wonder for your pooch to explore. After you've camped in Big Bend for a few days, you'll find it difficult to be indoors. You'll be feeling the same call of the wild that's bred into a dog's bones.

The National Park Service operates three campgrounds in the park, all of which charge $7 per night. Reservations are not accepted. You drive around the campground until you find an empty site you and your hound can agree on, then go to the self-registration station at the campground entrance, fill out the necessary paperwork, and deposit your money. Signs at the park entrances and at intersections leading to campgrounds notify you if sites are available. Remember to bring the correct change; it's a long way to a bank, and dollar bills are more valuable here than they are most places.

The Rio Grande Village Campground has 100 very shady sites along the river. Rest rooms and water are available in the campground, and the nearby store has coin-operated showers. A short nature trail leads from the campground along the Rio Grande, but your pooch is not allowed on it. Do not make the mistake a recent visitor did. She tied her poodle at the trailhead while she took the walk. When she returned, a javelina was standing beside an empty leash, licking his chops. This campground is 20 miles east of the Panther Junction Visitor Center via a paved road.

The Chisos Basin Campground's 63 sites offer high-altitude camping in a bowl surrounded by mountains on all sides. This is one of the prettiest campgrounds in Texas, and, therefore, one of the first to fill up. Sport and Samantha love the camp because it has rocks, trees, trash, and lots of visitors who fuss over cute dogs. Since the sun strikes this campground only a few hours a day, it remains the coolest in the park in summer; nights are downright chilly. Winter nights can bring temperatures below freezing; you'll be glad you brought along a hot-bodied hound to share your tent. Rest rooms and water are nearby.

Cottonwood Campground is very shady and pretty, thanks to the large trees for which it was named. The 31 sites sit beside the Rio Grande and are subject to flooding. However, your dog does have access to the river here. Chemical toilets are the only facilities.

Dogs are also allowed in the 50 primitive backcountry campsites, and these are Sport and Samantha's favorites. Somehow they sense that this is true wilderness camping, and it's up to them to keep Sally and me from being eaten by wild things (which, of course, never materialize).

Their desire to protect us is, I am sure, what makes them snuggle so close in the tent at night. There is no charge for camping at these sites, but you must obtain a permit at the Panther Junction Visitor Center. Sites may not be reserved.

Rio Grande Village RV Park is operated by a concessionaire. It has 25 RV sites, all with full hookups ($13). The sites lie along the Rio Grande and are not shaded, but there is a grove of trees nearby. Dogs must be leashed. The campground is 20 miles east of Panther Junction. For information contact Rio Grande Village, National Park Concessions, Big Bend National Park, TX 79834; (915) 477-2293.

There is a $10 per vehicle entry fee, good for a week. The northern entrance to the park is 40 miles south of Marathon on U.S. 385; from there it's another 29 miles to the visitor center. The western entrance is two miles east of Study Butte on Highway 118; from there it's 24 miles to the visitor center. The park is officially open 24 hours every day, but it was closed briefly several times in recent years due to federal budget crises. It's a good idea to call ahead, especially if there's a big budget battle going on in Washington. For more information contact the National Park Service, Big Bend National Park, TX 79834; (915) 477-2251.

• **The Post** 🐾 🐾 ½ 🐕‍🦺 See ❹ on page 34.

Your dog will have a lot more fun here than at most three-acre parks. The reasons? No county leash law and a spring-fed pond and stream running through the center of the park where your water dog can splash, swim, and play until it's time to flop and nap under one of the large trees shading the picnic ground. There's also a small playground and rest rooms, as well as barbecue pits and a dance slab.

A chain-link fence encloses most of the park, but the entrance remains open, so should your pooch spot one of the many cows or mule deer on the surrounding private property, you'll be able to keep her from pursuing. You may even see an elk come to water here; their numbers have been steadily increasing in recent years. When Sport and I last visited we saw several mule deer bucks and a bevy of does grazing just outside the park. The water also attracts a variety of birds, including some migratory waterfowl. It is a true West Texas oasis, and one of the few parks west of the Pecos where your pooch can run off leash.

To reach the park, turn south off U.S. 90 in downtown Marathon at the sign that says "County Park 5." Follow the road five miles to the park. (915) 837-2714.

RESTAURANTS

Cenizo Cafe: "Gesundheit!" said Sport when I told her where we were going to have lunch. Sport's manners are impeccable, but her Spanish is a little weak; she didn't realize that *cenizo* means "sage." This grayish shrub brightens the desert with purplish pink blossoms after rare rains. But we're here to talk about food, not flowers. You might expect to have to settle for just hot food in a town this remote; what you'll find instead is haute cuisine. Enter the adobe-walled patio and sit at one of the massive wooden tables made in Mexico; if it's late, you'll be greeted by the glow of a kerosene lantern on your table. Your hound will be intrigued by the collection of cow skulls on the wall; tell him to be patient—there are better things to chew on here than old bones. Of course, beef is de rigueur here in the heart of big ranch country, but the menu surprises with items such as quail, pork tenderloin, and a dish Sport and I agree is to die for (or at least to go for), a chile relleno stuffed with goat cheese. All soups and desserts are made on the premises. On U.S. 90 next to the Gage Hotel in downtown Marathon; (915) 386-4434.

Open Sky Cafe: Probably the last thing you'd expect to find in one of the most isolated spots in Texas is a restaurant where dogs are welcome. But perched on a hill overlooking the Rio Grande and the nearly defunct Mexican hamlet of La Linda is just that. The name comes from the fact that you eat outdoors at picnic tables under shade shelters made from ocotillo stalks. The menu of hamburgers and Tex-Mex dishes is simple but tasty and filling. The restaurant is 65 miles south of Marathon. Take U.S. 385 south to F.M. 2627 and go to the end of F.M. 2627. Turn right just before the bridge across the Rio Grande. (915) 376-2235.

PLACES TO STAY

Big Bend National Park: See Big Bend National Park on page 47 for camping information.

The Gage Hotel: Well-behaved small and medium-size dogs are very welcome at this historic two-story hotel with a modern adobe addition adjoining. (Large dogs may stay if they promise to be very, very good, cross their hearts and hope to die.) The 1927 part of the hotel has been fully restored to the period when a wealthy San Antonio cattleman built it so he'd have a place to stay when he came to visit his little place in the country—a mere 500,000 acres. The hotel is furnished in Southwestern and Mexican style; tell your pooch no gnawing on the rawhide chairs, please. Rocking chairs on the front porch afford a venue for one of the main forms of entertainment in Marathon, watching cars and trains go by. Even more pleasant are the courtyards in back, where fires burn in outdoor fireplaces on cool evenings. You and your pooch can warm your cockles and have some chips and salsa before dinner at the Cenizo Cafe next door.

Rooms in the historic part of the hotel range from $45 to $68, depending on whether you have a private bath or use the public one down the hall. The rooms draw their names from local landmarks: Santiago Peak, Chalk Draw, Javelina Gap, and Iron Mountain. Rooms in the new adobe addition all have private baths. Rooms without a fireplace are $100; those with a fireplace rent for $115; suites are $150. These rooms encircle a court-yard with trees, grass, and a fountain in the center and shaded benches all around. There's also a pool.

The Gage also manages Captain Shepard's Inn, a historic house with five rooms and a carriage house. Dogs are permitted here as well. Rates range from $85 for a room without a private bath to $105 for a room with a Jacuzzi and a private porch. The carriage house has two bedrooms, a bath, a kitchenette, a fireplace, and a living area and rents for $120 for up to four people.

Due to the remote location, reservations are strongly recommended. A 32-hour notice of cancellation is requested.

The hotel is on U.S. 90 downtown; there is no street address. P.O. Box 46, Marathon, TX 79842; (915) 386-4205 or (800) 884-4243.

Heath Canyon Ranch: Accommodations range from $27 to $59 at this former bunkhouse for mining company employees. The multiroom adobe building and the nearby mobile home can be configured different ways depending on your wishes. That is, you can rent just a room, or a couple of rooms with a kitchen, or a room with kitchen and bathroom. Tent camp-ing is $3 per person per night; RV sites with full hookups are $9. Dogs stay for no charge and can go for walks on the surrounding 622 acres. The Rio Grande runs along the southern boundary of the property, so there are swimming opportunities as well. The Open Sky Cafe (see page 51) is part of the complex. The ranch is at the end of F.M. 2627, about 65 miles south of Marathon. The address is Highway 2627 at Heath Cross-ing, Marathon, TX 79842-0386; (915) 376-2235.

STUDY BUTTE

Don't go embarrassing your pooch in front of the locals by pronounc-ing the name of this hamlet "Stuh–dee but"; the correct pronunciation is "Stew–dee byoot." It was named after a local miner, Will Study, not after what dogs do when they meet each other.

RESTAURANTS

La Kiva: Dogs would love to go into this steak and barbecue place, because it's built partly underground and eating out here would remind them of tunneling after rabbits or Samantha's favorite quarry, gophers. But of course they can't. Nor can they join you on the patio outside. How-ever, the restaurant is located in the Big Bend Travel Park, and all the campsites have picnic tables. Alert dogs will quickly realize they can order to go at the restaurant and eat in the campground or perch on the bank of Terlingua Creek, which runs along the edge of the site.

The restaurant is on Highway 170 a mile and a half west of Study Butte. Turn into the parking lot at the west end of the bridge over Terlingua Creek. (915) 371-2250.

Road Runner Deli: There are two ways to enjoy the deli sandwiches and gourmet coffees served up at this eatery. You can eat at the shaded tables in front or take a cue from the name and have them prepare you a meal you can carry away and eat while looking at the Big Bend scenery of your choice. This is not "ruffing it" food: offerings include Reuben, club, corned beef, and vegetarian sandwiches served with coffees such as Guatemala Antiqua, Kenya AA, and Yemen Matari. Located at the Study Butte Mall, on Highway 118 between its intersection with Highway 170 and the western entrance to Big Bend National Park. (915) 371-2364.

Terlingua Ranch Restaurant: Sit at one of the tree-shaded picnic tables in front while you share Mexican food, burgers, or a variety of home-style cafe dishes with your hound. The restaurant is located at the headquarters of the Terlingua Ranch resort. The entrance is about 16 miles north of Study Butte on Highway 118; from that point it's another 16 miles by dirt road to the restaurant. (915) 371-2416.

PLACES TO STAY

Big Bend Motor Inn, Mission Lodge, and Terlingua Oasis RV Park: All three of these properties are under the same management. Rooms are $60 to $125 at the motor inn, which has a swimming pool, and $45 to $75 at the lodge across the highway. At the RV park, rates are $15 for full hookups and $8 for tent sites. Each site has a picnic table and barbecue grill. Coin-operated showers, rest rooms, and a pool are nearby. Leashed dogs are allowed at campsites and in the shelters ($19) and three tepees ($19). The shelters resemble large doghouses, but the tepees look like the real thing. The policies regarding dogs are the same at all the properties: Dogs may not be left in rooms alone, they must be kept quiet, you must walk them away from the motel, and you are responsible for any damage they cause. There is a 25 percent charge for reservations canceled without seven days' notice. At the intersection of Highways 118 and 170. P.O. Box 336, Terlingua, TX 79852; (915) 371-2218 or (800) 848-2363 (reservations only).

Big Bend National Park: See Big Bend National Park on page 47 for camping information.

Big Bend Travel Park: Dogs are welcome as long as they are leashed.

The campground's 45 RV sites all have full hookups and rent for $12. Terlingua Creek runs along the east side of the campground, and dogs are allowed to explore the creekbed. Because of its location next to the creek, this is one of the most shaded campgrounds in the Big Bend area. It has the added advantage of an on-site restaurant, La Kiva, where you can order to go and eat in the campground (see page 52).

The campground is on Highway 170 a mile and a half west of Study Butte, at the west end of the bridge over Terlingua Creek. Box 146, Terlingua, TX 79852; (915) 371-2250.

Longhorn Ranch Motel: You'll pay $47 to $58 for a room here, but you and your pooch will want to spend most of your time outdoors. You two can hike or mountain bike the ranch's 12,000 acres, or take a guided jeep tour. The motel is 13 miles north of Study Butte. HC 65, Box 267, Alpine, TX 79830; (915) 371-2541 or (800) 510-7415.

Terlingua Ranch: Four cabins at this resort ranch accept dogs with a $10 deposit. They rent for $38, which may be the biggest bargain in the Big Bend. Why? Because the price includes walking privileges on the ranch's 1,100 miles of dirt roads. (This is a big ranch—over 200,000 acres.) You'll see desert, mountains, and lots of empty spaces. Dogs must be leashed, and you may not leave the roads, since the land on either side is privately owned. The entrance is about 16 miles north of Study Butte on Highway 118; from that point it's another 16 miles by dirt road to the headquarters. HC 65, Box 220, Alpine, TX 79830; (915) 371-2416.

Wildhorse Station: Cabins with kitchens and 237 mountainous acres for your pooch to roam rent for $50. Well-behaved dogs are welcome. The cabins are about four miles north of Study Butte on Highway 118. HC 65, Box 276-C, Alpine, TX 79830; (915) 371-2526.

DIVERSIONS

Teach your dog to be a bird hound: Jim and Barbara Hines lead guided bird-watching trips all over the Big Bend area, including on private land at the Terlingua Ranch just north of Study Butte. Their dog Yaqui, a golden retriever/Great Pyrenees mix, is an accomplished bird dog who will go along and help show your dog the ropes. Hint: It's not polite to point. (915) 371-2356.

Go gaga at a gallery: The Big Bend attracts two main types of people (not counting tourists): migratory ne'er-do-wells who flit in and out, and incredibly tough and talented people who love the land enough to endure its hardships while wresting a living from it. Among the latter group are six local artists who share gallery space at the Terlingua Artists' Alliance. The works for sale include pottery, paintings, jewelry, and sculptures made from materials scavenged from the desert. Dogs in arms or small dogs on leash may shop with you; the last time I visited, at least one work of art featured a dog. The gallery is open Friday, Saturday, and Sunday afternoons from September through May. Located on Highway 170 about 1.5 miles west of Highway 118; (915) 371-2371 or (915) 371-2312.

TERLINGUA

Terlingua is one of those paradoxes of the Big Bend, a ghost town that teems with life. The whole town is owned by a private foundation run by Bill Ivey. His long-term goal is to restore the entire town as it was when quicksilver mines operated here, from about 1900 to 1942. Ironically, this peaceful little town furnished the mercury for the primers in America's bullets in two world wars. The only explosive material produced here today is the chili concocted at the world championship chili cook-offs held each November.

Dogs go pretty much where they want in Terlingua, since there is no town government and no county leash law. This is not to say that your dog can run wild in Terlingua (some people have made that very mistake, to their sorrow). If your pooch brought home notes from canine kindergarten that included phrases such as "Does not play well with others" or "Does not respect the property of others," you would be well advised to keep him on a leash while visiting. Terlingua dogs (and their owners) stand firm when guarding their territory. Even though Terlingua calls itself a ghost town, many of the houses are occupied. Do your sightseeing from the roads; walking among or climbing on the ruins is not allowed. However, you are welcome to walk to the old church, abandoned mine workings, and other sites in the town, including the historic cemetery.

RESTAURANTS

Starlight Theater Restaurant and Bar: Angie Dean and her friendly staff will be happy to serve you and your pooch at one of the benches out front, which have a magnificent view of Terlingua ghost town and the Chisos Mountains. Be prepared for company: There are a lot of local dogs roaming loose, and they become very friendly when they smell food. This restaurant is deservedly known as one of the best in the Big Bend. The T-bone and filet mignon steaks are big sellers, but a runaway local favorite is the boneless pork chop in chipotle sauce, a spicy concoction whose principal ingredient is smoked, dried jalapeño peppers. You can also have chiles rellenos, grilled catfish, grilled chicken salad, or desserts such as Key lime cheesecake, bourbon pecan pie, or chocolate raspberry bash, a pie whose chief ingredient is scrumptiousness. While you're waiting for your dinner, check out the dog paw prints in the concrete ramp leading to the rest rooms. There's gotta be a story behind those.

The restaurant is on the porch in Terlingua ghost town; (915) 371-2326.

PLACES TO STAY

Big Bend National Park: See Big Bend National Park on page 47 for camping information.

DIVERSIONS

Pet your pooch on the porch: One of the main forms of entertainment in Terlingua is sitting on the porch that runs across the length of the downtown storefronts, talking with friends and making frequent trips inside the Terlingua Trading Company for cold drinks. As many as 15 local dogs may show up for one of these porch parties, and out-of-town dogs are welcome, too. Nights when a full moon rises over the Chisos Mountains to the east may inspire some world-class howling; even dogs have been known to join in.

Rattle some bones: Dogs love visiting cemeteries. There's always the chance something interesting will turn up. Digging never enters their minds, I'm sure. (Samantha, who pursues gophers with a dedication that can only be described as diabolical, is looking at me with that "Yeah, right," expression.) This historic cemetery contains the graves of mine workers and local residents from Terlingua's boom days. Some of the markers are works of art.

The cemetery is at the junction of the two main roads into Terlingua from Highway 170.

Track down a ghost: A ghost town ought to be full of ghosts, and Terlingua probably has its share. A two-story barracks-like home broods on a hill overlooking the ghost town. It was built for Chisos Mining Company owner Howard Perry in 1906. Perry lived regally while paying workers a dollar a day to slave in his quicksilver mine, which underlay the town. He was not well loved. Pam Ware lived in the house for several years. "The mansion is supposedly haunted by a disgruntled worker who comes by looking for Perry," Pam says. "I would hear walking on the second floor and feel a presence. But it was a great place to live. I never closed the windows, because there were barn swallows living inside. One night a dust devil came inside, tore the sheets from my bed, and flung the clothes from the closet—I thought I was having a poltergeist!"

Follow the road from downtown Terlingua west to the mansion. Walk on past the mansion to the arroyo, and you'll reach the remains of the Chisos Mining Company smelter in about a quarter mile. People worked like dogs here; your hound may shiver if petted by one of their ghosts.

JEFF DAVIS COUNTY

Hot dogs, listen up. Jeff Davis County has the highest overall altitude in the state, averaging better than a mile above sea level. The mean annual temperature is a pleasant 60 degrees Fahrenheit. Bring your person here and chill out.

FORT DAVIS

Nestled in the Davis Mountains, Fort Davis is the highest town in Texas, and it's the perfect place to take an overheated hound during the dog days of August. Daytime highs will likely be only in the 70s or 80s, and nights are cool enough to make you want to snuggle with your schnauzer. The pace is slow here, the people are friendly, the scenery beautiful, and the local dogs abundant and free-roaming. There is no leash law, but due to the presence of traffic, javelinas, and mountain lions, keeping your canine close is advised. Leashes are required at both the state park and the national historic site here.

PARKS, BEACHES, AND RECREATION AREAS

• **Davis Mountains State Park** 🐾🐾½ *See* **⑤** *on page 34.*
Mountain vistas dominate this 2,678-acre park, views which will be lost on your canine friend. However, leashed dogs will be happy to accompany you on walks, and while you savor the scenery, they will just as intently survey the smells left by such residents as javelinas, deer, and mountain lions. Yes, there are mountain lions here, and payment of the entrance fee neither guarantees seeing a mountain lion nor being protected from being eaten by one.

A 4.5-mile walking trail connects the state park with the Fort Davis National Historic Site on the edge of the town of Fort Davis. This moderately difficult trail threads its way along valley floors for most of its length. However, dogs are barred from trails in the national historic site, so you will have to end your trip at the scenic overlook about 2.5 miles from the beginning. The view from the scenic overlook is well worth the trip. (If you prefer, you can drive to it following Park Road 3A.) You'll glimpse snatches of the town of Fort Davis in mountain passes to the east, and there's a fine view of mountains in all directions. Directly beneath you to the south, in the narrow canyon with vertical rock formations lining its walls, was the site of the original Fort Davis, which was destroyed by Indians during a period of abandonment.

A second scenic overlook also offers spectacular views of the valleys to either side. From here you'll also spy whitewashed Indian Lodge, a park motel where dogs are banned, as well as distant McDonald Observatory. The white dome-topped structures housing some of the world's most powerful and (scientifically speaking) productive telescopes are clearly visible atop Mount Locke, 13 miles (by road) to the west. To the south you'll spot what is claimed to be the largest collection of greenhouses in the world. They produce just one thing: tomatoes. Tomatoes are one of the few foods Samantha is not wild about.

Several picnic areas with tables and fire rings dot the park, but my favorites are the ones along Scenic Drive. They hang off the sides of the ridge; you can see for many, many West Texas miles. Most offer the bonus of being shaded by small Emory oak or juniper trees. Birds will occupy many of those trees; ask for a bird list at park headquarters. When you spot that red-naped sapsucker or gray catbird (out of his seat for a moment), you'll be able to check it off.

Camping in the park is allowed along a normally dry wash that joins Limpia Creek just outside the park. Most of the sites are shaded at least partially by oak trees. All have shaded picnic tables and combination fire rings/barbecue pits. Rest rooms with showers serve the area. Although the area is fairly open, the sites are spaced well apart. The 27 RV sites with full hookups are $13; the 343 sites with water and electricity are $11; and the 33 tent sites with water nearby go for $8. Your campsite may be visited by a herd of javelinas around dawn or dusk. Keep a firm grip on your pooch's leash if this happens; the little piglike creatures have razor-sharp tusks and do not hesitate to use them if threatened. Rattlesnakes also inhabit the park.

Reservations are strongly recommended and must be made by calling (512) 389-8900 between 9 A.M. and 6 P.M. Monday through Friday. You can reserve a type of site, but not a specific campsite. Spaces are handed out on a first-come, first-served basis on arrival.

State parks require that dogs be kept on a six-foot leash. Dogs may not enter any park building and may not be left unattended.

No matter when you visit, bring along some warm clothes. Park elevations range from just under to just over a mile above sea level, and even summer nights can be quite cool. Your pooch might appreciate it if you buy a bundle of firewood at park headquarters and light a cozy fire for her to snuggle up to.

There is a $3 per person entrance fee. The park is three miles west of Fort Davis on Highway 118. The office is open from 8 A.M. to 5 P.M. The park closes at 10 P.M. except to overnight guests. (915) 426-3337.

• **Fort Davis National Historic Site** 🐾 *See* ❻ *on page 34.*

History hounds will enjoy a stop here, even though they must remain on a six-foot leash and may not enter any building. Still, sniffing piles of coyote and fox dung on a parade ground once trod by the black infantry and cavalry soldiers who won West Texas from the Comanche and Apache Indians is enough to stir any dog's patriotic blood—or at least excite her sniffer, especially if the pile is fresh, which is likely. Dogs are not allowed on the trails into the mountains and valleys beyond the restored fort buildings, but they won't mind. Mountain lions roam those areas, and these big cats are ones dogs should meet only in their dreams. Meeting one in real life would be a nightmare, or maybe a nightcat.

A free brochure acquaints you with the history of the fort and includes a map identifying the restored buildings and ruins. Fort Davis was a key post in the battle to wrest the American West from the Indians, and it was also a stop on the stage road between San Antonio and El Paso. Its location on the banks of Limpia Creek, at the mouth of a canyon with vertical rock formations looking like thousands of soldiers standing at attention, makes the fort one of the most scenic in all the West. Your pooch will probably find the huge cottonwood trees at the picnic ground near the entrance the most interesting feature.

Admission is $2 per person. Fort Davis is on Highway 17/118 at the northern edge of the town of the same name. It is open from 8 A.M. to 5 P.M. from Labor Day through Memorial Day and from 8 A.M. to 6 P.M. during the summer. It closes on Christmas. (915) 426-3224.

RESTAURANTS

Indian Emily Cafe: The patio out front is the perfect place to observe the traffic on Highway 118—which will probably include a few town dogs out for a stroll—while you dine on burgers, chicken-fried steak, enchiladas, or fajitas. On Highway 118 north at Cemetery Road; (915) 426-2166.

Limpia Hotel Dining Room: Proprietors Lanna and Joe Duncan, mom and pop of Mancha (Spanish for spot) the dog and Gato (Spanish for cat) the cat, also own the Limpia Hotel next door. They invite you to leave your dog in your room while you eat, tie him to a tree in the courtyard between the hotel and the dining room, or order to go and eat at one of the benches in the courtyard while your pooch sniffs the savory herbs in the herb garden, ignoring your dinner and leaving you to eat in peace. Yeah, right. As if any dog worthy of the name is going to stand by without drooling as you eat a chicken-fried beef tenderloin, new potatoes mashed with the skins on, seafood, homemade biscuits, Joe's homemade pie, or Rio Grande chicken—a chicken breast charbroiled and then garnished with green chilies and jack cheese. On Highway 118 at the town square; (915) 426-3241.

Pop's Grill: Local variations on the burger comprise the menu here:

Pop's Belly Buster, a double-meat, double-cheese burger; the West of the Pecos, known elsewhere as a bacon cheeseburger but served here with onion rings; and the South of the Border burger, made with jalapeño jack cheese, chilies, and southwestern sauce. There's also the standard assortment of fried vegetables—potatoes, mushrooms, and okra—and ice cream. Eat at the picnic tables out front or, for a little more quiet, go around back to the picnic tables on grass where your pooch can lounge leash-free as you eat—Fort Davis has no leash law. And there's no ordinance about table manners, either. Enjoy. On Highway 118 north directly across from the entrance to Fort Davis National Historic Site; (915) 426-3195.

PLACES TO STAY

Davis Mountains State Park: See Davis Mountains State Park on page 57 for camping information.

Fort Davis Motor Inn: Rooms are $49 to $60 here; dogs stay free, but your room will be inspected for damage when you check out, and if your pooch has been a bad boy, you'll pay. There are a couple of acres out back extending to a creek where you can take Rover for a romp. The motel also has 14 RV sites with full hookups that rent for $12.50. The motel is on Highway 17 about a mile north of downtown. Box 1124, Fort Davis, TX 79734; (915) 426-2112 or (800) 80-DAVIS/803-2847.

Limpia Hotel: This historic, two-story hotel has been accepting guests since shortly after the turn of the century, but it's never been more well appointed than now. For one thing, owners Joe and Lanna Duncan were ably assisted in running the hotel in their early years by Mancha the dog and Gato the cat. Nowadays Mancha and Gato have moved to smaller but more private quarters at Joe and Lanna's home, but their place has been taken by Cinco, a champagne-colored cat who now rules as the resident innkeeper. Your pooch is still welcome at the Limpia, however. Any dog may stay for a $10 per night fee and a little sucking up to Cinco. Included are snoozing privileges in front of the fireplace in the parlor, sunning rights on the enclosed veranda, and cat-watching from the front porch, where *gatos* generally fear to tread because of the row of rocking chairs. Rooms are $68 to $125. The Duncans also rent the Limpia Cottage, a house on four acres at the edge of town, for $110 per night for up to four people. The yard is not fenced, and mountain lions have been seen just behind the house, so they advise keeping a close watch on your dog. In fact, when I last visited, a poodle had recently been attacked and fatally slashed by a javelina at the hotel downtown. Also available is the Mulhern House, which has three units ranging in price from $79 to $89 per night. Its one-acre yard is fenced, but not dog-tight. Dogs pay the $10 per night fee at both these properties as well. The Limpia Hotel, where you check in for all rentals, is on Highway 118 at the town square. Box 1341, Fort Davis, TX 79734; (915) 426-3237 or (800) 662-5517.

Prude Guest Ranch: Leashed dogs are welcome in the RV campground and on the trails of this family-owned ranch. They'll be welcomed by ranch dogs Clod, Mariah, and Echo. Sites with full hookups are $12.50; sites with water and electricity only are $8.50. P.O. Box 1431, Fort Davis, TX 79734; (915) 426-3202 or (800) 458-6232.

DIVERSIONS

Get high with your hound: The highest paved road in Texas ends atop Mount Locke at the University of Texas McDonald Observatory, and leashed dogs can visit but not go inside any building. You and a friend can take turns enjoying the view from the parking lot with your dog while the other takes a self-guided tour of the 107-inch telescope, which is active only at night. Guided tours ($3) take place daily at 9:30 A.M., 10:30 A.M., 11:30 A.M., 1 P.M., 2 P.M., and 3 P.M. At the visitor center at the base of the mountain, you and your pooch can attend a free star party every Friday, Saturday, and Sunday night starting about an hour after sunset. While you look through the little end of a telescope at the wonders of the universe, your dog can sneak up behind you and put a cold, wet nose in the precise spot that will cause the loudest exclamation. You may come up with a whole new appreciation for black holes and big bangs. To reach the observatory, go about 14 miles west of Fort Davis on Highway 118. Turn right onto Spur 78 and follow it a mile and a half to the top of the mountain. Large RVs or vehicles towing trailers should not attempt this climb due to steep grades and sharp curves. For more information, contact Box 1337, Fort Davis, TX 79734; (915) 426-3640.

Visit D.C.: No, they haven't moved the nation's capital to West Texas, although that wouldn't be a bad idea—it would save the expense of shipping all that B.S. up north. The D.C. in question here is Dixie Chicken, a Jack Russell terrier/Corgi cross who hangs out with mom Marilyn Caldwell at Javelinas and Hollyhocks, a nature store with an eclectic collection of stuff from around the world. Rubber snakes, lizards, and bugs are hot items, as are children's toys, mounted butterflies, and jellies. They also have books on birds, the Big Bend, and area history. Sport's favorite and mine, though, was the raccoon jigsaw puzzle.

But you were wondering about D.C.'s name, right? As with most mysteries (at least those about dogs), the answer is simple once you know it. D.C. and Marilyn once attended Texas A&M University in College Station, and a local eatery called the Dixie Chicken was Marilyn's favorite hangout. I made the mistake of mentioning to Marilyn that I was a graduate of Texas A&M's greatest rival, the University of Texas at Austin, and she then had D.C. perform the pièce de résistance from her repertoire of tricks. Holding a piece of dry dog food aloft in front of D.C.'s adoring eyes, Marilyn intoned, "D.C., would you rather be a Tea-Sipper [a term of derision used by A&M students to refer to University of Texas students] or a dead dog?" at which D.C. promptly sank to the floor and rolled onto her side.

Javelinas and Hollyhocks is at 107 Highway 118 only because, as Marilyn explained, they bought the used front door for the shop in Comfort and the number came on it; there are no house numbers in Fort Davis, nor street names. It's right across the highway from the Limpia Hotel; (915) 426-2236.

VALENTINE

DIVERSIONS

Heart your hound: Every year in February the post office in tiny Valentine (population 214) gets a rush of business. People from all over the United States send their Valentines to Postmaster Maria Carrasco for special hand canceling and remailing. You can win the heart of that special pooch by sending him or her a Valentine carrying the special postmark from Valentine, Texas. Send your addressed, stamped cards (with a return address, please) to Postmaster, Valentine, TX 79854–9998. Allow two weeks for remailing and delivery. Do this every year and collect the special imprints, which are designed by local schoolchildren, selected by the city council, submitted to the local postmaster, and approved by the powers that be in Washington, D.C. Postmaster Carrasco says the design usually involves hearts, but she can recall ones involving cacti and cowboy hats. So far there's not been a cancellation mark depicting a dog, she says, but the idea has been planted. If she starts seeing a lot of Valentines addressed to Fido, Rover, and Buster Dog, who knows what could happen? For information, call (915) 467-2912.

PRESIDIO COUNTY

STATE WILDLIFE MANAGEMENT AREAS

See the National and State Forests/State Wildlife Management Areas chapter starting on page 621 for important information and safety tips on visiting these areas with your dog.

• **Las Palomas Wildlife Management Area—Ocotillo Unit** 😺 😺 🐕
See page 626 for a description of Las Palomas Wildlife Management Area.

CANDELARIA

DIVERSIONS

Take your dog to the end of the line: Candelaria is one of those places that seems so far removed from the ordinary world as to be almost surreal. A school, a tiny general store, and a few scattered dwellings huddle at the end of the paved road. Park at the general store (there's no sign; it's the building with the gas pump out front) and walk half a mile south along the dirt road (past the rusting bulldozer) to the Rio Grande, which is just a narrow channel a few feet wide. The international "bridge" here is a homemade affair depending on some automobile frame members, fraying cable, angle iron, and rotting boards to keep you from getting your feet wet. Across the river about a mile is a small Mexican village, but while you may want to walk carefully across the bridge and back just to say you crossed, visiting the village is not recommended. Drug smugglers have been known to use this crossing, and it's best to mind your own business and not tarry.

You can follow a dirt road past the end-of-pavement marker in front of the general store and reach the Rio Grande a couple of miles farther on. The river may not be flowing due to irrigation upstream. If it is, when you reach the International Boundary and Water Commission gauging station, park and take your pooch for an international swim.

MARFA

PARKS, BEACHES, AND RECREATION AREAS

• **Activity Center Park** 🏃 *See* ❼ *on page 34.*

Covering only about 15 acres, this little park is mostly taken up by a large activity center and baseball fields, but there is a small, tree-shaded picnic ground on one side of the entrance road and an open grassy area on the other side. Rest rooms and a small playground make this a good rest stop for people as well as for leashed pooches.

From U.S. 90 West, turn north onto the first street west of the Dairy Queen, cross the railroad tracks, and turn into the park just past the large yellow building housing the activity center. There were no street signs when I last visited. Open from dawn to dusk. (915) 729-4315.

• **Fidel Vizcano Park** 🐾 *See* ❽ *on page 34.*

This park contains about 50 acres, most of which are taken up by a roping arena and athletic fields. However, there are some small trees, lots of grass to roam, and two shaded picnic tables. The roping arena is a good place for leashed city dogs to sniff some stuff they don't see too often.

From Highway 17 just south of the courthouse, go two miles east on F.M. 1112 to the park. (915) 729-4452.

• **Travis E. Self Memorial Park** 🔥 *See* ❾ *on page 34.*

This long, skinny park takes up about two acres, but it has trees, a walking path, a picnic area, and a playground. The eastern part of the park is fenced, but dogs are required to be on leash.

The park is behind the United States Post Office. From U.S. 90, go north on Highway 17 about a quarter mile to the post office; turn right onto F.M. 1112 at the sign for the fairground. When I last visited, there were no street signs. Open from dawn to dusk. (915) 729-4315.

PLACES TO STAY

El Paisano Hotel: Some might say this hotel has gone to the dogs since 1955, when Elizabeth Taylor, Rock Hudson, and James Dean stayed here during the filming of *Giant.* They'd be right: the hotel now has three resident dogs, and they welcome your pooch as long as she is housebroken. Rates run from $80 for a standard room to $125 for a suite with a kitchen. Alas, the hotel was remodeled in the 1970s, and the rooms are no longer as they existed in 1955. Any dreams you had about sleeping in a movie star's bed will have to remain just that. 207 North Highland Avenue, P.O. Box Z, Marfa, TX 79843; (915) 729-3145.

Holiday Capri Inn: You actually get two motels in one here, since the same people own and operate the Thunderbird Motel across the street. However, all arrangements are made through the office here. Any size dog is welcome; there are no fees or deposits. Rooms are $45 to $47. On U.S. 90 West. P.O. Box 575, Marfa, TX 79843; (915) 729-4326.

FESTIVALS

Marfa Lights Festival: You might not drive all the way to Marfa to look for the mysterious lights that are said to appear about two nights out of three, but throw in a street dance and arts and crafts booths on the courthouse square, and it's worth the trip. The festival takes place Labor Day weekend; for a schedule of events call the Chamber of Commerce at (915) 729-4942 or (800) 650-9696.

DIVERSIONS

Light up your life: For over 100 years, mysterious lights have appeared in and around the Chinati Mountains south of Marfa, and for just as long people have been trying to explain them. The lights go on, and so do the explanations, none of which have proved satisfactory. Everything from mirages to swamp gas to piezoelectricity has been suggested, but nothing has been proven. A recent theory suggests that the latter two may combine to form at least some of the lights. The idea is that methane or other combustible gas in sedimentary layers of rock deep in the mountains seeps outward and is ignited by piezoelectricity generated in quartz formations above.

Whatever the cause, the Marfa Mystery Lights are the biggest—and only—show in town, and people come from around the world to see them. The lights dance, zip, advance, recede, dim, hover, brighten, and disappear. They are said to appear on average two out of three nights. Sport and I must have been there on the third night when we went to see them. The only lights we saw were from trucks parked beside the road while the drivers napped. There is a public viewing area on the south side of U.S. 90 about nine miles east of Marfa. Look to the right of the red beacons on the radio tower to the south. For information, call (915) 729-4942 or (800) 650-9696.

Make your dog a Giant fan: I'm not talking windmills or baseball here. The movie *Giant* was partly filmed on a ranch west of Marfa. You can impress your pooch with your knowledge of movie trivia by driving 21 miles west of town on U.S. 90 and pulling into the roadside picnic area just past the Air Force aerostat installation. (It's the dirigible with the radar dome underneath that resembles a pregnant guppy.) Look southeast at the ranch headquarters a couple of miles away. The framework of telephone poles you see just to the left of the buildings are all that remain of the facade of the ranch house in the movie. The rest of the lumber was used to build doghouses, barns, and other vital structures on the ranch. Sport was not impressed, but she did want to chase the pronghorn antelope across the fence and the tumbleweeds blowing across the highway.

Sing the blues: Let your hound howl along as you sing "Oh, lonesome me," while driving the loneliest road in Texas. From the western edge of Marfa, take F.M. 2810 south. The pavement ends after 32 miles, and from that point it's another 20 miles by dirt road to F.M. 170 at Ruidosa. Locals know this as the Pinto Canyon Road, since it passes through a gorge by that name. The views of the canyon and the Chinati Mountains are fine, and the experience of driving the whole way without seeing another person (which is likely) is sure to get your adventurer's blood stirring. Take time to stop along the way and just listen to the silence. You'll cross a creek where your pooch can get a drink, and when you get to Ruidosa, you can do the same at the little store there in the bend of the highway, beside the crumbling ruins of an adobe church. The last time I visited, there was a very friendly local dog eager to be petted.

PRESIDIO

Author James Michener is said to have called Presidio his favorite town in Texas. He did so because of the town's past, not because of what is here today. Even dogs, who need no more than a semi-fresh roadkill to fascinate them, can become bored here.

But boredom is a matter of perspective and expectations. History hounds like Michener are fascinated by the fact that this area at the junction of the Rio Grande and Rio Conchos has been inhabited for thousands of years. Hounds like Sport are fascinated (and horrified) by the fact that this little town is frequently America's hot spot, registering temperatures well over 100 degrees Fahrenheit for days on end. Couple that with the fact that shade is scarce, and dogs would be advised to visit during the cooler months. There's not much for a dog to do but pant and dream of an accident involving an ice-cream truck.

PARKS, BEACHES, AND RECREATION AREAS

• **Big Bend Ranch State Natural Area** 🐾½

See page 43 for a description of Big Bend Ranch State Natural Area.

RESTAURANTS

La Escondida: The name of this restaurant means "hidden" in Spanish, and it is well chosen, since the place is a little hard to find. However, the search will be worth it. You and your pooch can dine in the outdoor courtyard on shrimp, brisket, or Mexican food. To find the restaurant, drive north on U.S. 67 to Cibolo Creek, just outside town. Take the first ramp to the left after crossing the creek and follow the signs and red ribbons to the restaurant. (915) 229-3719.

2

AMARILLO/
THE PANHANDLE

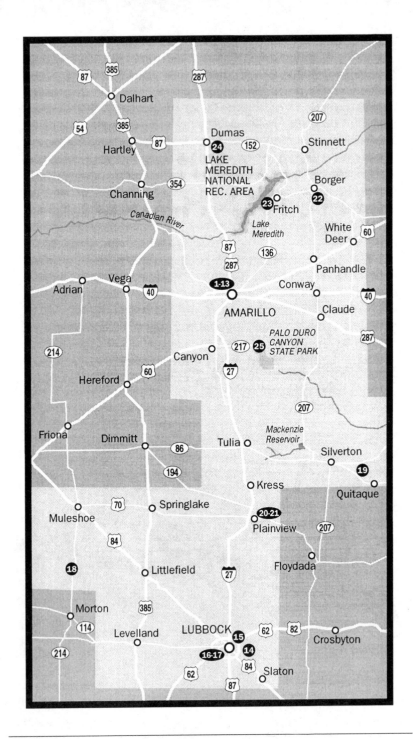

AMARILLO/ THE PANHANDLE

It's easy to dismiss the Panhandle as flat, dull, and far away from anything. Even people who've lived there have sometimes failed to connect with the magic. An executive for a large oil company, when explaining why he and his family were moving elsewhere, once described Amarillo, the Panhandle's principal city, as "a large truck stop."

That wasn't fair, as people who know Amarillo realize. Despite the popular conception of the Panhandle as a treeless plain, you will find an abundance of trees in Amarillo, as well as red-brick streets in historic neighborhoods just made for walking your pooch while admiring the architecture.

And all the good stuff isn't in Amarillo. Dogs will find the rest of the Panhandle to be much more than a place with a few towns where a dog can take long naps in the backseat while featureless miles roll by and then sniff a few tires in a parking lot during rest stops. In fact, two of the best places in all of Texas to take a dog are in the Panhandle, even though leashes are the rule everywhere.

Panhandle weather confounds and delights people and dogs who've never visited there. Much of the Panhandle lies in the region known as the High Plains. Note the word "high." Elevation in Texas increases as you travel north and west from the coast, and humidity decreases. The higher altitude and lower humidity make for some of the most pleasant weather in the state. Nights are agreeably cool even in the summer, which is considerably shorter than in regions farther south. We've been snowed on in Amarillo as late as the first of April and as early as the first of October. It has long been a dream of Sport, Samantha, and myself to find a way to bottle Panhandle August nights and sell them to the sweaty masses in Houston yearning for a break from the dog days of August. We'd call it Air of the Dog, and we'd make a fortune.

Panhandle people are some of the friendliest in the state, even though the idea of the traveling dog has yet to become firmly established here. Sport and I took pleasure in meeting exceptional people like Santa Marquez, manager of a drive-in restaurant in Dumas, who looked at us as though we were stupid when we asked if dogs were allowed to eat at the tables out front. "Of course dogs are welcome to eat here," she said. "Dogs are customers, too. Buy her a big burger and fries and let her sit right out there at a table and eat."

We also found places where your pooch can go on trail rides, watch clouds of migrating waterfowl, and hike some of the most scenic country in the whole state. Two of Texas's premier state parks, a national monument, and a national recreation area offer plenty of outdoor recreation for dogs. A number of smaller parks and wildlife refuges offer camping, wildlife viewing, picnicking, and hiking. If your pooch is a motor head, you can travel the Canadian River bottom in a four-wheel-drive vehicle from Lake Meredith all the way to the New Mexico border, a straight-line distance of some 60 miles. Take your camping gear and spend days exploring places where the feet of few pooches have been before.

Unfortunately, you and your pooch will have to eat lots of burgers while you are in the Panhandle. The severe winter climate and often boisterous winds mean that relatively few restaurants offer outdoor seating, and those that do—outside of Amarillo, the canine culinary capital of the Panhandle—are generally of the drive-in burger variety. However, we have yet to meet a hound hesitant to halve a hamburger.

We'll start with Amarillo and Lubbock, the two major cities in the Panhandle, and then branch out into other areas county by county.

AMARILLO

Amarilloans take pride in living in the "Queen City of the Panhandle," but it's much more than that. As one of the first cities to develop on the Great Plains, Amarillo became the commercial and cultural center not only for the Texas Panhandle but also for parts of Oklahoma, Kansas, New Mexico, and Colorado. And while dogs may not care about culture per se, they know that cultured people tend to treat dogs with *savoir vivre*. Therefore, dogs get treated pretty good in Amarillo. While there are no leash-free areas, dogs are welcomed in area parks, hotels, and restaurants.

PARKS, BEACHES, AND RECREATION AREAS

• **Belmar School Park** 🐾 *See* ❶ *on page 68.*

You may have to share this 14-acre park with kids on recess from the adjacent school, but what dog doesn't enjoy being fussed over by a bunch of squealing third-graders? The park is conveniently located along Interstate 40 and has a three-quarter-mile paved jogging trail circling large expanses of grass where soccer fields rule. There's no shade and no water, but there is a chemical toilet. You are responsible for cleaning up after your pooch, who must wear a leash.

From Interstate 40, exit on Coulter Road and take the eastbound access road to Hansford Street and the beginning of the park. All Amarillo city parks are closed from midnight to 5 A.M. (806) 378-3036.

• **El Alamo Park** 🐾½ *See* ❷ *on page 68.*

This is another of those parks convenient to Interstate 40 which has some other assets in addition to easy access. Large Siberian elm trees shade the part along the freeway, and we saw a couple of pooches with leashes flying in the breeze romping through the grass along a small drainage. Your pooch will have to stay on his leash to satisfy the law, however. The park has picnic tables with barbecue grills, rest rooms, and a playground as well as tennis courts and a softball field. You are responsible for cleaning up after your pooch.

From Interstate 40, take the Ross-Osage exit and follow the westbound frontage road to Roberts Street, where you'll take a right. You'll have to park on Roberts Street, as both streets paralleling the freeway are one-way eastbound. Closed from midnight to 5 A.M. (806) 378-3036.

• **Ellwood Park** 🐾🐾 *See* ❸ *on page 68.*

As downtown parks go, this one is spacious at 27 acres. In addition to athletic fields, it has lots of open, grassy spaces well shaded by large Siberian elms. When we last visited, it also had a healthy population of street people, but your leashed pooch should assure you freedom from being panhandled. If not, you might want to consider trading up to a larger, meaner-looking dog. The park also has playgrounds, rest rooms, picnic tables, and water. A paved jogging trail of 1.4 miles circles the park. When we last visited, a dalmatian puppy was eagerly towing his owner about. As at all Amarillo city parks, you are responsible for cleaning up after your pooch.

The park is at Park Place and Washington Street just south of downtown. Hours are from 5 A.M. to midnight. (806) 378-3036.

• **Gene Howe Park** 🐾🐾 *See* ❹ *on page 68.*

One small corner of this 20-acre park will be of most interest to your leashed pooch: the southwest one, where a wonderfully weedy pond beckons dogs to get their paws muddy while they see what they can flush out of the brambles. There are trees and grass aplenty, too, and picnic tables, rest rooms, and playground. Horseshoes, anyone? There is a place to pitch shoes as well. Your pooch would probably prefer you play with an old pair of tennies—they are easier on the teeth when fetched. You are responsible for cleaning up any doggy messes.

The park is at the intersection of Northeast 15th Avenue and Martin Road and is open from 5 A.M. until midnight. (806) 378-3036.

• **Lake Meredith National Recreation Area** 🐾🐾🐾½

See Lake Meredith National Recreation Area on page 92.

• **Martin Road Softball Complex** 🐾 🐾 *See* ❺ *on page 68.*

Despite the fact that the city designates this 52-acre site as a softball complex, this is a dog's park. It has a small lake with a resident goose population to bark at, grassy areas to prowl, weedy areas to explore, and trees to hike a leg on. For you, there are picnic areas, playgrounds, and rest rooms. You and your leashed pooch can share the half-mile jogging trail. Just across Martin Road, the next street to the east, is 20-acre Gene Howe Park, so if there are too many softball freaks here, you don't have to look far to find a more peaceful place. You are responsible for cleaning up after your pooch.

The park is at the intersection of North Mirror Road and Northeast 15th Avenue. It is closed from midnight until 5 A.M. (806) 378-3036.

• **Medical Center Park** 🐾 🐾½ *See* ❻ *on page 68.*

Your pooch may not be sick, but she'll love visiting this park located in the heart of Amarillo's medical complex. The 53-acre park stretches along both sides of an arroyo on Amarillo's west side, and leashed dogs will find much to delight in here. Just outside the park, the arroyo is typical High Plains terrain—semiarid, rocky, and stubbled with short grasses. In contrast, the manicured park contains a lake populated with geese and ringed with trees, a 1.5-mile paved jogging trail, several playgrounds, and picnic tables with barbecue grills. It's the ideal place for a pooch to spend some time while a person she knows visits the people vet. Clean up after your pooch or be subject to a $200 fine.

The park is located along both sides of Wallace Street between Southwest Ninth Avenue and Hagy Boulevard. From Interstate 40, exit on Coulter Road and go north on Coulter to Wallace; turn right and proceed to the park, which begins about half a mile down. The park is closed from midnight until 5 A.M. (806) 378-3036.

• **Oliver-Eakle Park** 🐾 *See* ❼ *on page 68.*

Just 2.5 acres make up this park, but the person for whom it is named looms much larger in Amarillo history. While your leashed pooch will want to check out the fountain, the large Siberian elm trees, and the picnic tables in the park, you'll find the Texas Historical Marker interesting. It tells the story of Melissa Dora Oliver-Eakle, who moved to Amarillo in 1895 and was one of its first real estate developers, always signing her name M. D. Oliver-Eakle because of prejudice against women in business. She built many of the homes in the area around the park as well as Amarillo's first skyscraper, a 10-story building downtown. Dog owners are responsible for picking up after their canine friends.

The park can be found at Southwest 28th Avenue and Polk Street, just off Interstate 27; take the 26th Avenue exit. It is closed from midnight until 5 A.M. (806) 378-3036.

• **Olsen School Park** 🐾 *See* ❽ *on page 68.*

Both you and your leashed pooch will be relieved when you find this six-acre park just south of Interstate 40. It has not only a small picnic area and playground but also rest rooms, a short paved jogging trail, and quite a few shade trees. Water is also available. You must clean up after your pooch.

From Interstate 40, exit at Bell Street and follow the eastbound frontage road to Anna Street. Turn right on Anna and follow it to Emil Street. Turn left and go one block to the playground/rest room area of the park. The park is closed from midnight until 5 A.M. (806) 378-3036.

• **Sam Houston Park** 🐾½ *See* ❾ *on page 68.*

The 14 acres of this urban park are well utilized, containing a variety of athletic fields as well as a 0.3-mile walking trail, but there's still plenty of open, grassy area for a leashed pooch to exercise, and the park is ringed by large Siberian elm trees, so there's napping and leg-hiking space, too. A few picnic tables with barbecue grills, rest rooms, and a playground complete the facilities. Water is available at the rest rooms. You are responsible for removing doggy doos.

The park is located at the corner of Line and Western Streets and is closed from midnight to 5 A.M. (806) 378-3036.

• **Southeast Regional Park** 🐾 🐾½ *See* ❿ *on page 68.*

Dogs were running loose everywhere when we visited this park, despite the city ordinance requiring leashes. Two sopping wet German shepherds left the small lake in the park and jumped into the back of their pickup truck while two dogs of indefinite ancestry (that's politically correct talk for mongrels) continued to race up and down the shoreline sniffing every clump of grass. The official size of this park is 337 acres, but only about 30 acres seemed to be usable when we were there. Much of the rest is undeveloped and heavily overgrown in weeds. There are rest rooms, picnic tables, playground, and a fishing pier on the small lake. Swimming and wading are not permitted in the lake, but that didn't stop the dogs we saw. There's lots of grass and small trees; this park will get better with time. You are responsible for cleaning up after your pooch.

The park entrance is off Southeast 46th Avenue just east of its intersection with Osage Street. It is closed from midnight until 5 A.M. (806) 378-3036.

• **Southwest Regional Park** 🐾½ *See* ⓫ *on page 68.*

A 128-acre park in the city should be just what every leashed dog is looking for. This is the perfect example of a modern planned urban park. It has 1.5 miles of paved jogging trails, brightly colored playgrounds, rest rooms, athletic fields, water fountains, and winding roads that take you by all of them to ample parking lots. But to a dog, it's just plain boring. It's too neat, too well planned, too well kept. Trees dot the perfectly flat park, all obviously planted about the same time and in such a manner as not to intrude on the soccer and softball fields. There are no weedy areas to sniff, no nut-bearing trees that might harbor a squirrel. Apartment-dwelling city dogs or traveling dogs desperate to get out of the car will welcome a stop, but they won't want to tarry long. In addition to requiring that dogs remain leashed, the city requires their human companions to remove all waste. There are trash cans available, but bring your own scooper.

The park is at Southwest 48th Avenue and Bell Avenue. From Interstate 27, exit on Bell Avenue and follow it north to the park. The park is closed from midnight until 5 A.M. (806) 378-3036.

• **Sunrise Park** 🐾 *See ⑫ on page 68.*

Booming into Amarillo from the east with a pooch whose eyeballs are floating and who's whining in your ear, you will surely welcome the sight of this 11.5-acre park with grass and trees for her and rest rooms for you. There are a few picnic tables with barbecue grills scattered around, and since the parkland includes a school, there's also playground equipment. As at all Amarillo parks, you are responsible for scooping.

From Interstate 40, exit at Eastern Street and drive four blocks north to Southeast 14th Avenue. Turn right and go one block to Tudor Street; turn left and you're there. The park is closed from midnight until 5 A.M. (806) 378-3036.

• **Thompson Memorial Park** 🐾🐾🐾½ *See ⑬ on page 68.*

If you and your leashed pooch are able to visit only one park in Amarillo, let it be this one. For starters, it's big—584 acres. In addition, the neatly mowed expanses of grass are heavily shaded by hundreds of large Siberian elm trees, and there are three—count 'em, three—lakes with grassy banks that permit pooches to get to the water. Between two of the lakes is a stone-paved spillway with swift-rushing water that just demands a pooch wet her paws as well as her whistle, even though people are forbidden from wading or swimming. We saw a yellow Lab wade right in up to her belly and then race off to hike a leg on a nearby tree. Her owners were picking up trash in the park; whether they were exempt from the leash law or just ignoring it, we didn't ask. We don't mind cutting a little slack for folks who keep the parks nice for the rest of us. (How's that for a sneaky introduction to the fact that you are responsible for cleaning up after your pooch in city parks?)

If your pooch isn't into chasing the squirrels darting about, perhaps he'll be more interested in barking at the ducks and geese on the lakes—they are suckers for a handful of crackers or other food tossed into the water. As you might expect in a major park, there are scores of picnic tables with barbecue grills, rest rooms, playgrounds, and a mile-long jogging trail.

The park is adjacent to U.S. 87/287 on the north side of Amarillo; exit Northeast 24th Avenue and go west one block to the entrance. The park is closed from midnight until 5 A.M. (806) 378-3036.

RESTAURANTS

The Bagel Place: The name says it all. You and your pooch can share a concrete doughnut at one of the benches in front. 2807 South Western Street; (806) 353-5985.

Bennigan's: This trendy place with a trendy menu—appetizers, burgers, salads, Mexican dishes, and more—welcomes you and your pooch at the benches out front. 3401 Interstate 40 West; (806) 358-7409.

The Black-Eyed Pea: "People are welcome to tie their dog to one of the trees in the grassy area outside while they eat, or they can eat at one of the benches out front," the dog-friendly manager said. "We'll even send out some water for a dog." Southern-style cooking is the thing here, as in hearty meals featuring meat and potatoes, but lighter fare is available, too. 3820 Interstate 40 West; (806) 355-9816.

Chili's Bar and Grill: The world championship chili cook-off in Terlingua, Texas, inspired the menu and decor of this chain of restaurants, but there's more than chili to be had, including ribs, quesadillas, salads, and burgers. You and your pooch can share on one of the benches out front. 3810 Interstate 40 West; (806) 379-6118.

Fenderz Bar and Grill: Have a burger at a table on the elevated deck right in front overlooking a busy street. 3605 Olsen Boulevard; (806) 358-6767.

Gardski's Restaurant and Bar: Benches on the covered walkway outside this eatery give you and your pooch a sheltered spot to share a burger, salad, fajitas, steak, or nachos. In the Wellington Square complex at Interstate 40 and Georgia Street; (806) 353-6626.

Macaroni Joe's Pasta House: If Italian food is for you, you'll find it here. In mild weather the restaurant sets up tables on the covered walkway; at all times there is a covered bench where you and your pooch can have your linguine or perhaps reenact the spaghetti-eating scene from *Lady and the Tramp.* In the Wellington Square complex at Interstate 40 and Georgia Street; (806) 358-8990.

Outback Steakhouse: Grab your meat-hungry hound and head for this popular steak house. Tell the greeters you have a pooch for a date and they will bring a tray and serve you at one of the benches out front. (Watching the cars whiz by on the freeway is the Outback version of television.) All they ask is that you keep your dog leashed and under control. (The sight of all those juicy steaks can drive some dogs wild.) The menu includes chicken and fish dishes, too. 7101 Interstate 40 West; (806) 352-4032.

Schlotzsky's: Sandwiches and pizzas on sourdough baked fresh daily will make you and your pooch glad there is a bench on the covered walkway outside where you can eat. 1619 South Kentucky Street in the Wellington Square complex; (806) 359-4445.

Sonic Drive-In: If this burger, fries, and hot-dog chain of drive-in eateries really wants to increase its business, maybe it ought to get Benji to do its commercials instead of Frankie Avalon. ("Who?" barked Sport. See what I mean?) The following locations welcome dogs at their tables in front: 7417 West 34th Avenue, (806) 352-4221; 3600 South Washington Street, (806) 355-0445; 2707 South Georgia Street, (806) 354-2238; and 1714 South Western Street, (806) 351-0022.

Wienerschnitzel: Down a dog at the tables out front. Down, I say, down! Good dog. 2801 South Western Street; (806) 355-7971.

Zest-E-Burger: Guess what you and your pooch will eat at the tables out front. 2418 Amarillo Boulevard East; (806) 376-9491.

PLACES TO STAY

A & A Longhorn Trailer Park: Dogs must be leashed. Both RV and tent sites are $10. The park is located at Interstate 40 and Arnot Street; take Exit 60. 17000 Interstate 40 West, Amarillo, TX 79121; (806) 359-6302.

Best Western: Rooms are $76 to $81 for you, plus $10 for your dog. 1610 Coulter Road, Amarillo, TX 79106; (806) 358-7861.

Big Texan Steak Ranch Motel: Your pooch will be fascinated to know that the chief claim to fame of this hotel is that it is next door to the Big Texan Steak Ranch restaurant, which offers a 72-ounce steak with all the trimmings free to anyone who can eat it within one hour. Unfortunately, this offer is not open to dogs. However, if you and your pooch station yourselves just outside the door and look like you are starving, there should be a steady parade of well-stuffed doggy bags emerging, if you catch my drift. Rooms are $45 to $65, and there is a $20 deposit for dogs. 7701 Interstate 40 East, Amarillo, TX 79104; (806) 372-5000 or (800) 657-7177.

Budget Host: Rooms are $40 to $50. Any size dog is welcome with a

$10 deposit. 2915 Interstate 40 East, Amarillo, TX 79104; (806) 372-8101 or (800) 283-4678.

Comfort Inn West: Your dog is welcome, but you may not leave her unattended in the room. Rooms are $42 to $90. 2100 South Coulter Road, Amarillo, TX 79106; (806) 358-6141 or (800) 228-5150.

Econo Lodge Suites: Rooms are $54. Dogs are allowed in smoking rooms only; there is a $5.65 fee. 1803 Lakeside Drive, Amarillo, TX 79104; (806) 335-1561 or (800) 847-6556.

Hampton Inn: "We have absolutely no fees, deposits, or size limits. Just bring your dog!" said the cheery reservations clerk. Rooms are $49 to $71. 1700 Interstate 40 East, Amarillo, TX 79103; (806) 372-1425 or (800) 426-7866.

Interstate Motel and Campground: Campsites are $11. 7401 Amarillo Boulevard West, Amarillo, TX 79016; (806) 355-9987.

KOA Amarillo: RV sites go for $20 to $22; tent sites are $17. Dog owners are expected to pick up after their pooches. 1100 Folsom Road, Amarillo, TX 79107; (806) 335-1792.

Lake Meredith National Recreation Area—Rosita Flats: The Rosita Flats area is for four-wheel-drive recreation, and the last time we checked, dogs were four-wheel drive. This primitive area with no facilities other than chemical toilets is designated for off-road use of four-wheel-drive vehicles. A labyrinth of rutted trails laces the bed of the Canadian River and assaults nearby hills. If you and your pooch enjoy blasting down dirt trails and through shallow water in four-wheel drive, you'll love this place. If you like, you can drive and camp all the way to the New Mexico border in the riverbed. There seems to be only two rules: Helmets and leashes no longer than six feet are required. Otherwise, you are free to walk or drive in the river—only inches deep at normal levels—or anywhere else you please. Camping is permitted, but there are no facilities; the only water available is in the river. There is plenty of shade from large cottonwood trees, and the sandy riverbank provides lots of waterside camping spots. Many people park under the bridge and walk upstream in the shallow river. Cottonwood trees shade the narrow channel, and small side canyons sometimes offer surprises. Sport and I found a small waterfall pouring into a fern-shrouded pool.

At the Canadian River crossing of U.S. 87/287, turn east on a dirt road at the south end of the bridge. Drive two miles to the center of the Rosita area. (806) 857-3151.

Northview RV Park: RV sites are $12. 100 West Mobley, Amarillo, TX 79108; (806) 381-1059.

Overnight Trailer Inn: "We're glad to see dogs come," said the owner.

"The only thing we ask is that they be kept inside at night so there's no barking." RV sites are $22. 900 Lakeside Drive, Amarillo, TX 79118; (806) 373-1431.

Radisson Inn—Airport: Small dogs are welcome. Rates are $69 to $89. A credit card imprint or a $100 deposit is required for your pooch. 7909 Interstate 40 East, Amarillo, TX 79104; (806) 373-3303 or (800) 333-3333.

Travelodge East: Rates are $45 to $55. 3205 Interstate 40 East, Amarillo, TX 79104; (806) 372-8171 or (800) 255-3050.

DIVERSIONS

See stupid people tricks at Cadillac Ranch: People do nutty things. Dogs know this. People eat juicy steaks and sometimes don't even bother to throw a starving dog the bone. They let cats live in the house and then blame the dog for fleas. Such is life. Well, as they say, art imitates life, and Cadillac Ranch is an example of the crazy things people do sometimes. Local eccentric Stanley Marsh III, who obviously has more money and time than worthwhile things to do, had 10 tail-finned Cadillacs half-buried in a field along Interstate 40 on the western edge of Amarillo. Supposedly they are inclined at the same angle as the sides of the Great Pyramid in Egypt. It's considered a work of modern art (!?), and you and your leashed pooch can walk into the field to view them close up if you like. (If your pooch hikes a leg on one of them, perhaps it's because the Egyptians considered cats sacred. Or maybe he is an art critic. Or maybe he just needed to go.) As you drive around town you'll notice many diamond-shaped signs saying things like "This Sign Is Art," "Wild Horses," "We Eat the Dead Cafe—Exit 1 Mile," and "Rich, Retired, Overfed." The aforesaid Mr. Marsh is responsible for those, too. People in Amarillo humor him. They're not sure if he's crazy or just a little odd. In Texas, you try not to mess with people like that.

Heading west from Amarillo, exit Interstate 40 at Soncy Road and continue on the frontage road to the next overpass, at Helium Road. Turn left under the overpass and proceed east on the frontage road about a quarter mile to a turnout at a break in the barbed-wire fence. (There's a sign for the Soncy Road exit right at the parking area.) Follow the path 200 yards to the cars. Heading east into Amarillo, exit Helium Road and stay on the frontage road to the parking area.

Live it up at Llano Cemetery: Dogs love cemeteries. They are such good places to dig for bones. Your leashed pooch is welcome to enjoy the trees, grass, and ponds at this site as long as he does not chase the ducks and geese on the ponds (or dig for bones). Sport and Samantha are proud of this cemetery because mom Sally Victor and dad Larry

Hodge did the research that got this cemetery listed on the National Register of Historic Places, the first cemetery in Texas to be so honored. Another item of interest regarding this place is that it holds the grave of a man named Smithee, the name Hollywood moviemakers credit as the director of any movie so bad the real director does not want to be identified with it—a real dog, in other words. Supposedly the name Smithee was chosen because no real person was named that. Well, there was at least one, and he's buried here.

The entrance is on Southeast 27th Avenue just east of Interstate 27 (exit at 26th Avenue and go east; it joins 27th Avenue just before going under the railroad overpass). The cemetery is open weekdays from 8 A.M. to 5 P.M. and weekends from 8 A.M. to 4 P.M. (806) 376-4538.

Pull for the dog: Go by the Wellington Square complex, Building D, and check out the bronze sculpture of the boy and his dog engaged in a tug-of-war in the covered area at the southeast corner of the building. It's by artist Ann LaRose, and even your dog will think it's cute. It looks so real Sport wanted to swap end-sniffs. At the corner of Interstate 40 and Kentucky Street, just east of the Ambassador Hotel.

Torture your terrier: There's one sure way to inflict severe psychological trauma on a dog: take him shopping at PetsMart. Any store that offers 720 kinds of dog food qualifies as a torture chamber for the pooch who wants to eat everything in sight (like our Samantha). Then there are those neat collars and spiffy leashes and the grooming area and— yikes!—the vet. PetsMart is a one-stop shopping center for dogs, and your pooch is welcome to choose her own toys, food, and other creature comforts herself. All you have to do is pay the bill. And drive her there. You are the one with the car keys, right? PetsMart in Amarillo is at 2800 Soncy Road; (806) 351-1171.

LUBBOCK

Lubbock suffers by comparison to its sister city in the Panhandle, Amarillo. (Detractors would say Lubbock suffers by comparison to anywhere. Lubbock has long been the butt of jokes such as the one about the person with six months to live whose doctor advised her to move to Lubbock. "Will I live longer?" she asked. "No, but it will seem like a year," the doctor replied.) Such stories tend to play up Lubbock's negatives and ignore its positives. Unfortunately, for dogs there are few positives. Dogs must be leashed everywhere, and we could find few places that actually welcomed them. For dogs, anyway, Lubbock seems destined to remain a stop on the way to someplace better.

PARKS, BEACHES, AND RECREATION AREAS

• **Buffalo Springs Lake** 🐾🐾½ *See* **⑭** *on page 68.*

The Texas Panhandle is full of surprises, and this spring-fed lake is one of them. Private homes take up much of the waterfront, but there's still plenty of lakeside camping and picnic areas. For leashed dogs, the best part of the park is the Llano Estacado Audubon Society Nature Trail, a 1.7-mile double loop that descends 155 feet—a dizzying distance on the pancake-like plains—to a wooded river bottom along the North Fork of the Double Mountain Fork of the Brazos River (try saying that 10 times very fast!). Ask for a trail brochure at the entry gate. The narrow, rocky trail has lots of switchbacks that had Sport and I wondering at times who was leading whom. We met a family with two collies frisking free, making me feel guilty for having Sport on a leash, but that's the rule. The trail affords excellent views of the lake, the pocket of trees in a bowl-like depression below the dam, and the encroaching subdivision of expensive homes on the far shore. The lakefront is largely unsuitable for walking, since heavy vegetation prevents access in most places, and dogs are not allowed on the swimming beaches or in the water. The lake and associated vegetation attract birds such as northern harriers, red-tailed hawks, roadrunners, mockingbirds, robins, painted buntings, scis-sor-tailed flycatchers, and yellow-billed cuckoos.

The park has three camping areas, all next to the lake and all well shaded by large trees. Tent camping with no water or electricity is $10 and is permitted anywhere within the designated area. The 50 sites with water and electricity are $12, and 30 sites with full RV hookups are $15. Reservations are not accepted.

Admission is $2.50 per person. The park is six miles east of Interstate 27 on East 50th Street, which becomes F.M. 835. It's open 24 hours a day. For more information, contact Buffalo Springs Lake, Route 10, Box 400, Lubbock, TX 79404; (806) 747-3353.

• **Mackenzie Park** 🐾🐾 *See* **⑮** *on page 68.*

Formerly a state park, this 248-acre site was turned over to the city because the state lacked funds to maintain it—and it's still suffering from lack of TLC. Sport and I dropped by for a pit stop, and she—on the required leash—completed her business promptly. Large expanses of grass and many trees make the park a traveling dog's delight. However, you may want to take care of any personal needs before you enter. After driving around a while, we finally found a rest room, but its floor was awash in some unknown liquid, and the overflowing toilet was inoperative. Peeeyuuuu!

The chief attraction is the prairie dog town, a space of about two acres enclosed by a low concrete block fence, inside which the members of an active—very active—colony of prairie dogs graze, keep watch for soaring hawks and hungry-looking dogs, and fascinate visitors with their industrious demeanor. Sport said watching all that running about and barking made her tired. This from the dog who will bark all night at a raccoon or skunk in the yard.

In addition to ample space for a leashed dog to walk, the park has picnic tables with grills, playground equipment, a golf course, and athletic fields. When we last visited, the city of Lubbock was constructing new facilities and upgrading old ones; perhaps that will solve some of the problems we found.

From Interstate 27, take Exit 4 and follow the signs to the park; it adjoins the freeway. The park is open from sunrise to midnight. (806) 775-2687.

• **Tech Terrace Park** 🐾 *See* ⑯ *on page 68.*

Spanning 18 acres, this park appeared to be the in place for a Sunday afternoon romp for Lubbock dog lovers when Sport and I visited. Despite a sign warning of a $200 fine for failure to keep dogs leashed, we saw a number of free-roaming canines happily chasing Frisbees, running, jumping, and rolling in the grass. There's plenty of shade for resting weary dogs, too.

The park is on Flint Avenue between 23rd and 25th Streets, just south of the Texas Tech University campus. It is open from sunrise to midnight. (806) 775-2687.

• **Wagner Park** 🐾 *See* ⑰ *on page 68.*

This nine-acre park is just south of the Texas Tech University campus and has plenty of grass and trees to occupy the leashed pooch, plus a playground, rest rooms, and a few picnic tables. At 26th Street and Flint Avenue, the park is open from sunrise to midnight. (806) 775-2687.

RESTAURANTS

Buffalo Springs Lake Marina Restaurant: Chow down on a burger or hot dog at one of five shaded lakeside picnic tables or a half dozen benches. There's no address; just follow the Pony Express Trail from the entrance to the marina. (806) 741-0758.

Jim Dandy Drive-in: Have a hamburger at one of the shaded tables out front. 2601 Clovis Road; (806) 762-4012.

Josie's Restaurant: You and your *perro* can share Tex-Mex food at one of the shaded tables out front. 212 University Avenue; (806) 747-8546.

Sonic Drive-In: This national chain serves up burgers, fries, and hot dogs. You and your pooch can eat at the tables out front at the following

Lubbock locations: 4611 34th Street, (806) 797-1626; 5722 Fourth Street, (806) 785-3121; 8010 University Avenue, (806) 748-0055.

Tommy's Famous Burgers: Eat at one of the tables under the trees in the parking lot. 117 University Avenue; (806) 763-5424.

PLACES TO STAY

Astro Motel: Rooms are $34 to $40. Dogs stay for a $25 deposit. 910 Avenue Q, Lubbock, TX 79401; (806) 765-6307.

Buffalo Springs Lake: See Buffalo Springs Lake on page 80 for camping information.

Days Inn—University: Rooms are $45 to $50. Pets must be kept in a carrier. 2401 Fourth Street, Lubbock, TX 79415; (806) 747-7111 or (800) 325-2525.

Holiday Inn Lubbock Plaza: Dogs under 20 pounds are welcome. Rooms are $84 to $94. 3201 South Loop 289, Lubbock, TX 79423; (806) 797-3241 or (800) 465-4329.

KOA Lubbock: "Pets er happiest with ther' owners. Please leash 'em and walk 'em outside our campground tree line boundries [sic] or in the designated pet walkin' area. Plastic baggies er great fer accidents. Areas IN and NEAR main buildings, playground, telephones, sidewalks, rest rooms, etc. are off limits to pets." The above is a direct quote from the campground brochure. It also bore such admonitions as "Washin' yur horse an drainin yur oil ain't allowed" and "Our children 'n pets er special! Campers 'n your guests, keep them horses at a walk (5 mph) please." There are 78 RV sites ($19), some with small trees; 10 tent sites ($16); and two cabins ($26). Dogs are permitted in cabins if yew kin brang yoresef to clean up after 'em. Sorry. Sport (or the devil) made me do it. The campground is in northwest Lubbock at the intersection of U.S. 84 and Kent Road. 5502 County Road 6300, Lubbock, TX 79416; (806) 762-8653.

Motel 6: All Motel 6s allow one small pooch per room. The rate is $38. 909 66th Street, Lubbock, TX 79412; (806) 745-5541.

Residence Inn by Marriott: Rates range from $45 to $105. Dogs must pay a $75 cleaning deposit. 2251 South Loop 289, Lubbock, TX 79423; (806) 745-1963 or (800) 331-3131.

Super 8 Motel: Rooms are $48 to $59. Dogs stay for a $25 deposit. 501 Avenue Q, Lubbock, TX 79401; (806) 762-8726 or (800) 800-8000.

Townhouse Inn: Rooms are $37; dogs stay for a $10 deposit. 4401 Avenue O, Lubbock, TX 79412; (806) 747-1677.

Village Inn Motel: Any old hound is welcome. Rooms are $50. 4925 Brownfield Highway, Lubbock, TX 79407; (806) 795-5281.

FESTIVALS

Buddy Holly Music Festival: If you love Buddy Holly music and your pooch loves sniffing around food booths and mooching handouts from total strangers, you'll want to be in Lubbock on the first weekend in September. Outdoor concerts featuring Buddy Holly songs and food booths serving up tasty treats will be along Avenues F, G, and H between 18th and 19th Streets. For information, call (806) 749-2929.

Fourth on Broadway: Celebrate the Fourth of July with a parade, street fair, concert, and fireworks display July 4 on Broadway between University Avenue and Avenue Q. For information, call (806) 749-2929.

Lights on Broadway Holiday Festival: Get your pooch in the mood for Christmas (and perhaps glean a few hints about what she'd like under her tree) the first weekend in December. Christmas lights, Christmas music, and Christmas goodies all point toward the biggest holiday of the year for dogs. It all happens at Broadway and University Avenue. Call (806) 749-2929 for information.

DIVERSIONS

Collar your collie: Dogs love getting new collars and then showing them off to all their buddies. "I have a new collar," you can almost hear them say. "My collar is prettier than your collar." But, when asked about their new collars, they typically reply, "Oh, this old thing? Well, yes, those are diamonds. You're still wearing that one from last year, aren't you, dear? Zircons look so nice on you. I must be going now. I have an appointment to have my nails done at PetsMart." PetsMart is the on-Earth version of Dog Heaven. Dogs can shop there for food, fashion, and fun items as well as books on how to train their humans. The Lubbock store is at 6801 Slide Road; (806) 798-0717.

Take your buddy to see Buddy: A heroic-size bronze statue honors Lubbock's most famous son, rock and roller Buddy Holly. Walk of Fame bronze plaques honor other West Texans who have made significant contributions to the entertainment industry. Your pooch can tread on the greats and howl over their sad fates. Is there a country-and-western tune in there somewhere? Arooooooooo! Check it out at Eighth Street and Avenue Q.

BAILEY COUNTY

MULESHOE

PARKS, BEACHES, AND RECREATION AREAS

• **Muleshoe National Wildlife Refuge** 🐾 🐾 ½ *See* ⑱ *on page 68.*
This 5,809-acre wildlife refuge—the first of its kind in Texas—pre-

serves some of the few playa lakes untouched by agriculture, surrounded by an unspoiled short-grass prairie ecosystem. When full, the three playa lakes furnish 600 acres of water for use by migrating waterfowl. The diversity of plants and animals this habitat supports led to the refuge being designated a Registered Natural Landmark. As you might expect, dogs must be leashed. The good news is the leash can be up to 20 feet long. Even better, admission is free.

Sport and I last visited in early fall, before the annual migration brought the 100,000 or so sandhill cranes and thousands of geese, but we found the prairie dog town quite interesting enough. You can drive right into it, and the little critters sit at the entrances to their burrows and bark fiercely at you, so be sure you have firm control of your pooch. Sport was desperate to catch one.

The sandhill cranes, however, are the chief attraction. From early October until February, the refuge harbors one of the largest concentrations of these birds in North America. Their raucous honks fill the skies with a wild melody that stirs the soul. In addition, 282 species of birds have been spotted here since the refuge was established in 1935; obtain a list at the refuge office.

A small campground/picnic area allows you and your pooch to spend the night being serenaded by the waterfowl, but be advised that these birds hold uproarious slumber parties every night; they do not sleep. The camping is free, but the 13 sites offer only a picnic table and a mowed area. Water and composting toilets complete the amenities; there is no shade.

A nature trail begins by the campground rest rooms and passes through a wooded area that's a good place to observe nesting birds such as mourning doves, horned larks, loggerhead shrikes, and northern mockingbirds. You'll probably find walking the refuge roads (closed during the migration season) more interesting and rewarding, since you will be able to observe the waterfowl on the various lakes.

The refuge is 20 miles south of Muleshoe on Highway 214. Turn west onto a gravel road at the refuge sign and follow it two miles to the visitor center, which is open Monday through Friday from 8 A.M. to 4:30 P.M. The visitor center lobby remains open 24 hours; you can pick up a bird list and brochure there. Visitor registration is required, though entrance is free. For more information, contact P.O. Box 549, Muleshoe, TX 79347; (806) 946-3341.

PLACES TO STAY

Economy Inn: You and your pooch can stay in a smoking room for $32. There are no fees or deposits for dogs. 2701 West American Boulevard, Muleshoe, TX 79347; (806) 272-4261.

Heritage House Inn: No fees, but no fleas is the rule at this motel. Dogs are definitely welcome here. "Some dogs are better behaved than children," the clerk told us. (As if we didn't know that.) There's a guest laundry and a heated pool, as well as a large area behind the motel for walking your pooch. 2301 West American Boulevard, Muleshoe, TX 79347; (806) 272-7575 or (800) 253-5896.

Muleshoe National Wildlife Refuge: See Muleshoe National Wildlife Refuge on page 83 for camping information.

Valley Motel: Clean dogs may stay here for free, but only for one or two nights. Rooms are $36. 1515 West American Boulevard, Muleshoe, TX 79347; (806) 272-4279.

BRISCOE COUNTY

QUITAQUE

Texas abounds with place names that mystify nonnatives and confound those who would follow accepted rules of pronunciation. Many a tongue has tripped over names like Mexia, Elgin, Waxahachie, Pontotoc, and Canutillo. But Quitaque gave even locals so much trouble that long ago they settled on a most undoglike pronunciation: "Kitty–kway." Just to be sure strangers get it right, the name is spelled out phonetically on roadside signs as you enter town. Even with the feline slant, dogs are still welcome here. Sport and I rubbed noses with a trio of local good old dogs in the parking lot of the town's one convenience store.

Dogs interested in etymology (and what dog isn't?) love speculating about the meaning of the name *Quitaque,* an Indian word. One explanation is "end of the trail," which seems quite appropriate in view of the fact that trails are one of the big attractions here. Another story says the word refers to two local buttes that resembled piles of horse manure. That explanation stinks. Still another story says the name is a slightly corrupted version of the name of a local Indian tribe whose name was translated by settlers as "whatever one steals." Perhaps your pooch can offer a better explanation. Sport suggested that the name refers to a dock where trainloads of cats brought to this area for dogs to chase were unloaded, but then she's a terrible punster.

Quitaque marks the midpoint of the second longest hiking trail in Texas, the 65-mile Caprock Canyons State Park Trailway. Serious hikers (as well as mountain bikers and horseback riders) can travel from South Plains, east of Plainview, all the way to Estelline, northwest of Childress.

Along the way the trail traverses the rolling Lower Plains, crosses the rugged Caprock escarpment, and stretches across the table-flat High Plains. There's even a 742-foot segment through an abandoned railroad tunnel. If the thought of walking 65 miles makes your dog's dogs whine, you can choose from five trails within Caprock Canyons State Park ranging from 1.5 to 5.5 miles.

PARKS, BEACHES, AND RECREATION AREAS

• **Caprock Canyons State Park** 🐾 🐾 🐾 ½ *See ⑲ on page 68.*

If your long-legged pooch likes to really stretch her legs (even though it must be on a leash), she'll love this 13,906-acre park and its 16 miles of trails.

The fascinating geology of the park began 250 million years ago, when the area was a series of mudflats and salt pans on the shore of a shallow, receding sea. By the time another 50 million years had passed, dinosaurs roamed a tropical lake basin here. A mere 2.5 million years ago, now-extinct zebras, giant tortoises, cheetahs, beavers, saber-toothed tigers, mastodons, and, yes, wild dogs hunted around an ancient lake. Only 10 thousand years ago, Native Americans hunted bison near the present Lake Theo. At that time the rim of the Caprock was perhaps half a mile closer to the lake than it is today. It's hard to believe, but millions of years ago the Caprock extended nearly to the site of present-day Fort Worth, nearly 200 miles to the southeast. Indians were attracted to the area by abundant game, clean springwater, firewood, chert for making arrowheads, and the shelter the canyon walls provided from winter winds. Some 500 years ago, this land was the home of the Apaches, who had no horses but used large dogs as beasts of burden. In historic times the parklands were part of the famed JA Ranch, a partnership between pioneer trail driver Charles Goodnight and Scot John Adair. One of Goodnight's passions was saving the buffalo he and other ranchers displaced from the Great Plains. Fittingly, the park today is home to the largest buffalo herd in the state park system. Pronghorn antelope also roam the park, and golden eagles winter here.

Within the park are 16 miles of hiking trails; a total of about 90 miles are planned. These trails vary from easy walks through fairly level terrain to strenuous climbs to the heads of canyons. Obtain a park map at headquarters; it shows contour lines that will help you estimate the relief of the trail(s) you plan to hike. There is water available for your pooch on some of the trails, but you should carry a supply for yourself. Do be aware when hiking portions of the trails in the bottoms of canyons that thunderstorms upstream can produce dangerous flash floods. Be aware of the weather and be prepared to move to a place of safety if rain comes. Sport and I saw one place where water had recently flowed six feet deep in a small draw we were hiking. Also be aware that rattlesnakes are found in the park.

Sport and I hiked a portion of the 5.5-mile Upper Canyon Trail and found it ideal for a warm September day. We walked in the bed of the South Prong of the Little Red River, which was flowing clear, cool water that Sport found quite drinkable as well as splashable. She hit a hot raccoon trail not long after we dropped into the canyon and had to be forced to stop tracking and admire the intricate lacy patterns of gypsum deposits in the red canyon walls. Sport's passion is zoology, not geology. We also found some deer tracks and sent a few lizards skittering across the rocks. Since walking the bottom of the canyon requires crossing and recrossing the stream numerous times and much of the time you are walking on rocks that can turn and slip, waterproof footwear with good ankle support is a must for walking this trail. At its midpoint this trail climbs sharply to Fern Cave, a high point from which you can see literally for a hundred miles. If you are really into scenic views and don't mind walking another four miles, follow the Haynes Ridge Overlook Trail, which branches off from the Upper Canyon Trail about a quarter mile southeast of Fern Cave. Following the high ridge leads to another scenic overlook with a view that stretches for miles. To make a complete loop back to the trailhead near the Little Red Camp requires hiking another 1.5 miles along the Canyon Loop Trail, making the total trip seven miles.

The five-mile Lower Canyon Trail also begins at the Little Red Camp and follows the beds of both the South and North Prongs of the Little Red River for much of its length. The trail joins the Canyon Loop Trail and returns to the trailhead after a total trip of 6.5 miles.

The Eagles Point Trail connects a parking area on the park road about half a mile east of the Little Red Camp with the park road spur to Lake Theo. The one-way length of this trail is two miles. Eagle Point is a prominence of the Caprock about half a mile from the northern end of the trail. It offers a sweeping view of the eastern half of the park. If you wish to walk some of the trails halfway, contact the park office about their shuttle service. Charges range from $5 to $7 per person; reservations are required.

The park offers a number of camping areas. Because this park is far from any major city, reservations are usually not necessary except on weekends and holidays. However the standard policies apply: Reservations must be made by calling the central reservation number, (512) 389-8900, between 9 A.M. and 6 P.M. Monday through Friday. Reservations are strongly recommended, and a deposit is required in order to guarantee a reservation. Specific sites may not be reserved; they are available on a first-come, first-served basis upon arrival. Dogs must remain on a six-foot leash and may not be left unattended or enter any park building.

The Honey Flat Camp gets half credit for being well named. It is flat, but we found nothing particularly sweet about it. Thirty-five campsites, some with water ($10) and some with water and electricity ($12) are generously spaced among a thick screening cover of mesquite and juniper. Each site has a shaded picnic table with barbecue grill. A playground and rest rooms with showers are also available.

Less developed but more to the liking of Sport and myself was the Little Red Camp, a walk-in tent camping area with 10 sites perched on a bluff overlooking the South Prong of the Little Red River. Each site ($9) has a shaded picnic table; the area is served by a composting toilet (no water, electricity, or showers). Campsites are only a few steps from the parking lot, are well screened from each other by vegetation, and offer superb views of the red canyon walls looming nearby. This campground is also an excellent jumping-off place for the Upper Canyon Trail, the Lower Canyon Trail, and the Canyon Loop Trail.

Another trailhead for the Upper Canyon Trail is at the South Prong Camp. The 20 walk-in tent sites ($8) each have a fire ring and a lantern post. There is no water or electricity, and it's a pretty good hike to the composting toilet. However, the campground is set amid a thick growth of mesquite trees whose green leaves contrast beautifully with the rich red of the canyon walls and the deep blue of the sky. For some reason this campground was thickly populated by a species of grasshoppers that looked dull gray until they flew, when they revealed brilliant orange wings and made a loud clattering sound. They rarely flew more than three or four feet, making them seem to be an easy catch. But try as Sport might, she could never catch one. Usually as she headed for one, another would spring up in front of her and lead her in another direction. Finally, panting and hot, she gave me a disgusted look as if to say, "I didn't really want to catch one, anyway."

If you truly enjoy getting away from it all, the park has four primitive camping areas accessible only by backpacking ($9); reaching these requires hiking from as little as a mile to as much as 15 miles. Be sure to check with a park ranger before striking out for one of these isolated sites; it's a good idea to plan a definite period for your stay and leave your expected return date with the rangers. Then be sure to show up on time so they won't come looking for you.

The park may be closed for public hunts at various times during the months from October through January; call ahead if you plan to travel to the park during that time.

The park is 3.5 miles north of Highway 86 in Quitaque on F.M. 1065.

Entry costs $2 per person. The office is open from 8 A.M. to 5 P.M. The gate doesn't close; there is an honor box at headquarters used to collect camping and day-use fees when the office is closed. (806) 455-1492.

PLACES TO STAY

Caprock Canyons State Park: See Caprock Canyons State Park on page 86 for camping information.

FESTIVALS

Fall Foliage Tour: Colorful leaves may leave your pooch wondering what all the fuss is about, but while you're appreciating the colorful displays of autumn, your dog can rubberneck at an antique tractor show, flea market, arts and crafts booths, pumpkin painting and carving, country music along Main Street, and mountain bike races. It happens the third Saturday in October in downtown Quitaque. For information, phone (806) 455-1492.

National Trails Day Celebration: Dogs won't recognize sleepy little Quitaque during this event, what with a parade, a hot-air balloon launch at sunrise, a chili cook-off, a motorcycle race, arts and crafts booths, motorized tours along the trailways, and various other festivities. It all takes place in downtown Quitaque on the first Saturday in June, and leashed dogs will revel in every minute. For information, phone (806) 455-1492.

SILVERTON

PLACES TO STAY

Lake Mackenzie: This municipal water supply lake has such steep canyon walls surrounding it that little shoreline is available for recreation or camping. However, the park does have 38 RV campsites with water and electricity ($7 plus $2 per person entry fee). Each site has a shaded picnic table and a barbecue grill. Rest rooms with showers are available, although they are not located near the camping areas. Reservations are advised for the RV sites. Tent camping ($2 per site plus $2 per person entry fee) is permitted almost anywhere you choose, except that you may not occupy an RV site unless you pay the $7 fee. Dogs must remain on leash, but they are permitted to go in the water at lake access points, mainly around boat ramps.

Most campsites offer sweeping views of the 900-acre lake and the spectacular canyon walls enclosing it. The lake occupies part of Tule Canyon, which is famous in Texas history for having been explored by the Spanish conquistador Francisco Vásquez de Coronado, who camped here in 1541. American soldiers camped here in 1874 before attacking a band of Comanches in the Battle of Palo Duro Canyon.

The lake is on Highway 207 seven miles north of its intersection with Highway 86, four miles west of Silverton. For information contact the Mackenzie Municipal Water Authority, Route 1, Box 14, Silverton, TX 79257; (806) 633-4326.

HALE COUNTY

PLAINVIEW

PARKS, BEACHES, AND RECREATION AREAS

• **City Park** 🐾🐾 *See* ❷⓿ *on page 68.*

The 40 acres of neatly mowed grass shaded by a thick sprinkling of Siberian elm trees provide a traveling pooch plenty of room to work off the excess energy built up by too many hours in the car, even though she must remain on leash. Located on a major thoroughfare, the park also offers picnic tables, barbecue grills, and rest rooms. A small drainage through its center may have a little standing water, weedy cover, and perhaps even some fresh dirt for your pooch's olfactory titillation. There's also a playground and water fountains.

The park is located in central Plainview at the intersection of U.S. 70 and Milwaukee Street. It's open from daylight to 10 P.M. (806) 296-1162.

• **Givens Park** 🐾½ *See* ❷❶ *on page 68.*

If your pooch likes the wide-open spaces the Panhandle is known for, he'll love romping across the 37 acres of this gently rolling, grassy, mainly treeless park. It's made to order for the insecure pooch who loves to roam but doesn't want to get lost. (Since he must remain leashed, there's no danger of that happening here.) There's a playground, picnic pavilion, water fountain, and rest rooms. Due to freezing weather, the rest rooms are closed from November 1 until Easter.

The park is located just off Interstate 27 Business Route on Campbell Street; turn east on West 16th Street and follow it two blocks to the park. Park hours are daylight to 10 P.M. (806) 296-1162.

PLACES TO STAY

Best Western Conestoga Inn: Rooms are $51 to $59; small dogs (under 10 pounds) stay free. 600 North Interstate 27, Plainview, TX 79072; (806) 293-9454 or (800) 528-1234.

Days Inn: Small and medium-size dogs are preferred, but clean, well-behaved big dogs may stay as well. Rooms are $52; there's a $4 per night fee for your pooch. 3600 Olton Road, Plainview, TX 79072; (806) 293-2561.

Holiday Inn Express: Rooms are $56. Small dogs stay for free. 4005 Olton Road, Plainview, TX 79072; (806) 293-4181 or (800) 465-4329.

HUTCHINSON COUNTY

BORGER

PARKS, BEACHES, AND RECREATION AREAS

• **Huber Park** 🐾 **1/2** *See* ㉒ *on page 68.*

Dogs must remain on leash in this 17-acre city park, but there isn't much for a dog to do here anyway except attend to necessary business. Most of the park is given over to people facilities such as playgrounds, basketball courts, and a picnic pavilion. There is space with grass and trees for the pooch who needs a stretch-and-sniff break. You'll have to make do with chemical toilets.

Adjacent to the park is a 16-space RV campground with water and electrical hookups. The sites abut Main Street; only a narrow strip of grass separates them from the street, and on the other side is a parking lot. The upside? Camping is free. There is a donation box at the information kiosk by the dump station, but there are no official fees. Tent camping is not permitted. Reservations are not accepted.

The park lies at the intersection of Highway 136 and South Main Street on Borger's south side. It is open 24 hours. For information, contact the Borger Parks and Recreation Department, P.O. Box 5250, Borger, TX 79008; (806) 273-0922.

RESTAURANTS

Mr. Burger: Burgers and fries are on the menu here; eat at the table out front. 205 South Cedar Street; (806) 274-3551.

Sonic Drive-In: Like many Sonics, the Borger outlet has a table out front where you can eat your burger and fries. Unlike most Sonics, you have to look hard to find this one, as Main Street isn't the main street in Borger anymore. 1006 North Main Street; (806) 273-5521.

PLACES TO STAY

Huber Park: See Huber Park above for camping information.

The Inn Place of Borger: Small, well-trained dogs are welcome; bigger dogs may stay if they pass muster with the manager. (Any motel located on Bulldog Boulevard just has to accept dogs, right?) The modern, two-story motel has a place to walk dogs out back. It's a little hard to find the entrance unless you know the trick: Turn west off Highway 136 (Cedar

Street) at the McDonald's just north of the intersection of Highways 136 and 207. 100 Bulldog Boulevard, Borger, TX 79007; (806) 273-9556.

DIVERSIONS

Blowin' in the wind: Windmills symbolize the Texas Panhandle, and rightfully so, for it was the invention of the water-pumping windmill that made the settlement of the Great Plains possible. The water table in most places is several hundred feet below the surface, making hand-dug wells impractical and restricting settlement to the banks of flowing streams. It is only fitting that J. B. Buchanan, "Mr. Windmill," lives in the Texas Panhandle in northwestern Hutchinson County. Buchanan has been collecting windmills for years, and his backyard sprouts one of the best private collections in the country. When the Smithsonian Institution needed a specimen of a particular windmill in good condition, they came to J. B. Buchanan. 'Nuff said. Buchanan is serious about keeping his 15 or so windmills in good shape; despite being near about 80 years of age, he still climbs the towers to keep them oiled and greased. He welcomes visitors, especially those with dogs interested in windmills. And what dog could resist a water-related piece of machinery with not one but four places to hike a leg? Windmills beat fireplugs all hollow. To view the collection, follow Highway 136 north from Borger to its intersection with F.M. 281. Turn west on F.M. 281 and go about a mile. You'll see the windmills behind the house on the south side of the highway.

FRITCH

PARKS, BEACHES, AND RECREATION AREAS

• **Lake Meredith National Recreation Area** 🐾🐾🐾½
   See ㉓ on page 68.

At 44,977 acres, this national recreation area is the largest block of public land in the Texas Panhandle. Dogs must stay on leash, but they are allowed to go into the water, and there are plenty of places for them to do so. Lake Meredith was formed by damming the Canadian River; the recreation area completely surrounds the 15-mile-long lake and extends another 10 miles up the river. Side canyons around the lake itself generally have steep walls that limit access to the water, and the surrounding countryside is flat and mostly treeless. For a dog, therefore, the most interesting part of the recreation area lies along the river channel upstream of the lake. Dense vegetation near the river harbors a variety of wildlife from deer to wild turkeys to songbirds. Huge cottonwood trees and wild plum thickets fill the canyons, and pronghorn antelope roam the plains beyond.

You and your pooch are permitted to roam on foot anywhere within the boundaries of the recreation area, and the dirt roads in the McBride Canyon and Plum Creek areas are ideal for walking. Horseback riding is permitted in certain areas, as are mountain biking and even off-road use of four-wheel-drive vehicles. But perhaps the best walking of all—for people and pooches—is in the river itself. The Canadian has a sandy bed, and the water is normally only a few inches deep. It's ideal for splashing along, wiggling your toes in the dirt. Dogs will want to walk forever, but theoretically they must stop at the New Mexico boundary, about 60 straight-line miles upstream. Since the Canadian River is a navigable stream, under Texas law its bed is public land and you are free to travel it as long as you stay within the normal limits of the stream.

There is no admission fee to the recreation area, and camping is free as well. Reservations are not accepted; stays are limited to 14 days. Where you choose to camp will depend largely on whether you want to enjoy the water or the hiking. Information on our favorite camping spots is given below and on pages 94 and 95.

Headquarters is in Fritch on Highway 136. Office hours are 8 A.M. to 5 P.M. For information, contact the Superintendent, Lake Meredith National Recreation Area, P.O. Box 1460, Fritch, TX 79036; (806) 857-3151.

PLACES TO STAY

Lake Meredith National Recreation Area—Bugbee Canyon: Primarily a fishing area, Bugbee Canyon has a sandy beach at normal water levels. You can camp on a beach in the shade of large cottonwood trees. From Fritch, go north on F.M. 697 to Sanford, turn left onto F.M. 1319; follow it to F.M. 3395, go left to Bugbee Drive, turn left, and follow the road into the canyon.

For information, contact the Superintendent, Lake Meredith National Recreation Area, P.O. Box 1460, Fritch, TX 79036; (806) 857-3151. Office hours are 8 A.M. to 5 P.M. Campground quiet hours are 10 P.M. to 6 A.M.

Lake Meredith National Recreation Area—Cedar Canyon: Camping is secondary to windsurfing in Cedar Canyon, a small beach area covered mostly by two large parking lots. About 15 picnic tables hug the shoreline or huddle under a small grove of cottonwood trees. Rest rooms and water are available. This area will be quite crowded on summer weekends and holidays; if you and your pooch seek solitude, you'll be happier elsewhere. There is a swim beach where leashed dogs are allowed in the water. To reach the campground, follow Highway 136 east from park headquarters one-half mile to Fritch Fortress Road, go 2.7 miles to High Plains Road, turn right and continue 1.2 miles to the intersection with Sanford-Yake Road, then turn left and go 0.4 miles to a ranger station.

There turn left and follow the road half a mile to the campground.

For information, contact the Superintendent, Lake Meredith National Recreation Area, P.O. Box 1460, Fritch, TX 79036; (806) 857-3151. Office hours are 8 A.M. to 5 P.M. Campground quiet hours are 10 P.M. to 6 A.M.

Lake Meredith National Recreation Area—Fritch Fortress: This camping area is more developed than most around the lake, with 10 sites with shaded picnic tables and fire rings perched on a bluff a hundred feet above the lake. The view of the blue lake ringed with red canyon walls is spectacular, but the steep cliffs prevent access to the water except at the boat ramp. When we last visited, the rest room serving the area had been closed due to vandalism and replaced with chemical toilets. Fresh water for the area is available at the trailer dump station. To reach the campground, follow Highway 136 east from park headquarters one-half mile to Fritch Fortress Road. Turn left and follow this road 3.5 miles.

For information, contact the Superintendent, Lake Meredith National Recreation Area, P.O. Box 1460, Fritch, TX 79036; (806) 857-3151. Office hours are 8 A.M. to 5 P.M. Campground quiet hours are 10 P.M. to 6 A.M.

Lake Meredith National Recreation Area—Harbor Bay: There are approximately 33 campsites in a half-moon around—what else—Harbor Bay. Most sites have a picnic table, garbage can, and fire ring. Chemical toilets serve the area; there is no water except for that in the lake, and that is the main attraction of this camping area. The shore slopes gently down to the water, and most campsites are, literally, at water's edge. In fact, when we last visited, the lake level was higher than normal and some picnic tables were awash. A few of the sites are shaded by cottonwood trees and are always snapped up first. Water dogs will love this campground, with or without shade. Any time the heat gets to be a problem, the lake is right there to cool off in. The campground is 1.5 miles west of Fritch on Lakeview Drive.

For information, contact the Superintendent, Lake Meredith National Recreation Area, P.O. Box 1460, Fritch, TX 79036; (806) 857-3151. Office hours are 8 A.M. to 5 P.M. Campground quiet hours are 10 P.M. to 6 A.M.

Lake Meredith National Recreation Area—McBride Canyon: Chief Ranger Dale Thompson says McBride Canyon is the prettiest country in the Texas Panhandle outside Palo Duro Canyon, and I wouldn't disagree. Red canyon walls give way to sandy flats shaded by huge cottonwood trees. Camping is where you find it along dirt roads. Picnic tables, barbecue grills, and chemical toilets are the only facilities.

The road into the canyon can present a problem during wet weather. There is a slippery red clay hill to negotiate just as you enter the canyon, but that's not the worst of it. Heavy oil field trucks make daily trips into the canyon and churn up huge mudholes during rainy spells. Check at park headquarters in Fritch if you are in doubt about road conditions. The access road for the campground is 6.3 miles south of Fritch on Highway 136. Turn at the sign for Alibates Flint Quarries National Monument and follow this paved road 3.2 miles to an intersection; turn left and go another 2.7 miles to the entrance to the canyon, where the paved road ends. Dirt roads lead to campsites over the next two miles.

For information, contact the Superintendent, Lake Meredith National Recreation Area, P.O. Box 1460, Fritch, TX 79036; (806) 857-3151. Office hours are 8 A.M. to 5 P.M. Campground quiet hours are 10 P.M. to 6 A.M.

Lake Meredith National Recreation Area—Sanford-Yake: The Sanford-Yake campground is the most highly developed of all those around the lake, with about 60 sites, each with a shaded picnic table and barbecue grill. There is a rest room, and water is available. The sites are on a bluff high above the lake, and most are surrounded by expanses of mowed grass. A number of the sites have one or two trees nearby. Views from some of the sites are expansive, while others are tucked into small depressions that block views of the lake but afford some privacy. To reach the campground, follow Highway 136 east from park headquarters one-half mile to Fritch Fortress Road, go 2.7 miles to High Plains Road, turn right, and continue 1.2 miles to an intersection with Sanford-Yake Road; turn left and go 1.4 miles to the campground.

For information, contact the Superintendent, Lake Meredith National Recreation Area, P.O. Box 1460, Fritch, TX 79036; (806) 857-3151. Office hours are 8 A.M. to 5 P.M. Campground quiet hours are 10 P.M. to 6 A.M.

DIVERSIONS

Make a quarry your quarry: Thousands of years ago, First Americans came to the red bluffs above the Canadian River to mine the high-quality, rainbow-hued flint that occurs only here. Tools and dart points of this prized stone have been found all over North America, indicating that it was a valuable commodity traded among many tribes. No doubt much of that flint was carried by the dogs the pre-horse Indians used as beasts of burden. Today the quarries lie within Alibates Flint Quarries National Monument, and you and your leashed pooch can visit to learn more about your common heritage. You can see the outcrops of flint and the pits where the First Americans mined it. A park ranger may give a flint knapping demonstration to show how flint was made into tools. Guided tours leave the Bates Canyon ranger station every day at 10 A.M. and 2 P.M. from Memorial Day through Labor Day, at other times by appointment. From Fritch, drive south 6.3 miles on Highway 136 to Cas Johnson Road. A park service sign marks the turnoff. Drive west on Cas Johnson for 3.2 miles to a fork in the road; go right and drive two miles to the ranger station. For reservations or information write to Superintendent, Alibates Flint Quarries National Monument, P.O. Box 1460, Fritch, TX 79036; (806) 857-3151.

MOORE COUNTY

DUMAS

Dumas takes pride in the fact that its name was made nationally known in the 1940s by a song called "I'm a Ding Dong Daddy from Dumas," which was recorded and made popular by Phil Harris, bandleader for the Jack Benny radio show. Caricatures of a cowboy—the "Ding Dong Daddy"—and a cowgirl—"Ding Dong Dolly"—were made up to serve as the community logo.

In these more politically correct times, a lawsuit would be the more likely result. The lyrics to the song are, quite frankly, awful. Every verse exalts men and insults women. Here's a sample:

I'm a Ding Dong Daddy from Dumas,
You ought to see me do my stuff.
I'm a jug jugglin' Jasper
From Flat Fork Flats, and
You ought to see me strut.
I'm a corn huskin' huskie,
Got a gal called Cleta,
She's a flip flop flapper
But her brains are in her feet.

Ahem. Sport and I decided to put our heads together and come up with some new words. See if you like our version better.

I'm a Ding Dog Doggy from Dumas,
You ought to see me do my stuff.
I'm a cat chasin' canine
From the great state of Texas,
You ought to hear me ruff.
I tree raccoons all night, and
Hunt for fleas all day.
I'm a Ding Dog Doggy from Dumas,
You ought to see me do my stuff.

Now, Sport and I admit that's pretty bad song writing, even for a dog and an old goat, but we did manage to get through a whole verse without demeaning anybody, which is more than can be said for the original. Maybe we'll inspire Dumas to adopt a new icon and upgrade its image.

Interestingly (to me, anyway—Sport dozed off as soon as we stopped talking about raccoons) there is a continuing dispute as to who actually wrote the song and as to whether it is about Dumas, Texas, or Dumas, Arkansas. Researchers have turned up information supporting both sides, and the two Dumases (Dumi?) periodically slug it out in the press, each claiming to be the true and only home of the real "Ding Dong Daddy." Ye gads.

PARKS, BEACHES, AND RECREATION AREAS

• **Lake Meredith National Recreation Area** 🐾🐾🐾½
See Lake Meredith National Recreation Area on page 92.

• **Noel McDade Park** 🐾 *See* ㉔ *on page 68.*
Hemmed in by a complex of athletic fields, the four acres or so of this urban park are still friendly to leashed dogs. There's a nice balance between playground and picnic areas and open, shaded, grassy spaces where a dog can run. For the dog who needs structure, there's even a quarter-mile paved jogging path. Rest rooms and water are available.

From U.S. 87/287, turn east on 14th Street and go six blocks to Durrett Avenue and the park on your right. The park is open 24 hours. (806) 935-4101.

PLACES TO STAY

Best Western: Rooms are $57 to $67. Dogs under 25 pounds may stay for free, but only in rooms with an outside entrance. 1712 South Dumas Avenue, Dumas, TX 79029; (806) 935-6441.

Holiday Inn Express: All well-trained dogs are welcome, but the management of this new hotel requests that you bring along a blanket for your dog to lie on. As if you'd go anywhere without Bowser's binkie. Rooms are $69. 1525 South Dumas Avenue, Dumas, TX 79029; (806) 935-1177.

Lake Meredith National Recreation Area—Blue Creek Bridge: Think of this part of the national recreation area as an inland beach. The sandy banks and bed of Big Blue Creek provide a place where you and your leashed pooch can walk, swim, wade, or roar through the water in your four-wheel-drive vehicle. The sand here can be treacherous when dry; be sure your vehicle is capable of handling it before driving too far into the area. (A tip: If you do get stuck, let part of the air out of your tires to improve traction; drive slowly to the nearest service station and replace it.) The creek bottom is thickly shaded with cottonwood trees and makes an ideal walking path. You can hike about two miles upstream from the bridge to the boundary of the public land.

Primitive campsites are available scattered among the trees, and picnic tables, garbage cans, fire rings, and chemical toilets are provided. You can camp on the creek bank or back among the trees. However, if you camp here, do expect people to come roaring along in four-wheel-drive vehicles from time to time.

From U.S. 87/287, travel east on F.M. 1913 for 18.2 miles to the Blue Creek Bridge. There is no sign on the highway marking either the bridge or the camping area. Access to the area is a dirt road at the north end of the bridge.

For information, contact the Superintendent, Lake Meredith National Recreation Area, P.O. Box 1460, Fritch, TX 79036; (806) 857-3151. Office hours are 8 A.M. to 5 P.M. Campground quiet hours are 10 P.M. to 6 A.M.

Lake Meredith National Recreation Area—Blue West: Two camping areas at Blue West let you choose between sites offering privacy and lake access and those with scenic views of the lake. The Chimney Hollow site has about 20 primitive campsites at the lakefront. Some are literally at the water's edge. Picnic tables, fire rings, garbage cans, and chemical toilets are the only facilities. There's not much shade, but some sites are fairly well screened by surrounding vegetation. The other camp sits atop a high bluff overlooking the lake and has about 40 shaded picnic tables with barbecue grills scattered across a hilltop. Chemical toilets serve campers there.

To reach the Blue West Area, from U.S. 87/287 follow F.M. 1913 east for 15.2 miles to the National Park Service sign at the turnoff; proceed another 2.5 miles to the entrance. For the first camping area, turn left onto the dirt road 2.5 miles from F.M. 1913. For the second, leave F.M. 1913 at the entrance and follow the paved road for four miles.

For information, contact the Superintendent, Lake Meredith National Recreation Area, P.O. Box 1460, Fritch, TX 79036; (806) 857-3151. Office hours are 8 A.M. to 5 P.M. Campground quiet hours are 10 P.M. to 6 A.M.

Lake Meredith National Recreation Area—Plum Creek: If you and your pooch like solitude, you'll likely find it at the Plum Creek recreation area, which is situated in the canyon carved by the creek that gave the area its name. The bed of the creek, although hemmed in by weeds and tall grass, is heavily shaded by cottonwood trees. Their green leaves, the blue sky, and the red clay of the surrounding hills form a scene even a dog will find beautiful. Six-foot leashes are the rule here as everywhere in the national recreation area.

In addition to the creek channel, dirt roads in the area provide good walking opportunities, winding through stands of brilliant sunflowers. Walk quietly and you might surprise a deer or a wild turkey.

A primitive campground with about 15 sites—picnic table, barbecue grill, and garbage can included—lies at the end of the access road. Chemical toilets are also available. There is no water. The free sites sit atop a level knoll overlooking a heavily wooded bottom along the creek.

From U.S. 87/287, go east on F.M. 1913 for 12.3 miles; turn right at the national recreation area sign onto a paved road and follow it 6.1 miles to an intersection with an information kiosk. Make a sharp right onto a dirt road and go another 1.6 miles to an intersection; take the right fork and continue 0.4 miles to the campground.

For information, contact the Superintendent, Lake Meredith National Recreation Area, P.O. Box 1460, Fritch, TX 79036; (806) 857-3151. Office hours are 8 A.M. to 5 P.M. Campground quiet hours are 10 P.M. to 6 A.M.

Motel 6: "During pheasant hunting season, we have a lot of dog guests," the manager said. Rooms are $42. 1701 South Dumas Avenue, Dumas, TX 79029; (806) 935-9644.

Texhoma Park: The city of Dumas offers free overnight camping for RVers; travelers with leashed dogs are welcome. The 24 sites have electrical and water hookups, and while they are located in a parking lot, there is a two-acre park with trees, grass, a playground, and rest rooms adjacent. Reservations are not accepted. Located on U.S. 87 north at Twichell Avenue. (806) 935-4101.

FESTIVALS

Dumas Dogie Days: No, you literary dogs, the middle word in the name of this festival is not misspelled. The name "dogie" applies to a motherless calf. This festival does not celebrate four-legged creatures who bark and instead honors the pioneer ranchers of the area. Actually, it's just a good excuse for a parade, carnival, rodeo, and dance. Your leashed pooch can enjoy the outdoor activities with you. The festivities are held on Main Street and at Noel McDade Park, 14th Street and Durrett Avenue, the second weekend in June. For information, call (806) 935-2123.

RANDALL COUNTY

CANYON

PARKS, BEACHES, AND RECREATION AREAS

• **Palo Duro Canyon State Park** 🐾 🐾 🐾 1/2 *See* ㉕ *on page 68.*

Your leashed pooch will be fascinated to know that visiting this park puts him on the location of some of the most stirring events in Texas history. (Okay, so dogs don't give a well-gnawed bone about history. Let him take a nap.)

Palo Duro Canyon was visited by the Spanish explorer Francisco Vásquez de Coronado in 1541 as he searched for the Seven Cities of Gold. Some folks say the feast of thanksgiving he and his men held here was America's first. Later, the Comanche Indians used the canyon as a refuge and hunting place. (Yes, the Spanish came first. Only after the Comanches got horses from the Spanish did they venture here. But the Indians had dogs before they had horses. So there.) It was here in 1874 that U.S. army troops defeated the Comanches under Quanah Parker and forced them to accept reservation life in Oklahoma. Two years later, Charles Goodnight drove the buffalo from the canyon and moved in a herd of longhorns. You can see a reconstruction of the dugout Goodnight lived in during his first winter in the canyon just past the Hackberry Camp.

Two walking trails take you to one of the park's premier attractions, Lighthouse Peak, a tall rock formation jutting from the canyon wall. The Lighthouse Trail is a 4.5-mile round-trip path that is easy walking. The more challenging Running Trail winds nine miles to the same destination. The Lighthouse Trail heads at river crossing No. 2, where Park Road 5 and Alternate Park Road 5 split; the Running Trail begins just across the road from the Hackberry Camp and joins the Lighthouse Trail about midway.

Sport and I hiked the Lighthouse Trail on a breezy, overcast September day. The well-worn path varies in width. In places it's wide enough to drive on; in others, grass tickles your ankles as you walk by. The path is mostly level, climbs in and out of a usually dry ravine several times, and has no steep climbs unless you choose to press on to the very base of the Lighthouse rather than view it from a distance. Half a mile in, you'll be at the base of a massive red sandstone formation with another formation similar to the Lighthouse on its left end. Take a good look. If it's not worth walking another four miles to see basically the same thing, turn around here. At the 1.5-mile point, look to the left before descending into the draw. The Lighthouse is visible in the distance. Still want to go on? We did, and along the way we met a group of a dozen Japanese exchange students. Sport was surrounded in an instant, and the amount of tail-wagging, head-patting, ear-fondling, and nose-beeping that ensued would have been disgusting if it had not been so doggone cute. When Sport and I finally got to where we could get a good look at the Lighthouse, we could see it is really two very similar formations jutting from the same base. The slightly larger one in front always gets its picture in magazines, but I'd never realized there were two. The smaller one gets no publicity and no respect. I'm sure the thought flashed through Sport's mind as the words came out of my mouth: "I guess the other one is the Doghouse."

It's easy to see why Palo Duro Canyon has attracted so many different people over the years. It's not as big as the Grand Canyon, but, hey, you don't have to drive all the way to Arizona to see it, either. Red canyon walls soar as high as 1,500 feet above the winding Prairie Dog Town Fork of the Red River. As you approach the canyon across the table-flat plains, there is no warning of its presence until an arm of the canyon suddenly gnaws at the shoulder of the highway, falling away almost straight down. You enter the canyon by the same route by which Goodnight brought in his herd of longhorns. The road quickly adopts the bed of the Prairie Dog Town Fork of the Red River as its path, crossing the stream six times in the next eight miles. Scattered along the way are seven camping areas with a total of 146 sites.

Farthest from headquarters is the Mesquite Camp ($12). Nineteen tent sites, each with a shaded picnic table, fire ring, barbecue grill, water, and electricity are served by a rest room with showers. The sites are fairly open, giving campers excellent views of the canyon walls pressing in closely all around. A covey of half-grown scaled quail greeted us as we pulled in, skittering across the road like nervous leaves. Later a cottontail rabbit hopped casually by, and a roadrunner streaked up the road in hot pursuit of a tasty lizard. Coyotes howled during the night, reminding us of the wisdom of state park rules against leaving your pooch tied outside your tent or vehicle at night.

It was here we met Blaine and Pat Lewallen of Canyon, who were acting as campground hosts. In real life this retired couple works to save racing greyhounds—Pat used her retirement money to build the greyhound barn where 39 rescued dogs now live. Tuffy, a 14-year-old who was their first rescue, shared their camping trailer with them. If you are interested in helping save retired racing greyhounds from destruction, contact Save the Greyhound Dogs, Inc., P.O. Box 8981, Essex, VT 05451; (800) 327-7843.

The Juniper Camp ($14), accessed by Alternate Park Road 5, has 20 pull-through sites designed for RVs. Mesquite and juniper trees provide some privacy, but most of the sites are fairly open. Each site has a shaded picnic table, fire ring, water, and electrical hookups. As with all the other campgrounds, the Prairie Dog Town Fork of the Red River is just steps away. Dogs are allowed in the water as long as they remain on leash.

The Cactus Camp ($8) consists of seven primitive tent sites, each with a shaded picnic table and fire ring. A water faucet serves the area, and there is a rest room at a nearby parking area for the Cottonwood picnic site, where we saw a flock of wild turkeys doing their morning grooming. The park road runs through the center of this camping spot, which has steep, rugged cliffs on one side and the river bottom on the other.

The Sunflower Camp ($8) has 18 tent sites scattered among a thick grove of cottonwood and hackberry trees along the river. When we last visited, this campground was closed for the removal of sand deposited by a flood. On a previous trip we were entertained by wild turkeys wandering through the campground on their way to water in the river. Each campsite has a picnic table, fire ring, and lantern pole, and all are shaded by trees. This is a great campground for water people and water dogs—when it's not flooded. There is a rest room with showers for the area, but individual sites have no water or electricity.

The Fortress Cliff Camp ($8) has 18 primitive tent sites, each with a shaded picnic table and a fire ring. Water is available in the area, but there are no rest rooms. The sites are nestled in a thickly wooded mesquite flat along the river and showed signs of recent flooding on our last visit. Some of the sites are fairly private due to the heavy growth all around, and since it lies between two low-water crossings of the river, it will appeal to dogs who like to rough it and play in the water.

The Hackberry Camp ($12), despite its name, has 33 sites with water and electricity, most of which are shaded by mesquite or cottonwood trees. Five of the sites are pull-throughs suitable for trailers; the others are usable by tenters or RVers. A rest room with showers serves the area, which sits in a horseshoe bend in the Prairie Dog Town Fork of the Red River. Just across the road from this campground is the trailhead for the nine-mile round-trip Givens, Spicer, and Lowry Running Trail, which hooks up with the Lighthouse Trail.

The Sagebrush Camp ($14) has 30 sites, two of which are pull-through, all with water and 50-amp electric service. In comparison to the other campgrounds, this newest of the lot is absolutely sterile. Sites are closely spaced, most are not screened from adjoining sites, and there is not a tree worthy of the name. The sites were obviously laid out for efficiency rather than aesthetics; we hope the practice ends here. At the time we last visited there were no rest rooms or showers, but a facility was planned.

Reservations for campsites at all state parks must be made by calling the central reservation number, (512) 389-8900, between 9 A.M. and 6 P.M. Monday through Friday. Reservations are strongly recommended, and a deposit is required in order to guarantee a reservation. Specific sites may not be reserved; they are available on a first-come, first-served basis upon arrival.

Dogs must be kept on a six-foot leash, may not enter any park building, and may not be left unattended. You may be requested to show proof of current rabies vaccination.

The park is located about 12 miles east of Canyon on Highway 217.

From Amarillo, take Interstate 27 south to Highway 217 and go east eight miles. The park closes at 10 P.M. except to overnight guests. The entry fee is $3 per person. (806) 488-2227.

RESTAURANTS

Fat Boys Bar-B-Que: Try the beef, sausage, ham, or German dog at this place where co-owner Terry Marler says, "If it was up to me, you could bring your dog inside." Instead, you'll have to eat at the table out front. As a bonus, there is a city-owned RV park just behind the restaurant where you can water and dewater your pooch. 104 23rd Street; (806) 655-7363.

The Fountain: Lite is the word used to describe the menu here, from sandwiches to salads to baked potatoes to daily lunch specials. You can sin a bit with Blue Bell Ice Cream, however. Eat at one of the tables on the covered sidewalk out front. On the courthouse square at 404 15th Street; (806) 655-0348.

Goodnight Trading Post: Located in Palo Duro Canyon State Park (see page 99), this combination souvenir shop, grocery store, and restaurant has a lunch counter that serves breakfast, lunch, and dinner. There is an outdoor patio area with several picnic tables where owner Joe Walsh says you and your pooch are welcome to dine. Rib eye steaks are the house specialty; your pooch will surely approve. The outdoor eating area is well hidden by shrubbery to the southeast of the building. Just circle around to the right of the building as you approach it from the parking lot and follow the mowed path. There is no table service; tie your dog outside while you go in and order. The trading post is about a mile from the park entrance on your left; (806) 622-3327.

McDonald's: Just how many outlets of this humongous international chain have you seen where you and your pooch could share a table right out front? Not many, we'll wager. This one has a table out front because smoking is not allowed in the restaurant, and a regular customer wanted to be able to have a cigarette with his morning coffee, so he bought a table (painted the correct shades of yellow and red) and put it out front. You and your pooch are welcome to use it, but if a guy with a cup of coffee and a cigarette sits down beside you, don't ask him not to smoke—it's his table. 200 23rd Street; (806) 655-9502.

Schlotzsky's: Try the famous original sandwich on fresh sourdough bun or see what new item they've cooked up. Eat at the covered table out front. 901 23rd Street; (806) 655-2867.

Sonic Drive-In: Burgers, fries, and foot-long hot dogs are the everyday fare. Eat at the tables out front. 1007 23rd Street; (806) 655-3661.

PLACES TO STAY

Buffalo Lake National Wildlife Refuge: The centerpiece of this 7,664-acre wildlife refuge once was a lake that attracted thousands of migrating and wintering waterfowl, but upstream dams and declining rainfall now keep the lake dry most of the year. The lake can still hold some water in wet years, but the often-dry lakebed detracts from the recreational charm of the place. Dogs must be on a 20-foot leash here, but you might want to consider this as a backup camping site in case Palo Duro Canyon State Park is full, which it often is. While you're here you might catch a glimpse of one of the 333 species of birds sighted on the refuge; hawks in the fall and neotropical birds in the spring and fall are the main attractions. You can't beat the price: for a $2 entrance fee per vehicle, you can camp at one of 24 tree-shaded campsites along Tierra Blanca Creek. Rest rooms are available, as is water. Each site has a picnic table and a barbecue pit. The catch? An automatic locking gate clangs shut at 6 P.M. from October 1 until March 31, and at 8 P.M. from April 1 until September 30, and doesn't open until 8 A.M. You can exit via a one-way gate. P.O. Box 179, Umbarger, TX 79091; (806) 499-3382.

City of Canyon RV Park: A shady grove of hackberry trees almost hides this little campground just off the main north-south street, and many people never know it's there. That's too bad, because the camping costs only $5. All 30 sites have water and electricity. Pay at the on-site registration box. Reservations are not accepted. Dogs must be leashed. The park is at the corner of North Second and 21st Streets. For information, contact the city of Canyon at 301 16th Street, Canyon, TX 79015; (806) 655-5003.

Goodnight Inn: This motel-type inn charges $40 to $95. Dogs stay for $5 each per night. It's on the southern edge of town on U.S. 87. Route 2, Box 142, Canyon, TX 79015; (806) 655-1132 or (800) 654-7350.

Palo Duro Canyon State Park: See Palo Duro Canyon State Park on page 99 for camping information.

DIVERSIONS

Play cowboy with your cowdog: You and your pooch can both get a taste of cowboy life by going on a trail ride to the Lighthouse or an overnight campout complete with cookouts at dinner and breakfast. You furnish your own camping gear and dog food, and everything else is included in the $75 price for the trail ride or the cookout; a minimum of six riders is required for both. Make reservations by contacting Joe Walsh at Route 7, Box 4-11, Amarillo, TX 79118; (806) 488-2760, (806) 622-3327, or (806) 488-2786.

3
AUSTIN/ NORTHERN HILL COUNTRY

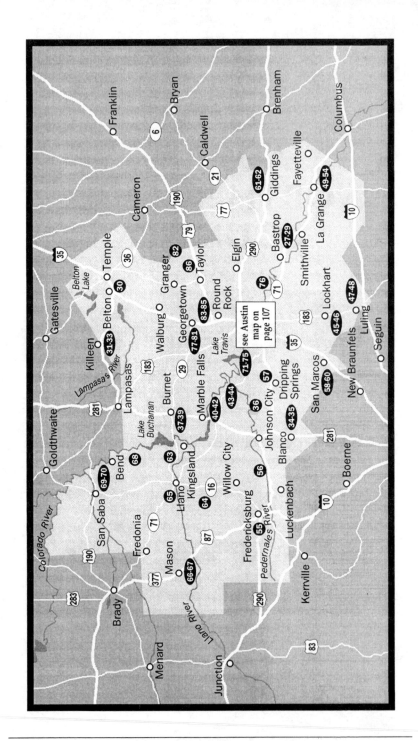

AUSTIN AREA MAP

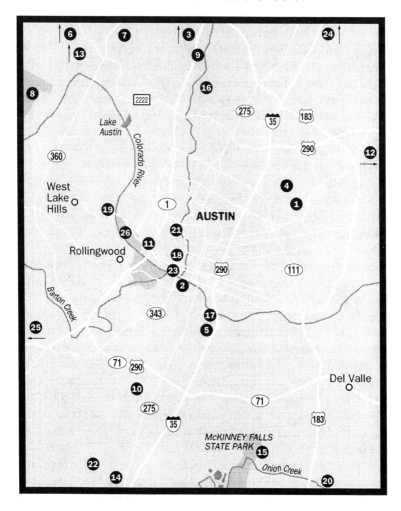

AUSTIN/NORTHERN HILL COUNTRY

Nature blessed Austin with a bounty of trees, streams, and varied landforms. The city sits astride the Balcones Fault, which millions of years ago quaked and uplifted the area to the west. The Colorado River and countless creeks carved the shattered edge of the resulting plateau into the blue-tinged hills for which the city is famous. Three major geographic regions of North America divide Travis County into distinctly different biomes rich in diversity of plants and animals. There's a lot for a dog to sniff here.

But nature's blessing—or at least humans' response to it—was also a curse. If the old saw is true that we always hurt the thing we love, Austin has been loved nearly to death. Who wouldn't want to live in such a wonderful place? And people wanting to move here to live have been Austin's undoing. (In their defense, it must be added that many of them are dog lovers, and your pooch will find the welcome mat out at many area hotels and restaurants.)

As a former resident of Austin and a lifelong student of Texas history, I think I am qualified to state that the state's capital city is on a collision course with the 21st century. When I first moved here in the early '60s to attend The University (even today the University of Texas at Austin is generally regarded as the One and Only), Austin was still basically a small town that just happened to be the center of state government and higher education, if not culture. How small was it? For starters, Interstate 35 wasn't finished around 15th Street, Ben White Boulevard had one service station and no strip shopping centers on it, U.S. 183 north was a pleasant country highway, Oak Hill was out in the boonies, and no one had ever heard of Mopac, much less Loop 360. Downtown had no high-rise buildings except the Capitol.

The pace of change continues to accelerate, and while the damage being done to the environment surpassed nature's ability to heal it years ago, few seem to care or even to have noticed. Someday there will be a reckoning, and Austin's worst fear will be realized: It will have become another Houston.

All of which is to say the growth of the last three decades has been rapid, disruptive, and quite unkind to the environment that attracted people to move here in the first place. Asphalt, concrete, and people in too big a hurry to get to places that didn't exist a dog's lifetime ago have pretty well destroyed the character of the town I knew then.

But, we come to praise Austin, not to bury it. The people who live here and those who move here in hordes every day will take care of the latter soon enough. In the meantime, a dog can have a pretty good time here. The city does have a dozen leash-free areas, even though only two are marked with identifying signs, and that only because local dog lovers paid for the signs and saw to it they were put up. (Two of these areas are not included in this book; one is hard to find, and the other runs along an unfenced railroad right-of-way.) The same creeks that gnawed ragged gashes in the hills and still make Austin a dangerous place to drive when it rains created perfect places for greenbelts and walking trails, and dogs lucky enough to live in Austin have some great recreational areas. The Colorado River and the chain of lakes west of Austin are ringed with additional parks, a number of which offer leash-free swimming and hiking for hounds.

We'll start with Austin and then cover the surrounding counties in alphabetical order.

AUSTIN

PARKS, BEACHES, AND RECREATION AREAS

• **Airport Leash-free Area** 🐾 🐕 *See ❶ on page 107.*

Imagine a piece of sun-baked property about five acres in size with a busy city street along one side, an airport parking lot on the other, an overgrown, impenetrable creek bisecting it, and an abandoned apartment complex abutting the creek. If you were a dog-hating City Hall bureaucrat who'd been bugged a lot lately by dog lovers asking for more leash-free land for pooches, could you think of a use to which such a star-crossed chunk of public property could be put? You bet you could. That's probably not the way this area got designated as leash-free, but the result is the same. There are some nice post oak trees on the grounds, but did I mention the large storm sewers emptying into the bermed area that takes up most of the usable space, which tells you the area could be flooded from time to time? All this was lost on Sport, who just enjoyed nosing about under the trees and running unfettered, but the point is that when it came time to hand out leash-free areas, Austin dogs sometimes had to take the hind teat, as the old saying goes. The area is not fenced and there is no water, so the only thing that kept it from getting the fireplug was the leash-free designation. Hey, they're trying down at City Hall. Very trying, sometimes.

From Interstate 35, drive east on East 51st Street about a mile and a half to its intersection with Manor Road. (You'll come to Old Manor Road first, but keep going. That's not it.) Turn right on Manor Road and cross the bridge across Tannehill Creek; just beyond you'll see four 30-foot metal towers that are part of the airport's traffic control system. Park in the graveled area outside the chain-link fence. The best part of the leash-free area runs from that point east to the sign for airport remote parking. The park is open from 6 A.M. to 10 P.M. (512) 499-6700.

• **Auditorium Shores** 🐾 🐾 🐾 ½ 🐕 *See ❷ on page 107.*

The area along Town Lake between South First Street and Bouldin Avenue sits directly north of Palmer Auditorium and comprises about 10 acres. Your pooch is free to roam off leash as long as she remains in sight and under your direct control. You are responsible (under penalty of a $500 fine) for removing and disposing of any little social mishaps. In addition to wide-open spaces to frolic and shade trees under which to recoup, the site offers a number of other amenities. There are rest rooms and water fountains at the parking lot. Down at the lakefront is a gazebo dedicated by former First Lady Lady Bird Johnson (you remember her—she was married to a guy who liked to hold his dogs up by their ears. Oh, yeah, he was president of the United States, too).

Samantha and Sport take special pride in this gazebo, because it was built by a local women's professional organization, Women in Construction, a group to which their mommy, Sally Victor, once belonged. However, these callous canines were much more interested in the lily pond near the gazebo with a little stream trickling out of it and running the few yards to the lake. This was just the thing two hot water dogs were looking for on a steamy July day, and they went for it. Then we discovered, a few yards farther on beside the playground (for kids, not for dogs) the shower installed for the use of joggers on the hike and bike trail. Samantha loves to bite at flowing water, and this country girl almost became a city dog on the spot. Wowza! An outdoor shower where dogs and their people can shower together! It's almost kinky, and these two fell into the spirit with no urging. Then Samantha found and fell to on a rotting pigeon carcass under the bridge, and we knew things were back to normal. You can take the dog out of the country, but you can't take the country out of the dog. If your pooch is prone to molest mallards, be aware there is a flock of ducks that hangs around under the bridge. The skies may not be cloudy, but discouraging words may be called for.

Auditorium Shores is on the south side of Town Lake. From Interstate 35, take Riverside Drive west to South First Street. Immediately after crossing South First Street, turn right into the parking lot. The leash-free area is between Riverside Drive, Town Lake, and the next street to the west, Bouldin Avenue. The park is open from 6 A.M. to 10 P.M. (512) 499-6700.

• **Balcones District Park** 🐾🐾🐾 *See* ❸ *on page 107.*

Sport and I both love surprises, and this 51-acre urban park in North-west Austin gave us a big one: a half-mile-long walking trail in the bed of a branch of Walnut Creek, with a spring thrown in to boot. At first glance the park seemed pretty ho-hum, with the usual collection of picnic tables, volleyball and basketball courts, and a scattering of trees around a swimming pool. But as we drove to the park, we crossed a bridge over a small creek and I thought I saw what appeared to be a paved trail along the creek bank, so we put Sport on the required leash and went to investigate. We were so glad we did. Climbing down a steep incline beside the bridge over Duval Road, we descended to the creekbed and found the beginning of a concreted trail. The canopy of oak and elm trees overhead completely blocked the sun, and although the day was hot and the creek dry, Sport and I had the bit of the spirit of adventure in our teeth, and we struck off down the trail.

About a quarter mile later, we met a red-haired young lady with two dogs of indeterminate ancestry in tow. Actually, their leashes dangled from her hand as the two pooches caromed from one side of the trail to the other, noses to the ground. Obviously this trail made a lot of scents to them. "They love it down here," she said apologetically, "and there's hardly ever anybody on this trail, so I let them off the leash." One of the dogs kept running back down the trail and disappearing behind a bush, from which then came splashing sounds. Sport and I investigated and found the reason: a cheery little spring bubbling from the base of the limestone bluff, forming a pool the size of a washtub. It was just the size of the tub we keep filled with water for Sport and Samantha at home, and Sport plopped right in. A ruffle of ferns growing from the cliff and a mat of moss extending across the path told us the spring flows all the time. The water forms several larger pools in the solid limestone creekbed, making the spot ideal for cooling your feet while your pooch satisfies her water needs. Sport and I returned to the car refreshed and a little glad that no sign marks the trail. We wanted to keep it our little secret.

The park is in Northwest Austin just northwest of the intersection of Loop 1 and Duval Road. Exit Duval Road from Loop 1 and go west; take the first street to the right, Amherst Drive. The park entrance is on your right. Park hours are 6 A.M. to 10 P.M. (512) 499-6700.

• **Bartholomew Park** 🐾 *See* ❹ *on page 107.*

The 57 acres in this park will be of only minimal interest to dogs. However, it is adjacent to Robert Mueller Airport, so dogs who fly in and have tired wings might want to take a leashed jaunt along Tannehill Creek or do a few stretching exercises in the shade of one of the pecan trees. When Sport and I visited last, construction crews making improvements to the park had it so torn up we weren't quite sure if it would still look like a park once they got all the pieces back together. However, Sport and I have a general rule that the level of a dog's interest in park improvements is inversely proportional to the amount of concrete used, so we don't hope for much.

Bartholomew Park is at the intersection of East 51st Street and Berkman Drive in northeast Austin. Park hours are 6 A.M. to 10 P.M. (512) 499-6700.

•Blunn Creek Greenbelt 🐾🐾🐾 *See ❺ on page 107.*

Austin is blessed—or cursed, depending on your point of view—with many creeks. These creeks can cause flooding problems at times, but mostly they provide pockets of quiet and nature in the midst of urban sprawl. The Blunn Creek Greenbelt is a case in point. This ribbon of creek channel choked with huge oak and pecan trees connects Little Stacy Park and Big Stacy Park, both oriented toward the swimming pool and playground crowd. But between the two is two-thirds of a mile of graveled trail hugging the creek channel, and you and your leashed pooch will enjoy every inch of it. This is especially true because this little park shelters more squirrels per square inch than any other place Sport and I visited on our travels. The little buggers beg for scraps at your picnic table and dart across the path and up trees in hot pursuit of squirrel sex or whatever it is they are after when they play ring-around-the-rosy on tree trunks. Poor Sport almost got dizzy from swiveling her head from side to side trying to keep up with all the action. Then two big black Dobermans appeared off leash with their human companion, and Sport switched from dreaming of possible offensive actions against the squirrels to watching those two big bruisers very carefully.

While you can park just about anywhere on the streets girding the long, skinny greenbelt, Sport and I seek off-street, shaded parking any time we can get it. Parking near rest rooms is available at both swimming pools. However, we chose to follow Sunset Lane south along the east side of the greenbelt to a point where it dead-ends behind an elementary school's playground. A footbridge across the creek leads to the walking trail, and a few yards downstream of the bridge, Sport found a good place to wade into the creek to cool off and have a drink.

From Interstate 35, exit onto Woodland Avenue and go west. You'll reach the greenbelt area in about a mile. Turn left onto Sunset Lane just before you cross the bridge and follow it about a block to where it dead-ends at a turnaround. Park in the shade at the end of the footbridge. Park hours are 6 A.M. to 10 P.M. (512) 499-6700.

•Bob Wentz Park at Windy Point 🐾🐾1/2 *See ❻ on page 107.*

Windsurfers are the main clientele at this 211-acre park, and dogs are barred from the part of the park where most of these wind heads hang out. However, leashed dogs are free to roam the rest of the property. And howlelujah, they are allowed to remove their leashes to take a dip in Lake Travis. "It just gets too hot out here in the summertime not to let them go in the water—even though the water temperature is 86 degrees," says the friendly park ranger, herself a dog lover. A graveled path sprinkled frequently with picnic tables and benches winds along the shore, and the views of the lake and Mansfield Dam are spectacular. Entry to the park costs $5 per vehicle, and the gates are open from 8 A.M. to 8 P.M.

Turn left (west) off Ranch Road 2222 on Oasis Bluff Road, then take a right at the stop sign onto Comanche Trail. Follow the signs to the park entrance on your left. The park is open sunrise to sunset. (512) 473-9437.

• **Bull Creek District Park** 🐾🐾🐾½ 🐕 *See* ❼ *on page 107.*

As soon as we turned onto the street leading to this park, Sport perked up. Trees crowded close in from both sides and formed a canopy overhead. Sport's hunting dog genes kicked in, and she began scanning the bushes for possible quarry. Then we splashed through a low-water crossing, and when Sport saw three dogs running, jumping, and swimming in Bull Creek, she did something she almost never does: she gave that begging whine that says, "Puh-leeeeeze, puh-leeeeeeeeze let me go and I promise never to gnaw the curtains or scratch the door or bark under the window all night ever again." While I took that with a tub of salt, I pulled into the parking lot and opened the door so Sport could bound down to the creek and join in the fun.

Only a small part of this 48-acre park has been set aside as a leash-free area, but big fun is had there. Park in the parking lot on the north side of Bull Creek. The leash-free area is designated by signs and includes the huge oak trees shading the creek bank and the creek itself. The creek flows across limestone and gravel and is generally shallow, but some deeper pools allow the water dog to practice her breaststroke. There are rest rooms and a few picnic tables where you can while away the time while your pooch plays with the other dogs running barefoot in the park. Sport was also fascinated by a young dachshund perched atop a picnic table watching a squirrel on a nearby stump. She drippingly investigated a group of people doing tai chi on a concrete slab across the creek while their dogs played in the water. This is a park where your dog will never get bored.

Bull Creek is quite subject to flooding during rains, and gates across Lakewood Drive deny access to the park during floods. Respect the signs and do not try hiking into the park; your pooch may love to swim, but it's a short shot down the creek into Lake Austin, and a pooch swept away by floodwaters could well be gone forever.

The park is just off Loop 360 (Capital of Texas Highway) on Austin's west side. From Ranch Road 2222 just east of its intersection with Loop 360, turn north on Lakewood Drive and follow it to the park entrance on your right. There is no gate to the park, but a 10 P.M. to 5 A.M. curfew is in effect, and the park has been designated a crime-free area, which means it gets close scrutiny by the local gendarmes. (512) 499-6700.

• **Emma Long Metropolitan Park** 🐾🐾🐾½ 🐕

See ❽ on page 107.

This popular park has 1,147 acres, only 70 of which are developed. That's the bad news; the good news is that while your pooch must remain leashed in most of the park, there is a leash-free area.

The developed portion along Lake Austin sees the most usage, but on weekdays the park is almost deserted. Huge pecan and cottonwood trees shade open, grassy flats great for the energetic pooch to burn off a few calories dragging you along behind. Along the shoreline, willow trees weep in sympathy with the leashed pooch, but your water dog may go in the water on leash as long as she is outside the designated swimming area, which is near the snack bar and rest rooms at the south end of the park.

Hiking can be an adventure at Emma Long. A sign at the park entrance advises you of the dearth of improved camping trails and invites you to follow any of the numerous deer trails at your own risk. Sport can follow brushy deer trails with ease and loves to, but I persuaded her with a few Herculean tugs on the leash to join me on the improved Turkey Creek Trail, a one-mile (one way) trail that is within the leash-free area. Parking for this trail is between the entrance gate and the honor booth where you pay your entrance fee. You'll pass the trailhead on your right just as you get to the bridge over Turkey Creek. Continue on another hundred yards to the marked parking area on your right; a trail outlined with limestone rocks guides you back to the trailhead. Keep your pooch on leash until you cross the creek, which is one boundary of the leash-free area. Sport and I saw a cottontail and two young buck deer in velvet, but she was most interested in the hundreds of small conical depressions in the loose soil of the trail from which little jets of sand erupted. I scooped up one of the patches of sand and blew the dirt away, revealing to Sport's amazed eyes an ant lion, or what we called a doodlebug when I was a kid. These little insects scurry around backward and dig the depressions in the sand as ant traps. Sport was fascinated. Or maybe she was just bored. When she stands there with her head down and her eyes closed, it's hard to tell if she is concentrating or sleeping. But she was attentive to my story about my childhood, winning her enough brownie points for a drink of water when we got back to the car, since the creek was dry.

If you and your pooch are up for a little more adventure and want to enjoy spectacular views of Lake Austin, park just past the entrance booth at City Park Drive and Pearce Road and walk north (to the right of the road) into the leash-free area. The best views of the lake are from atop the bluff. "It's really beautiful up there," says Susan Blackledge, park supervisor for the City of Austin, which administers the park. "However, it can be dangerous if you get too close to the edge and fall off the bluff. I usually suggest that people stay away from this area."

The camping area has 20 sites with water and electricity, clustered at the north end of the park. These rent for $10. The 50 tent sites have water nearby and go for $6. Many of the tent sites back up to a wooded hillside and have some shade; others are scattered among huge cottonwood trees where several tents may share a shady place. It's first-come, first-served. To illustrate the popularity of this park on weekends, park rules specify that you must physically occupy your site to keep someone else from grabbing it. It can go beyond that. While Sport and I were checking it out, we overheard a telephone conversation at the snack bar: A man was reporting how one of his camping neighbors woke him up in the night eating leftovers out of his cooking pots! Apparently not all the streetpeople live on Austin streets. Most parks warn against leaving food out because of wild animals; here you sometimes have to watch out for the people. The park is staffed 24 hours a day, so if you have problems, there is help nearby. Your pooch may have a chance to practice his guard dog techniques, however.

Entrance costs $3 per vehicle Monday through Thursday and $5 on weekends and holidays. The park is west of Loop 360 off Ranch Road 2222. From Loop 360, drive half a mile west on Ranch Road 2222 to City Park Road; turn left and go about six miles to the park entrance. The gates are open from 7 A.M. to 10 P.M. (512) 346-1841.

• **Far West Boulevard Right-of-Way** 🐾🐾½ 🐕

See ❾ on page 107.

The politicians who run things around here are famous for not being able to make up their minds, or for changing them once projects are well under way. It's a good thing for pooches that a planned extension of Far West Boulevard over Loop 1 to tie into Shoal Creek Boulevard never got built due to neighborhood concerns about increased traffic. (And a legitimate concern it was, too; Sport and I nearly got run off the road numerous times by speeding, aggressive drivers in sport utility vehicles who seem to leave their manners behind when they get in their cars. Lighten up, people. Be more like a dog.) The section of right-of-way for the street that never got built covers about 25 acres and contains a couple of floodwater retention ponds, so there is a healthy growth of trees in the bottom area beneath a high berm enclosing the ponds. A concrete walkway about a quarter-mile long makes a loop beginning and ending on the west side of the area next to the railroad tracks, where there is a graveled parking area. The city keeps an area about three feet wide on either side of the walkway mowed, so there is room for your pooch to "tend to bidness," as we say in Texas.

There are several ways to reach the leash-free area. If you are west of Loop 1 and wish to walk, you can use the Far West Boulevard overpass to access the pedestrian walkway across the Missouri-Pacific Railroad tracks; the walkway leads directly into the leash-free area. To use the loop trail off Great Northern Boulevard, turn west off Shoal Creek Boulevard onto Foster Lane (which runs one block south of Anderson Lane and parallel to it). Follow Foster Lane to its intersection with Great Northern Boulevard and turn left; the northern end of the loop trail is nine blocks south. You can also park in the 6900 block of Shoal Creek Boulevard (between Stoneway Drive and Dover Court); a concrete pathway connects to the loop trail. Park hours are 6 A.M. to 10 P.M. (512) 499-6700.

• **Garrison District Park** 🐾🐾½ See ⑩ on page 107.

Good things do come in small packages might be the lesson of this city park, although 40 acres isn't minuscule for a park located in a congested area. Your leashed pooch won't care much for the pool, playground, and athletic fields, but he will love the expansive picnic area that takes up about half the park. Hundreds of live oak trees shade every square foot of ground and provide more opportunities to tangle a six-foot leash than you would dream possible.

To reach this park at 6001 Manchaca Road (that's pronounced MAN-shack by locals), exit Interstate 35 at William Cannon Drive and go west on William Cannon about 2.5 miles. Turn right (north) on Manchaca Road and go half a mile to the park entrance on your right. The park is open from 5 A.M. to 10 P.M. (512) 441-2772.

• **Johnson Creek Greenbelt** 🐾🐾 See ⑪ on page 107.

This slightly more than one-mile trail is notable chiefly for making creative use of what would otherwise be a pretty useless area: the underside of Loop 1. The concrete-surfaced trail (with a mowed strip of grass on either side) begins beneath the knot of freeway bridges where West First Street and Loop 1 meet and travels parallel to Loop 1 in the bed of Johnson Creek. Even though the whoosh of cars overhead is constantly with you, the contrast between the noisy traffic above and the trees, creek, and limestone bluffs all around you is calming. The trail ties into the far more popular Town Lake Trail beneath the Loop 1 bridge, where a map depicts the trail system and a chart shows the distances to various points on the trails to help you plan your hikes. There's a shower and portable toilets here, too. We visited in summer when the adjacent Austin High School was not in session and had no trouble finding a shaded parking spot under the West First Street bridge next to the Austin High School Tennis Center. Because school was closed, the rest rooms were locked up, but the water fountain on the north side of the building worked, and Sport and I had a good cool drink. As at other city parks, leashes are required.

From Loop 1 heading south, take the Lake Austin Boulevard exit, but instead of turning onto that street, go straight ahead on Atlanta Street (parallel to Loop 1). After one block turn left onto Veteran's Drive and go under Loop 1; the parking lot for the tennis center is on your left. Park hours are 6 A.M. to 10 P.M. (512) 499-6700.

• Lake Walter E. Long Metropolitan Park 🐾🐾 *See* ⑫ *on page 107.*

At 1,147 acres, this would appear to be a big park, but large chunks of land are taken up by a power plant lake and an exposition center. As for the rest, your leashed pooch can eat with you in the shaded picnic areas and even go for a swim in the lake, but there's not much else to do. There were a couple of soppy, free-roaming Labs with their people the last time Sport and I visited, but then Labs are simple dogs given to simple pleasures. Sport requires more mental stimulation, such as the occasional squirrel or rabbit to consider making a dash for, but we didn't see a single one of either.

The park is east of Austin at Lake Walter E. Long, often called Decker Lake by old-timers like myself. From U.S. 290 East, go south on F.M. 3177 to Decker Lake Road. Turn left and follow Decker Lake Road to Hog Eye Road and take another left to the park entrance. The entry fee is $3 per vehicle Monday through Thursday and $5 Friday through Sunday and holidays. Park hours are 6 A.M. to 10 P.M. (512) 499-6700.

• Mansfield Dam Park 🐾🐾½ *See* ⑬ *on page 107.*

Your pooch will have to stay on his leash until he gets in the water at this 65-acre county park, but once he's in the water he can swim unfettered. Unfortunately, the best swimming areas for dogs are on either side of the boat ramp, which is extremely busy on weekends and holidays.

Primitive camping is available for $10, and there are no designated sites, so you may camp anywhere you wish or can find a spot. Reservations are not accepted. The most popular sites are along the waterfront of Lake Travis, but the most heavily shaded and private places are on the other side of the entry road. It's still just a couple of hundred yards to the water, and your pooch will appreciate the shade as you nap the day away, since there's not much else to do here.

The park is on Mansfield Dam Road; turn right off Ranch Road 620 at the west end of Mansfield Dam. Entry to the park costs $5 per vehicle. The park is closed from 10 P.M. to 7 A.M. (512) 473-9437.

• **Mary Moore Searight Metropolitan Park** 🐾🐾🐾
   See ⑭ on page 107.

The 344 acres of this park feature a two-mile walking trail along Slaughter Creek. Begin at the parking lot and follow the paved path to the right. Pets are required to be leashed, but when we last visited, we met a man with two hulking free-ranging dogs he said loved it there. We could see why. Soon after leaving the parking lot the trail traverses a creek that usually runs, but even in dry weather the solid limestone bed of the stream holds a large shaded pond just to the right of the trail crossing. It's perfect for wading (for people) or wading and drinking (for dogs). If your pooch tires of the trail and sniffing through the thick brush, you can scout for lost tennis balls around the courts. There's also a disc golf course; maybe you'll get lucky and find a lost Frisbee. We saw two men, a woman, and a dog head out on the course. We didn't stick around to see who won.

From Interstate 35, take Slaughter Lane west about a mile and a half to the entrance on your left. Open from dawn to dusk. (512) 499-6700.

• **McKinney Falls State Park** 🐾🐾🐾½ *See ⑮ on page 107.*

The popularity of this park on the southern outskirts of Austin—most evident on weekends and holidays—is well deserved. Your leashed pooch will enjoy the three-mile paved walking trail and the three-quarter-mile natural Smith Rockshelter Trail, even though she will look at you with pleading eyes when you tell her she is not allowed in the water anywhere in the park, especially since you are. Swimming in Onion Creek is a fine way to spend the dog days of summer. Williamson and Onion Creeks join in the park, and there are two falls areas that offer room for sunning on rocks as well as swimming. The swimming areas may be closed following rains.

There is one other trail, a three-mile mountain bike trail, but a park ranger counseled against trying to walk it. "You can't hear those things coming," she said. Of course, she hasn't walked the trail with a sharp-eared pooch. Still, your pooch will have plenty of squirrels, trees, and bushes to entertain her. The Smith Rockshelter Trail passes through a limestone overhang where Native Americans once lived. This trail begins behind the park visitor center.

The 84 campsites with water and electricity ($12) have rest rooms with showers nearby. The sites are spaced about 50 yards apart, and the surrounding elm and hackberry trees are so thick you may never see your neighbor. The sites are laid out in typical state park fashion around looped drives. There are eight primitive walk-in sites ($7) along Onion Creek. You'll have about a 250-yard hike from the parking lot north of the group dining hall. There is water at the primitive camping area. Reservations for campsites at all state parks must be made by calling the central reservation number, (512) 389-8900, between 9 A.M. and 6 P.M. Monday through Friday. Reservations are strongly recommended, and a deposit is required in order to guarantee a reservation. Specific sites may not be reserved; they are available on a first-come, first-served basis upon arrival. The standard state park policies regarding pooches apply: Dogs may not enter any building. They must remain on a six-foot leash and may not be left unattended.

The park is on the southeast side of Austin. From Interstate 35, take Ben White Boulevard east to its intersection with Burleson Road. Turn right (east) onto Burleson Road and follow it to McKinney Falls Parkway. Turn right on the parkway and follow it to the park entrance. To reach the park from Highway 71 or U.S. 183, take U.S. 183 south from its intersection with Highway 71. Turn right onto Burleson Road and follow it to McKinney Falls Parkway. Turn left onto the parkway and follow it to the park entrance. Entry costs $2 per person. The park is closed from 10 P.M. to 8 A.M. except to overnight guests. (512) 243-1643.

• **Northwest Park** 🐾 🐾 ½ *See* ⑯ *on page 107.*

Taking Sport to Northwest Park brought back memories of a previous life when my kids were young and would be waiting for me every summer day when I got home from work, primed to ask, "Can we go swimming?" Off we would go to Northwest Park's swimming pool for an hour. The swimming pool is still there, but today's Northwest Park is considerably different from what it was 25 years ago, and the change is all for the better as far as your dog is concerned. Following a disastrous 1980 flood on Shoal Creek (which runs along the west side of the 30-acre park) a massive excavation project lowered the western part of the park some 10 feet to form a flood retention pond. This part of the park serves as a parking lot during normal times, but there is also a landscaped pool along the creek channel where giant lily pads grow. You'll like those, with their huge white blossoms the size of a hat, but your leashed pooch will prefer the graveled trail around the edge. The water level is just perfect for getting a drink or going for a cooling plunge. The rest of the park is packed with playground equipment and picnic areas, but the acre or two of grassy berms surrounding the pond furnish dogs with myriad opportunities for sniffing. There are even some trees where your boy dog can engage in leg-lifting exercises.

The park is in northwest Austin just off Burnet Road between Allandale Road and West Anderson Lane. From Burnet Road, turn west onto Greenlawn Parkway and go one block; turn left onto Daugherty Street and take the first right onto Albata Street, which dead-ends into the park. Park hours are 6 A.M. to 10 P.M. (512) 499-6700.

• **Norwood Estate** 🐾 🐾½ 🐕 *See* **17** *on page 107.*

Situated where Interstate 35 crosses Town Lake (the Colorado River), this three-acre park couldn't be better located for the traveling pooch. If you don't have time to enjoy Austin's other leash-free areas, this one will at least let you get out of the car, stretch those legs, and polish up the old tennis-ball chasing skills. The fenced park is stocked with volunteer-provided jugs of water, bowls, plastic poop bags, and a supply of very well-used tennis balls. Most of the park is shaded by pecan trees, and while heavy use has worn the grass in some areas, there is still plenty of space for your pooch to do her thing. You are responsible for removing and disposing of waste and keeping your pooch under voice control, but that's it.

Adjacent unfenced parkland requires your pooch to be on a six-foot leash, but the views of Town Lake and the downtown skyline will so charm your dog that he will ask to take in the sight every time. It's especially lovely in early morning and evening.

From Interstate 35, take the Riverside Drive exit and go west on Riverside Drive to the first turn-in to the right (about 100 yards). The chainlink fence on your right encloses the leash-free area. Park anywhere along the curb. At the locked gate, go up the incline to its left; the entrance gate is about 20 yards down the fence. Park hours are 6 A.M. to 10 P.M. (512) 499-6700.

• **Pease Park** 🐾 🐾 🐾 *See* **18** *on page 107.*

Dogs love parties, and this 42-acre park is home to one of the most famous of all, the annual Eeyore's Birthday Bash held in late April. Named for the bashful donkey in the Winnie-the-Pooh tales, this craziness is just an excuse for a party, as if one were needed. The rest of the year Pease Park is a family place where leashed pooches and their people can picnic, swim, swing, hike, play disc golf or volleyball, and generally just enjoy this long, skinny park stretching all the way from 15th Street to 24th Street, where the leash-free part of the Shoal Creek Greenbelt begins. This parkland was once part of a plantation belonging to Elisha M. Pease, who was governor of Texas before the Civil War.

While the park is quite visible from Lamar Boulevard, there is no parking along that busy thoroughfare. From Lamar Boulevard between 12th and 15th Streets, take Enfield Road west and immediately turn right onto Parkway Road. It will intersect with Kingsbury Street in about a block. Park along Kingsbury Street to enter the park. Park hours are 6 A.M. to 10 P.M. (512) 499-6700.

• **Red Bud Isle** 🐾🐾🐾 🐕 *See ⑲ on page 107.*

This peninsula below Tom Miller Dam is only a couple of acres, but for the dog it offers fun out of all proportion to its size. The attraction is water—clear, clean, cool water being released from Lake Austin into Town Lake. Your pooch can run leash-free as long as you keep her in sight and under voice control. This shouldn't be difficult even with thick underbrush and large cypress and sycamore trees crowding the shoreline, because the shoreline is exactly where your pooch will be. Sport the water dog took one look at the inviting emerald green water and belly-flopped in. She is a strong swimmer, but the swift current was a bit much even for her. If your pooch is lacking in swimming skills or neglected to bring his swim fins, take him to the west (right) side of the island, where the current is much weaker. There are lots of little trails leading to barely submerged rocks your pooch can use as diving boards and you can use as cooling footrests for soaking your weary feet.

From Interstate 35, take Sixth Street west until Fifth and Sixth Streets converge at Loop 1; go straight ahead and the street will become Lake Austin Boulevard. Follow Lake Austin Boulevard to Red Bud Trail and turn left. You'll see the park on your left just after you cross the first bridge. The park is open from 6 A.M. to 10 P.M. (512) 499-6700.

• **Richard Moya County Park** 🐾🐾🐾 *See ⑳ on page 107.*

"Is this a park or a pecan orchard?" Sport and I wondered as we pulled into this 100-acre park drenched in pecan trees from large to small. The answer seems to be it's a bit of both. Two miles of hiking and biking trails wind among the pecan groves along the banks of Onion Creek. You and your leashed pooch will find many footpaths leading to choice spots along the tree-shaded creek where you can go wading. Picnic tables abound, as do squirrels attracted by pecans, so keep a firm grip on your pooch's leash. Watch out for snakes in the dense undergrowth along the creek. Playgrounds, group picnic areas, and softball fields dominate about 60 acres of the park, but the remaining 40 acres just cry out to be explored by adventurous canines. Rest rooms and drinking water are available. The park can be crowded on weekends.

The park is 1.5 miles east of U.S. 183 on Burleson Road. From Interstate 35, go east on Highway 71 (Ben White Boulevard) to U.S. 183. Take U.S. 183 south to Burleson Road and turn left. The park is open from 7 A.M. to 9 P.M. in the summer; it opens later and closes earlier the rest of the year. (512) 473-9437.

• **Shoal Creek Greenbelt** 🐾🐾🐾½ 🐕 *See ㉑ on page 107.*

Shoal Creek runs along Lamar Boulevard west of the University of Texas campus in central Austin, and a three-mile surfaced trail follows the creekbed from its intersection with the Town Lake Trail at Cesar Chavez Street (West First Street) to Seiders Spring Park at 38th Street. About half a mile of that trail (the portion between 24th and 29th Streets) is a designated leash-free area, and it's a dandy. To begin with, there is a shaded parking area (very important to Sport, who hates to get into a hot car and burn her feet on hot seats) off Lamar Boulevard north of 24th Street. Going either direction on Lamar, watch for an old concrete bridge crossing the creek on the west side of the street. It's officially the 2600 block of Shoal Creek Boulevard, but it's just a little loop off the west side of Lamar. At the southern end of the block-long area is a low stone wall and a sign designating the spot as an exercise area for dogs. When Sport and I last visited, only two of the 12 leash-free areas in the city were marked, so we appreciated the sign very much. Even better, a sign along the trail warns bicyclists to "Reduce Speed—Dog No Leash Area." Wow! For once dog rights were being acknowledged.

This portion of the greenbelt is beautiful, hemmed in by the creek and Lamar Boulevard on one side and limestone bluffs on the other with the tree-shaded trail in the middle. There's usually water in the creek to play in and drink, and benches now and again invite you to stop and contemplate the future of dogdom while your oblivious pooch just goes about being a mutt. Dogs love exploring the bushes and chasing the squirrels, who have perfected the ability to reach the safety of a tree at the last possible moment.

At the southern end of the exercise area a post holds a white plastic bag full of other plastic bags just above a trash can. If you can't guess what they are for, check out the bulletin board holding copies of "Trail Dirt," the newsletter of the Austin Metropolitan Trails Council. The Shoal Creek Greenbelt has its own organization, the Shoal Creek Greenbelt Coalition, thanks to the efforts of the likes of Joan Bates, an attorney for the Texas Department of Health and mother of Pluto, Cowboy, and Caitlyn. (Two of those are dogs and one is a daughter. You figure out who is who.) The group is working to provide poop stations and a bulletin board to handle all the dirt from and about dogs on the trail. If you want to help, you can contact Joan at (512) 371-1892 or Inga Van Nynatten at (512) 473-9383.

The parking area for the trail is on the west side of Lamar Boulevard about two blocks north of 24th Street. Park hours are 6 A.M. to 10 P.M. (512) 499-6700.

• **Slaughter Creek Metropolitan Park** 🐾🐾½ *See* ㉒ *on page 107.*

This 545-acre park is largely undeveloped, which means it's great for dogs. Soccer fields constitute most of the built environment; the rest is limestone hills and creek bottom studded with oak and juniper trees. Your leashed pooch can explore along the creek or follow unmarked trails winding through the brush.

From Interstate 35, follow Slaughter Lane west about six miles to the park entrance. The park is open from 6 A.M. to 10 P.M. (512) 499-6700.

• **Town Lake Metropolitan Park** 🐾🐾🐾 🖐 *See ㉓ on page 107.*

The choicest parts of this 509-acre park stretching on both sides of Town Lake from Tom Miller Dam in west Austin to Longhorn Dam in east Austin are right where they should be, downtown where the people are, for this is a people park. The park has over 10 miles of hiking trails on both sides of the river, and these get almost constant use. Leashed dogs can and often do accompany their mommies and daddies along these trails, which are served by water fountains, open-air showers, and rest rooms. You are responsible for cleaning up after your pooch under penalty of a $500 fine, and from the looks of the trails, most people do just that.

The views of Town Lake and the city skyline account for much of the park's popularity, but few would use these trails were Austin not a town where fit is in and jogging is a way of life for many people and their pooches. Your pooch couldn't care less about the 17 athletic fields for everything from rugby to softball, but she will appreciate the many trees, especially the ornamental apple and cherry trees when they bloom in the spring.

Parking is not a problem for many users of this park because they work in downtown Austin and just change into their jogging clothes and trot over. You and your pooch will find it easiest to park at the Auditorium Shores parking lot on the south side of Town Lake at the intersection of South First Street and West Riverside Drive. (This is also a leash-free area.) Another good parking lot with some shaded spots is by the Austin Parks and Recreation Department offices on the south side of Town Lake at the intersection of West Riverside Drive and South Lamar Boulevard. Turn west off Lamar Boulevard into the parking lot. The Town Lake Trail runs by both these lots. Park hours are 6 A.M. to 10 P.M. (512) 499-6700.

• **Walnut Creek Metropolitan Park** 🐾🐾🐾½ 🐕
See ㉔ on page 107.

This North Austin park best illustrates the biggest problems facing would-be leash-free dogs in Austin: uncertainty as to where leash-free areas are, and ambivalence toward the whole concept. "I'm really not clear myself where the leash-free area is, and because we've had some problems with loose dogs out there, I don't really want to advertise it," said the park supervisor for the City of Austin. Of the 12 leash-free areas in the city, only two have signs posted identifying them as such. This 293-acre park labors under an additional burden: confusing street signage. The ordinance describes the leash-free area as being bounded on the north by Cedar Bend Drive, but no street is identified as such by signs. To make matters worse, there is a street labeled Cedar Bend Drive on the city map, but when you visit the park, the street signs say that street is Old Cedar Lane. "We call the street entering off North Lamar Boulevard North Cedar Bend Drive," the supervisor said. "I don't recommend people going out there with their dogs, because I'm not sure where the leash-free area is. I'd have to research it." When directly asked to do so, she agreed, but the whole episode epitomized the status of leash-free dogs in Austin—they don't get much respect. You and your pooch can help improve the situation by asking that signs demarcating leash-free areas be posted and by being on your very best behavior when you visit.

The outcome of our quest for knowledge was this: The official interpretation of the leash-free area is the part of the park to the south (left) of the road as you enter the park from North Lamar Boulevard. Park in the lot by the swimming pool and hike down the hill to the graveled access road running parallel to Wells Branch. Turn right (south) and explore to your heart's content. Wells Branch (on your left) joins Walnut Creek (straight ahead) near the park's southeast corner. A maze of trails crisscrosses the leash-free area. Some lead to pools in Wells Branch. Others wind across meadows and down to Walnut Creek's heavily overgrown banks.

From Interstate 35 north, turn west onto Yager Lane. At the first intersection, turn left (south) onto North Lamar Boulevard. The park entrance road (which had no street sign when we last visited) is on your right about half a mile south, just past the traffic light at Dillingham Lane. Park hours are 6 A.M. to 10 P.M. (512) 499-6700.

• **Windmill Run Park** *See* ㉕ *on page 107.*

This neighborhood park of 50 acres is in the midst of a good old boy/ good old dog neighborhood. When Sport and I pulled in to check it out, a couple of good old boys were barbecuing at the picnic site nearest the parking lot—the prime spot for checking out any cute females who might be coming to walk. They had a good old mutt with them—think of him as a conversation starter—and sure enough, the object of their intentions showed up in tow of a large hound type not long after. None of them were very interested in us as we checked out the picnic tables, playground, and softball field spread among junipers and tall grass. It's a semi-wild kind of place, with a veneer of civilization thinly masking the wild inner core—sort of like your dog. There are no trails as such, and no water or rest rooms, but Sport enjoyed nosing about for a few minutes and carefully selecting that special place for a squat.

From U.S. 290 west of Oak Hill, turn north on Scenic Brook Drive and follow it about half a mile to Kirkham Drive—there's a sign for the park. It's open from sunrise to sunset. (512) 473-9347.

• **Zilker Park** 🐾🐾🐾 ◀● 🐕 *See ㉖ on page 107.*

About 60 acres of this most famous of Austin parks have been set aside as a leash-free romping ground. Well, okay, it hasn't been set aside only as that: On summer evenings and weekends the huge grassy expanse with pecan trees around the edge is overrun by crazed men and women chasing wildly after bouncing balls, yelling and jumping and banging into each other. No wonder Sport the unsophisticated country dog thought she'd discovered some kind of newfangled city dog with two legs and a ponytail. Sport does not speak soccer. There is a rocky outcrop on the western end of the area where dogs who loved the movie *Out of Africa* can lounge, lionlike, contemplating the view of Town Lake and the Austin skyline and perhaps lost loves from another time long ago when men were men and women were women and dogs were dogs. A dense growth of trees along the Town Lake shoreline harbors critters worth investigating.

At the northeast corner of the soccer field area, slip your pooch's leash on and venture across Lou Neff Drive to the observation point bearing the same name. It offers a spectacular view of downtown Austin and Town Lake. Catch a full moon rising over the city just after sunset and you and your pooch will both feel like howling at it. If you and your pooch would like to see more of the lake, keep the leash on and strike out along the hike and bike trail running between the water's edge and the railroad tracks. It runs for 10 miles along both sides of the lake.

There are water fountains in the soccer field area where you can water your pooch if you have a bowl or cup. Also popular with two Labs we saw were the beach volleyball courts on the west end. There's something about wriggling around on your back in loose sand that satisfies an urge that overwhelms every dog now and then.

Your pooch can enjoy the rest of the park with you as long as he remains on his leash. There is lots of shade and grass for lounging, but the energetic pooch may prefer to tackle the 7.5-mile Barton Creek Greenbelt Trail that begins just west of the swimming pool, which is, alas, off-limits to dogs. This trail winds along the bed of Barton Creek and offers no water save for that found in the creek. The trail is naturally surfaced and rocky in spots.

From Interstate 35, take the Riverside Drive exit and follow Riverside Drive to its intersection with Barton Springs Road. Turn left and follow

Barton Springs Road to Zilker Park. The leash-free area is to your right immediately after you cross Barton Creek. Take the first right after crossing the bridge and follow the one-way drive that circles the leash-free area; it leads to several parking lots. The first parking area (on your right) serves a picnic area open only to leashed dogs. Try the second parking lot (on your left). It has some good shade trees and a water fountain nearby. The park is open from 5:30 A.M. to 10 P.M. (512) 472-4914.

RESTAURANTS

Amy's Ice Creams: You and your pooch may share a cup or a cone at the bench out front. The ice cream is made right here in Austin and caters to special tastes, but the manager groaned, "Lord, no," when I asked if they made any special flavors for dogs. Oh, well. Maybe someday there will be a Pork Chop Puree or a Doggy Bone Cookie Dough. 3500 Guadalupe Street; (512) 458-6895.

Back Yard Burgers: The setting is almost surreal: a wooden deck with green plastic tables and chairs clustered in the shade of huge live oak trees—in the parking lot of a busy shopping center. But then that's Austin, and this is a place where you and your pooch can share a burger and fries while contemplating rejoining the traffic on Loop 1. 2505 West Parmer Lane; (512) 836-1170.

Boar's Head Bar and Grill: The friendly staff will be pleased to serve your pooch a drink—as long as it's what the hound in Walt Kelly's "Pogo" comic strip referred to as "aitch-two-oh." But given the choices available from this extensive menu that well represents the "Austin mix" of sandwiches, burgers, pasta, salads, and Tex-Mex, your pooch will be quite content on the big outdoor patio. 700 West Sixth Street; (512) 472-2739.

Dirty Martin's Place: "No killer dogs, please," requested the befuddled person who answered the phone at this Austin institution where burgers, fries, onion rings, and cold beer have attracted a loyal following for decades. You and your leashed, well-behaved pooch may eat at one of the shaded tables out front. 2808 Guadalupe Street; (512) 477-3173.

Emma Long Metropolitan Park Snack Bar: On weekends and holidays you and your pooch can share yet another of the "best burgers in Texas" at one of half a dozen picnic tables on the patio out back, overlooking the lake. The snack bar is at the swimming beach in Emma Long Metropolitan Park. The park is west of Loop 360 off Ranch Road 2222. From Loop 360, drive half a mile west on Ranch Road 2222 to City Park Road; turn left and go about six miles to the park entrance. (512) 346-1831.

The Green Mesquite: There's more to this place than meets the eye in more ways than one. The two green benches out front caught my eye, but then I found there is also a patio out back where dogs are allowed.

Plus, the sign says "BBQ and More," and the "more" includes chicken-fried steak, burgers, and Cajun food, so you and your pooch should do well here. 1400 Barton Springs Road; (512) 479-0485.

Little City Espresso Bar and Cafe: Dogs will be fussed over and get special attention at both locations. "We will be glad to bring some water for a thirsty pooch," the owner said. Each location has six outside tables where sandwiches, pastries, and bagels are served along with specialty coffees. 3403 Guadalupe Street, (512) 467-2326, and 916 Congress Avenue, (512) 476-2489.

Magnolia Cafe: Two locations of this popular eatery welcome you to tie your pooch just outside the patio while you dine. 2304 Lake Austin Boulevard, (512) 478-8645, and 1920 South Congress Avenue, (512) 445-0000.

Mesa Hills Cafe: "We have probably the most beautiful gazebo in the city of Austin, and we have no problem with you eating out there with your dog," the owner said. Sport didn't care so much about the great view, but she was impressed with the Mexican food, burgers, and salads. Well, maybe not with the salads. 3435 Greystone Drive; (512) 345-7423.

Mojo's Daily Grind: If your dogs are tired, a pause for a cup of exotic coffee and a pastry will put the prance back in those paws. You can eat at the tables out front. 2714 Guadalupe Street; (512) 477-6656.

Nick's Great Pizza: This place is open only Friday through Sunday, but you and your pooch can share a pizza at one of the shaded picnic tables out front. The friendly owner will serve up water on request. 11302 F.M. 2222; (512) 331-4471.

Pizza Nizza: Dog-loving owners with four pooches of their own are more than happy to have you and your leashed pooch dine on pizza and pasta at one of 14 patio tables. "Be sure to put in the book that we'll be happy to bring water for people's dogs," the friendly manager said. 1608 Barton Springs Road; (512) 474-7590.

Romeo's: They love dogs here but request that you tie your pooch to the patio fence outside the dining area. The Italian dishes range from pasta to pizza. 1500 Barton Springs Road; (512) 476-1090.

Ruta Maya Coffee House: If your pooch has always longed to have a cup of java and a pastry or sandwich on the loading dock of a former warehouse, this is the place where you can fulfill her fantasy. 218 West Fourth Street; (512) 472-9638.

Schlotzsky's: Only a few of these homegrown Austin sandwich shops have outside seating where a person with a pooch may enjoy a unique sandwich created right here in town. The old dogs among us remember when all sandwiches were toasted in an oven at the sole location on South Congress Avenue; now it's a franchise operation. We found two shops with outside seating: 2205 East Riverside Drive, (512) 443-6518, and 2003 Guadalupe Street, (512) 472-8381.

Sfuzzi: You and your pooch may want to dress up to eat at one of the two white-linened tables on the sidewalk. The menu is classy, too, ranging from pizza and pasta to poached salmon and "broasted" chicken. And the name? We're wondering, too. Pronounced quickly, it sounds suspiciously like one of Sport's sneezes. 311 West Sixth Street; (512) 476-8100.

Smoky J's: "Oh, there's no problem at all if you want to bring a dog—in fact, the owner has one that stays around," the clerk said. "Bring your dog's water bowl or we'll give you a cup for water." Eat your barbecue at one of the covered outside tables. 7008 North F.M. 620; (512) 331-4888.

Spaghetti Warehouse: This place pioneered the idea of converting rundown warehouse space into upscale dining in Austin, and while they do not have table service on the sidewalk out front, you and your pooch may order to go and eat at one of the tables there. The name describes the menu pretty well. 117 West Fourth Street; (512) 476-4059.

Sweetish Hill: Your pooch will love you forever for taking him to this Austin institution where sandwiches are just a sideline to the real reason for its existence: cakes, cookies, brownies, and other sinfully rich delights. 1120 West Sixth Street; (512) 472-1347.

Texas Picnic Company and Bakery: Food to go of the sandwich and sweet variety is the deal here. Just outside the front door, steps descend to the Waller Creek Trail, a one-mile downtown pedestrian path where you and your pooch can eat at a shaded bench and then pay for that pastry with some exercise. 605 Sabine Street; (512) 473-2518.

Thundercloud Subs: You and your pooch can enjoy sandwiches that are fresh made to your order and stuffed with everything from cold cuts to avocado (Sport likes hers with alfalfa sprouts) together on the deck out back at the F.M. 620 location or at the tables out front on Burnet Road. 6920 North F.M. 620, (915) 335-3663, and 5401 Burnet Road, (512) 467-9438.

Upper Crust Bakery: You can have a sandwich for lunch or bakery items any time at one of the tables out front. That goes for your leashed friend, too. 4508 Burnet Road; (512) 467-0102.

Waterloo Brewing Company: You and your pooch may sit at one of the four tables out front and wolf down a sandwich or burger while you quaff a beer brewed on the premises. 401 Guadalupe Street; (512) 477-1836.

Waterloo Ice House: The menu is typical Austin eclectic: burgers, tacos, burritos, chicken sandwiches, chicken-fried steak. You and your pooch may eat on the covered patio. The management requests that your pooch remain tied at your table. 1106 West 38th Street; (512) 451-5245.

Wheatsville Co-op: Hairy legs are always in style and welcome here, whether they come two or four to a customer. The emphasis is on healthy, primarily vegetarian, fare, which you and your pooch may share at one of the tables out front. If your pooch has been pining for hummus or falafel or just a crust of good old hearty sourdough wheat bread, this could be his spot. 3101 Guadalupe Street; (512) 478-1164.

Wylie's Bar and Grill: A potpourri of good food—stuffed pork chops with rosemary potatoes, quesadillas, burgers, tortilla soup, fajitas, burgers, salads—awaits you and your pooch on the patio on the side of this popular eatery. 400 East Sixth Street; (512) 472-3712.

PLACES TO STAY

Austin Capitol KOA: Dogs must be kept on leash, and owners must clean up after them. Dogs are not allowed in cabins. Campsites are $32. Reservations are accepted. 7009 South Interstate 35, Austin, TX 78744; (512) 444-6322 or (800) 284-0206.

Austin Executive Lodging: Rates are $45 to $75 daily, but if you've fallen in love with Austin and can't bear to leave, you might want to rent for a month or so. "We have a variety of fully furnished apartment homes throughout Austin. We are locally owned and operated, and we love dogs," the manager said. There is a $250 deposit for pooches, $100 of which is nonrefundable, plus a $10 per day charge. P.O. Box 201494, Austin, TX 78720; (512) 795-0051 or (800) 494-2261.

Bel-Air Motel: If you want to be close to St. Edwards University, as perhaps you might if your pooch is a big Dallas Cowboys fan and wants to attend their summer training camp, this motel will put you nearby. Rooms are $40. There is a $5 per day fee for dogs. 3400 South Congress Avenue, Austin, TX 78704; (512) 444-5973.

Best Western—Atrium North: Rooms are $55 to $85. Small dogs only may stay here. 7928 Gessner Drive, Austin, TX 78753; (512) 339-7311 or (800) 468-3708.

Best Western Seville Plaza Inn: Small, housebroken dogs may stay here. Rooms rent for $55 to $63. 4323 South Interstate 35, Austin, TX 78744; (512) 447-5511 or (800) 528-1234.

The Brook House Bed-and-Breakfast: Any size dog is welcome as long as you take her for needful walks in the alley out back; otherwise, she can join you in the yard. This is a very peaceful neighborhood just north of the University of Texas. Your room has a VCR, so you can rent *Old Yeller* and bawl your eyes out. Rooms are $75 to $99. 609 West 33rd Street, Austin, TX 78705; (512) 459-0534.

Carrington's Bluff Bed-and-Breakfast: Rooms rent for $59 to $109. As long as your dog is well behaved and housebroken, he is welcome. This inn is just west of the University of Texas campus. 1900 David Street, Austin, TX 78705; (512) 479-0638.

Clarion Inn: You and your pet will share a smoking room. When you check in might be a good time for your pet to look small, well-behaved, and precious. The inn has an exercise room. Rooms are $75. 2200 South Interstate 35, Austin, TX 78704; (512) 444-0561 or (800) 434-7378.

Corporate Lodging Suites: If you and your pooch like the suite life, one of these properties at various locations around Austin may be just what you're looking for. That is, if your pooch weighs no more than 25 pounds and can pay a fee ranging from $75 to $150 depending on the property. Suites are $99 to $139. 4815 West Braker Lane, Suite 516, Austin, TX 78759; (512) 345-8822.

Doubletree Guest Suite Hotel: Rooms rent for $115 to $190 at this hotel convenient to downtown and the Capitol. Dogs 25 pounds and under are welcome for a $5 fee. 303 West 15th Street, Austin, TX 78701; (512) 478-7000 or (800) 424-2900.

Doubletree Hotel Austin: Room rates are $69 to $180, and there's a $25 deposit for dogs. Imprinting your credit card lets your pooch up to 25 pounds stay here; the room will be inspected before you check out. The hotel has an airport courtesy van. 6505 North Interstate 35, Austin, TX 78752; (512) 454-3737 or (800) 222-8733.

Drury Inn Highland Mall: The room rate of $75 includes breakfast. This hotel also has an airport courtesy van and accepts pets under 20 pounds for free. 919 East Koenig Lane, Austin, TX 78723; (512) 454-1144.

Drury Inn North: Rooms are $78 to $84. Dogs up to 20 pounds may stay at no extra charge. 6711 North Interstate 35, Austin, TX 78752; (512) 467-9500.

Emma Long Metropolitan Park: See Emma Long Metropolitan Park on page 114 for camping information.

Governor's Inn Bed-and-Breakfast: This inn is just west of the University of Texas campus. As long as your dog is well behaved and housebroken, she is welcome. Rooms rent for $59 to $109. 611 West 22nd Street, Austin, TX 78705; (512) 479-0638.

Habitat Suites Hotel: Ahhh, shopping! This hotel is adjacent to one of Austin's premier shopping malls and is also centrally located just off Interstate 35. There is a $25 pet fee; only small dogs are allowed. Rates are $107 to $147. 500 Highland Mall Boulevard, Austin, TX 78752; (512) 467-6000 or (800) 535-4663.

Hawthorn Suites Central: Rooms rent for $79 to $159. Small dogs pay a $50 fee, which may be increased if there is damage. 935 La Posada Drive, Austin, TX 78752; (512) 459-3335 or (800) 527-1133.

Hawthorn Suites South: Rates range from $79 to $149. Dogs pay $50 for the first day and $5 each day thereafter. There is a health club for the people among you. 4020 South Interstate 35, Austin, TX 78704; (512) 440-7722 or (800) 527-1133.

Hudson Bend Camper Resort: Small dogs may stay here if they are leashed at all times, picked up after, and not left unattended. The resort has waterfront access to Lake Travis. Sites rent for $18. Reservations are required. 17317 West Beach Road, Austin, TX 78734; (512) 266-1562.

Mansfield Dam Park: See Mansfield Dam Park on page 117 for camping information.

McKinney Falls State Park: See McKinney Falls State Park on page 118 for camping information.

Motel 6—Airport: One small pooch per room is welcome. Rooms are $44. 5330 North Interstate 35, Austin, TX 78751; (512) 467-9111.

Motel 6—Central: Rooms are $49. All Motel 6s allow one small pooch per room. This one offers an airport courtesy van. 8010 North Interstate 35, Austin, TX 78757; (512) 837-9890.

Motel 6—North: Rooms are $42. All Motel 6s allow one small pooch per room. 9420 North Interstate 35, Austin, TX 78753; (512) 339-6161.

Motel 6—South: Rooms are $42. All Motel 6s allow one small pooch per room. 2707 South Interstate 35, Austin, TX 78741; (512) 444-5882.

Pecan Grove RV Park: Sites, which are for self-contained RVs only, rent for $20. Each campsite may have one dog under 15 pounds. Reservations are suggested. 1518 Barton Springs Road, Austin, TX 78704; (512) 472-1067.

Quality Inn Airport: Your room will set you back $50. Pooches pay a onetime $25 fee. The inn has a courtesy airport van and a health club. 909 East Koenig Lane, Austin, TX 78758; (512) 452-4200 or (800) 221-2222.

Red Lion Hotel Austin Airport: Aroooo! This first-class hotel accepts *dogs only!* Well, people belonging to dogs can stay, too. But no cats are allowed. Rates are $89 to $129. Dogs must plunk down a $20 deposit or their credit card. The hotel has a courtesy airport van as well as health club. 6121 North Interstate 35, Austin, TX 78752; (512) 323-5466 or (800) 547-8010.

FESTIVALS

Canterbury Faire: Somewhere in her cells your pooch no doubt harbors at least a few genes from a heroic dog who saved fair maidens in distress and guarded her master's European castle from roving bands of brigands. Awaken those medieval memories locked in her subconscious by snapping on her leash and taking her to this reincarnation of those ancient days. She'll think she's in merrie olde Englande as she gnaws a turkey leg, listens to music played on traditional instruments, and watches demonstrations of martial arts of those times. You'll want to buy her a handmade coat of arms or perhaps a jerkin for yourself. The local greyhound club will be there, so your pooch won't feel conspicuous. Slow, perhaps, but not conspicuous. The festival is held in early April in Waterloo Park, at the intersection of 12th and Trinity Streets. For information, call (512) 327-7622.

Zilker Kite Festival: In early March dogs are barred from part of their leash-free area at the Zilker Park soccer fields so kite enthusiasts can see whose kite flies higher or better or is just plain bigger. However, there's plenty of room left over for dogs interested in watching slightly heavier-than-air craft. It's a pretty safe bet there will be some kites decorated like dogs and cats—something about tails just inspires creativity. The park is at 2100 Barton Springs Road. For information, call (512) 478-0905.

DIVERSIONS

Accessorize your Akita: Austin is one of those places where people wear their jewels with their jeans; don't humiliate your hound by taking him out in public without first stopping by PetsMart for the latest in haute "coature." The in-store veterinary clinic can polish his pearly whites, the grooming shop can make his coat shine, and the two of you can pick out just the right collar, bandanna, or fashion-statement leash to complete The Look. Dogs shop for themselves here; you're along just to pick up the tab. The two Austin stores are at 1628 Ohlen Road (512-835-7212) and 5400 Brodie Lane (512-892-3297).

Catch a tutu with your Toto: Austin's ballet company best struts their stuff at a series of outdoor performances beginning in early June at the Zilker Hillside Theater. You and your leashed, well-behaved pooch can share a blanket and a picnic and soak up some culture whether either of you can dance on your toes or not. The show is free. 2100 Barton Springs Road; (512) 892-1298.

Climb every mountain: Psssssst! Mount Bonnell isn't just for lovers anymore. Some folks claim it's only 100 steps or so to the top of this peak towering above the city, but your leashed pooch will swear it's more like 400. The view from the top is hands down the best to be had of Austin, Lake Austin, and the hills to the west. At night it's even more spectacular. Just be careful not to get too close to the edge and fall off; every year someone does and has to suffer for hours (or die painfully) until emergency medical crews can make the retrieval. Do not throw a stick over the edge and shout "Fetch!" unless you never want to see your pooch again. 3800 Mount Bonnell Drive; (512) 499-6700.

Ford every stream: Construction of a highway bypass diverted traffic on Ranch Road 620 from Mansfield Dam, and the former roadbed is now open to pedestrian traffic only. You and your leashed pooch can trudge as many of the more than 7,000 feet of the dam as you like. Rising over 250 feet above the bed of the Colorado River, the dam is an excellent vantage point from which to view Lake Travis and the surrounding countryside. Okay, it's more of a cityside now. But the view is still nice. The dam is on Ranch Road 620 about midway between Highway 71 and U.S. 183.

Get thee to a punnery: O. Henry was one of America's foremost short story writers, and he lived in Austin for a time. Early each May he is honored (dubiously, perhaps) with a pun-off, a contest whose object is to tell the story that will elicit the most groans from the audience. Leashed pooches may attend; so far there have been no canine contestants. The O. Henry Pun-off is held on the grounds of the O. Henry Museum, 409 East Fifth Street; (512) 472-1903.

Put your basset in the Bastille: As the only state in the Union to have existed for any extended period as an independent nation, Texas is therefore the only state to have a foreign embassy dating from that period (the 1840s). The French Legation was the home of the French chargé d'affaires to the fledgling Republic of Texas, and as with many frontier matters, diplomatic affairs tended to be a little rough around the edges, conducted as they were by people who were described as "men with the bark on." Not the dog kind of bark, of course—tree bark. Anyway, relations between the two countries became strained when the Frenchman failed to pay a hotel bill run up while his official residence was being constructed. Then the innkeeper's pigs—by accident, no doubt— found their way into the Frenchman's bedroom, where he discovered them munching on official papers. Ordering his manservant to repel the porcine pirates with a pitchfork, the Frenchman flew into a snit that had international repercussions.

Today the French Legation celebrates Bastille Day each mid-July with food booths, gourmet wines and pastries, fencing demonstrations, French singing, and other events you and your leashed pooch are welcome to attend. Dogs have acted as wedding attendants at nuptials held on the grounds, so they are not strangers to these parts. No pigs, please. 802 San Marcos Street; (512) 472-8180.

Show your pooch some bloomers: The Zilker Botanical Center offers a visual and olfactory feast for both canine and human eyes and noses. If you and your pooch are at each other's throats after too many hours in the car, a visit to the Oriental Garden can soothe the savage beast in both of you. Isamu Taniguchi, a Japanese immigrant who suffered much from discrimination during World War II, personally built the garden as a peace offering to his adopted country. The winding paths, serene views, and trickling streams calm the soul, just as he designed them to. There is so much to sniff and savor here that your pooch may forget—and forgive—the leash. That's in the spirit of this little sanctuary in the midst of urban bustle.

Also part of the Botanical Center is the Rose Garden, built and kept by the Austin Garden Club. This is a popular site for weddings; your pooch can be your best dog here on that special day just as he is every other day. Also part of the complex is an early log schoolhouse and a pioneer log cabin. The buildings are locked, but you can peek in the window to see how dogs of long ago lived. I explained to Sport that the choice spot in front of the fireplace was reserved for the brave hunting dog who protected her home from bears and mountain lions and marauding raccoons bent on destroying the corn crop. She gave me that dog look that says, "Being directly descended from a long line of such heroic canines and having watched *Old Yeller* besides, I knew that."

The Zilker Botanical Center is located at 2220 Barton Springs Road; (512) 477-8672.

Sing a song of summer: Leashed pooches are welcome at a series of summer musical productions at the Zilker Hillside Theater beginning in July. It's outdoors, it's free, it's hot—well, everything can't be perfect, even in a dog's world. 2100 Barton Springs Road; (512) 397-1464.

Spam it up: Spam neatly illustrates the fact that people and dogs have entirely different ideas about what constitutes good food. (Of course, a rotting skunk carcass in the backyard serves the same function.) The annual Spamarama features the mystery meat people would rather heat than eat, but dogs think it's wonderful straight out of the can. To them it's high-class Alpo. No recipe is too disgusting to be entered in this cooking contest as long as the main ingredient is—yuk!—Spam. Leashed pooches may well find they are offered more samples than even a dog's stomach can stand. Sport Dog's advice is to bring your own dog food—at least you'll know what's in it. The cook-off is usually held on the Saturday closest to April 1. For dates and location call (512) 416-9307.

Tell the vet to buzz off: "Pets are absolutely welcome at The Herb Bar," says Twila Willis, owner and herbalist who is mother to a 110-pound bloodhound. "We always give dogs a treat when they come in, as well as some bottled water." Twila says that pretty much anything you can do for yourself herbally, you can do for your pet, using smaller doses. She uses herbs and essential oils to repel fleas and other critters. To get rid of an infestation, she suggests pyrethrum flowers or diatomaceous earth. The best-sounding remedy was a flea powder made of bay, rosemary, sage, and pennyroyal leaves, all of which are natural insect repellents. "It makes your dog smell like a sachet," Twila says. She recommends the book *Natural Insect Repellents for Pets, People, and Plants,* by Janette Granger. You and your pet may shop in person or by mail for the herbs and the book; request a catalog from The Herb Bar, 200 West Mary Street, Austin, TX 78704; (512) 444-6251.

Throw a dog writer a bone: When *Old Yeller* author Fred Gipson went to that big kennel in the sky, his bones were laid to rest in the State Cemetery in Austin, near his old friends Walter Prescott Webb and J. Frank Dobie. The three graves are just downhill and northeast a bit from Stephen F. Austin's grave. Go by the cemetery at East Seventh and Comal Streets and drive the shortest state highway—F.M. 165—that goes from the entrance to the little knoll where the graves are located. Then you and your leashed pooch can take a doggy treat over to Fred's grave just to let him know dog lovers everywhere still care. A cemetery worker said it would be fine to leave edible treats at the grave. "If it gets to be a problem, we'll pick them up," he said. However, Sport and I suspect the squirrels will get there first. The cemetery is bounded by East Seventh, East 11th, Navasota, and Comal Streets, east of Interstate 35. Follow East 11th Street to the entrance. (512) 478-8930.

Wish a jackass happy birthday: We're not talking about your boss, here. This is about one of the most beloved fictional characters of all time, Eeyore. You remember Eeyore—the gloomy donkey in the Winnie-the-Pooh stories. On the theory that Eeyore needs cheering up once a year (and that any old excuse will do for a party), well-wishers—many in appropriate costumes—descend on Pease Park in late April each year for what is perhaps *the* defining rite of spring for students at the University of Texas at Austin. The best part is that your pooch will think the party is for *him.* This is a cheap date; it's free, and once you've been, your pooch will know how to wrap a maypole and act silly.

From Lamar Boulevard between 12th and 15th Streets, take Enfield Road west and immediately turn right onto Parkway Road. It will intersect with Kingsbury Street in about a block. Park along Kingsbury Street to enter the park. (512) 499-6700.

BASTROP COUNTY

Bastrop County has one main thing going for it: It's close to Austin, but it's not Austin. Still largely rural, the county is somewhat insulated from the hustle and bustle of the big city. And while dogs must remain on leash in every park in the county, the parks are some of the prettiest in the state.

BASTROP

Bastrop is a charming riverside city with a long and proud history, but it's not very hospitable to dogs. None of the local motels or restaurants welcome your pooch. However, some of the best camping in Central Texas is just outside town in Bastrop State Park, so you can still enjoy the area's main attraction, the Lost Pines.

PARKS, BEACHES, AND RECREATION AREAS

• **Bastrop State Park** 🐾🐾🐾½ *See ㉗ on page 106.*

Sport and Samantha are suckers for a love story, probably because they are (usually) such lovable pooches themselves. In the section on Choke Canyon State Park, Sport and Samantha learned how Larry and Sally decided they liked each other well enough to get married. Bastrop State Park is where they did it. Yep, on a cold February 14 about 100 dog years ago, Larry and Sally stood in front of a blazing fire in the Bastrop State Park Rectory (built in the 1930s by the Civilian Conservation Corps) and snapped leashes on each other. (Dogs must remain on a six-foot leash in the park, but Larry and Sally cut each other a little more slack.)

This 3,504-acre park is graced with the Lost Pines, a relict stand of loblolly pine trees that dates back thousands of years to a time when Texas was cooler and wetter (and dogs were wilder and viciouser). Dogs who don't know better would swear they were in East Texas. There's something about a pine forest that really turns dogs on. Maybe it's the thousands of tall, straight trunks reaching for the sky, just begging to have a leg hiked on them. Maybe it's the soft carpet of pine needles blanketing the ground, just begging to be squatted on. Maybe it's the pungent smell of pine rosin assaulting sensitive canine nostrils. Or maybe it's the mysteriousness of the dark stillness that envelopes the adventurous dog as he seeks out the forest's secrets. Whatever it is, your pooch will love Bastrop State Park, particularly since it is just made for exploring on six feet.

The 8.5-mile Lost Pines Hiking Trail within the park has two trailheads along Park Road 1A. One is about 250 yards south of the intersection of Park Road 1A with Park Road 1C, which joins Bastrop State Park (see above) and Buescher State Park (see page 139). The trailhead is across Park Road 1A from the parking area for a CCC–built scenic overlook. The other trailhead leaves from a parking area along Park Road 1A just across from the Copperas Creek Camping Area. Obtain a trail map and rules when you enter the park. There are no designated campsites along the trail, but you may camp anywhere you choose once you pass a primitive road about half a mile from the Copperas Creek trailhead and a mile from the scenic overlook trailhead. Be careful where you pitch your tent and where you let your leashed pooch explore: there is a rank abundance of poison ivy along the trail, and it's a long walk back while the line "You're gonna need an ocean of calamine lotion," keeps running through your head. Be prepared to battle ticks, chiggers, and mosquitoes, too. The trail traverses creek bottoms and hilltops, running for much of its length along the top of a ridge trending east and west in the park ("So it's for ridgeback hounds?" Sport asks hopefully.) Along the northern leg of the loop trail a little more than two miles into the walk is a scenic overlook that lets you see mile after mile of pine trees falling away on descending slopes. It's a good place to just sit with your arm around your pooch and reflect on things that make life worth living. Sharing an experience like this with your dog is one of them. Taking your shoes off and letting your hot spots cool is another.

While your pooch is banned from the most highly sought-after accommodations in the park, the charming CCC–built sandstone cabins, you can share a campsite in one of two campgrounds. The Copperas Creek Camping Area would be my choice, as it has 28 sites with water and electricity and seven with water only spaced well apart under an open canopy of large pine trees, and not only does the Lost Pines Hiking Trail have one of its trailheads there, but also a nature trail connects this area to the park's other camping area. This campground near the park pool has a day-use picnic area as well as 25 trailer sites with water and electricity and 11 tent sites with water only. There is no chance for privacy here, for while the campsites are shaded by pine trees, there is no understory of screening brush, and picnickers and swimmers will be coming and going (noisily) all day and into the night. Sites with water and electricity are $12; those with water only are $9. The park also has a golf course if you are so inclined; the pro shop number is (512) 321-2327.

Reservations for campsites at all state parks must be made by calling the central reservation number, (512) 389-8900, between 9 A.M. and 6 P.M. Monday through Friday. Reservations are strongly recommended, and a deposit is required in order to guarantee a reservation. Specific sites may not be reserved; they are available on a first-come, first-served basis upon arrival.

While you're here, Dr. Deborah Douglas, author of *Gone for the Day: Family Fun in Central Texas*, prescribes a session of box-top sledding on pine needles. All you need is a piece of cardboard, a pine-needle-covered slope, courage, and a temporary absence of common sense. Sit on your cardboard and push off. Take your pooch along. If she has long, floppy ears that will stand out in the breeze, the effect is heightened. If she has a rotund tummy that will cushion your impact with a pine tree that won't get out of your way, that's even better.

The park is on Highway 21 about one mile east of Bastrop, or you may enter the park by following Park Road 1C from Buescher State Park. There is a $3 per person entry fee, but if you enter through Buescher State Park, that $2 entry fee will get you into this park as well. The park is open 24 hours. (512) 321-2101.

PLACES TO STAY

Bastrop State Park: See Bastrop State Park on page 136 for camping information.

FESTIVALS

Old Iron Bridge Outdoor Market: Towns with historic old iron bridges like to show them off as much as some people do their historic old dogs. This mid-October arts and crafts festival started out being held on the old iron bridge across the Colorado River but was moved to Fisherman's Park because of safety concerns. Still, you and your leashed pooch will enjoy shopping and snacking on the bank of the Colorado.

My grandfather, Burl Mason, ranched in Bastrop County when there was only a wooden bridge across the Colorado, and each year he drove a herd of cattle to Bastrop to the railroad. One year he was getting ready to put the herd onto the bridge to cross when a young woman said she did not want to wait until after the herd crossed; she was in a hurry to get to town. My grandfather tried to talk her into waiting, but she went ahead. When she was about halfway across, the herd of longhorns broke loose and ran for the other side, overtaking her. She had to crawl out on the end of a loose bridge plank and hang on for dear life while the thundering herd stomped and bellowed across, bouncing her high into the air. When the cowboys got to her, she was so scared they had to pry her fingers off the board one by one.

Fisherman's Park is just upstream from the old iron bridge at the intersection of Willow and Farm Streets. (512) 321-2419.

DIVERSIONS

Get hysterical: Texas is full of what my wife Sally Victor calls "hysterical historians," she being one herself. Such people look at old houses with the same longing with which a hungry pooch eyes a rib eye steak hanging half off the kitchen counter. Bastrop is a visual feast for dogs who appreciate historic buildings. It has 131 sites listed on the National Register of Historic Places in the very first multiple resource nomination in the United States. You and your leashed pooch can view these structures by taking a walking tour of the historic district. The Chamber of Commerce has a brochure and map. 927 Main Street; (512) 321-2419.

ELGIN

PLACES TO STAY

Ragtime Ranch Inn: A sheltie named Rags runs this place (which is named after him), and since he doesn't like to make beds or scrub toilets, he lets Roberta Butler and Debbie Jameson hang out here, too. "Here" is a fourplex bed-and-breakfast inn on 37 acres where your pooch is welcome to run leash-free to her heart's content. She can even chase one of the six resident cats. "They know how to take care of themselves," Roberta says, waving at the abundant trees located just a short cat sprint apart. The ranchette has pastures where horses roam, woods where raccoons and foxes and squirrels and other fascinating critters live, and even a pond for water dogs. "Dogs love it here—they can haul butt and have fun," Roberta says. After they've had their fun, you can use one of the hoses strategically located at each corner of the building to hose them off before they join you inside on the queen-size beds (two per room) or lounge in front of the fireplace. That's after you've rocked a while on the porch that wraps the building, of course. There's even a doggy shower room adjacent to room number 1. It's a screened-in area with water hose and floor drain where really dirty dogs can get a good hosing down. Doggy towels are yours for the asking, although some regular customers bring their own and a bed top cover as well, to spare the house linens and help make sure they are allowed to come back. A word to the wise should be sufficient.

Dogs pay nothing for all this luxury, but there is a $20 deposit to cover any little mishaps brought on by an excess of happiness. Rooms are $95. From Elgin, take F.M. 3000 east 3.2 miles to County Road 96; turn right and go 1.3 miles to County Road 98 (also marked Ragtime Ranch Road). Turn left onto County Road 98 and follow it half a mile to its end to reach the ranch; ignore the stop sign on the chain-link fence at the mobile home on your right about halfway there. It's just there for decoration. P.O. Box 575, Elgin, TX 78621; (512) 285-9599 or (800) 800-9743.

SMITHVILLE

PARKS, BEACHES, AND RECREATION AREAS

• **Buescher State Park** 🐾 🐾 🐾 ½ *See* ㉘ *on page 106.*

If your dog loves trees (and what dog doesn't), he's going to love this 1,017-acre park and its 3,504-acre neighbor, Bastrop State Park. Due partly to their proximity to Austin but largely because of their great natural beauty, these are some of the most popular parks in the state. Therefore, you and your leashed pooch may find the parks quite busy on weekends and holidays. On weekdays, though, you two will be able to walk miles of wooded trails in splendid isolation.

The trails are very special. The dominant tree in the area is a stand of loblolly pines that are relicts of cooler, wetter days when pine forests extended much farther west in Texas than they do today. This isolated pocket of evergreens sprawls across Buescher and Bastrop State Parks; because they are more than a hundred miles from their cousins to the east, they are known as the Lost Pines. The historical-minded dog may be interested to know that the Governor's Mansion in Austin was built using lumber from this forest. But if your pooch doesn't care about that, she will love exploring trails totally shaded by pines, each footfall muted by a thick litter of pine needles. You can amaze your pooch by engaging in an activity made possible by the hilly terrain and the pine needles: box-top sledding. Just take along a piece of cardboard big enough for you (or you and your pooch) to sit on. Find a steep, needle-covered slope as free of obstacles as possible. Sit down on your cardboard, grasp your pooch (or her leash) firmly, and push off. Your Texas toboggan will get to the bottom of the hill, as country folks say, right quick. Barring any chance encounters with a tree, of course.

Walking dogs can roam a 7.7-mile dirt trail that leaves from a trailhead at the Lakeview Camping Area at the southern end of the park and parallels Park Road 1C. The trail crosses the road at several places; parking places let you access portions of the trail. A map of the trail is obtainable from park headquarters.

The park has a large day-use picnic area with screened shelters (as in all state parks, dogs are not allowed in any park building). Dogs are not allowed in the 30-acre lake that occupies the area between the picnic and camping areas. The Cozy Circle Camping Area has 14 sites designed for trailers or RVs; all sites have water and electricity ($9). The Oak Haven Camping Area has 25 sites with water and electricity ($9) located in an area well shaded by trees, and surrounding vegetation screens the sites from each other, which are not spaced very far apart. The Lakeview Camping Area has 25 sites located under large trees, but the entire area is very open, with little ground cover vegetation. Sites have water only and rent for $6. The neatest thing about this camping spot is the large picnic pavilion built of native sandstone and local lumber by the Civilian Conservation Corps during the 1930s. There is a fireplace at each end, one facing the inside of the open building, and the other facing the outside. You and your pooch can bring along some firewood (gathering wood is prohibited in the park) and cuddle beside a cozy fire. Toasted marshmallows, anyone?

Reservations for campsites at all state parks must be made by calling the central reservation number, (512) 389-8900, between 9 A.M. and 6 P.M. Monday through Friday. Reservations are strongly recommended, and a deposit is required in order to guarantee a reservation. Specific sites may not be reserved; they are available on a first-come, first-served basis upon arrival. Entrance to the park costs $3 per person, which also covers entry to Bastrop State Park, located 10 miles away via Park Road 1C.

From Smithville drive two miles northwest on Highway 71, then go north on Highway 153 for half a mile to enter Park Road 1. The park is closed from 10 P.M. to 8 A.M. except to overnight guests. (512) 237-2241.

• **Rocky Hill Ranch** 🐾 🐾 🐾 *See ㉙ on page 106.*

Sometimes you run into a place that just doesn't fit into a nice, neat category. Rocky Hill Ranch had me scratching my head for a while. Is it a recreation area, a campground, or a restaurant? The confusing answer is that it is all three. However, since recreation is their main thing and everything else that goes on there revolves around that, we're including it here. (Besides, every dog I know considers eating and sleeping to be the ultimate in recreation.) Your pooch must remain on leash, but there are few other places we found where you can walk 30 miles of trails together on 1,200 acres of pine- and oak-studded hills, camp beneath the shade of an oak grove, and pig out on the covered porch of a country cafe without ever stepping off the property. Resident dogs Shebe (a Lab) and Lassie (guess what) greet you as you drive in.

Rocky Hill Ranch was designed for mountain bikers intent on destroying their bikes and themselves by plunging down hills and skidding around trees, but such tomfoolery seems to appeal to people who like dogs (Is there a connection here?), so owner Grey Hill opens the premises to all leashed dogs and their owners, whether they ride bikes or not. The trails are divided into three levels of difficulty for the bikers, but the guidelines serve well for hikers, too: Green-marked trails have gentle slopes; blue trails offer steeper hills and stream crossings; black trails are very steep and rugged. The trails bear such names as Fat Chuck's Demise, E-Z Pickens Trail, and my favorite, Fofenique Trail. Naturally, I had to ask about that one. "It's named for the Fofenique Indians," Grey Hill deadpanned. "They camped here at Camp Fofenique." AAAAARRRRRGGGGGHHHHH! There are also jeep trails for you and your pooch to walk if the idea of meeting a crazed biker flat-out at the bottom of a steep hill does not appeal to you.

The camping area is very primitive, consisting of an area cleared of brush and weeds and shaded by trees. Crude picnic tables dot the grove, but they are the sum total of the facilities. No water is available at the campground. When we last visited, construction was under way on screened shelters where dogs will be allowed. Tent camping is $4 per person, and there is a $6 per day fee for using the trails.

Food is available at the Rocky Hill Cafe and Saloon, which hugs the base of a tremendous oak tree hung with Spanish moss. The menu features half-pound burgers (you and your pooch can share one and both have plenty to eat) and sandwiches.

The ranch is on Highway 153 just west of its intersection with Highway 71 north of Smithville. P.O. Box 655, Smithville, TX 78957; (512) 237-3112.

RESTAURANTS

Rocky Hill Cafe and Saloon: See above.

PLACES TO STAY

Buescher State Park: See Buescher State Park on page 139 for camping information.

Cedar Owl Bed-and-Breakfast: You and your cowdog can stay in your own cabin with a fenced yard (but no gate) on this ranch where mature, well-behaved, housebroken dogs are welcome. Your dog can even be off leash inside the yard as long as she is under your direct control. The cabin rents for $125. The owner will take your credit card number and charge you for any doggy damages. Route 1, Box 300, Smithville, TX 78957; (512) 360-4894.

Katy House Bed-and-Breakfast: Sallie Blalock and family (which includes a golden retriever and a Welsh corgie) welcome you and your pooch to stay in one of two rooms with outside access. "The reason we don't allow them inside is because that's where our dogs are," Sallie says. Sallie specifies that you must make prior arrangements before bringing your pooch, you are responsible for any damage, and your pooch may not be left alone. As if. There is no dog fee; rooms are $75 to $95. 201 Ramona Street, Smithville, TX 78957; (512) 237-4262 or (800) 843-5289.

Rocky Hill Ranch: See Rocky Hill Ranch on page 141 for camping information.

FESTIVALS

Cavalier Dayes of Texas: The Rocky Hill Ranch hosts this Renaissance festival featuring artisans, musicians, and costume-clad hobbyists who engage in simulated duels, jousts, falconry demonstrations, and other medieval pursuits each year near the end of March and the first of April. It takes place at the ranch on Highway 153 just west of its intersection with Highway 71 north of Smithville. Call (512) 237-3112.

BELL COUNTY

Bell County is a place in a hurry to go nowhere. Interstate 35 splits the county from north to south, giant Fort Hood sprawls to the west, and the rush to get somewhere else dominates life here. It's not a restful or particularly friendly place to take a dog. Still, you may find yourself passing through and in need of a place to sleep or dewater your pooch. The concept of outside seating at restaurants seems to have barely penetrated these parts; bring a lunch.

BELTON

PARKS, BEACHES, AND RECREATION AREAS

• **City of Belton Park and Ride Facility** 🐾½ *See* ㉚ *on page 106.*

The five acres or so of this combination parking lot and park front Interstate 35, making it an ideal spot for a quick stop to dewater your pooch. There are rest rooms for people, too, under the shade of large pecan trees. Open grassy areas invite your pooch to romp, and a creek flowing along the north side of the park adds ambience for people and sniffing opportunities for dogs.

The park is at the intersection of the Interstate 35 access road and Confederate Park Street. Exit at Central Avenue. There is no phone.

RESTAURANTS

The Park Drive-In: Share a burger with your beagle at the picnic tables under the pecan trees and then go for a stroll in the tiny park across the street. The restaurant is just west of downtown at South Davis Street and West Avenue A; (254) 933-7400.

PLACES TO STAY

Live Oak Ridge Park: This U.S. Army Corps of Engineers campground on a cove of Lake Belton is nicely shaded with live oak trees. By design, there is no playground and no picnic area; all the campsites are rigged for RVs, and there is no swimming beach, which means it attracts a more mature crowd. Your senior-citizen pooch will fit right in.

The 40 sites go for $14 a night, which includes water and electricity and the use of rest rooms with showers. All the sites are well shaded and have a picnic table and barbecue pit.

From Highway 317 two miles north of Belton, take F.M. 2305 west one mile, then go south one mile on F.M. 2271. 99 F.M. 2271, Belton, TX 76513; (254) 780-1738.

KILLEEN

PARKS, BEACHES, AND RECREATION AREAS

•**Community Center Park** 🐾 *See* ③ *on page 106.*

Athletic fields, parking lots, and buildings smother most of this 139-acre park, but the weedy, brushy fringe along Nolan Creek on the north side beckons the leashed pooch.

Located on South Young Street a quarter mile north of Business U.S. 190, the park is open from 9 A.M. to 7 P.M. (254) 526-0550.

•**Conder Park** 🐾 *See* ③ *on page 106.*

The best part of this 30-acre park is the marshy pond populated by ducks on the south end. It feeds a small creek running through the center of the park, where mowed grass and live oak trees share the space with a playground, picnic tables, and rest rooms. You and your leashed pooch can tramp across the two footbridges over the creek looking for trolls. Park rules require you to pick up after your dog.

The park is at Business U.S. 190 and Conder Street. Hours are 9 A.M. to 7 P.M. (254) 526-0550.

•**Long Branch Park** 🐾½ *See* ③ *on page 106.*

This 77-acre park seemed to be the favorite of local dogs; we saw several leashed pooches taking their owners for a jaunt along the jogging trail here. The gently rolling terrain has few trees, but there is a creek running through the center of the park, although its banks were steep, weedy, and muddy. For people, there are picnic tables, barbecue grills, rest rooms, and a playground. Park rules require you to keep your dog on a leash and pick up after her.

At the corner of East Rancier and Branch Streets, the park is open from 9 A.M. to 7 P.M. (254) 526-0550.

RESTAURANTS

Mr. Sub: "Bring all the dogs you want!" the manager said. At least those that like submarine sandwiches are welcome to eat with you at one of the covered tables out front. 716 West Veterans Memorial Boulevard (Business U.S. 190); (254) 634-7438.

Red Lobster: Order to go and eat on the bench out front. 1001 West Central Texas Expressway (U.S. 190); (254) 526-7335.

Taco Cabana: Don't tell your pooch this is a chain restaurant and she'll be glad to share Tex-Mex with you on the patio. Or maybe she's into chains 'n' tacos. 1002 West Central Texas Expressway (U.S. 190); (254) 519-2842.

BLANCO COUNTY

The county, river, and town of the same name (Spanish for "white") likely are so called because of the white limestone that predominates. President Lyndon B. Johnson was born here, and his memory lives on among dog lovers for his habit of holding his beagles up by their ears to show them off. The county itself isn't much friendlier to dogs, who must remain on leash and are barred from the water at one of the county's two state parks. Dogs are totally forbidden at the Lyndon B. Johnson National Historical Park in Johnson City, but after hearing how LBJ treated his hounds, Sport didn't want to visit there anyway.

BLANCO

PARKS, BEACHES, AND RECREATION AREAS

• **Blanco State Park** 🐾 1/2 *See* ㉞ *on page 106.*
This 105-acre park is built for water lovers, but those of the four-legged kind are not welcome. Not only must dogs be kept on a six-foot leash, but they must stay out of the water and all park buildings as well. The park stretches for nearly a mile along both sides of the Blanco River, which runs through the town of the same name. Large pecan trees shade riverside picnic tables and barbecue grills where you and your pooch can have a cookout. Water is available, as are rest rooms and playgrounds.

Just after crossing the low water bridge to the campground, turn left onto a gravel road. A few yards on is a parking area; beyond the barricade a short hiking trail leads along the riverbank. It was suitably weedy for Sport; she found lots to sniff. The trail passes under the U.S. 281 bridge, which was festooned with cliff swallow nests when we visited. Parents darted in and out, bringing insects to their young. Sport watched the ceaseless activity for a while and concluded, I think, that being neutered has its advantages.

The small, tree-shaded campground overlooks the river; it is laid out in typical state park fashion with sites closely spaced around a loop drive, but there is a grassy area in the center where you can walk your pooch. Sites with full hookups are $14; sites with water and electricity (including tent sites) are $12.

Reservations for campsites at all state parks must be made by calling the central reservation number, (512) 389-8900, between 9 A.M. and 6 P.M. Monday through Friday. Reservations are strongly recommended, and a deposit is required in order to guarantee a reservation. Specific sites may not be reserved; they are available on a first-come, first-served basis upon arrival.

The park entrance is on the north side of the Blanco River at the U.S. 281 crossing. The entry fee is $3 per person. The park closes at 10 P.M. except to overnight guests. (830) 833-4333.

• **Town Creek Nature Trail** 🐾 *See* ㉟ *on page 106.*

Park at the southeast corner of the town square and amble along a short trail that follows a channelized creekbed. Large pecan and willow trees overhang the trail, which branches several times and crosses the creek on footbridges. The narrow trail with lots of vegetation all around provided Sport with many sniffing opportunities.

Just across the first footbridge, the trail forks at a park bench. The right fork takes you to the Blanco River and the east end of a day-use picnic area in the state park. The left fork leads by one of the most magnificent live oak trees any dog ever hiked a leg on. Sport was awed. Then she spotted the biggest cat she'd ever seen (other than our own resident cat, Comet the 15-pound wonder) and lost interest in the tree. She normally would not dream of chasing a cat, but this brindle tabby looked too much like a raccoon. I was glad I had a firm grip on the leash.

The park is at the intersection of Pecan and Third Streets, on the southeast corner of the square. There is no phone.

RESTAURANTS

Blanco Valley Health Coffee and Juice Bar: Sit at one of four tables on the sidewalk and sip a cup of organic coffee, cappuccino, latté, espresso, or brevé; fresh-squeezed carrot, wheat grass, or fruit juices; Italian sodas, or fruit smoothies. "One of my regular customers brings his weimaraner in for frozen yogurt and has me put it in a bowl so they can share," says owner Sherri Stockman. 608 Fourth Street; (830) 833-2483.

Pecan Street Bakery and Cafe: Have a breakfast taco, homemade pastry, burger, or quiche at one of two outside tables or two benches at this cozy little place on the southeast corner of the square. 306 Pecan Street; (830) 833-5737.

Phil's BBQ and Deli: Sport and I passed by Phil Anderson's smoking pit on our way to picnic at Blanco State Park. That was a mistake Sport will not soon let me forget. After lunch we dropped by to inquire if pooches were welcome at the five tables under the pecan trees along Town Creek. "Dogs are not only welcome; I'll bring them some meat scraps," Phil smiled. I could feel Sport's accusing stare even before I looked at her. Yep, I was in deep doggy doo. I'd fed her a corner of a salami sandwich when she could have been dining on brisket. A dog does not soon forget things like that; I had to put up with mournful sighs for a hour as we trucked on down the road. If barbecue isn't on your menu, try a deli sub sandwich, a burger, a salad, or fried catfish.

And speaking of things fried, the brave hearts among you may wish to sample one of Phil's Phried Phrickers. "It's a battered, deep-fried Snickers bar," Phil explains. "This is probably the only place in the country where you can get one." No doubt.

Phil's is located on U.S. 281 just north of the Blanco River at 115 Main Street; (830) 833-2139.

PLACES TO STAY

Blanco State Park: See Blanco State Park on page 145 for camping information.

DIVERSIONS

Flea to the market: The Blanco Flea Market, a collection of antiques and collectible dealers housed in a funky old store, welcomes small dogs as long as they are kept in arms. "One of our dealers brings her Pomeranian into the store in a basket," the clerk said. "But even our owners won't bring their big dogs in." You and your cuddly canine may find just that accent piece you've been looking for—there's not much that isn't for sale here. Fifth and Pecan Streets; (830) 833-2204.

Track down a dinosaur: Sport has one of the biggest, blackest, wettest dog noses I've ever had the pleasure of rubbing. That king-size sniffer is wasted on tracking down raccoons when it was meant for bigger things— like dinosaurs. Sport had her chance to track down a sauropod near Blanco, and your pooch will enjoy doing so, too. The bonus is getting to frolic in the Blanco River at the same time. Follow F.M. 1623 west from its intersection with U.S. 281 in downtown Blanco. About three and a half miles from town, turn south (left) on County Road 103. Park at the end of the bridge and walk left (downstream) in the riverbed, making sure not to trespass on private land away from the river. Look for three-foot-long depressions with raised edges. Sport sniffed. She was not impressed. Even her supersensitive nose was not up to the challenge of following a 120-million-year-old scent trail.

JOHNSON CITY

Don't try to take your pooch to the Lyndon B. Johnson National Historical Park here; she is not welcome. Instead, head out to Pedernales Falls State Park, where at least a leashed pooch can go for a swim. And for heaven's sake, don't sound like some out-of-touch tourist and pronounce the name as it's spelled. For some reason, the name is pronounced PERD-uh-nal-is. I know, I know, by the same line of reasoning there ought to be a breed of dog called the Saint Barnyard, but there it is. Live with it. This is Texas. We may be wrong, but do it our way.

PARKS, BEACHES, AND RECREATION AREAS

• **Pedernales Falls State Park** 🐾🐾🐾½ *See* **③⑥** *on page 106.*

Your dog will find much to love about this 5,212-acre park in the heart of the Texas Hill Country. It has trails to walk, hills to climb, trees galore, and miles—literally miles—of river to swim. The only drawback is that your pooch must remain leashed at all times. You will likely see free-roaming pooches and be tempted to let yours join them, but resist the urge. "We may bar dogs from the park in the future if people don't keep them on leash," the park superintendent warns.

Swimming is what this park is all about, and as long as your pooch remains on her six-foot leash, she is free to enjoy the four miles of riverfront beach with you. The swimming area is reached by taking the first road to the right past the campground. A trail about 200 yards long stretches from the parking lot (with rest rooms and cold-water shower out front) to the river. The climb is steep and slippery. You may notice your pooch holding his head to one side as you go down, and you may feel a touch of vertigo as well. Soon you realize that all the trees in the hundred-foot-deep gulch lean downstream. There is a good reason for this. The Pedernales, a typical Hill Country stream, has a mercurial temperament, quick to rise and quick to fall. Periodic flash floods sweep the canyon; the cypress trees along the river and the oaks and junipers on the canyon walls have all been sculpted by rushing water and given a permanent tilt. The realization that the canyon can be completely filled with raging torrents makes you appreciate the warning signs throughout the park telling you that when the flood warning sirens sound, you should vacate the river bottom areas immediately.

To gain the best appreciation for the power this measly little river can muster at times, hike the Falls Trail—a short, easy walk—to an observation point overlooking the Pedernales Falls. The trail winds through a cedar brake dotted with oak trees, ideal habitat for the endangered golden-cheeked warbler, which nests in the area in the spring. Suddenly the limestone strata fall away rapidly, sending the river tumbling down rock slides and through narrow chutes. At low water the river disappears into slots cut over the ages; at flood stage the rapids here rival any in North America. Sport and I hiked down to the riverbed to wiggle our toes in a sandy beach deposited by some past flood, but we kept an ear peeled for the warning siren.

To get a taste of the sublime pockets of beauty this park holds, take the nature trail that leaves the park's one campground near campsite 21. Park at the head of the trail and head downhill. The park calls this a quarter-mile nature trail; after hiking it on a well-developed June afternoon, Sport and I decided it was considerably longer than a quarter of a mile and was misnamed as well. It ought to be called a natural trail, because what trail making has taken place has been done mainly by the feet of people and dogs using the trail. It is steep, very rocky, poorly marked, and extremely twisting. Yet it is well worth the effort, for at its midpoint is an overlook from which you can see the Twin Falls, a limestone grotto shaded by cypress and oak trees. Ferns droop from limestone cliffs, and the sound of running water does its best to drown out the calls of songbirds. Sport wanted to do a triple somersault off the overlook above the pool, but the area is closed to visitors because they have loved it nearly to death in the past, causing soil compaction and damaging the vegetation. Watch carefully as you hike this trail, because it is easy to miss a turn. In many places the only clue you have that you are on the trail is the faint depression in the ground left by those who passed before you.

For a more challenging hike, take the 7.5-mile Wolf Mountain Trail, which begins at a parking lot reached by taking the first right-hand turn after you leave park headquarters. This is a very rugged trail that traverses several streambeds and climbs steep, rocky hills. There is a spring at the farthest point of the trail from the parking lot where a thirsty pooch can take a drink and cool down for the return journey. Dogs are not allowed to stay overnight in the primitive camping area about two miles from the start of the trail. In addition, they are banned from the trail in the park designated for equestrian use.

The person who designed the campground deserves an award from whatever group recognizes excellence in the art of packing people into parks without making them feel like sardines. The campsites ($16) are spacious, well screened from each other by oak, mesquite, and juniper trees, and have electricity and water. Most of us would be happy to have a backyard as large and inviting. Your pooch will have plenty of room to dewater, sniff around, and generally feel woodsy. Don't be surprised if you catch him gazing longingly at checked flannel bandannas the next time the two of you go shopping for clothes. This park will make your pooch fall in love with the outdoors.

Reservations for campsites at all state parks must be made by calling the central reservation number, (512) 389-8900, between 9 A.M. and 6 P.M. Monday through Friday. Reservations are strongly recommended, and a deposit is required in order to guarantee a reservation. Specific sites may not be reserved; they are available on a first-come, first-served basis upon arrival.

The park is located nine miles east of Johnson City on F.M. 2766. If you are coming from Austin, it's closer to take F.M. 3232 north from U.S. 290. The entrance is at the intersection of the two highways. Entrance costs $4 per person. The park opens at 8 A.M. and closes at 10 P.M. except to campers. (830) 868-7304.

RESTAURANTS

The Feed Mill: The Feed Mill is exactly what its name implies, and more. This former eyesore blossomed under the care of artist Charles Trois into a complex of shops, restaurants, a winery, a petting zoo—a labyrinth beckoning leashed dogs to explore. Around every turn is another piece of old farm equipment or oddity waiting to be sniffed. "This is a pretty dog-friendly place," a shop owner told us, inviting us in. Tom Burks welcomes dog lovers to come inside his winery and sample his wares; he also offered the use of the tables just outside for people who want to order to go at the Feed Mill Cafe upstairs. Your pooch won't let you miss the Feed Mill: Samantha started barking wildly as soon as she spotted the giant inflatable King Kong swaying atop the building. 103 West Main Street (U.S. 290); (830) 868-7299.

PLACES TO STAY

Pedernales Falls State Park: See Pedernales Falls State Park on page 148 for camping information.

Save Inn: All good dogs are welcome here for $5 per night. Rooms are $41 to $46. 107 U.S. 281/290 South, P.O. Box 610, Johnson City, TX 78636; (830) 868-4044.

BURNET COUNTY

At the risk of overusing a phrase that is already a classic cliché, Burnet County may be one of Texas dog lovers' best-kept secrets. The Colorado River cuts through live-oak-clad pink granite hills, making for some of the prettiest scenery in the state. Dams along the river create a chain of lakes abutted by public recreation areas, four of which permit unleashed pooches to hike, swim, and investigate scent trails left by the abundant wildlife.

BURNET

PARKS, BEACHES, AND RECREATION AREAS

•**Hamilton Creek Park** 🐾 🐾 *See* ㊲ *on page 106.*

This urban park just southwest of the intersection of the two main highways serving Burnet sprawls along the banks of Hamilton Creek. A one-mile (round-trip) sidewalk lets leashed pooches get their exercise mostly in the shade and always just a step away from the water, although the channelized creekbed does not invite drinking or dipping.

From U.S. 281, turn west on Jackson Street, which is two blocks south of the intersection with Highway 29. Go two blocks to a parking area for the park. The park is open 24 hours. (512) 756-6093.

• **Inks Lake State Park** 🐾 🐾 🐾 ½ *See* ❸❽ *on page 106.*

This 1,202-acre park is a Texas treasure. Wrapped around five promontories projecting into Inks Lake, the park is strewn with pink granite outcrops cloaked in a thick fuzz of live oaks, mesquites, and junipers. Your leashed pooch will love rubbing noses with the many white-tailed deer that wander unafraid in the campgrounds. These deer will literally eat out of your hand, although caution should be exercised, especially during the fall rut, when males can become aggressive.

The northern two-thirds of the park is most popular with campers and swimmers in the summertime, since it has several protected coves that are designated swimming areas. Your pooch, who must remain on leash throughout the park, is not allowed in the water or adjacent to the swim beaches in this area. In addition, dogs are banned from the screened shelters and may not be left tied outside.

A network of improved hiking trails—nearly six miles in all—winds among the campsites in the southern third of the park and extends across Park Road 4. These trails are an excellent place to view the park's abundant wildlife. Obtain a park map when you check in; it shows the hiking trails and distances between points. Trailhead signs mark the beginnings of trails, but when Sport and I last visited the signs were badly in need of maintenance and were hard to read. Plus they are very hard to uproot and drag along with you. Get the map.

Campsites in the northern half of the park have water and electricity ($15). Perhaps because this part of the park is the best for swimming and is therefore quite popular, sites are packed closely together. Many are shaded by trees, but the emphasis here is on efficient use of space. Screened shelters rent for $20, but your pooch is not allowed inside and cannot be left outside. Campsites in the southern half of the park—reached by turning left when you leave the park headquarters—have water but no electricity, but they are more widely spaced and are more likely to be shaded by trees. They go for $10. You and your water dog will be most happy in campsites 300 through 349. Many of these sites back up to the shoreline. The water is only a few feet away, and your leashed pooch is free to swim and splash until she has worked up the world's biggest outdoor appetite. Hot dog, anyone? All improved camping areas are served by rest rooms with showers.

If you and your wilderness pooch want to camp with the critters, the Pecan Flats Trail Camp ($8) lies half a mile north of Park Road 4. Park on the left just past park headquarters and follow the hiking trail a mile to the first campsite and a mile and a half to the farthest from the parking lot. The numbered sites are laid out in a half-moon pattern about 100 yards apart.

Reservations for campsites at all state parks must be made by calling the central reservation number, (512) 389-8900, between 9 A.M. and 6 P.M. Monday through Friday. Reservations are strongly recommended, and a deposit is required in order to guarantee a reservation. Specific sites may not be reserved; they are available on a first-come, first-served basis upon arrival.

From Burnet go west on Highway 29 six miles to Park Road 4 and follow the signs three miles to the park. The entry fee is $3 per person. The park closes at 10 P.M. to all except overnight guests. (512) 793-2223.

• **Tommy White Park** 🐾 *See* ③⑨ *on page 106.*

There are about five acres in this park, most of which are given over to people pursuits. However, a picnic area right behind the swimming pool is a handy relaxing place for a stressed-out car pooch who is fed up with you not stopping to ask directions. Next to the shaded picnic area is an open field of about an acre where a leashed pooch can work off her frustrations and get ready for more miles.

The park is on Highway 29 about half a mile west of its intersection with U.S. 281. Turn right at the next driveway after the Ho-Jo Inn entrance. It's open 24 hours. (512) 756-6093.

RESTAURANTS

Burnet County BBQ: You and your hungry pooch can share one of the two picnic tables in the covered area to the left of the entrance. 616 Buchanan Street (Highway 29 West); (512) 756-6468.

PLACES TO STAY

Inks Lake State Park: See Inks Lake State Park on page 151 for camping information.

Sundown Motor Inn: Rooms are $35 to $45. There is no fee for housebroken dogs to spend the night. 205 North Water Street (U.S. 281), Burnet, TX 78611; (512) 756-2171.

FESTIVALS

Burnet Bluebonnet Festival: There are probably few prettier places on Earth than the Texas Hill Country during the spring wildflower season, and Burnet celebrates this annual blooming event with a mid-April arts and crafts festival. Your leashed pooch is welcome to attend as long as he does not complain too much about looking at hundreds of handmade craft items, nearly every one of which is adorned with the Texas state flower. Call the Chamber of Commerce for dates, locations, and specific events: (512) 756-4297.

DIVERSIONS

Circle the wagons: Fort Croghan was established in 1849 to protect settlers from the Indians, who did not appreciate having the prettiest part of Texas taken away from them. You and your leashed pooch can visit the outdoor exhibits (but not the museum), including log and stone cabins built by area settlers in the 1850s and the powder magazine of the old fort. Admission is by donation. If you and your pooch visit during Fort Croghan Day in mid-October, you can watch folks dressed in period costumes bake bread in a wood cook stove, churn butter, quilt, shear sheep, make lye soap, or feed sorghum cane into a press and boil the juice into syrup. Particularly attentive pooches might beg a sample. Sport much prefers the syrup to the lye soap. Having had my mouth washed out with the latter a time or two when I was young, I agree completely. 703 Buchanan Drive (Highway 29 West); (512) 756-8281.

Feel young again at the Burnet Antique Mall: Whenever I feel old, I just pop into the nearest antique store, and in a few minutes I feel rejuvenated. Most of the stuff inside is much older than I am. Sometimes Sport and I find an antique tin to add to the family collection. Sport and Samantha favor new tins themselves, as they often come with goodies inside to be shared with well-behaved puppies. Small dogs held in arms may browse until they find just that perfect antique for their doghouse. 206 South Main Street; (512) 756-7783.

Mind your Ps and Qs at Suzy Q: I would neither have written this book nor visited Suzy Q if I had never met Dr. Deborah Douglas of San Antonio. (Sport just dozed off. She could sense a story coming and somehow knew it would not involve a raccoon.) When the publishers of this book began looking for someone to write it, they first contacted the aforesaid Dr. Douglas, who had recently published an excellent travel guide to the Texas Hill Country and has a writing style every bit as witty and irreverent as my own. For some reason she preferred to take care of her medical practice instead of writing this book, but she did recommend yours truly for the job. So here I am. And here you are, standing on the sidewalk in front of Suzy Q, wondering what all this has to do with you. I'm getting to that. In her book, Dr. Douglas recommended this store as her favorite place in Texas to shop for clothes, and after having visited (leaving Sport outside; only small dogs in arms are allowed inside), I have to say the woman has good taste. And not just because she recommended me. The store has very nice Southwestern wear as well as gourmet coffees and teas. 132 South Main Street; (512) 756-8246.

MARBLE FALLS

PARKS, BEACHES, AND RECREATION AREAS

- **Camp Creek Primitive Recreation Area** 🐾🐾🐾 🐕
  See **40** *on page 106.*

Your pooch will love running leash-free among the hundreds of huge pecan trees in this 500-acre park. What she won't love is the steep shoreline of Lake Travis that makes it difficult to cool off after all that romping. There are miles of dirt roads to hike. One has been converted to a strictly hiking trail; an information kiosk and parking area is on the right shortly after you enter the park. There is no entrance fee.

Camping is free, too, at a five-acre lakeside campground maintained by Burnet County. About a dozen picnic tables, all shaded by huge pecan trees, several fire rings, and a dumpster compose the facilities. The surrounding vegetation is dense, so the lack of sanitary facilities should pose no inconvenience to someone accustomed to scooping dog poop.

The park is eight miles east of Marble Falls off Ranch Road 1431. Turn right (south) on County Road 343 and follow it about half a mile to the park, which is open 24 hours. (512) 473-4083 or (800) 776-5272.

- **Johnson Park** 🐾🐾 *See* **41** *on page 106.*

Dogs must stay on leash in this city park, but the grass is so invitingly green and neatly mowed, the trees are so lush, and Falls Creek is so cool they won't mind too much. The day-use only park has shaded picnic tables, a playground, swimming in the creek, barbecue pits, and rest rooms.

From U.S. 281, turn west on First Street just before the bridge across Lake Marble Falls. In one block turn left on Avenue H; after another block turn right on Yett Street. (When your pooch whines, "Are we Yett there?" for the jillionth time, you can truthfully answer in the affirmative.) The park is open for day use. (830) 693-3615.

- **Shaffer Bend Primitive Recreation Area** 🐾🐾🐾½ 🐕
  See **42** *on page 106.*

"Free" is the operative word at this Lower Colorado River Authority park. There is no entry fee, camping is free, and your pooch may run sans leash everywhere except in the camping areas, which are few in number and marked only by fire rings. This is an isolated, secluded, 535-acre park where you can lounge on the bank of Lake Travis—which at this point is only a couple of hundred yards wide—in the shade of huge pecan trees or swim in the lake off one of the sandy beaches reached by unpaved roads.

Exploring the roads is one of the charms of this park. Sport and I turned down a promising looking dirt track off the main graveled road and immediately found ourselves in a grove of large pecan trees. Sport was thinking raccoon until the herd of deer bolted from the deep shade. Much of the park is brushy and weedy, which makes for great sniffing, but such areas can harbor rattlesnakes, ticks, and poison ivy.

Shaffer Bend has more than a mile of frontage on Lake Travis, and most of the campsites overlook the river bottom. If you camp here, be aware of the fact that Lake Travis is a flood control lake, and its level can go up quickly due to heavy rains upstream. Be ready to move to higher ground, or better yet, camp there in the first place if the weather promises rain. Some of the ungraveled roads in the park may become impassable in wet weather, since they negotiate boggy bottomland and cross creeks.

Shaffer Bend is on the north side of Lake Travis nine miles east of Marble Falls on Ranch Road 1431. From Ranch Road 1431 turn right (south) on County Road 343A and follow the pavement about a mile. The unmarked entrance to the park is on your right just at the pavement's end. It is open 24 hours. (512) 473-4083 or (800) 776-5272.

PLACES TO STAY

Best Western Marble Falls Inn: Small dogs only may stay at this brand-new, two-story motel. There is lots of grass around for necessary strolls. Rooms are $60 to $75. 1403 U.S. 281 North, Marble Falls, TX 78654; (830) 693-5122 or (800) 528-1234.

Camp Creek Primitive Recreation Area: See Camp Creek Primitive Recreation Area on page 154 for camping information.

Shaffer Bend Primitive Recreation Area: See Shaffer Bend Primitive Recreation Area on page 154 for camping information.

SPICEWOOD

PARKS, BEACHES, AND RECREATION AREAS

• **Grelle Primitive Recreation Area** 👣 👣 👣 🐕

See ㊸ on page 106.

If 400 acres of leash-free Hill Country woodland with half a mile of Lake Travis shoreline for swimming and a two-mile sure-'nuff rugged hiking trail is what your pooch is looking for, this park fills the bill. The $3 per vehicle entry fee gets you and your pooch this and more, for primitive camping here is free. Only fire rings and the occasional portable potty mar the natural landscape. Live oak groves and dense juniper thickets hide large numbers of white-tailed deer. Your pooch is free to roam off leash anywhere except in the camping area as long as he remains under your direct control.

Somehow this park just lacks the charm of some of the other primitive recreation areas operated by the Lower Colorado River Authority on the north side of Lake Travis. In addition, the park is much more popular and heavily used due to its proximity to Austin. Sport and I are not antisocial—we get along with each other tail-waggingly well—but we just prefer a little more solitude than this park offers on weekends. Weekdays the park is nearly deserted.

The two-mile (one way) hiking trail begins at a portable potty at the southernmost campsite and climbs up a steep hill right away. That pretty well sets the tone of the trail, but how else would you get those spectacular views of the lake? Of course, when we last visited it was a hot July day, and the lake was a mere ghost of its usual self, so both the trail and the views of the lake were somewhat lacking. We hope to get back when the drought is over.

The park is on the south side of Lake Travis just outside the hamlet of Spicewood. Take Highway 71 west from Austin to Spur 191 at Spicewood. Turn right (north) on Spur 191 and go about a mile to Spicewood; turn right on County Road 404 and follow it about a mile to its intersection with County Road 412. Watch carefully for this turn to the left, as it comes just over the brow of a hill. Turn left onto County Road 412 and go about half a mile to the park entrance. Entry costs $3 per vehicle. It is open 24 hours. (512) 473-4083 or (800) 776-5272.

• **Muleshoe Bend Primitive Recreation Area** 🐾 🐾 🐾 🐕
  See **44** *on page 106.*

At something over 900 acres, this may be the biggest park in the Lower Colorado River Authority's system of primitive recreation areas, but biggest is not always best, even in Texas. Sport and I found little to quarrel with, but not a lot to get excited about, either. There is a fine walking trail which takes off through a chain-link gate just behind the entrance information kiosk. The trail leads you to bluffs overlooking Lake Travis, and the view is spectacular. However, we were much more interested in the many white-tailed bucks in velvet we saw throughout the park as we traveled the maze of well-maintained gravel and dirt roads. Sport and I both find deer beautiful to watch, and we share a love for them as well. We both think they are delicious.

Camping is free at the primitive lakeside campsites, the best of which are marked by fire rings. Others are simply a mound of blackened rocks under a particularly nice shade tree. All have views of the lake, which had receded nearly half a mile when Sport and I visited in the middle of a drought. Normally, campsites are just a long leash away from the lake, and the camping area is the only place your pooch is required to be adorned with her leash. Throughout the rest of the park, she may roam sans leash as long as she is under your direct control.

This park is not an easy one to find. Just remember to turn right at every opportunity, and you won't go wrong. From Highway 71 west of Austin, take Paleface Ranch Road to the north. It will become Burnet County Road 404 just after you pass Hayne Flat Road and enter Burnet County. After about another mile, turn right on County Road 414. In about a mile, jog hard right at the sign advertising hang gliding lessons and continue on to the entrance to the Ridge Harbor subdivision, where County Road 414 takes another sharp bend to the right. In about a mile, the pavement will end. Immediately turn right onto the gravel road and go another quarter mile to the park entrance. The entry fee is $3 per vehicle. It is open 24 hours. (512) 473-4083 or (800) 776-5272.

PLACES TO STAY

Grelle Primitive Recreation Area: See Grelle Primitive Recreation Area on page 155 for camping information.

Muleshoe Bend Primitive Recreation Area: See Muleshoe Bend Primitive Recreation Area on page 156 for camping information.

CALDWELL COUNTY

Sometimes leash laws are a good thing. That's the case in Caldwell County, where one of the chief attractions is some of the most scrumptious barbecue any dog ever lapped a lip around. Loose dogs and unguarded meat just do not mix well. Around dogs like Samantha, the fastest jaws in the West, even guarded meat is not safe.

Besides barbecue fit for the dog who would be king, Caldwell County's other chief asset is Cookie, the public relations dog at Lockhart State Park. Your pooch will have to stay on leash at this and all other parks in the county, but Cookie alone makes a visit worthwhile.

LOCKHART

This town is noted as being the home of one of the best barbecue places in Texas, Kreuz Market (that's pronounced "kreytz"). Unfortunately, your pooch cannot enter this hallowed hall, but you can order to go and chow down at a couple of local parks that are ideal for the purpose. At Lockhart State Park you'll meet Cookie, one of the smartest, most playful Labrador retrievers in Texas. Okay, she is THE smartest and most playful, as well as the cutest. If you don't believe me, ask Cookie's mom, Charlotte Mercer, who will probably take your money as you enter the park. When I last visited, Cookie turned the charm up

---

full blast, retrieving an empty Famous Amos cookie package from a park garbage can so she could entice me into a game of keep-away. Cookie is very good at keep-away. But then she's also very good at having her tummy scratched. Go by and pay her a visit. She's expecting you.

You'll have to keep your pooch on leash at all times here, but if you feed him barbecue for every meal, he'll forgive you.

PARKS, BEACHES, AND RECREATION AREAS

• **Lockhart Municipal Park** 🐾 🐾 1/2 *See* ⑮ *on page 106.*

Sport and I headed out of Austin in a hurry early one morning, and by the time we got a half-hour down the road, Sport remembered she had some urgent business she had not attended to. So we pulled into the first park we saw when we got into Lockhart. Then Sport didn't want to leave. She's a sucker for clear, clean creeks with banks shaded by large pecan, oak, and willow trees. She knows that's just the sort of place where raccoons, squirrels, and other interesting-smelling critters hang out. Even though she had to remain on leash, Sport had a fine time exploring along the quarter mile or so of creek that forms the southern border of this 41-acre park. There's also a small fishing lake where some boys were trying their luck, a playground, picnic tables, tennis courts, rest rooms, and some athletic fields.

The park is at the intersection of U.S. 183 and City Park Road on the north side of Lockhart. It is open from sunrise to 10 P.M. (512) 398-6452.

• **Lockhart State Park** 🐾 🐾 🐾 1/2 *See* ⑯ *on page 106.*

Bigger isn't always better, even in Texas. This 263-acre park where your pooch must remain leashed is a small park by any standard, but it stands head and shoulders above all other Texas state parks as being, without doubt, the dog-friendliest park in Texas. The reason is Cookie, a four-year-old Lab. "Cookie is not just the park dog, she's our public relations person—and she does a really good job," says Cookie's mom, Charlotte Mercer. Charlotte is the park's administrative technician. Cookie feels right at home in the park because she is the second generation of her family to grow up there. Her father, Bear, belongs to the park superintendent and also grew up in the park.

Most of the park is taken up by a nine-hole golf course, which gets a lot of repeat customers. Cookie has a lot of fans among them. "People ask for Cookie before they ask to talk to us," Charlotte says. Cookie's favorite part of the park is the creek that runs through its center. Thickly shaded by elm trees, the creek has lots of pools to splash in and overgrown banks to explore. You may see deer, coyotes, foxes, raccoons, opossums, armadillos, nutrias, rabbits, squirrels, and a variety of birds. There can also be the occasional rattlesnake, so beware. A picnic area with tables and barbecue grills is located along one branch of the creek.

All the standard state parks regulations regarding dogs apply. Dogs must remain on a six-foot leash and may not enter any park building. Dogs may not be left tied outside a tent or RV, or be left unattended at any time.

The small campground is one reason the park has a reputation as being a quiet, peaceful place. There are 10 RV sites with water, electricity, and sewage hookups that rent for $12 a night. Ten tent sites with water and electricity go for $10. These sites are located along the creekbank and are heavily shaded by trees. A rest room with showers serves the camping area. There is also a swimming pool, and fishing is allowed in the creeks. Plum Creek is spring-fed and crosses the golf course area, leading to an unusual rule for this park: No fishing in fairways!

Reservations for campsites at all state parks must be made by calling the central reservation number, (512) 389-8900, between 9 A.M. and 6 P.M. Monday through Friday. Reservations are strongly recommended, and a deposit is required in order to guarantee a reservation. Specific sites may not be reserved; they are available on a first-come, first-served basis upon arrival.

From U.S. 183 one mile south of Lockhart, go west on F.M. 20 for two miles to Park Road 10. There is a $2 per person entry fee. The park closes at 10 P.M. except to overnight guests. (512) 398-3479.

RESTAURANTS

Golden Fried Chicken: "Sure! No problem!" the manager said when I asked if Sport and I could share one of the two covered tables out front. And yes, Sport demands her chicken be deboned and her french fries cooled off. Hold the ketchup, please. 640 South Colorado Street (U.S. 183 South); (512) 398-4442.

Texas Burger: Order a meat-and-bun for your pooch and share one of the five covered picnic tables out front. 1118 South Colorado Street (U.S. 183 South); (512) 398-5241.

PLACES TO STAY

Leisure Camp and RV Park: Dogs are recognized as being part of the family here, which means not only that they are welcome but also that you must take responsibility for them and clean up after them. Dogs must be kept on leash any time they are outside, and they may not be tied outside. There is a walking area for dogs, and they are not allowed in the San Marcos River, which runs by the camp. Tent sites are $11; sites with water and electric hookup are $15; screened shelters are $30. The campground is 12 miles southwest of Lockhart in Fentress. P.O. Box 277, Fentress, TX 78622; (512) 488-2563.

Lockhart State Park: See Lockhart State Park on page 158 for camping information.

LULING

As Sport and I neared Luling, the car began to smell. We both stared out the window with that demeanor that says, "I don't smell anything. Do you smell anything?" The closer we got to town, the ranker the smell became. But the reason is not what it often is when traveling dogs beg too many samples of unfamiliar foods. Luling is an oil town—literally—and the black stuff comes out of the ground saturated with a healthy dose of odoriferous gas. About 200 pump jacks dot the town, doing their part in keeping you and your traveling pooch on the go. Many have been decorated with fanciful depictions of animals; Luling may be the only town in Texas whose oil wells form the basis of a tour.

Your pooch must remain on leash while in Luling, but she is welcome at the town's biggest annual event, the Watermelon Thump, as well as at other festivals. And then there's that barbecue. . . .

PARKS, BEACHES, AND RECREATION AREAS

• **Northside Park** ⛲ *See ㊾ on page 106.*

This eight-acre park has a playground, pool, picnic tables, rest rooms, and some grassy areas where your leashed pooch can take care of urgent business, but it is almost totally lacking in charm. The picnic tables are shaded by trees, but it's not the kind of place you'd go to spend time with your dog.

From U.S. 183, turn west on Trinity Street and go two blocks to Park Avenue. Turn right into the park, which is open 24 hours. (830) 875-2481.

• **Southside Park** 🐾 *See ㊽ on page 106.*

Only marginally better than Northside Park on the other end of town, this park at least has a pleasantly shaded riverbank where your leashed pooch can disembark and sniff a few trees before finding that special spot she's looking for. There's only about an acre to survey, so it won't take her long. The big disappointment is that very steep banks prevent you and your pooch from making your way down to the water. There is a water faucet at the end of the park farthest from the highway, however.

The park is on the east side of Highway 80, on the north side of the San Marcos River. It closes at 10 P.M. (830) 875-2481.

RESTAURANTS

City Market Barbecue: This famous barbecue joint makes its own sausage and serves it up hot off the pit. Eat at one of the benches under the trees across the street. 633 East Davis Street; (830) 875-9019.

Luling Bar-B-Q: Dine with your doggy at one of the benches across the street. 709 East Davis Street; (830) 875-3848.

Wood Stop Country Store and Cafe: Barbecue is wonderful. Barbecue is manna. Barbecue is nigh unto a religion in Texas. But—can you keep a secret?—even the most thoroughly Texan dog sometimes wants to eat something besides tender, juicy, lip-smacking-good meat. Well, okay; it's you who has to have something different once in a while. The Wood Stop will please both you and your pooch, because they have not only barbecue but also burgers, steaks, and fish, all of which you and your pooch can eat on their covered gazebo out back. 401 North Mesquite Street (Highway 80 North); (830) 875-5415.

PLACES TO STAY

Coachway Inn: Rooms are $38 to $45. Small dogs only may stay here; there is no charge. 1908 East Pierce (U.S. 90/183 East); (830) 875-5635.

FESTIVALS

Luling Watermelon Thump: "There's no policy on dogs yet," the Chamber of Commerce manager told me ominously. This longtime late-June celebration of one of the county's juiciest assets—even counting those oil wells—recently moved to the downtown area behind a fence, so it's possible that at some point dogs may be excluded. This would be a shame, as dogs can thump right along with the best of them. At least their tails can. Your pooch probably won't be interested in most of the events—rodeo, golf, bowling tournaments, and the crowning of the Thump Queen, but she's sure to love the street dances (doh-si-doh your Doberman), arts and craft fair, flea market (Sport and Samantha are forever picking up bargain fleas), food booths, and seed-spitting contest. (The world record of 68 feet, 9 $\frac{1}{8}$ inches was set way back in 1989; if your pooch hopes to break it, she'd better start practicing right now.) The event is held in the 600 block of East Davis Street in downtown Luling. For information, call (830) 875-3214.

Night in Old Luling: You'll like the arts and crafts show and the classic car show; your pooch will enjoy getting all decked out and taking part in the pet parade. It all takes place in mid-October each year in the 600 block of East Davis Street in downtown Luling. For information, call (830) 875-3214.

DIVERSIONS

Jack around: Luling was built on top of an oil field, and pump jacks nod and hum all over town—in parking lots, in people's front yards—wherever the precious black gold was found. Pump jacks are not the prettiest thing to have sitting on your property, so local citizens decided to dress them up with painted designs. There's one decorated like a grasshopper, and another like Tony the Tiger. At one time all the pump jacks were so adorned, but time took its toll on the paint and the enthusiasm of the volunteers, and many of the "oil paintings" have been taken down, including the one that featured a dog (Snoopy, of course, the world's most recognizable cartoon canine). However, the paintings may be redone and "rehung," so check around to see what's up. If Snoopy reappears, he'll probably be in his old location, in the parking lot on the south side of the Super S grocery store at the intersection of Highway 80 and Crockett Street. Your pooch would be pleased to have his picture taken there, you can be sure.

Veg out: Take your pooch shopping at the open-air Farmer's Market in the 700 block of East Davis Street (at the intersection of U.S. 183 and Highway 80). Vendors sell local watermelons and produce (as available seasonally) out of stands or the backs of their pickup trucks.

FAYETTE COUNTY

As every dog knows, sometimes the truth is stranger (and more interesting) than fiction. Fayette County provided the venue for a famous episode in Texas history that never made the history books but inspired a Broadway play and a movie: *The Best Little Whorehouse in Texas.* Yep, it was right here in rural Fayette County that the madams and misses of the Chicken Ranch plied their trade in what was said to be the oldest continuously operating brothel in the United States, dating to 1844. Its operations were tolerated by the local sheriff, who solved many a case using information leaked by patrons caught with their pants down— figuratively as well as literally. The house got its name during the Great Depression, when a lack of ready cash and the need to feed a stable of hungry fillies led the owner to institute a policy described in *The New Handbook of Texas* as (I kid you not) "one chicken for one screw." The respected reference work states that not only were the girls well fed, but also the Chicken Ranch became an exporter of both live chickens and eggs. And that despite the fact that no doubt at least one egg-sucking dog lived under the porch.

The Chicken Ranch closed in 1973 following an exposé on Houston television by Marvin Zindler, who would finish behind a dog-beater in a popularity contest in La Grange to this day. In one of those tacky twists that could only happen in Texas, two Houston lawyers bought the ranch and moved part of the building to Dallas, where it served as a restaurant, called the Chicken Ranch, that served mainly chicken dishes. In an even weirder twist, the hostess at the restaurant was the last madam of the La Grange operation. Who says Texans have no sense of propriety?

For the dog who is not interested in the seamy side of life, the county has three leash-free areas. However, even the dog who ordinarily would not give a worn-out tennis ball for a history lesson will want to visit one historic site in the county: the very first roadside park in Texas. Any dog whose self-respect, not to mention traveling privileges, has been saved by the fortuitous appearance of a roadside park will definitely want to take a respectful squat here.

FAYETTEVILLE
FESTIVALS

Lickskillet Days: If there ever was a festival with a name dogs could identify with, this is it. The community of Fayetteville was once known as Lickskillet. Each mid-October, food and arts and crafts booths take over the town in celebration of those days of old. Fayetteville is east of La Grange on F.M. 955. For information, call (409) 968-5756.

LA GRANGE

There must be something in the water in La Grange: every single motel in town accepts dogs. This is good not so much because you need a place to sleep, but because you and your pooch will have a haven where you can hole up while you sample every kind of kolache this town is famous for: cheese filled, prune filled, apricot filled, peach filled—I could go on and on, but as I am writing this at a distance of 150 miles from those doughy delights, it's too painful. You'll have to eat in your room, because the restaurants that serve kolaches don't have outside seating. But did you really want anyone to see you eating all those sweets you said you were giving up? Hmmmm? I thought not. Sport and I recommend the kolaches at the Bon Ton Restaurant (on Highway 71 West), Lukas Bakery (on the square), and Weikel's Store and Bakery (Highway 71 West). They're all good—for your soul if not for your body.

When you start feeling guilty about all that sugar you've consumed, head for one of the area parks where leashed dogs may roam, or visit the Rice-Osborne Bird and Nature Trail, where your overindulging pooch can atone somewhat for her gluttonous behavior by running leash-free. This is punishment?

PARKS, BEACHES, AND RECREATION AREAS
• City Park 🐾1/2 *See* ㊾ *on page 106.*
This approximately one-acre park has Colorado River frontage with

a grassy, pecan-tree-shaded picnic area where you and your leashed pooch may take a break. When Sport and I last visited, neither the light nor the water in the men's room were working, but Sport didn't seem to mind. Fortunately for a thirsty dog, the water faucet beside the large pecan tree directly in front of the rest room building did spew forth a cooling stream.

From Highway 71 go north on Washington Street to Pearl Street. Turn left and go one block to Main Street. Turn right and go two blocks to Hanacek Road. Turn left to get to the park, which closes at dusk. (409) 968-5806.

• **Colorado River Boat Ramp and Picnic Area** 🐾 *See* **50** *on page 106.*

Highway river crossings often provide the only public access to public waterways in public-land-poor Texas. A case in point is this pretty little parkette nestled below the old Colorado River bridge. Its reason for being is a public boat ramp, which also provides river access for you and your leashed pooch. About an acre of grass, shaded partly by trees and partly by the bridge, gives you and your pooch a place to stretch and get out of the car for awhile. Picnic tables, barbecue grills, and portable toilets are the amenities.

The park is below the Highway 71 bridge at the Colorado River. Turn right at the public boat ramp sign and descend beneath the bridge. The park is open 24 hours. There is no phone.

• **Monument Hill and Kreische Brewery State Historical Parks** 🐾 🐾
See **51** *on page 106.*

You get two parks for the price of one here, but the total acreage is only about 40. However, within that small space are packed two walking trails, picnic areas, a monument to and graves of heroes of Texas's fight for independence, and the remains of a historic brewery. You and your leashed pooch can gain quite a bit of knowledge about Texas history, the early brewing industry, and native Texas plants.

Dogs love buried bones, and few places in Texas have more historic collections of bones than this park, although we must hasten to add that while respectful contemplation of the remains is encouraged, digging is strictly forbidden. Buried here are the remains of about 50 Texans killed in two separate campaigns against Mexico following the Texas Revolution. The bones were moved here in 1848 and are principally those of men from Fayette County. Sport and I walked the half-mile interpretive trail that takes visitors past the grave site and the nearby ruins of a brewery that once occupied the site. Approaching the grave and monument, we saw a little building that looks something like a guardhouse. We peeked inside and saw a guest registry. Sport Dog is now enshrined in history as one of the visitors signing the guest book. With a little help from me, of course.

The view of the Colorado River and the town of La Grange from the scenic overlook just past the monument is awesome and well worth a much longer walk. Farther on is a pay telescope; if you have binoculars, take them along to enjoy the view. For Sport, though, the two highlights of the walk were yet to come—her idea of a scenic overlook is a tree limb loaded with raccoons. As we approached the overlook of the ruins of the brewery, three buzzards erupted from a tree just a dozen feet away. If there's one thing that gets Sport more excited than raccoons, it's buzzards, and she went crazy barking at them. Then we visited the second best part of the tour, the water fountain and faucet located where the brewery overlook spur trail takes off from the main path. We both had a good drink.

The park is located on the outskirts of La Grange just off U.S. 77 South. From the intersection of U.S. 71 and U.S. 77, go south on U.S. 77 one mile to Spur 92. Turn right on Spur 92 and follow it to the entrance. Entry costs $2 per person. Hours are 8 A.M. to 5 P.M. (409) 968-5658.

• **Park Prairie Park** 🐾 🐕 *See ⑤② on page 106.*
Lake Fayette's 2,420 acres serve as the cooling lake for the Fayette Power Plant, pumping electricity for Austin's air conditioners, toasters, curling irons, and electric fences restraining dogs. Yikes! This park is one of two access points for the lake, which due to its warm waters is a favorite with fishers, the main users. However, if you have a yen to camp by the water, there are primitive campsites ($7). No reservations are accepted. The camping area straddles the boat ramp and is shaded by trees; thick grass grows to the water's edge. Your pooch is required to be on leash in the camping area only, but there isn't much place else to roam. Dogs can swim in the water off leash, however.

And what about that odd name? The park is named after the nearby rural community of Park Prairie. So it's Park Prairie Park. Sort of like Snoop Doggy Dog was named for—oh, forget it.

To reach the park, take Highway 71 to Highway 159 in La Grange; follow Highway 159 east about 7.5 miles to County Road 196. Turn right on the county road and follow it to the park entrance. The entrance fee is $4. The park is open 24 hours a day. (409) 249-3344 or (800) 776-5272.

• **Rice-Osborne Bird and Nature Trail** 🐾 🐾 ½ 🐕
See ⑤③ on page 106.
Dogs on Lower Colorado River Authority lands are required to be leashed only in campground areas. That's good news for your pooch, because he can romp and play along this 2.5-mile lakeside nature trail

winding through 20 acres as long as you keep him company. There is no admission charge. The trailhead is at the entrance gate to Oak Thicket Park, which is primarily used as a boat-launching facility and is only open from 5 A.M. Saturday until 6 P.M. Sunday. That means you and your pooch can wander in solitude any weekday. Park at the entrance gate and walk to your heart's content.

To reach the park, take Highway 71 to Highway 159 in La Grange; follow Highway 159 east about 9.5 miles to the entrance to Oak Thicket Park. A sign beside the entrance gate marks the trailhead. The park is open 24 hours. (409) 249-3971 or (800) 776-5272.

• **White Rock Park** 🐾🐾🐾 🐕 *See ⑤④ on page 106.*

After a long day in the car, Sport bailed out and hit the ground running, rolling, and barking at this 30-acre leash-free park that requires dogs to be "under owner's control" according to the sign at the entrance. Whether Sport was under control at the moment was debatable. Sometimes a dog's just gotta be a dog. Then we discovered that the park also has a mile-long walking trail, picnic tables with barbecue grills, a rest room, and—best of all—a concrete walkway that leads down the Colorado River bank to a set of concrete steps descending into the water and, just a few steps farther on, a wooden deck. Both are shaded by large pecan trees. A water dog could spend all day here diving into the water, running up the bank to roll in the dirt, running over to the deck to jump up on her owner, running back to jump into the water . . . . The park also has athletic fields; if you venture there it would be best to leash your pooch.

From Highway 71 east of downtown, turn right (southeast) on Lester Street (it runs right along the cemetery fence) and follow it until it makes a T with Eblin Street. Turn left on Eblin Street and go one block to South Mode Lane; turn right and follow it to the park entrance sign. The park is open from 7 A.M. until dusk. (409) 968-5806.

PLACES TO STAY

Carter Motel: Rooms are $24 to $34. Well-behaved dogs may slide on in for a $25 deposit. 243 Ellinger Road, La Grange, TX 78945; (409) 968-8331.

Cottonwood Inn: Rooms are $28 to $38. There is a pool and a restaurant. 1494 Highway 71 West, La Grange, TX 78945; (409) 968-3175.

Northpointe Executive Suites: Any size executive dog may enjoy the amenities of a two-story townhouse suite with pool and tennis courts, and an enclosed dog run. Rooms are $44. There is no pet fee, but you are responsible for any damage. 202 Northpointe Avenue, La Grange, TX 78945; (409) 968-6406.

Park Prairie Park: See Park Prairie Park on page 165 for camping information.

River Valley Motor Inn: Rooms are $35 to $55. Small dogs only are welcome here at no fee. Working dogs may use the fax and copy machines. 1611 Business 71 West, La Grange, TX 78945; (409) 968-8314.

DIVERSIONS

Make a pilgrimage with your pooch: In the late 1800s many European immigrants settled around La Grange, and their influence is felt in many ways today. Besides kolaches, one of the most interesting is an assortment of rural churches in southern Fayette County. Lacking the funds to build the chapels of their dreams, the immigrants built modestly but decorated interiors lavishly, painting plain wooden columns with feathers to look like marble and splashing angels across ceilings. Four of these churches are open daily to the visitor, but our favorite time to go is on Saturday, when you may happen upon the organist practicing hymns for the morrow. Dogs will not mind waiting outside for you, since all the churches have grassy, shaded grounds around them.

From La Grange, go south on U.S. 77 to its intersection with F.M. 1383. Follow F.M. 1383 east 3.5 miles; turn right on Mensik Road (County Road 471) and go one-tenth of a mile to Ammansville's St. John the Baptist Church. Its white exterior with black roof is austere, in stark contrast to the soft pink color scheme of the interior. Notice the stair railings and columns painted to resemble marble. Outside, your pooch will enjoy the spacious lawn with a water faucet conveniently located at the base of the utility pole to the right of the entrance.

Continue south from Ammansville on F.M. 1383 for 5.3 miles; turn right on Piano Bridge Road (County Road 480) and go one-tenth of a mile to Saints Cyril and Methodius Church in Dubina. The subdued white and gray exterior gives no hint of the lavish interior dominated by rich blues. The stations of the cross are extraordinarily ornate. While the locked gate inside the entrance doors prevented us from going farther than the vestibule, there were a couple of bonuses. First was the friendly gray and white dog who dashed up to greet us, begging to be petted and then waiting patiently for us to come out and administer round two. The second was something you'll not see often: the original version of the porta potty. Not so discreetly tucked into some trees west of the church are two privies labeled "Muzske" (men) and "Zenske" (women). These afford you and your pooch the rare opportunity to squat together. As we headed off for the next church, we were escorted to the edge of town by a gray and white streak who had obviously done this before.

From Dubina, follow County Road 480 west. In 1.9 miles it becomes

F.M. 615, which is paved. Continue another 2.6 miles to U.S. 77; go across on County Road 440 and continue 1.6 miles to St. Mary's Catholic Church in High Hill. This imposing red-brick structure is the most lavishly decorated and appointed of all the painted churches. The altar is amazing.

From High Hill, continue 2.5 miles south on F.M. 2672 to U.S. 90 in Schulenburg; turn right and go 8.4 miles to F.M. 1295; turn left and drive 0.7 miles to St. Mary's Church in Praha. This limestone church also has a highly decorated interior; the angels soaring above the elaborate altar make it my favorite. Tell your pooch the little stone house by the parking lot is not a doghouse; it's a grotto. There is plenty of shade across the parking lot at the covered pavilion, and the little white house beside the pavilion is just what you hoped: a modern rest room.

For information and a map showing the locations of the painted churches, contact the La Grange Area Chamber of Commerce, 171 South Main Street, La Grange, TX 78945; (409) 968-5756 or (800) 524-7264.

Spring into summer: When winter rains cometh, wildflowers follow in the spring, and Fayette County roadways offer some of the best viewing in the state. Picture your pooch in a patch of primroses, Indian paintbrush, bluebonnets, or other varieties of wildflowers blanketing the area. The La Grange Area Chamber of Commerce furnishes information on the best places and dates to see an abundance of blossoms. For information, call (409) 968-5756 or (800) LA GRANGE/524-7264.

Take a historic squat: How many times has a strategically located roadside park saved your pooch's life, not to mention the upholstery of your car? Fayette County offers traveling dogs a unique opportunity: they can take a squat in the very first roadside park in Texas. The park is 12 miles west of La Grange on the south side of Highway 71. A Texas Historical Marker tells its tale.

GILLESPIE COUNTY

Gillespie County is one of the most hospitable in the state—but not to dogs. There isn't a leash-free area in the whole county. However, the welcome mat is out for pooches at a number of area motels, bed-and-breakfasts, restaurants, and stores. Your pooch can eat, sleep, and shop right along with the hordes of people doing the same.

FREDERICKSBURG

Penny Reeh, former director of the Fredericksburg Convention and Visitors Bureau, is fond of saying that this Gillespie County town's popularity as a tourist destination is due to three things: a dead president

(Lyndon B. Johnson), a dead admiral (Chester Nimitz), and a big rock (Enchanted Rock). While dogs might love to sniff all three of those things—especially the dead bodies—there's a lot more in Gillespie County for the traveling pooch to like. Specifically, you and your pooch can luxuriate in sumptuous bed-and-breakfasts, gobble up some of the finest German cooking west of the Black Forest, and put your noses to the ground in search of bargains that would make a Scottie proud.

"Grow where you are planted" might well have been the motto of Fredericksburg's founders. German immigrants sowed the seeds of civilization in 1846, and the town took root in the rocky Hill Country soil. Today visitors reap the harvest of a rich cultural heritage carefully tended and cultivated for a century and a half. More than anything else, desire to experience that heritage draws people from all over the world to Fredericksburg, making it one of the most-visited cities in the state.

Diane Smith teaches history as she takes people (and their pooches) on carriage rides through the historic neighborhoods. "People wonder about the really wide Main Street," she says. "Early Fredericksburg had a lot of freighters who used oxen, which can't back up as a team. So the street was made wide to give them room to turn around. Also, the Germans were very neat people, and the wide street let them park their teams in the middle of the street and keep the sides clean for walking."

The sharp-eyed Sport wondered why the first letters of street names going east from the center of town spell "All Welcome," and those going west spell "Come Back." The blame appears to lie with the local Lions Club, which took on the project of naming the streets and installing street signs sometime after 1933.

Marcia Dietz runs Dietz Bakery with her husband. She sums up what makes Fredericksburg special. "This is a rural Texas town that happened to be settled by German people. Some visitors expect Fredericksburg to be a little piece of Germany, with people wearing lederhosen. But that's not what Fredericksburg is. We are Americans who have kept a lot of the German traditions."

And one of the nicest of those traditions is expressed in a word used frequently in Fredericksburg: willkommen. You'll find that word applies to dogs as well as humans.

PARKS, BEACHES, AND RECREATION AREAS

• **Lady Bird Johnson Municipal Park** 🐾 ½ *See* 55 *on page 106.*
Your leashed dog can play in Liveoak Creek, which runs through this 340-acre park, and there is a shaded picnic area with room to roam, but the bulk of the park is for people activities—a golf course, putting greens, driving range, swimming pool, baseball fields, volleyball, and tennis courts.

A shaded campground with rest rooms and showers is laid out in neat rows primarily for the convenience of RVers. Sites with hookups are $13; tent sites are $6. Reservations are accepted. Rules governing dogs are strictly enforced: Dogs must be on leash at all times. They may not be left unattended in or out of an RV or tent. They may not be left tied outside even if the owner is inside. Dogs may not enter any building on the site. Only two dogs are allowed per campsite. Owners must clean up after their dogs immediately.

The park is three miles south of Fredericksburg on Highway 16. The office is open from 7 A.M. until 10 P.M. except during daylight savings time, when it closes at 11 P.M. (830) 997-4202.

RESTAURANTS

Altdorf Restaurant: Ask for a table next to the fence around the patio and tie your dog nearby so you can slip her some of your bratwurst, sauerbraten, or sandwich. "We take water to thirsty dogs all the time," the manager said. 301 West Main Street; (830) 997-7865.

Auslander Restaurant: Your leashed pooch is welcome to join you at your table on the patio, and friendly waitpersons know what to do when a thirsty dog shows up. "We see a lot of thirsty dogs in the summer," the manager said. Circle the block and park in back; that's also where the patio is. The eclectic menu includes German, Mexican, Greek, and American foods. 323 East Main Street; (830) 997-7714.

The Plateau Cafe: How dog-friendly is this place with 20 tables in their garden dining area? "A lady was just in here wanting to get food to go because she had three dogs with her. I told her to come on in," the manager said. The staff loves to water leashed, thirsty dogs. You'll like the Texas-size chicken-fried steak, the garlic-flavored mashed potatoes, or one of the German specialties. 312 West Main Street; (830) 997-1853.

PLACES TO STAY

Alfred Haus: If a little yellow house on the back side of a 240-acre ranch sounds like the kind of getaway your harried husky has been pining for, the Alfred Haus is for you. Located nine miles outside Fredericksburg on a working ranch where cattle, llamas, and emus roam, the ranch has a four-acre fishing pond you may use (bring your own gear). This is the perfect place for your pooch to work out those kinks in his cast. No breakfast is provided, but there is a fully equipped kitchen with coffee and teas furnished. The house rents for $74 with a two-night minimum on weekends. Make reservations through Gastehaus Schmidt, 231 West Main Street, Fredericksburg, TX 78624; (830) 997-5612.

The Baag Farm House Bed-and-Breakfast: This frame house was built in the 1920s as a wedding gift for the daughter of a previous owner of this property near Luckenbach. Painted blue with white trim, the house sets off the white wicker porch furniture. Yes, there's a porch for your pooch to nap on, which she'll need to do after exploring the adjoining 35-acre pasture. Rooms are $85. Make reservations through Gastehaus Schmidt, 231 West Main Street, Fredericksburg, TX 78624; (830) 997-5612.

Comfort Inn Motel: The $64 rate includes a continental breakfast. This motel with tennis courts also has a vacant lot out back where you can exercise your leashed pooch. Notify the manager you have a dog; leaving it in the room alone is verboten. 908 South Adams Street, Fredericksburg, TX 78624; (830) 997-9811.

Country Inn: Any size dog is welcome here, where there is a big yard for walking your leashed friend. Rooms are $35 to $45. The inn is located on U.S. 290 at the west city limit, with no street address. Route 2, Box 98, Fredericksburg, TX 78624; (830) 997-2185.

Fredericksburg KOA: Two dogs are allowed per RV site ($18.75) but not in cabins. Dogs must be leashed at all times. A grassy field is available for needful visits, and there are all kinds of exotic animals to bark at in the adjoining pasture. Reservations are accepted. It's located five miles east of Fredericksburg on U.S. 290. Route 1, Box 238, Fredericksburg, TX 78624; (830) 997-4796.

Frontier Inn: This small 11-unit motel takes any housebroken dog and provides an extra sheet to protect the bedspread so you and your pooch can snuggle like you do at home. There's a vacant lot out back to walk your leashed dog as long as you promise to clean up after him. Rooms are $33 to $44. The inn is located on U.S. 290 at the west city limit, with no street address. Route 2, Box 99, Fredericksburg, TX 78624; (830) 997-4389.

Indiana House Bed-and-Breakfast: All you transplanted Hoosier dogs listen up: You can get a taste of Yankee-land by staying in this log cabin, which really did come from Indiana. Situated next to a barn and surrounded by live oak trees, the house is fully furnished with antiques. The master bedroom has a four-poster bed and a fireplace. Outside are 35 acres to roam; legendary Luckenbach is just a few miles down the road. The house rents for $115. You can make reservations through Settler's Crossing, 104 Settler's Crossing Road, Fredericksburg, TX 78624; (830) 997-2722 or (800) 874-1020.

Lady Bird Johnson Municipal Park: See Lady Bird Johnson Municipal Park on page 169 for camping information.

Miller's Inn: This motel's owner is not wild about dogs, but he will accept small and medium-size dogs "because we think a lot of our guests." Motel rooms are often in short supply in Fredericksburg, so you and your leashed pooch may wind up here. Be nice and maybe someday dogs will not only be tolerated but actually welcomed. Rooms are $32 to $50. 910 East Main Street, Fredericksburg, TX 78624; (830) 997-2244.

Oakwood RV Park: This pretty, tree-shaded campground accepts no large dogs, does not tolerate dogs left alone, and requires that you clean up after your leashed pooch. Campsites are $23. Reservations are accepted. The park is two miles south of town on Highway 16 at F.M. 2093. Route 2, Box 218B, Fredericksburg, TX 78624; (830) 997-9817.

Pioneer Homestead Bed-and-Breakfast: Slap a coonskin cap on your pooch's noggin and head for this 1800s log cabin built by German immigrants. Two of the three bedrooms have queen-size beds and a fireplace, just the cozy kind of place to curl up in while dreaming of the exciting hunt to come tomorrow—antique hunting, of course. The Pioneer Homestead is furnished in 18th- and 19th-century antiques, from the rugs on the original wood floors to the numerous accent pieces. You and your pooch may roam the adjacent 35-acre pasture as well. The Pioneer Homestead is located in the country east of Fredericksburg and near Luckenbach. It has been featured in both *Country Living* and *Country Homes* magazines. Rooms are $115. Make reservations through Settler's Crossing, 104 Settler's Crossing Road, Fredericksburg, TX 78624; (830) 997-2722 or (800) 874-1020.

Rocky Top Bed-and-Breakfast: Your leashed pooch can explore 22 acres, rub noses with horses, goats, and potbellied pigs, and take a dip in the creek for the bargain price of $5. You can put your exhausted pal to sleep in your $70 room. The inn is located eight miles north of town at 7910 F.M. 965. Route 4, Box 221, Fredericksburg, TX 78624; (830) 997-8145.

Schmidt Barn Bed-and-Breakfast: We've all probably seen times when, viewing puddles in the floor or the tattered corner of an expensive counterpane, we've wanted to thunder at our transgressing canine, "You're sleeping in the barn tonight!" This is your chance to make good on that threat—except staying at the Schmidt Barn is a treat, not a punishment. This 1860s German limestone barn has been transformed into one of Fredericksburg's premiere bed-and-breakfasts. Antique furniture inside is complemented by the fragrant herb and flower garden just outside the door. Nearby, you and your pooch can dally away the day in a wooden swing under a huge live oak. The resident cats will greet you; they adhere strictly to the Golden Rule. (They will also climb in your car and go to sleep; if you don't want to arrive home with an extra furry body, roll your car windows up.) Schmidt Barn has been featured in several travel guides as well as *Country Living* and *Travel & Leisure* magazines. Dogs under 20 pounds may share the barn with you for $10 each per night. You'll pay a very reasonable $85. Make reservations through

Gastehaus Schmidt, 231 West Main Street, Fredericksburg, TX 78624; (830) 997-5612.

Sunset Inn Motel: Small, leashed dogs are welcome. There is a dog walk out back. Rooms are $39 to $44. 900 South Adams Street, Fredericksburg, TX 78624; (830) 997-9581.

Von Heinrich Home Bed-and-Breakfast: Fredericksburg is famous for its B&Bs, and the Von Heinrich Home is one good reason why. This 1787 Pennsylvania Dutch *fachwerk* house was reconstructed on a 35-acre site just a few miles down the road from the legendary Luckenbach. (*Fachwerk* refers to the type of construction in which a hewn log framework is erected and then infilled with stones mortared together.) You and your pooch may lounge in front of the fireplace in the living room, bake a batch of doggy treats in the kitchen, visit with the donkeys and sheep outside, or just veg out under the vine-covered arbor. There's even a Jacuzzi built for two. Fully furnished with antiques, the Von Heinrich Home has been featured in both *Country Living* and *Country Homes* magazines. Rooms are $119. Make reservations through Settler's Crossing, 104 Settler's Crossing Road, Fredericksburg, TX 78624; (830) 997-2722 or (800) 874-1020.

DIVERSIONS

Get carriaged away: Diane Smith and her toy poodle Scamper love telling dogs all about Fredericksburg's history as their horse-drawn carriage creaks and rumbles along neighborhood streets. Diane says she has never had a canine customer bail out in pursuit of a cat, so your pooch still has a chance to be first should your grip slip on the leash. If you feel lucky, check the daily schedule posted on the barn door behind the Altdorf Restaurant at 301 West Main Street, but Diane recommends you call her for a reservation at (830) 997-2211.

Pound the pavement: You and your pooch cannot "do" Fredericksburg without joining the masses endlessly migrating along the sidewalks from one end of Main Street to the other and back. There are at least 67 antique stores, boutiques, galleries, and assorted other shops in this town that probably accounts for more credit card charges per capita than any other burg of its size in Texas. If you and your pooch leave town without at least one thing you never knew you could not live without until you saw it, you will be the first to do so. Actually, you'll be the second. Exactly why Sport wanted a 12-foot-long dining table made of recycled jarrah wood railroad ties from South "Arfrica" I will never know—there's no way it would fit in her doghouse—but she had to moan and bitch all the way home, because the $9,878 price tag would have put her way over the credit limit on her charge card.

Fortunately, there are lots of more affordable things to buy in

Fredericksburg if the lucky dog just knows where to look. Here are a few shops we found that welcome four-footed shoppers; you can probably get in a lot more by asking politely and maybe whining just a little.

Valerie Durst at Something Different welcomes dogs if held in owners' arms. Walk by the shop's display windows (115 East Main Street; 830-997-2734) and see if the colorful and stylish clothes for women (and a few for men) don't tempt you to hoist your husky and go inside. The Secret Garden (102 East Main Street; 830-997-5507) lured Sport with its air of mystery and racks of fine female fashions, but since small dogs only are allowed inside, I had to drag this 75-pound Rhodesian Ridgeback on down the street to Texas Wines, Etc. (214 East Main Street; 830-997-5780), where the friendly manager poured me a sample of the Hill Country's finest and brought Sport a bowl of water, commiserating that "It's too hot to leave a dog outside." Sport said it was some of the finest water she'd ever drunk, with overtones of opossum toes, just a hint of horse slobber, and a fishy finish. My wine was every bit as good. Drinking always puts Sport in a mellow mood, so next we headed for the Dulcimer Factory (155 East Main Street; 830-997-2626) and stood on the sidewalk outside listening to some fine mountain ditties banged out on a hammer dulcimer while smaller dogs in owners' arms sashayed into the store. Sport felt more at home when we went into Hill Country Lodge (229 East Main Street; 830-997-9933), where all well-behaved dogs are welcome to browse the rustic Adirondack-style home furnishings and antler art. The only thing the store lacked to look like an upscale hunting camp was a hound dog sprawled out asleep on the floor, but I managed to get Sport outside just before she nodded off. We got back to our country roots at the Texas Trading Company (329½ East Main Street; 830-990-8927), which features Texas primitive furniture. Owner Dorothy Good asks that only small dogs in arms shop at these stores and at her Mexican imports shop, El Nicho (124 East Main Street). After all that shopping, Sport and I dragged our tender dogs to Fredericksburg Bakery (141 East Main Street; 830-997-3254) where we sat on one of the five benches out front and happily shared a sweet roll and a double dip of vanilla ice cream.

Sniff a snootful: Send yourself and your pooch into sensory overload as you wander the star-shaped herb and flower garden of the Fredericksburg Herb Farm. Then sample the goodies from the tea room at a shaded picnic table. There are enough smells here to overwhelm a bloodhound's sniffer—and they are all wonderful. The small in-town farm is a few blocks south of West Main Street. Follow Milam Street six blocks south of Main Street to Whitney Street and turn right. 402 Whitney Street; (830) 997-8615.

LUCKENBACH

DIVERSIONS

Feel no pain: You and your leashed pooch can get a preview of what Dog Heaven must be like by visiting the inspiration for the Waylon Jennings/Willie Nelson song "Let's Go to Luckenbach, Texas." There is absolutely nothing to do in this wide spot on a loop road except lie around in the shade, drink, listen to music, and tell lies. (Sport says, "What's your point?") Nevertheless, you can't be considered a true Texan until you've visited the Alamo, spent the night in Dalhart, and taken your dog to Luckenbach. Sport thinks there is nothing finer than dozing in the shade under the big tree out behind the combination general store/post office/bar listening to the clinking sounds made by yuppies from San Antonio pitching washers. "We love dogs—we have them ourselves," the manager says.

From Fredericksburg, drive 5.5 miles east on U.S. 290, then go south on F.M. 1376 for 4.5 miles. The highway sign for Luckenbach gets stolen as fast as a new one gets put up, so if you cross Grape Creek without having seen a sign, turn around and go back; take the first left after you cross the creek. Some kind of silliness is always happening in Luckenbach; call (830) 997-3224 for information and a recorded schedule of events.

STONEWALL

PARKS, BEACHES, AND RECREATION AREAS

• **Lyndon B. Johnson State Historical Park** 🐾 *See ⑤⑥ on page 106.*
Sport thought there would be lots for a dog to do at this 733-acre park, since former president Lyndon B. Johnson fancied himself a dog lover. She was less than thrilled to learn that one of LBJ's more famous stunts was to hold his dogs up by their ears. (Judging from the size of his ears, perhaps LBJ's mother did the same to him.) Sport was disappointed to learn that pooches must remain on leash—as at all state parks—and may not enter any buildings or go on any of the tours. However, she decided the price was right: there is no entrance fee. There is a 1.25-mile nature trail affording a view of some penned wildlife, but Sport, a free-roaming dog herself, prefers to look at wild things that are truly wild. If you're a dog, mostly you'll just stand around in this park waiting for your person to utter those magic words "Kennel up," so you can leave.

People tend to find the park considerably more interesting, so you may want to take a dog-sitter along and take turns exploring what it has to offer. This will definitely be a requirement if you wish to visit any of the National Park Service facilities connected with LBJ, because dogs are totally banned there.

Lyndon B. Johnson State Historical Park is a day-use park where you can enjoy historical study, picnicking, nature study, fishing, hiking, and viewing part of the state's Texas longhorn herd. The park is famous for its spring wildflower display.

The visitor center contains memorabilia from President Johnson's boyhood, pictures from the presidential years, and photos of famous guests at the nearby LBJ Ranch. Attached to the visitor center is the Behrens Cabin, a two-room dogtrot cabin built by German immigrant H. C. Behrens during the 1870s. (Your dog can't go inside, but he will be interested to know this style cabin got its name because the open space between the two rooms was where the dogs hung out.)

The Sauer-Beckmann Farmstead, located east of the visitor center and off the nature trail, is a living history farm. Life on the farmstead is presented as it was in 1918. Park interpreters wear period clothing and do the farm and household chores as they were done at that time.

Bus tours of the LBJ Ranch are conducted by the National Park Service and start at the state park visitor center.

There is a picnic area with a rest room and a playground where poochsitters can wait for other members of the party.

The park is located two miles east of Stonewall on U.S. 290. Enter on Park Road 52. Park buildings are open from 8 A.M. to 5 P.M. except Christmas. The grounds are open until dark. (830) 644-2252.

PLACES TO STAY

Stonewall Motel: Rooms are $31 to $35; mobile homes rent for $106 weekly or $400 monthly. There's a large exercise area, where dogs must remain leashed. The motel is on U.S. 290 in Stonewall. Box 808, Stonewall, TX 78671; (830) 644-2661.

WILLOW CITY

Hill Country wildflower displays can be spectacular, and lots of folks think one of the prettiest drives in Texas is the Willow City Loop, which spurts off Highway 16 some 13 miles north of Fredericksburg, passes through the hamlet of Willow City, and winds along country roads past some of the Hill Country's most scenic granite mountains. Unfortunately, the beauty of the drive is mostly lost on dogs, who must content themselves with keeping a sharp eye out for cows, deer, and raccoons shuffling across the road. About the only thing you can do when those bored snuffles start exploding from the rear seat is look for a place where you can stop and eat. We found two country places your dog will love.

RESTAURANTS

Harry's on the Loop: Have some barbecue at the table on the front porch or at one of half a dozen tables under the big pecan tree out back. Even though Harry's is in a rural community, the owner requires dogs be kept on leash because some local dogs turned out to be less than friendly. From Fredericksburg, go north 13 miles on Highway 16; turn right on F.M. 1323 and go three miles. (830) 685-3553.

Rabke's: Rabke's isn't a restaurant, it isn't in Willow City, and it's well off the beaten path, but it is about as Texas as a place can get. You get your food wrapped in butcher paper and take it outside to eat or try to drive with one hand, eat with one hand, and fend off a hungry pooch with the other hand (something's wrong with this picture). This family-owned business, located on a ranch, makes the best eye-of-round beef jerky your pooch ever mooched a piece of. Some folks prefer the turkey jerky to the beef; at less than half the price of the beef, you'll probably want to let your pooch eat turkey as she wonders, "Where's the beef?" You are welcome to tie your dog outside as you go in to make your selection, "If it can get by our dogs," jokes Beverly Haas. Beverly also says you and your pooch are welcome to take your purchase down to the creek in front of the store and munch away with your feet in the water "as long as you ask permission first." Those of you with three hands can just get back in the car and go.

From Fredericksburg, drive north 13 miles on Highway 16; turn left (west) on Eckert Road and go four miles. From Enchanted Rock State Natural Area, go south seven miles on F.M. 965 and turn left on Crabapple Road at the bridge over Crabapple Creek. At 2.7 miles, bear right at the fork; in another half mile turn left (east) on Eckert Road. Rabke's is another mile up on your right. (830) 685-3266.

HAYS COUNTY

This rural county on the outskirts of the Austin metropolitan area suffers more from people pollution than anything else. There are few parks, and none of those are leash-free. All the parks are located inside towns, which lessens their appeal considerably.

DRIPPING SPRINGS

PARKS, BEACHES, AND RECREATION AREAS

• **Founders' Memorial Park** 🐾½ *See* ㊲ *on page 106.*

I know you always ask your pooch before you leave anywhere, "Do you need to go?" And the answer is always the same, "I'm fine." And then you get 10 miles down the road and the whining starts, and then the desperate nudging of the head against your arm, and finally the pleading looks that say, "Aren't you ever going to stop and dewater me?" Founders' Memorial Park in Dripping Springs is made for dogs like that heading west from Austin. While your pooch must remain on a six-foot leash and cannot enter any of the park buildings, he can take the break he should have taken before leaving home. This 30-acre park has a swimming pool, rest rooms, a playground, and plenty of open space (and even a few trees).

From the intersection of Ranch Road 12 and U.S. 290, drive north on Ranch Road 12 about half a mile to the park entrance on your right. The park is open from 9 A.M. until sunset. (512) 858-4725.

RESTAURANTS

Hamburger Hill Restaurant: The name tells the story of the menu, but you have to try these burgers to appreciate them. The best way is to select from a variety of ingredients and "build your own" as you would a pizza. You and your leashed pooch are welcome to share one of the tables on the outside deck if you promise not to chase the resident cats. If you want shade, order to go and eat at the roadside picnic area just east. 290 Sportsplex (U.S. 290 West); (512) 858-4164.

SideSaddle BakeHouse: Grab a burger or other sandwich or have the chicken-fried steak at one of the four covered tables or two tables on the open deck out front. Finish off with a huge cookie or a wedge of pie from the bakery. The restaurant is on the south side of U.S. 290 just west of its intersection with Ranch Road 12. (512) 894-4001.

DIVERSIONS

Be a swinger with your springer: Stop in at Hill Country Swings and take home a hand-crafted porch swing (love-seat models are available so your adoring pooch can worship you as you swing), compost bin, or hand-crafted basket. Manager Lisa Patton brings her dog to work with her every day and invites you and your pooch to stop in, visit, and even have a complimentary dish of water. 709 U.S. 290 West; (512) 858-5207.

SAN MARCOS

PARKS, BEACHES, AND RECREATION AREAS

• **Bicentennial Park/Children's Park** 🐾 🐾 1/2 *See* 🜲 *on page 106.*

If parks had hips, that's where these two would be joined. Instead, the six or so acres of these two parks share a parking lot. Your leashed pooch can visit the shaded, grassy picnic areas in either park, but she will much prefer to hike a hundred yards up the graveled path into Bicentennial Park and jump into the clear, cool San Marcos River. When Sport and I visited there were people tubing and canoeing in this spring-fed river that rises in town and runs right through it. Hmmm. I wonder if there's a movie in there somewhere.

The parks are at the intersection of C. M. Allen Parkway and Comal Street. There is an 11 P.M. park curfew. (512) 754-7275.

• **City Park** 🐾🐾½ *See ㊾ on page 106.*

This park of about 10 acres spans both sides of the San Marcos River and offers grassy banks, shaded picnic sites, and a graveled walking trail where you and your leashed pooch can roam—just not very far. There is a snack bar, bathhouse, and tube rental operated by the Lions Club here.

The park is at the end of Jowers Access Road, off Aquarena Springs Boulevard. Follow the blue and white City Park signs; there were no street signs when we last visited. There is an 11 P.M. park curfew. (512) 754-7275.

• **Ramon Lucio Park/Rio Vista Park** 🐾🐾½ *See ㊿ on page 106.*

The spring-fed San Marcos River unites these two parks that are side by side along a major thoroughfare, divided only by the street on which you enter. Ramon Lucio Park is covered by athletic fields, but Rio Vista Park lives up to its name. Huge pecan trees shade both the river and nearby picnic tables. You and your leashed pooch can picnic or swim in the river. There are also tennis courts and a pool. The two parks together contain about 36 acres.

The parks are at the intersection of C. M. Allen Parkway and Cheatham Street. There is an 11 P.M. park curfew. (512) 754-7275.

RESTAURANTS

Bubba's Bar-B-Q: "Just call ahead or let me know you have a dog when you get here so I can put Brisket, the restaurant cat, in a safe place before you come around to the deck out back," requested a cheerful Bubbette when we called. And if you haven't figured it out by now, any place that combines the name Bubba with barbecue is serious about serving good-old-boy portions of ribs and brisket—the cow part, not the cat. 119 East Hutchison Street; (512) 392-6111.

Grins Restaurant: You can tie your pooch to a tree right beside the outside deck where you'll be munching on burgers, chicken, or a variety of health-conscious dishes. 802 North LBJ Drive; (512) 396-0909.

Palmer's Restaurant and Bar: Invite your pooch to wear her white gloves and join you in the open-air courtyard of this upscale restaurant for soup 'n' salad, burgers, sandwiches, or Tex-Mex cuisine. 216 West Moore Street (Ranch Road 12); (512) 353-3500.

PLACES TO STAY

Days Inn: Small dogs only (sorry, Sport Dog) may stay free. Rooms are $39 to $75. 1005 North Interstate 35, San Marcos, TX 78666; (512) 353-5050 or (800) DAYS INN.

Executive House Hotel: Small dogs only are accepted; there are no fees. Rooms are $55 to $85. 1433 North Interstate 35, San Marcos, TX 78666; (512) 353-7770.

Howard Johnson: All dogs are accepted on payment of a $60 deposit, $50 of which is refundable. Rooms are $49 to $86. 1635 Aquarena Springs Drive, San Marcos, TX 78666; (512) 353-8011 or (800) I-GO-HOJO.

Motel 6: Rates are $34 to $36. All Motel 6s allow one small pooch per room. 1321 North Interstate 35, San Marcos, TX 78666; (512) 396-8705.

FESTIVALS

Bluebonnet Kite Festival: You and your pooch will have loads of fun making a kite decorated like a cat, and your pooch will love barking at it as you fly it. Actually, your kite doesn't have to look like a cat to be in this festival where food and games share the billing with kite flying. The late-April festival is just an excuse to take advantage of spring zephyrs. ("Is that a white cat with black stripes?" Sport wants to know.) The festival takes place on the grounds of the Butler Manufacturing Plant, 2301 North Interstate 35. For information, call (512) 396-2374.

Chilympiad: Rumor has it that you will see as many dogs as you will people acting crazy at this statewide chili cook-off. The dogs help maintain balance, I suppose. Beauty pageants, arts and crafts, food booths, and live music compete with the serious business of brewing up the hottest, tastiest pot of chili, which was, as every Texas dog knows, declared the state dish by the Legislature in 1977. Particularly charming pooches have been known to mooch samples. If your pooch is one, it may prove helpful to know that while water will not put out the fire in your mouth, milk, butter, or beer will. The cook-off is held in late September at the Hays County Exhibit Building, Interstate 35 south at Clovis Barker Road. For information, call (512) 396-5400.

Summerfest: The Fourth of July means live patriotic music, children's games, speeches by politicians (borrrring!), and fireworks all across this land of yours, mine, and our dogs. For location and information, call (512) 396-6080.

DIVERSIONS

Hark in the park: Thursday evenings from June through mid-August, pack a picnic basket and a ragged old doggy blanket, and head for Juan Veramendi Park at the intersection of Hopkins Street and C. M. Allen Parkway for a free concert. Your pooch will not be allowed to sing along, but he will learn some new tunes to perform in the shower at home. For information, call (512) 396-2325.

LEE COUNTY

I grew up in Lee County, way over in the western part jutting into an angle between Bastrop and Williamson Counties. Partly as a result, I've always been partial to sandy soil and post oak trees, both of which Lee County has in abundance. The combination makes Lee County a candidate for dog paradise, but unfortunately, there are few public places to take a dog. However, what it lacks in quantity, it makes up for in quality. The Nails Creek Unit of Lake Somerville State Park is a fine place to take a dog, even though she must remain on leash.

STATE WILDLIFE MANAGEMENT AREAS

See the National and State Forests/State Wildlife Management Areas appendix starting on page 621 for important information and safety tips on visiting these areas with your dog.

• **Somerville Wildlife Management Area** 🐾🐾½

The bottomlands along Yegua Creek and the post-oak-covered uplands adjacent provide cover and food for feral hogs and mourning doves, and Flag Pond holds waterfowl in the winter. Your hunting hound can accompany you off leash while hunting doves or waterfowl or lounging in camp; otherwise, he must be leashed. Hunting hogs with dogs is not allowed. See page 627 for a description of the area.

GIDDINGS

PARKS, BEACHES, AND RECREATION AREAS

• **City Park** 🐾 *See ㉛ on page 106.*

Like many small-town city parks, this expanse of seven acres or so is given over mostly to athletic fields, but there are some open grassy areas and shaded picnic tables with barbecue grills, as well as a playground. There is also a reputed quarter-mile walking trail, but other than a white stripe painted on the pavement, we could find no sign of one other than the two signs telling us the city is not responsible for accidents. Hmmmmm. I suppose it would be difficult to prove in court that one hurt oneself on a trail that does not exist, but then I have missed a few episodes of *The X-Files*. You and your pooch will most enjoy the part of the park at its east end; turn right as you enter and curve around the complex of athletic fields. There is plenty of shade and grass here, and water is available. Rest rooms are located in the green building at the baseball field.

The park is just north of U.S. 290 on Montgomery Avenue. It's open 24 hours. (409) 542-5739.

• Lake Somerville State Park—Nails Creek Unit 🐾🐾🐾½
See ⑫ on page 106.

Saying this park only has about 900 acres is like saying a wasp's stinger is just a little bitty thing. The Nails Creek and Birch Creek Units of this park lie on opposite sides of the lake and give access to some 5,000 acres of public land surrounding Lake Somerville. Twenty-one miles of improved trails enable hikers, bikers, and horseback riders to circle the west end of the lake and connect the two units. A trail within the Nails Creek Unit forms a loop and also connects to the main trail. You may access this narrow, sandy trail from either the equestrian-use area just past the park entrance or from a trailhead kiosk just before you get to the boat ramp. Dogs must remain on leash within the state park and on the trail system. The gently rolling terrain traversed by the trail is heavily wooded in most places by post oak trees growing in great profusion, but you will find hickory trees, yaupon, and several other varieties of oaks as well. Virtually all these trees are deciduous, so this country is at its prettiest in spring and summer. The trail also passes along and through numerous creek bottoms, and wildlife, including white-tailed deer and feral hogs, is abundant. While the sandy soil grows sandburs, the camping areas and trail are generally free of them. In the spring, the section of trail between the Nails Creek Unit and Flag Pond (a five-mile round-trip) is noted for its wildflowers.

While the 13-mile Somerville Trail itself poses no difficulty for hikers, the lack of potable water throughout its length means you must carry enough water for your own use. Well water for your pooch is available at two of the six primitive campgrounds along the trail, Newman Bottom and Wolf Pond. Newman Bottom is about five miles from the Nails Creek trailhead; Wolf Pond is some four miles from the Birch Creek trailhead. Lake Somerville itself is not a reliable source of water for hikers, as it lies miles from most points on the trail and is subject to drawdown in droughts. All primitive campsites along the trail ($4) have chemical toilets. A map of the trail system available at park headquarters locates all the facilities along the trail, which is a one-lane graveled road.

The Nails Creek Unit has 40 campsites with water and electricity ($9).

The sites are well spaced among post oak trees; all are shaded, and most offer considerable privacy. The sandy soil means that you will be reminded of camping at the beach: sand will be in everything from food to sleeping bags, and your pooch will delight in bringing it inside. There are 10 tent sites with water nearby ($6) in the vicinity of the boat ramp, but these sites are very open, with little shade, and when we last visited the lake level was so low it was half a mile to the water. It's better to pay the extra $3 and have a nice, shaded, private campsite in the trees. When the lake level is normal, some of the sites are within 50 yards of the water's edge, so your leashed pooch won't have far to go to take a dip. All sites with water and electricity are served by rest rooms with showers; the primitive sites have rest rooms only. Reservations for campsites at all state parks must be made by calling the central reservation number, (512) 389-8900, between 9 A.M. and 6 P.M. Monday through Friday. Reservations are strongly recommended, and a deposit is required in order to guarantee a reservation. Specific sites may not be reserved; they are available on a first-come, first-served basis upon arrival.

To reach the Nails Creek Unit, drive north on Highway 180 about 15 miles from its intersection with U.S. 290 six miles east of Giddings. The park entrance fee is $2 per person. Park hours are 8 A.M. to 10 P.M. (409) 289-2392.

PLACES TO STAY

Lake Somerville State Park—Nails Creek Unit: See Lake Somerville State Park on page 182 for camping information.

LLANO COUNTY

Llano County is blessed with some of the prettiest scenery in the whole state. Eons ago magma welled up beneath layers of limestone, bending and fracturing the rock. Then erosion stripped away the soft limestone and revealed pink granite. Embarrassed by the exposure, perhaps, Mother Nature dressed herself in live oak and mesquite trees and threw a shawl of wildflowers around her shoulders. The Colorado River bounds Llano County on the east, and dam-builders in the 1930s created lakes that delight water-loving pooches and their owners.

Llano County boasts one of Texas's premier state parks and a number of private lakeside campgrounds, and while dogs must remain on leash everywhere in the county, they will be so bedazzled by the beauty all around them they will scarcely notice. You, of course, will suffer early onset of arthritis from having your arms repeatedly yanked from their sockets by a rubber-necking dog enjoying all the views.

Keep your dog on a leash when you visit Llano County, and not just because it's required by law. Llano County literally bristles with deer and, in the fall, with deer hunters, who take a dim view of free-ranging dogs. The only thing worse than seeing your pooch bound out of sight pursuing a fleeing white-tail would be hearing the boom of a deer rifle a few seconds later.

BUCHANAN DAM

PARKS, BEACHES, AND RECREATION AREAS

• **Black Rock Park** 🐾🐾 *See ⑥③ on page 106.*

This approximately 20-acre park operated by the Lower Colorado River Authority occupies a point of land projecting into Lake Buchanan. A gravel beach where your dog can run leash-free as long as she is outside the camping area edges the sparkling shoreline. The park has a playground and rest rooms.

Campsites occupy the bulk of the park, and your pooch must remain leashed in the camping area. However, she will be so tired from swimming and playing fetch in the water she will never notice her tether while she's sleeping. Camping is $7 per night. Most campsites are shaded with large oak, willow, cottonwood, or juniper trees and have a picnic table and barbecue grill.

From the intersection of Highways 29 and 261 on the western edge of Buchanan Dam, take Highway 261 north 2.5 miles to the park entrance. Entry costs $5 per vehicle. (The honor system is in effect. Pay at the lockbox at the entrance.) The park is open 24 hours. (800) 776-5272.

PLACES TO STAY

Black Rock Park: See Black Rock Park above for camping information.

Lake Point Cottages: Alan and Sherri Crawford run more than just your typical lakefront motel. They've remodeled the quaint 1940s-era cottages sitting among scattered live oaks just upstream from Buchanan Dam and made them into a lakeside resort. You and your leashed pooch will have lots of grass to visit, and the lake is just steps away whenever a cooling dip is called for. Most cabins have fully equipped kitchens. There is a $10 per visit dog fee, and pooches may not be left alone in rooms. Rates are $45 to $80 with a two-night minimum stay; one-night stands will cost you $5 extra. Sport wanted to stay in cabin 2, because that's where the 1995 remake of the movie *Lolita* was filmed. She thought it would be neat to sleep in the same bed as Melanie Griffith. Hmmmm. She might be right.

The reservations policy reflects the resort nature of Lake Point Cottages. Reservations from April through September must be for two nights. Holiday weekends during that time require three-night stays. A 50 percent deposit or a credit card number is required to hold a reservation. There is a 14-day cancellation period.

Other services available include canoe, paddleboat, and personal watercraft rentals, guided fishing trips, sight-seeing excursions, and waterskiing instruction. Your pooch is welcome on fishing and sight-seeing trips. Waterfront RV and tent camping sites are also available for $15 per night.

Lake Point Cottages is on Highway 29 half a mile west of Buchanan Dam. Route 1, Box 22, Buchanan Dam, TX 78609; (512) 793-2918.

Shady Oaks RV Park: This private 23-acre campground is just below Inks Dam on the Colorado River and enjoys 1,700 feet of river frontage. It caters primarily to fishers, with lighted fishing docks and a boat ramp. You and your leashed pooch can rent a boat ($15 per day) or just sit in the shade and enjoy the breeze blowing up the Colorado River valley. Closely spaced RV sites ($15) and tent sites ($10) nestle beneath huge oak trees. Rest rooms with showers, a recreation room, and laundry are available.

Dogs must remain on leash at all times. They may not be left unattended either in an RV or tent or in a campsite. "If your dog poops, you scoop," the rules state. Dogs are not allowed inside any park building.

The park is about 2.5 miles south of Highway 29 on County Road 301. Turn south at the west end of Inks Lake Bridge and follow the signs. P.O. Box 725, Buchanan Dam, TX 78609; (512) 793-2718.

KINGSLAND

PLACES TO STAY

Kingsland Lodge: This waterfront resort greets you with huge live oaks at the entrance. Neat smoke-blue cottages with front porches face constant-level Lake Lyndon B. Johnson a hundred yards away. Pooches must remain on leash at all times and may not be left alone in cabins. There is no fee for dogs; cabins rent for $52 to $120 per night. There is a three-night minimum from May through September. RV hookups are available at $24 per night. Turn off F.M. 1431 at the El Rio gas station. "The name of the street is Campa-Pajama Lane," manager Pauline Denney says, "but there's no sign and no one would believe the name anyway." Really? P.O. Box 69, Kingsland, TX 78639; (915) 388-4830.

Lake LBJ Motel: This one-story motel-type unit on F.M. 1431 half a mile south of Kingsland has a large mowed lawn out back for walking dogs. Rooms are $35 to $42. Route 2, Box 139, Kingsland, TX 78639; (915) 388-4571.

DIVERSIONS

Slab your Lab: Pack a picnic lunch, drinks, and lots of sunscreen and take your water-loving pooch to The Slab, a popular swimming area just outside town where the Llano River runs over granite outcrops. There are no facilities, but you can splash and lounge to your heart's content. Be sure to stay within the river channel so you won't trespass on private property. From F.M. 1431 in Kingsland, take F.M. 3404 west 1.3 miles to the river crossing. Park at the turnout on either side of the road at the east end of the low-water bridge.

LLANO

Llano is a quiet little town split by a river of the same name. It is famous in Texas for two things: deer hunting and barbecue, both of which are among the best to be had anywhere. In November and December more than 16,000 deer hunters descend on the county, an invasion that resembles a military operation in more ways than one as four-wheel-drive vehicles occupied by gun-toting, camouflage-clad men and women roam the countryside. The resulting carnage makes carnivorous canines fairly quake in anticipation of juicy morsels of venison, and they are not disappointed. Deer season is Sport and Samantha's favorite time of the year. The other 10 months it's Diet City.

Fortunately, Llano's barbecue pits smoke and sizzle all year 'round. This is real Texas barbecue, slow-cooked in outside pits over mesquite coals. It is impossible to drive through Llano without passing at least one barbecue place, so take pity on that starving dog beside you and stop. You can eat at outside tables or get your barbecue to go and defend it from your starving pooch until you get to a roadside picnic area. And when looking for a roadside picnic area, remember that their locations are marked by little blue dots on official Texas highway maps, so finding one isn't difficult.

PARKS, BEACHES, AND RECREATION AREAS

• **Enchanted Rock State Natural Area** 😾 😾 😾 *See* 🙽 *on page 106.*
Enchanted Rock State Natural Area consists of 1,643 acres on Big Sandy Creek. The entrance is in Gillespie County, but the bulk of the park is in Llano County. The rock is a huge, pink granite boulder that rises 425 feet above ground and covers 640 acres. Its summit stands 1,825 feet above sea level. It is the second largest batholith (underground rock formation uncovered by erosion) in the United States. Enchanted Rock was designated a National Natural Landmark in 1971 and was placed on the National Register of Historic Places in 1984.

As at all Texas state parks, pooches must remain joined to their owners by leashes no longer than six feet. This sometimes onerous restriction is comforting at Enchanted Rock, for here you will appreciate the security of having your brave guard dog close by. When she pricks up her ears or perhaps droops her tail, she is probably hearing sounds that you cannot hear—sounds people once believed were made by ghosts. Indians believed the weird creaking and groaning noises were made by spirits, but geologists say they result from the rock's heating by day and contracting by night.

Enchanted Rock can be a delight for the hiking dog with tough paws and a big canteen. The rock absorbs and holds heat, so even in cooler months be careful your pooch doesn't overheat. Four miles of hiking trails wind through the granite formations, which are liberally sprinkled with oak, pecan, elm, and mesquite trees. Squirrels, armadillos, rabbits, and lizards dart about. Turkey vultures roost and soar around the rock, and Sport never saw a buzzard she wouldn't bark at. White-tailed deer are common, and the park's bird life is varied and abundant.

Sport and I prefer the Summit Trail, which climbs to the very top of Enchanted Rock. It begins at a parking lot reached by turning right immediately after you pass the park headquarters. You can water your pooch at one of several drinking fountains at the parking lot or at the creek at the beginning of the trail if it is running. The well-marked trail passes through tumbled boulders the size of freight cars before climbing steeply to the top. The view from the top is worth the huffing and puffing it takes to get there. You look down on the entire park and surrounding area. Sit down and rest while you enjoy the view and tell your pooch how a Texas Ranger pursued by Indians saved his scalp by climbing to the top of the rock, lying down, and picking off Indians as their heads appeared. Lie down on your tummy beside your pooch, put your head on your paws, and watch fellow visitors come into view, and you'll see how it worked. Other people will think you're nuts, but then maybe they haven't heard this story.

Enchanted Rock is the place I chose to take my children on their first camping trip, and after 20 years the magic is still there. Shaded and secluded, the walk-in campsites ($9 per night) cluster along Sandy Creek at the base of Little Rock, itself a huge granite batholith. Facilities include rest rooms with showers nearby, tent pads, picnic tables, and fire rings. Hike-in primitive sites ($7) in three other areas have composting toilets. It's a two-mile walk to any of them. Your pooch would probably prefer the Moss Lake primitive camping area, reached by the Echo Canyon Trail. It is near a pond where a hot dog can take a dip.

Reservations for campsites at all state parks must be made by calling the central reservation number, (512) 389-8900, between 9 A.M. and 6 P.M.

Monday through Friday. Reservations are strongly recommended, and a deposit is required in order to guarantee a reservation. Specific sites may not be reserved; they are available on a first-come, first-served basis upon arrival. The park may be closed for public hunts to remove excess deer at times during the fall.

From Llano, take Highway 16 south for 14 miles then go west eight miles on F.M. 965. From Fredericksburg, go north 18 miles on F.M. 965. Entry costs $3 per person. The park office is open from 8 A.M. to 5 P.M. on weekdays and until midnight on summer weekends. The park closes at 10 P.M. except to overnight guests. (915) 247-3903.

• **Robinson Llano City Park** 🐾½ *See* ㊲ *on page 106.*

Most of this park is occupied by a golf course. About the only things for the leashed dog to do here are wolf down some barbecue at one of the picnic tables, take a trot and a squat along the riverbank, and nap under a live oak tree. The Llano River borders the property, but the steep bank makes it difficult for a leashed pooch to wet a paw.

Camping is permitted in a fenced-off area adjacent to the rodeo arena, but Sport could see no reason why anyone would pay $8 to stay on a bare, treeless rectangle of dirt without so much as a picnic table to shade a weary dog. You may make a reservation by calling the Chamber of Commerce at (915) 247-5354 from 8 A.M. to 5. P.M. on weekdays, but reservations are not needed unless there is a rodeo going on, and why would anyone not directly involved want to camp next door to a bunch of rowdy cowboys ridin', ropin', and yellin' half the night? (Cowdogs excepted, of course.) On weekends the honor system is in effect; leave your money in the lockbox on site.

The park is two miles west of the courthouse square on F.M. 152. It is open 24 hours. (915) 247-5354.

RESTAURANTS

Cooper's Old Time Pit Barbecue: People drive a hundred miles just to eat at Cooper's, and once you and your pooch have chowed down on succulent pork ribs, juicy sirloin steak, tender brisket, or savory *cabrito* (goat) at one of the shaded outdoor picnic tables, you will never again be able to travel through the Hill Country without your pooch emphatically slamming her paw on Llano's location on the map and drooling all over you. Chocolate chip cookies may send telepathic messages to Snoopy, but Cooper's barbecue will speak to your pooch with a voice of thunder. 604 West Young Street; (915) 247-5713.

Crabapple Crossing Country Store: Texas-size barbecue sandwiches served on a shaded porch beside Crabapple Creek make this spot a popular one with visitors to Enchanted Rock State Natural Area. It's located four miles north of the park on Ranch Road 965; (915) 247-4260.

Laird's Bar-B-Q: "Lots of dogs eat here," says the owner. The deck holding two picnic tables is tiny, but the taste is as big as Texas. 1600 Ford Street; (915) 247-5234.

PLACES TO STAY

Badu House: Samantha's Mom (Sally Victor) researched and wrote the text for the Texas Historical Marker for the Badu House. Samantha would like to take the credit, but this was years before she arrived to begin the process of slowly destroying our home and everything in it. Small dogs and well-behaved, housebroken dogs of any size may stay here at no charge in the kennel out back. Rooms range from $65 to $95. 601 Bessemer Street, Llano, TX 78643; (915) 247-1207.

Best Western: Small dogs only are allowed, but there is no fee. Rooms are $36 to $61. 901 West Young Street, Llano, TX 78643; (915) 247-4101 or (800) 346-1578.

Chaparral Motor Lodge: Rooms at this motel are $35. 700 West Young Street, Llano, TX 78643; (915) 247-4111.

Enchanted Rock State Natural Area: See Enchanted Rock State Natural Area on page 186 for camping information.

Robinson Llano City Park: See Robinson Llano City Park on page 188 for camping information.

DIVERSIONS

Round up a rare rock: Llanite, a brown granite with blue and pink feldspar crystals, occurs only in Llano County. Rock hounds drive nine miles north of Llano on Highway 16 and hunt for it in the highway right-of-way where the road cuts through a hill a quarter mile north of the Babyhead Cemetery. Your pooch is a rare gem; let her prove it by sniffing out a handsome specimen.

Track down a bargain: Sport sprang to attention when she spotted the stuffed red fox in the window of Lillie's Antiques. I was more interested in the antique cracker tin. "My dog (Gee Gee the poodle) is in here. As long as your dog and mine are congenial, come on in," invited owner Lillie Craven. You and your pooch can shop this historic, multiroomed old building on the bank of the Llano River for all kinds of antiques and collectibles. 303 Bessemer Street (Highway 71/16); (915) 247-4618.

MASON COUNTY

I can flatly state that Mason County has the prettiest scenery in the state, has the friendliest people, and is more deserving of visitation by dogs and dog lovers than any other place on the face of the Earth. I can say these things not just because Sport, Samantha, Comet the Cat, Sally, and I live here, but because they are true.

Pretty scenery is pretty much wasted on dogs, of course, as are friendly people who are not providers of food, ear-scratching, and ball-throwing on a daily basis. So what is it about Mason County that makes it so special to dogs and dog lovers?

Mason County was the home of Fred Gipson, a writer who probably made more people blubber over a dog story than any other person in history. The story was *Old Yeller*, and the hero of that story was a real Mason County dog. Every pooch should make a trek to Old Yeller country at least once during his lifetime, just as every Muslim should make a pilgrimage to Mecca. Your pooch will be thrilled to know he is walking the same ground as the author of his favorite dog story. You and your pooch will want to visit the Mason County M. Beven Eckert Memorial Library, which houses an exhibit honoring Fred Gipson in its foyer. You'll be interested in the displays telling the story of Gipson's career; your pooch will probably be more interested in the trees and grass outside. That's okay. Fred was a dog man. He'd understand. Of course, he might have a little trouble with the fact that dogs are not allowed into the exhibit about one of the most famous dogs of all time.

While the city of Mason has a leash law, the surrounding county does not. That's the good news. The bad news is that Mason County has few public places to take a pooch. There are a few points providing public access to the Llano River, but like most of the Hill Country, Mason County is deer, sheep, and goat country, and free-roaming dogs are not tolerated by area ranchers or hunters. If you take your pooch to the river area listed below, be sure she can be trusted not to wander before slipping the leash off.

FREDONIA

RESTAURANTS

Fredonia General Store: You and your pooch can munch a burger or chicken-fried steak (and even a piece of homemade pie that's really homemade) on the bench out front or at the picnic table nearby. The historic old general store houses the local post office and is somewhat of a community center as well. It's the kind of place that doesn't look natural unless it has a hound dog or two sleeping on the porch. Take F.M. 386 north from the courthouse square in Mason 16 miles to Highway 71. Just before the intersection, turn east at the Fredonia sign. Take the first right and immediately turn left into what passes for downtown. The Fredonia General Store is on the south side of the street. (915) 429-6243.

PLACES TO STAY

Heart of the Heart Guest Cabin: Does your pooch like lazing on the porch? Napping in front of a wood stove? Watching deer browse all around? This ranch cabin has a porch with a panoramic 30-mile view and all the solitude any city-weary pooch could ask for. Any size housebroken pooch is welcome for a $10 deposit. You'll pay $80. The cabin is located three miles from Fredonia in northern Mason County. For information, reservations, and directions, call (915) 429-6222.

MASON

PARKS, BEACHES, AND RECREATION AREAS

• **Fort Mason Park** 🐾 🐾 *See* **36** *on page 106.*

This 128-acre park on the edge of town is owned by the county but operated by the city, so the City of Mason's leash law applies. Mason's dogcatcher drives a worn-out pickup truck and has two bad knees, but he still manages to corral his share of errant canines, so keep your pooch restrained while you explore the short walking trail that winds among the trees behind the rodeo ground and dance slab.

Large pecan trees shade the campground ($8 per night) which backs up to the golf course; rest rooms and showers are available. Pay at the lockbox at the entrance to the camping area. Your pooch can watch you chase the little white ball around or take a short snooze; it's just a nine-hole course.

The park is on U.S. 87 at the south city limits and is open 24 hours. Reservations may be made by calling City Hall at (915) 347-6449 or (916) 347-6656.

• **James River Crossing of the Llano River** 🐾 🐾 🐕
See **37** *on page 106.*

The Llano River is one of those Texas streams classified as navigable, which means you and your pooch can enjoy the water as long as you can get to it without trespassing on private property. Fortunately, a number of highways cross the Llano, making it possible for you to use the public right-of-way for parking and river access. The James River Crossing of the Llano is one of Sport and Samantha's all-time favorite spots on hot summer days. Samantha—the dog who will eat anything—wades around and bobs for river moss while Sport swims and explores the bushes for varmints. You and your pooch are free to roam and romp off leash as long as you stay in the water or within the floodplain of the river. (It would be a good idea to stay off the center stripe of the highway, too.) This is not a problem here, as the river divides and flows around a large island, which you can drive to from the roadway. Sport and Samantha like the area on the west side of the highway best. The water there is shallow, the current is not too swift, and you can park at the water's edge so lazy pooches don't have to walk more than five steps before they are standing belly deep in water.

This is a popular fishing and camping spot. Camping is totally primitive with no facilities, no fees, no reservations, no nuttin' except lots of water for dogs to play in and lots of bushes to sniff and lots of picnic remains to munch. If you camp, be aware that both the Llano and the James River (which joins the Llano just upstream) flow through rocky hill country terrain that does not hold much water when it rains. A rainstorm upstream can lead to a rapid rise in the river, which could endanger campers on the island. If you are camping on the island, be aware of the weather and be ready to move to higher ground if the water begins to rise.

From the intersection of U.S. 87 and F.M. 1723 at the south city limits of Mason, drive 2.5 miles south on F.M. 1723 to its intersection with F.M. 2389. Go west on F.M. 2389 for 4.5 miles to the Llano River. Gravel paths on both sides of the highway lead to popular fishing and camping spots on the island. The area is open 24 hours; there is no phone.

RESTAURANTS

Willow Creek Cafe: The huge front doors and vast expanse of glass tell you the historic old building housing this eatery was built for some purpose other than a restaurant. In fact, it was one of Mason's early auto dealerships. The dining area was once the new car showroom, and flivvers mounted the ramp out front (it's still there, too) and rolled right in the front door. Today Cindy Morris and crew serve up burgers big enough to choke a Doberman, outstanding quesadillas, chicken-fried steak, and even fresh pizza. The homemade pies and bread will make you never want to go home. Order to go and eat at one of the benches on the shaded sidewalk while you watch life pass Mason by. 102 Fort McKavett; (915) 347-6124.

PLACES TO STAY

Fort Mason Park: See Fort Mason Park on page 191 for camping information.

Hasse House Ranch Bed-and-Breakfast: This historic 1880s German farmstead sits on the bank of Willow Creek, surrounded by 320 acres of pasture where your pooch can sniff deer tracks, wade in the creek, and even—as Sport and Samantha did—put a raccoon up a tree while following the self-guided nature trail. Keep a sharp eye out for rattlesnakes, just one reason the owner requests you keep your pooch leashed any-time she is outside the yard fence. Dogs are not permitted inside the house, but the fenced yard and big front porch are all any country-loving, full-moon-baying dog could want. The whole house is yours for $90 a night unless you opt to pay $5 extra for the full continental breakfast featuring goodies from Mason's Busy Bees Bakery. Go for it. Bypass surgery isn't that big a deal anymore. The Hasse House Ranch is six miles east of Mason on Highway 29. For information write P.O. Box 58, Mason, TX 76856; (915) 347-6463.

Hill Country Inn: Any size dog is welcome to stay for free as long as she is housebroken. Rooms are $37 to $43. 336 Fort McKavett, Mason, TX 76856; (915) 347-6317.

James River Crossing of the Llano River: See James River Crossing of the Llano River on page 191 for camping information.

SAN SABA COUNTY

If another county in Texas ever inspired both a love note to a nut written by English poet Alfred, Lord Tennyson, and the name of one of America's most popular breakfast cereals, it has escaped the attention of both myself and Sport, the sharp-eyed history buff. As we tooled around San Saba County, Sport and I both remarked on the abundance of majestic pecan trees—but for vastly different reasons. I love to eat pecan pie and pecan pralines, and Sport likes to, well, let's just say that for a girl dog, she performs leg-lifts nigh perfectly. Yet we were not the first to admire the pecan trees of San Saba County, and thereby hangs a tail—er, tale.

Pecan trees are native to Texas, and the ones in San Saba County were remarked on by early Spanish explorers. However, the nuts from native trees are quite small and devilishly hard to extract the makings of a pecan pie from. It took an Englishman, Edmund E. Risien, to unlock the potential of Texas pecan trees. Risien left his native Kent in 1872 and arrived in San Saba in 1874 with a dollar and a half in his pocket and a desire to succeed in his heart. In one hour he had a job; the next morning his first task was to build coffins for two men who had been hanged. He knew he wasn't in England anymore, Toto.

Always looking for a way to make a buck, Risien took an interest in improving the native pecans. He offered to pay five dollars for the best five pounds of pecans brought to him. Then he craftily bought the land at the junction of the San Saba and Colorado Rivers where the tree that produced them stood. (Sport said this is getting boring, so I should either jump a raccoon out of that pecan tree or get to the point.) Risien then went nuts about developing improved varieties of pecans, budding, grafting, pollinating, and otherwise getting involved in the sex life of trees until he came up with some 20 kinds of paper-shelled pecans.

(Okay, Sport, get ready. Here it comes.) Risien promoted his large-meated, easy-to-shell pecans by sending samples to famous people. One batch went to Alfred, Lord Tennyson, who responded with a handwritten note dated March 19, 1892: "It is very kind for you to have thought of sending me nuts from your beautiful Pecan tree & I thank you most sincerely. My gardener shall try & make them grow here. We consider the Walnut the best among our nuts I think, but to us your Pecan nuts seem better still. May you live long & happily and see your Pecan tree flourish!"

Risien also exhibited pecans arranged in a grapelike cluster at the Chicago World's Fair, and a gentleman named C. W. Post was so impressed he came to San Saba to visit Risien and tour the pecan groves. After he went home, Post decided to name a crunchy new cereal he was working on (energetic tail-wags, please) Grape-Nuts. (If only Post had showed more gratitude, your pooch might even now be sitting at your feet begging for the dregs of your bowl of Risien Bran.)

San Saba County is still the acknowledged pecan capital of the world, and the bottomlands along the San Saba and Colorado Rivers sprout hundreds of thousands of pecan trees. These trees grace the parks and campgrounds you and your nutty pooch can visit while you are here, though few such places be. And, your pooch will not be happy to learn, she must remain on her leash everywhere in the county. However, San Saba County offers a number of places where the water-loving dog can splash, swim, and slurp in some of Texas's cleanest rivers. Take your swim togs when you visit.

BEND

PARKS, BEACHES, AND RECREATION AREAS

• Colorado Bend State Park 🐾 🐾 1/2 See ⑥⑧ on page 106.

Dogs doomed to dwell with faint-hearted humans take note: Visiting this park takes some perseverance. Access to the Bend area itself is via narrow, twisting farm-to-market highways that, even though they wander through beautiful Hill Country, tax the patience of the city-dweller accustomed to freeways. Then, when you finally reach the bend in the road that is Bend, you must drive another 10 miles on washboard dirt tracks to reach the park headquarters. Along the way you will likely have to stop a time or two to let grazing cattle get out of your way, for much of the route is through unfenced rangeland. Samantha regards the matter of cows in the road as a bonus, since she loves nothing better than bounding from front seat to back over and over as she barks madly at cows we drive by. Just be aware that for some reason black cows, especially, love to sleep in the road, so if you must drive at night, be extra careful.

Rest assured, though, that the drive is worth the trouble as well as the $2 per person entry fee. Colorado Bend State Park's 5,000-plus acres occupy some of the best of the northern Texas Hill Country. The park has six miles of river frontage, two spring-fed creeks, and rolling uplands gashed by rocky canyons. Nearly 12 miles of hiking trails—actually old ranch roads—are open to leashed dogs and their owners. (You may have to share the Riverside and Upper Gorman Creek Trail with mountain bikers, but the Spicewood Springs Trail is for hikers only.) Best of all, riverside campsites shaded by huge oak, elm, and pecan trees invite lazy days that would make Huck Finn look downright industrious. Wildlife watchers can count on seeing numerous white-tailed deer. Endangered golden-cheeked warblers and black-capped vireos nest in the park in the spring, and bald eagles winter and fish along the river.

Texas state parks forbid the use of a leash longer than six feet, and dogs may not be left unattended (which includes being tied outside) or taken into any park building. Dogs may not enter the water at a designated swimming area or enter the beach adjacent to a swimming area. (If an area is designated for swimming, there will be signs so stating. Otherwise, your dog is free to splash all she wants as long as she does not interfere with other swimmers.)

Colorado Bend State Park offers primitive camping only, with two large riverside camping areas available on a first-come, first-served basis; no reservations are accepted. There are no individual sites; in true Texas style, you stake your claim to a spot and defend it, paying $7 a night for the privilege. There are no hookups, but water is available at the park office and midway of the main camping area, and chemical toilets are provided. A primitive camping area is accessible by hiking a bit over a mile down the Upper Gorman Creek Trail, on your right about a mile inside the park entrance.

Colorado Bend is infested with feral hogs as well as white-tailed deer and will be closed from time to time for what Texas writer Deborah Douglas calls "seasonal wildlife pruning" in her book *Gone for the Day: Family Fun in Central Texas*. Call ahead before planning a trip to the park during August, October, November, and December. When you do visit, take care to keep a tight grip on your leash in case your pooch wants to chase after a hog or a deer. The hogs can be deadly on dogs.

During February and March the park may be infested with fishers there for the annual run of white bass going up the Colorado River to spawn, so expect crowded conditions, especially on weekends. Of course, if your pooch likes to fish, he would rather visit then than at any other time. Intent anglers, however, may take a dim view of a shallows-thrashing canine.

Sport and I last visited on a hot (101 degrees) June day, and we much preferred sharing the hiking trail along the river over having the upland trails to ourselves. Most of the trail is shaded by huge pecan trees, and the river is never more than a few steps away, making it easy for both of us to plunge in for a cooling drenching. The riverside trail has the added advantage of eliminating the need to carry water for your pooch.

Bend is located 19 miles east of San Saba on F.M. 580. From San Saba, take U.S. 190 east about four miles to F.M. 580 and follow the signs 13 miles to Bend. From Bend, follow signs along County Road 294 and County Road 257 (unmarked) four miles to the park entrance and another six miles to the park office. Entry costs $2 per person. The office is open from 8 A.M. to 5 P.M. The park closes at 10 P.M. except to overnight guests. (915) 628-3240.

PLACES TO STAY

Barefoot Fishing Camp: Take your shoes; the name comes from the owners, not from the dress code. Leashed dogs are welcome. Cottonwood, mesquite, and pecan trees shade campsites in the RV park and along the river. Some campsites are at the water's edge along three miles of river frontage where you and your pooch may fish, sunbathe, or curl up together with a copy of *Old Yeller.* Day use is $3 per person; primitive camping costs $3 per person, and RV sites are $12. This campground is located on private land in a bend of the Colorado River. The owners shut down during November and December to harvest pecans. The gates are locked from 10 P.M. to 7 A.M. From the intersection of F.M. 580 and County Road 294 in Bend, follow County Road 294 for 3.5 miles to the entrance. (915) 628-3395.

Colorado Bend State Park: See Colorado Bend State Park on page 194 for camping information.

Sulphur Springs Fishing Camp: Leashed dogs may camp with their owners along the grassy banks of the Colorado River, shaded by pecan and mesquite trees. Rent a tube and raft the rio, admiring the view of the limestone bluffs across the river. Dog-paddle quietly, and you may sneak up on a deer. Your angling canine can even go fishing. Since the owners have 6,000 pecan trees, they close for the harvest during November and December, but even in sunny Texas most dogs are content to forgo swimming in winter. Campers pay a $3 daily entrance fee and $1 per night per person; dogs may freeload. Follow Country Road 294 six miles from its intersection with F.M. 580 in Bend. P.O. Box 44, Bend, TX 76824; (915) 628-3252.

SAN SABA

PARKS, BEACHES, AND RECREATION AREAS

• **E. E. Risien Park** 🐾🐾½ *See ㊉ on page 106.*

Guesses at City Hall about this park's size ranged from 15 acres to about 20. However, the size of the park will not matter to your dog. What she will be excited about are the huge pecan trees shading every square inch of the park and the San Saba River running along its north side. Knotted ropes dangling from tree limbs overhanging the water invite swimming, even though dogs must remain on leash. The park has picnic tables, barbecue grills, a playground, drinking fountains, and rest rooms.

Even Sport could see that this was the best place in San Saba County to camp, so we were both dumbfounded to learn that camping is not permitted in the park except during special events. Meanwhile, campers broil in the sun a quarter mile away in Mill Pond Park. It's a doggone shame.

The park is three-quarters of a mile east of the courthouse square on U.S. 190. Hours are 8 A.M. to 10 P.M. (915) 372-5144.

• **Mill Pond Park** 🐾½ *See ㊉ on page 106.*

This 71-acre city park is crammed with athletic fields, a playground, a museum, and a swimming pool, but it does offer a short nature trail and a few grassy areas where a car-weary pooch can stretch his legs while on his leash. Best of all, there is a spring-fed pond that spills into a winding creek with low, grassy banks just made for a quick dip. It's a great area for water dogs, even though it is only a few dozen yards long. After Sport spent the better part of a day cooped up in the car, she thought it was quite spacious.

In contrast, the camping area's lack of charm makes it stick out like a big old tick on a dog's ear. Designed for RVs, it has 20 sites arranged in neat rows among fledgling trees. Picnic tables sit under a covered pavilion. Sites with water and electricity are $11 a night; tent sites are $4. No reservations are accepted. Pay fees at City Hall (303 South Clear Street) weekdays from 8 A.M. to 5 P.M.; a worker collects fees at the park on weekends.

The park is half a mile east of the courthouse square on U.S. 190. Hours are 8 A.M. to 10 P.M. (915) 372-5144.

PLACES TO STAY

Mill Pond Park: See Mill Pond Park above for camping information.

DIVERSIONS

Swing on the bridges of San Saba County: Not many counties in Texas can boast of even one historic suspension bridge. San Saba County has two, and your pooch will love the sway of the bridge and the click of her toenails as she trots across weathered planks high above the water. San Saba County has no leash law, so your unfettered pooch can tramp along the bridges and associated country roads and sniff every interesting bolt, boulder, and bunny trail.

Sport enjoys cultural comparisons, and she was rapt as we sat beside Indian grinding holes at the south end of the Regency suspension bridge and looked across the Colorado River just as First American lookouts did, watching for the buffalo herds on their southward migration. As I told her how Indian dogs pulled loaded travoises on the trek, she gave me that "You've got to be kidding" dog look. But my story about buffalo hunts and dogs gorging on scraps and having mounds of bones to gnaw had her whooping. Now the only suspension bridge across the Colorado River, the Regency bridge dates from 1939. From the intersection of U.S. 190 and Highway 16 in San Saba, go north two miles on Highway 16 to F.M. 500; go west on F.M. 500 some 15 miles to County Road 114; turn right and go one mile to the bridge. Park at a turnout beneath the cable on the south end of the bridge; the Indian grinding holes will be in the large granite boulder 10 feet from your front bumper.

San Saba County's second suspension bridge is known as the Swinging Bridge or the Beveridge Bridge. This fragile-looking bridge that resembles a Tinkertoy project has endured since 1896, when the Flinn, Moyer Bridge Company of Weatherford, Texas, accepted the challenge of spanning the San Saba River. From the intersection of U.S. 190 and Highway 16 in San Saba, drive west on U.S. 190 to Ninth Street. Turn right and go to China Creek Road; take a left and drive 1.4 miles to the bridge.

Tree your intended: Dogs know that people are a couple of sacks of dog food shy of a load, and the Wedding Oak is proof of that fact (for Sport, anyway). "Why would anyone want to get married standing under a tree on the side of a dirt road?" Sport wanted to know. She knows that trees have one supreme purpose: to hold raccoons. She inspected the trunk and branches for raccoons and lost interest when she found none. I explained the unneutered facts of life to her, but she remained skeptical. One thing is certain: If you want to get married under the Wedding Oak with your mystified pooch as your attendant, all you have to do is convince a minister or justice of the peace that you know what you are doing. From the intersection of U.S. 190 and Highway 16 in San Saba, drive west on U.S. 190 to Ninth Street. Turn right and go to China Creek Road; take a left and drive one mile to the tree. It's the big green thing.

TRAVIS COUNTY

In addition to the 12 leash-free areas in the city of Austin, Travis County offers four more in rural areas, making it one of the best counties in Texas for a dog to live or visit. In fact, the only four-paw park we found in all of Texas is right here in Travis County. Lake Travis is the most popular recreation spot for people and dogs and can be quite crowded on weekends and holidays, but on weekdays you and your pooch will have plenty of privacy. And, if you are willing to drive a few extra miles to one of the primitive recreation areas operated by the Lower Colorado River Authority, you and your pooch will have to contend with far fewer people any day of the week.

BRIARCLIFF

Briarcliff began as a resort area on Lake Travis. It was a bit before its time and was not a financial success. It gained notoriety when country-and-western singer Willie Nelson bought it because he wanted its golf course. Dog lovers revere it because of nearby Pace Bend Park, the best leash-free park in the state.

PARKS, BEACHES, AND RECREATION AREAS

• **Pace Bend Park** 🐾🐾🐾🐾 🐕 *See ⑦ on page 106.*
This 1,520-acre park has it all: water where pooches can swim, trails where they can run off leash, and campgrounds where they can snooze away the night under a star-studded Texas sky. The entire park is on a peninsula jutting into a hairpin bend in Lake Travis, with steep bluffs on one side offering spectacular campsites hanging off the sides of cliffs and views of the setting sun, and on the other side, gentle grassy slopes descending to the water over which tomorrow's glowing orb will ascend. A park like this just inspires one to bombastic, if not poetic, verbiage. (Sport is giving me that "Do I know you?" look from the backseat.)

The hiking trails take up the high ground running down the center of the peninsula. While they are not well maintained, they pose no problem to the rugged outdoor dog whose thoughtful owner carries a supply of water for both on hikes. The trails loop around some rugged hills and tackle other steep ascents head-on, but from the top you can see water on both sides of you and advancing condominiums to the east.

There are some 400 primitive campsites ($10), but almost all those on the west side of the park (to your left as you enter) sit high atop steep bluffs and offer no access to the water. Sport and I much preferred the camping area at the tip of the peninsula at Kate's Cove and Johnson Cove. Big post oak trees shade the picnic tables and barbecue grills or fire rings, while a grassy bank slopes to the water's edge. The pooch under direct control may visit with other like members of his species, swim, and watch the deer that wander by on their way to drink at the lake. There are rest rooms, but no water is available. Drinking water is available in the park at Tatum Cove. Since this park is extremely busy on weekends and holidays, it's a good idea to bring an ample supply of water so you don't have to stand in line waiting to fill your jug.

The improved camping area has but 20 sites ($15), but water and electricity are available, as are rest rooms with showers.

The park is reached by taking Highway 71 west from Austin to Ranch Road 2322. Turn right on Ranch Road 2322 and follow it to the park entrance. Entry to the park costs a paltry $5 per vehicle. The park never closes. For reservations or information, call (512) 473-9437.

PLACES TO STAY

Pace Bend Park: See Pace Bend Park on page 199 for camping information.

LAGO VISTA

PARKS, BEACHES, AND RECREATION AREAS

• **Arkansas Bend Park** 🐾 🐾 *See ⑫ on page 106.*

This Travis County park is only 195 acres, but it sits on a point jutting into Lake Travis and offers some spectacular views from shaded campsites along the water. Dogs must remain on leash except when they are in the water, which will likely be often. Even though the lake was very low when Sport and I last visited, leaving vast ugly expanses of lake bottom exposed, there was more than enough water to excite Sport the normally unflappable water dog.

Campsites are scattered along a maze of rocky roads winding along the points of land jutting into the lake (fees are $10 per night). Most are shaded by live oak and juniper trees. Picnic tables and barbecue grills are standard equipment, but bring your own water, or at least a large container for water. There are faucets at the park entrance that promise water but delivered none when Sport and I last visited. Both composting toilets and those of the totally repulsive portable kind are available. This campground is somewhat isolated and just a cut above primitive, but if you and your pioneer dog like roughing it, you'll like it here.

From Interstate 35 take U.S. 183 north 13.5 miles to Ranch Road 1431. Go left (west) on Ranch Road 1431 for 11.3 miles to Lohman Ford Road. Take this road south 4.5 miles to Sylvester Ford Road; turn left and follow the road about two miles to the park entrance. Entry costs $5 per vehicle. Hours are 7 A.M. to 10 P.M. For reservations or information, call (512) 473-9437.

RESTAURANTS

The Fairway Pizza and Grill: "Lots of people bring their dogs in the gate by the front porch and let them run around in here while they eat," the owner said. There was a resident cat asleep under one of the picnic tables shaded by juniper trees, so it would probably be appreciated if your pooch stayed on her leash while you have pizza, calzone, chicken-fried steak, or a sandwich. 7405 Lohman Ford Road, Lago Vista, TX 78645; (512) 267-2112.

PLACES TO STAY

Arkansas Bend Park: See Arkansas Bend Park on page 200 for camping information.

TRAVIS PEAK

PARKS, BEACHES, AND RECREATION AREAS

• **Gloster Bend Primitive Recreation Area** 🐾🐾🐾 🐕
*See **73** on page 106.*

With the exception of the lakeside camping area, your pooch is free to run leash-free over this 600-acre park consisting of oak- and juniper-covered hills with over a mile of Lake Travis shoreline. That's easier said than done; the steep, rocky hillsides are thickly cloaked in oak trees and that bane of Austin allergy sufferers (and the source of great wealth for Austin's allergists), the mountain juniper. No facilities are provided other than a boat ramp, fire rings at choice campsites, composting toilets, and trash collection points. The park was deserted the day Sport and I visited except for a man and woman going through the dumpster collecting aluminum cans. Digging in the trash was right down Sport's alley, but I persuaded her to accompany me to the lake for a dip and a tour of the camping area. The campsites are scattered along primitive roads; some would have been 50 feet from the water had the lake not been abnormally low due to drought. Other sites we looked at were high atop a hill overlooking the lake. All had ample shade, and even though the day was warm, a steady breeze cooled us off. Sport and I agreed that since there is no camping fee, it is not a bad deal at all. The park is pretty far from Austin's madding crowds, but bluff-top homes just across the lake were a constant reminder of what we were escaping.

From Interstate 35 take U.S. 183 north 13.5 miles to Ranch Road 1431. Go left (west) on Ranch Road 1431 for 17 miles to Singleton Bend Road. Turn left (south) onto this road and follow it three miles to the park. Entry costs $3 per vehicle. The park is open 24 hours. (512) 473-4083 or (800) 776-5272.

• **Turkey Bend Primitive Recreation Area** 😋 😋 😋 ½ 🐕
See **74** *on page 106.*

Sport fell in love with this park as soon as she saw the large stands of post oak and live oak trees, many festooned with moss and grapevines, that were obviously made for the sole purpose of concealing raccoons. The 400 acres of this park have been left largely undeveloped, which is just what the raccoon-seeking hound would prefer. Sport had a grand time sniffing out possible hiding places.

A loop trail accessed from a trailhead about a quarter mile inside the park entrance gave our legs a real workout but rewarded us with views of the lake and surrounding hills that stretched out for miles. Park at the large graveled parking area to the left immediately after passing the entrance station where you pay your fee. The trail winds through dense juniper thickets where deer lurk, and equestrian use of the trail is encouraged, so if there is a horse trailer in the parking lot and your pooch shares Samantha's love of chasing large quadrupeds, you might want to take a leash along, even though none is required. This is also rattlesnake and poison ivy country.

The no-fee primitive camping areas provide fire rings only, but some were located in groves of oak trees so dense I began quoting from Robert Frost's "Stopping by Woods on a Snowy Evening": "The woods are lovely, dark and deep. . ." You have not seen a bored dog until you have quoted poetry not involving eating, sleeping, or chasing cats to one while standing on the bank of a sky-blue lake on a hot summer day. We slipped the leash off so Sport could have a swim; dogs are required to be on leash only in the camping areas, which take up but a minuscule portion of the park. If you can do without a fire ring, you can camp on the grassy lakeshore; when Sport and I last visited, Lake Travis was so low a couple hundred yards of shoreline were exposed.

From Interstate 35 take U.S. 183 north 13.5 miles to Ranch Road 1431. Go left (west) on Ranch Road 1431 to Shaw Drive, about 9.5 miles west of Lago Vista. Turn left (south) onto Shaw Drive and follow it two miles to the park entrance. There is a $3 per vehicle entry fee. The park is open 24 hours. (512) 473-4083 or (800) 776-5272.

PLACES TO STAY

Gloster Bend Primitive Recreation Area: See Gloster Bend Primitive Recreation Area on page 201 for camping information.

Turkey Bend Primitive Recreation Area: See Turkey Bend Primitive Recreation Area on page 202 for camping information.

VOLENTE

PARKS, BEACHES, AND RECREATION AREAS

• **Sandy Creek Park** 🐾 🐾 *See* 🆖 *on page 106.*

This 25-acre park is basically a small campground containing about 30 sites with picnic tables and barbecue grills, almost all heavily shaded with juniper and live oak trees. Rest rooms and water are available. Campsites carry a $10 price tag and are available on a first-come, first-served basis. The shoreline here is steep, so dogs may have difficulty taking advantage of the Travis County park policy that permits them to be off leash in the water. Otherwise, they must remain leashed.

From U.S. 183 in Cedar Park, take Ranch Road 1431 west two miles to Lime Creek Road; turn left and follow this road six miles to the park entrance. The entrance fee is $5 per vehicle. Hours are 9 A.M. to 7:30 P.M. (512) 473-9437.

PLACES TO STAY

Sandy Creek Park: See Sandy Creek Park above for camping information.

WEBBERVILLE

PARKS, BEACHES, AND RECREATION AREAS

• **Webberville Park** 🐾 🐾 🐾 ½ 🐕 *See* 🆖 *on page 106.*

The Colorado River kisses the edge of this 135-acre park where your pooch can roam leash-free as long as he remains within your sight and under voice control. There is no fee for the use of this park, which is a popular picnicking and boat launching site. The picnic area covers most of the park and is heavily shaded by large pecan trees. There are a couple of playgrounds, rest rooms, and water fountains. The park also has softball and volleyball fields if your pooch has athletic tendencies. Unfortunately, the steep riverbanks prevent use of the river for swimming, although there is a fishing pier. You and your pooch can walk two miles of graveled trails that snake through the picnic area. Checking out the picnic tables for any lingering scraps occupied Samantha the perennially starving dog for half an hour before I realized she would never leave of her own accord and called for her to kennel up. Meanwhile a chow took over as he and his family wandered by.

The park is three miles east of Webberville off F.M. 969. Turn right (south) onto Webberwood Road and follow the signs to the park. Entrance is free. The park is open 9 A.M. to 7:30 P.M. from March 1 through April 30 and September 10 through October 31; 8 A.M. to 9 P.M. from May 1 through September 9; and 9 A.M. to 6 P.M. from November 1 through the end of February. (512) 473-9437.

WILLIAMSON COUNTY

Until just a few years ago, Williamson County was a rural enclave where people moved to escape the pressures of nearby Austin. Today Williamson County is just another Austin suburb, even though it struggles to hang on to its small-town image. The county has a surprising number of parks, but—not surprisingly—dogs must remain leashed in all of them. In addition, the rapid urbanization of the county has resulted in a hardening of attitudes toward dogs in recent years, and while many places in the county still welcome dogs, increasingly they are merely tolerated.

STATE WILDLIFE MANAGEMENT AREAS

See the National and State Forests/State Wildlife Management Areas starting on page 621 for important information and safety tips on visiting these areas with your dog.

• **Granger Wildlife Management Area** 🐾 🐾 ½

Hunting hounds will find much to pursue here. Dogs may be used to hunt coyotes and furbearing animals such as raccoons and foxes, but not feral hogs. You and your pooch may team up to hunt a variety of waterfowl and migratory game birds as well as squirrels. The San Gabriel River bottom and the shores of Lake Granger range from open fields to dense thickets. Camping is available in nearby U.S. Army Corps of Engineers parks (see below). See page 626 for a description of the area.

GEORGETOWN

PARKS, BEACHES, AND RECREATION AREAS

• **Blue Hole Park** 🐾 🐾 ½ *See* **77** *on page 106.*

High-diving daredevil dogs will love this park. Your chicken-hearted dog will, too. The six-acre park is named for a swimming hole on the South San Gabriel River at which a favorite people activity is diving from a 30-foot limestone bluff into the water. Your sensible, level-headed, leashed pooch will probably be content to enter the water in a more conventional manner. There are picnic tables, barbecue grills, and a rest room scattered among the dense trees on the hillside overlooking the swimming area. This very popular area with young people will be quite crowded on weekends and holidays, but on weekdays you and your pooch will likely have it all to yourselves. A hike and bike trail meanders along the river, departing from the park's east end to connect with VFW Park and San Gabriel Park; total length of the loop trail is about two miles.

From the intersection of Austin Avenue and Second Street, drive west on Second Street one block to Rock Street; take a right and go one block to the park. The park is open from dawn to dusk. (512) 930-3595.

• **Cedar Breaks Park** 🐾 🐾 *See ⑱ on page 106.*

Sport Dog lives in Mason County, the heart of Texas white-tailed deer country, and she thought she'd seen a lot of deer. Then we visited the U.S. Army Corps of Engineers parks around Lake Georgetown, and we saw more deer than we have ever seen anywhere else in Texas. It seemed that every picnic and camp site had at least one deer. It was mid-July, and pairs of spotted fawns were everywhere. I was glad Sport had to be leashed; otherwise, she might not have been able to resist temptation. Sport and Samantha love deer. They think they are delicious.

The 230-acre park projects into Lake Georgetown on two promontories, and in some places—notably the campground area—the banks are too steep to permit easy access to the water. However, the 41 picnic sites, each with shade shelter and barbecue grill, sit on an easy-sloping shore that will make it easy for your pooch to wet her whistle, her tummy, and anything else she cares to submerge. After she comes out of the water on her leash, she will give you a shower when she shakes off.

There is no entry fee to the park, but your pooch incurs certain other obligations upon entering. He must remain on a leash "under six feet in length" and may not go upon swimming beaches. You must remove any animal waste.

The 16.6-mile Good Water Trail begins at a parking area on the west side of the road just past the park entrance. This trail takes you into a heavy cedar brake where springtime might find endangered golden-cheeked warblers nesting. However, the surface of the trail consists of small, loose rocks, many with sharp edges. Unless you have heavy footwear with strong ankle support and your pooch has tough paws, you might want to pass this trail up and hike along the grassy lakeshore instead. However, if you and your pooch are up for a challenge, pack your camping gear and strike out. The trail is marked with mileposts and winds along the lake, passing through several primitive camping areas before ending on the opposite side of the lake at Russell Park. The only water on the trail is at Tejas Camp, at mile 11, so be sure to carry plenty of water. Other primitive camping areas are Cedar Hollow, between miles 4 and 5; Sawyer, between miles 6 and 7; and Walnut Springs, at mile 15. Hikers are asked to check in and out with park rangers at Cedar Breaks Park, Tejas Camp, and Russell Park. Obtain a trail map when you enter Russell or Cedar Breaks Park.

If you hike the trail between October and early January, be aware that part of it passes through a wildlife management area where public deer hunts may be taking place. Check with park rangers and exercise extreme caution. Also, be aware that Russell Park, the terminus of the trail, is closed from October 1 through March 31, so you will have to arrange to be picked up outside the park entrance. Leaving your vehicle parked on the county road is not recommended.

The park has 64 campsites with water and electricity ($18) laid out in a loop on a promontory offering good views of the lake from most sites. Many of the sites are only a few feet from the edge of a steep cliff overlooking the lake. These offer spectacular views of the sunset as well as water-skiers. The sites were designed with camping trailers or RVs in mind, but most have heavily shaded, level areas where you can pitch a tent. There are two rest rooms with showers in the campground. To make reservations, call (800) 284-2267; there is a $6.50 fee.

The park is west of Georgetown off F.M. 2338. From Interstate 35, drive west on F.M. 2338 just over three miles, then turn left on Cedar Breaks Road and follow it two miles, crossing the dam, to get to the picnic and camping areas. Entrance is free. The park is open from 6 A.M. to 10 P.M., and the gate to the campground is locked each night at 10 P.M. (512) 930-5253.

• Jim Hogg Park 🐾 🐾 See ⑦⑨ on page 106.

This 198-acre park is basically two large campgrounds in the middle of a deer refuge. Sport and I counted 63 deer while checking out the 148 campsites with water and electricity. (Sport says I counted two fawns twice, but even if I did, you get the point: There is a tremendous number of deer in this park.) There is no entry fee, but there are no day-use areas, either. As I said, camping is the main thing here. Some of the campsites offer double hookups for RVs so you and a friend can share a space.

The campsites ($18) are laid out in two large loops so that about half of them have excellent views of the lake. The promontory on which the campground sits runs north and south, so the sun rises over the lake. Junipers are the dominant vegetation, although there are some small oak trees struggling to compete for a patch of sky and grow into big oak trees. Meanwhile, the overpopulated resident deer attempt to eat everything, even the junipers. It's no wonder the park is closed from time to time in the fall to allow public hunts to try to keep deer numbers in line with the carrying capacity of the land.

Campsites 1 through 78 are open all year, while sites 79 through 148 are open only from April 1 through September 30. To make reservations, call (800) 284-2267; there is a $6.50 fee.

From Interstate 35, take F.M. 2338 west six miles to Jim Hogg Road. Turn left (south) onto Jim Hogg Road and go two miles to the park. There is no entry fee. The park is open from 6 A.M. to 10 P.M., and the gate to the campground is locked each night at 10 P.M. (512) 930-5253.

• **Russell Park** 🐾🐾🐾 *See ⑳ on page 106.*

Entry to this day-use-only park of 255 acres will set you back $3 per vehicle, but the price includes the use of what park employees call "The Doggy Beach," a picnic area with four shaded tables with barbecue grills where your leashed pooch can have a swim and a hot dog—er, tube steak. The Doggy Beach is officially picnic area 3. Dogs are banned from the swimming beach area, picnic sites 57 through 66. Signs posted at the entry to the beach bear the hated dog in red circle with slash symbol.

From Interstate 35, go west on F.M. 2338 about seven miles to F.M. 3405. Turn left (south) on F.M. 3405 and go one mile to County Road 262; take another left onto this road and go a mile to the park entrance. The park is open from 6 A.M. to dusk from April 1 to September 30. (512) 930-5253.

• **San Gabriel Park** 🐾🐾🐾 *See ㉑ on page 106.*

The 100 acres of this park border the first three-quarters of a mile of the San Gabriel River. Your trivia-loving pooch will be interested to know that the North and South Forks of the San Gabriel join at the western boundary of the park, just upstream from where the hike and bike trail bridge crosses. This trail connects with VFW Park and Blue Hole Park, both upstream, and offers about two miles of concrete-paved surface. San Gabriel Park has lots of open spaces for your leashed pooch to wander, but he will likely gravitate toward the water. A low dam at the east end of the park backs up the river to make a dandy people swimming hole complete with ropes hanging from limbs over the water so you can take a plunge into the cool, clear water. However, for dogs the water is probably best downstream of the dam, where about 150 yards of parkland remain before the river exits the park. The water in this stretch is shallow, slow-moving, and ideal for letting a leashed pooch wade and drink. Huge pecan trees shade a graveled parking area just past the low-water bridge below the dam.

The usual playgrounds, picnic tables, and barbecue grills complete this urban park. Rest rooms and drinking fountains are also available.

The park is easily accessible from Interstate 35. Take Exit 262 for Williams Drive (F.M. 2338) and go east on Williams for two blocks to its intersection with Austin Avenue, then turn left. Take the first right, onto

Stadium Drive; the park is past the athletic fields. It is open 24 hours. (512) 930-3595.

RESTAURANTS

Cianfrani Coffee Company: You and your pooch can get your caffeine and share a muffin at one of the four sidewalk tables while you observe happenings on the square. 715 Main Street; (512) 869-7030.

Courthouse Cafe and Creamery: "We're famous for our chicken tortilla soup, which I'm making right now," said Karen, the owner, when I called. "We have two tables and a bench, all covered by an awning, on the sidewalk out front where people and their dogs can eat. In fact, we'll even tear the top off a Styrofoam food-to-go container and bring a dog a drink." Karen is a dog owner herself and knows how to please pooches. The menu features Karen-made soups, salads, sandwiches, and hand-dipped Blue Bell ice cream. 805 South Austin Avenue; (512) 863-9755.

PLACES TO STAY

Claibourne House Bed-and-Breakfast: Small, well-behaved dogs are welcome at this inn with a fenced yard where they can roam leash-free. Rooms are $85 to $95. 912 Forest Street, Georgetown, TX 78626; (512) 930-3934.

Comfort Inn: "Small, clean, family-member type dogs are welcome," the manager said. Rooms are $60 to $70, and there's a $5 pet fee. 1005 Leander Road, Georgetown, TX 78628; (512) 863-7504.

Days Inn: No barking dogs left alone in rooms is the only requirement here. Room rates are $44 to $56. 209 North Interstate 35, Georgetown, TX 78628; (512) 863-5572.

Cedar Breaks Park: See Cedar Breaks Park on page 205 for camping information.

Jim Hogg Park: See Jim Hogg Park on page 206 for camping information.

FESTIVALS

Fourth of July Family Festival: Probably the most fun part of this festival is the children's parade, an event that inspires people to dress up dogs and kids in patriotic outfits that would make the Founding Fathers blush with pride. There's also a free fishing derby for kids; pooches are allowed to observe. Food booths and a variety of rides will entertain your pooch, and the speeches will probably put her to sleep. It's held on the Fourth of July in San Gabriel Park, at the intersection of Austin Avenue and Stadium Drive. For details, call (512) 930-3535.

Mayfair: Food, fun, and games in the park let you and your leashed pooch celebrate the coming of spring. The event is held in early May at

San Gabriel Park, at the intersection of Austin Avenue and Stadium Drive. For information, call (512) 930-3545.

Scarecrow Festival: If your pooch loves to dress up and go trick-or-treating (and what Halloween hound doesn't?), he'll have a grand time mooching his way around the square while admiring the costumes on all the other dogs. The festival is held in late October on the square, at the intersection of Eighth and Martin Luther King Streets. For information, call (512) 930-3545 or (800) 436-8686.

DIVERSIONS

Be peachy-keen: Some outings with your pooch are sweeter than others. Take your hound to the Schwegmann Orchard and he will have his choice of 1,800 peach trees to hike a leg on while you pick your own fruit and try not to think about how the trees are irrigated. "We have two dogs of our own, so we have to ask people to keep their dogs leashed," says Kathy Schwegmann. With 30 acres of fragrant fruit to explore, only pooches with the sourest of dispositions should complain. The orchard is open for picking in June and July. For information and directions to the farm, call (512) 863-3314.

Eat a square tomato: Okay, the tomatoes aren't square, but the courthouse square is the location of a Farmer's Market each Thursday from May through October. Your pooch will love all those fresh-from-the-farm smells, and we're not just talking fresh fruits and vegetables. There are all those tires on all those pickups to be sniffed, and the soles of farmers' shoes are an olfactory library of fascinating lore to a dog. Meanwhile, you can score some cucumbers, peaches, melons, or other goodies to share later. It's held on the courthouse square, at the intersection of Eighth and Martin Luther King Streets. (512) 863-8706.

Get all dolled up: Jan Hagara loves her Pomeranian, so it's only natural that she would welcome your dog at the factory outlet store selling her line of collectible porcelain dolls and figures. Even better, some of the figurines themselves include dogs. Your pooch will love shopping for her own image immortalized in porcelain. Before going inside it might be well to explain to your tail-wagger that some of these dolls sell for as much as $2,000, so she should take plenty of cash inside with her or be very, very careful not to wag her tail when someone walks up to her and says, "Oh, what a beautiful dog." Otherwise, things could turn ugly very quickly. Jan Hagara Outlet is at 40114 Industrial Park Circle; take Exit 264 off Interstate 35 north of Georgetown. Industrial Park is on the east side of the highway; the outlet store is in the blue buildings. (512) 863-3072.

Go native: Robbin Voight and her cats Spunky and Tigger say it is fine for you and your leashed pooch to visit Bird's Nest Farm, where you can see display gardens of native plants and herbs and buy some as well. If your pooch is into herbalism, she'll want to take plenty of spending money along. Call for hours and directions: (512) 863-4877.

Go on a power trip: Your dog will be absolutely thrilled to visit this outdoor museum featuring antique farm equipment, including about 150 old tractors. "You can bring half a dozen dogs if you want to, as long as they don't hike a leg on me," said Ray Miller, who put the collection together with brother Louis. That shouldn't be a problem with all those big tires around. Millers' Mechanical Mart is at 806 East Eighth Street; (512) 863-5060.

Light up your life: The Candle Factory specializes in hand-dipped candles; you and your small pooch are welcome to shop the showroom as long as your dog is in your arms or on her leash. Then you can go home and burn the candle at both ends. 4411 South Interstate 35; (512) 863-6025.

GRANGER

PARKS, BEACHES, AND RECREATION AREAS

• **Taylor Park** 🐾🐾🐾 *See* **82** *on page 106.*

Dogs love ghost stories, especially bloody ones told around a campfire under a full moon with plenty of blood-curdling howls hurled into the night at unexpected moments. Aroooooo! This Lake Granger park has a 1.2-mile hiking trail that furnishes the stuff of which campfire legends are made. The Comanche Bluff Trail begins at a parking area and rest room reached by taking the second left after you enter the park. Just a couple hundred yards down the trail sits the Hoxie Bridge, and thereby hangs the tail, er, tale. The bridge was built over the San Gabriel River about 1900, but a great flood in 1921 washed it a quarter mile downstream. Convicts from the state penitentiary at Huntsville were brought in to rebuild it, and one, a reputed troublemaker, was shot in the head by a guard and his body hung in a tree as a warning to the others. The spirit of the unburied prisoner was said to have terrorized local residents for years, always appearing on a Friday night during the full moon. (Perhaps overlong stays at end-of-week happy hours had something to do with the ghostly appearances.) Finally a local priest's prayers laid the spirit to rest. The bridge was dismantled in 1979 and rebuilt at its present site in 1982, where it now serves as a footbridge on the Comanche Bluff Trail. Encroaching vines and trees give the bridge a foreboding appearance even today—watch out for that ghost.

If you and your leashed pooch hike the trail early or late in the day, keep a lookout for coyotes, bobcats, foxes, and squirrels. All these are merely of academic interest, but if you should happen upon a feral hog (wild boar), avoid it by whatever means necessary. The lake surrounded by heavy brush in the midst of an agricultural area produces ideal habitat for these vicious creatures that can make dog burger out of your pooch.

There is no entry fee for day use of this 395-acre park, which means that you and your leashed pooch may use the picnic area at no charge. The shaded tables with barbecue grills sit atop an elevated promontory overlooking the lake.

The 48 campsites with water and electricity ($10 except those that will accommodate two RVs, which are $14) are also atop a promontory. Both the picnic area and the campground reflect the character of the Blackland Prairie as well as the preoccupation with and love of bulldozers by the U.S. Army Corps of Engineers. That is to say, the sites sit in a neatly scraped area with planted grass and fledgling trees, surrounded by much larger and more lush native vegetation. This is a campground with little character and less privacy. It doesn't even offer decent views of the lake.

The camping area does overlook the Hoxie Bridge on the Comanche Bluff Trail, so you and your leashed pooch can sit around the campfire making s'mores and telling ghost stories and howling at the moon until quiet time begins at 10 P.M. Each campsite has a shaded picnic table and barbecue grill. There is a rest room with showers in the area.

From Highway 95 south of Granger, go east on F.M. 1331 to the park entrance on your left. Entrance is free. The park is open from 6 A.M. to 10 P.M. For camping reservations, call (512) 859-2668.

PLACES TO STAY

Taylor Park: See Taylor Park on page 210 for camping information.

ROUND ROCK

Until recently, Round Rock was a small country town on the outskirts of Austin noted chiefly for being the place where the famous outlaw and train robber Sam Bass met his fatal bullet a century ago. Then the high-tech boom hit, and the factories located where land was cheap and taxes were low. Round Rock spread faster than a computer virus on the Internet.

Round Rock's growth stresses the community as the people there struggle to develop solutions to problems that did not exist just months before. Dogs are among the casualties. When Sport and I asked for a copy of park regulations regarding dogs, we were told that a just-passed ordinance bars dogs from going within 100 feet of "any organized event."

Not only will your softball-loving pooch have to hang up her catcher's mitt when she visits Round Rock, she won't be able to attend any street festivals, either. The news regarding parks isn't much better. While there are three where a dog can go to get away from all the traffic and people, she must remain on leash at all times, and may not approach within the aforesaid 100 feet of any organized event taking place in a park.

PARKS, BEACHES, AND RECREATION AREAS

• **Henry S. McNeil Community Park** 🐾🐾 *See ㉝ on page 106.*

This park just off the frontage road of busy Interstate 35 is a welcome relief from all those miles of asphalt. Only about 20 acres, the park is thickly wooded with live oak trees and has a rest room, playground, water fountain, picnic tables, barbecue grills, and softball fields. Your pooch is not permitted within 100 feet of the softball fields when there is a game going on, but she'll be too busy sniffing around the brushy banks of Chandler Branch on the south side of the park to notice. Squirrels provide other visual stimuli.

Southbound on Interstate 35, exit at Ranch Road 1431 and cross over. Turn right onto the two-way frontage road; the park entrance is just south of the exit ramp. Northbound on Interstate 35, exit at Ranch Road 3406 and follow the two-way frontage road about a mile to the park entrance. Hours are 6 A.M. to midnight. (512) 867-6442.

• **Memorial Park** 🐾1/2 *See ㉞ on page 106.*

The main thing to recommend the three or so acres of this urban park is that it is just off Interstate 35 and may be the salvation of the traveling dog about to humiliate himself. Your leashed pooch may find relief among the trees and rocks in the bed of Brushy Creek. If your pooch likes history at all, she will be fascinated by the round pedestal-like limestone formation in the creekbed by the ruins of the old bridge. This is the round rock that gave the city its name. Off-street parking is nil, so you'll have to park on the street and dodge traffic to get down to the low-water crossing, from which you can access the creek.

Exit Interstate 35 at Ranch Road 620 and take that road west for just one block. Turn right on Chisholm Trail and go one block; when you cross the low-water bridge you are in the park. Hours are 6 A.M. to midnight. (512) 867-6442.

• **Old Settlers Park at Palm Valley** 🐾🐾 *See ㉟ on page 106.*

Only a tiny portion of this 427-acre park is of interest to the leashed dog. Most of the acreage is given over to grass and only grass—no trees, no interesting humps to stand on, no nothing. In addition, dogs are banned from going within 100 feet of "any organized event," so there will be times when a good part of the park will be off-limits entirely. However, most of those events take place where a dog wouldn't want to go anyway—leave bare and ugly places to the people, we always say.

To find the dog-friendly part of the park, follow the entrance road, Harrell Parkway, past the soccer fields. Shortly you'll come to a knoll behind which hides a small lake with a streamer of willow trees tailing off its north end. Your pooch can drink or swim at the lake and hike with you along a trail that follows the tree line. This is virtually the only shade in the park. A few picnic tables and barbecue grills hug the shoreline as well, and there is a rest room here and a playground. However, there is also a group pavilion, and when Sport and I last visited, tents were being set up all over the knoll for an upcoming festival; you may find yourselves banned from the rest room, playground, and picnic areas.

The park is 2.5 miles east of Interstate 35 on U.S. 79. Hours are 6 A.M. to midnight. (512) 867-6442.

RESTAURANTS

Round Rock BBQ: As at many such places, pork stars on the menu here, but the usual assortment of barbecued meats and sides is available. You and your pooch have your choice of three picnic tables. 1310 Round Rock Avenue; (512) 255-7447.

PLACES TO STAY

Best Western: Rooms are $65 to $85. Dogs stay free, but a credit card imprint is required in case of damage; otherwise, pay a $5 fee. 1831 North Interstate 35, Round Rock, TX 78664; (512) 255-3222 or (800) 528-1234.

TAYLOR

Taylor may be the only city in Texas whose sewer system was paid for by dogs. Of course, people actually paid the money, but dogs played a vital role. Early in the town's history a political genius hatched a scheme designed to rid the town of loose dogs and lessen the stench resulting from lack of a sewer system. According to the official city history, town leaders hired a small boy to catch stray dogs and bring them to a pound set up on the town square. Each time he delivered a dog, he got a quarter. Each time an owner arrived to reclaim a dog, the fee was a dollar, which included a numbered brass collar tag. Taylor must have had an awful lot of dogs, because the story is the money paid for completion of the town's first sewer system. The corollary to this story should be that the young boy became wealthy and went on to found a home for indigent dogs, but for some reason the history is silent on this point.

Taylor nevertheless owes a debt of gratitude to dogs, which may explain why many public events are open to pooches. The city does still have a leash law, but dogs are welcome to attend a variety of festivals. There's not much else for a dog to do here, however.

PARKS, BEACHES, AND RECREATION AREAS

• **Murphy Park** 🐾 🐾 *See* **86** *on page 106.*

This approximately 40-acre urban park is heavily given over to human pursuits—a swimming pool, athletic fields, and picnic grounds—but there is room left over for a car-weary pooch to go for a leashed walk, hike a leg on one of the numerous trees, and even take a drink from the small lake.

From U.S. 79, turn west on West Lake Drive and go about a quarter mile to the entrance on your left. The park has an 11 P.M. curfew. (512) 352-5003.

FESTIVALS

National Rattlesnake Sacking Championship: If you want to give a bad case of the shivers to your pooch, snap on a strong leash and take him to this festival featuring snake handling. Yikes! There's also an arts and crafts show (where perhaps you can buy your pooch that rattlesnake skin collar he's been pining for), food (including rattlesnake meat), sky diving demonstrations, and a car rally. The festival is held in early March (while it's still cold enough for the snakes to be sluggish) at Murphy Park, on West Lake Drive just west of U.S. 79. For information, call (512) 365-1533.

Optimist Crappie Tournament: No, it's not what you think. The crappie is a fish, and the object is to catch more of them than anybody else. Get your pooch a fishing pole and take her fishing—it's the ultimate bonding experience. Held in early April on Lake Granger. From Highway 95 north of Taylor, go east on F.M. 1331 to the park entrance on your left. For information, call (512) 352-6364.

WALBURG

RESTAURANTS

Walburg Restaurant and Biergarten: Okay, you German shepherds, dachshunds, and wolfhounds, put on your lederhosen. We're going to a real German restaurant you're going to love. The patio out back seats 400 people, there's live German music on weekends, and the menu is stuffed with dishes featuring sausage, sauerbraten, wiener schnitzel, chicken cordon bleu, and other European specialties designed to delight doggy diners. Best of all, dogs of any breed are welcome at this big old restaurant in a little old town. Bring your appetite: The food is excellent, you get a lot of it, and if you drop something on the ground, there's a dog right there to take care of it. From Interstate 35 north of Georgetown, take Exit 268 and head east four miles on Farm Road 972. The restaurant is the big building with all the cars out front. (512) 863-8440.

4

BROWNSVILLE/ LOWER RIO GRANDE VALLEY

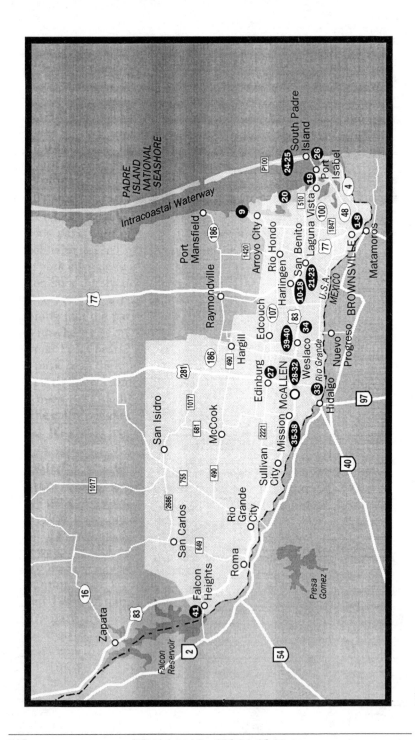

BROWNSVILLE/LOWER RIO GRANDE VALLEY

The Lower Rio Grande Valley—usually referred to simply as "The Valley"—is unique for two reasons: its subtropical climate and its location on the border with Mexico. This is as far south as you can go and still be in Texas. Or, to look at it the way the majority of the people here do, this is as far north as you can go and still be in Mexico.

The warm winters, along with the availability of water from the Rio Grande for irrigation, make The Valley one of Texas's chief agricultural centers. Vegetables and citrus fruits are the main crops, along with tourists seeking relief from winter's chill. As many as 75,000 people from frozen climes like Kansas, Iowa, and Minnesota migrate here each winter. They generally celebrate Thanksgiving at home before heading south, returning in time to file their income tax in April.

The Winter Texans, or snowbirds, add much to the flavor of The Valley. If as you drive along you overtake a dually pickup truck with four silver- and blue-haired individuals and one white toy poodle inside, tooling along in the middle of the road at some speed far below the limit, you have without a doubt met some Winter Texans. On the other hand, the friendly grandmother type you meet striding briskly along a nature trail in a park with a Pomeranian at her side will also likely be a Winter Texan. Ditto for the people ahead of you in the checkout line at the grocery store.

The region's dependence on agriculture and tourism, both seasonal endeavors, is partly responsible for this area having a high unemployment rate. Incomes are low, a fact reflected in many ways, one of which is the quality of the parks you and your pooch will be able to visit. Most parks here are small, and maintenance is sometimes lacking. Low incomes also translate into less money being spent on pets, and The Valley has a continuing problem with rabies due to unvaccinated domestic animals. Be sure your dog is fully protected before you bring him.

Don't get the impression you can't have a good time with your dog in The Valley. Some of the state's finest beaches are here, and there are some excellent wildlife refuges and state parks that welcome dogs. Beach bum dogs and bird-watching dogs will find few places better to roam. Eating out will be more of a problem. Almost no restaurants have outside seating due to the humid climate, a summer that goes on almost all year, and the Texas addiction to air-conditioning.

BROWNSVILLE

Sport, Samantha, and I traveled tens of thousands of miles and visited towns in every corner of Texas (and most of the rounded-off places), and nowhere did we find a better place than Brownsville for a dog to get lost. If all those whining puppies are getting on your nerves, Mom and Pop Dog, you can disappear across the border here and pretend you are young, wild, and carefree again.

Actually, Brownsville is such a great place for a dog to get lost because of Sarah Manrrique, the city's animal control supervisor. This woman will leave no empty leash dangling sadly from a dog owner's hand if she can help it. She runs advertisements in the newspaper seeking to put lost dogs and their people back together. She's used the information on collar tags to call out-of-state veterinarians to get prescriptions for obviously ill dogs. She urges all dog owners to leave a temporary Texas address with their hometown veterinarian so she can contact them should their hound somehow turn up in her custody. And listen up, panting pooches: She has outfitted her animal control officers with air-conditioned trucks—meaning air-conditioned back where the dogs ride as well as up front. The trucks also carry the legend "If I had a city tag on, I'd be home now."

Of course, no one wants or expects a dog to get lost, but take a dog to a strange town where margaritas flow as plentifully as water, and, well, stuff other than magic happens. So if you or your dog have plans for one of you to get blotto and wander off, wear your tags and do it in Brownsville. Sarah oversees the untimely demise of between 5,000 and 6,000 unfortunate pooches every year, and she'd rather the number were zero. She definitely does not want your dog to become a statistic. She publishes a pet's guide to Brownsville, which states, in part, "We ask that you walk your owner on a leash so as not to lose them. Also, wear identification tags in case you are picked up so we can contact your owner. Remind your owner to leave a forwarding address with your veterinarian at home, or have your owner teach you how to dial collect from the nearest phone."

Ironically, Brownsville probably had more loose dogs than any other city my controlled canines and I visited. Sarah told me this continues a long Brownsville tradition and quoted a soldier from a century ago who stated that the place ought to be called Dog Town because of the number of dogs wandering the streets. Nevertheless, the city does have a leash law, and your pooch is expected to obey it. Otherwise, he will have to answer to Sarah.

PARKS, BEACHES, AND RECREATION AREAS

• Central Avenue Park 🐾 *See* ❶ *on page 218.*

Although it's only about an acre and a half, leashed dogs will find this to be a pretty little park. It's packed with trees, picnic tables, basketball courts, and playground equipment, but there's still plenty of grass and lots of shade.

The park is at the intersection of Central Avenue and Boca Chica Boulevard. Hours are 8 A.M. until midnight. (956) 542-2064.

• Gonzalez Park 🐾½ *See* ❷ *on page 218.*

The 40 or so acres of Antonio Gonzalez Park lean heavily toward parking lots, a pool, and athletic fields on the south end, but the northern half welcomes leashed dogs with plenty of grass and open space. There are lots of picnic tables and a playground, but little shade.

From F.M. 1419, go south a block and a half on 28th Street to the park entrance. Hours are 8 A.M. until midnight. (956) 542-2064.

• Lincoln Park 🐾🐾 *See* ❸ *on page 218.*

This park of about 30 acres would be a water dog's delight if the banks of the two *resacas* (lakes that were once river channels) it contains sloped more gently to the water. Still, there's plenty for a leashed dog to like, with lots of trees and grassy areas and even some small inclines to drag you up and down. Footbridges across the *resacas* make it possible to walk both sides of the banks, so if your pooch is one of those who always wants to know what's on the other side, you can show her. Picnic tables dot the long, skinny park, and there is some playground equipment scattered about. Palm and mesquite trees provide welcome shade. As everywhere we went in Brownsville, we saw lots of dogs roaming around loose.

Although the park grounds appeared peaceful and well tended, the rest room buildings all had their doors boarded up and were covered in what appeared to be gang graffiti. Taking your dog with you to this park appears to be a good idea for more reason than one.

The park is at the intersection of U.S. 77/83 and Highway 4 (International Boulevard). Hours are 8 A.M. until midnight. (956) 542-2064.

• Morningside Park 🐾🐾 *See* ❹ *on page 218.*

Brownsville is a city of *resacas*—old channels of the Rio Grande long since abandoned by the river and now curving, palm-lined lakes scattered throughout town. This park of about 50 acres fronts one of those *resacas,* and there's a mowed path to lead your leashed hound right down to the water. The park and its numerous picnic tables get lots of shade from mesquite, hackberry, and anaqua trees. Athletic fields take up most of the center of the park, but they're fenced to keep the players inside, out of the way of the leashed dogs enjoying the rest. Several playground areas will keep small-dog owners occupied. There are also lots of grassy slopes for romping.

The park is about a mile and a half south of Boca Chica Boulevard on Morningside Road. Hours are 8 A.M. to midnight. (956) 542-2064.

• Porter Park 🐾1/2 See ❺ on page 218.

The 12 acres of this park next to the Gladys Porter Zoo sit in the bend of a *resaca* and are cut into several chunks by streets and parking lots serving the pool, community theater, shuffleboard courts, and activity center, but the fringes bordering the water are great for leashed dogs. Rows of palm trees shade much of the park, and a sidewalk skirts much of the *resaca*. Sport and I saw lots of ducks and wading birds in the water, but the steep banks made it hard for a dog to grab a drink without getting a total dunking in the process. A large playground and lots of picnic tables make this a pleasant spot to spend time.

Dean Porter Park is at the intersection of East Sixth and Ringgold Streets, just a block west of U.S. 77/83. Hours are 8 A.M. until midnight. (956) 542-2064.

• Portway Acres Park 🔥 See ❻ on page 218.

The main features of this park of about two acres are the children's playground painted in shocking shades of red, blue, and yellow and the large population of neighborhood dogs, some constrained by fences and some roaming freely in flagrant violation of the city leash law. Judging from what Sport and I saw when we last visited, there will be plenty of trash to sniff around the half dozen picnic tables, and the sprinkling of mesquite and palm trees adds additional appeal for boy dogs. Sport is one of those female dogs who squats or hikes, depending on her mood. This was her first chance to hike her leg on a palm tree, and she took it.

The park is just south of Highway 48 on Brownsville's east side. Turn south on Central Avenue and go one block to Austin Road; turn left and go three blocks to the park. Hours are 8 A.M. until midnight. (956) 542-2064.

• Sabal Palm Grove Sanctuary 🐾 🐾1/2 See ❼ on page 218.

Sport and I agree that these 527 acres are among the most special in Texas. When the first Spanish explorer sailed up the Rio Grande, he described a vast palm forest extending up the river for tens of miles. Today only 32 acres of this virgin forest remains, all here within this sanctuary. Never cleared for agriculture like the remainder, this tiny forest is a library of life, a living record of what the Lower Rio Grande Valley was like before humans came along and "improved" it.

Sport, of course, was not impressed by all this. Like other leashed dogs who visit, her primary interest was in sniffing and exploring the jungle-like growth along the Forest Trail. Dogs who visit can do something they can do nowhere else in Texas: experience a tropical woodland with all its exotic birds and animals, some of which occur now here else in the United States. To say there are some unique smells here is not exaggerating. Bobcats, coyotes, and coral snakes (beware!) are known to exist on the sanctuary, and the endangered ocelot and jaguarundi may make nocturnal appearances your hound's talented sniffer will discern. The sanctuary's extensive bird list includes species rarely seen farther north, such as the chachalaca, green jay, buff-bellied hummingbird, and kiskadee flycatcher. A photo blind extending over a *resaca* (a lake that was once a river channel) along the Forest Trail will get you close to many of the birds, especially wintering waterfowl. You can get a trail guide keyed to numbered posts along the trail at the visitor center.

The Native Trail, only 0.4-mile long, winds through an area outside the sabal palm forest; a trail guide identifies plants used by First Americans. This trail takes you to the Rio Grande, whose waters today are almost totally drained for a variety of uses, primarily irrigation.

Sport and I walked the Forest Trail, since this sanctuary is, after all, about the sabal palms. Vegetation crowds in on both sides of the narrow dirt path, and the towering palms block the sky. Spanish moss drapes many trees, and now and again a fallen tree across the path required we clamber over—not an easy task when the leash and I went over and Sport went under. Sport tugged insistently at the leash whenever she spotted a side trail leading to the *resaca,* which had its own blend of sights and smells. Once we found an area where some unknown creature had feasted on seedpods fallen from the palm trees. I don't know what it was, but Sport spent five minutes carefully sniffing the ground, the seedpods, and the bushes.

To reach the sanctuary, take U.S. 77/83 to Highway 4 (International Boulevard). Go east on Highway 4 to F.M. 1419 (Southmost Road) and turn right. Drive 5.7 miles to Sabal Palm Road; turn right and go one mile to the sanctuary entrance. The entry fee is $3. Hours are sunrise to sunset. The visitor center is open from 8:30 A.M. to 5:30 P.M. (956) 541-8034.

• **Washington Park** 🐾 1/2 *See* **8** *on page 218.*

Trees and grass cover almost every bit of the approximately 10 acres of this downtown park, and old-fashioned streetlights line its sidewalks. It's a great place to stretch your legs while you dewater your leashed pooch. There's a large fountain in the center of the park where you can also rewater your pooch. Picnic tables offer the possibility of a romantic lunch in the park with comestibles from one of the neighborhood eateries nearby, none of which have outside seating. Sport and I spotted a *panadería* (bakery) and a *tortillaría* (tortilla factory) as well as a *taquería* (taco stand). Sport, however, was more interested in the queue of school-children at one end of the park, having learned from experience that kids are suckers for a cute dog with big brown eyes and soft, floppy ears. Why buy lunch when you can brown-bag it out of somebody else's lunch sack? Dogs have no pride. They'll bum a bite from anybody. At least Sport will—politely. Samantha demands and snatches.

The park is at the intersection of East Seventh Street and Madison Street. Hours are 8 A.M. until midnight. (956) 542-2064.

PLACES TO STAY

The Rio Grande Valley has more than 500 RV and mobile home parks with somewhat more than 66,000 sites. Virtually all of them permit dogs; most also cater to the semipermanent residents known as Winter Texans, many of whom leave their dwellings here year-round. *The Park Book*, available free from area chambers of commerce, lists the parks by name and by city. You may also obtain a copy by mail by sending $2 to Les Johnson, Route 7, Box 508, Harlingen, TX 78552.

Citrus Motel: Dogs may stay in cottages (which have kitchenettes) but not in regular rooms and must be on leash any time they are outside the room in consideration of the resident cats, the manager said. There is no fee or deposit. Cottages are $40 to $60. 2054 Central Boulevard, Brownsville, TX 78520; (956) 550-9077.

Grande Motel: "Dogs must be housebroken. Beyond that, we're real liberal. We're pet people ourselves," said the manager. "Most people who travel with dogs have had them for a while, and they are members of the family, and we treat them as such." The manager also stressed that this is a small, very clean family-run motel. There are no deposits or fees for dogs; rooms are $32. 2004 Central Boulevard, Brownsville, TX 78520; (956) 541-1961.

Motel 6: All Motel 6s permit one small pooch per room. Rooms are $40. 2255 North Expressway, Brownsville, TX 78520; (956) 546-4699 or (800) 466-8356.

CAMERON COUNTY

ARROYO CITY

PARKS, BEACHES, AND RECREATION AREAS

• **Adolph Thomae Jr. Park** 🐾1/2 *See* ❾ *on page 218.*
The one thing the nearby Laguna Atascosa National Wildlife Ref-

uge (see page 230) fails to offer visitors is the opportunity to spend the night in that wonderful wilderness. This 57-acre park at least partly fills that void, though in doing so it violates the very solitude one wishes to experience. In short, it's a compromise between the way we'd like the world to be and the way it must be. Dogs understand this subtlety, especially since the same kind of paradox requires them to be on a six-foot leash here.

The park was actually carved from the wildlife refuge, and a mile-long trail lets you and your dog experience snippets of it, even though you're never more than a few steps from the park road. Even so, Sport and I had gone only five steps down the trail when we found our first coyote poop. Javelinas are also common here, and mountain lions are present on the adjacent refuge, so keep your buddy close. Maybe he'd prefer a four-foot leash.

Activities in the park center around fishing, with two lighted fishing piers, a bank fishing area with electrical outlets, and boat ramps. However, there are also two day-use picnic areas and a playground.

There are 35 RV campsites with full hookups ($15) and 10 tent sites with picnic tables only ($12). A tent at a site already occupied by an RV is charged an additional $12 per night. Almost all the sites have at least some shade, and rest rooms with showers are nearby. The RV sites only may be reserved, and these may be occupied for up to six months at a time. The weekly rate for these sites is $85; monthly is $210.

The park is three miles east of Arroyo City on F.M. 2925. There is a $4 per vehicle entrance fee. Hours are 6 A.M. to 10 P.M. in summer and 6 A.M. to 9 P.M. in winter. (956) 748-2044.

PLACES TO STAY

For information on RV and mobile home parks, see the Places to Stay section for Brownsville on page 224.

Adolph Thomae Jr. Park: See Adolph Thomae Jr. Park above for camping information.

BAYVIEW

DIVERSIONS

Make your dog see red: Take your hound to the four-acre citrus orchard of Lee Earls and pick your own juicy, sweet Rio Red grapefruit. If you're not sure which ones to choose, Lee will have his black Lab, Ebony, advise. (Peewee and Fluffy, the shih tzus, supervise from the fenced yard where Ebony will go if your dog isn't friendly.) Lee says your pooch can run off leash as long as you keep her under control. She can also rub noses with a cow, chickens, goats, and emus. Oh, and if your dog doesn't like grapefruit, Lee also sells live or fresh-dressed rabbits. Yum. Grapefruit are ripe for picking from November to June. (Is this a great place, or what?) From the intersection of F.M. 510 and F.M. 2480, go north on San Roman Street about half a mile to number 124; signs will guide you when fruit is available. (956) 233-3386.

HARLINGEN

PARKS, BEACHES, AND RECREATION AREAS

• **Dixieland Park** 🐾 1/2 *See* ❿ *on page 218.*

Your leashed dog will be humming "On a clear day, you can see forever" under his breath as he bustles about the flat-topped hill overlooking a 90-acre reservoir across the road from this 20-acre park. The uniformly shaped hill looks suspiciously like the dirt from the hole now filled with water. There's a thin scattering of mesquite trees, a large covered group picnic pavilion, and grass, grass, grass. Dogs are not allowed in the reservoir area across the road from the park.

The park is about two miles south of U.S. 83 on Dixieland Road. It's a handy place to stop and dewater your dog after you've collected reams of tourist literature from the Texas Department of Transportation Travel Bureau, which you'll pass by on the way. The park is closed from midnight to 7 A.M. Sunday through Thursday and from 1 A.M. to 7 A.M. Friday and Saturday. (956) 472-8870.

• **Hugh Ramsey Nature Park** 🐾 🐾 1/2 *See* ⓫ *on page 218.*

When Sport and I last visited, this 54-acre park along the Arroyo Colorado was having birthing pains. The concept is good: separate nature and jogging trails winding through a thick tangle of mesquite, native brush, and prickly pear cactus. Leashed dogs will find lots of thorny plants to learn to avoid. Sport and I opted for the nature trail, a loop covering a little more than a quarter mile with a photo blind near its midpoint on the arroyo. We'll reserve final judgment until we've seen it again. The broad, graveled path is bounded on either side by a cleared strip some 50 feet wide over which runs a tangle of drip irrigation pipes. The area is covered in a thick layer of wood-chip mulch. For a nature trail, it was one of the most unnatural we've seen. Numerous plantings—of native species, we hope—were just taking root.

The jogging trail, a narrow dirt path with lots of weeds and trees encroaching on both sides, seemed a great deal more natural. It leaves the parking lot beside the composting toilet. Unfortunately, it had rained shortly before our arrival, and before we had gone 10 yards down the path, the black, sticky mud had all six of our feet balled up to twice their normal size. We had to turn back or learn to walk on muddy stilts.

The park is on Ed Carey Drive where it crosses the Arroyo Colorado. The entrance and parking lot are about three-quarters of a mile south of the intersection of Ed Carey Drive and Harrison Avenue (Highway 106). The park is closed from 9 P.M. to 6 A.M. (956) 472-8870.

• **Iwo Jima Memorial** 🐾 🐾 *See* **⑫** *on page 218.*

A dog's idea of a significant event in history is the time he managed to filch a rib eye steak off the kitchen counter and escape undetected. But even dogs should visit this heroic monument depicting the raising of the American flag on the island of Iwo Jima during World War II. The memorial is the original working model from which the bronze in Washington, D.C. was cast. It sits on the parade ground of the Marine Military Academy, flanked by the grave of one of the soldiers memorialized and by trees planted in memory of other Marines who have died in the service of their country.

Leashed, respectful dogs are welcome to view the memorial from the sidewalks surrounding it while you contemplate the sacrifices made by millions of Americans to keep our country free. No story is more poignant than that of Pfc. Ira Hayes, the figure at the rear of the group with his hands upraised. Hayes is one my favorite characters in American history, a Pima Indian whose life was immortalized in "The Ballad of Ira Hayes." Listen to this song about the forgotten hero's ghost lying in a lonely ditch before you visit the memorial, and if you don't leave with tears in your eyes, you're too hard-hearted to own a dog.

The memorial is at 320 Iwo Jima Boulevard, a block east of F.M. 507 at Valley International Airport. Hours are 10 A.M. to 4 P.M. Monday through Saturday and 1 P.M. to 4 P.M. Sunday. (956) 412-2207 or (800) 365-6006.

• **Lon Hill Park** 🐾½ *See* **⑬** *on page 218.*

This park is part of a complex of fairgrounds, swimming pools, baseball fields, and an auditorium, so the acreage, 73, is misleading. Only about 15 acres on the south side of Fair Park Boulevard are suitable for leashed dogs. However, this part of the park is most pleasant, with plenty of shade from anaqua and mesquite trees, picnic tables, a large playground, and lots of well-mowed grass. One of the nicest parts is the butterfly and hummingbird garden, a small area planted with flowering shrubs. Some hardy blossoms braved the cool temperatures of January when Sport and I last visited, although the winged creatures they were intended to attract were absent. We would have plucked an orange off the tree in the garden, but taller visitors than we had beaten us to the fruit. This was the last park Sport and I visited in the city, and she was heartbroken that we had found not one single squirrel or raccoon, but she concealed her grief quite valiantly, settling for sniffing a few garbage cans.

The park is on Fair Park Boulevard a quarter mile west of its intersection with Commerce Street. If coming from U.S. 77 north, exit on Fair Park Boulevard and go half a mile east to the park. It's open 24 hours a day. (956) 472-8870.

• **McCullough Park** 🐾 *See* ⓮ *on page 218.*

This is about as wild as it gets in Harlingen. The park's 1.5 acres snuggle in a bend of the Arroyo Colorado alongside a busy street, but upon entering the park via a dirt road, you climb a hill that quickly drops off on the other side to the stream. The park is completely undeveloped, but when Sport and I last visited, the grass was mowed. There are some scattered mesquite trees on the upland part, and the arroyo bank wears a thick stubble of weeds and carrizo cane. Dogs must be leashed.

The park is at the intersection of Ed Carey Drive and South 25th Street at the south end of a bridge. Turn west onto a dirt road into the park opposite the sign for South 25th Street. The park is open 24 hours. (956) 472-8870.

• **McKelvey Park** 🐾 1/2 *See* ⓯ *on page 218.*

Sport bounded out of the car eagerly at this park of 11 acres along the banks of the Arroyo Colorado. She knew the thick growth of trees along the water meant the possibility of raccoons, and we headed straight for it. Clouds of mourning doves lifting off the hillside beside the playground distracted us, though, and then Sport decided to do a leg-lift on a palm tree, and then the scent from the shaded picnic tables wafted our way, and we spent half an hour and never did find out if there were raccoons in the arroyo or not. The park terrain is rolling and mostly open, but the area along the arroyo is muddy and weedy—just the thing for a dog tired of sniffing asphalt.

The park is at the intersection of U.S. 77 Business and Commerce Street. You must be heading north on U.S. 77 Business to be able to enter the parking lot beside a large apartment complex. The park is open 24 hours. (956) 472-8870.

• **Pendleton Park** 🐾 1/2 *See* ⓰ *on page 218.*

This 47-acre park had just what Sport and I were looking for: open rest rooms for me and lots of trees for her. (Sport can't decide whether she's a squatter or a hiker and oscillates between patches of grass and trees.) Robins and mourning doves peppered the grass, but as in all other Rio Grande Valley parks we visited, there was a severe shortage of squirrels. Nothing adds spice to a park like an infuriated squirrel barking at the dog barking at him. The park has playgrounds, picnic tables, athletic fields, and a small, boggy pond at its southwest corner. Sport wanted to explore its muddy banks, but I restrained her, because the black, sticky mud here clashes with the car's seat covers, not to mention my clothes. Sometimes a leash is a good thing.

The park is at the intersection of F.M. 507 (Morgan Boulevard) and Grimes Avenue. The entrance is on Grimes Avenue just north of the intersection. The park is open 24 hours. (956) 472-8870.

• **Victor Park** 🐾 **1/2** *See* ⑰ *on page 218.*

This 40-acre park is ideally situated for the traveling dog heading to the beach at South Padre Island with her sunscreen and surfboard. It doglegs around a bend in the U.S. 77/83 access road just south of where those two arteries intersect. Much of the area is taken up by fenced athletic fields, but there's still lots of open grassy spaces and scattered groves of mesquite trees for the leashed dog to survey. Picnic tables and playgrounds are located near the highway; you don't even have to pull into the park if you don't want to. The rest rooms by the baseball fields were locked when Sport and I last visited.

The entrance is at the intersection of U.S. 77/83 and M Street. The park is open 24 hours. (956) 472-8870.

• **Windsor Park** 🐾 *See* ⑱ *on page 218.*

This charming little park covers only about two acres, but it is nicely shaded by large, grotesquely twisted mesquite trees and has two playgrounds and several picnic tables. A leashed terrier was busy visiting the picnic tables and hiking his leg on the black garbage barrels. Despite the fact that it was mid-January when Sport and I last visited, we found many red-breasted robins seeking worms in the grass. Spring was already on the way to the Lower Rio Grande Valley.

The park is at the intersection of 77 Sunshine Strip (U.S. 77 Business) and East Fillmore Avenue. It's open 24 hours. (956) 472-8870.

RESTAURANTS

Applebee's Neighborhood Grill and Bar: Steaks, burgers, and pork ribs headline the menu. Dogs are welcome to join you at the bench in front. 1519 West Harrison Street; (956) 425-5544.

Church's Fried Chicken: Not many outlets of this national chain have tables by the street, but this one does. Dogs are welcome to join you outside for their preference of white meat or dark. 921 West Tyler Street; (956) 423-7494.

PLACES TO STAY

For information on RV and mobile home parks, see the Places to Stay section for Brownsville on page 224.

Horizon Inn: Rates are $31 to $40. Dogs pay $10 per night. 325 North Highway 77, Harlingen, TX 78552; (956) 428-0888.

La Quinta Inn: Dogs up to 25 pounds are welcome for no fee or deposit. Rooms are $76 to $83. Free continental breakfast and airport transportation are included. 1002 South Expressway 83, Harlingen, TX 78550; (956) 428-6888 or (800) NU-ROOMS/687-6667.

Motel 6: All Motel 6s allow one small pooch per room. This one charges $36 for a room. 224 South Expressway 77, Harlingen, TX 78552; (956) 421-4200 or (800) 466-8356.

Save Inn: Rooms are $32 to $44. Dogs pay $10 each per night and must leave a $15 damage deposit. 1800 West Harrison Street, Harlingen, TX 78550; (956) 425-1212.

LAGUNA VISTA

PARKS, BEACHES, AND RECREATION AREAS

• **Roloff Park** 🐾 *See* ⑲ *on page 218.*

It's possible to pack a lot into three acres, and that's what's happened here. Fortunately, leashed dogs can enjoy most of it. The park has a view of Laguna Madre, but no access to the beach. However, there is a mesquite grove shading a picnic area and playground, and about half the park is open and grassy. If your Lab wants to practice his lob, there's a fenced tennis court. Tennis bracelets are optional.

The park is at the corner of F.M. 510 and Saunders Street, behind the city hall and library. Hours are sunup to sundown. (956) 943-1793.

PORT ISABEL

PARKS, BEACHES, AND RECREATION AREAS

• **Laguna Atascosa National Wildlife Refuge** 🐾 🐾 ½ 🐾
See ⑳ *on page 218.*

"Me Tarzan, you Dog," I told Sport as we entered this huge wildlife refuge. Its 45,187 acres are a jungle of interspersed wetlands and some of the last remaining native South Texas thorny brushland. This diverse habitat supports a wide variety of mammals, including the rare ocelot and jaguarundi, and more than 400 species of birds. The refuge welcomes leashed dogs everywhere except in the visitor center. There is a $2 per vehicle admission fee. Sport the hunting dog was quite proud to find that our possession of a migratory bird hunting and conservation stamp admitted us free, and she didn't have to make retrieves in cold water. As if.

Despite its size and the abundance and variety of its wildlife, especially birds, there's not a lot for a dog to do here. The 15-mile Bayside Tour Loop does give hounds the chance to wet their paws in the Laguna Madre. Be aware that while part of this drive is paved, those parts were badly potholed when Sport and I last visited. Don't take this drive if you are in a hurry. About two miles from the beginning, the drive passes along a beach. Park at one of the roadside turnouts and take your dog for a romp in the water. Sport bounded out eagerly when she spotted the water but was quickly distracted by debris washed in from the ocean. Timbers, trash, and coyote tracks competed for her nose on the hard-packed sand. While she sniffed and marked a number of spots, I used my binoculars to scan small islands offshore and was rewarded with the sighting of a pair of roseate spoonbills. Farther on, just past the Red-head Ridge Overlook, we discovered the reason for its name. Hundreds of redheaded ducks blanketed the surface of a small lake. For some reason a totally different kind of duck frequented Pelican Lake, where we saw no pelicans. Instead, thousands of bottom-feeding ducks did a constant tip-up routine, showing their white bottoms and orange feet while grabbling for food on the bottom.

Sport and I also visited the Laguna Atascosa, a lake named for its muddy color when disturbed by winds. On the day we visited, thousands of American coots dotted the milky waters, making the lake look like nothing so much as a bowl of heavily peppered cream gravy. (Sport agrees with this description. To be fair, we were both hungry at the time, and the breakfast of biscuits and gravy we'd had hours before was only a very fond memory.) The 1.5-mile Lakeside Trail runs alongside this pond, but the height of the brush prevents you from seeing much of the lake itself. However, 50 yards from the parking lot, Sport and I found a fresh mound of coyote scat, which entirely satisfied Sport. If you want to see the birds on the water, the free telescope at the observation point at the parking lot is your best bet. If you are quiet and move slowly as you walk along the trail, you'll see many birds in the brush. You may also see a deer, javelina, or feral hog. Avoid the latter, which can cheerfully inflict fatal wounds on a dog. Alligator Pond, a quarter of a mile south of the overlook, usually has one or more alligators in residence and should be avoided. They can be aggressive and love the taste of dogs and small children.

Other walking trails on the refuge include the one-eighth-mile Kiskadee Trail and the 1.5-mile Mesquite Trail, both of which start near the visitor center. Both trails have considerable shade and pass by shallow ponds where your pooch can splash, provided there is no sign of alligators about. The Paisano Trail is a one-mile paved path running through thick brush alongside the Bayside Tour Loop. Its location between the Laguna Madre and the Laguna Atascosa makes this a good birding trail. The longest of the refuge trails is the 3.1-mile Moranco Blanco Trail. This primitive trail leaves the Bayside Tour Loop a short distance past the Redhead Ridge Overlook and winds along the bay. The refuge brochure promises you'll see yucca in bloom in spring; when Sport and I last visited, it was mid-January, and many of the yuccas were already in bloom despite freezing weather the week before. Folks in deep South Texas have a different concept of the seasons. Winter, when it comes at all, is a couple of days in December or January. Spring begins sometime in December and lasts until April, when summer arrives and stays until spring.

From Highway 100 between Harlingen and Port Isabel, go north on F.M. 510 for 5.4 miles to a Y. Veer to the right and continue 6.6 miles to the visitor center. There is a $2 per vehicle admission fee. The refuge office is open from 8 A.M. to 4:30 P.M. Monday through Friday. The visitor center is open from 10 A.M. to 4 P.M. Thursday through Monday from October through April and on weekends only in May. It is closed from June through September. You may drive the tour roads every day from sunrise to sunset. (956) 748-3607.

RESTAURANTS

Church's Fried Chicken: Dogs like Sport and Samantha are cheap dates at this place. Sport likes wing tips, while Samantha adores corncobs. Eating out with these two is not pretty, although the crunching and smacking, mixed in with the occasional territorial growl, make it pretty noisy. Here you can hide in the little gazebo out back. Keep a firm grip on your pooch; there's a parking lot cat competing for groceries. 1706 Highway 100; (956) 943-8592.

PLACES TO STAY

For information on RV and mobile home parks, see the Places to Stay section for Brownsville on page 224.

SAN BENITO

PARKS, BEACHES, AND RECREATION AREAS

A special warning is in order about taking your dog to San Benito parks. The city council there may, in case of a rabies emergency, require that all dogs be confined to their owner's property. Each period of confinement ends after 30 days. After carefully reading the ordinance, I find that no exception is made for walking your dog in the park or on public streets. Before visiting San Benito, it would be advisable to call City Hall at (956) 399-5344 and make sure a dog rabies emergency is not currently in effect.

• **John F. Kennedy Memorial Park** 🐾 ½ *See ㉑ on page 218.*
Has your hound been complaining that she hasn't had enough room

to run lately? This park gives you the opportunity to put a stop to her—to use the polite word—complaining. It runs about a mile along Fresnos Resaca just west of downtown. Trees, picnic tables, and playgrounds line the water's edge for the entire length of the park. Leashed dogs may enjoy the park, but neither you nor they may go into the water, which supplies the city.

To reach the park, take Highway 345 north from U.S. 77/83. Go seven blocks to Stenger Street; turn left and go four blocks across the *resaca.* Turn right onto Freddy Fender Street; this puts you in the middle of the park, which stretches along the *resaca* in both directions. The park is closed from 10 P.M. to 8 A.M. (956) 399-5344.

• **Landrum Park** 🔥 *See ㉒ on page 218.*

A gaudy red, blue, and yellow playscape is the centerpiece of this little park that is only one city block square. However, there are a few trees and a paved walking path as well as several picnic tables with barbecue pits. Maybe your pooch will find a bone to gnaw after she takes care of business.

From U.S. 77/83, go north one block on Highway 345 to Swanson Street. Turn right and go two blocks. The park is closed from 10 P.M. to 8 A.M. (956) 399-5344.

• **Stookey Park** 🐾 *See ㉓ on page 218.*

A dog won't find much to get excited about in this park of about 100 acres. There is plenty of open grassy space to ramble, but that's about it. The few trees are small and scattered, the site is almost completely flat, and large chunks of the park are covered with athletic fields, a pool, a playground, and an activity center.

From U.S. 77/83, go west on F.M. 448 a mile and a half to Stookey Road. Turn left (south); the park is on the left, a quarter mile ahead. The park is closed from 10 P.M. to 8 A.M. (956) 399-5344.

PLACES TO STAY

For information on RV and mobile home parks, see the Places to Stay section for Brownsville on page 224.

SOUTH PADRE ISLAND

South Padre Island pioneered the concept of fun in the sun in Texas. The idea caught on so well that the sleepy little burg of some 30 years ago is now a seaside beehive bristling with hotels, condominiums, and shops. Fortunately, dogs are still welcome here, even though they must be leashed.

Beaches attract visitors year-round, but spring and summer are the busy times—especially March and April, when spring-breakers descend in hordes. The wild beach parties that resulted in boozed-up underage hounds engaging in wet T-shirt contests have been toned down by better law enforcement, but you'll still be better off visiting at another time, since motel rates double then. This community's dependence on tourism makes the people hospitable. Dogs are welcome the length of the island, and that's better than 30 miles of surf, sand, and sun. Arooooo!

PARKS, BEACHES, AND RECREATION AREAS

• **Andy Bowie Park** 🐾 🐾 *See* **㉔** *on page 218.*

This 125-acre park is what pampered beach bum dogs are looking for. The section east of Park Road 100 has a concession stand (open seasonally), rest rooms, showers, a children's playscape, barbecue grills, and a large covered picnic pavilion. Access to the beach is by foot only.

The beach gets heavy use from the bikini-and-beach-blanket crowd during summer months and is totally inundated during the annual spring break madness in March and April. Dogs who want to be alone with their people should investigate the less-developed Edwin Atwood Park less than two miles to the north (see below).

Directly across Park Road 100, on the south side of the South Padre Island Convention Centre, is the balance of the park, which features a 1,500-foot boardwalk over part of the Laguna Madre. Bird-watchers and bird dogs should take along binoculars and their "Petey" and see how many feathered friends they can identify.

The park is on Park Road 100 at the northern edge of the town of South Padre Island, 3.8 miles from the causeway. The entrance fee is $2 per vehicle. Hours for day use vary by season but generally are 7:30 A.M. to 5 P.M. in winter and until 8 P.M. in summer. (956) 761-2639.

• **Edwin Atwood Park** 🐾 🐾 *See* **㉕** *on page 218.*

This northernmost park on South Padre Island is small—only seven acres—but it is the access point for 28 miles of beach that you and your leashed pooch are free to explore. The only facilities are rest rooms and a picnic pavilion at the park entrance.

The first 10 miles or so of beach are accessible by two-wheel-drive vehicles; after that you'd better have all-wheel drive, the park ranger said. Dunes may harbor coyotes and other wildlife, but they are off-limits to you and your dog; you must restrict your activities to the beach. Camping is permitted for no extra fee, but you must camp on the beach. Sand and water dogs will find plenty to keep them busy here. Surf fishing and shelling are popular with the two-legged crowd.

The park is on Park Road 100, about 5.5 miles north of the causeway. There's a $2 per vehicle daily entrance fee plus a $2 beach clean-up fee, 50 cents of which will be refunded if you return a full litter bag before the park office closes. Hours for day use vary by season but generally are 7:30 A.M. to 5 P.M. in winter and until 8 P.M. in summer. (956) 761-2639.

• **Isla Blanca Park** 🐾1/2 *See* ㉖ *on page 218.*

What can you say about a 150-acre park that has nearly 600 RV campsites? Well, for one thing, you'll see lots of RV-dwelling snowdogs trotting their snowbirds around the 1.5-mile paved walking and biking trail or, more likely, towing them up and down the beach. Winter Texans (snowbirds) migrate south and colonize the park from November through March, and they bring their pooches (snowdogs) with them.

Dogs must be leashed, and you must have a poop container visibly in your possession while walking your dog. Pooper-scoopers are available in the park office. Dogs are not allowed in rest rooms, but otherwise they are free to go anywhere in the park.

The park occupies a point of land between the Gulf of Mexico on one side and the Laguna Madre on the other. Consequently, you are never more than a couple of hundred yards from the mile-long beach. Dogs may go on the beach and into the water as long as they are leashed. All the beach area is given over to swimming, walking, and picnicking; the camping areas are located in the interior of the park. The walking/biking trail loops around the RV campground, with end points at the beach.

This is a highly developed park with rest rooms, showers, a bait and tackle shop, laundry, concession stands (open seasonally), and restaurants. The emphasis is on semipermanent residence rather than recreation. Many dogs enter in the fall and don't come out until spring, when they go back to Illinois or Minnesota or whatever part of the tundra whence they came. Brrrrr.

The RV campground makes full use of the space available while still allowing a little patch of grass for each site. Shade is unknown, despite a smattering of palm trees. Sites with full hookups rent for $16, or $18 if you want cable television and $15 if you want water and electricity only. Tent sites with parking, rest rooms, and showers are $12. Primitive walk-in tent sites with rest rooms nearby are $16. You may add a tent at a RV site for an extra $8.50 per night. Sites may be occupied for up to six months at a time.

Reservations for RV sites may be made up to a year in advance of arrival but must be made in person or by mail; no telephone reservations are accepted. A deposit is required equal to the weekly rate for the total number of weeks reserved or one month's rent, whichever is less. (Weekly rates are $90; monthly rates are $235.) Daily reservations are not accepted.

Turn right when you get off the causeway onto the island and go half a mile to the park entrance. The park has a daily entrance fee of $4 per vehicle, but this is waived for campers. For more information or to make a reservation, contact Cameron County Park System, P.O. Box 2106, South Padre Island, TX 78597; (956) 761-5493.

RESTAURANTS

McDonald's: If your pooch doesn't know what the menu here is, either she is not from this planet or does not watch television. Have your burger and fries at one of the tables out front. 908 Padre Boulevard; (956) 761-4999.

Naturally's Veggie Cafe: If the salad bar doesn't interest your carnivorous canine, perhaps she'll perk up for a garden burger or a bowl of vegetarian chili. Join her at a table out front. 3112-A Padre Boulevard; (956) 761-5332.

The Pantry: This strip shopping center cafe serves up homemade soups, salads, sandwiches, and burgers to discriminating dogs at the tables in front. No huffing and puffing are needed to get service; this is the *pantry,* not the pantery. 708 Padre Boulevard (in Franke Plaza); (956) 761-9331.

Rovan's Bakery and Restaurant: From sweet rolls to ribs, this restaurant has what it takes to please the hungry hound. Portions are large, and the service is friendly and fast. Breakfast is served all day; lunch specials and pit barbecue hit the plate at 11 A.M. Park in back and eat at one of the benches outside the rear entrance. 5300 Padre Boulevard; (956) 761-6972.

Subway: The sandwiches and salads are the same as you'll find at any other location—cold cuts, tuna, turkey, veggie, meatball—but this shop has something most of the others don't, tables on a little deck out front where you can eat with your pooch. 2100 Padre Boulevard; (956) 761-6700.

Taco Bell: Pooches who are used to getting their food out of a bag will think the production-line Mexican food here is pretty good. It is, too. Your hound can eat with you at one of the tables out front. If you want to see something funny, try the trick I pulled on Sport here: Give her a taco. After a recent unfortunate encounter with a spiny visitor at home, she thought it was some kind of porcupine sandwich. There was this crunchy stuff on the outside guarding the juicy meat on the inside. 2000 Padre Boulevard; (956) 761-4456.

TCBY Yogurt: Dogs do not know that frozen yogurt is not ice cream. Be kind to their hearts and waistlines (and yours) while you share a cone, sundae, or shake at a sidewalk table. 410 Padre Boulevard (in Fiesta Plaza); (956) 761-2921.

Whataburger: You won't have to eat just a burger at this chain restaurant. It's open 24 hours and serves breakfast as well as burgers and fries.

Samantha wags her tail furiously whenever she spots the big orange W on the sign. Whatadog. Eat at the tables out front. 105 West Retama (on Padre Boulevard); (956) 761-7862.

Yummies Coffee Shop: Tell your pooch to put off his shoes from off his feet before heading for the sidewalk table; he treads on sacred grounds. Share some cappuccino, espresso, or frozen yogurt before heading out to inspect and douse a burning bush. 708 Padre Boulevard (in Franke Plaza); (956) 761-4907.

PLACES TO STAY

South Padre Island is a beach resort area, which means you can expect to pay higher rates from Memorial Day through Labor Day. However, you do not want to go to South Padre Island during the months of March and April unless you are a college student. The entire island will be taken over by students on spring break, and while they are generally better behaved (and fewer in number) than they were a few years ago, traffic will be horrible, all the restaurants will be jammed, and motel rates will be about double the normal high season rates quoted below.

For information on RV and mobile home parks, see the Places to Stay section for Brownsville on page 224.

Best Western—Fiesta Isles: Rooms are $48 to $99. Dogs put down a $25 deposit. This inn is not on the beach. 5701 Padre Boulevard, South Padre Island, TX 78597; (956) 761-4913 or (800) 528-1234.

Days Inn: Rooms are $49 to $79. There is a $25 fee per visit for dogs. This inn is not on the beach. 3913 Padre Boulevard, South Padre Island, TX 78597; (956) 761-7831 or (800) 329-7466.

Edwin Atwood Park: See Edwin Atwood Park on page 234 for camping information.

Isla Blanca Park: See Isla Blanca Park on page 235 for camping information.

Motel 6: Rooms are $36 to $50. All Motel 6s accept one small pooch per room. This inn is not on the beach. 4013 Padre Boulevard, South Padre Island, TX 78597; (956) 761-7911 or (800) 466-8356.

Seabreeze Beach Resort: Condominium units are $105 to $150 per day, with a three-day minimum. Dogs pay a $50 fee. The resort has beach access. 5400 Gulf Boulevard, South Padre Island, TX 78597; (956) 761-1541 or (800) 541-9901.

Sea Grape Motel: Dogs 25 pounds and under are welcome. This inn is not on the beach. Rooms are $35 to $60. 120 Jupiter Lane, South Padre Island, TX 78597; (956) 761-2471.

Surf Motel: Rooms at this beachfront motel are $49 to $79. Dogs 25 pounds and under must put down a $50 deposit. 2612 Gulf Boulevard,

South Padre Island, TX 78597; (956) 761-2831 or (800) 723-6519.

Tiki Condominium Hotel: You'll pay $83 to $105 for a room in this condominium a block from the beach. Dogs under 20 pounds may stay for a $30 fee. 6608 Padre Boulevard, South Padre Island, TX 78597; (956) 761-2694.

FESTIVALS

Ruff Rider Regatta: Sail into the sunset with your Irish setter on this two-day, 150-mile race from South Padre Island to Corpus Christi in late August. There are categories for one-person and two-person boats. Call for rules and entry fees: (956) 761-3052 or (800) SO-PADRE.

Sand Castle Days: What could be more embarrassing than watching your dog bound into the middle of an elaborate sand castle just completed by its proud creators? Use the leash and it won't happen. You and your pooch can watch professionals pack and sculpt the gritty stuff or you can build your own pitiful imitations of their amazing creations. Every dog wants a castle for a doghouse or a waterfront image of himself; give it to him and you might even win a prize. The event is held on the beach in mid-October. For information, call (956) 761-3052 or (800) SO-PADRE.

South Padre Island Easter Egg Hunt: Dress up your pooch in her Easter outfit and tune up her sniffer for this annual hunting of the eggs held around Easter. Call for the date and location: (956) 761-3052 or (800) SO-PADRE.

South Padre Island Labor Day Beach Volleyball Tournament: Your dog's neck will be sore from watching the balls flying back and forth. Early September is a fine time to be on the beach, whether playing volleyball or just bod-watching. There are categories for men, women, and coed play. For information and entry fees, call (956) 943-6060.

HIDALGO COUNTY

EDINBURG

PARKS, BEACHES, AND RECREATION AREAS

• **Memorial Park** 🐾 *See ㉗ on page 218.*

I'd wager there is more playground equipment per square foot in this park of about three acres than in any other that Sport and I visited. Fortunately, there was still room for a few trees, some grass, and rest rooms.

The park is at the intersection of East Sprague Street and U.S. 281. It is closed from 10 P.M. to 6:30 A.M. (956) 381-5631.

RESTAURANTS

Schlotzsky's: The tables out front are the perfect venue to enjoy a sandwich I can be up front about: It's one of the best you'll ever lip-wrestle your dog for. A variety of cold cuts and cheeses piled atop a sourdog (make that sourdough) bun make this sandwich unique. 1704 West University Drive; (956) 316-3354.

PLACES TO STAY

Echo Hotel and Conference Center: Dogs are welcome as long as they are housebroken and are not left unattended; you will be responsible for any damages. Rooms are $36 to $43. 1903 South Closner Street, Edinburg, TX 78539; (956) 383-3823.

M^cALLEN

PARKS, BEACHES, AND RECREATION AREAS

• **Bill Schupp Park** 🐾 *See ㉘ on page 218.*

This is a pleasant little park of about 25 acres, with a fitness track around its perimeter and lots of picnic tables, barbecue pits, and trees in the middle. When I last visited, two unleashed, law-breaking Pekingese were exercising their mom on the track. Two playgrounds, two volleyball nets, and rest rooms complete the facilities.

From U.S. 83, drive north on Highway 336 about three miles. The park is at its intersection with Zinnia Avenue. Side-by-side signs declared the park to be closed from 11 P.M. until 7 A.M. or from 10 P.M. to daylight. (956) 682-1517.

• **Cascade Park** 🐾 *See ㉙ on page 218.*

Only the southern end of this park of about five acres is open to dogs, the rest being occupied by a pool and athletic fields. Picnic tables and a playground sprawl among mesquite trees. Perhaps the park's best feature is its location near the airport and the Hilton Hotel.

From U.S. 83, go south about a mile on Highway 336. The park is at the intersection of Highway 336 and Bales Road. Hours are 7 A.M. to 11 P.M. (956) 682-1517.

• **Las Palmas Park** 🐾 *See ㉚ on page 218.*

This little park of about two acres appeals to lots of kinds of dogs. The timid pooch will be happy to see the community police station on the east side of the park. The pooch facing his golden years will be comforted by the senior citizen activity center to the north. Academically challenged dogs could hang around the adult learning center on the west side hoping a few scraps of knowledge would come their way. For the totally self-centered dog who only wants to run and play, there's the open

---

grassy area with trees, picnic tables, and a jogging track on the southern half of the park. And then there is the park's namesake, a twin row of stately palm trees lining the entry drive. Boy dogs will bark for joy.

From U.S. 83 Business, go north on F.M. 1926 (North Depot Street) about a mile to Quince Street. Turn left and go two blocks; the park is at the intersection of Quince Street and North 25th Street. Hours are 7 A.M. to 11 P.M. (956) 682-1517.

• **McAllen Nature Center** 🐾 1/2 *See* ㉛ *on page 218.*

A subtropical jungle of mesquite trees and prickly pear cactus covers most of this park's 25 acres, but graveled walking trails loop throughout, making it a walking dog's delight. Cottontail rabbits scuttling through the underbrush added spice when Sport and I last visited. This is also a good birding spot due to the thick tangle of native brush. There is a rest room, but it was badly in need of cleaning and restocking with supplies when we were here.

The part of the park nearest the entrance has been cleared of brush to make room for picnic tables under the trees. There were two jarring notes: One was the prevalence of what seemed to be gang graffiti on the nature trail signposts, which had no interpretive information in place. Graffiti had also been painted on many trees. We also noted a considerable amount of traffic both in cars and on foot that seemed to be totally unrelated to the park's purpose. That is, these people did not seem to be here to commune with nature. Some were carrying parcels and seemed to be headed for the border a few miles away. Others just seemed to be there. This is a good place to have a dog with you, it seems. Sport and I didn't feel unsafe or uncomfortable, just alert. Our advice is to look it over, and if you don't like what you see, leave.

The park is at 4101 West U.S. 83 Business. It is open from 8 A.M. until 6 P.M. in the winter, 7 P.M. in the summer. (956) 682-1517.

• **Municipal Park** 🐾 1/2 *See* ㉜ *on page 218.*

This is a good-sized park of about 60 acres, but it must have been designed by a former professional pie slicer. By the time pieces had been allocated to a pool, playgrounds, athletic fields, and parking lots, the smallest slice was left over for people and dogs. Only the southwest corner of the park—an area of about five acres—offers much room for a pooch to roam. However, it's shady and grassy there, and picnic tables, barbecue grills, rest rooms, and a small playground make it an all-purpose place. A rotund water tower bearing the legend "McHi Bulldogs" and a picture of a suitably snarling dog looms over this end of the park. It didn't take a bulldog to cow Sport; she met her match in a gaggle of pushy grackles raiding a garbage can. Sport decided that she, like society, has no use for these obnoxious birds.

From U.S. 83, drive north on Bicentennial Boulevard about two miles. The park is at the intersection of North Bicentennial Boulevard and Quince Street. It is closed from 11 P.M. to 7 A.M. (956) 682-1517.

• **Santa Ana National Wildlife Refuge** 🐾 🐾 *See* **33** *on page 218.*

Dogs are more tolerated than welcomed on this 2,080-acre refuge, but the rules permit leashed dogs, and dogs pay their taxes, so they ought to visit. Otherwise, they'd miss out on some of the best walking trails in the Lower Rio Grande Valley. There was no admission fee when Sport and I last visited, but a park ranger gloomily predicted one would be imposed soon. By the time you read this you may be required to show proof of rabies vaccination for your pooch. We were also subjected to a harangue about not leaving dogs in parked cars. The kind of knucklehead who would leave a dog in a parked car probably will not read this book, but if you spot a pooch left in a car, you can notify refuge personnel and the owner will be ticketed. I would appreciate it if you would not mention I told you to do so. Sport and Samantha eat a lot of dog food, and I need to sell all the books I can.

This refuge is known for the number and variety of birds you can see here, including many that are found no farther north in the United States. Bring binoculars, your bird book, and snacks and water for you and your pooch. Temperatures even in winter can be quite warm, and water is not available on the trails. Water and rest rooms are available at the visitor center.

The refuge has 12 miles of trails ranging from 0.3 to two miles in length, a seven-mile drive, and about three miles of service roads open to foot traffic. If the visitor center is closed when you arrive, look for a refuge map at an information board under the canopy. The well-marked trails meander through dense vegetation in the Rio Grande floodplain. Dogs must stay on the trails and are not permitted to go into the water. Ticks, coral snakes, chiggers, and mosquitoes bedevil visitors who forget to bring insect repellent; don't forget yours. Refuge employees warned us about one other potential hazard, illegal aliens crossing the Rio Grande. If you take the Wildlife Management Trail, you may meet some of these people in the vicinity of Pintail Lake. Some visitors have been harassed and asked for money. Having your dog with you should be very comforting if you walk this trail. There is something about bared teeth that makes people with unfriendly intentions much easier to get along with.

Several of the refuge's 11 trails loop around small lakes and have photo blinds where you can hide while you watch the wildlife. All the trails, the service roads, and the refuge drive are open to foot traffic every day from sunrise to sunset. The seven-mile refuge drive is open to vehicle traffic only on Tuesdays and Wednesdays from 9 A.M. to 4 P.M. The other five days of the week, a tram takes visitors on this drive, but dogs are not allowed.

The refuge entrance is on U.S. 281 a quarter mile east of its intersection with F.M. 907. The visitor center is nominally open from 9 A.M. to 4:30 P.M., but hours may change seasonally or with staffing problems. It's best to call ahead. The visitor center is closed Christmas Day and New Year's Day. (956) 787-3079.

RESTAURANTS

Church's Fried Chicken: I like white meat; Sport likes dark meat; Samantha likes anything as long as it's food, and some things that aren't, such as greasy bags. We make a good team eating out—there's nothing left to make a mess. Here we chowed down on chicken, coleslaw, and corn on the cob at the covered tables out front. It was good. 620 South 10th Street; (956) 686-6701.

Taco Bell: The menu of fast-food Tex-Mex is constantly changing at this national chain, but you can always count on getting tasty frijoles, burritos, tacos, and other dishes. There's a patio out front where your leashed pooch can join you. 420 South 10th Street; (956) 994-0700.

Taco Cabana: Girl dogs like this chain of Tex-Mex restaurants because it's painted in their favorite shade of pink. At least that's what Sport tells me. I'm sure the mountainous plates of nachos we've shared on several outlets' patios had nothing to do with her opinion. There are two locations here that welcome dogs on their patios: 1010 South 10th Street (956-630-2888) and 3815 North 10th Street (956-618-2227).

PLACES TO STAY

For information on RV and mobile home parks, see the Places to Stay section for Brownsville on page 224.

DIVERSIONS

Polish that pooch's pearly whites: It's happened again. In her rush to pack her bag for this trip, your absentminded hound left her toothbrush and toothpaste behind in the bathroom of the doghouse at home. What to do? Get thee to PetsMart. If a dog needs it or could want it, PetsMart has it, and your leashed canine can march right in and shop for it herself. And this store has a new reason to shine those nippers to a blinding white: a pet portrait studio where you can get that perfect picture of your poodle. 420 East Expressway 83; (956) 618-2203 (main) or (956) 687-7832 (portrait studio).

MERCEDES

PARKS, BEACHES, AND RECREATION AREAS

• **Kennedy Park** 🐾 *See* ㉞ *on page 218.*

The early-morning welcoming committee at this 20-acre park was a yawning mixed-breed dog who politely investigated our tires before moving on. Sport took a leashed tour of the playground and picnic tables at one end of the long, skinny park before pronouncing it acceptable by squatting. There are a few mesquite trees for boy dogs and a couple of baseball fields for dogs who appreciate sport. Not you, Sport.

To reach the park, exit U.S. 83 on F.M. 491 and go south about five blocks to U.S. 83 Business. Turn right and go eight blocks to Frances Avenue. Turn left and go three blocks to the park. It is open 24 hours. (956) 565-3114.

MISSION

PARKS, BEACHES, AND RECREATION AREAS

• **Anzalduas Park** 🐾🐾 *See* ㉟ *on page 218.*

Parks along the Rio Grande are rare, but this one would be popular with dogs even if it were somewhere else. In fact, the river is there for looking at only—swimming is not allowed. Dogs love the place because it is 96 acres of grass and trees punctuated by picnic tables and barbecue grills. On a busy weekend, the smells are enough to drive a dog insane. Perhaps that's why dogs are required to be leashed.

Large parts of the park are completely shaded, and there are rest rooms and playgrounds. There's a boat ramp for boating dogs and a fishing pier for those who prefer to transfer their catfish directly from the hook to the grill.

As you enter the park, you cross a floodway used to divert water from the Rio Grande into a relief channel. The park closes when flooding occurs.

To reach the park, follow F.M. 494 south from U.S. 83 in Mission. Three miles after you cross F.M. 1016, turn left at the sign onto an unnamed road. The park entrance is 0.4 miles farther on. There is a $4 per vehicle entrance fee. Hours are 6 A.M. to 8 P.M. (956) 585-4509.

• **Bentsen–Rio Grande State Park** 🐾🐾🐾 🦴 *See* ㊱ *on page 218.*

I had heard of the elusive South Texas brush country bird called the chachalaca before visiting here, but I'd never seen one. Thanks to Sport, I was almost involved in a chachalaca murder before we left this 588-acre park on the Rio Grande. More on that later.

The park is a bird-watcher's paradise, as became clear to Sport and me as we slowly drove through the RV camping area. Makeshift bird feeders perched on nearly every picnic table, and grapefruit and orange halves were impaled on nearly every available branch. Groups of people with binoculars peered into the brush, while others just as intently focused on images in camera viewfinders. Sport and I got out to see what all the fuss was about. It turned out it was almost about us.

The center of attention was a large group of chachalacas—brownish, chicken-sized birds that looked remarkably like a neighbor's chicken with which Sport had recently had an unfortunate (for the chicken) but tasty (for Sport) encounter. It was midafternoon, and the bowl of food Sport had dawdled over that morning was a distant memory. These chickens looked tame and tasty to her, and it took some rather sharp jerks on the required six-foot leash to convince her that these were not chickens, and that should she grab one, there were at least 25 people in earshot who would pounce on us and hold us until the park ranger arrived. Dogs, like children, know just what to do to humiliate you in public.

Chachalacas are but one of the many birds and other animals that make people flock to this park. Green jays, the groove-billed ani, the altimira oriole (we saw one of its socklike nests hanging from a branch above the park road), coyotes, bobcats, ocelots, jaguarundis, skunks, armadillos, badgers, and javelinas all inhabit the park. And, remind your dog, they are all protected by state law. So far dogs have come out the losers, park rangers told me. Two dogs had recently been sprayed by skunks, an experience Sport has had more than once.

While you'll see many birds lured into the camping area by seeds and fruit put out by visitors, the park also has three nature trails that lead by ponds and *resacas* that hold water at times. The Rio Grande Trail (1.9 miles) has a spur that takes you to the bank of the Rio Grande, where you may see migratory creatures of another kind heading north. While Sport and I were at the parking area for the Singing Chaparral Nature Trail (one mile) near the park entrance, three young men carrying their belongings in plastic bags passed by on the park road. It's best in such situations simply to mind your own business, which Sport and I did. We did hike the Singing Chaparral Nature Trail, but my principal impression was of the rear end of a dog with her nose glued to the ground.

The park sits partly on wooded lowlands along the river and partly on drier chaparral brushlands higher up, and it's hard to find a place in the park that is not shaded all day. A day-use picnic area lies along the main park road before you get to the camping areas. The 78 RV sites all have shade, a picnic table, barbecue grill, and lantern post. They rent for $14 from November through April and $12 from May through October. The 64 water-only sites ($8 year-round) are similarly equipped. Each area has rest rooms with showers, but only the water-only sites have a playground nearby. The latter sites are considerably more open and crowded than the RV spaces, but they do have the advantage of being on the bank of a *resaca,* which makes it easy for fishing dogs to bring home their supper. (Dogs are allowed to go into the water as long as they remain on leash, although steep banks can be a problem.) The RV area surrounds a dense thicket with a small pond in its center, and it was here that bird life was so abundant on the day Sport and I visited.

Reservations for campsites must be made by calling (512) 389-8900 between 9 A.M. and 6 P.M. Monday through Friday. You may reserve a type of site but not a particular campsite. Sites are assigned on a first-come, first-served basis on arrival.

As at all state parks, dogs are not allowed to go into any park building. They may not be left unattended and must be kept inside your tent or vehicle at night. Wearing a six-foot leash is required.

To reach the park, follow U.S. 83 Business west of Mission to F.M. 2062. Turn south on F.M. 2062 and go 2.6 miles to the park entrance. The entry fee to the park is $2 per person per day. The gate is open from 7 A.M. to 10 P.M., when the park closes except to overnight guests. (956) 585-1107.

• La Lomita Chapel 🐾 *See ❸❼ on page 218.*

A small chapel dating from the mid-19th century is the focal point of this park of about two acres. Religious dogs may want to take a moment to meditate or perhaps pin a prayer to the bulletin board inside the chapel, but most leashed hounds will prefer to explore the surrounding shaded picnic ground. There are rest rooms in the little white building beside the parking lot.

From the intersection of F.M. 1016 and F.M. 494, go 2.1 miles west on F.M. 1016 and turn left onto an unnamed dirt road. Go 0.2 miles to another unnamed road and turn right. In a quarter mile, when you get atop the levee, turn left to the entrance. The park closes at 7 P.M. (956) 580-8760.

• Oblate Park 🐾 *See ❸❽ on page 218.*

Only a city block square, this tree-shaded park with tennis courts in the center and an ornate bench will serve well for the leashed pooch in dire straits.

From Highway 107 north, turn right on East 12th Street and go four blocks to the park. The park is open from daylight until 7 P.M. (956) 580-8760.

RESTAURANTS

Pepe's River Fiesta: Your hound will likely declare this restaurant on the Rio Grande his favorite place to eat out in all of South Texas. First of all, there are cats lurking in the bushes at the entrance, which always stimulates a dog's appetite. (A cat in the parking lot is to a dog what salsa on guacamole is to a person.) Second, multilevel decks with shaded tables overlook the Rio Grande—you can even arrive by boat if you choose. And third, the menu features all the things dogs love: nachos, sandwiches, salads, fried chicken and catfish, hamburgers, Mexican food, and barbecue. There are daily lunch specials, too. Just so things never get boring, there's a dance floor and two open-air bars. This is a popular hangout of Winter Texans. From the intersection of F.M. 1016 and F.M. 494, go 2.1 miles west on F.M. 1016 and turn left onto an unnamed dirt road. Go 0.2 miles to another unnamed road and turn right. In a quarter mile, when you get atop the levee, drive straight ahead to the restaurant. (956) 519-2444.

PLACES TO STAY

For information on RV and mobile home parks, see the Places to Stay section for Brownsville on page 224.

Bentsen–Rio Grande State Park: See Bentsen–Rio Grande State Park on page 243 for camping information.

WESLACO

PARKS, BEACHES, AND RECREATION AREAS

• **City Park** 🐾🐾 *See ❺ on page 218.*

Sport and I didn't see any other dogs at this approximately 60-acre park, but we did spot something we saw at no other park in Texas: a little girl and her parents walking their pet rabbit. The white bunny with pink eyes and black ears and nose hopped, grazed, and played chase with the little girl. I sat in the car with Sport and studiously avoided calling attention to the rabbit until the people left. Only then did I snap on the leash and take Sport for a walk. Sport loves to chase wild rabbits, and although I've never seen her catch one, I didn't want this rabbit to be her first.

This is a well-planned park with athletic fields separated from picnic tables, playgrounds, and open spaces. The trees are small and furnish no shade worthy of the name, but some of the picnic tables have roofs. Water is available at faucets painted blue, and there are rest rooms.

The park is on Airport Road midway between U.S. 83 and U.S. Business 83, about five blocks from either one. It is closed from 11 P.M. to 7 A.M. (956) 973-3172.

• **Harlon Block Park** 🐾½ *See ❻ on page 218.*

Sport and I really liked the sentiment expressed on a sign at the entrance to this park of about 40 acres: "You don't stop playing because you grow old. You grow old because you stop playing." This sounded like a park built by people who understood dogs.

While much of the park is reserved for the use of people who would rather try to hit a ball with a stick and run around a square instead of throw a ball for dog, there's lots of room for the latter activity among the picnic tables, playgrounds, and trees.

From U.S. Business 83, go west on Sixth Street three blocks to the park. It's closed from 11 P.M. to 7 A.M. (956) 973-3172.

RESTAURANTS

Church's Fried Chicken: Your dog's gotta love eating on the patio. 205 West U.S. 83; (956) 968-5611.

Frontier Restaurant: Choose from Tex-Mex or American food offerings, order to go, and eat at one of the benches in front. 3022 East U.S. 83; (956) 968-6384.

STARR COUNTY

RIO GRANDE CITY
PARKS, BEACHES, AND RECREATION AREAS

• **Falcon State Park** 😊😊 *See ④ on page 218.*

If your dog doesn't do winters well, this 573-acre park may be just what he's looking for. Its location on the Rio Grande in deep South Texas means that winter makes only brief, infrequent appearances here. When Sport and I last visited on a mid-December day, a wild olive tree at park headquarters was blooming and loaded with fruit. Later, we met a Winter Texan dog, Henrietta III, who spends every winter in the park with her folks, Clint and Dee Metz, who don't do northern Michigan winters, either. We disturbed Henrietta in the midst of some important business outside the park recreation hall, and the chunky, coal-black cocker spaniel growled at us, looking and sounding like a miniature bear. "She does that only when she's interrupted while doing her business," Dee said. The rest of the time, Henrietta is the soul of hospitality as she helps welcome visitors to the snack bar the Metzes run in the recreation hall (see the Restaurants section on page 249).

Falcon State Park is a favorite destination of Winter Texans because of its mild winters. It's also favored by birders, who have the opportunity to see many tropical species never seen farther north in the United States. Two nature trails in the park take you into the brush surrounding the lake where wildlife viewing is best. The trails are short, easy walks, but snakes and thorns are present. Keep your leashed pooch well in hand on the trails, especially if she is not familiar with prickly pear, tasajillo, and other kinds of cactus she may (ouch!) run into.

Within the park is Falcon Lake, which is used primarily as a holding tank for irrigation water destined for use farther downstream and whose levels can fluctuate widely. The day-use picnic areas at water's edge when the lake is full may be fully a quarter mile away when it is low. However, since there is no designated swimming area in the park, your pooch is free to go into the water wherever he likes, as long as he remains leashed. There are lots of opportunities for the water dog to wander the shoreline, especially when the lake is low and the water's edge is far from the brush. Four promontories jut into the lake, making for lots of shoreline.

The park campground has 62 campsites suitable for RVs. Those with full hookups rent for $10; those with water and electricity only are $9. The sites are fairly closely spaced and, due to a lack of screening vegetation, not very private. Each site has a picnic table with shade shelter, barbecue grill, and lantern post. Some have birdhouses. This park is a good place to hang bird feeders around your campsite; you'll attract lots of feathered friends for close-up viewing. Forgot yours? Just take a two-liter soft drink container, cut "windows" in its sides about halfway up, fill it with birdseed, and hang it from a bush. If you make it, they will come.

The tent camping area has about 17 sites ($6), each with a picnic table with shade shelter, barbecue grill, and water nearby. There is no natural shade and no privacy at these sites. There is a nice view of the lake, but there's a nice view of all the other campsites as well, including yours. Better by far are the 24 screened shelters, which rent for $15. While your pooch is not allowed inside, these shelters are spaced well apart and are screened from each other by the surrounding brush. Each has a picnic table and ceiling fan inside and water faucet, barbecue grill, and fire ring outside. You may not leave your dog tied outside at night, but if she doesn't mind sleeping in the car or travels with her own pup tent, you'll both be happy here.

For reservations, call (512) 389-8900 between 9 A.M. and 6 P.M. Monday through Friday. You may reserve a kind of campsite but not a particular site. Dogs may not enter any building, may not be left unattended, and must be on a six-foot leash at all times.

From Rio Grande City, go west on U.S. 83 about 20 miles to F.M. 2098, then go southwest three miles to Park Road 46. There's a $2 per person entry fee. The office is open from 8 A.M. until 5 P.M.; the park closes at 10 P.M. except to overnight guests. (956) 848-5327.

RESTAURANTS

Falcon State Park Snack Bar: This isn't really so much a restaurant as it is a community center for the Winter Texans and their dogs who spend about six months here each year. Clint and Dee Metz, assisted by their cocker spaniel Henrietta III, dish out burgers and Mexican food and organize a number of activities to keep people and pooches from getting bored. Every Saturday morning you and your pooch can have all the pancakes you can handle for $2; there are picnic tables outside where you can eat. Tuesday nights the Metzes serve up full dinners, and on Thanksgiving and Christmas they serve the traditional bounty. They also have occasional free hayrides through the park; dogs are welcome at those and the dinners that precede them. The snack bar is at the park recreation hall; there is no phone.

PLACES TO STAY

Falcon State Park: See Falcon State Park on page 247 for camping information.

5

CORPUS CHRISTI/ THE COASTAL BEND

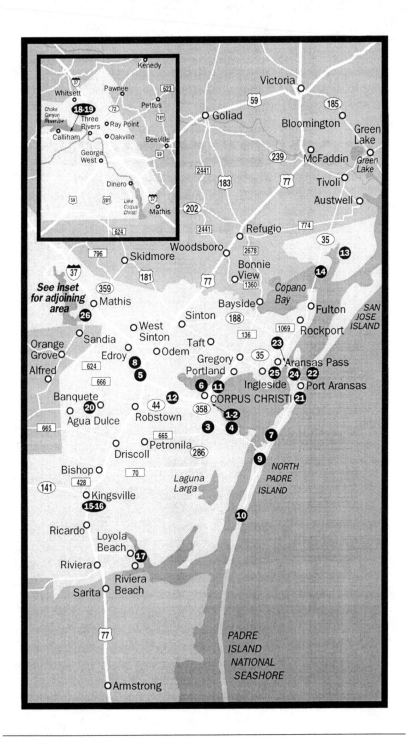

CORPUS CHRISTI/ THE COASTAL BEND

If not for a fluke of history, residents of most of this part of Texas would call their dog by saying something like, "Venga aquí, perro!" Way back in 1836 (that's over 1,100 dog years ago), Texas declared its independence from Mexico, which claimed the Nueces River was the southern boundary of Texas. A few years later, Texas claimed the Rio Grande—much farther south—was the boundary. After Texas joined the United States in 1845, the U.S. and Mexico fought a war over the boundary and General Zachary Taylor's army bivouacked in Corpus Christi before moving down to Brownsville, where the first shots of the war were fired. Corpus Christi became part of the United States, not Mexico, but many dogs here are still bilingual.

We'll start with the city of Corpus Christi and then cover the surrounding counties and cities in alphabetical order.

CORPUS CHRISTI

Corpus Christi and surrounding Nueces County offer a variety of experiences for pooches. The South Texas brush country is famous for producing large white-tailed deer, javelinas, and coyotes. It's a great place for dogs to observe wildlife. But the main attraction of Nueces County is the Gulf seacoast. Dogs from the dry, dusty inland just can't get over seeing all that water. We've found a fitting variety of places for you and your pooch to visit, from tangled river bottoms to beaches that stretch virtually unbroken for almost a hundred miles. There's buried Spanish treasure to sniff out and even one island where your pooch can frolic sans leash.

Corpus Christi, the main city in Nueces County, bills itself as the Sparkling City by the Sea, but dogs don't care much about that. They'd rather know that this is a place where you can sniff a dead fish one minute and help build a sand castle the next. They'd rather you didn't tell them they have to stay on a leash virtually everywhere in the county, but they'll be so busy having fun they won't mind very much.

PARKS, BEACHES, AND RECREATION AREAS

• **Blucher Park** 🐾 🐾 ½ *See* ❶ *on page 252.*

This tiny park—about the size of a small city block—lies directly behind the city's main library and is a hidden downtown treasure. When

Sport and I visited in spring, it was crowded with bird-watchers exclaiming over Nashville warblers, Lincoln sparrows, blue grosbeaks, golden-fronted flickers, and painted buntings. Birds migrating between North and South America funnel through coastal Texas, making it one of the top birding areas in the world. "The migration is near its peak," one birder told us in mid-April. Blucher Park, with its flowing creek and dense stands of mesquite, hackberry, and elm trees, is a boy dog's dream as well a bird haven highly regarded by local birders. It was made to order for bird dogs.

Pathways paved with environmentally friendly wood mulch wind through a profusion of trees and flowering shrubs. Sport enjoyed sniffing the various flowers, but she was especially intrigued by a large cavity in the trunk of a giant hackberry tree, which she was convinced held her favorite quarry, a raccoon. She circled the tree, looking up eagerly, until I praised her for finding the raccoon and then dragged her away by the required leash. Birds drink from the creek, but since it flows through a heavily populated area and gathers runoff from streets and parking lots as well as lawns treated with all kinds of chemicals, pooches would be better served by drinking elsewhere.

Fine old homes from the 1880s line Carrizo Street, which borders the park on its west side. Several front yards hold signs inviting birders to continue their expedition into the backyard of the home, but you and your pooch would probably be wise to ask permission before accepting the invitation.

The park is bounded by Blucher, Tancahua, Kinney, and Carrizo Streets. From Interstate 37, exit on Tancahua Street and turn right. Follow Tancahua to Kinney Avenue, turn right, go one block, and turn right on Carrizo Street. Park anywhere in the 100 block of Carrizo. The park is open from sunrise to sunset. (512) 880-3461.

• **Cole Park** 🐾 🐾 ½ *See* ❷ *on page 252.*

The extensive grassy areas in this 43-acre park wedged between Ocean Drive and Corpus Christi Bay begged Sport to spread her floppy ears and run free, but alas, as in all Corpus Christi city parks, leashes are required. Nearly a mile long, it has steps midway that descend to a gravel beach strewn with enough trash to make it a delight for beachcombing hounds. Sport and I passed, though, preferring to look at passing ships through the pay telescope. A sign at the park entrance scolds, "Dogs on Leash Only," although we saw a black Lab romping about unfettered and splashing in the surf. Sport thought the scattered palm trees looked vaguely like fireplugs, but being a female, she wasn't quite sure what they signified. She was content to bark at the seagulls and mourning doves flitting about.

The elaborate playscape looked like fun, but dogs are banned so we had to be content with sitting at one of the nearby picnic tables and watching unleashed children scamper all over it. On weekends you and your pooch can purchase a snack at the concession stand; you will be comforted to find that the concession building has rest rooms. The view of the Corpus Christi skyline curving around the bay, with the carrier USS *Lexington* in the background, is enough to make any landlubbing pooch dream of becoming a sea dog. Unfortunately, dogs are not permitted on the swimming beach.

Despite being near downtown hotels and a major residential area, Cole Park is mostly deserted except on weekends. Weekdays, your pooch will be able to do his thing virtually unobserved by human eyes (surely you don't look, do you?), and you can wield your pooper-scooper with plenty of elbow room. This you will definitely want to do, as Corpus Christi has a city ordinance with a big bite (up to a $500 fine) for failure to clean up after your pooch.

Should you attempt to visit Cole Park on a day when it is crammed with too many adults for your privacy-loving pooch, continue down Ocean Drive. Periodically for the next several miles there are small waterfront parks that offer no facilities and, consequently, attract few people. Your dog, however, will find plenty of grass and room to roam on leash.

The park has a 10 P.M. curfew. From southbound Interstate 37, turn right on Shoreline Drive and follow it until Ocean Drive joins from the left. At that point the beginning of Cole Park is on your left, just past the Holiday Inn. There are several parking areas. (512) 880-3461.

• **Corpus Christi Botanical Gardens** 🐾🐾🐾 🐾

See ❸ on page 252.

A doggy diamond in the ruff, this 110-acre farm is slowly being transformed into a garden center. Trotting along on her leash, as all dogs must here, Sport was confounded when she saw the sign "Vine Arbor" backed among mesquite trees where there were no vines. Hiking along the trail marked "Palapa," we crossed a footbridge and descended to a flat along Oso Creek, where we saw another sign that read "Fruit and Nut Orchard," although no trees bearing edible goodies were in sight. "Aha!" I said. "Woof!" declared Sport. We both realized at the same time that the gardens are still very much in progress and that the signs designate where things will be someday. So we happily struck off for the Bird Tower (along the wood-mulch-paved Bird and Butterfly Trail), where we climbed to the top of the tower overlooking a 12-acre pond. Sport pointed out the sign below that read, "Aquatic Garden," and we gave each other a knowing wink.

Park benches along the Bird and Butterfly Trail offer resting places, and numerous hydrants supplied with hoses for watering plants (but, on the day we visited, no water) promise every walking dog's dream: a drink every 50 yards and countless trees to hike a leg on or squat behind. We also took the Nature Trail but don't recommend it; even on a dry day our feet quickly gummed up with sticky black clay. We did find one pork chop bone and three piles of coyote poop, so it wasn't a total loss. Bushes and trees with identification tags affixed foretold a self-guiding nature walk that will answer every dog's question about what kind of bush she is squatting behind. Inquiring dog brains want to know.

The botanical gardens are people-friendly, with a visitor center, children's playground and garden, composting demonstration area (better known to dogs as a scratch-and-sniff facility), and community garden. On weekends you and your pooch may find gardeners laboring away on their little plots; your veggie-loving pooch may be able to mooch a carrot. Dogs love carrots—they crunch almost exactly like little baby bunny bones.

One of the best parts of the garden lies behind the white picket fence just across South Staples Street from the visitor center. Lush gardens surround a renovated 60-year-old farmhouse. Beyond is the old barn (alas, gray sheet metal instead of weathered wood) and a picnic area with two tables. Follow the road past the greenhouses to the Mesquite Trail, guarded by a "Watch for Snakes" sign. Along this one-mile loop, signs identify native plants, and shaded benches let you rest your weary dogs. The dense South Texas brush screens the view of the subdivision across the way. Sport and I learned the names of many South Texas plants, which we promptly forgot when a javelina (a small piglike creature with sharp tusks and a nasty attitude) emerged from the Oso Creek bottom and darted across the trail in front of us. Although the seclusion of the area may tempt you to slip off the leash and let your pooch run free, resist the urge. Abundant coyote and javelina tracks indicate the dense brush conceals a host of critters that would like to make a meal of a tender, juicy pooch.

Because the botanical gardens were unfinished when Sport and I visited, the entry fee was waived. However, at some point in the future you can expect to pay a $2 fee for adults ($1.50 if you're 65 or older) and $1 for children aged five to 12.

The Corpus Christi Botanical Gardens are at 8510 South Staples Street. Southbound from South Padre Island Drive (SPID to locals), take the South Staples exit and turn right. The entrance is just past the first big curve to the right after you leave SPID. The gardens are open Tuesday through Sunday from 9 A.M. to 5 P.M. and on Thursdays until 8 P.M. (512) 852-2100.

• **Hans A. Suter Wildlife Area** 🐾 ½ *See* **4** *on page 252.*

The Hans A. Suter Wildlife Area was named for the man who led the drive to preserve Oso Bay for wildlife. (Sport was intrigued by the name *oso*, which is Spanish for bear. I explained that a bear is kind of like a Texas-sized raccoon. She wondered if we'd see one so she could rescue me from it.) Despite the bear connection, the attraction here is birds. Gulls of all stripes (and no stripes), ducks, terns, skimmers, roseate spoonbills, and any of about 500 species of winged creatures either live here or pass through on their annual migrations. Visitors and their leashed dogs must stay on the paved trails and boardwalks, but an early morning stroll (or, with a dog, start, stop, sniff, and lunge) around the tidal flat with hundreds of birds flying, darting, and screaming about you is a great way to wake up. The area's 70 acres stretch for half a mile along the bay and include an athletic complex (where there are rest rooms) across Ennis Joslin Road.

A boardwalk leads to a beachfront viewing area where your retriever will be absolutely aquiver at the sight of all those roseate spoonbills, pelicans, ducks, and wading birds waiting to be fetched. If your dog isn't clued in to shorebirds, the information kiosk at the parking area at the intersection of Nile Road and Ennis Joslin Road is worth a visit. Also at the parking lot are two shaded picnic tables.

While there is comparatively little room to roam, the sounds of the shorebirds are much more pleasing to the ear than the cries of hordes of children begging their parents for *raspas* (fruit-flavored shaved ice cones) at Cole Park. The wildlife area is generally much less crowded on weekends than the bayfront parks along Ocean Drive, but during peak bird migrations in spring and fall, you and your pooch will share the area with birders.

From downtown Corpus Christi, take Ocean Drive to Alameda Street. Turn right on Alameda, then in about a block go left on Ennis Joslin Road. From Interstate 37, take Highway 358 (Padre Island Drive) south and exit on Ennis Joslin Road. Turn left onto Ennis Joslin. The park entrance and a parking lot are at the intersection of Ennis Joslin and Nile Roads. The park is open daily from sunrise to sunset. (512) 880-3461.

• **Hazel Bazemore County Park** 🐾 🐾 ½ *See* **5** *on page 252.*

If your dog wears hiking boots, she'll love these 77 acres of steep mesquite- and hackberry-cloaked hillsides—some cordoned off and marked unsafe—which fall away into the Nueces River bottom. The park has numerous shaded picnic tables with barbecue pits and expansive grassy areas where, sadly, dogs must remain leashed. Even if your dog forgot to bring his binoculars, he will enjoy the nature pond (go left at the park office), which has enclosed photo/birding blinds overlooking a two-acre pond heavily used by resident and migrating waterfowl. Bwana Beagle will want to wear her jungle hat at the nature pond, for the thick brush along the trails will make her feel as if she is on safari. Labs and golden retrievers may prefer the photo blind whose trail begins on the left side of the children's playground area, since it sits right on the water.

Down by the riverside, tree-shaded banks offer the opportunity to wet a fishing line while relaxing at a picnic table. Signs warn "Danger: Deep Water," so if your doggy is tempted to take a dip, hold on tightly to the leash. This park also offers excellent birding, and you may have a close encounter of the raptor kind, as Sport and I did when a hawk buzzed our heads. Which one of us she thought she could carry off and eat we were not sure.

Up on the rugged hillsides, you and your pooch can gambol along the River Bend Nature Trail. A brochure available at the park office identifies numbered plants along the way. A scenic overlook lets you view the river bottom, an apartment complex, and a truly ugly electrical transmission line. Don't pass up the overlook: On the rare occasions when it rains too much in Texas, the river bottom area may be closed due to high water, and this may be as close as you and your pooch will get.

The park is on County Road 69, a fact that will do you no good whatsoever to know, since it is not marked. From southbound Interstate 37, take the U.S. 77 exit and follow the frontage road to F.M. 624; turn right on this road and go three-quarters of a mile. Turn right between the canal and the huge, ugly electrical transmission line. The park entrance is half a mile down, just past a residential area.

The park office is supposed to be open daily from 8 A.M. to 5 P.M., but when Sport and I visited it was locked from about 10:30 A.M. to noon. The park is open 24 hours daily. (512) 949-8121.

• **Heritage Park** 🐾 🐾 *See* **6** *on page 252.*

Pooches love feeling secure and being in touch with their roots, as your historical-minded, leashed companion will as you wander the paved, shaded walkways winding among two city blocks filled with restored homes from Corpus Christi's past. Who knows, one of your pooch's ancestors may once have lolled away on hot summer days under the porch of one of these buildings. No matter how serious a scholar of historic architecture your pooch is, she can't go inside the buildings, but there are grassy lawns on which to romp. The rose garden is sized and arranged to host small weddings, complete with arched pergolas and rose-lined walkways. If Sport ever finds a dog who deserves her, she wants to get married here.

Public rest rooms and benches offer human comfort, and one of the historic homes houses a tearoom where you and your pooch can dine (see Jeron's Tea Room on page 265).

From southbound Interstate 37, turn left on Chaparral Street and proceed to the park on your left in the 1500 block, about four blocks from the freeway. The park is open daily from sunrise to sunset. (512) 880-3461.

• **Mustang Island State Park** 🐾🐾½ *See* **❼** *on page 252.*

Another day, another beach—in this case about five miles' worth just north of Padre Island National Seashore. You can't drive the beach between these two parks because of a pass connecting the Gulf of Mexico with Corpus Christi Bay. The drill here is the same as at other state parks: Dogs are welcome as long as they are leashed. This includes going into the water, although dogs are not allowed in swimming areas designated for people. That's okay. Your pooch would probably prefer not to bare her bod in front of a horde of strangers, which is what you are likely to find at this popular (with people) park. For enjoying these crowded conditions you are privileged to pay an entry fee of $3 per person.

Texas state parks forbid the use of a leash longer than six feet, and dogs may not be left unattended (which includes being tied outside) or taken into any park building. Dogs may not enter the water at a designated swimming area or enter the beach adjacent to a swimming area.

Walking, digging, and swimming are the order of the day at this 3,703-acre state park. Local legend has it that pirate Jean Laffite buried some of his treasure on Mustang Island, so if your pooch digs up what looks like a chest full of gold and jewels, don't make her cover the booty back up. When you get all sandy, sticky, and sweaty, you and your pooch can rinse off at an outdoor freshwater shower. Then picnic at one of the shaded tables in the day-use area while you count your gold doubloons.

Camping is allowed in two places. You will pay $12 to sleep in the developed camping area, which resembles a paved parking lot with picnic tables, rest rooms, and showers. Sheltered somewhat from the Gulf winds by sand dunes, this area is a popular feeding site for industrial-strength mosquitoes. Somewhat better is the open beach camping area, which offers a view of something besides your neighbor's RV, along with chemical toilets, rinsing showers, and potable water. The price is better, too, at $7. The downside to camping in this spot is that you and your pooch will feel like sardines on busy weekends, when as many as 300 campsites crammed onto a 7,000-foot stretch of beach are filled with people. Sport, who has 28 acres to roam at home, tends to feel a little cramped under such conditions.

Reservations for campsites at all state parks must be made by calling the central reservation number, (512) 389-8900, between 9 A.M. and 6 P.M. Monday through Friday. Reservations are strongly recommended, and a deposit is required in order to guarantee your reservation. You cannot reserve a specific site; they are available on a first-come, first-served basis upon arrival.

You may access the park from Corpus Christi via Padre Island Drive, which becomes Park Road 22 as you exit the city. Continue to Highway 361 and turn left. From Port Aransas, take Highway 361 south for 14 miles to the park entrance. The gates are open from 7 A.M. to 10 P.M.; office hours are 8 A.M. to 5 P.M. For more information, contact P.O. Box 326, Port Aransas, TX 78373; (512) 749-5246.

• **Nueces River Park** 🐾 See ❽ on page 252.

The main thing to recommend this park wedged between Interstate 37 and the Nueces River is its convenience for the cross-legged dog and her owner who have done as many miles as they can do since they did their last doo. There's grass for her and public rest rooms for you.

You'll also find a free campground (no hookups, but water is available)—a good illustration of the old adage that you get what you pay for. You are welcome to camp anywhere except on the soccer field, if that tells you anything. If not, consider that the other main activity here besides kicking a ball around in semiorganized mayhem is fishing in the Nueces River, so you may have to share your campsite with a determined angler or three. No reservations are required; pick up your free camping permit (good for up to three days) at the Corpus Christi Visitor Center in the park, which is open 24 hours daily. Sport advises you to squat and move on.

Traveling either way on Interstate 37, take Exit 16; the park is on the west side of the highway. (512) 241-1464 (visitor center); (512) 880-3461 (Corpus Christi Parks and Recreation Department).

• **Padre Balli County Park** 🐾🐾½ See ❾ on page 252.

Approximately two miles of Gulf beachfront give your leashed pooch plenty of space to romp and play in the water. Other than dog-watching (which Sport pronounced to be fine), there's little to do but walk on the sand, splash in the water, and dig in the dirt. Sounds like a dog's life. There is no entry fee, and parking is free inside the marked areas at the swimming beach and Bob Hall Fishing Pier, but if you want to drive down the beach a bit and get away from the madding crowd, your pooch will have to shell out $6 for a one-month beach parking permit or $11 for a yearlong one. The only other fee involved with using this park is one you'll gladly pay: 25 cents for a cold, freshwater shower. You and your pooch can share the showers to rid yourselves of that icky, sticky I've-been-to-the-beach feeling.

This park and the island on which it sits were named for a Spanish priest, Padre José Nicolás Balli. Around 1800, the king of Spain granted Balli the entire 100-mile-long island stretching from Corpus Christi Bay to the mouth of the Rio Grande. The island became known as Padre Balli's Island and, later, simply Padre Island.

Padre Balli would be amazed to see what changes two centuries have wrought in his beloved island, especially when he got to the campground located in the park. Imagine a campground designed by a person who stripes supermarket parking lots for a living and you've got a pretty good picture of this facility: row after row of campsites (66 in all; no reservations accepted) jammed so close together you can feel your neighbor's dog panting on you. You and your pooch do not want to camp here, paying $10 for a site with water and electricity or $4 for a spot with neither. If beach camping is your thing, you'll want to buy a beach parking permit and pay $4 for the right to stake out your own spot on the oceanfront so you both can commune with nature, or at least avoid being stepped on in the dark.

There is another reason to opt for a primitive campsite on the beach. Dogs in the know are aware that mosquitoes infest areas behind the dunes (where the campground is) because those spots are shielded from the wind, while the steady Gulf breeze sweeps the beach free of pesky bloodsuckers. Though Sport can handle the occasional flea or tick with her usual equanimity, she and I both lose our cool when attacked by a cloud of biting insects. There are no public rest rooms on the beach, but if by now you haven't learned from your dog what to do when nature calls in an isolated area and you can't wait until facilities are available, be more observant. Just take along a plastic bag with a roll of toilet tissue, a garden trowel, and a book of matches. The trowel is to bury stuff; the matches are to burn the used toilet tissue.

When you set out to find your private place on the beach, you will discover that travel on the beach is one-way north of the visitor center, set up so that traffic approaching from Corpus Christi must travel south on the beach. If you want to camp on the beach north of the visitor center, you must obtain your permit, get back on Park Road 22, and go back toward town to access the beach. South of the visitor center, beach traffic runs two ways.

From Interstate 37, take Padre Island Drive, which will become Park Road 22. Continue past Beach Access Road 5 to the park entrance on your left. The office is staffed 24 hours a day. (512) 949-8121.

• **Padre Island National Seashore** 🐾🐾½ *See* ⑩ *on page 252.*

Although Padre Island National Seashore is actually located in Kleberg, Kenedy, and Willacy Counties, we're including it here because the only vehicular access is from Corpus Christi, in Nueces County. For a bit of park history, see Padre Balli County Park on page 260.

If you're a dog, life's a beach on Padre Island. Then again, your dog might want to pronounce "beach" slightly differently, since pooches must be leashed along the entire 65 miles of beach in the park. Dogs are not permitted in the Malaquite Beach Visitor Center, nor on beaches with signs designating them as swimming areas. Elsewhere, even swimming dogs must be leashed.

The entry fee of $4 per car entitles you and your pooch to do few doggy deeds except play on the beach. You can walk the Grasslands Nature Trail, a three-quarter-mile loop, but abundant mosquitoes and the threat of meeting a rattlesnake on the trail detract somewhat from the experience. Birding may reward the visitor with sightings of many tropical species rarely seen farther north in the United States, including the green jay and the caracara—get a complete list at the visitor center—but if your dog is anything like Sport, her attention span is rather short when it comes to looking at birds instead of chasing them. Perhaps if she used binoculars. . . .

Sport took considerably more interest in the sea turtles. She is a laid-back dog, and the turtles' pace suited her better than that of darting kestrels. Five species of sea turtle visit Padre Island. The most commonly seen are the loggerhead and green sea turtles. Others are the endangered Kemp's ridley, leatherback, and hawksbill. Sea turtles nest on the park's beaches from April through September. If you and your pooch spot a nesting turtle, report it to park rangers. Hatchlings stranded on the beach will likely not survive; your pooch can become a hero by taking the baby turtle to a ranger, who will turn it over to a woman who provides care.

Sport considers herself quite the water dog and is a strong swimmer, but use caution when swimming with your dog on Padre Island. A strong undertow flows parallel to the beach and can be hazardous. Also, while in the water, be on the lookout for one of the sea's nastiest denizens, the Portuguese man-of-war. This beautiful blue jellyfish is often seen floating in the water or washed up on the beach, where it looks like a partially deflated balloon. It can inflict painful stings on you and your pooch. If stung, mix unseasoned meat tenderizer and water into a paste and rub on the wound.

Winds and water combine to deluge Padre Island beaches with almost every ounce of seaborne trash dumped into the Gulf of Mexico.

When Sport and I last visited, an oil spill near Galveston, hundreds of miles away, was washing up on the beaches. Millions of little globules of crude oil speckled the beaches and collected on our paws. Take along some baby oil or a spray can of WD-40 to remove tar and oil from shoes and footpads.

As if all those hazards weren't enough, the camping canine must worry about coyotes. The farther south you venture into four-wheel-drive territory, the more likely you are to encounter your pooch's wilder cousins. But this is a dog-eat-dog world, park rangers point out. "Do NOT leave your dog unattended," a ranger warned us. "Coyotes will eat her." While I cringed at the thought and Sport bared her teeth at the very idea of being gobbled up (or perhaps at the serious tone of the ranger's voice), it occurred to us that a dog on a tether must look very much like lunch on a string to a coyote. We vowed to stick very close to each other day and night. Sport loves sleeping inside tents anyway.

By now you are probably wondering why anybody would go to a park where trash, tar, turtles, and dog-eating beasts dominate the beaches. For your dog, the question is a good one. There's not much for a dog to do here except walk on the beach, splash in the surf, and dig in the sand, all of which she must do while leashed. You, however, can enjoy birding, surf casting, searching for seashells on the shore, and watching the sun rise over the ocean as you sip your morning coffee—all experiences made richer by the companionship of a camping canine. So tell your dog to stop whining and let you have a good time. Otherwise, cheaper brands of dog food can be had, you know.

The only fee campground ($5) in the park is three-quarters of a mile south of the ranger station. The Campground Designer from Hell plopped about 50 concrete picnic tables in the middle of a paved parking lot between the dunes (Keep Out!) and the beach. Sport covered her eyes with a paw when she saw it. "Zis iz campink?" she howled. "Dey haf vayz to mek you enchoy it," I replied. Then we left, unswayed by the fact that the area offers rest rooms and cold showers.

Primitive camping (no fee) is allowed at Bird Island Basin, a marginally more inviting spot. No showers are provided, and the toilets are of the charming chemical kind. At least here you and your pooch can camp at water's edge—just be sure you know where the high tide mark is. We saw a school bus converted into a camper that had misjudged by about six feet and was well mired.

Bird Island Basin is a popular windsurfing area, which some dogs find quite entertaining. On weekends the beach is packed solid—sometimes two or three deep—with cars, campers, people, tents, beached surfing gear, etc. If you and your pooch must camp here, try to find a spot in the short stretch of beach extending beyond the turnoff to the boat ramp. The ramp is heavily used on weekends by fishers heading south to Baffin Bay in pursuit of speckled sea trout and redfish, and the steady stream of vehicles pulling rattling boat trailers by your campsite will begin well before daylight. A poodle does need his beauty rest.

You and your dog will enjoy camping at Padre Island much more if you slip away south down the beach as far as your vehicle type and your courage permit. The farther you go the fewer people and other dogs you will see, but be aware that you must have four-wheel drive to venture very far south of the vehicle barrier separating Malaquite Beach from South Beach. Camping is primitive and free, but if you get stuck in the sand, the National Park Service, which you and your dog support with precious tax dollars, will make no effort to extricate you. They will collect your poor, bleached bones, but you'll have to call a wrecker to retrieve your car. Should you make it all 60 miles from the end of the pavement before getting stuck, your towing bill will be enough to make you howl louder than a dog who's been told she can't go with you to a meat market that offers samples.

From Corpus Christi, head south on Padre Island Drive, which becomes Park Road 22 when you reach the island. Or, for a beachy adventure, drive the eight miles of sand between Padre Balli County Park and the national seashore. The park is open 24 hours. The visitor center operates 9 A.M. to 6 P.M. from Memorial Day to Labor Day and 9 A.M. to 4 P.M. the rest of the year. For more information, contact 9405 South Padre Island Drive, Corpus Christi, TX 78418; (512) 937-2621.

• **The Watergarden** 😊 ◀● *See* ⑪ *on page 252.*

This giant circular fountain with grass and walkways all around is just the place to take the stymied pooch who can't make wee-wee. The sounds of 150 nozzles gushing in unison and water tumbling down stepped waterfalls are sure to do the trick. A thirsty pooch can probably poach a sip, but wading is a no-no. You'll enjoy sitting on one of the 12 park benches under the pergola while your canine companion naps, dreaming of rescuing you from a raging rapid. About two acres of grass surround the water garden, which sits amid the Art Museum of South Texas, the Corpus Christi Museum of Science and History, and the Civic Auditorium, none of which admits dogs. Dogs are also banned from the ships of the Columbus fleet—replicas of the *Niña, Pinta,* and *Santa Maria*—which are on display here as well. If your pooch growls about such medieval admissions policies, remind her that when the upstart Columbus first set foot in the so-called New World, dogs were already here—along with the other First Americans. Sniff.

The Watergarden is in the 1800 block of North Chaparral Street. From southbound Interstate 37, turn left on North Chaparral and follow it half a dozen blocks to a sign directing you to the parking lot. Be advised that the fountain may be turned off when there is a water shortage, which can happen just about any summer. The park is open daily from sunrise to sunset. For information, call the Corpus Christi Parks and Recreation Department at (512) 880-3461.

• **West Guth Park** 🐾 *See* **⑫** *on page 252.*

"What a disguthting name," I lithped as Thport and I pulled off the freeway for a pit thtop (okay, enough already) at this 80-acre park, which is basically a large playground for people. Bike trails are verboten to dogs, who must remain on leash throughout the park. Among the facilities are a swimming pool, golf course, picnic tables, children's playground, barbecue pits, and a small pond with ducks and geese to feed, so the family pooch and her squad will find plenty to do. Unfortunately, while there are scattered trees and lots of open, grassy areas, most of the facilities are clearly geared toward people who engage in organized activities rather than toward pooches yearning to breathe free. Still, the park is right on the freeway and may be just what the pooch with crossed legs is looking for.

From southbound Interstate 37, take Exit 9 for Up River Road/Rand Morgan Road. (There is another exit for twisting Up River Road where it crosses the freeway again, but you want Exit 9.) Immediately turn right (almost a U-turn) onto Up River Road; the park entrance is 100 yards ahead on your left. There is a sunset curfew. (512) 880-3461.

RESTAURANTS

Che Bello: Have a sandwich, croissant, biscotti, espresso, or *affogato* with your pooch at one of seven outside tables or five benches scattered about. Keep a tight grip on your pooch: resident parking-lot cats roam the area looking for handouts, and a six-foot-tall plywood figure of a cat (who works for the nearby Cat House, a shop devoted to silly kitty stuff) dominates the patio. Gift shops are all around, but your pooch would probably prefer a slurp from the fountain. In the Water Street Market at 320-C William Street; (512) 882-8832.

Jeron's Tea Room: Sport the hound dog felt quite the yuppie puppy while dining at the lone table on the porch of this sandwich/quiche/soup-n-salad place, but your plebeian pooch may prefer to take her lunch to one of the park benches scattered about Heritage Park. If you can't make lunch, try afternoon tea Tuesday through Thursday, although it is so hard for dogs to crook their pinkies when sipping tea. 5830 McArdle Street; (512) 980-1939.

Landry's Seafood House: Looks can be deceiving. This place is so big and fancy we were almost afraid to ask if dogs were allowed on the outside deck, which has a magnificent view of the downtown Corpus Christi skyline across the marina. Howlelujah: The answer was not only yes, the manager was very friendly and acted downright pleased to have us. (Alas, the deck is open only during the summer months.) You and your pooch can chow down on "Peaux Boy" sandwiches, burgers, or shrimp and oyster baskets. 600 North Shoreline Drive (on the Peoples Street T-Head); (512) 882-6666.

Marker 37 Marina: Park your pooch at one of 10 covered picnic tables and order a Mother Clucker's grilled chicken breast sandwich ("The Biggest Breasts in Town," the sign boasts). They must be good, since that is the entire menu. There's no view, but the manager loves dogs. After dining, you can watch the fishing boats come in. 13317 South Padre Island Drive (exit immediately after crossing the JFK Causeway bridge and look for the marina's name atop its roof in three-foot-high white letters); (512) 949-8037.

Pier 99: "Cool," said the manager when Sport and I told him we were working on a guidebook for dog lovers. "We love dogs. If people want a bowl of water for their dog, we'll bring it. We just don't have dog food."

This place may be as close to doggy dining paradise as it gets in Texas. We had a clue when we spotted the coin bank in the shape of a dog's face beside the cash register for donations to the local humane society. Then we saw the patio with some 30 tables and a spectacular view of the Corpus Christi skyline and the carrier USS *Lexington* anchored just 150 yards away. Some tables are shaded, some sit on concrete, others sit on sand where your pooch can dig in and snooze while dreaming of a Beach Bum burger, Cajun shrimp, or chicken-fried steak.

Take U.S. 181/Highway 35 north from Interstate 37, cross the Harbor Bridge, and take the exit for the Texas State Aquarium/USS *Lexington.* Follow the signs for the *Lexington* to 2822 North Shoreline Drive; (512) 887-0764.

Water Street Seafood Company: Fresh seafood straight from the Gulf of Mexico stars on the menu at this establishment where you and your pooch can chow down at one of eight tables under a pergola out front (except during winter). Manager Jill Reed says the ambience is nicest around dusk. That's also when the parking-lot cats come out; keep a tight leash on your dog. Order from the "to go" menu at the hostess desk just inside. "Once some people from Mexico brought in a little dog in a carrier, and I kept it for them at the register," confided the cashier. But to comply with the letter of the law, your pooch should remain outdoors. In the Water Street Market at 309 North Water Street; (512) 882-8684.

PLACES TO STAY

Days Inn: Small dogs only are accepted. You'll pay $54 to $72, which includes a continental breakfast for you. Sorry, pooches, it's dog food for you. 901 Navigation Boulevard, Corpus Christi, TX 78408; (512) 888-8599 or (800) 325-2525.

Embassy Suites: A $10 per day fee will get any size dog a room here. You'll need to fork over from $89 to $139 for yourself. 4337 South Padre Island Drive, Corpus Christi, TX 78411; (512) 853-7899 or (800) EM-BASSY/362-2779.

Gulf Beach II Motel: The official policy allows small pets only, but well-mannered big dogs often charm their way in. Grassy fields on three sides and a beach on the other will appeal to your pooch as much as the three-level sundeck and proximity to the Texas State Aquarium will to you. Rates are $60 to $66. 3500 East Surfside Boulevard, Corpus Christi, TX 78402; (512) 882-3500 or (800) 882-3502.

Hampton Inn: If the thought of sleeping next door to a dog racetrack won't keep your pooch awake nights dreaming of liberating her oppressed brethren, you might stay here. Small dogs are welcome; un-attended dogs must be kept in a carrier. Room rates are $64 to $80. 5501 Interstate 37, Corpus Christi, TX 78408; (512) 289-5861.

Holiday Inn Corpus Christi Airport: Even your jumbo-jet-sized dog is welcome. Rates are $69 to $76. 5549 Leopard Street, Corpus Christi, TX 78408; (512) 289-5100 or (800) HOLIDAY/465-4329.

Holiday Inn Emerald Beach: "We get a lot of people who travel with their dogs. They are just like part of the family," says the reservations clerk. With a public beach on one side, an open field on the other, and Cole Park just a couple of blocks away, this is a doggone friendly place for your peripatetic pooch. Any size dog is welcome. Rates are $89 to $135. 1102 South Shoreline Boulevard, Corpus Christi, TX 78401; (512) 883-5731 or (800) HOLIDAY/465-4329.

Howard Johnson Marina Hotel: Dogs under 18 inches tall may stay here for $10 per night, plus $49 to $129 for their human traveling companion. 300 North Shoreline Boulevard, Corpus Christi, TX 78401; (512) 883-5111 or (800) 883-5119.

La Quinta Inn—North: No dogs over 25 pounds are allowed. (Shucks, our cat weighs almost that much.) Room rates are $69 to $76. 5155 Interstate 37, Corpus Christi, TX 78404; (512) 888-5721 or (800) NU-ROOMS/687-6667.

La Quinta Inn—South: Don't assume all hotels with the same name have the same rules: this La Quinta allows pets up to 40 pounds. Rates are $59 to $75 (proving that sometimes more is less). 6225 South Padre

Island Drive, Corpus Christi, TX 78412; (512) 991-5730 or (800) NU-ROOMS/687-6667.

Motel 6: All Motel 6s allow one small pooch per room. There are two locations in Corpus Christi. Rates are $34 for the inn at 845 Lantana Street, Corpus Christi, TX 78408; (512) 289-9397. Rooms are $49 at 8202 South Padre Island Drive, Corpus Christi, TX 78412; (512) 991-8858.

Mustang Island State Park: See Mustang Island State Park on page 259 for camping information.

Nueces River Park: See Nueces River Park on page 260 for camping information.

Padre Balli County Park: See Padre Balli County Park on page 260 for camping information.

Padre Island National Seashore: See Padre Island National Seashore on page 262 for camping information.

Red Roof Inn: Walk your dog in the field out back. Rates are $25 to $55. 6301 North Interstate 37, Corpus Christi, TX 78409; (512) 289-6925 or (800) 843-7663.

Surfside Condominium: If you and your pooch are planning on visiting Padre Island, why not stay on the island? This condominium hotel is located near Padre Balli County Park (see page 260) and Padre Island National Seashore (see page 262) and is just a few miles from Mustang Island State Park (see page 259). Nothing feels better than a hot shower and clean sheets after a day at the beach, and for just $3 a night, any size dog can share them with you. Your room will cost from $85 to $110. 15005 Windward Drive, Corpus Christi, TX 78418; (512) 949-8128 or (800) 548-4585.

FESTIVALS

Harbor Lights Festival: The annual Harbor Lights Festival and Boat Parade is a dog-friendly event. The name is pretty much self-explanatory, and as you might expect, it takes place in early December. If you have been very good this year, your pooch might let you hold one end of his leash and go with him. For information, phone (512) 985-1555.

DIVERSIONS

Shop for shrimp, then paddle your own canoe: The Peoples Street T-Head in downtown Corpus Christi is *the* place to get the freshest shrimp you and your seafood-loving dog will ever lap lips over. Shrimpers hawk their daily catch each afternoon, and prices vary with market conditions, your bargaining skills, and the power of pleading pooch eyes. Across the street, at Beach Boat Rentals, you can rent a paddleboat or motorboat—no, your seafaring pooch won't be the first to do the dog paddle in one of these craft. Expect to pay about $15 per half hour. There's no street address; just follow Shoreline Drive to the Peoples Street T-Head (a T-shaped jetty that forms a protected harbor for the marina). There's no phone, either. Apparently, these folks do not want the IRS or anyone else to find them.

Visit the vet and like it: When Sport and I first spotted the South Side Animal Hospital as we blazed by on our way to the beach, we did a double take. The fenced, AstroTurfed playground out front looked familiar, though there were no golden arches in sight. It's obviously designed for children, but when we asked the friendly veterinary assistant if dogs were allowed to use the playground while their traveling companion ate lunch or shopped, he said, "Whatever will go in there can have at it." Fittingly, from the parking lot you'll see almost every variety of fast-food emporium known to the kitchen-challenged: Long John Silver's, Taco Bell, Subway, Whataburger, Grandy's, and Bill Miller Bar-B-Q. You can grab a meal, whip into the South Side Animal Hospital, and shoo your pooch into the play area while you eat in the air-conditioned waiting area inside (keeping a watchful eye through the large windows), or you can sit on a stool in the play area. Then you and your pooch might want to shop for doggy treats or a new flea collar or spruce up at the grooming shop in back. 6940 South Padre Island Drive, Corpus Christi, TX 78412; (512) 993-7388.

Mall your malamute: What dog doesn't like to go shopping? Unfortunately, Texas law bars pooches from the most fascinating stores of all, those that sell people food. However, you and your pooch can max out both your charge cards at PetsMart, which is kind of like a Wal-Mart for dogs. (Okay, it's for cats and fish and birds and hamsters and stuff, too, but who cares?)

Take your leashed pooch to PetsMart and you will learn things about your dog's preferences you never dreamed of. For example, Samantha likes to bark at cows, but shy Sport was the one who lusted after a leash in the black-and-white Holstein cow pattern. And I never suspected Samantha loved puns until she started rolling in the aisle in front of the doggy greeting cards, making noises like a Doberman who's just tried to swallow a 20-foot leash. Okay, as the dog who will attempt to eat anything, maybe she *was* choking on a leash.

A PetsMart spree can be educational for your dog, too. Sport's jaw dropped when she found out they carry 720 kinds of dog food. (Her look clearly said, "I knew you'd been holding out on me.") Her chest swelled with pride after she counted nine aisles devoted to dog stuff and only three for cats. I was certain I heard her snicker when we passed by a sign promising "Paws-Itively Low Prices." As we went by the book section (books about dogs, not for them), I could see she was already planning which of the stylish collars in the next aisle over she would wear to book signings. As a short-haired pooch whose daily grooming consists of jumping into a tub of water and then rolling in the sand, she was fascinated by the poodle getting clipped in the grooming area; as a recent recipient of a rabies vaccination, she was forgiven for baring her teeth as we went by the veterinarian's office.

The Corpus Christi PetsMart is located in Moore Plaza, which fronts on South Padre Island Drive, at 5214 Blanche Moore Drive; (512) 993-8882.

ARANSAS COUNTY

In a state in which somewhere around 97 percent of the land is privately owned, Aransas County is an anomaly, with about 86 of its 252 square miles of land contained in a national wildlife refuge and a state park. That 34 percent sounds like a lot, but as the saying goes, "100 percent of nothing is still nothing." That's math even a dog can understand, and when your pooch discovers that he must remain on his leash everywhere he goes in this county, he may well growl.

Karankawa Indians once roamed this coastal area, rubbing themselves with alligator grease to ward off the huge mosquitoes. Two of the three still roam here; we'll bet a rawhide chew your pooch can figure out which. Keep your tasty friend on her leash at all times so she won't become an alligator snack. Alligators have been known to attack dogs even in the presence of humans.

You and your dog will have a good time if you enjoy looking at wildlife, art, and big trees. The time of year you visit will likely influence how you feel about the experience. The Texas coastal climate is delightful in fall, winter, and spring, but the heat and humidity can be nigh unbearable in summer. That's why the area is popular with Winter Texans, people from colder climes who make this part of Texas their home during the more temperate months. You and your pooch will probably meet a lot of folks and dogs from other states while you're here. Just remember the Texas motto: Friendship.

ROCKPORT-FULTON

These two coastal towns are joined at the hip, so to speak. If you don't look carefully, you'll miss the signs indicating you've passed from one to the other. The Rockport-Fulton area is the birding capital of Texas and is known worldwide for its abundance and variety of birds. It's also a center for art and fishing.

Rockport has a split personality when it comes to its leash law as well. While dogs must remain on an eight-foot leash in the city's public parks, in all other places they are considered to be under restraint if they are at heel beside a "competent person" and obedient to that person's commands. Therefore, your pooch can trot proudly beside you down city streets without being leashed as long as he remembers which of you is in charge. The ordinance also specifically makes the owner of a dog responsible for picking up and disposing of waste properly. Fines can be as much as $200, making a $5 leash or a five-cent plastic bag seem cheap by comparison.

PARKS, BEACHES, AND RECREATION AREAS

• **Aransas National Wildlife Refuge** 🐾 🐾 ½ 🐕
   See ⑬ on page 252.

If there is one thing Sport the Rhodesian Ridgeback loves to do, it's hunt raccoons. Therefore, she instantly fell in love with this 54,829-acre wildlife refuge when a large raccoon ambled across the road in front of us as we approached the visitor center. Later, exploring on her leash, she saw javelinas, alligators, deer, and a rare, endangered whooping crane and sniffed a multitude of feral hog tracks, but I could tell that after the first encounter she always had one eye peeled for another raccoon. There's something about a dog in alert mode that's unmistakable.

Even for the leashed dog, there is plenty to enjoy in this coastal wild-life wonderland. Most of the refuge is a peninsula jutting into San Antonio Bay. Low-lying tidal marshes frequented by nearly 400 species of birds alternate with slightly higher grasslands and groves of live oaks. This creates a great deal of what wildlife biologists call "edge" habitat that sustains a huge variety of wildlife. Sport didn't care about that. She just knew there was an incredible variety of things to sniff, bark at, and yearn to chase along the trails: rabbits, squirrels, coyotes, armadillos, quail, deer, turtles, frogs, bobcats, alligators, snakes. Well, forget chasing the last three.

Besides the requirement that dogs must remain leashed, the refuge was a slight disappointment in one other respect: Most of the acreage is not open to visitors. A 16-mile paved driving loop leads to a half dozen walking trails ranging from 0.3 to 1.4 miles in length, but that's it. The rest of the refuge is reserved for the animals who live there, as it should be. Actually, Sport and I found quite enough to keep us busy and entertained without venturing into the deep bush. We saw great views of San Antonio Bay, armadillos scuttling through the brush, deer browsing tree lines, and even—from half a mile away—a very rare whooping crane. It was a good day.

Rangers at the visitor center seem to take pleasure in recounting for you all the bad things that can happen to your pooch here, but it's for Bowser's own good. "Keep your dog on a leash and near you," a ranger told us. "We have had dogs eaten by alligators." Rattlesnakes, alligators, ticks, mosquitoes, javelinas, and vicious feral hogs are just some of the critters that you and your pooch need to avoid. Fortunately, that's not difficult to do, except in the case of the mosquitoes and ticks.

After driving up from Rockport, Sport and I chose to begin our visit with a picnic. (Why is it that dogs would much rather eat yucky stuff they find on the ground instead of the carefully prepared goodies you drag out of the ice chest?) You'll see picnic tables on your left just after leaving the visitor center on the driving tour. Nestled among live oak trees, the tables are very inviting, but pass them by. Just over a mile farther, a much bigger picnic ground offers many large live oaks, a view of the bay, barbecue pits, rest rooms, and a water faucet.

Sport and I decided to hike the mile-long Hog Lake Trail first. Sandy and shady, the trail wound around a pond whose edges bore signs of extensive feral hog rooting. Back at the parking area, we crossed the road to the Big Tree Trail, named for the 400-year-old live oak near its midpoint. Sport was far more interested in another large tree with many hollows that she was convinced hid a whole herd of raccoons. Farther on, a pond was ringed with tracks of deer, coyotes, and large feral hogs. The trail breaks out of a thicket at the edge of the bay and forks. A boardwalk to the left leads to a marsh area where you can observe people wade-fishing far offshore. Back at the fork, the other trail returns you to the parking lot.

We almost passed up the observation tower because the long concrete ramp to the top looked daunting. Fortunately, we changed our minds. Your dog may not be interested in climbing the ramp (it took me 141 steps; Sport's four legs required somewhat more), but you should be. The view of San Antonio Bay and Mustang Slough alone are worth the climb, and from November through April you stand an excellent chance of seeing a whooping crane. Only about 150 of these magnificent birds exist in the wild. We saw one feeding in the shallows along Mustang Slough. There are free telescopes atop the tower and rest rooms below.

From Rockport, take Highway 35 north to F.M. 774 and turn right. Follow the zigzagging route to F.M. 2040, which leads to the entrance; large signs mark each turn. The refuge is open daily from 6 A.M. to 6:30 P.M. For more information, contact the refuge at P.O. Box 100, Austwell, TX 77950; (512) 286-3559.

• **Goose Island State Park** 🐾 🐾 🐾 *See* ⑭ *on page 252.*

This 314-acre park sits at the junction of three bays: Aransas, Copano, and St. Charles. But that's not why dogs like it. Rather it's because the park is home to the Big Tree, the state champion coastal live oak. The Big Tree is reached by taking, of all things, Palmetto Street from the park entrance. Encircled by a chain-link fence to protect it from climbing kids and leg-lifting dogs, its personal one-acre lawn is covered with wild-flowers in the spring. Sport was awed by its size: 35-foot trunk circumference, 89-foot crown spread, 44-foot height, and nine main branches, each larger than most trees.

At more than 1,000 years of age, this tree has seen its share of dogs come and go. We watched a leashed Brittany haul her owner around the sidewalk circling the tree, keeping her nose pressed to the ground and never giving the tree a glance. Obviously it was a girl dog, since boy dogs are completely captivated by the possibilities. The mowed lawn around the tree gives plenty of room for a leashed romp.

As if the Big Tree were not enough, a nature trail winding through a camping area passes thousands of trees, making boy dogs feel totally inadequate. So many trees, so little time.

The park offers two camping areas, one on the beach and one sequestered among groves of live oaks. Campsites in the beach area are crowded together, and the shade shelters painted a sick shade of seafoam green made both Sport and I go "(B)arf, (b)arf." The one redeeming factor is the stiff sea breeze, which keeps the mosquitoes inland, at the wooded camping area. At either area, sites with water and electricity are $11; tent sites are $8.

Despite the mosquitoes, which can be combatted with insect repellent—strongly advised, happy dogs abound in the wooded camping area, because it obviously was planned by a person who put dogs first. Campsites are well spaced and scattered among huge live oak trees, mostly screened from each other by underbrush. The paved roads winding among the trees and a one-mile unpaved walking trail are plenty to satisfy your pooch's need for a post-prandial promenade.

Reservations for campsites at all state parks must be made by calling the central reservation number, (512) 389-8900, between 9 A.M. and 6 P.M. Monday through Friday. Reservations are highly recommended, and a deposit is required in order to guarantee your reservation. You cannot reserve a specific site; they are available on a first-come, first-served basis upon arrival.

Texas state parks forbid the use of a leash longer than six feet, and dogs may not be left unattended (which includes being tied outside) or taken into any park building. Dogs may not enter the water at a designated swimming area or enter the beach adjacent to a swimming area.

The park is 10 miles north of Rockport off Highway 35. Turn right on Park Road 13 and follow it to a T intersection; turn right again and proceed to the headquarters. The park closes at 10 P.M. except to overnight guests; the office is open 8 A.M. to 5 P.M. (512) 729-2858.

RESTAURANTS

Rudders Bar and Grill: Dine with your dog at one of the five patio tables inside Rockport's Austin Street Station, a minimall of shops inside a restored building. Sport mooched a margarita shrimp and pronounced it lip-smacking, nose-licking, tail-wagging good. No dogs are permitted after 6 P.M. 415 South Austin Street; (512) 790-7245.

PLACES TO STAY

Anthony's by the Sea Bed-and-Breakfast: Dogs of any size may stay here and run leash-free in the large, fenced backyard. The employees may even dog-sit if you need some alone time. Rooms are $75 to $85. 732 South Pearl Street, Rockport, TX 78382; (512) 729-6100 or (800) 460-2557.

Bayfront Cottages: Any controllable dog is accepted. Rates are $45 to $48. 309 South Fulton Beach Road, Fulton, TX 78358; (512) 729-6693.

Best Western Inn by the Bay: Big dogs are welcome, but only in smoking rooms. Rates are $56 to $62. 3902 Highway 35 North, Fulton, TX 78358; (512) 729-8351 or (800) 235-6076.

Goose Island State Park: See Goose Island State Park on page 272 for camping information.

Hunt's Court: Rockport has been lost in time for quite a while, and the abundance of "courts" and "cottages" is evidence of that. These bright green and yellow cottages are on the waterfront. No large dogs are accepted. Rates are $59 to $119. 725 South Water Street, Rockport, TX 78382; (512) 729-2273.

Key Allegro: Every home here has a boat slip, and the views of the bay are magnificent. Some condominium owners allow dogs to stay in their properties if they pay a $100 deposit per furry head. A two-night minimum stay at $110 to $140 per night is required. 1809 Bayshore Drive, Rockport, TX 78382; (512) 729-2772.

Kontiki Beach Motel: This three-story waterfront motel has no size limit on dogs. There is a $5 fee per dog per stay. Rooms are $55 to $85. 2290 Fulton Beach Road, Fulton, TX 78358; (512) 729-4975 or (800) 242-3407.

Laguna Reef Hotel and Suites: This beachfront hotel only takes small dogs. A $40 deposit is required, and there's a $5 nightly fee per pooch. Rooms are $50 to $220. 1021 Water Street, Rockport, TX 78382; (512) 729-1742 or (800) 248-1057.

Sandollar Resort Motel: Dogs 20 pounds and under may stay for $5 per night each. People pay $47 to $59. 919 North Fulton Beach Road, Fulton, TX 78358; (512) 729-2381.

Sportsman Manor: Your manorly sporting dog of any size is welcome. Rooms are $36 to $44. 4170 Highway 35 North, Fulton, TX 78358; (512) 729-5331 or (800) 224-6684.

Village Inn: Unattended dogs are not allowed in rooms, but you wouldn't do that to your precious pooch, anyway. There is a $5 nightly fee per dog. Rooms are $45 to $90. 503 North Austin Street, Rockport, TX 78382; (512) 729-6370 or (800) 338-7539.

FESTIVALS

Fiesta en la Playa: Even dogs without Chihuahua blood will enjoy eating Mexican food and listening to Tejano music at this Labor Day weekend fiesta. Leashed *perros* are welcome on the festival grounds around the Rockport-Fulton Area Chamber of Commerce at 404 Broadway Street in Rockport. For more information, call (512) 729-6445 or (800) 242-0071.

Fulton Oysterfest: Oysters may not be a big deal to your pooch, but they are to the folks around here who make their living gathering and serving these briny dollops of the deep. You and your leashed pooch can compete in oyster-shucking and raw oyster-eating contests if you like, or just enjoy the booths offering food, arts and crafts, and entertainment.

Usually held in early March, the festival allows well-behaved, leashed dogs to participate in the goings-on at Fulton Navigation Park. For information, call (512) 729-6445 or (800) 242-0071.

Holly Days Festival: What pooch doesn't like to do his Christmas shopping in a carnival-like atmosphere complete with a Santa Claus to whom he can whisper his secret desires? Shop 'til you drop or eat 'til you pop along South Austin Street in downtown Rockport in early December. Dogs must remain on leash. For information, call (512) 729-6445 or (800) 242-0071.

Rockport Art Festival: Rockport is a haven for artists who, along with artists from across the Southwest, showcase their work each year in an open-air festival. Your pooch may not fancy the background jazz or the aerobatic show, but he's sure to appreciate the food booths.

Leashed dogs are welcome. The festival is held in early July on the grounds surrounding the Rockport-Fulton Area Chamber of Commerce, at 404 Broadway Street in Rockport. For information or this year's dates and schedule of events, call (512) 729-6445 or (800) 242-0071.

Rockport Seafair: Has your pooch been crabby lately? Then she won't want to miss the crab races and crab beauty contest at the Rockport Seafair, not to mention the fresh seafood, gumbo cook-off (samples may be mooched), music, parade, and arts and crafts booths. She must remain on her leash, but other than that she can have all the fun a dog can handle.

The festival takes place in mid-October on the grounds around the Rockport-Fulton Area Chamber of Commerce, at 404 Broadway Street in Rockport. For information, call (512) 729-6445 or (800) 242-0071.

DIVERSIONS

Get all fired up: Some of America's greatest heroes have been dogs, and your patriotic pooch will enjoy the Fourth of July fireworks display if she's not afraid of such things.

Brave—or deaf—leashed dogs are welcome. You may watch the fireworks reflected in the waters of the bay, but you'll have to do so from outside Rockport Beach Park, where dogs are banned. Park wherever you can along Broadway Street or Fulton Beach Road. For information, call (512) 729-6445 or (800) 242-0071.

Strut your stuff: You and your canine jogging companion can join in the annual Whooping Crane Strut, which offers the choice of a 5-K walk and a 5- or 10-K run. Held in early April, the events begin near Fulton Navigation Park. Call (512) 790-9622 for this year's starting line locations and date.

Teach your dog to read: Pat's Place is a rather nondescript name for a bookstore, but dogs can't read anyway. Sport and I were attracted by the drawing of a dog reading a book in their advertisements. While you shop for a trashy novel to take to the beach, "I'll give your thirsty dog a drink," says co-owner Mary Kay Farnsworth. Your dog can also pick out a best-seller to gnaw on. And just across the patio is Rudders Bar and Grill (see page 274), where the treats run more toward food for the tummy than for the mind. Reading makes dogs really hungry (then again, what doesn't?).

Pat's Place is in the Austin Street Station, 415 South Austin Street, Suite C, in Rockport; (512) 729-8453.

Paint your pooch: Rockport has quite a colony of artists, and several galleries offer not only paintings for sale but also painting lessons. Van Dogs love to pose for portraits (especially if they are painted by old masters), and classes last as little as three hours. If your painting doesn't turn out to look much like your pooch, you can always hang it in the doghouse. Collect your palette-packing pooch and hie you off to one of the following galleries.

The Rockport Artists' Gallery features the work of local artists and craftspeople in its consignment shop and offers painting classes. Your leashed pooch can mingle with the five dogs of one of the owner's daughters. It's at 414 South Austin Street, Rockport; (512) 729-0600.

Estelle Stair (pronounced star) was one of the moving forces in establishing Rockport as a haven for artists, and her name graces the gallery she helped found. Lisa Baer, niece of the late Estelle, says she would appreciate your nonbarking dog being kept on a leash, as would the two resident cats, Scrabble and Foxtail. The Estelle Stair Gallery offers painting classes at 406 South Austin Street, Rockport; (512) 729-2478.

The Simon Michael Gallery was the first in Rockport and is just the place to take the fidgety dog who's absorbed about as much culture as he can. Small dogs may be carried into the gallery, but even they would probably prefer to be tied to one of the numerous trees shading the expansive grounds, though we don't recommend doing this for too long. There's another reason to leave pooches outdoors while you shop: Simon Michael is a prolific artist, and $5,000 paintings are stacked all around the floor. There is no sign saying "If you hike a leg on it, you buy it," but you don't want to risk hearing that dreaded trickling sound in this gallery. 510 East King Street; (512) 729-6233.

Worm your way into your dog's heart: City dogs and their country cousins will feel right at home at Moore Than Feed, a combination feed store and antique shop in Rockport. "Our customers regularly bring their dogs into the shop," says owner Melvin Moore. "One lady brings her duck—he walks up the steps and in the door right behind her." Web-footed customers and lots of breakables on low shelves are two good reasons to keep your pooch leashed in the store, even though Moore says, "Bring in your dog—she's not going to hurt anything. That's why we've got bare wood floors." Even better are the picnic tables outside in the oak tree grove, where you and your canine companion are welcome to have a picnic. (The place for barbecue in Rockport—Mac's—is down the street a few blocks toward town.) Your dog will love munching on brisket while watching ducks parade into the feed store. And yes, they do sell worm pills.

Moore Than Feed is located at 902 West Market Street in Rockport; (512) 729-4909.

KLEBERG COUNTY

Ask anybody anywhere in the world to name the most famous ranch they can think of, and if they don't answer "The King Ranch," I'm a Saint Bernard. The King Ranch is one of the largest ranches in the world today—about 825,000 acres—and is headquartered in Kleberg County. It owns almost the entire county, and parts of several others, a fact that should wipe that silly grin right off your pooch's face, since, with one tiny exception you'll read about later (see Diversions on page 280), the

King Ranch does not allow other people's dogs to set paw on any of its property.

However, you and your pooch need not skulk out of the county with your tails between your legs. Ironically, two of the only places we found in the entire region where your dog can run off leash are located right here in Kleberg County. Even more ironically, one of those places, the B Bar B Ranch Inn Bed-and-Breakfast (see page 279), is located on land that once belonged to the King Ranch. So when your pooch gets that faraway look in her eyes as she squats for her morning ritual at the B Bar B, consider what she's probably thinking: "There is justice, after all."

KINGSVILLE

Kingsville owes its beginnings to a remarkable woman, Henrietta King, wife of King Ranch founder Richard King. At the time of his death in 1885, the ranch had 500,000 acres of land and $500,000 in debt. By the time Mrs. King died in 1925, the ranch was debt-free and had more than doubled in size. Much of this success can be attributed to the efforts of her son-in-law and ranch manager, Robert J. Kleberg.

Mrs. King was a visionary who saw the need for settlement of South Texas, and she encouraged the building of railroads and towns. Kingsville was at first a company town in every way. Mrs. King was financially involved in the real estate company that sold lots to settlers, the lumber company that built their homes, the ice company that cooled their tea, the publishing company that printed their newspaper, the power company that generated their electricity, and the companies that processed the cotton they grew. She built or gave land for nearly every church and school in town. When Henrietta King sneezed, the whole town said, "Gesundheit!" and dogs howled and hid under the porch.

The King Ranch no longer operates as an independent fiefdom (though some might argue that point), but it still wields considerable economic, political, and social power in Kingsville.

PARKS, BEACHES, AND RECREATION AREAS

• **Dick Kleberg Park** 🐾½ *See* ⓑ *on page 252.*

"All pets must remain on leash at all times. Unleashed pets will be picked up by Health Dept. and owners will be fined," reads the largest sign at the entrance to this 360-acre park. "I know people like to let their dogs run, but we had a man badly mauled by a loose dog, and we can't have that happen again," the park manager said.

Kingsville's leash law specifies that dogs are allowed off leash if they are at heel and obedient to command. The county commissioners considered adopting a leash law in 1995 but declined. Therefore, it would take a legal beagle to determine upon what authority the sign is based, but it's probably best not to press the issue. Keep your pooch leashed. The two of you won't want to linger long anyway. Most of the park's grassy areas are devoted to athletic fields, there is little shade, and it felt unfriendly to dogs. Sport did enjoy doing her business with what I thought was just a hint of an editorial flourish.

From the U.S. 77 bypass south, exit on F.M. 1717 and follow it to the park entrance on your left. The park is open from 7:30 A.M. to 11 P.M. (512) 595-8591.

• **The Mesquite Grove** 🐾🐾🐾 🐕 *See* **16** *on page 252.*

This little park on the edge of the Texas A&M University Kingsville campus covers only an acre or so, but it ranks high because it is one of the few places we found in the Corpus Christi area where your dog can run off leash. Well, actually, the city ordinance specifies that your dog must be on a leash or at heel and obedient to command, so you'll have to run along with her. There are plenty of shade trees, grassy areas, picnic tables, and water faucets. You and your pooch can celebrate his off-leash romp with a good guzzle.

From U.S. 77, drive west on Highway 141 past the visitor information center and turn right on North Seale Street. Go to the end (the second stop sign), turn right, and park on the street. The park is open 24 hours. (512) 593-3606.

RESTAURANTS

Young's Pizza: The eatery is far better known for its wide variety of sandwiches and stuffed "patooties" than it is for pizza. You and your pooch can dine at one of four picnic tables on the covered patio. A friendly waitperson will bring a thirsty dog a bowl of water if asked. 625 West Santa Gertrudis Street; (512) 592-9179.

PLACES TO STAY

B Bar B Ranch Inn Bed-and-Breakfast: Your traveling pooch will want to come here again and again. While you relax in your room or the hot tub, she can loll in the shaded kennel out back (dogs are not permitted in the rooms). Then both of you can wander the surrounding 80 acres leash-free, as long as she is under close supervision. Owners Luther and Patti Young encourage people to bring their dogs. They ask only that you remember this is a working ranch, cows are expensive, and chasing them is not permitted. If your pooch wants to learn all about quail hunting, she can stay at the hunting kennel with the ranch's 75 or so quail dogs, where she can swap yarns with the troops. She can also rub noses with Omar the 400-pound, tame feral hog. The $85 to $125 rate includes a gourmet breakfast for you. From Kingsville, take U.S. 77 south to County Road 2215 and turn left. Follow the gravel road to the sign that points to the inn. Route 1, Box 457, Kingsville, TX 78363; (512) 296-3331.

Econo Lodge/Quality Inn: Your dog is welcome as long as she is housebroken. There is a $20 to $25 deposit depending on the size of your pooch. Rates are $39 to $45. 221 South U.S. 77 Bypass, Kingsville, TX 78363; (512) 592-5251.

Get & Go Travel Center/Holiday Inn: Trained dogs under 30 pounds are welcome if they are willing to stay in a kennel. This motel is on the southern outskirts of town, so there is plenty of room for a stroll. Rates are $44 to $54. 3430 South U.S. 77 Bypass, Kingsville, TX 78363; (512) 595-5753 or (800) 465-4329.

Howard Johnson: "No very big dogs, please," says the manager, holding a hand about thigh-high. Rates are $39 to $51. 105 South U.S. 77 Bypass, Kingsville, TX 78363; (512) 592-6471.

Motel 6: All Motel 6s permit one small pooch per room. Rates are $27 to $39. 101 North U.S. 77 Bypass, Kingsville, TX 78363; (512) 592-5106.

FESTIVALS

South Texas Ranching Heritage Festival: Your dog will want to wear her bandanna and cowboy boots and hat to this celebration of the Hispanic influence on ranching in Texas. Actually, as your cowdog can probably tell you, Hispanics didn't just influence ranching, they invented it, shaped it, and developed a way of life other late-arriving Europeans adopted as their own. Cowboy food, cowboy crafts, and cowboy songs and games will make your pooch puff her chest out with pride to be a Texan, even if it's only for a little while. Most of the events take place outdoors, so there's plenty of opportunities for leashed dogs to learn about their Western heritage. If you are not yet cowed and feel spurred to get further details about this late-February fling, call (512) 595-2819.

DIVERSIONS

Be treated like visiting royalty at the King Ranch: Well, actually, your pooch will only be tolerated here while you are enjoying a tour of this fabulous Texas legend. But no Texan (or those misfortunate enough not to be) should miss the chance to visit the world's most famous ranch. Your pooch can't enter the visitor center to see the video, and she can't go on the bus tour, but if you bring a friend who will stay with your dog in the shaded visitor center area, you can take turns seeing it all and tell your pooch about it later. The $7 tour lasts about an hour and a half. The King Ranch Visitor Center is on Highway 141 just west of Kingsville and is open 9 A.M. to 4 P.M. daily except Sunday, when hours are noon to 4 P.M. P.O. Box 1090, Kingsville, TX 78364; (512) 592-8055.

RIVIERA

If you ask for directions, don't pronounce the name of this town the way the French do the name of their famous resort area. In these parts it's pronounced rih-VEHR-uh. And while I can't list the Brush Country Inn located in Riviera in the Restaurants section because it has no outside dining for you and your pooch to share, I can say that you must eat here at least once before you die.

The Brush Country Inn is one of the last places in Texas to serve an authentic, gen-yoo-wine chicken-fried steak (the King Ranch's Calera Camp Cookhouse is another, but it will be a very cold day in South Texas before you eat there) fixed the way it ought to be—"sliced thin and fried hard," as humorist Will Rogers liked his. Order the Brush Country Saddle Blanket, and shortly you will hear a pounding noise coming from the kitchen as the cook tenderizes a whole round steak by hammering it with a mallet. When served, the steak will hang off all sides of the platter and feed two people with ample scraps and a bone left over for a deserving dog. Forget what your doctor told you about fat, cholesterol, and all the other stuff that's bad for you but tastes so good and have one. It's an experience you won't be able to repeat any time soon, and your loving pooch would want you to have it. Order to go and eat in the parking lot if you must.

PARKS, BEACHES, AND RECREATION AREAS

• **Kaufer-Hubert Memorial Park** 🐾🐾🐾 *See* ⑰ *on page* 252.

This five-acre park is primarily designed for picnicking on the shores of Baffin Bay, but its many mesquite trees, water faucets, and grassy areas serve the weary traveling dog as well. The park is fully equipped for human visitors, too, with rest rooms, picnic tables, barbecue grills, a boat ramp, fishing pier, playground, and a sweeping view of the bay. Virtually deserted on weekdays, it can be quite busy on weekends and holidays when the fishing crowd comes out. Baffin Bay is a hot spot for summer anglers trying for redfish and speckled trout.

Sport swapped end-sniffs with a free-roaming black Lab and a fishing-pier Chihuahua, but we hesitated to remove her leash. While county commissioners declined to enact a leash law in 1995, the county parks and recreation department takes the view that dogs should remain on leash.

From U.S. 77, take F.M. 628 east approximately nine miles to the park, which is open from 8 A.M. to midnight. (512) 297-5738.

PLACES TO STAY

Seawind RV Resort: Not just for recreational vehicles, this bayside campground has 20 tent sites with water. "About three-fourths of our campers have pets," the manager says. An unfenced dog walk where dogs must remain leashed runs across the back of the campground, and Kaufer-Hubert Memorial Park is just across the street. RV sites are $16 nightly; tent sites are $10. From U.S. 77, take F.M. 628 east approximately nine miles. Route 1, Box 67D, Riviera, TX 78379; (512) 297-5738.

LIVE OAK AND McMULLEN COUNTIES

These two counties are treated together because Choke Canyon Reservoir and Choke Canyon State Park—the only attractions here—spread across both.

My wife, Sally Victor, and I remember Live Oak and McMullen Counties and Choke Canyon State Park not because of the abundant wildlife but because this is where we discovered we loved each other enough to stay together under less than ideal conditions.

Not long before we married, we attended a Texas Archaeological Society field school here. The dam had not yet been built, and we were acting as grunts for the archaeologists searching for and recording evidence of prehistoric inhabitants. The first evening a huge thunderstorm roared through, blowing over tents, soaking everything, and raising the humidity to 100 percent plus. The next day the temperature also topped 100 as we were digging in the mud with trowels and toothbrushes. In the evening we dragged our blistered hands and aching backs into camp, where we were greeted by Texas-sized mosquitoes that could bite through the two layers of denim in our jeans pockets. Nights were still, hot, and humid, especially inside a little plastic tent.

After a week of that, we decided that we could probably get through whatever else life could throw at us, and we got married. (Sport and Samantha, who were not even gleams in Sally's eyes at that point, are sitting reading this over my shoulder and saying, "Awwwww.")

Sport and Samantha were also interested to learn that the tiny McMullen County town of Tilden was originally known as Dogtown because all the ranchers thereabouts in the early days had packs of cowdogs who followed them into town. After a wild Saturday night, they would all head back for the ranch, ear-chewed, hungover, and ready for another week of chousing longhorns.

STATE WILDLIFE MANAGEMENT AREAS

See the National and State Forests/State Wildlife Management Areas appendix starting on page 621 for important information and safety tips on visiting these areas with your dog.

• **James E. Daughtrey Wildlife Management Area** 🐾 🐾 🐾
This part of the South Texas brush country has been enriched by the addition of Choke Canyon Reservoir to the environment. Your outdoor dog can accompany you here on dove and quail hunting trips or on fishing expeditions as long as she remains leashed while not hunting or in camp. See page 626 for a description of the James E. Daughtrey Wildlife Management Area.

THREE RIVERS

PARKS, BEACHES, AND RECREATION AREAS

• **Choke Canyon State Park—Calliham Unit** 🐾 🐾 🐾
See ⑱ *on page 252.*
Choke Canyon State Park has a split personality—it is divided into three units (two of which are normally open to you and your leashed dog) divided by a 26,000-acre reservoir. The Calliham Unit is the larger of the two, at 1,100 acres.

Texas state parks forbid the use of a leash longer than six feet, and dogs may not be left unattended (which includes being tied outside) or taken into any park building. Dogs may not enter the water at a designated swimming area or enter the beach adjacent to a swimming area.

The Calliham Unit is known among wildlife watchers statewide for the amount and variety of animals you and your pooch can see up close in their native habitat. White-tailed deer are especially numerous. Sport and I watched a group of seven feeding casually under oak trees no more than 50 feet away. Javelinas and alligators, both of which can be hazardous to a dog's health, also reside here. Under no circumstances should you leave your dog unattended or sleeping outside your vehicle or tent.

Signs warn against feeding javelinas, which can become aggressive, but park rangers said visitors are allowed to bring corn and feed the deer. Use caution even with deer. Put the corn on the ground a short distance away, and do not attempt to feed deer from your hand.

Choke Canyon Reservoir is the chief water supply for the city of Corpus Christi, and in dry years your "lakeside" campsite may be a quarter mile from the nearest water. However, most of the sites offer a great view of the lake when it has water in it. You'll also see signs reading

"Beware of Alligators" and then, almost as an afterthought, "No swimming in this area." No kidding.

There are three distinct camping areas, with different facilities and fees. A walk-in tent camping area on the shore of a 90-acre catch-and-release fishing lake has some tree-shaded sites, while others have shade shelters. There are rest rooms but no showers. Sites are $9.

The multiuse camping area is a mesquite-shaded flat atop a promontory overlooking the lake. It offers good views in exchange for no privacy. A wild turkey hen wandered through as Sport and I checked it out. This area has rest rooms and hot-water showers. Sites with water and electricity are $14. The trees in this campground were alive with birds, and we saw several bird feeders cleverly made by cutting the side panels out of gallon milk jugs. Take along some birdseed and put out a feeder to attract birds to your campsite. If you make it, they will come.

The screen shelter area offers accommodations that Sport compared to giant, plush doghouses. Alas, dogs are barred from entering, and it is against regulations to tie a dog outside. If you wish to enjoy one of these pleasant little "cabinettes" with interior lights, ceiling fan, electrical outlets, and small front porch, you may have to pitch a pup tent outside and sleep there with your pooch. Screened shelters are $20.

Reservations for campsites at all state parks must be made by calling the central reservation number, (512) 389-8900, between 9 A.M. and 6 P.M. Monday through Friday. Reservations are strongly recommended, and a deposit is required in order to guarantee your reservation. You cannot reserve a specific site; they are available on a first-come, first-served basis upon arrival.

The Calliham Unit is 11 miles west of Three Rivers on Highway 72. Turn north on Park Road 8 to the headquarters, which is open from 8 A.M. to 5 P.M. The park gates are open from 5 A.M. to 10 P.M. The entry fee is $3 per person. (512) 786-3868.

• **Choke Canyon State Park—South Shore Unit** 🐾🐾½
   See ⑲ on page 252.

Covering 385 acres, this is the smaller of the two units open to dogs at Choke Canyon State Park.

South Texas brush—mesquite and huisache, mainly—separates grassy areas from the lake. There's not much for a dog to do here other than walk a short birding trail. Sport found it fascinating because it dives into the old Frio River channel, preempted when the dam was built and now being reclaimed by brush and trees draped with Spanish moss. A confirmed water dog, Sport had never before been able to walk on the bottom of a river without getting her paws muddy and drawing cross looks when she tracked mud all over the car seats. There is a boat ramp where a leashed dog can take a short dip except during times when large volumes of water are being released and going into the water is forbidden.

Follow park signs to the camping area below the dam. Just before you drop off the dam, there is a shaded scenic overlook where you can watch the lake extinguish the setting sun. The campground has a good scattering of trees. Sites with water and electricity are $14; tent sites are $9. Walk-in group tent camping with no facilities is $7 for eight or more people. There are numerous water faucets, and a nearby day-use picnic area has water, rest rooms, and a beach area where your leashed dog can cool off in the water away from any swimmers who might be present.

Reservations for campsites at all state parks must be made by calling the central reservation number, (512) 389-8900, between 9 A.M. and 6 P.M. Monday through Friday. Reservations are strongly recommended, and a deposit is required in order to guarantee your reservation. You cannot reserve a specific site; they are available on a first-come, first-served basis upon arrival.

Texas state parks forbid the use of a leash longer than six feet, and dogs may not be left unattended (which includes being tied outside) or taken into any park building. Dogs may not enter the water at a designated swimming area or enter the beach adjacent to a swimming area.

The South Shore Unit is on Highway 72, four miles west of Three Rivers. The office is open from 8 A.M. to 5 P.M. The park closes at 10 P.M. except to overnight guests. The entry fee is $3 per person. (512) 786-3538.

RESTAURANTS

Nolan Ryan's Waterfront Restaurant: Eat while rocking in one of the chairs on the front porch and enjoying the view of the lake. This fisher-oriented place offers a full, hearty menu. It's located next to Nolan Ryan's Bass Inn—Choke Canyon (see below); (512) 786-4938.

PLACES TO STAY

Choke Canyon State Park—Calliham Unit: See Choke Canyon State Park on page 283 for camping information.

Choke Canyon State Park—South Shore Unit: See Choke Canyon State Park on page 284 for camping information.

Nolan Ryan's Bass Inn—Choke Canyon: Small dogs may stay in rooms, and there is a kennel out back for large dogs. A deposit is not normally required, but the manager may request one at her discretion. This inn is located in the country, 7.5 miles west of Three Rivers on Highway 72, and has plenty of room for a leashed pooch to roam. Rates are $51. Box 129, Three Rivers, TX 78071; (512) 786-3521.

NUECES COUNTY

If not for a bold move by the fledgling Republic of Texas in the 1830s, Texas dogs would have to get a visa and (yikes!) shots to visit this area. After Texas gained its independence from Mexico, that country claimed the Nueces River was the boundary between the two countries. So Texas simply passed a law saying the boundary was the Rio Grande and grabbed the real estate. For a while the dispute was like two dogs fighting over a bone neither really wanted, but Texas eventually prevailed, a lucky thing for Texas dogs. Some of the best dog beaches in the state are right here, even though leashes are required.

BANQUETE

PARKS, BEACHES, AND RECREATION AREAS

• **John J. Sablatura Park** 🐾 🐾½ *See* ⓴ *on page 252.*

This 20-acre county park is a canine oasis in oft-parched South Texas. We've frequently driven right by it while going from Corpus Christi to family property farther west, because the part you can see from the road looks unpromising, surrounded as it is by extensive farm fields. This time Sport and I stopped, and we were glad we did. The park is almost totally shaded by large mesquite trees and has extensive grassy areas for the conducting of important dog business. Sport had to wear her leash, but there was a creek bottom to explore, and that made up for it. Water faucets—painted yellow—dot the park, as do picnic tables and barbecue pits. Even if the park is closed, you can still take a rest break here, as the portion nearest the highway is not fenced and has a good place to pull off the busy highway safely.

The park is one mile west of Banquete on Highway 44. Gates are open 24 hours daily; the office is open from 8 A.M. to 5 P.M. For more information, contact P.O. Box 18608, Corpus Christi, TX 78480-8608; (512) 949-8122. The park office number is (512) 387-7686.

PORT ARANSAS

Port Aransas is one of my favorite places in Texas to visit, and Sport and Samantha give it dewclaws up, too. It's a tiny little town whose existence depends on tourists and fishers, and the residents know how to make both feel welcome. There are probably more good places to eat per capita here than any other town in Texas, although only one welcomes dogs. Best of all, Port Aransas offers access to miles and miles of beaches where dogs can sun, dig, sniff, roam, and just generally be the worthless beach bums that they are—and fit right in.

With one exception, leashes are required, but somehow being on a leash while eyeball to eyeball with a sharp-beaked heron or saber-clawed jetty cat doesn't seem such a bad idea. Sport could stay for days just smelling the sea air, splashing in the surf, letting her ears blow free in the wind, and examining all the olfactory wonders that wash up on the beach. Come to think of it, that's what I like about the place, too.

If you and your dog are intrepid adventurers, or if you simply must have a few hours during which the two of you are not connected by an umbilical cord, Port Aransas is the gateway to the only leash-free beach in the area, St. Joseph's Island. You can be castaways for as long as you like on this uninhabited finger of land accessible only by boat. Fortunately, a shuttle boat runs daily from the marina area in Port Aransas.

Dogs are always titillated by tales of the seamy side of life—due no doubt to their preoccupation with things that smell rotten—and the "Port A" of today gives no clue that this sweet little burg was the last stronghold (as far as we know) of organized illegal gambling in Texas. Until just a few decades ago the town could be reached only by ferry, and ferry service ended around midnight and did not resume until early the next morning. That made Port A perfect for people who liked to conduct their business, shall we say, free from fear of being bitten by the law. Locals told Sport and me that cooperative state and local officials allowed as many as 25 gambling houses in Port A to operate undogged by the law as long as minors were barred. A deputy sheriff stationed at the ferry landing turned back teenaged would-be sun-worshippers, and the money and liquor flowed all night, every night.

Today's Port A is a family place given over to the enjoyment of sun, surf, and sand, but I'm told there are a few unhappy souls who still think that when gambling ended, Port A went to the dogs.

PARKS, BEACHES, AND RECREATION AREAS

• **Mustang Island State Park** 🐾 🐾 ½
See page 259 for a description of Mustang Island State Park.

• **Port Aransas Park** 🐾 🐾 ½ *See* **㉑** *on page 252.*
Sport is always ready to go to the beach one more time, so we headed for Port Aransas Park, covering 167 acres on Mustang Island on the outskirts of town. Swimming, picnicking, camping, and beachcombing—all leashed activities for dogs—are the order of every day. Somehow Sport never gets bored with any of them, especially swimming and picnicking. There's something about a frisk in the water that makes a pooch ravenous.

Campsites with water and electricity ($15) and beach campsites ($6) are available. In either case you will sleep in close proximity to water and other people. Shaded picnic tables at both classes of sites do provide welcome relief from the sun for a pooch and her person. A word of warning: If you park anywhere on the beach outside the marked area and do not display an official beach parking permit on your vehicle, you will be cited, and the last time we checked, the fine was $50. Buy your $6 permit at the Chamber of Commerce office (on your right just as you get off the ferry) and avoid becoming a fugitive.

This beach has always been a favorite of mine because of the graffito that once graced a sign on the approach road. The sign read, "Dangerous Undertow. Watch Your Children." Underneath, in shaky spraycan hand, some wag had added the single word "disappear." It's no longer there, perhaps the only example of its kind that not only was not offensive but also served a useful purpose. The mental image it conjured probably saved more than one kid's life.

To reach the park, stay on Cotter Avenue after you leave the ferry and follow it all the way to the beach. When you must turn or become waterborne, take a right to the park office. The park is open 24 hours. (512) 749-6117.

• **St. Joseph's Island** 🐾🐾🐾 🐕 *See ㉒ on page 252.*

St. Joseph's Island is a rarity in Texas: private land where your pooch can run leash-free. A wealthy Texas family owns the island and permits pooches and their people to visit its southern end, opposite the town of Port Aransas, up to a fence marking the beginning of their cattle ranch. The chief attractions are excellent shelling, beachcombing, and solitude.

As you might expect, this paradise isn't perfect. The only access to the island is by boat. If you and your nautical pooch left yours at home, you can take the Jetty Boat from Port Aransas. It makes scheduled trips approximately hourly until noon and every two hours in the afternoon. Your pooch will hardly be able to wait for the short ride to end so she can run sans leash—keeping in mind that there are rattlesnakes on the island. You also need to take along all the food, water, and anything else you and your pooch will need for the duration of your stay, which can include overnight camping if you wish.

Camping is totally primitive. There are no designated sites, no fees. You just pick a spot and camp. It's the closest you and your dog will ever get to returning to those days soon after the dawn of dog time when humans and canines first lay down together to share the warmth of a campfire. Howling at the full moon rising over the Gulf of Mexico is a good way to express your feelings about this place.

The owners of the island ask that you clean up after yourself and your pooch. Respecting their wishes will help keep this gem of an island open for future beach bum dogs.

Board the Jetty Boat ($8.95 round-trip for people; dogs ride free) at Woody's Sports Center, 136 West Cotter Avenue, Port Aransas, TX 78373; (512) 749-5252.

RESTAURANTS

The Quarterdeck: Tie your dog in a shaded area just outside the covered deck dining area and let the friendly staff take care of her while you eat at one of 20 tables overlooking the harbor. "We will bring a thirsty dog a bowl of water and pet her if she's cute—and I've never seen an ugly dog," says owner Pru Miller. 914 Tarpon Street; (512) 749-4449.

PLACES TO STAY

Lone Palm Motel: Medium and small dogs are preferred, although larger ones may be permitted at the manager's discretion. The pet fee is $5 per day, and dog owners are responsible for any damage. Room rates are $25 to $50. 306 South Alister Street, Port Aransas, TX 78373; (512) 749-5450.

Mustang Island State Park: See Mustang Island State Park on page 259 for camping information.

Paradise Isle Motel: Big dogs are okay if they are well behaved. There is a $10 fee per dog per day. A large lawn where you can walk your dog on leash has shaded picnic tables and barbecue grills. Rates are $35 to $65; rooms with a kitchen are $10 extra. 314 Cut-off Road, Port Aransas, TX 78373; (512) 749-6993.

Port Aransas Inn: Your pooch had better be on her best behavior here: drug-sniffing police dogs live next door. There is a fenced grassy exercise area behind the pink, three-story motel, but your well-behaved dog under 20 pounds must remain leashed. A $10 deposit is required if paying by cash, and you must notify the motel that you are bringing a dog. The beach is a five-minute walk away. Rates are $39 to $89. 1500 11th Street, Port Aransas, Texas 78373; (512) 749-5937.

Port Aransas Park: See Port Aransas Park on page 287 for camping information.

Seahorse Lodge: The canine-friendly owner of these 12 cottages has two Chihuahuas; perhaps that's why she requests no large dogs and no more than two per room. She also stresses that dogs are not to be left unattended in rooms. Each cottage has two bedrooms and plenty of grassy areas around. The beach is just two blocks away. There is a $5 daily charge for your pooch. You'll pay $70. A two-night minimum stay is required. 503 Avenue G, Port Aransas, TX 78373; (512) 749-5513.

Sunday Villas: Two of the units in this complex of raised beach houses will take any size dog; the others accept dogs under 25 pounds only. You and your pooch will have two or three bedrooms and a fully equipped kitchen. An unfenced dog walking area and the nearby beach are available to leashed dogs. There is a $20 cash fee per dog for flea control, and no more than two dogs per unit are allowed. Rates are $120 to $168. 1923 South 11th Street, Port Aransas, TX 78373; (512) 749-6480 or (800) 638-6236.

DIVERSIONS

Dog your ship as it comes in: Port Aransas is the place where all the ships that dock at ports from Corpus Christi to Rockport must enter and leave the Gulf of Mexico. As a result, there is a lot of ship traffic, and the dog who witnesses an oil tanker steaming by at close range will long remember the sight. To get the best view of the ships, follow Cotter Avenue from the ferry landing all the way to the beach. A mile-long jetty provides enough front-row seats to the ship parade for all the dogs in Texas. Since the jetty is also a popular fishing spot, there are a number of jetty cats working the area, making it a virtual certainty that your pooch will see at least one thing of interest. (Jetty cats are feral felines who hang out on the pink granite jetties, living by their wits, their claws, and the largess of fishers who toss them unwanted hardhead catfish. Dogs should beware—these are tough cats.) This is a perfect spot to watch the sun set over the water. Take a cool drink for both of you and watch as the sea slowly swallows the sun's golden orb and night clutches the Texas coast to its watery breast. (Sport asked if she could write something, so I let her, but after that bombastic blizzard, I have banished her from the keyboard forever.)

Peek at plankton: You and your leashed, well-behaved pooch can take a two-hour cruise aboard the *Duke* and learn loads about denizens of the deep. You'll watch dolphins and birds for a while. Then the crew will pull a plankton net behind the boat and haul the catch aboard to be viewed through small hand-held microscopes. Next it's on to bigger things. A small shrimp net brings in crabs, shrimp, and a variety of fish, which are dumped into an on-board, hands-on tank for viewing and touching. Sport cowered when a crab advanced on her nose, waving his pincers, but then Sport cowers at almost anything. Bring food and water for you and your pooch and $15 for your fare. Pooches ride free and get all the plankton they can eat.

The *Duke* docks at Woody's Sports Center, 136 West Cotter Avenue; call (512) 749-4795 or (512) 749-7559 for a cruise schedule, rates, and reservations.

SAN PATRICIO COUNTY

Irish wolfhounds, take note: San Patricio County was the site of an early colony of Irish settlers, and a few historic buildings from that era can still be found in the little town of San Patricio. Leashed dogs can stroll the streets and muse upon their roots.

ARANSAS PASS

PARKS, BEACHES, AND RECREATION AREAS

• **Aransas Pass Community Park** 🐾½ *See ㉓ on page 252.*

For a few minutes, Sport and I felt pretty good about this 100-acre park devoted mostly to athletic fields, open grassy areas, and ponds where a leashed dog could disport herself. Then we saw the sign near the children's playground, and I started reading it aloud to Sport: "No alcoholic beverages. *No* camping. *No* glass containers. *No* hunting. *No* firearms. *No* profanity. *No* peddling. *No* littering. *No* wading. *No* swimming. *No* fishing." Sport's head and tail drooped lower and lower with each no, and then came the coup de grace: "All animals leashed at all times." I looked at Sport and added, "And *no* fun," and we stayed *no* longer.

From Highway 361 heading east, turn right on East Johnson Avenue. The park is on the waterfront in sight of the highway. It is open from 8 A.M. to 10 P.M. (512) 758-5301.

• **Coastal Birding Trail** 🐾🐾 *See ㉔ on page 252.*

The Coastal Birding Trail is not a park per se but a series of coastal areas from Beaumont to Brownsville designated as prime bird-watching areas. This part of the trail actually lies in Nueces County, but since the only vehicular access is through Aransas Pass (which lies in Nueces, San Patricio, and Aransas Counties), we are including it here.

Because we are back in Nueces County, that entity's strict leash law applies throughout the five-mile stretch of highway from Aransas Pass to the Port Aransas ferry landing. Your pooch will yearn to splash in the water that lies 100 yards distant on either side of the road, and as long as he remains on the leash, it's okay. You'll have to share the beach with fishers and campers, since these tidal flats are a popular bay-fishing area. That has its benefits, too, as there will be plenty of rotting fish for your pooch to delight in, or perhaps a crab, pelican, heron, or seagull.

While you're here, drive on to the ferry. Here Sport discovered a distinct pleasure at being afloat, although she did bark madly at the dolphins that piloted our boat across the Gulf Intracoastal Waterway. The ferry is free, operates 24 hours a day, and utterly severs the connection between the hustle and bustle of the outside world and the laid-back atmosphere of Port Aransas. People say that "Port A" lives on island time, but Sport prefers to think of it as lazy-dog-in-the-sun time. On weekends and holidays the wait for the ferry may not be worth the trip: by the time you've baked in the sun for an hour and a half, it may take more than the tranquillity of Port Aransas to soothe your jangled nerves. Signs along the highway advise you of how long the wait for the ferry will be. If you must stop more than two miles from the ferry landing, it's quicker to turn around and go back to Corpus Christi, where you can take the Crosstown Expressway to South Padre Island Drive, which intersects Highway 361.

The Coastal Birding Trail, designated by brown and white signs with the outline of binoculars, lies along both sides of Highway 361 between Aransas Pass and the Port Aransas ferry landing. It is open 24 hours. For information, write the Aransas Pass Chamber of Commerce, 452 Cleveland Boulevard, Aransas Pass, TX 78336; (512) 758-2750 or (800) 633-3028.

PLACES TO STAY

Homeport Inn: A big, vacant, mowed lot out back is available for walking your cooped-up dog. Any size dog can stay here by paying a $20 fee. Rooms are $34 to $59. 1513 West Wheeler Street, Aransas Pass, TX 78336; (512) 758-3213.

Seabreeze Motel: The manager laughed when I asked if he allowed dogs. "We've got retrievers and Labs here right now," he explained. "We don't have a size limit as such. We look at the dog, and if its size is within reason, it can stay." The motel sits on 3.5 acres where you can walk your pooch, and all rooms have full kitchens. Rates are $35 to $53, plus $3 for the dog. 1404 South Commercial Street, Aransas Pass, TX 78336; (512) 758-3014.

INGLESIDE

PARKS, BEACHES, AND RECREATION AREAS

• **Live Oak Park** 🐾🐾🐾 *See* ㉕ *on page 252.*

Thousands of live oak trees jam this 90-acre park, presenting the boy dog with a dilemma: which to use? The sandy soil feels good between both human and canine toes. A short nature trail begins near the playground equipment and winds through a dense live oak grove. It's just the thing for an explorer dog: narrow, dark, and mysterious. There are no interpretive signs for humans, but you wouldn't be able to read them anyway. You'll be hanging on for dear life to your leashed dog as she forges ahead into the mini-wilderness.

Other amenities include a disk golf course (try playing that with a leashed pooch!), playground equipment, rest rooms, picnic tables, barbecue pits, and water faucets by the rest rooms and big barbecue pit. Take the dirt road to the right at disk golf "hole" number 2 to a large open, grassy area with a pond where your leashed pooch can take a dip.

Ingleside animal control officer Joe Ramirez stressed the $500 fine for having a dog with no proof of rabies vaccination, but he seemed almost apologetic for the city's leash law. "If there is a problem, we will have to enforce the leash law," he said, implying that the well-behaved pooch just might be able to sneak off the leash for a bit and get away with it. But we don't advise trying. Joe might be watching.

From eastbound Highway 361, turn right (south) on F.M. 1069. On the southern outskirts of town turn left onto Sherry Avenue and go two blocks to the park entrance. The park is open 24 hours. (512) 776-2517.

DIVERSIONS

Dance with dolphins: You know your super pooch has super powers. Let her prove it by using her as a dolphin divining device. Erv and Sonja Strong, owners of Dolphin Connection, say their dog Pete can hear dolphins long before they can be seen. If other passengers do not object, you can take your dog on a boat ride to meet the dolphins of Corpus Christi Bay. The dolphins put on displays of aquatic acrobatics and often approach the boat to be petted and speak face to face with your pooch. Reservations are required; call for prices and directions. Route 1, Box 185, Ingleside, TX 78362; (512) 776-2887.

MATHIS

PARKS, BEACHES, AND RECREATION AREAS

• **Lake Corpus Christi State Park** 🐾🐾 *See ㉖ on page 252.*

"Oh, wowza, 365 acres!" Sport exulted as we pulled into this park after a too-long drive. She was promptly crushed when she learned that not only was she forbidden to run free or swim, she could not even go near the beach or fish from the pier. (And she's just learned to handle her fly rod.)

Texas state parks forbid the use of a leash longer than six feet, and dogs may not be left unattended (which includes being tied outside) or taken into any park building. Dogs may not enter the water at a designated swimming area or enter the beach adjacent to a swimming area. Just how broadly the state defines "adjacent" no one was able to explain to Sport and me, so we suggest you check with park rangers for their interpretation, since they will be the ones enforcing the regulation. Some are more sympathetic than others.

So much room is taken up by picnic and camping sites that few unclaimed grassy spaces remain for walking your leashed pooch, but the park is laced with roads that make convenient loops, so there is no excuse for becoming a couch pooch during your visit. The picnic area/swimming beach gets a cooling breeze blowing across the lake most of the year and also has numerous water faucets where a thirsty pooch can slake her thirst. Sport likes to drink directly from the faucet, but in deference to human users not accustomed to drinking after a dog, it's best to bring along a small bowl. Forgot yours? No problem. The bottom cut from a large plastic soft drink bottle makes a cheap, lightweight, recyclable water bowl, and a recycling center—where you can dispose of your bottle or scrounge around for one to make a bowl—is located at the park entrance. Your pooch can have her bowl and help save the environment, too.

Basically, this park is one big tree-shaded lakeside campground. There are 48 RV and trailer campsites with water and electricity, 60 tent sites with water nearby, and 25 screened shelters inside which pets are not allowed. Don't be tempted to sleep inside and tether your dog outside: South Texas is home to coyotes and javelinas (small piglike animals with large tusks), both of which have been known to snack on small dogs left outdoors. In addition, Texas state park regulations forbid unattended pets and define such as "A pet that is unaccompanied or not under immediate control. Pets tied or secured outside of camping equipment or buildings are not considered under immediate control." You and your pooch will enjoy many hours of togetherness in Texas state parks.

Many campsites are secluded, screened from other campers by the ubiquitous South Texas brush. Boy dogs will be ecstatic to see that virtually every campsite picnic table is shaded by a tree. Many campsites offer views of the lake. Sites with water are $8; with water and electricity, $14; with water, electricity, and sewage hookups, $16; screened shelters are $20.

Reservations for campsites at all state parks must be made by calling the central reservation number, (512) 389-8900, between 9 A.M. and 6 P.M. Monday through Friday. Reservations are strongly recommended, and a deposit is required in order to guarantee your reservation. You cannot reserve a specific site; they are available on a first-come, first-served basis upon arrival.

From southbound Interstate 37, take the Highway 36/359 exit. Follow Highway 359 west to Business 359, then take Business 359 west to its junction with F.M. 1068. Turn right on F.M. 1068, which turns left after just one block, then follow this road to Park Road 25. Or, from northbound Interstate 37, take Exit 34 and follow the brown and white park signs on Highway 359 west to Park Road 25.

Park gates are open from 5:30 A.M. to 10 P.M.; the office is open from 8 A.M. to 10 P.M. April through August and until 5 P.M. the rest of the year. The park entry fee is $3 per person. (512) 547-2635.

PLACES TO STAY

Lake Corpus Christi State Park: See Lake Corpus Christi State Park on page 293 for camping information.

6

THE DALLAS–FORT WORTH METROPLEX

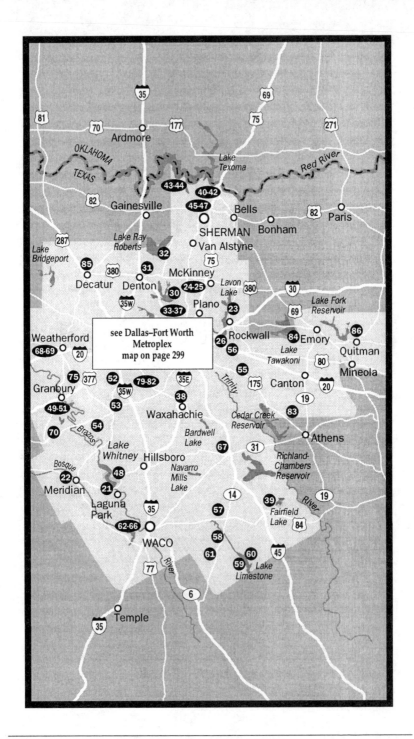

DALLAS–FORT WORTH METROPLEX

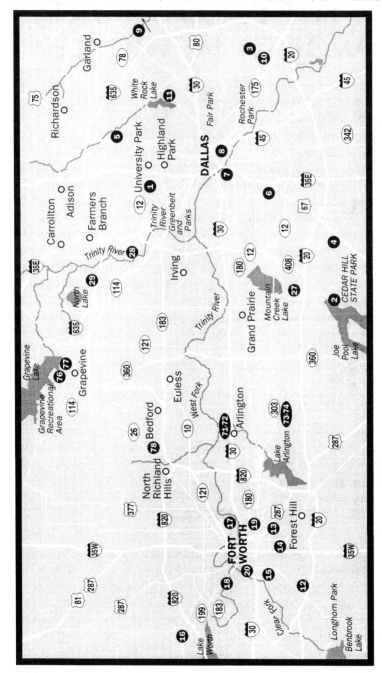

THE DALLAS–FORT WORTH METROPLEX

The Metroplex offers everything a dog could want except lots of places to romp off leash. We did find one leash-free area in Dallas, one in Hood County, and three in Limestone County, but other than that, your pooch must remain tethered. On the other hand, there are some magnificent parks in this region. Dallas and Fort Worth straddle the line between East Texas, with its abundant rainfall and trees, and West Texas, a higher, flatter, drier region. The resulting differences in elevation and vegetation mean parks offer a great variety of scenery. The region's demand for water resulted in dams being built on virtually every stream of any size, so that many parks—even in cities—include access to a lake as one of their charms. Many other parks include greenbelt areas along creeks.

One of the nation's largest lakes—Texoma—is a short drive north of the Metroplex and is a center for outdoor recreation. Perhaps as popular with big-city dogs are the small towns around the Metroplex, many of which have made determined efforts to retain their charm and appeal. Weekend and holiday visits to these towns reward harried hounds with a breather from the faster pace of city life. There's time to stop and smell the roadkills here without becoming one yourself.

To help you find the best places to take your pooch in the Metroplex, we'll start with the cities of Dallas and Fort Worth. Then we'll cover the smaller towns in surrounding counties (in alphabetical order). You should be able to drive to any of the places listed in a couple of hours. Convincing your pooch to return to the city may take a little longer—if there's one thing pooches say more often than "Are we there yet?" it's "Do we have to go already?"

DALLAS

Dallas is one of the 10 largest cities in the United States, but it isn't nearly as cosmopolitan as one might expect—at least not where dogs are concerned. Only one city park is leash-free, and then only during off-peak hours for human use. However, given the fact that most humans here spend a good part of their lives locked inside their cars during the daily commute, perhaps Dallasites feel that people are more in need of places to run and breathe free.

The automobile is almost as necessary to life in Dallas as is air, and that may be a good thing, for you and your pooch will need wheels to get to the best area parks, most of which lie outside the city. One of the best of all Texas state parks for dogs—Cedar Hill State Park—is just minutes from downtown. The very dog-friendly Dallas Nature Center is also just a short trip by car. Only slightly farther afield is huge Lake Texoma and some of the best camping in Texas at Eisenhower State Park. Numerous recreation areas and resorts ring the lake, offering something for the pooch who wants to be pampered as well as for the dog who wants to "ruff" it. Dallas dogs may just be among the luckiest in Texas, because they have some of the best weekend getaway spots in the state from which to choose, even though they must remain leashed at all of them.

PARKS, BEACHES, AND RECREATION AREAS

• **Bachman Lake Park** 🐾🐾½ *See* ❶ *on page 299.*

This 205-acre park surrounding a lake is just minutes from Texas Stadium and right at the north end of Love Field's main runway. Plane-watching pooches can do their thing (leashed) here as at few other places. The planes come so close to the park's south side you can recognize your friends' faces in the little windows as they taxi into position for takeoff. And they can see your dog's tail wagging good-bye.

When a plane lands, your pooch will go crazy as it passes less than a hundred feet overhead. I thought Sport was going to have a heart attack. She loves to bark at planes, but she'd never been so close to one, and she was not nearly so brave when the shrieking monsters seemed about to swoop down and grab her up.

The three-mile paved walking trail around the lake gets steady use by people and their pooches from nearby neighborhoods. Sundays are especially busy days; expect the park to be jammed. However, there is lots of open space with trees, picnic tables, playground, and rest rooms. The shore slopes gently to the water and then drops off sharply the last couple of feet to mud—sort of an industrial-strength bathtub ring. If you don't mind muddy paws in the car (or you travel prepared to deal with dirty feet), your pooch will enjoy exploring the water's edge for interesting bits of urban debris.

The park is at West Northwest Highway (Loop 12) and Lakefield Drive. It is closed from midnight until 6 A.M. (214) 670-4100.

• **Cedar Hill State Park** 🐾🐾🐾½ 🐾 *See* ❷ *on page 299.*

Were it not for the onerous leash law common to all state parks, this 1,810-acre park would rate four paws, paws down. It has everything the urban dweller and his dog could ask for: close proximity (the kids won't ask "Are we there yet?" more than once before the answer is yes), outstanding campsites, miles of dog-accessible beaches, boating and fishing on 7,500-acre Joe Pool Lake, scenic views, five miles of hiking trails, an off-road biking area with eight miles of trails, and even an agricultural history center.

When Sport and I last visited in mid-October, leaves were splashing red and yellow and gold across the hillsides. From mid-October through mid-November should be an ideal time to visit if you enjoy the colorful displays of fall. Call the park number below for information about fall color.

As you might expect, the park with something for everyone and his dog attracts almost everyone and his dog. Fortunately, the spacious facility seems equal to the task. Even on a mid-October weekend, the busy season, there were actually a few campsites available. The park was abuzz with people and dogs, though. In one campground we saw more pink bicycles and Pekingese than I knew existed. Personal watercraft sprouted from behind every four-wheel-drive sport utility vehicle. Yet the day-use areas of the park, which offer some great beaches for dogs, were almost deserted.

The same could not be said of the hiking trails. The popular Talala Trail, a 2.5-mile interpretive trail, bore heavy traffic. A brochure available free at park headquarters introduces walkers to a variety of native plants and animals that appear along the trail. Sport was gratified to see that raccoons appear on the list, along with armadillos, bobcats, cottontails, and coyotes. I was more interested in the native grasses such as big and little bluestem, and birds like the migratory painted bunting, a winged rainbow sometimes seen in the park. The trail is easy walking, and water is available at the trailhead between the entrances to the Hog Wallow and Coyote Crossing Camps. (Mmmmmm. Don't those sound interesting.) Primitive camping ($7) is allowed along the trail.

Another primitive camping area ($7) is along the Pond Trail, which heads at a parking area on the south side of the road just west of the entrance to the Coyote Crossing Camp. The 2.5-mile trail has a spur to a scenic overlook of the lake and the advancing suburbs of Dallas.

Although dogs are not allowed on the designated swimming beach on the loop road encircling the Lakeview Camp, they are free to enjoy the water on leash everywhere else in the park. Every camping and day-use area of the park has excellent beaches for dogs. The sandy shores slope gently to the water, and the beaches are generally free of rocks and grass. There may, on occasion, be a dead fish to add olfactory interest.

If the attractions of this park stopped here, it would be pretty much like a lot of other state parks located on lakes. But this place has something special: the Penn Farm Agricultural History Center. Originally about 1,100 acres, the farm included the present parklands as well as bottomlands that are now truly bottomlands: they are at the bottom of Joe Pool

Lake. First settled about the time of the Civil War, the farmstead contains almost all the buildings erected by the Penn family for the next 100 years. And judging from the numerous pieces of old horse-drawn farm equipment displayed, most of that remains as well. I was patient with Sport as she carefully compared one pile of horse manure's scent to another in the barnyard area; Sport was patient with me as I poked, prodded, and peered until I figured out how the McCormick reaper worked. Trails through the underbrush carried us to windmills, log barns, a smokehouse, and a farmhouse. Ghostly remnants of old stacked-rail fences lurked in the thickets reclaiming former pastures and fields. It's a good place for your city dog to gain an appreciation for her country cousins.

Camping is a major activity at the park, and while the 355 campsites share some similarities, the different campgrounds have subtly different natures. (All campsites except the primitive backpack sites are served by rest rooms with showers and have a picnic table, barbecue grill, fire ring, and lantern post.) The Shady Ridge and Eagle Ford Camps have sites with water and electricity ($12). Located in a hilly part of the park, the sites are very heavily shaded and screened from each other by trees and brush. Premium waterfront sites go for $15. The area has two fishing piers. There is a good beach area for dogs; if you want a campsite close to water, try for numbers 52 through 56 or 100 through 108.

The Lakeview Camp's 71 sites ($12) seemed to be very popular with families with dogs. The elevated campground has good views of the lake and is somewhat more open than the other campgrounds. Perhaps that's why families like it—they can keep an eye on the kids. Dogs are not allowed in the swimming area at the lakefront below this campground.

Perhaps the best lake views are from the sites on the loop of the Hog Wallow Camp ($12). This fairly open, level area offers a choice of campsites that front the lake (numbers 263 to 270) or that back up to a heavily wooded peninsula jutting into the lake (numbers in the 240s and 250s). The beach here is excellent for dogs; rates for premium lakeside campsites are $15.

Variety is also the hallmark of the 75-site Coyote Crossing Camp. Sites 281 through 301 sit atop a hill overlooking the lake, with the lower numbered sites being located in very dense vegetation that makes them quite private. Sites 302 through 355 are on a fairly open plain beside the lake, at the foot of a hill. Regular sites are $12; rates for premium sites by the water are $15.

As at all state parks, dogs are not allowed in any park building or on the beach at designated swimming areas. Dogs must remain on a six-foot leash and may not be left unattended.

Reservations for campsites at all state parks must be made by calling the central reservation number, (512) 389-8900, between 9 A.M. and 6 P.M. Monday through Friday. Reservations are strongly recommended, and a deposit is required in order to guarantee a reservation. Specific sites may not be reserved; they are available on a first-come, first-served basis upon arrival.

The park is 15 miles south of Dallas on F.M. 1382. Entrance costs $5 per person. The park is closed except to campers from 10 P.M. to 8 A.M. The office is open daily from 8 A.M. to 5 P.M. (972) 291-3900.

• **Crawford Park** 🐾½ *See* ❸ *on page 299.*

You and your leashed pooch will get a lot more than 69 acres of fun out of this park, because it's joined at the hip—at the creek, actually—with the 196-acre Samuell-Elam Park, and a paved walking trail links the two. Crawford Park is largely given over to soccer fields, although a small stand of pine trees in the middle is a pleasant visual surprise and also gives your hound's sniffer something different to savor. If you have a loved one in the nearby Southeastern Methodist Hospital, this is a good place to come and take a break from being serene and supportive. In other words, have a howling good time and go back refreshed.

The park is at 8700 Elam Road, at the intersection of Prairie Creek Road and Elam Road. Hours are 6 A.M. to midnight. (214) 670-4100.

• **Dallas Nature Center** 🐾🐾🐾 *See* ❹ *on page 299.*

Imagine a place just seven acres short of one square mile in size. A place where seven miles of trails carry you through distinctly different habitats at elevations that vary over 200 feet from lowest to highest. A place where flowers, trees, and sky compete for the eye of the beholder. A place with signs at the entrance that read, "Slow. Squirrels Crossing." A place where dogs are welcome. A place that charges no admission fee (but does request a $3 per car donation). A heavenly place you don't have to die to get to. It's not a canine version of paradise; it's the Dallas Nature Center.

This is a place that teems with life in more ways than one. It is a nature preserve with prairies, wildflowers, and wetlands. But it's also a place where people come to seek refuge from the bustling metroplex at the bottom of the hill, a dozen miles and one world away. And they bring their dogs. On leash, it is true, but what hound doesn't feel safe, secure, and loved when near its human? (Macho dogs will deny it to the death, but inside every hero dog is a lapdog yearning to nap with his head tucked under your arm.)

Nine trails, three of which prohibit dogs, present different aspects of this ecologically varied area. Millions of years ago movement along a fault line raised the Austin Chalk 220 feet above the Eagleford Shale, forming a west-facing bank of hills and dividing the bottomlands from the top lands. The resulting biological diversity defines the character of the various trails, which range from a mere quarter mile to 2.5 miles round-trip. You can buy a trail map for 25 cents at the headquarters or use it for free if you return it. One of the most enjoyable ways to see the trails, however, is by taking one of the regularly scheduled guided walks with a naturalist. Fees are generally $2 for members and $4 for non-members; call the number below for the current schedule. Your leashed pooch is welcome to accompany you on these walks. There are even night walks, when your pooch will have a better chance of spotting some of the center's furry four-footed inhabitants.

If wildflowers appeal to your pooch, try the Little Bluestem Trail, which meanders through a wildflower prairie. This is a flat walk of only a quarter mile round-trip, but in spring and fall (rains willing), you'll see a bountiful display of blooms. One of the most popular trails with dogs as well as people is the Cattail Pond Trail, a 1.5-mile trek with an observation platform offering a spectacular view of Joe Pool Lake. On a clear day you can see . . . Fort Worth. You may have some trouble explaining to your pooch why there are no cats, or even parts of cats, at Cattail Pond. There's always hope, of course. Be forewarned that this trail requires descending the Mountain Creek Escarpment, the equivalent of a 25-story building, and then getting back up again either by backtracking or by taking the connecting Fossil Valley Trail. The latter trail is steeper and more difficult. It is 2.5 miles round-trip, and while it offers great views of the countryside, you'll be spending most of your time watching your feet on the steep slopes.

The Cedar Brake Trail dives through a mysterious stand of mature juniper trees (known everywhere in Texas as cedar trees) and climbs some of the center's steepest slopes. The 2.5-mile round-trip also crosses Possum Haw Creek four times; your pooch will have plenty of chances to wet her whistle.

For a longer (2.25-mile) but easy hike, take the Escarpment Road Trail, an old ranch road that connects with the Cattail Pond Trail and lets you visit this premier spot in the park without having to negotiate steep slopes. For a quick, easy sampler of the different types of terrain and vegetation the center offers, hike the 0.75-mile Possum Haw Trail. The name alone should keep even easily bored dogs alert.

Dogs are not permitted on the Butterfly, Mulberry, and Bluebonnet Trails.

The center is two miles south of Interstate 20 at 7171 Mountain Creek Parkway. Entry is free. It's open from dawn to dusk. (972) 296-1955.

• **Fair Oaks Park** 🐾 *See ❺ on page 299.*

This 233-acre park is located near Presbyterian Hospital. Leashed pooches can picnic with you, walk the paved trail, or just hang out under the trees. There's a playground, basketball court, and baseball fields. The park has a chemical toilet but no water.

This park is one of a series of parklands that run continuously along White Rock Creek for about six miles but have different names—Moss Park, Flag Pole Hill Park, Lake Highland Park, Norbuck Park, and even White Rock Lake Park. The White Rock Trail connects the parks with a paved hiking and biking path. Parks along the way have rest rooms, water, and picnic grounds. The entire route is shaded by large trees.

The park is located at 7600 Fair Oaks Drive. Hours are 6 A.M. to midnight. (214) 670-4100.

• **Kiest Park** 🐾🐾½ *See ❻ on page 299.*

Dogs were running everywhere when we visited this 258-acre park—some on the required leash, some not. The unleashed dogs were sniffing and humping each other on a baseball field, while the leashed ones were enjoying a paved multiuse trail that winds through the grounds. The gently rolling, heavily wooded terrain, wildflower areas, and location in a south Dallas residential area combine to make this a very popular place for a morning stroll. There are also athletic fields, shaded picnic grounds with barbecue grills, a playground, and rest rooms in the park, as well as a healthy population of squirrels. Since it's near the union of U.S. 67 and Interstate 35E, it's also a handy spot to dewater your hound before you get into the more congested downtown area, where rush hour freeways can become parking lots and trap you and a dog desperate to keep appointment with a fire hydrant. (When such things happen to us, Sport and I inspect the tires. It doesn't take long for her to take the hint.)

From either Interstate 35E or U.S. 67, exit on Kiest Boulevard and go west one mile. You can access the hiking trail by turning right onto Rugged Drive and taking the first left, or you can continue on West Kiest Boulevard to the first right, Conservation Drive, and enter the park there. The park is open from 5 A.M. to midnight. (214) 670-4100.

• **Lake Cliff Park** 🐾🐾 *See ❼ on page 299.*

There's not much to this park except a small lake and the surrounding green space, but it's a pleasant oasis for a leashed pooch. Gently rolling terrain, lots of trees, and a grassy bank sloping to the water's edge make this a place where dogs can have a good time.

It's located at East Fifth Street and Blaylock Street. Park along Blaylock Street. The park is closed from midnight to 5 A.M. (214) 670-4100.

• **Old City Park** 🐾🐾½ 🐕 *See* **8** *on page 299.*

Tell your pooch this collection of 37 restored historic homes, buildings, and shops from the 19th century is an outstanding outdoor architectural museum, and she will probably not even twitch an ear. Tell her that she can visit on her leash from 10 A.M. to 4 P.M. weekdays and noon to 4 P.M. on Sundays ($5 entrance fee for you), and she may give out a yawn. But mention that at all other hours this is a leash-free facility, and she will bound up asking, "When can we go?" The park is convenient to downtown and to several hotels and is a popular early morning and evening dog-walking spot. The leash-free policy will remain in effect unless there are problems, the park manager said, adding that bringing along your pooper-scooper would be one good way of assuring that problems do not arise. Or lurk in the grass waiting for an unwary victim to step in the wrong place. The park is closed from midnight to 5 A.M. 1717 Gano Street; (214) 421-5141.

• **Robertson Park** 🐾½ *See* **9** *on page 299.*

You'd think a 251-acre park surrounded by water on three sides would rate high even if dogs must remain on leash, which is the case here. But this park is basically a boat ramp and a hayfield with a few picnic tables scattered around. There are only a few widely scattered trees. We did see a chow and his owner, but they were sitting at a picnic table, and neither seemed to be having a lot of fun. However, the park does have a saving grace: It's the location of the Bayview Marina, where you and your pooch can dine at a waterside table. (See the Restaurants section on page 308.)

The park is at Interstate 30 and Dalrock Road. It is closed from midnight to 6 A.M. unless you are fishing or boating. (214) 670-4100.

• **Samuell-Elam Park** 🐾🐾 *See* **10** *on page 299.*

Located right next to Crawford Park, this 196-acre park is an example of one of the times when bigger is better. You and your leashed pooch can travel the paved walking trail that runs through both parks, but this is where you'll want to come to picnic in the shade of the oak trees or ride the merry-go-round. There is a rest room here, too. Prairie Creek divides the two parks, and the dense stand of post oaks along its near half-mile course through the park should allow any pooch to tree a squirrel or spot a raccoon. Or she can follow the lead of a toddler we saw trying to catch one of the many grackles looking for morsels in the picnic area. The best part of the park for dogs, however, is the southern half, which is totally undeveloped and consists of a post oak woodland laced with dirt trails that wind among the trees. Just head past the soccer fields into the wilds of southeast Dallas.

The park is at the intersection of Elam Road and Prairie Creek Road. It is closed from midnight until 6 A.M. (214) 670-4100.

- **White Rock Lake Park** 🐾 🐾 ½ *See* ⑪ *on page 299.*

Dogs love greenbelt parks, even when they must remain on leash, as is the case with all but one Dallas park. Greenbelts by definition occupy land that periodically floods, resulting in lots of grass and weeds, large trees, and an emphasis on structures that will be minimally damaged by flooding, such as walking trails. White Rock Lake Park has 1,873 acres of lakeside park plus another 498 acres of greenbelt linking it to other parks along White Rock Creek—Lake Highland Park, Norbuck Park, Flag Pole Hill Park, Moss Park, and Fair Oaks Park. All this open green space dedicated to the outdoor pleasures of dogs and their people lies just northeast of downtown, and we saw plenty of evidence that everyone from rollerbladers to a group of old codgers playing dominoes in a pavilion takes advantage of it. Dogs will love splashing in the shallows of the lake and eyeing the flock of pelicans roosting on stumps in mid-lake. Squirrels abound, as do other brush-dwelling critters such as opossums and raccoons. Keep a firm grip on the leash and resign yourself to the fact that your pooch will go on sniffing all day if you let her.

The White Rock Trail, a paved two-lane multiuse trail, runs through the complex of parks.

The official address of the park is 8300 South Garland Road. However, you can access the complex of parks at numerous points off East Northwest Highway, North Buckner Boulevard, and South Garland Road. Perhaps the best way to pick a spot from which you and your pooch can set out to enjoy the park is to take East Lawther Street from its intersection with North Buckner Boulevard and East Northwest Highway. From that point south, East Lawther Street runs along the shore of White Rock Lake, passing numerous places where you can park and access the greenbelt or parks. The park is closed from midnight to 6 A.M. (214) 670-4100.

RESTAURANTS

Bayview Marina: Manager Pam Helton says the deli sandwiches are the big favorite here, but you and your leashed pooch can also have a burger, sub, hot dog, or chili cheese fries at one of the covered tables beside the water. We bet your pooch will vote for the fries. There's something vaguely visceral about them. The restaurant is in Robertson Park on Lake Ray Hubbard at 600 Cooke Drive; (972) 412-1977.

Blind Lemon: Get here before 10:30 P.M., when this restaurant turns into a Deep Ellum nightclub, and you and your pooch can sample what the management calls American brew food—burgers, pizza, and pepper steak—or splurge on glazed salmon or roasted duck. (Deep Ellum is the center for Dallas folks who favor alternative lifestyles.) You may sit at the sidewalk tables, but your pooch will have to be tied outside the railing. 2805 Main Street; (214) 939-0202.

Chuy's: Spice up your pooch's life by taking her out for Tex-Mex. Sit on the patio outside. 4544 McKinney Avenue; (214) 559-2489.

Gator's: American and Tex-Mex food—and fried alligator tail, too—are served at the sidewalk tables. 1714 North Market Street; (214) 748-0243.

Going Gourmet: The menu leans toward the Italian and features pasta, lamb, chicken, pork, and beef dishes that any dog would be proud to eat on the outside patio. 4345 West Northwest Highway; (214) 350-6135.

Good Eats Cafe: If six kinds of mesquite-grilled chicken breast don't sound good to you, perhaps you'd like fajitas, tuna, salmon, chicken-fried steak, or even chicken-fried chicken. Eat on the patio. 4727 Frankford Road; (972) 447-0624.

Good Eats Grill: You'll meet lots of dogs at the outdoor patio, and there's a reason: They really do serve good eats here. Choose from mesquite-grilled chicken or fish, chicken-fried steak, or the wide selection of vegetables. The all-veggie plate is one of the top sellers. 3888 Oak Lawn; (214) 522-3287.

The Green Elephant: This restaurant is for dogs hungry enough to eat a you-know-what. You and your pooch will be served American food, burgers, and sandwiches (but no elephant) on the patio. 5612 Yale Boulevard; (214) 750-6625.

Jake's Old-Fashioned Hamburgers: Eat at one of the tables on the patio. 10226 Garland Road; (214) 319-6060.

La Petite Maison: "We have a very charming patio right out front where you can eat with your dog," the manager said. "That's very Parisian." She described the menu as French provincial: sandwiches, pasta, paté, duck's breast, filets, and other "simple" foods from the French countryside. Wear your beret and take your manners along, because this is a fine restaurant and you'll be right out front where everybody can see you. 2917 Fairmount Street; (214) 855-0700.

Lombardi's: Sit at one of the tables next to the fence and tie your pooch on the outside while you eat Italian food, seafood, steak, or chicken. You might even slip your friend a bite now and again. 311 North Market Street; (214) 747-0322.

LuLu's Bait Shack: Cajun-style seafood served on the patio will satisfy your pooch's desire for something different that doesn't come out of a sack and go "clunk" when it hits her food dish. 2621 McKinney Avenue; (214) 969-1927.

San Francisco Rose: Dining dogs must be tethered to the railing and remain outside the patio, but they won't feel left out. The wait staff and managers love dogs and will bring them water and tell them what good doggies they are and all that stuff you won't have time for while you're digging into burgers, nachos, salads, sandwiches, or the blue plate special. 3024 Greenville Avenue; (214) 826-2020.

Sonny Bryan's Smokehouse: Your pooch will love you forever for taking him to this Dallas dining institution for barbecue. Eat on the patio outside and, if your pooch becomes overly enthusiastic at the sight (and smell) of hearty portions of ribs and brisket, tie him to the fence around the patio and slip him a morsel every now and again. 302 North Market Street; (214) 744-1610.

Spaghetti Warehouse: You just might meet the manager's golden retriever as you have Italian food at one of the sidewalk tables on the former loading dock. 1815 North Market Street; (214) 651-8475.

Tony Roma's: Ribs are what this chain restaurant is famous for, but they also have soups, salads, sandwiches, chicken, and other dishes. Your pooch will be crushed if you order anything without a bone in it. Dine at the sidewalk tables. 310 North Market Street; (214) 748-6959.

PLACES TO STAY

Bed-and-Breakfast Texas Style: This reservation service represents properties all over Texas, some of which accept dogs. Rates start at $65. For information write to 4224 West Red Bird Lane, Dallas, TX 75237; (972) 298-8586 or (800) 899-4538.

Cedar Hill State Park: See Cedar Hill State Park on page 301 for camping information.

Crown Plaza Hotel: Room rates range from $79 to $185. This hotel charges pooches a $125 deposit at check-in and refunds $100 if there is no damage. 7800 Alpha Road, Dallas, TX 75240; (972) 233-7600 or (800) 922-9222.

Harvey Downtown Dallas Hotel: Pets may not be left unattended in rooms, which rent for $129 to $159. Dogs up to 25 pounds are accepted, but they must pay a $125 deposit, of which a hefty $100 is nonrefundable. 7050 Stemmons Freeway, Dallas, TX 75247; (214) 630-8500 or (800) 922-9222.

Harvey Hotel—Dallas: Pets may not be left unattended in rooms, which rent for $109 to $139. Dogs up to 25 pounds are accepted, but they must pay a $125 deposit, of which a hefty $100 is nonrefundable. 7815 LBJ Freeway, Dallas, TX 75251; (972) 960-7000 or (800) 922-9222.

Hawthorn Suites—Market Center Hotel: Rates are $125 to $159. Pooches under 50 pounds pay a onetime charge of $50. 7900 Brookriver

Drive, Dallas, TX 75247; (214) 688-1010 or (800) 527-1133.

Hotel Crescent Court: Rooms range from $195 to $1,550. (You read correctly: $1,550 per night.) There is a $50 fee for dogs. 400 Crescent Court, Dallas, TX 75201; (214) 871-3200.

La Quinta Inn—East: Rooms range from $67 to $73. Dogs under 25 pounds stay free. 8303 East R. L. Thornton Freeway, Dallas, TX 75228; (214) 324-3731 or (800) NU-ROOMS/687-6667.

The Mansion on Turtle Creek: Rooms are from $425 to $1,750. Dogs up to 30 pounds are welcome and cost $50 per visit. 2821 Turtle Creek Boulevard, Dallas, TX 75219; (214) 559-2100 or (800) 527-5432.

Radisson Hotel and Suites: Rooms are $129 to $159. There is a $50 deposit for dogs, of which $25 is refundable. 2330 West Northwest Highway, Dallas, TX 75220; (214) 351-4477 or (800) 333-3333.

Ramada Hotel at the Convention Center: Rooms are $150. 1011 South Akard Street, Dallas, TX 75215; (214) 421-1083 or (800) 527-7606.

Ramada Hotel—Market Center: Rooms are $59 to $99; dogs must leave a $75 deposit. 1055 Regal Row, Dallas, TX 75247; (214) 634-8550.

Residence Inn Marriott Hotel—Market Center: Suites are $120 to $160; dogs cost $50 extra. 6950 North Stemmons Freeway, Dallas, TX 75247; (214) 631-2472 or (800) 331-3131.

Residence Inn Marriott Hotel—North Central: Suites are $79 to $160. Dogs pay a onetime fee of $60. 13636 Goldmark Drive, Dallas, TX 75240; (972) 669-0478 or (800) 331-3131.

Renaissance Hotel—Dallas: Rates are $149 to $189. Dogs must weigh no more than 15 pounds. 2222 North Stemmons Freeway, Dallas, TX 75207; (214) 631-2222 or (800) 468-3571.

Sheraton—Dallas: Rates are $59 to $129. Dogs weighing 50 pounds or less pay a $150 deposit, which will be refunded upon checkout unless there is damage. 1241 West Mockingbird Lane, Dallas, TX 75247; (214) 630-7000.

FESTIVALS

St. Patrick's Day Parade: Irish wolfhounds, listen up! Have your person dye you green and you'll be the hit of the parade down Greenville Avenue on St. Paddy's Day. Or just come as you are, blend into the crowd, and hope someone drops a hot dog. The festivities take place in mid-March. For information, call (214) 368-6722.

DIVERSIONS

Git along, little dogies: The largest sculptural group in the world is this herd of 70 bronze steers and three cowboys plodding along what actually once was a cattle trail. ("Dogie" was the name given to orphan calves.) Dogs are noticeably absent—they had to remain home to guard the ranch. If your pooch is like Samantha and likes to bark at cows, he'll go stratospheric here. The sculpture is still growing; there may be even more cows when you visit. It's at Pioneer Plaza, at the corner of Young and Griffin Streets.

Go off the West End: The West End Historic District is rich in historical buildings, and its street life pulsates with old-fashioned street vendors, sidewalk cafes, and surrey service. There's no telling what adventures may befall you and your leashed pooch as you stroll along. The West End is on the west side of downtown along Market Street, Pacific Avenue, Woodall Rodgers Freeway, and McKinney Avenue and is near hotels, the convention center, and the West End Market Center. (214) 720-7107.

Go off the deep end: Deep Ellum is the center for Dallas folks who favor alternative lifestyles. (One such person we met told Sport and me that *we* were the ones with the alternative lifestyles.) If your pooch wants to watch you get your ears or some other (actually any other) body part pierced or tattooed, this is the place. Shops, restaurants, and clubs attract a clientele that makes for extremely interesting people-watching, especially after 10 P.M. Deep Ellum is located along Elm Street just east of downtown.

Go for broke: Even Dallas billionaire Ross Perot is afraid to take his dog shopping at PetsMart. There are just too many temptations, what with more than 700 kinds of dog food and hundreds of other things pooches can't bear to live without. Shop with your pooch, have her groomed, or take care of those neglected vaccinations at the veterinary clinic. As far as dogs are concerned, this place beats Wal-Mart paws down, even if billionaire founder Sam Walton did name his store brand of dog food after Ol' Roy, his favorite hunting dog. There are two PetsMart stores in Dallas: 13656 Preston Road (972-386-4791) and 6301 Abrams Road (214-349-9071).

Hold the cheese, please: The Swiss Avenue Historic District contains fine examples of Georgian, Spanish, Mediterranean, English Tudor, and Prairie School homes. Show your pooch where the rich dogs of yesteryear lived. The homes are on Swiss Avenue between Fitzhugh and La Vista Streets.

Take a sashay in a surrey: Dogs are welcome to share a surrey ride through the West End Historic District with members of their own party. Rides are about $30. Board at Market and Munger Streets in the West End. (214) 946-9911.

FORT WORTH

Fort Worth has a flavor distinctly different from Dallas, its mega-neighbor to the east. Dallas is upscale; Fort Worth is down-home. You might think that would mean Fort Worth would be a great place for a dog. If so, you've been reading too many 40-year-old issues of *The Saturday Evening Post* with Norman Rockwell covers. In Texas in general, the more sophisticated the town, the more friendly it is for dogs. Often it's in small-town rural Texas where dogs are merely tolerated and people who travel with dogs are regarded as a little odd, and Fort Worth clings doggedly to its small-town, cowtown heritage. When we called the Fort Worth Parks and Recreation Department and asked if any of the city parks had a leash-free area for dogs, the woman on the phone hooted and said, "In Fort Worth? You've got to be kidding." As for festivals, she said that Fort Worth has a policy of discouraging dogs at outdoor events.

Fort Worth has some good parks for dogs, even though the city's leash law applies everywhere. The best of the lot is the Fort Worth Nature Center and Refuge, which is just minutes from downtown.

PARKS, BEACHES, AND RECREATION AREAS

• **Boaz Park** 🐾 🐾½ *See* **⑫** *on page 299.*

The Fort Worth Parks and Recreation Department probably isn't particularly proud of Boaz Park, but it's great for a leashed dog looking for a scruffy, rugged spot right beside the road. The park lies mostly along creekbanks heavily overgrown with elm trees. Rutted turnouts bear testimony to periodic flooding. Beware of this park in wet weather. Some of those ruts looked like there might still be a car at the bottom of them.

The unkempt nature of much of the park is just the thing for the dog too long deprived of disgusting and/or dead things to sniff. When Sport found a dead opossum beside the road, I could almost hear her say, "Yessss! This is a park I can really get my teeth into." For you, the charm will be harder to find. There are a few picnic tables scattered about, but not much else. Just enjoy the good time your pooch is having.

From U.S. 377 South just north of Interstate 20, turn onto South Z. Boaz Park Drive. Closed from sunset to sunrise. (817) 871-5700.

• **Cobb Park** 🐾 🐾 🐾 *See* **⑬** *on page 299.*

This is a great city park for leashed dogs, but Sport and I had an experience here that took some of the shine off. As we drove around the park, we followed a road to a turnaround by an athletic field. Bounding across the grass toward us came a large black and white hound, wagging its tail, obviously abandoned and thinking its owner had come to pick it up. As it got closer, we could clearly see its ribs. This was a dog slowly starving. I looked at the sleek, well-fed, much-loved dog in the front seat beside me and knew I had to do something. I dug through our camping box and came up with a can of beans and franks. Seconds later the lost hound was having his first square meal in quite some time. He never even looked up as we drove off, feeling guilty for not being able to do more. Looking back, I think of that dog and know there must be many more like him, separated from their humans by choice or by chance. It is to those unknown, homeless dogs that this book is dedicated in hopes that someday all good dogs will have a good home.

Leashes are the rule here as in all Fort Worth parks, but that law seems to be ignored as often as the "right lane must turn right" signs. At the playground area we saw a mother dog and two pups—well fed, thank goodness—walking near the creek that runs north to south through the heavily wooded park. If your dog likes the water, drive south on Cobb Park Drive to the southern end of the park and park on the gravel at the intersection with the Redbud Trail. A few yards down the Redbud Trail is a low-water crossing where your pooch can cool off in the pool. I wouldn't recommend letting him drink the water, since one never knows what kind of chemicals can be in urban runoff. The park has lots of roaming area and a few picnic tables, but we found no water other than the creek. The only rest room facility was a chemical toilet at the playground.

The park is on U.S. 287 just southeast of downtown; exit Cobb Park Drive, which reaches the park in just a block. The park is closed from sunset to sunrise. (817) 871-5700.

• **Echo Lake Park** 🐾 *See* ⓮ *on page 299.*

Ordinarily a park with a lake right beside a freeway would rate pretty high, but we were put off by signs posted all around the small lake warning against fishing in it because of contamination. The grassy banks give easy access to the water, but I wouldn't let Sport so much as wet a whisker in there. The park is about equal parts parking lot, contaminated lake, and playground, but it does have rest rooms and lots of shaded picnic tables. Just don't go near the water unless it's to feed the large flock of ducks. Dogs must be on leash in all Fort Worth city parks; here it's a downright good idea.

From Interstate 35W, take Exit 47 (Ripy Road) and go north on the access road about half a mile to Echo Lake Park Drive and the entrance. The park is closed from sunset to sunrise. (817) 871-5700.

• **Forest Park** 🐾 🐾 *See* ⓯ *on page 299.*

Downtown Fort Worth parks somehow promise more than they deliver, and this one along the Clear Fork of the Trinity River is no exception. Leashed dogs will find lots of grass and large trees and open space along the river, and plenty of squirrels to eye diabolically, but there's just not much to do but walk around a bit, squat, and say, "Well, I guess that's it." There are no mini-jungles to explore, no paths winding through the bushes from which one may flush a raccoon or tiger. Too much space—for a dog's taste—is given over to picnic tables and zoos and botanical gardens and other stuff that dogs find boring not only because they are barred from entering. There is one place with easy access to the river here, under the railroad bridge at the north end of the park, and your pooch may enjoy a dip.

The park is at the intersection of South University Drive and Colonial Drive. It is closed from sunset to sunrise. (817) 871-5700.

• **Fort Worth Nature Center and Refuge** 🐾 🐾 🐾 ½ 🐾
   See 🔟 *on page 299.*

Try to imagine 3,500 acres of lakeside wilderness with 25 miles of hiking trails, all just minutes from downtown, where you and your leashed pooch can roam for free. Give up? Then go to the Fort Worth Nature Center and Refuge. It's real. The center is northwest of town on Lake Worth, and its prairies, marshes, and mixed hardwood forest remain much as they were when settlers first saw them. To help preserve the wilderness nature of the park, dogs must remain on leash and you must pick up after them. Other than that, your only responsibility is to have a good time.

Your first stop should be the Hardwicke Visitor Center, where you can pick up a trail map and discuss with one of the staff members what kinds of things you'd like to see, and how that might affect which trails you choose. Of the dozen trails, nine begin at the visitor center. The trails range in length from 775 feet to seven miles, with most being about two to three miles. Each trail is well marked with signposts using a different symbol for each trail. This is a good thing, since many of the trails intersect, and without the signposts you might find yourself endlessly looping about feeling like the guy stuck on the Boston subway in the Kingston Trio song "The MTA."

You and your pooch could meet a variety of wildlife on your walk, so keep a firm grip on the leash. The refuge is home to white-tailed deer, wild turkeys, bobcats, coyotes, red and gray foxes, raccoons, opossums, rabbits, and armadillos as well as a variety of birds. You can buy a bird list at the visitor center for a quarter. Be especially watchful of your pooch if you take the Prairie Trail, which passes by a 60-acre pen containing a small herd of not-so-small buffalo. "The buffalo don't like dogs—keep her away from the fence," workers warned.

Since the refuge borders the Trinity River and rises to the uplands surrounding it, the trails take you through a variety of habitats. Along the river, marshes predominate, and the Greer Island Trail crosses a levee to a forested island of about 50 acres, a former hill that was mostly submerged when the river was dammed to form Lake Worth. The Marsh Boardwalk Trail gives you a close-up view of a wetlands ecosystem. The Canyon Ridge Trail lives up to its name by climbing in and out of canyons. This scenic trail is three miles long one way and is the only hilly trail on the refuge.

While the trails provide hours of walking pleasure, Sport and I also enjoyed driving the roads of the refuge. We were there in mid-October, and many of the trees were shedding their leaves. On some stretches of road, a canopy of trees joined overhead and the breeze sent a golden rain of leaves down onto the pavement. We just had to get out and walk in the downpour.

If you want to learn as you walk, you and your leashed pooch are welcome to go on free guided walks held a couple of times a month. Call the visitor center for dates and details.

The refuge is four miles west of Interstate 820 on Highway 199; exit at the sign and follow the frontage road north about 50 yards to Buffalo Drive; turn right and follow the signs to the visitor center. Admission is free. The refuge is open from 9 A.M. to 5 P.M. Tuesday through Saturday and from noon to 5 P.M. on Sunday except from Memorial Day to Labor Day, when it opens weekdays at 7 A.M. It is closed on Monday. 9601 Fossil Ridge Road; (817) 237-1111.

• **Gateway Park** 🐾 🐾 *See* **17** *on page 299.*

Every city should have a park on a major highway at the edge of town for the dog who forgot to go before she left home, or who left home so long ago she can hardly remember whether she's a squatter or a hiker. Gateway Park fills that need for dogs entering Fort Worth from the east on Interstate 30. No more than 60 seconds will elapse between the time you spot the exit sign for Beach Street and your pooch freezes in the appropriate position with that look of intense relief on her or his face. Just slip the leash on before your dog bolts from the car.

The park is located along the West Fork of the Trinity River, which means that much of it is in the floodplain. That explains the large pecan trees common in the park. It also explains the partially demolished and trash-laden deck projecting over the river at the Riverbank Road picnic area. Sport and I had hoped to wet our paws in the water here, but a series of steps leading down the riverbank ended in midair about four feet above water level. Whether the river had taken the rest, or the builders never found the next page of the blueprints, or the construction money ran out we may never know. It was a bigger disappointment to Sport than to me, since she had a hankering for water and we found none anywhere else in the park.

There are a few picnic tables in the park, and a paved walking trail along the river, but other than a large complex of athletic fields with a few chemical toilets nearby, not much else.

From Interstate 30, exit on Beach Street and go north about half a mile to the park entrance, Gateway Park Drive. The park is closed from sunset to sunrise. (817) 871-5700.

• **Rockwood Park** 🐾½ *See ⑱ on page 299.*

A golf course hogs most of this park along the West Fork of the Trinity River, but there's a nice strip of grass and lots of trees between the golf course and the river. Leashed dogs can take a break here and perhaps sniff around the few picnic tables for lost goodies. More likely you'll have to let your pooch know that he is wasting his time trying to catch one of the many squirrels darting about. They seem to like to bury nuts on the greens and fairways of the golf course.

The park is at the corner of Highway 199 (Henderson Street) and Northwest 18th Street. It's closed from sunset to sunrise. (817) 871-5700.

• **Sycamore Park** 🐾🐾½ *See ⑲ on page 299.*

This park will delight even the leashed dog. Yes, leashes are the rule here, even though as we entered the park we met four tough-looking bruisers running loose. On closer examination two of them turned out to be obviously nursing females, so maybe we'd just stumbled into a canine kaffeeklatsch instead of a rumble. At any rate, the park is big enough that Sport and I left them to their pursuits and went on to another part of the park, where we took a stroll on a paved path winding along a flowing creek. The park is heavily wooded with large oak and pecan trees, and fascinating beards of brush skirt the creek and associated drainages, so there is plenty for pooches to explore. There's also a playground and water, but we found no rest rooms. The southern end of the park is taken up by the baseball stadium for nearby Texas Wesleyan University, so there's plenty of parking. The only negative we found was that because of ballpark traffic on game days, all the streets in the park are one way, making it a little inconvenient to get around. Take one wrong turn and you're out of the park.

From Interstate 30, exit on Beach Street and drive south to East Rosedale Street; turn right and go one block to the park entrance. The park is closed from sunset to sunrise. (817) 871-5700.

• **Trinity Park** 🐾🐾 *See ⑳ on page 299.*

For the pooch visiting the Cultural District or downtown who is in desperate need of dewatering, try this park that stretches nearly two miles along the Clear Fork of the Trinity River just west of downtown. It's crammed with large trees, hundreds of squirrels, a playground, picnic tables, and walking trails.

From Interstate 30, exit at University Drive and go north one block to the entrance. The park is closed from sunset to sunrise. (817) 871-5700.

RESTAURANTS

Coffee Haus: Five different coffees daily, hot chocolate, lattes, and desserts will get your heart pumping; saucer and blow at one of the sidewalk tables. 404 Houston Street; (817) 336-5282.

Houston Street Bakery: This downtown bakery serves up java and sweets all day and sandwiches for lunch. Eat at a sidewalk table. 201 Commerce Street; (817) 870-2895.

J & J Oyster Bar: Your pooch will have lots of canine company at the picnic tables out front. "We get lots of dogs, especially in the summer," the manager said. "We'll even bring them a bowl of water." But will giving your poor starving pooch a measly bowl of water be fair while you are eating oysters on the half shell, boiled shrimp, or fried fish? 612 University Drive; (817) 335-2756.

Jason's Deli: Two Fort Worth locations welcome you and your pooch for deli sandwiches. You'll be served at the tables in front at 5443 South Hulen Street; (817) 370-9187. You can eat at the sidewalk tables at 6244 Camp Bowie Boulevard; (817) 738-7144.

La Madeleine: The "casual French" menu here—served up at sidewalk tables—leans toward salads, soups, sandwiches, and quiche. 6140 Camp Bowie Boulevard; (817) 732-4656.

Marble Slab Creamery: Lap up your ice-cream confections at the sidewalk tables. 312 Houston Street; (817) 335-5877.

Papa John's Pizza: Have your pepperoni with extra cheese at one of the tables in front. 4900 Camp Bowie Boulevard; (817) 738-8100.

Ruffino's: Our informants recommend the lasagna and the veal chops at this very nice Italian restaurant where you and your pooch can eat on the patio. 2455 Forest Park Boulevard; (817) 923-0522.

Sardine's Ristorante Italiano: So your hound has been bugging you for Italian food? Specifically, *zuppa de pesce*? Bring her here, sit at a sidewalk table, and order a hearty portion of this house specialty: scallops, clams, sole, and redfish in a spicy tomato sauce. Or stick to more traditional favorites such as spaghetti or linguine. Dieting? They'll prepare low-calorie, low-fat, or vegetarian dishes on request. Don't be restricted by the menu. They boast that if they have the ingredients for what you want, they'll make it. 3410 Camp Bowie Boulevard; (817) 332-9937.

Spaghetti Warehouse: What could be more Italian than eating spaghetti with meat sauce or linguine with clam sauce at a sidewalk table? The view will be of the historic Stockyards area instead of the

Leaning Tower of Pisa, but dogs won't mind. 600 East Exchange Avenue; (817) 625-4171.

Starbucks Coffee: Get your caffeine and sugar while your pooch sips a complimentary bowl of water. Some Starbucks locations have special dog bowls; here you'll have to settle for whatever the manager can rustle up. She brings her own dog here. 6115 Camp Bowie Boulevard; (817) 735-1580.

TCBY Yogurt: The secret is out. Dogs supposedly out walking their owners to help them lose weight somehow manage to end up having a vanilla cone at one of the tables in front. "We have a lot of regular customers who are dogs," the manager said. 6008 Camp Bowie Boulevard; (817) 738-7306.

Tommy's Hamburgers: Stroll around Stockyards Station, a collection of shops and restaurants, to work up an appetite, then stop in for a burger on the covered patio. 140 East Exchange Avenue; (817) 625-6654.

Whataburger: Have a burger at a sidewalk table. 400 Houston Street; (817) 332-1578.

Whiskers Catfish and Oyster Bar: Dine on seafood on the covered patio in Stockyards Station. 140 East Exchange Avenue; (817) 625-1070.

PLACES TO STAY

Holiday Inn South: Rooms are $85. Small dogs are allowed; owners are responsible for any damage. "We do have a policy that a $20 deposit is required, but that's not rigidly enforced," the manager said. "We look at the dog and decide." 100 Alta Mesa Boulevard East, Fort Worth, TX 76134; (817) 293-3088 or (800) 465-4329.

La Quinta Inn—Northeast: Rooms are $74 to $79. Dogs under 25 pounds stay free. 7920 Bedford-Euless Road, Fort Worth, TX 76180; (817) 485-2750 or (800) NU-ROOMS/687-6667.

La Quinta Inn—West: Rooms are $74 to $79. Dogs under 25 pounds stay free. 7888 Interstate 30, Fort Worth, TX 76108; (817) 246-5511 or (800) NU-ROOMS/687-6667.

Ramada Inn Fort Worth Downtown: Rooms are $93 to $113. Dogs under 10 pounds are welcome. 1701 Commerce Street, Fort Worth, TX 76102; (817) 335-7000 or (800) 272-6232.

Ramada Inn Midtown: Rooms are $72. Dogs stay for $10 each. 1401 South University Drive, Fort Worth, TX 76107; (817) 336-9311 or (800) 336-3000.

Residence Inn by Marriott: Rooms are $83 to $125. Dogs pay $5 each per night for up to six nights; for seven or more nights, there is a one-time fee of $60 per dog. 1701 South University Drive, Fort Worth, TX 76107; (817) 870-1011 or (800) 331-3131.

DIVERSIONS

Boogie with the buffalo: You and your leashed pooch can take part in either the 10K Buffalo Boogie or a two-mile fun walk at the Fort Worth Nature Center and Refuge in mid-April. 9601 Fossil Ridge Road, Fort Worth, TX 76135; (817) 237-1111.

Shop with your sheltie: Your dog's nose is his primary way of learning about the world around him, and boy, can he get a noseful (and a graduate degree in consumer economics) at PetsMart, the store where dogs shop right alongside their people. Whether you need a new leash, a comfy bed filled with cedar chips, or just a bag of industrial-strength rawhide chews to save your new Italian-made loafers, PetsMart has it. Fort Worth has three stores: 1300 Green Oaks Road (817-377-8676), 4800 Southwest Loop 820 (817-731-4353), and 8350 East Freeway Boulevard (817-460-2772).

Track the long twin silver line: You and your pooch can howl old Bob Seeger and the Silver Bullet songs as you ride the Forest Park Train. Dogs are welcome as long as they are leashed and don't try to jump out. People pay $3; dogs ride free. The train is in Forest Park at South University Drive and Colonial Drive. (817) 336-3328.

BOSQUE COUNTY

LAGUNA PARK

PARKS, BEACHES, AND RECREATION AREAS

• **Lake Whitney** 🐾 🐾 *See* ㉑ *on page 298.*

The U.S. Army Corps of Engineers maintains 10 campgrounds around the lake. Dogs are required to be on leash. The Soldier's Bluff Park Campground at the western end of the dam in Laguna Park is a rare jewel among Corps of Engineers facilities, which generally look like they were designed by someone with a bad toothache. About 15 very large campsites lurk in the shade of a sprawling live oak grove. Each has a picnic table, barbecue grill, and lantern post. There's lots of room for a pooch to roam, and the lake is just a few yards away. When we last visited in mid-October, there was no entrance fee and no camping fee, but as soon as electricity is installed the rates will be $16 for sites with water and electricity and $12 for sites with water only. Currently camping is first come, first served, but that may change in the near future; call ahead.

Headquarters for the lake, where you can obtain a map of the lake and the campgrounds, is on Highway 22 half a mile north of Laguna Park. Parks are closed from 10 P.M. to 6 A.M. except to overnight guests.

For more information write P.O. Box 5038, Laguna Park, TX 76634; (254) 694-3189.

PLACES TO STAY

Lake Whitney: See Lake Whitney on page 320 for camping information.

MERIDIAN

PARKS, BEACHES, AND RECREATION AREAS

• **Meridian State Park** 🐾 🐾 *See ㉒ on page 298.*

This park is tiny for a state park—only 502 acres—but it seems bigger than that. Part of the reason is a park road that loops, winds, twists, turns, and climbs around the small lake in the center of the park. The other reason is the dense forest of oak and juniper trees that prevents you from seeing more than a few feet. Leashed dogs will think they are in the deep, dark woods. In fact, we saw more dogs here for the number of campsites than at any other state park. We spotted four dogs among the 29 campsites, all properly chained and lounging by the campfire on a cool October morning. This is a good place for a dog to lead a dog's life.

Four trails totaling about five miles take you all the way around the lake and into a large undeveloped section where endangered golden-cheeked warblers may be observed during the nesting season from mid-March until early July. If you have been hankering to notch your binoculars for this species, this park may be the place to do it. A heavy cover of oak and juniper trees growing on steep hillsides forms prime habitat for these migratory neotropical birds. You'll find the trails on the park map you get when you check in. The Shinnery Ridge Trail, a 1.7-mile loop, is an easy walking, paved trail that is also suitable for wheelchairs. It traverses a high ridge above the lake that is good golden-cheeked warbler habitat. The information board at the trailhead was of special interest to me, since it holds a number of metal signs that I helped make some 25 years ago. I'd always wondered what happened to them and proudly tried to point them out to Sport, but she was more interested in the pair of squirrels holding drag races in the road.

If you are looking for a day-use park to go picnicking, this place would not be a good choice. The picnic area is at lakeside, and it does have a playground, but there are only a handful of tables and space is limited.

Camping, on the other hand, is this park's strong suit. The only drawback—or, perhaps, the chief advantage—is the small number of sites. There are six tent sites with no water in the area ($6), and these are some of the most appealing. They sit beside the lake and are located far away from the rest of the park facilities. Park personnel expect your pooch to stay out of the lake despite the fact that the only designated swimming area—where state regulations forbid dogs—is at the playground. The eight tent sites with water nearby go for $8. Seven back-in multiuse sites with water and electricity are $11, and eight pull-through sites are $12. There are also 11 lakeside screened shelters that rent for $20, but your pooch is banned from these and may not be left tied outside.

Reservations for campsites at all state parks must be made by calling the central reservation number, (512) 389-8900, between 9 A.M. and 6 P.M. Monday through Friday. Reservations are strongly recommended, and a deposit is required in order to guarantee a reservation. Specific sites may not be reserved; they are available on a first-come, first-served basis upon arrival. The standard state park regulations for dogs apply. They must be kept on a six-foot leash and may not be left unattended. Dogs may not enter any park building.

The park is two miles west of Meridian on Highway 22. It closes at 10 P.M. except to overnight guests. The park office is open from 8 A.M. to 5 P.M. except on summer Fridays, when it remains open until 10 P.M. The entry fee is $2 per person. There is no gate; late arrivals may register for camping at a self-pay station at park headquarters. (254) 435-2536.

PLACES TO STAY

Meridian State Park: See Meridian State Park on page 321 for camping information.

COLLIN COUNTY

LAVON

PARKS, BEACHES, AND RECREATION AREAS

• **Lavon Lake** 🐾🐾 *See ㉓ on page 298.*

The U.S. Army Corps of Engineers operates 16 parks around this 21,000-acre lake. As is typical of Corps of Engineers parks, they are small, but all have access to the water. Dogs must be leashed in all the parks and in the water. However, the primitive nature of many of the parks, particularly those that have a boat ramp and a chemical toilet as their only facilities, means that you and your pooch will probably be able to enjoy them by yourselves.

Several of the parks offer primitive camping ($7). Lavonia Park has 38 sites with water and electricity ($15) and 15 tent sites ($9). From Highway 78 in Lavon, follow the signs one mile west to the park. East Fork Park has 50 sites with water and electricity ($15). From Wylie, go east on

Highway 78 three miles; turn left at the sign and follow the signs three miles to the park. Parks are closed from 10 P.M. to 6 A.M. except to overnight guests. For information and a map, write to 3375 Skyview Drive, Wylie, TX 75098; (972) 442-3014.

PLACES TO STAY

Lavon Lake: See Lavon Lake on page 322 for camping information.

MᶜKINNEY

McKinney is one of those places where nothing big ever happened but lots of little things did. That's what makes it interesting. You'll be interested to know that Jesse James and his gang hid out in McKinney when things got too hot for them elsewhere. The house standing at 616 West Virginia Street belonged to a cousin of the James brothers, and they stayed here a number of times. Your dog will be more interested in the house at 1104 South Tennessee Street, which played the haunted house in one of the all-time best dog movies ever made, *Benji*. (At least Sport and Samantha thought it was good. They like happy endings, and when I start howling at the end of *Old Yeller,* so do they.)

Your dog must remain on leash here, but there are so many things for them to do with you they'll hardly notice. In fact, special events centered around dogs were being planned by the Downtown McKinney Association as this book was being written.

PARKS, BEACHES, AND RECREATION AREAS

• **Erwin Park** 🐾 🐾 ½ *See* ㉔ *on page 298.*

This 212-acre park has just about everything a dog could ask for: wooded areas, open spaces, walking trails, and ponds. For you, there's a picnic area, rest rooms, and a playground.

The park is at 4300 County Road 1005. Hours are 7 A.M. to 10 P.M. (972) 542-2676.

• **Towne Lake Park** 🐾 🐾 ½ *See* ㉕ *on page 298.*

The first thing we saw when we pulled into this 108-acre park right on U.S. 75 was a leashed beagle joyfully leading his owner along the 1.2-mile paved jogging path, which is lighted for night use. (This latter fact was of special interest to Sport Dog, who knows that raccoons come out at night.) The trail circles a 22-acre lake ringed with picnic tables and barbecue grills. There's also a playground and fishing dock, paddleboats for rent, and pecan trees to provide plenty of shade and venues for leg-hiking exercises. The resident geese honk and flap their wings at any dog who approaches too close, as Sport found out. She only wanted to be friendly.

The park is at U.S. 75 and Parkview Drive. Hours are 7 A.M. to 10 P.M. (972) 542-2676.

RESTAURANTS

El Chico: Eat Tex-Mex at the bench out front. This chain restaurant claims to have started the Tex-Mex craze, though lots of folks will challenge that. 1222 North Central Expressway; (972) 548-7526.

Herby's Soda Fountain: Wash down your cheeseburger or chicken salad sandwich with a creamy milkshake at one of the sidewalk tables. 210 North Tennessee Street; (972) 548-7632.

Sonny Bryan's Smokehouse: You'll feel like you're back in grade school as you eat your barbecue in one of the old school desks out front, but school lunches were never like this. 318 North Central Expressway; (972) 562-5484.

PLACES TO STAY

Comfort Inn: Rooms are $49 to $62. Dogs under 25 pounds stay free. 2104 North Central Expressway, McKinney, TX 75070; (972) 548-8888 or (800) 221-2222.

Lighthouse RV Resort: Rates are $22 to $24 for full hookups. Tent sites are $15. There's a dog walking area for leashed pooches; owners are expected to take care of any needed cleanup. The resort is at U.S. 75 and Highway 121. P.O. Box 350, Melissa, TX 75454; (972) 838-4600 or (800) 844-2196.

FESTIVALS

HarvestFest on the Square: Held the first Saturday in October, this street fair features arts and crafts, food, and live entertainment on the courthouse square at Louisiana and Kentucky Streets. For information, call (972) 542-0163.

Mayfair on the Square: The same zany folks who bring you the offbeat activities of the Downtown McKinney Association (see Diversions below) enlist the aid of crafters, antique dealers, food purveyors, and musicians to welcome spring to North Texas the third Saturday in May. The street fair takes place around the courthouse square at Louisiana and Kentucky Streets. For information, call (972) 542-0163.

DIVERSIONS

Bark if you like art: Puff out those chests with pride, pooches. The first work of public art commissioned to decorate a downtown wall features (Ta-daaa) a dog. Painted by local artist Jake Dobscha in 1994, the approximately 30-foot-wide by 20-foot-tall mural depicts a hunter and his redbone hound at the end of a day afield. It's a little tricky to find, though, since it's at the corner of a one-way street and a one-way alley, and most people sail right on past without ever seeing it. To be sure you don't miss it, go west on Virginia Street from the courthouse square; the second street from the square is Wood Street, which is actually an alley. The mural is on the west-facing wall of the building at the corner of Virginia and Wood Streets. The best thing to do is park and walk into the alley.

Be a ninny in McKinney: Actually, you can be anything you want to be in McKinney, thanks to the free-wheeling atmosphere generated by the Downtown McKinney Association, a group of crazy people masquerading as owners of shops around the courthouse square. In most Texas towns Halloween comes but once a year. Downtown McKinney merchants play dress-up nearly every weekend. You and your leashed pooch may stumble into such semiorganized silliness as the Raucous Caucus (held before election day), the World's Largest Snipe Hunt, James Bond Day, Texas Heroes Day, a '50s party, or a celebration relating to some generally recognized holiday, none of which is allowed to pass unmolested. When we last checked, they were even thinking about adding some sort of dogfoolery just for pooches. There's music, window decorations, contests, and costumes geared to each week's theme, so your pooch will never be bored by a repetition of something he's seen before.

Everything happens around the courthouse square downtown. For the skinny on what's going down in McKinney this weekend, call (972) 542-0163.

PLANO

PLACES TO STAY

Harvey Hotel—Plano: Pets may not be left unattended in rooms, which rent for $115 to $159 nightly. Dogs up to 25 pounds are accepted, but they must pay a $125 deposit, of which a hefty $100 is nonrefundable. 1600 North Central Expressway, Plano, TX 75074; (972) 578-8555 or (800) 922-9222.

Spring Creek Village RV Park and Campground: Only RV sites are available; they rent for $20. Dogs must stay inside. 29-A Rose Lane, Plano, TX 75074; (972) 423-6704.

DIVERSIONS

Get a new leash on life: Don't be bored in Plano—go shopping! PetsMart has everything your dog ever dreamed of and more. Not only that, she can prance proudly into the store and shop right along with you. Maybe you can even teach her to push the shopping cart. 3115 West Parker Road; (972) 867-5626.

DALLAS COUNTY

ADDISON

PLACES TO STAY

Hampton Inn: Rooms are $57 to $78. Small dogs only may stay here. 4555 Beltway Drive, Addison, TX 75244: (972) 991-2800.

Harvey Hotel: Pets may not be left unattended in rooms, which rent for $140 to $185. Dogs up to 25 pounds are accepted, but they must pay a $125 deposit, of which $100 is refundable. 14315 Midway Road, Dallas, TX 75244; (972) 980-8877 or (800) 922-9222.

Homewood Suites: Apartment-style suites with kitchenettes are $107 to $172; your pooch will pay $50 extra. 4451 Belt Line Road, Addison, TX 75244; (972) 788-1342 or (800) 225-5466.

Motel 6: Rooms are $48. All Motel 6s allow one small pooch per room. 4325 Belt Line Road, Addison, TX 75244; (972) 386-4577.

GARLAND

PARKS, BEACHES, AND RECREATION AREAS

• **Woodland Basin** 🐾 *See ㉖ on page 298.*

Jones Park stretches along the western side of Lake Ray Hubbard, but much of it is inaccessible by land. This little pocket of perhaps 50 acres is a tangle of weeds and trees with a quarter-mile boardwalk nature trail. Leashed dogs and their owners can learn the names of some native trees from signs along the path. When we last visited, the path was suffering from lack of maintenance, but it gave us a welcome opportunity to get out of the car and stretch our legs. It will do the same for you.

The park is at 18000 East Miller Road; park at the west end of the bridge. It's closed from midnight to 6 A.M. (972) 205-2750.

RESTAURANTS

Sonic Drive-In: This branch of the national chain allows you and your pooch to have a burger and fries at an outside table. 1210 West Miller Road; (972) 278-1224.

GRAND PRAIRIE

PARKS, BEACHES, AND RECREATION AREAS

• **Mountain Creek Lake Park** 🐾🐾 *See ㉗ on page 299.*

You've heard of split-level houses (at least, if you were alive during the '60s you have). This 750-acre park is a split-level, too. Its different parts have different characters. The northern part, on the western shore of Mountain Creek Lake, is a manicured urban park with golf course, playground, acres of mowed grass, scattered mesquite trees, and a paved jogging trail with exercise stations periodically placed along its one-mile length—the Mountain Fitness Trail. We didn't see any joggers (or mountains, either) on our last visit, but there were two unleashed mixed-breed dogs hanging about (despite the fact dogs are supposed to be leashed) and two women on horseback. A woman and her chow were the only users of the jogging trail. There is easy access to the lake, but the signs warning not to eat the fish because of contaminated water persuaded us not to go for a sip or a dip. This northern part of the park is at the intersection of Lakeview Drive and Hardy Road, off Southeast 14th Street about 1.2 miles north of F.M. 1382.

The southern part of the park has a totally different character. Soccer fields take up most of it, and when we were there last on a Saturday morning, peewee soccer was in full swing. It's a great place to watch kids play, if that's your thing. However, dogs like Sport prefer to nose around in brush and trash piles, and both are to be found here under the power transmission line on the north side. Follow the dirt track underneath the transmission line to a weedy, unkempt part of the park with an illegal dump along a boggy slough. Again, signs warn against eating fish from these waters, so we kept our distance. At the southern end of the soccer field is a small shaded, well-kept picnic area. Rest rooms and water are available at the soccer fields.

The park is on F.M. 1382 about 0.8 miles north of Interstate 20. Hours are 6 A.M. until midnight. (972) 237-8100.

PLACES TO STAY

Traders Village RV Park: Sites are $16 to $20. Dogs must be leashed at all times and are not allowed in any buildings or the swimming pool area. Dogs must be walked in the designated area; owners must clean up after their pets in other areas should the need arise. Dogs may not be left unattended at any time or left outside at night, and noisy dogs will be asked to leave immediately. Grrrr. 2602 Mayfield Road, Grand Prairie, TX 75052; (972) 647-8205.

IRVING

PARKS, BEACHES, AND RECREATION AREAS

• **California Crossing Park** 🐾 1/2 *See* 28 *on page 299.*

This small park near Las Colinas has lots of squirrels roaming a well-tended lawn shaded by large oak trees—just the place for a leashed pooch to take a break. There's also a National Guard armory with a couple of tanks out front if your pooch fancies military things. Watching *Patton* too many times can do strange things to a dog.

The park is at the corner of Luna Road and California Crossing. Hours are from dawn to dusk. (972) 721-2501.

• North Lake Park 🐾🐾½ *See ㉙ on page 299.*

Sport and Samantha have a passion for barking at things that fly. Anything the size of a buzzard or bigger begs to be barked at, including airplanes. I suppose planes are just another big bird to them. (Or perhaps they look at them the same way as the cannibal mother explaining airplanes to her child: It's like lobster—hard on the outside but very tasty on the inside.) If your pooch shares this fixation on flight, he'll love this park of about 600 acres just north of Dallas–Fort Worth International Airport. The flight path for planes taking off and landing from this, the world's busiest airport, is just west of the park, and a steady stream of 727s, 747s, and L1011s parades past. Even better, there's a wind farm just to the south with three giant windmills turning lazily in the breeze, and if that doesn't get your pooch excited, nothing will.

If the location of the park near an airport gave you a clue to the fact that it is pretty flat, congratulations. You're really paying attention. You get a treat and a pat on the head. Vast expanses of mowed grass stretch between scattered mesquite trees. Picnic tables with barbecue grills also dot the landscape. Your leashed pooch can get to the water easily almost any place around the lake—it's flat, remember?

Not long after entering the park, we began to suspect that most of the budget had been spent on signs, and when we went in search of the 1.5-mile hiking trail promised by one sign, our suspicions were confirmed. We could find no trail. Either all the money got spent on signs, or one of several locked gates prevented us from reaching the trailhead. But no matter. You and your pooch can walk almost anywhere in the park.

The park is at 13300 Belt Line Road, just north of Interstate 635. It is closed from one hour after sunset to 6:30 A.M. according to one of the many signs we saw, but several access gates to the park were locked at mid-morning the day we visited. (972) 721-2501.

RESTAURANTS

The Black-Eyed Pea: Order your Southern home-style cooking to go and eat on the bench out front. 3601 Belt Line Road; (972) 255-0563.

Southern Recipe: Dogs eat here all the time, the manager said. Take your pooch and join the regulars at the picnic tables on the patio. The menu lives up to the name: chicken-fried steak, chicken-fried chicken, pot roast, meat loaf, sandwiches, and burgers. 2101 West Rochelle Street; (972) 252-2003.

Texas Bar and Grill: Your pooch will think he's in Venice when you take him to eat on the outdoor patio here. It overlooks the Mandalay Canal in the Las Colinas development. The menu includes everything from steaks to pasta. 220 East Las Colinas Boulevard; (972) 869-2007.

PLACES TO STAY

Drury Inn: Small dogs are welcome as long as their traveling companions don't leave them unattended in rooms. Rates are $95, which includes breakfast. 4210 West Airport Freeway, Irving, TX 75062; (972) 986-1200 or (800) 325-8300.

Four Seasons Resort and Club: This is an extremely posh hotel where you and your pooch will both be pampered, for a price. Rates are $295 to $340; guests may use the golf course, tennis courts, health club, and other facilities. Leashed dogs up to 30 pounds are welcome. 4150 North MacArthur Boulevard, Irving, TX 75038; (972) 717-0700 or (800) 332-3442.

Hampton Inn: Bring your dog if she's under 20 pounds; otherwise call ahead to check with the manager. Rooms are $75 to $90. Dog owners are responsible for any damages. 4340 West Airport Freeway, Irving, TX 75062; (972) 986-3606 or (800) 325-8300.

Harvey Hotel—DFW: Dogs may not be left unattended in rooms, which rent for $159 to $195. Dogs up to 50 pounds are accepted, but they must pay a $125 deposit, of which $100 is refundable. 4545 West John Carpenter Freeway, Irving, TX 75063; (972) 929-4500 or (800) 922-9222.

Harvey Suites—DFW: Pets may not be left unattended in rooms, which rent for $139 to $190. Dogs up to 50 pounds are accepted with a $125 deposit, of which $100 is refundable. 4550 West John Carpenter Freeway, Irving, TX 75063; (972) 929-4499 or (800) 922-9222.

Homewood Suites: Rates are $124 to $184; dogs are $50 extra. 4300 Wingren Drive, Irving, TX 75039; (972) 556-0665.

Motel 6: Rooms are $39. All Motel 6s allow one small pooch per room. 510 Loop 12 South, Irving, TX 75060; (972) 438-4227.

Red Roof Inn—DFW North: Rates are $59 to $64. Small dogs only may share your room. 8150 Esters Boulevard, Irving, TX 75063; (972) 929-0020 or (800) 843-7663.

Red Roof Inn—DFW South: Rates are $50 to $65. All dogs are welcome. 2611 West Airport Freeway, Irving, TX 75062; (972) 570-7500 or (800) 843-7663.

Sheraton Grand Hotel: Rates are $145 to $175. Small dogs are allowed for a $25 fee. 4440 West John Carpenter Freeway, Irving, TX 75063; (972) 929-8400 or (800) 345-5251.

DIVERSIONS

Go for a gallop: The nine bronze mustangs splashing through a pond surrounded by a granite plaza form not only the world's largest equestrian sculpture but also a sight sure to amaze even your jaded jet-set pooch. Dogs might even be able to sneak a dunk and a drink. The Mustangs of Las Colinas are at Williams Square, 5205 North O'Connor Boulevard; (972) 869-9047.

Charge like the Light Brigade: Whip out that credit card and brandish it high as you and your pooch storm through the doors of PetsMart and into the Valley of 600 (actually, make that 720) Kinds of Dog Food. If your pooch can't find what she wants here, she can probably get along without it. But she'll still want to go shopping with you at a store where dogs are not only welcome, they're positively worshipped. After all, at this store, dogs are at the top of the food chain. 4005 West Airport Freeway; (972) 255-0027.

DENTON COUNTY

AUBREY

PLACES TO STAY

The Guest House Bed-and-Breakfast: This two-bedroom cottage with a fenced yard rents for $85. You must leave a $150 deposit for the pleasure of bringing your furred friend. Dogs must be in a pet carrier when left behind in a room. 5408 Highway 377 South, Aubrey, TX 76227; (940) 440-2076.

CARROLLTON

PLACES TO STAY

Sandy Lake RV and Mobile Home Lodge: RV sites are $15 to $22; tent sites are $12. Dogs must be leashed at all times and may not be left outside. Owners must clean up after their dogs should an accident occur off the designated dog walk. Noisy dogs are not permitted. Unattended dogs will be impounded at the owner's expense. 1915 Sandy Lake Road, Carrollton, TX 75006; (972) 242-6808.

THE COLONY

PARKS, BEACHES, AND RECREATION AREAS

• **Hidden Cove Park** 🐾🐾🐾 *See* **30** *on page 298.*

Dogs must be kept on a six-foot leash here, but with 720 acres of land next to a 29,700-acre lake to explore, even fettered pooches manage to survive quite nicely. The park is located on a large promontory jutting into the lake, and its gentle slopes and thick groves of mesquite trees are a welcome relief from the miles of table-flat cotton fields one passes on the way. A day-use area has shaded picnic tables and barbecue grills scattered among mesquite trees overlooking the lake, and there's plenty of room for Rover to rove.

A three-mile hiking trail begins at a turnaround at the west end of the park (past campsites 29 and 30). The mowed dirt path winds across a not particularly interesting mesquite flat to the lakeshore. Primitive backpack camping ($5) is available along the trail.

The park has 50 multiuse campsites ($16), each with a shaded picnic table, barbecue grill, fire ring, water, and electricity. Rest rooms with showers are nearby. The campsites range from totally exposed with close neighbors to fairly secluded sites located among elm trees on the lake. If the park is not busy, you may be able to choose your site. Reservations are accepted (though not for a particular site).

Most of the 38 screened shelters ($28) have a view of the lake; many are just feet from the water at normal lake levels. Each also has a fire ring, barbecue grill, picnic table, electrical outlet, interior light, water, and lantern post. Rest rooms with showers serve each area. Those numbered in the 50s were personal favorites: nicely shaded by trees, they also offered a view of the lake. Unlike the screened shelters at state parks (which this used to be before the city took it over), your pooch is allowed to stay with you inside the shelters. In fact, the park superintendent told me the only building dogs are not allowed to enter is the group dining hall, where food is prepared. So live it up, inside dogs! This park will let your person treat you just like you're at home. Get off the bed!

The park is off F.M. 423 north of The Colony. Turn west onto Hackberry Road and follow its twisting progress 2.3 miles to the park. Signs mark the way. Entry fee is $5 per car. The park is open from 8 A.M. until 10 P.M. (972) 294-1155.

RESTAURANTS

Taco Bueno: You and your leashed pooch can wolf down your enchiladas on the patio right out front. 4904 Main Street; (972) 625-4101.

PLACES TO STAY

Hidden Cove Park: See Hidden Cove Park on page 330 for camping information.

DENTON

Small towns in Texas as a rule offer limited opportunities for having fun with your dog. Denton is the exception that proves that rule. Here you'll find not only a great urban park but also one of the best state parks for dogs. Plus, you and your leashed pooch will not only be welcome at one of the best events for dogs held anywhere, you'll be the star attractions. Denton's Dog Days of Summer puts pooches on a pedestal each June. Hundreds of dogs converge on the courthouse square for a festival at which every booth and event caters to canines.

PARKS, BEACHES, AND RECREATION AREAS

• **North Lakes Park** 🐾 🐾 ½ *See* ❸❶ *on page 298.*

By any standard, this park's 350 acres qualify it to be called a large urban park. While it has the usual assortment of athletic fields, playgrounds, picnic areas, and a pool, it has something else most urban parks don't: huge open expanses where a leashed dog can cavort. And while the overwhelming impression this park gives is one of neatly mowed grass and few trees, there are weedy drainage basins to explore, especially in the southern half. In the spring you and your pooch will both enjoy the wildflower prairie on the park's north side, you for its display of flowers and your pooch because the 50 or so acres of unmowed field make an ideal place for small, furry critters to hide. A walking trail winds through the wildflower prairie, and while we saw one bulldog and two English sheepdogs and their owners making happy tracks there, several other people and their dogs preferred walking the length of an earthen embankment running the width of the park, parallel to a paved walking trail. In short, no matter what your taste in trails, there's something here for you. Okay, so your pooch is in training to climb Mount Everest and was hoping to work on her high-altitude acclimatization. Sorry, you're in the wrong state.

The park is on both sides of Windsor Drive from Hinkle Drive to Bonnie Brae Drive in northwest Denton. From U.S. 380, go north on Hinkle Drive to Windsor Drive. The park is closed from 10 P.M. to 8 A.M. (940) 566-8270.

• **Ray Roberts Lake State Park—Isle du Bois Unit** 🐾 🐾 🐾 ½
See ❸❷ *on page 298.*

Warning: Bring your pooch here and she may never want to leave, even though she must remain on a six-foot leash. This is a dog's park, with sandy soil, beaucoup trees, and miles of hiking trails, all enveloped by 11 miles of shoreline, much of it easily accessible from campsites.

The Isle du Bois unit contains 1,397 of the park's 4,000 acres. Post oak trees are dominant, although you will find a fragrant pine from time to time. The only part of the park not heavily covered in trees is the day-use area. Many of its 192 picnic sites have shade shelters; all have barbecue grills. Water and rest rooms are available. There's also a playground for the kids and a swim beach, although dogs are banned from the beach.

There are plenty of other places for a leashed pooch to wet her paws, however. One of the best is in the Quail Run Camp, where a parking lot on the north side fronts the water. There's a great view of the lake, and the bank slopes gently down to the water.

Pick up a trail guide at park headquarters if you and your pooch want to do some serious walking. I wouldn't call it hiking; the terrain is too gentle for that. But with 4.5 miles of paved trails winding through the camping areas, and another 12 miles of dirt trails connecting the spread-out units of the park, you can rack up some miles. Sport and I much preferred the dirt trails, even though they must be shared with bike and horse riders. The loose dirt of the trail is easy on a pooch's paws, and there are always those periodic piles of pungent horse apples to be sniffed and wondered at—perhaps even marked. And should you meet a horse on the trail, well, it's always good for a big dog like Sport to see that there are four-legged critters even bigger than she is.

The camping here is among the best at any Texas state park. The amazing thing was that virtually every site was a good one. The 98 regular sites with water and electricity go for $12, and a select 17 waterfront campsites rent for $15. Sites with water only are $9. The Hawthorn and Wild Plum walk-in camping areas (55 sites total; $9) offer more privacy than the drive-in areas, and it's not a long walk to any campsite. However, while these camps have water and composting toilets, they are not served by a rest room with showers. Sport and I still liked them, because many of the campsites are just a few feet from the water, and mowed paths to the shore make bank fishing easy.

The Bluestem Grove Camp is designated for equestrian use (14 campsites; $9). Its large parking lot was littered with fascinating reminders of equine digestive processes when Sport and I last visited. We used the parking lot as a jumping-off place for two of the trails, the Jordan Park Trail and the Elm Fork Trail. These dirt trails wind along the lakeshore through heavy groves of post oak trees.

The Deer Ridge and Quail Run Camps ($12) cater to RVers and folks who need electricity as well as water. In keeping with their more developed character, these spots have rest rooms with showers. A paved walking trail connects them with each other and with the day-use area.

One of the things we appreciated most about this state park was that here we found something we hadn't seen at any other park. The headquarters has a notebook with maps of all the camping areas and a site-by-site list of every campsite, which tells, among other things, the degree to which each site is shaded. Leafing through the notebook is a good way to pick a campsite that meets your minimum requirements—say, near the water, in heavy shade, and not on the direct route between all the other campsites and the rest room. It's something we'd like to see at other state parks.

Since this is a state park, dogs must not only remain on leash at all times, they are also banned from entering any park building. They may not be left outside at night, nor may they be left unattended at any time.

Reservations for campsites at all state parks must be made by calling the central reservation number, (512) 389-8900, between 9 A.M. and 6 P.M. Monday through Friday. Reservations are strongly recommended, and a deposit is required in order to guarantee a reservation. Specific sites may not be reserved; they are available on a first-come, first-served basis upon arrival.

The park is located on F.M. 455 four miles west of its intersection with U.S. 377 (10 miles east of Interstate 35). Entry is $3 per person. The park office is open from 8 A.M. to 5 P.M. The park closes at 10 P.M. except to overnight guests. (940) 686-2148.

RESTAURANTS

Applebee's: Share a salad, fajitas, smothered chicken, steak, or pork riblets with your dog on the bench out front. 707 South Interstate 35 East; (940) 591-9353.

The Black-Eyed Pea: Southern-style home cooking heavy on the vegetables is what you and your pooch will share on the benches out front. 2420 Interstate 35 East; (940) 320-4140.

Giuseppe's Italian Restaurant: In addition to the usual seafood and pasta dishes, this restaurant in a charming two-story Victorian house specializes in northern Italian dishes with French-influenced sauces. You'll dine in doggy heaven: a table on the lawn. 821 North Locust Street; (940) 381-2712.

Good Eats Grill: Texas dogs who like Texas-style home cooking—chicken-fried steak, mesquite-grilled chicken and fish, fresh vegetables—will like eating with you on the patio here. 5812 Interstate 35 North; (940) 387-3500.

Outback Steakhouse: Practice your "G-day, mate," and take your hound for Australian-atmosphere steaks; eat on one of the benches on the front porch. You'll think you're in Alice Springs. ("Alice does what?" Sport asks.) 300 South Interstate 35 East; (940) 320-5373.

Sonic Drive-In: Have your burger and fries at one of the tables out front. 109 North Loop 288; (940) 484-2712.

Sweetwater Grill and Tavern: Head for the covered patio and plan to stay awhile. The huge menu features such items as jalapeños stuffed with shrimp or cheese, hand-breaded onion rings, quesadillas, chili, tortilla soup, beef tenderloin salad, grilled vegetable salad, burgers, a shrimp and bacon sandwich, seafood gumbo, baby back ribs, and—a personal favorite—a chicken-fried beef tenderloin sandwich. 115 South Elm Street; (940) 484-2888.

PLACES TO STAY

Econo Lodge: Rooms are $45; dogs pay a $25 deposit. 3116 Bandera Street, Denton, TX 76207; (940) 383-1681 or (800) 55-ECONO.

Exel Inn: Rooms are $42. Dogs under 25 pounds may share a smoking room with you. 4211 North Interstate 35, Denton, TX 76207; (940) 383-1471 or (800) 356-8013.

KOA Kampground: Prices are $19 for a tent site, $26 for an RV site, and $28 for a camping cabin. Small dogs only are accepted. All dogs must be leashed, may not be left unattended, and must be kept inside after 10 P.M. Owners must clean up after their dogs. 7100 South Stemmons Freeway, Denton, TX 76205; (940) 497-3353.

La Quinta Inn: Rooms are $67 to $78. Dogs under 25 pounds stay free. 700 Fort Worth Drive, Denton, TX 76201; (940) 387-5840 or (800) NU-ROOMS/687-6667.

Motel 6: Rooms are $40. All Motel 6s allow one small pooch per room. 4125 North Interstate 35, Denton, TX 76201; (940) 566-4798.

Radisson Hotel: Rates range from $89 to $99. Put down a $100 deposit or leave a credit card imprint and move your pooch right in. 2211 Interstate 35 East, Denton, TX 76205; (940) 565-8499 or (800) 333-3333.

Ray Roberts Lake State Park—Isle du Bois Unit: See Ray Roberts Lake State Park on page 332 for camping information.

FESTIVALS

County Seat Saturday: Leashed dogs whose companions will clean up after them are welcome to visit some 100 booths selling arts and crafts and to listen to live music from four stages. Admission is free to this western-theme event; put a red bandanna on your pooch and let her do-si-do. The event is held on the courthouse square at 110 West Hickory Street on the second Saturday in September. For information, call (940) 566-8529.

Dog Days of Summer: This event just for dogs and their people was the brainpuppy of Julie Glover, the assistant Main Street program manager, and was so successful it won a statewide award for the best downtown promotion of 1995. Leashed dogs and people who will wield a scoop if need be are admitted free. You can shop for doggy visors, gourmet bones, or homemade dog biscuits and get information from veterinarians, the humane society, and local kennels. There are dog training demonstrations, a dog parade, and a "Heinz 57" dog show in which every dog wins a ribbon. Groom your pooch before you come and have his portrait made—a "glamfur shot" for which a variety of costumes are furnished. If your pooch is contemplating a career change or perhaps needs advice on her love life, a gypsy will read her footpads and "foretail" her future. If you've ever wanted to be one of 900 pairs of dogs and dog owners putting on the dog, this is your chance. It's held on the court-house square, 110 West Hickory Street, the second Saturday in June. For information, call (940) 566-8529.

Texas Storytelling Festival: Storytellers from across the nation come to share their tales at this late-March event. It's a safe bet that a dog will figure in at least some of the stories. It's held at Civic Center Park, at Bell and Withers Avenues. For information, call (940) 387-8336.

LEWISVILLE
PARKS, BEACHES, AND RECREATION AREAS

• **Central Park** 🐾🐾 *See* ㉝ *on page 298.*

Whoever designed this five-acre urban park must have studied yin and yang at some time or another. The neatly mowed grass as you enter the park is balanced by the unruly brush in its interior. The open ex-panses on one side of the picnic ground are confronted by a dense grove of trees on the other. In the middle is a playground and picnic area where the forces of open and closed battle. At least that's the way it seemed to me. Sport, trotting along on her required six-foot leash, was much more impressed by the dozens of squirrels who were busily engaged in har-vesting pecans.

The balance between developed and undeveloped carries through-out the park. Rest rooms and water are available in the red-brick build-ing by the red-brick picnic pavilions, but just across the parking lot is a thick jungle of undergrowth laced with narrow footpaths just made for exploring. When Sport and I last visited, there were enough discarded fast-food containers in there to keep a dog busy sniffing all day.

The park is located at 1829 South Edmonds Lane. From Interstate 35E, take Highway 121 south to Valley View Drive. Turn right and fol-low Valley View Drive to Edmonds Lane. Turn right and go a block to the entrance. The park is closed from 11 P.M. to 6 A.M. (972) 219-3550.

• **College Street Park** 🐾 *See* ㉞ *on page 298.*

Conveniently located to Interstate 35E, this 12-acre park is mostly con-sumed by people things—a playground, pool, and athletic fields. How-ever, a delicious little band of trees and grass along a small drainage runs through the center of the park. Across the drainage is a picnic area. We found no water or rest rooms open, since the pool was closed. Dogs must remain on a six-foot leash; that's the rule at all Lewisville parks.

From Interstate 35E, exit at Main Street and drive north on the east frontage road two blocks to College Street; turn right and go two blocks to the park. The park is closed from 11 P.M. until 6 A.M. (817) 219-3550.

• Lewisville Lake Park 🐾 🐾 ½ *See ⑤ on page 298.*

Water dogs will find enough beach here to fulfill their every fantasy, even though they must remain on a six-foot leash. The day-use section of the 350-acre park ($3 per vehicle admission) encompasses four promontories jutting into the lake, and all have grassy banks that slope gently to the water's edge, where a sandy beach takes over. The only drawback is a lack of shade near the beach itself, but there are picnic tables with barbecue grills near the water in places; some of the best are at Sailboard Point. Dogs will enjoy visiting the rows of tall pine trees and picnic tables in the group picnic area. You never know what someone dropped while eating.

The campground seems to have been designed with schooling sardines in mind, since the sites are spaced as closely as possible. Most are shaded by pine or oak trees, but there is little elbow room, especially if you have four elbows. The 91 sites with water and electricity are $12; the 16 tent sites with picnic tables, barbecue grills, and water and rest rooms nearby are $6. Reservations are not accepted. The campground gate is closed from 11 P.M. to 7 A.M. No more than two pets are allowed per campsite, and owners must pick up after them. The most interesting feature of the campground is a grassy area with dozens of slabs of rock set upright in the ground; Sport thought they looked like Stone Age fire hydrants and treated them accordingly.

From Interstate 35E, exit at F.M. 407 and go east; you will immediately find yourself on Lake Park Road. To reach the day-use area, turn left onto Turtle Trail as soon as you enter the park. To reach the campground, go straight on Lake Park Road to Kingfisher Drive and turn left. (972) 219-3550.

• Raldon–Lake Cities Park 🐾 🐾 *See ⑥ on page 298.*

Greenbelt parks along creeks in urban areas are a dog's best friend, and this 12-acre park is no exception. It meanders through a neighborhood following the contours of a creek. Leashed dogs will enjoy hiking the segment of the Lewisville Trail found here. Or perhaps they will take a page from Sport's notebook and attempt to chase a large black cat we found sunning itself in a puddle of morning among a grove of elm trees. Sport normally gets along fine with cats, especially Comet the Resident Cat, but this one looked too much like a raccoon for its own good. There are plenty of squirrels, though, so Sport was easily distracted. The park has playgrounds scattered about, a few picnic tables, and some benches, but no other facilities. While the channelized creek had a little water running in it, I wouldn't let Sport drink it. There's no telling where that water had been.

The park has an entrance in the 200 block of Wildfire Drive, although the official address is 800 Foxwood Place. It's in one of those new subdivisions where nothing makes sense, if that explains anything. From Interstate 35E, exit at Fox Avenue and go west to Village Drive; turn left and go to Fox Creek Drive; turn left to Wildfire Drive. The park is closed from 11 P.M. until 6 A.M. (972) 219-3550.

• **Woods Park** 🐾1/2 *See* **㊲** *on page 298* .

I think of this as the 3-D park of Lewisville. A disc golf course lies along a drainage, and it's been bulldozed. You and your pooch (on her six-foot leash) can get a workout on the paved walking trail, but there's little else to do unless you like to run along the trail with your nose to the ground trying to detect where all the other walkers had been by sniffing clues left by their shoe soles. Since the principal purpose of this 30-acre park is to provide a flood-control greenbelt along a creek, there are few trees to impede the flow of water. The lack of timber didn't seem to detract from the fun for an unleashed whippet we saw leading its owners along the trail, nose to the ground.

The park is at Kirkpatrick Drive and Century Oaks Drive. From West Main Street, drive north on Kirkpatrick Drive to its intersection with Century Oaks Drive; park on the street along Century Oaks Drive. The official address is 1000 Arbour Way. The park is closed from 11 P.M. until 6 A.M. (972) 219-3550.

RESTAURANTS

Charlie's Restaurant on the Lake: After a hard day of waterskiing on Lake Lewisville, your pooch will be hankering for a burger, steak, or catfish. But she'd rather jump straight from the boat to the table. Here's a place where she can do just that—or you can come by car. It's at Pier 121 Marina. You and your pooch may dine on the patio overlooking the lake. Drive five miles east of Lewisville on Highway 121 and turn north on East Hill Park Road. Go another 1.4 miles to the marina entrance. (972) 625-4461.

Clyde's Old Time Hamburgers: We have it on good authority from a friend who lives in Lewisville that the hamburgers here are some of the best in the world. That explains why this is a popular dining-out spot for dogs: "Dogs eat here all the time," the owner said, and we could tell he didn't mean out of the garbage cans. You and your leashed pooch can check out the burgers at one of the tree-shaded tables on the patio on the side of the building. 136 Main Street; (972) 420-6995.

Razzoo's Cajun Cafe: There's a little open-air patio out back enclosed by a black metal fence. You and your pooch can chow down on seafood, chicken, steaks, fish, and oysters with an emphasis on spicy seasonings. 1990 South Stemmons; (972) 316-0326.

PLACES TO STAY

Comfort Suites of Lewisville: Rooms are $70 to $79. A $50 refundable deposit per visit lets any size dog stay here. 755-A Vista Ridge Boulevard, Lewisville, TX 75067; (972) 315-6464.

Hickory Creek Park: This U.S. Army Corps of Engineers park is for camping only; there are no day-use areas. It has 124 campsites with water and electricity ($12) and 10 primitive sites ($8). All sites have picnic tables, barbecue grills, and fire rings. Dogs must be leashed. The park is closed from 10 P.M. to 6 A.M. Currently camping is first come, first served, but that may change in the near future; call for up-to-date policies.

From Interstate 35E north of Lewisville, take Exit 457B and go west on Tuberville Road to Point Vista Road; turn left (south) to the park entrance. (972) 434-1666.

La Quinta Inn: Rooms are $70 to $81. Dogs under 25 pounds stay free. 1657 South Stemmons Freeway, Lewisville, TX 75067; (972) 221-7525 or (800) NU-ROOMS/687-6667.

Lewisville Lake Park: See Lewisville Lake Park on page 337 for camping information.

Residence Inn: Room rates are $99 for a studio to $149 for a two-bedroom. If your dog's back is lower than your knees, she can stay here for a $100 fee plus $10 per night. 755-C Vista Ridge Mall Drive, Lewisville, TX 75067; (972) 315-3777.

FESTIVALS

Western Week Festival and County Fair: Lots of fun things go on at this downtown street fair, but for dogs the highlight of the day has to be the wiener dog races. "We had 27 dogs entered before post time," tourism director Kim Dillon said. "However, by the time we started the races, more than 75 people had showed up with every kind of long, low-slung dog you can name. We ran dog races for hours. It was great." The festival is held in the 100 and 200 blocks of Main Street. For information on the dog races, contact the Humane Society of Lewisville at (972) 317-2555.

DIVERSIONS

GetSmart at PetsMart: You and your pooch can both learn a thing or two at this store where the two of you can shop for books on obedience training, check out the 700-plus kinds of dog food, have your nails clipped, or get one of those trendy new poodle cuts. All the smart dogs shop here. 2450 South Stemmons Freeway; (972) 315-2336.

Sail into the sunset: Leashed, well-behaved dogs are welcome to board the *Miss Lewisville* riverboat for a sight-seeing tour of Lake Lewisville. You'll pay $9; dogs ride free. The boat docks at 2 Eagle Point Drive. (972) 434-2500 or (800) 720-6822.

ELLIS COUNTY

WAXAHACHIE

Sport had mixed emotions when I told her we were going to Waxahachie to look at gingerbread. She remembers well the time she found a fresh-baked gingerbread loaf destined for donation to a local charity bake sale cooling atop the kitchen table. She remembers even better the fussing out she got for devouring half of it uninvited. She was both relieved and disappointed, then, to learn that the gingerbread in Waxahachie is the kind that decorates old houses, not the kind that tempts innocent dogs into lives of confectionery crime. Cotton bolls produced big fortunes for dozens of Waxahachians (Waxahachieites? Waxa-hachietonians? Waxahachiers?) around the turn of the century, and much of that wealth, rather than being spent on deserving dogs, was squan-dered on opulent houses. Is there no justice? At any rate, Waxahachie now claims to have 20 percent of the buildings in Texas listed on the National Register of Historic Places, and if any proof is needed that dogs got the short end of the stick, it is this: Not one of those structures is a doghouse. However, you and your pooch are welcome to look at the houses and speculate about the character of people who so shamelessly shafted their best friends.

Cotton was king in those days, and dogs still come off second best in Waxahachie. We did find a good park, but other entertainment is scarce, unless your pooch happens to appreciate historic architecture. In that case, enjoy. You'll find few better places in the state.

PARKS, BEACHES, AND RECREATION AREAS

• **Getzendaner Park** 🐾🐾 *See ㊳ on page 298.*

Pooches worn out from the strain induced by attempting to differen-tiate between Queen Anne and Eastlake Victorian houses will find plea-sures more to their liking in this 40-acre park. Playgrounds, rest rooms, and picnic tables nest within an unpaved circular fitness path with nu-merous exercise stations. Dogs can stretch and warm up before heading for the best part of the park for them, a wooded area with winding foot-paths along a creek. Park on the northwest side of the park beside the utility pole numbered 5, and take the footbridge across the creek. Huge bur and water oaks, cedar elms, and pecan trees cast a perennial shade inhabited by squirrels and other creatures of the woodland.

The park is on Grand Avenue two blocks west of U.S. 287 Business and has a 10 P.M. curfew. (972) 937-7719.

RESTAURANTS

1879 Townhouse: Have your scratch pancakes, Texas-size chicken-fried steak, roast beef, quiche, or grilled, fried, or Cajun catfish on the bench on the sidewalk. 111 South College Street; (972) 937-7261.

PLACES TO STAY

Comfort Inn: Rooms are $59. 200 North Interstate 35E, Waxahachie, TX 75165; (972) 937-4202 or (800) 228-5150.

FESTIVALS

A Faire on the Square: It's all very confusing to pooches: Each Thanksgiving weekend, Waxahachie celebrates a Victorian Christmas on the courthouse square with food, music, and buggy rides. But confused or not, she'll enjoy putting on her best Victorian leash and lace and taking part in the festivities, especially the traditional munching of the Christmas cookies. On the courthouse square at Main and Rogers Streets, one block east of U.S. 77 Business. For information, call (972) 937-2390.

DIVERSIONS

Feast on gingerbread: Admiring the historic architecture is the principal pastime in Waxahachie, and both walking and guided tours make it easy for you and your leashed pooch to do so. All tours start at the courthouse square and the 1895 J. Riely Gordon Ellis County courthouse, chosen by the American Institute of Architects as the most outstanding example of courthouse architecture of the period. Obtain tour brochures from the Chamber of Commerce office at 102 YMCA Drive, Waxahachie, TX 75168; (972) 937-2390.

FREESTONE COUNTY

FAIRFIELD

PARKS, BEACHES, AND RECREATION AREAS

• **Fairfield Lake State Park** 🐾🐾🐾 *See ㊴ on page 298.*

Conveniently located just an hour and a half's drive southeast of Dallas, this 1,460-acre park should be a favorite of every Metroplex mutt, even though dogs must be leashed here. Trees, trails, and wildlife abound. Straddling a transition zone between uplands and bottomlands and wrapping around a lake, this park's thick cover of fragrant humus will grab a dog by his nose and never let go. The variety of smells that must be explored will seem endless, so remind your pooch that he can't smell everything in one trip. You'll want to come back again and again anyway.

You will find the day-use area of little interest to you and your pooch. Because it contains a designated swimming area, several signs at its perimeter declare "Pets prohibited in this area." You'll have to picnic in the parking lot or at your campsite, but as you'll see, that won't be a hardship.

Bring your walking shoes, your binoculars, and your bird book. Nine miles of trails expose visitors to an abundance of furry and feathered creatures. Sport and I saw four deer along the trails and rafts of coots feeding in the shallows of the lake. You may spot raccoons, beavers, squirrels, waterfowl, or—in winter—a bald eagle. Be sure to keep an eye out for snakes, poison ivy, and bull nettle, however. The Big Brown Creek Trail, 4.5 miles one way, leads to a primitive camping area ($8) with a rest room. The trailhead is at a parking area just outside the park entrance. Two roads lead north here; you want the paved one, which is the second road as you go away from the park entrance. The graveled road leads to a cemetery. A free guide available at park headquarters and signs along the trail's first mile and a half will teach you the names of native plants. Pooches will want to check out the flowering dogwood, of course. In fall the flame leaf sumac lives up to its name, blazing crimson against a background of rust- and gold-colored oak leaves. Spring visitors can feast on wild blackberries growing in brambles among the trees. Just watch out for snakes and chiggers when berry-picking.

The Fairfield Lake Birding Trail begins at a parking area 1.4 miles past park headquarters and travels about a mile along the lakefront. The sandy trail delights dogs, who love the feel of sand between their toes and the gritty texture it adds to the seat covers in your car. The marshy cove around which the trail wraps harbors egrets, herons, and lots of coots. Raccoons grope the shallows for crayfish, and deer come to drink at twilight. There's a lot more than birds to be seen here.

As you drive the park road to the camping areas, you'll find there are two entrances to the Cooks Ferry Camp. Directly across from the second entrance is a leg of the Fairfield Lake Nature Trail. Farther on, you'll find the main trailhead and a parking area just past the entrance to the Post Oak Camp. This two-mile trail loops and branches as it traverses a promontory jutting into the lake. Birds and wildlife abound here as they do throughout the park, but this trail offers more sweeping views of the lake.

Camping is excellent due to the abundance of shade cast by large blackjack, post oak, sand jack, and water oaks. The latter can grow to a height of 80 feet but are still outstripped by the 10-story mockernut hickories. The Springfield Camp has 36 sites, each with a picnic table, barbecue grill, fire ring, and lantern post. There is water in the area, plus a playground and rest rooms with showers. Most of the sites rent for $8, but those on the water go for $10. You won't get much benefit from being on the water, however, as the shore is weedy and not inviting for walking. This camping area may be closed during some winter months.

The Cooks Ferry Camp is open year-round. It has 64 multiuse sites with water and electricity. Premium waterfront sites here rent for $15; the balance go for $11. There is a playground and two rest rooms, one with showers. The large, shady, fairly open sites all have a picnic table, fire ring, barbecue grill, and lantern post. The terrain is somewhat hilly, and several ravines cut through the campground. The shoreline is weedy and not suitable for walking or swimming.

For what Sport and I felt to be the best campsites, try the Post Oak Camp (closed in winter). The 35 spacious sites here have water and electricity and rent for $11, except for those at lakeside, which are $15. A rest room with showers and a playground serve the area. Our favorite site was number 108, which is located off a turnaround at one end of the campground. This huge campsite has access to the lake, and a deep ravine shields you from neighboring campsites. You'll almost think you have the park to yourself.

Reservations for campsites at all state parks must be made by calling the central reservation number, (512) 389-8900, between 9 A.M. and 6 P.M. Monday through Friday. Reservations are strongly recommended, and a deposit is required in order to guarantee a reservation. Specific sites may not be reserved; they are available on a first-come, first-served basis upon arrival.

State park rules for dogs apply here. Your pooch must be kept on a leash no longer than six feet, and you may not leave her unattended— as if. She may not enter any park building, and as noted above, is banned from the swimming beach and adjacent picnic area. Your pooch may go in the water anywhere else in the park as long as she is leashed.

From Fairfield, drive six miles northeast on F.M. 2570 to Park Road 64, then proceed to the park. Entry is $2 per person. The office is normally open from 8 A.M. until 5 P.M. but may be open later on weekends. The park closes at 10 P.M. except to overnight guests; the entrance gate is locked from that hour until 6 A.M. (903) 389-4514.

RESTAURANTS

Java Jack's Gourmet Coffee: Sandwiches, soups, salads, gourmet

---

coffees and espressos, milkshakes, and desserts are served up at side-walk tables. 125 South Mount Street; (903) 389-2331.

PLACES TO STAY

Fairfield Lake State Park: See Fairfield Lake State Park on page 341 for camping information.

GRAYSON COUNTY

DENISON

Huge Lake Texoma and its associated parks and recreation areas dominate the Denison area. The U.S. Army Corps of Engineers operates 41 public use areas around the lake, and concessionaires run at least 23 more, with over 1,100 campsites just on the Texas side of the lake. You can fish, ski, sail, or cruise the lake in a rented houseboat. Accommodations range from primitive tent camping through luxury resorts. One of the best state parks in Texas to take a dog fronts the lake just outside Denison. For information on Corps of Engineers campgrounds not reported on below, write the U.S. Army Corps of Engineers at Route 4, Box 493, Denison, TX 75020 or call (903) 465-4990. Information on privately operated facilities around the lake can be obtained from the Lake Texoma Association, Box 610, Kingston, OK 73439; (405) 564-2334.

PARKS, BEACHES, AND RECREATION AREAS

• **Eisenhower State Park** 🐾🐾🐾 *See ⑩ on page 298.*

Sport, Samantha, and I fell totally in love with this park, even though dogs must remain on leash here. The reason? We three agreed it has one of the best campgrounds in Texas, crowned by what is perhaps the single best campsite in the whole state. Even better, due to competition for customers between the Texas Parks and Wildlife Department and the U.S. Army Corps of Engineers parks in the area, the entrance fee to the park is only $1 per person, and camping fees are low, too.

The park is lush with trees, with elms and a variety of oaks predominating. Samantha, however, was captivated by the bois d'arc trees, which when we visited in mid-October were dropping their large green fruits that resemble tennis balls on steroids. Chasing tennis balls is Samantha's highest passion after eating, and she was beside herself when she saw all the "balls" on the ground. Nothing would do but to throw them for her. The nice thing about it was that since Samantha has never learned to bring back a ball once she's retrieved it, all I had to do was stand in the middle of a bunch of bois d'arc apples and fire away again and again until her tongue was hanging out.

The abundant vegetation also forms the basis for a nature trail along the first half mile or so of a four-mile hiking trail that connects all the park's campgrounds. Begin the nature trail at a parking lot just inside the entrance to the Armadillo Hill Camp. Numbered posts are keyed to a free brochure you can get from park headquarters. There's a bird checklist on the back of the brochure. The narrow dirt trail winds through dense stands of trees and crosses the park road five times, making it easy to hike in segments.

The park's six camping areas have 217 campsites and 35 screened shelters and are served by rest rooms with showers. As far as we could tell, there's not a bad campsite in the bunch. Some are closer together than others, especially in the Bois d' arc Ridge RV Camp, where sites with water and electricity rent for a mere $10. (There's that competition with the Corps of Engineers at work again.) Even though the sites are a little closely spaced for our taste, there is plenty of vegetation to screen one from another. The Armadillo Hill Camp has both water and electric sites ($9) and water-only sites ($6). These sites are heavily shaded, and many are quite spacious. They are on a high promontory offering views of the lake but no access to the shore.

Both the Fossil Ridge and Elm Point Camps are water-only sites for tents. Most sites are $6, but a few near the swim beach (closed to dogs, alas) have been designated as premium and go for $8. All have heavy shade; some offer views of the lake.

The Deer Haven Camp has 35 screened shelters ($20), and while they are well kept and shaded, keep in mind that park regulations forbid you from taking your dog inside and state that pets may not be left tied outside a shelter or tent at night. So you probably won't be interested in a screened shelter unless your pooch can be persuaded to bed down in your car.

Which brings us to the best campsite in Texas. We nominate number 179 in the Elm Point Camp. It's a tent site at the end of the road, on a promontory that juts into Lake Texoma. Twin tent pads (one for you, one for the dog tent) sit on either side of the picnic table. Trees shade the entire site all day, and waves break against the base of the 40-foot bluff on which it sits, lulling you to sleep. A chain-link fence guards against anyone falling over the edge. The view of the lake is one of the best in the park.

Reservations for campsites at all state parks must be made by calling the central reservation number, (512) 389-8900, between 9 A.M. and 6 P.M. Monday through Friday. Reservations are strongly recommended, and a deposit is required in order to guarantee a reservation. Specific sites may not be reserved; they are available on a first-come, first-served basis upon arrival. Other standard state park regulations also apply. Dogs must be on a six-foot leash and may not enter any park building or the swimming beach area.

To reach the park, follow U.S. 75 north from Denison to F.M. 91; turn left and go two miles to F.M. 1310; turn left again and go two miles to the park entrance. Entry costs $1 per person. There is no park gate, but the park is closed to all except overnight guests from 10 P.M. to 8 A.M. The park office is normally open from 8 A.M. to 5 P.M. but may be open as late as 10 P.M. on weekends and holidays. (903) 465-1956.

• **Loy Lake Park** 🐾🐾½ *See* ㊶ *on page 298.*

This park right on U.S. 75 makes a great rest stop for a car-weary pooch who doesn't mind staying on his leash. The approximately 100-acre park encircles a small lake with grassy banks sloping gently to the water, so a thirsty pooch can bravely take a drink of wild water and maybe even dip a paw in. We wondered about a sign at the entrance warning that the park will be closed in the event of ice, something we saw nowhere else on our travels. Does Denison have a problem with ice storms? Polar bears? Inquiring dog brains want to know. Buildings in the park bear the unmistakable imprint of the Civilian Conservation Corps, so there's some nice historic architecture nestled among the post oak trees. Rest rooms and water are available.

The county-owned park is at the intersection of U.S. 75 and Loy Lake Road. It's closed from 10 P.M. to 6 A.M. For information or to reserve facilities, call Bill Stone at (903) 463-1020.

• **Waterloo Park** 🐾🐾 *See* ㊷ *on page 298.*

Sport couldn't get over all the water in Denison parks. It seemed that every park we visited had a lake in the middle. This 148-acre park was no exception. Here, however, steep banks made access to the water somewhat of a problem. We had to be content with roaming a large grassy area and watching kids play in the playground. If we'd been there in summer, we could have rented a paddleboat ($3 per hour) and gone for a doggone delightful cruise. For a beautiful view of the lake, hike across the grass-covered earthen dam. Picnic tables and rest rooms are available.

The park stretches along Waterloo Lake Drive. From U.S. 75, take Loy Lake Road east; turn left onto Waterloo Lake Drive and follow it about a quarter mile to a parking area overlooking the lake. Hours are from sunrise to sunset. (903) 463-5116.

RESTAURANTS

Sonic Drive-In: Both locations will serve you and your pooch at their outside picnic tables. The tables are in back of the store at 2405 South Austin Street, (903) 465-2562. Eat at the tables out front at 3325 F.M. 120 West; (903) 465-5720.

PLACES TO STAY

Eisenhower State Park: See Eisenhower State Park on page 344 for camping information.

Ramada Inn: Rates are $45 to $70. Your pooch will snooze in comfort for a $25 deposit. 1600 South Austin Avenue, Denison, TX 75020; (903) 465-6800.

FESTIVALS

Grayson County Fair: Some days dogs feel like frisking about, and other days they'd rather just put on something comfortable and hang out. The Grayson County Fair has both kinds of dog days covered. You and your leashed pooch can dress up and take part in the pet parade, which awards prizes in such categories as pet looking most like owner, or your pooch can show off her athletic prowess by competing in the dog races sponsored by the local humane society. Later you can both stroll the midway of what is billed as the largest carnival in Texas, where you can pig out on cotton candy and throw your money away trying to win worthless prizes. The festival is held in Loy Lake Park, which is just west of the intersection of Loy Lake Road and U.S. 75; take Exit 67. For information, call (903) 465-1551.

GORDONVILLE

PARKS, BEACHES, AND RECREATION AREAS

• **Juniper Point Recreation Area** 🐾🐾🐾 *See* ㊸ *on page 298.*
This U.S. Army Corps of Engineers park is special to Texas hounds who've been forced to exist in Oklahoma and can hardly wait to get back across the Red River and take a good squat on Texas soil. Located at the Texas end of the bridge across the Red River, it's the first place your homesick hound can get out of the car and celebrate his return to Texas, even though he must do so on a leash.

As is unfortunately typical of Corps of Engineers parks, day-use areas have been deliberately kept to a minimum—in this case nonexistent. (Sometimes the Corps just doesn't seem to believe it ought to help people enjoy themselves.) Corps regulations require that if you so much as park at a designated campsite, you have to pay the camping fee. However, you are in luck here. Turn west off U.S. 377, which splits the park in two, into the Juniper Point West Recreation Area. On your left just after entering is a rest room with showers. Follow the paved road around to a sign with the hiking symbol. Turn left and then, in about 50 yards, left again into a lakeside camping area. As soon as you turn in, turn hard left again into the parking area for the Cross Timbers Hiking Trail. This 14-mile route follows the southern shoreline of Lake Texoma upstream all the way to the Paw Paw Creek Resort Area. The trail climbs in and out of creekbeds and up and down bluffs for the first three miles; expect to do some huffing and puffing and frequent resting of your dog. The trail is heavily eroded in places, and the ruts and rocks argue strongly for heavy footwear with good ankle support. Also, be sure to take plenty of water for you and your pooch; there is none along the route. With one of Texas's largest lakes right at your boot tips, you might be tempted to take along some water-treatment tablets and drink lake water, but it's not recommended. The Red River carries a large load of salt into the lake, making the water unfit for drinking according to the U.S. Public Health Service. There are two primitive camping areas along the trail.

The Juniper Point Campground, on the east side of U.S. 377, has 70 campsites laid out with exceptional sensitivity for a Corps of Engineers park. It looks like they actually left the bulldozer at home for a change. Some sites are right at the water's edge, while others are almost lost among dense stands of oak and juniper trees. Sites with electricity and water are $18; those with water only nearby are $13. Reservations are not accepted. The area is closed from November 1 through March 31.

Follow U.S. 377 north from Whitesboro for 14.3 miles to the bridge across the Red River. Entry is free. The campground is closed from 10 P.M. to 6 A.M. The gate attendant is on duty Monday through Friday from 8 A.M. to 10 A.M. and again from 4 P.M. to 10 P.M. Saturday and Sunday hours are 8 A.M. to noon and from 2 P.M. to 10 P.M. Contact the U.S. Army Corps of Engineers at Route 4, Box 493, Denison, TX 75020; (903) 523-4022.

• **Rock Creek Camp** 🐾 🐾 1/2 *See* **44** *on page 298.*

If you and your pooch really want to get away from it all for the day, try this isolated park, the farthest upstream on Lake Texoma. We'd avoid the concessionaire-operated campground and go to the picnic area—turn left at the sign directing you to the Shepard Air Force Base Recreation Area, then stay right. The area is a low-maintenance one, which means the grass may not be mowed and there are no facilities other than a unisex privy, but the shore slopes gently to the lake where a leashed pooch can swim. Dirt roads meander through cedar and oak trees, and you'll probably not meet a soul while walking.

From U.S. 377, go west on F.M. 901 for 1.8 miles. Turn north on Rock Creek Road and go 3.4 miles, then turn right on an unnamed road and go 0.2 miles; turn right onto another unnamed road and go 0.6 miles, then turn right on yet another unnamed road and go 0.1 miles to the entrance. The park is closed from 10 P.M. to 6 A.M. (903) 523-4308.

RESTAURANTS

Big Mineral Camp Snack Bar: Burgers and sandwiches fill the menu at this snack bar; eat at one of the tables on the covered patio out front. From Whitesboro, drive 14 miles north on U.S. 377, then go east on F.M. 901 for 1.8 miles; turn left onto Big Mineral Road and continue one mile; turn right onto Brady Road and go another 1.5 miles to the entrance. (903) 523-4287.

PLACES TO STAY

Big Mineral Camp: There are lots of resorts and campgrounds around Lake Texoma, but this one has to be one of the most dog-friendly, "Probably because we have a dog ourselves," says Lisa Barnett, who operates the camp with husband John. "You ought to see this place on weekends. There are dogs everywhere."

Big Mineral Camp has a marina, store, snack bar, fishing dock, and personal watercraft and boat rentals, so you and your pooch should not get bored while you're here. The camp has more than 100 shaded lakeside campsites ranging from tent sites ($5) to sites with electricity only ($8), sites with electricity and water ($10), and full hookups ($12). In addition, there are five mobile homes for rent from $38 to $150; your pooch is allowed inside as long as she does not get on the furniture.

From Whitesboro, drive 14 miles north on U.S. 377, then go east on F.M. 901 for 1.8 miles; turn left onto Big Mineral Road and continue one mile; turn right onto Brady Road and go another 1.5 miles to the entrance. P.O. Box 576, Gordonville, TX 76245; (903) 523-4287.

Cedar Mills Marina and Resort: Choose from tent camping ($10), lakefront RV camping ($20 to $25), or furnished cabins ($54 to $99). Your leashed, well-behaved pooch is welcome everywhere in this resort except at the restaurant. One mile south of the U.S. 377 bridge across Lake Texoma, turn east at the sign to the resort. Route 1, Box 37, Gordonville, TX 76245; (903) 523-4222.

Juniper Point Recreation Area: See Juniper Point Recreation Area on page 347 for camping information.

POTTSBORO

RESTAURANTS

Garcia's: This Mexican food restaurant closes from November to March, but during the rest of the year you and your pooch are welcome to dine at the outside tables. It's located at Loe's Highport Resort and Marina. From Pottsboro, follow F.M. 120 north to Highport Road and turn left at the Fina station. Follow the signs to the resort. (903) 786-4500.

PLACES TO STAY

Lighthouse Resort and Marina: You and your pooch may want to make this your home on Lake Texoma, since dogs of any size are welcome; there are no fees. You can rent a campsite with water and electricity for $20 or splurge and spend $60 to $200 on a cabin. The resort is 7.5 miles north of Pottsboro on F.M. 120. Route 2, Box 411, Pottsboro, TX 75076; (903) 786-2311.

SHERMAN

PARKS, BEACHES, AND RECREATION AREAS

• **Fairview Park** 🐾🐾 *See ㊺ on page 298.*

Although athletic fields heavily infest this park of about 20 acres, the northern part borders a creek, and a graveled jogging trail allows leashed dogs and their humans to exercise together. The thickly wooded creek bottom provides not only shade but also the opportunity for some spur-of-the-moment side trips after a squirrel beating a hasty retreat. The park has playgrounds, water, and rest rooms, too.

From U.S. 75, take Taylor Street west about a mile to the park. The entrance is on North Ricketts Street. The park is closed from midnight until 4 A.M. (903) 892-7344.

• **Hagerman National Wildlife Refuge** 🐾🐾½ *See ㊻ on page 298.*

The main purpose of these 11,000 acres (of which marsh and ponds cover about 3,000 acres) is to provide habitat for wildlife, but leashed pooches can enjoy long nature walks here with their favorite person as well. Working dogs are also welcome to accompany their quail- or dove-hunting human companion. When hunting, dogs are not required to be on leash.

While you and your pooch are welcome to walk the many miles of roads and trails on the refuge, you are not allowed to disturb any wildlife. Therefore, the wilderness areas of the refuge are off-limits to dogs. Unfortunately, a "No Dogs" sign may soon greet all visitors to the refuge, says ranger Jim Williams. "We're thinking of prohibiting dogs because we've had problems with unleashed animals in places such as the picnic area," he said. "However, if you keep your dog on its leash and stick to the roads and trails, there's no problem."

Walking the refuge's dirt roads and trails will likely be preferable to taking the nature trail near the refuge visitor center. When Sport and I last visited, the trail was poorly maintained. Weeds pressed in from both sides, and fallen tree limbs blocked part of the path. The trail runs along a swampy area, and industrial-strength mosquitoes attacked in squadrons. You'll also need to keep an eye out for fire ants, ticks, chiggers, and snakes. Nature had pretty well taken back the trail bearing her name. The five-mile Meadow Pond Road was a much more pleasant walk. It's a two-track dirt road closed to traffic and traverses the southwest quadrant of the refuge, crossing two creeks and passing by the pond from which it gets its name.

The payoff for braving the wilderness—and that's what this is—is the opportunity to see wildlife in large numbers. As many as 7,500 Canada geese stop over here during their annual migration, and they are joined by snow geese, white-fronted geese, Ross' geese, and a variety of ducks. Other wildlife you may see includes many songbirds, white-tailed deer, squirrels, rabbits, and—Sport's favorite—raccoons. October through March is the best time for viewing waterfowl. From April through June, white pelicans and other shorebirds pass through. Wading birds are common during the summer and early fall. A bird list for the refuge is available at the visitor center; it lists 316 species that have been seen on the refuge.

Finding the refuge requires traveling some unpaved roads. Several different routes are possible; the one presented here was chosen because it is the only one that does not require crossing a low-water bridge that normally is slightly under water and may be impassable at any time in a low-slung car. From U.S. 82, about 7.5 miles west of Sherman, turn north on Southmayd Road. Go 2.3 miles to Judge Elliot Road and turn right; continue 0.2 miles to Bennett Lane and turn left; from that point it is 1.2 miles to the refuge entrance sign, on your left. Signs guide you the remaining 2.6 miles to the visitor center, which is open from 7:30 A.M. to 4 P.M. Monday through Friday. You may travel the refuge roads and trails from dawn to dusk. The refuge is closed at times during October and November for deer hunts; call before planning a visit during those months. There is no entry fee. (903) 786-2826.

• **Herman Baker Park** 🐾🐾🐾 *See* 🐾 *on page 298.*

Trees, water, and grass attract dogs and people to this 49-acre park encircling a 34-acre lake. You can picnic at a shaded table and then work off those calories by hiking all the way around the lake. Or you and your pooch may prefer to just cool your heels in the creek below the dam. And speaking of the dam, what athletic pooch can resist the fun of running up the steep, grassy dam and then sliding back down again? Bring a piece of cardboard to slide on and you can join in the fun.

From Highway 56, go south one mile on Herman Baker Park Road to the entrance. The park is closed from midnight to 4 A.M. (903) 892-7344.

RESTAURANTS

Schlotzsky's Deli: The owner, who himself is owned by a dog, welcomes leashed pooches to eat at the patio tables out front. The menu consists of sandwiches; the Schlotzsky is an original creation featuring several kinds of meats on a sourdough bun any pooch would kill to have just a tiny piece of. 2902 U.S. 75 North; (903) 813-3354.

PLACES TO STAY

Best Western Grayson House: Rooms are $47 to $89. Dogs pay a $10 fee. 2105 Texoma Parkway, Sherman, TX 75090; (903) 892-2161 or (800) 723-4194.

Crossroads Inn: Rooms are $27 to $29. Dogs pay $3.50 each per night. 2424 Texoma Parkway, Sherman, TX 75090; (903) 893-0184.

Holiday Inn: Rooms are $79. Dogs pay no fees or deposits. 3605 U.S. 75 South, Sherman, TX 75090; (903) 868-0555 or (800) 465-4329.

Ramada Inn: Rates are $40 for people; dogs will pay $5. 401 South Sam Rayburn Freeway, Sherman, TX 75090; (903) 893-6581.

HILL COUNTY

STATE WILDLIFE MANAGEMENT AREAS

See the National and State Forests/State Wildlife Management Areas starting on page 621 for important information and safety tips on visiting these areas with your dog.

- **Aquilla Wildlife Management Area** 🐾🐾

Your dog can tag along and be helpful as you hunt doves, quail, squirrels, waterfowl, and rabbits. Feral hogs are present on the area and should be avoided; you are not allowed to hunt them with dogs. There are no camping facilities available. Your dog does not have to be leashed as long as she is hunting. See page 625 for a description of the area.

HILLSBORO

RESTAURANTS

Schlotzsky's Deli: This chain eatery began in Austin and built a reputation by making one fine sandwich. You and your pooch can sit at one of the picnic tables on the porch out front and decide whether the reputation is deserved. 200 Northwest Interstate 35; (254) 582-5155.

Texas Boy Bar-B-Q: The owner's reaction was pretty typical for small-town Texas when I asked if dogs could eat at the outside tables: stunned silence, followed by a chuckle, and then, "I've never been asked that before, but I don't see any problem." You and your pooch can munch on a barbecue sandwich or have a plate lunch with all the fixin's. 610 West Elm Street; (254) 582-2440.

PLACES TO STAY

Best Western: Rooms are $52. Small dogs only are allowed, but there is no fee or deposit. 307 Service Road Interstate 35, Hillsboro, TX 76645; (254) 582-8465.

Ramada Inn: Rooms are $60 to $65. Interstate 35 and Texas 22, Hillsboro, TX 76645; (254) 582-3493.

FESTIVALS

Bond's Alley Arts and Crafts Festival: Stroll the courthouse square with your leashed pooch the second weekend in June and you'll be surrounded by people selling arts and crafts. For information, call (254) 582-2481.

Cotton Pickin' Fair/Go Texan Days: Food booths, games, and the usual assortment of arts and crafts cluster around the courthouse the second Saturday in September. Leashed dogs may attend. For information, call (254) 582-2481.

WHITNEY

PARKS, BEACHES, AND RECREATION AREAS

• **Lake Whitney State Park** 🐾🐾 *See* **48** *on page 298.*

I was about to decide that this 955-acre park on the eastern shore of Lake Whitney was totally without charm when I met a woman crammed into a tiny car with two large dogs, both of whom wanted to share the driver's seat and window with her (and lick her ears). In answer to my question, she said, "They love this park. They got to see deer and," she glanced around to make sure no park personnel were around, "chase them." That's strictly forbidden, of course, since dogs must remain on leash here as at all state parks, but her story went far to erase my first impressions of the place. If dogs like it, who cares what I think?

The first thing that strikes you upon entering is that it is flat, very flat. In fact, an Air Force emergency landing field with a 2,000-foot runway and an even longer taxiway take up the entire center of the park. If you and your pooch like to fly your own plane on your weekend getaways, this park may be for you. Private planes are allowed to use the strip, which has a windsock as the only flying aid. Don't be surprised if your quiet weekend camping trip is interrupted by a fly-in or skydiving demonstration; call the park before going to see if an event is scheduled at the airstrip.

The lake is the chief attraction here, and we saw lots of tackle boxes sitting atop picnic tables in the campground. The day-use areas are small, but they do offer good views of the lake. If your pooch likes to wolf down lunch and then sleep it off in the shade while you catch up on your leisure reading or drown worms, you might like it here.

A couple of walking trails take you through wooded areas to the lakeside; chances are that you will see one or more white-tailed deer here or in the runway area early and late in the day. Remember: Chasing is not allowed! The longest trail, which heads on the main park road just before the boat ramp entrance, is just under a mile loop.

The 137 campsites are split up among seven areas, all but one of which is on a promontory. Unfortunately, even though many of the sites are near the water, a weedy shoreline does not invite you to the water's edge. Dogs are allowed in the water on leash everywhere except at the one designated swimming area at the picnic ground. Tent sites with water only rent for $8; sites with water and electricity are $12; sites with full hookups are $13.

All the campsites have this in common: Camping in one of them is like camping on your front lawn. Grass covers the level ground, there are some trees scattered about, and all your neighbors can see every move you make and vice versa. You almost expect to hear lawnmowers revving up on Saturday morning; it's that close to suburbia.

Reservations for campsites at all state parks must be made by calling the central reservation number, (512) 389-8900, between 9 A.M. and 6 P.M. Monday through Friday. Reservations are strongly recommended, and a deposit is required in order to guarantee a reservation. Specific sites may not be reserved; they are available on a first-come, first-served basis upon arrival.

The usual rules apply to dogs. They may not enter any park building, must remain on a six-foot leash, and may not be left unattended. This park may be closed at times during October through January for public hunts to remove excess deer; call ahead before scheduling a trip during those months.

To reach the park, take F.M. 933 from its intersection with Highway 22. Go 0.6 miles to F.M. 1244; follow that highway 2.3 miles to the entrance. There is a $2 entrance fee. The park closes at 10 P.M. except to campers. The office is open from 8 A.M. to 5 P.M. (254) 694-3793.

PLACES TO STAY

Lake Whitney State Park: See Lake Whitney State Park on page 353 for camping information.

HOOD COUNTY

GRANBURY

PARKS, BEACHES, AND RECREATION AREAS

• **Granbury City Park** 🐾 *See ㊾ on page 298.*

Only about four acres of this multiuse park are suitable for dogs. There are lots of trees and grass, picnic tables, and a playground. Water is available. Its chief attraction for the traveling dog is its location near downtown and along U.S. 377 Business.

The park is at the corner of West Pearl Street (U.S. 377 Business) and North Park Drive. It's closed from 10 P.M. to 5 A.M. (817) 579-1094.

• **Hunter Park** 🐾 1/2 *See ㊿ on page 298.*

Sport got her hopes up when I mentioned Hunter Park, but she was somewhat disappointed when she saw it. It's about 35 acres, but only a narrow strip along Lake Granbury has what this hunting dog is always looking for: lots of weeds, bushes, and trees among which she can sniff out the elusive raccoon. Most of the park is taken up by an open grassy area posted with signs stating "Grass lease—do not enter." However—and this is a big however to a dog—the operator of the park, the Brazos River Authority, has no policy requiring dogs to be leashed in the park. Suddenly that 35 acres looked a lot better to Sport, who loves a good swim. She headed straight for the sandy beach and was soon paddling happily about.

There are about 20 shaded picnic tables along the waterfront, each with a barbecue grill. Camping is permitted; there is no fee. Go north of the courthouse square about two miles on Highway 51; turn left into the park a quarter of a mile past the north end of the bridge over Lake Granbury. The park is open 24 hours. (817) 573-1407.

• **Lambert Branch Park** 🐾🐾 *See (51) on page 298.*

Three acres of doggy heaven describes this park just a block and a half off the courthouse square on North Houston Street. The shopped-out pooch can rejuvenate himself with a leashed romp in this hilly little tree-shaded park with a creek running through it. You'll like the footbridges over the creek and the shaded picnic tables. The park is closed from 10 P.M. to 5 A.M. (817) 579-1094.

RESTAURANTS

The Coffee Grinder: The owner was very excited to hear that her restaurant was going to be in this book, since she is originally from San

Francisco and loves Foghorn Press publications. (Dogs understand the need to butter up the editors once in a while; please be patient. Besides, she really did say that.) You and your pooch will be treated like royalty here whether you sit on the bench on the sidewalk in front or go around to the covered patio in back. The menu includes deli sandwiches, soups and salads, espresso, gourmet coffees, Italian sodas, gelato, and fresh fruit smoothies. 129 East Pearl Street; (817) 279-0977.

Dairy Queen: Get your fast-food fix at one of the tables out front. 512 West Pearl Street; (817) 573-3361.

Hennington's Famous Barbecue Palace: The courthouse square serves as the backdrop for this out-of-the-ordinary barbecue restaurant tucked under a building overhang. Five tables out front border but do not intrude on the sidewalk; you and your leashed pooch can dine undisturbed. The house speciality is an East Texas–style pork sandwich, but all the usual meats and sides are available. 110 North Crockett Street (on the east side of the square); (817) 279-1062.

Hennington's Texas Cafe: Order to go and eat at one of the benches out front. Grilled chicken salad; roasted garlic and goat cheese served with kalamata olives, roasted peppers, and Parmesan toast; "belly bustin'" burgers; shrimp and basil ravioli; chicken-fried steak; pecan wood-grilled beef tenderloin; or Atlantic salmon topped off with crème brûlée or lemon pound cake—the menu goes on and on. But you're ready to eat now, right? 121 East Bridge Street (in the Nutt House, on the north side of the square); (817) 573-8400.

Irby's Burgers and Catfish: The menu includes not only the items in the name but also chicken-fried steak and Mexican and German food. Eat at one of the tables out back overlooking the lake. 804 East Pearl Street; (817) 573-7311.

Merry Heart Tearoom: Tea and crumpets, anyone? Or perhaps a sandwich, soup, or salad? Eat at one of the benches out front. 110 North Houston Street (on the west side of the square); (817) 573-3800.

Nutshell Eatery, Bakery, and Creamery: Enjoy your cone or sandwich at the bench on the sidewalk in front. 137 East Pearl Street (on the south side of the square); (817) 279-8989.

Pop's Malt Shop: Have a chicken-fried steak dinner, club sandwich, or buffalo burger washed down with a creamy malt on the patio out front. 2113 East Highway 377; (817) 573-0336.

Rinky-Tink's Sandwich and Ice Cream Parlor: Eat one of this place's namesake creations at the bench out front. 108 North Houston Street (on the west side of the square); (817) 573-4323.

PLACES TO STAY

Best Western Classic Inn: Rates are $40 to $59. Small dogs only are welcome. 1209 North Plaza; Granbury, TX 76048; (817) 573-8874.

Derrick-Hoffman Farm: A mere $70 gets you and your pooch a turn-of-the-century cottage, furnished with antiques, on a 265-acre working farm. "Dogs are as well behaved—and as welcome—as people," says owner Jane Hoffman. "There's a lovely fenced yard around the house, and I encourage people to wander the mowed paths in the pasture." From Granbury, follow Highway 4 north four miles to Thorp Spring, then take F.M. 2580 north 6.9 miles to the gate on the left with a red bandanna. P.O. Box 298, Granbury, TX 76048; (817) 573-9952 or (800) 573-9953.

Hunter Park: See Hunter Park on page 355 for camping information.

Midway Pines Cabins and RV Park: RV sites rent for $14 at this campground 10 miles south of Granbury; cabins are $45. Dogs must be on leash when outside; they have four pine-shaded acres to explore. 9322 Glen Rose Highway, Granbury, TX 76048; (817) 573-0869.

Plantation Inn on the Lake: Rates are $63; small and medium-sized dogs may stay for $5 extra. 1451 East Pearl Street, Granbury, TX 76048; (817) 573-8846.

FESTIVALS

Old-Fashioned Fourth of July: Arts and crafts, games, parades, and fireworks over the lake at dusk take place the weekend of July 4. It's held on the courthouse square, at Pearl Street (U.S. 377 Business) and North Crockett Street. For information, call (817) 573-1622.

DIVERSIONS

Walk, walk, walk your dog: Granbury has a year-round 10K walk sanctioned by the American Volkssport Association. You can parade your pooch and rack up points at the same time. For the location and instructions, call (817) 326-2164.

JOHNSON COUNTY

BURLESON

PARKS, BEACHES, AND RECREATION AREAS

• **Chisenhall Park** 🐾 ½ *See* ❷ *on page 298.*

Leashed dogs may enjoy the mostly open 40 acres of this park or hike the moderately rugged 2.5-mile exercise trail, which runs along a creek.

There's also a playground, a swimming pool, rest rooms, and a picnic area here.

From Highway 174 South, go east on McNairn Road to the park entrance at 500 Chisenhall Park Lane. The park is open from 6 A.M. until midnight. (817) 447-3865.

RESTAURANTS

Arby's: Dogs love roast beef, and that's what Arby's is all about. Chow down at the table out front with your pooch. 801 Northeast Alsbury Boulevard; (817) 295-0043.

Fas Taco: Have your Tex-Mex at one of the tables out front while you ponder why the "t" is missing in the name. *¿Quien sabe?* 555 Southwest Wilshire Boulevard; (817) 295-0756.

Old Town Smokehouse: Sit at the bench out front and wolf down your smoked beef, turkey, ham, or sausage, or have a sandwich. 114 South Main Street; (817) 447-6366.

Taco Bell: Watch the latest television commercial to see what variation on Mexican fast food is on special this month, then have some at the table out front. 316 Southwest Wilshire Boulevard; (817) 295-6381.

PLACES TO STAY

Mockingbird Hill Mobile Home and RV Park: Pay $12, park your RV, and pick up after your dog and you'll both be welcome at this country campground. 1990 South Burleson Boulevard, Burleson, TX 76028; (817) 295-3011.

CLEBURNE

PARKS, BEACHES, AND RECREATION AREAS

• **Byron ("Buddy") Stewart Park** 🐾 🐾½ *See* ❸❸ *on page 298.*

This park is a little hard to get to, but it's worth the effort. It has a free campground and one of the best picnic areas for the dog-accompanied traveler we've found. There's also no entrance fee.

The picnic area lies along the Nolan River. Its banks are too steep to allow pooches to reach the water easily, although numerous tracks in the mud proved many had succeeded. Huge pecan trees shade the picnic ground, which covers perhaps 20 acres and has about 15 picnic tables and two pavilions. That leaves oodles of room for pooches to roam, which local laws require they do while leashed.

The campground suffers greatly by comparison. Its seven sites have no shade trees. Each site has a shaded picnic table and a barbecue grill—or would have had them if some had not been missing. The rest rooms consist of chemical toilets at the soccer fields across the road. But like we said, it's free.

The park is on the western edge of Cleburne on U.S. 67. The easiest way to reach it is to follow the "Hospital" signs off the highway and then, when you reach the hospital entrance, turn left to the park entrance a quarter mile down the access road. The park opens at sunrise and closes at midnight except to fishers and campers. (817) 645-0999.

• **Cleburne State Park** 🐾 🐾 *See* **54** *on page 298.*

This is a cozy park of 529 acres, and cozy is how you'll feel here. That's cozy the way Shakespeare put it: "Cabined, cribbed, confined, bound in." The park is long and skinny to begin with, and Cedar Lake takes up 116 acres. Nearly half the park is undeveloped rocky, juniper-covered hillsides. There's just not much room, and you'll find you are always bumping into other visitors.

There are two hiking trails in the park, the mile-long Spillway Trail and the 2.4-mile Coyote Run Nature Trail. Sport and I hiked the Spillway Trail, as its name promised a flowing stream and emerald pools, and perhaps a waterfall. Twenty yards into the walk we crossed a small limestone creekbed with little pools, and we looked forward to bigger and better things. Unfortunately, we didn't find them. The farther upstream we got, the drier the creek. Numbered markers along the Coyote Run Trail correspond to a trail guide available at park headquarters. It acquaints you with some of the local plants and animals and warns you about rattlesnakes and poison ivy.

If you like togetherness, you'll like this park's campgrounds. We saw lots of families with small children; many of them also had dogs. However, much of this park lacks charm for a dog. The 58 campsites are, with few exceptions, very close together and lacking in privacy. In fact, in the Cedar Grove Campground, many camping trailers were parked so close together you could literally stand between them, stretch out your arms, and touch both. Sport and I like a little more elbow room. All except six campsites have water and electricity, a picnic table, campfire ring, and rest rooms with showers nearby. These sites rent for $11 except for premium waterfront sites, which go for $14. Of these, the best are numbers 44 to 58. These sites are well shaded and relatively uncrowded. Many are at the water's edge, and the gently sloping bank gives easy access to the lake for fishing or swimming. Dogs are allowed in the water here, but they are banned from the swim beach in the day-use area. Our favorite sites, though, were the six primitive sites ($8), which have water and a rest room with showers nearby. These sites all back up to the lake, are very heavily shaded, and are almost totally screened from each other.

Reservations for campsites at all state parks must be made by calling the central reservation number, (512) 389-8900, between 9 A.M. and 6 P.M. Monday through Friday. Reservations are strongly recommended, and a deposit is required in order to guarantee a reservation. Specific sites may not be reserved; they are available on a first-come, first-served basis upon arrival.

Drive 10 miles southwest of Cleburne on Highway 67 to Park Road 21, then follow Park Road 21 for six miles. The gate is locked from 10 P.M. to 7 A.M.; late arrivals may get the combination to the gate by calling the park between 8 A.M. and 5 P.M. on their date of arrival. The entrance fee is $2. (817) 645-4215.

RESTAURANTS

The Purple Turnip: Sit on the terrace out front and be the center of attention as you have an apple-smoked pork tenderloin sandwich, portobello mushroom sandwich, vegetarian sandwich, crab cakes, or gourmet soups and salads. 104 North Pendell Place; (817) 558-6927.

West End Grill: The menu varies from barbecue to catfish. Eat on the patio. 1629 West Henderson Street; (817) 558-3663.

PLACES TO STAY

Byron ("Buddy") Stewart Park: See Byron ("Buddy") Stewart Park on page 358 for camping information.

Cleburne State Park: See Cleburne State Park on page 359 for camping information.

Days Inn: Rooms are $50. Dog owners must clean up after their pooches. U.S. 67 South at North Ridgeway Street, Cleburne, TX 76031; (817) 645-8836.

Gate 1 Motor Inn: Rooms are $39. Dogs must put up a $30 cash deposit or credit card imprint; the room will be inspected for doggy damage before checkout. 1836 North Main Street, Cleburne, TX 76031; (817) 641-3451.

Western Inn: Rooms are $38 to $40. Small dogs are welcome. 1411 East Henderson Street, Cleburne, TX 76031; (817) 645-4386.

FESTIVALS

Cleburne on the Rise Hot Air Balloon Festival: In late July or early August there's even more hot air than usual in Cleburne as dozens of colorful hot air balloons fill the skies competing for prizes in games such as "Hare and Hound." (Ask your hot air hot dog to explain it to you.) For landlocked leashed pooches, there's a carnival, food booths, and arts and crafts. The festival is held at the airport, 1650 Airport Road. For information, call (817) 645-2455.

KAUFMAN

PARKS, BEACHES, AND RECREATION AREAS

• **City Lakes Park** 🐾🐾½ *See* ⑤⑤ *on page 298.*

This park of about 100 acres doesn't get much respect—the official city map touts five area lakes but ignores the city's own parks—but for the leashed dog, it's not a bad place to visit. When Sport and I last made a dewatering stop there, city crews were busily clearing and burning brush. The lakes were almost dry, but there was a nice fringe of brush and weeds around the edge that held fascinating smells for Sport. Personally, I liked the wood smoke better. You won't find much shade here, as the park is mostly open grassland. There is a playground, rest rooms, and a picnic area.

The park is on Highway 34 about half a mile north of the city limits. It is open from sunrise to sunset. (972) 932-2216.

RESTAURANTS

Especially for You: Your pooch will feel special as she sits on the patio under the canopy sharing your soup and sandwich, daily blue plate special, or sinfully rich dessert. She'll think the place ought to be renamed Especially for Dogs. 100 West Grove Street; (972) 932-4274.

Sonic Drive-In: Sit at one of the picnic tables out front. What would burger-craving traveling dogs in Texas do without their friendly Sonic Drive-Ins? 214 East Mulberry Street; (972) 962-2445.

PLACES TO STAY

Countryside Inn: Rooms are $40 to $50. Dogs pay a $10 fee. 501 East Fair Street, Kaufman, TX 75142; (972) 932-2101.

DIVERSIONS

Get lit with your lassie: Join in the lighting up of the Christmas lights around the square the first weekend in December. Then shop for that special Christmas collar for your hound. It takes place on the courthouse square at Washington and Grove Streets. (972) 932-3118.

TERRELL

PARKS, BEACHES, AND RECREATION AREAS

• **Ben Gill Park** 🐾½ *See* ⑤⑥ *on page 298.*

Leashed dogs have a three-quarter-mile jogging trail to share with you, and there is a 2.5-acre lake whose waters sometimes spit up interesting subjects for sniffing. The playground is every kid's dream. This can be a busy park, with a swimming pool, tennis courts, athletic fields, and picnic area taking up most of the grounds. But dogs who had one too many cups of coffee before leaving home will be greatly relieved to find it.

The park is on West Moore Avenue (U.S. 80 West) half a mile east of its intersection with Highway 205. Hours are 6 A.M. to midnight. (972) 551-6604.

PLACES TO STAY

Classic Inn: Rooms are $35 to $39, which includes a continental breakfast. Small dogs may stay for a $25 fee. 1604 Texas 34 South, Terrell, TX 75160; (972) 563-1521 or (800) 346-1580.

Days Inn: Rooms are $48 except on the first Monday (and preceding weekend) of each month, when nearby Canton has its Trade Day. Then rates zoom to $85. Dogs pay $5 all the time. 1618 Texas 34 South, Terrell, TX 75160; (972) 551-2100 or (800) 325-2525.

FESTIVALS

July Fourth Celebration: It seems that nearly every city in Texas has some sort of Fourth of July celebration, and Terrell is no exception. However, Terrell goes to more trouble than most, with a community picnic, live music, skydivers, carnival, children's games, coloring contest, and a bike, trike, and wagon parade in which you will normally find a number of canine participants decked out in their best patriotic costumes. Held on July 4 in Ben Gill Park at West Moore Avenue (U.S. 80 West), half a mile east of its intersection with Highway 205. (972) 563-5703.

LIMESTONE COUNTY

Three leash-free parks are the good news about this county; the bad news is that all the parks are small. However, in a state where virtually all land is privately owned and there are few public places that allow dogs to run off leash, even small leash-free areas are big news to dogs. Two of the leash-free areas border Lake Limestone and offer free camping and swimming as well, so this could be just the weekend hideaway you and your dog have been looking for.

GROESBECK

PARKS, BEACHES, AND RECREATION AREAS

• Confederate Reunion Grounds State Park 🐾 🐾
See ⑤⑦ on page 298.

This day-use park really was used for what its name implies, reunions of veterans of what has been variously called (in the South), "the late unpleasantness," "the War for Southern Independence," "the War of Yankee Aggression," and (among certain four-legged segments of the population) "the War to Make Raccoon Hunting the National Pastime." Such subtleties are lost on dogs, however, who will be much more interested in park features such as Miss Mamie Kennedy's 1914 Confederate Flirtation Walk, a paved footpath along the Navasota River. Pay the entrance fee at the honor booth and take your leashed pooch for a flirtatious frolic in the park's 71 acres of woods.

Sport was far more interested in the squirrels feasting on the huge bur oak acorns than she was in the picnic ground or the 1893 dance pavilion. Unless there is a family reunion or wedding going on, you and your pooch will likely have the park to yourselves, there being no attendant on duty. There's a rest room, water faucets, a playground, and even a swimming hole on Jack Creek, making this a pleasant place to spend a summer day. Old dogs, like old soldiers, like to spend the afternoon snoozing in the shade after a big dinner-on-the-grounds of fried chicken, sliced tomatoes, fried okra, black-eyed peas, corn on the cob, scratch biscuits so light they float off the plate unless held down by big gobs of butter, peach cobbler good enough to make you slap your momma, and frosty glasses of iced tea. At least old Southern dogs do.

From Highway 14, go west 2.8 miles on F.M. 2705 to the park entrance. The road makes two 90-degree turns as it intersects, follows, and then leaves another farm-to-market highway; just follow the signs for F.M. 2705. Entrance costs $2. The park is open from 8 A.M. until 5 P.M. weekdays year-round and stays open until 8 P.M. on weekends from March through November. It is also open until 8 P.M. on weekdays from June 1 through Labor Day. (254) 562-5751.

• **Fort Parker State Park** 🐾 🐾 **1/2** *See* 🔢 *on page 298.*

This is a park with a split personality. Of its 1,485 acres, 750 lie under the waters of Lake Fort Parker, and 735 acres are rolling oak woodlands surrounding the lake. As at all state parks, your pooch must remain leashed. However, park personnel seemed downright friendly toward dogs compared to those at other state parks. "People are out here with their dogs all the time, and we just don't pay much attention to them," a park ranger said. In other words, the park treats dogs as though they are part of the natural order of things. It's too bad that attitude is met so seldom in our state park system.

The split personality theme carries over into the day-use area, which sits on a promontory extending into the lake. On one side of the service road is the main lake and the designated swimming area. Dogs are barred from the water and the picnic area adjacent. However, just on the other side of the road is another day-use area, also sloping down to an arm of the lake, and dogs are permitted here. Unfortunately, weedy, marshy banks prevent access to the water unless you don't mind having your tummy tickled by weeds. The Springs Trail begins at the footbridge in this area and runs about two miles past a historic cemetery, the group camping area, and a small spring-fed lake where trout fishing is allowed. Did your pooch pack her fly rod?

A second trail, under development when we last visited, will connect with Old Fort Parker two miles to the west. Birding is a popular activity along the trails; ask for a bird list at headquarters.

The campground has only 25 sites with water and electricity ($12). Ten screened shelters rent for $16, but dogs are not allowed inside. Of course, you may not—nor would you—leave your pooch unattended. All the campsites have a view of the lake, a picnic table, fire ring, and lantern post. A rest room with showers serves the area. While trees shade all sites, a lack of understory means you will have no privacy. And, the thick vegetation along the shoreline prevents access to the water. You may fish from a pier, however.

Ten primitive campsites ($6), each with just a picnic table and fire ring, hide in a thick tangle of trees and brush at the upper end of the lake. When we last visited only one faucet served the area, but more were planned. However, as it was littered with leaves and piles of brush from recent clearing operations, this was not an inviting campground when we saw it.

Reservations for campsites at all state parks must be made by calling the central reservation number, (512) 389-8900, between 9 A.M. and 6 P.M. Monday through Friday. Reservations are strongly recommended, and a deposit is required in order to guarantee a reservation. Specific sites may not be reserved; they are available on a first-come, first-served basis upon arrival.

Dogs must be kept on a six-foot leash and may not enter any park building. They must be kept inside a tent or vehicle at night, and you must pick up after them.

The park is on Highway 14 about six miles north of Groesbeck. There is a $2 entrance fee. The office is open from 8 A.M. to 5 P.M.; the park is closed except to campers from 10 P.M. to 8 A.M. For more information, contact Route 3, Box 95, Mexia, TX 76667; (254) 562-5751.

• **Limestone County Park No. 2** 🐾 🐾½ 🐕 *See* ⑤⑨ *on page 298.*

The mirror image of its twin on the north side of Lake Limestone, this 25-acre park has 10 shaded picnic tables with barbecue grills arranged on a curve of sandy beach. Dogs may run off leash here and at all parks administered by the Brazos River Authority. Camping is free. No reservations are required, but if you want to stay longer than a week, you must notify a ranger. Campers must also pick up their trash. Other than that, you and your pooch are free to run, splash, and play. That's the good news. On the other hand, there's not much shade, and most of the park resembles a well-mowed suburban lawn. However, Sport and I were captivated by a large yellow and white tomcat checking out the garbage cans for scraps. He looked a great deal like Sport and my favorite cat, Comet, who helps me write everything by napping atop my notes and who worked overtime on this book.

From F.M. 3371, just over six miles south of its intersection with Highway 164, turn east onto County Road 773; go 0.3 miles and turn left at the water treatment plant. The park is open 24 hours. (254) 729-3810.

• **Limestone County Park No. 3** 🐾½ 🦴 *See ⑩ on page 298.*

The best part of this 17-park is the beach, a sandy crescent on the north shore of Lake Limestone. Nine shaded picnic tables with barbecue grills, a small grove of oak trees, and a few acres of grass complete the tableau. His and her composting toilets sit atop the highest point in the park. Dogs may run off leash here and at all parks administered by the Brazos River Authority. Camping is free; no reservations are required, but if you want to stay longer than a week, you must notify a ranger. Campers must also pick up their trash.

The park is on F.M. 3371 five miles south of its intersection with Highway 164. It's open 24 hours. (254) 729-3810.

• **Old Fort Parker State Park** 🐾 🐾 🦴 *See ⑪ on page 298.*

This reconstructed frontier fort of the 1830s gives the pooch who loves rawhide in some form other than chews the opportunity to take part in re-creations of buckskin days when frontier Texans battled the Indians. In fact, that's just what happened here in 1836. A band of Indians attacked the fort, killing five and capturing five, the most famous of which was Cynthia Ann Parker, who grew up to marry a Comanche chief and give birth to Quanah Parker, the last Comanche war chief. You and your pooch can visit the site of the battle for just $2, and your pooch can even run leash-free inside the log fort's walls while you look at the cabins furnished with period furniture. It's likely that your pooch will make friends with Sally and Jimbo, the resident dogs at the fort, "and probably a couple of cats who live in the woodpile whose names we don't know because we can't get close enough to ask them," a park ranger told us.

For those of you who have been reading this guide for a while and are now reeling in shock from all those references to dogs being welcome at this state park while they are barely tolerated in others, an explanation is in order. Although this is a state park and was once run by the Texas Parks and Wildlife Department, it is now operated by the city of Groesbeck, which is considerably more enlightened when it comes to dogs. So let that girl roam and pretend she is a frontier dog protecting you from the Indians—or perhaps an Indian dog about to attack a settler dog. I suppose dogs can play cowdog and Indian dog.

Your pooch is also welcome to attend, on leash, historical reenactments held periodically at the fort. You and she can dress up in your best frontier garb and live as the pioneers did a century and a half ago. Dogs just love gnawing a big old bone beside a campfire. Call the park for information on scheduled events.

From Groesbeck, go north four miles on Highway 14; turn west onto Park Road 35 and follow it one mile to the park. Entrance costs $2. The park is open from 8 A.M. to 5 P.M. For more information, contact Route 3, Box 746, Groesbeck, TX 76642; (254) 729-5253.

RESTAURANTS

Sonic Drive-In: Does your pooch prefer Tater Tots or french fries? Conduct your taste test at the tables out front. 303 North Ellis Street; (254) 729-8989.

Susie's Restaurant: Order to go from a varied menu—chicken-fried steak, rib eye steak, chicken strips, grilled chicken, or fried shrimp—and eat on the benches in front. 301 South Ellis Street; (254) 729-5227.

PLACES TO STAY

Fort Parker State Park: See Fort Parker State Park on page 363 for camping information.

Limestone County Parks: See Limestone County Parks on pages 364 and 365 for camping information.

FESTIVALS

Christmas at the Fort: Indian descendants of Cynthia Ann Parker gather each December at the fort where she began her Indian life for a weekend of celebration centered around early Texas history. You and your leashed pooch can sample frontier cooking, listen to frontier music, watch Native American dances, and feel your blood stir to the beat of Comanche drums. It's held at Old Fort Parker around the second weekend in December. From Groesbeck, go north four miles on Highway 14, then turn west on Park Road 35 and follow it one mile. For information, call (254) 729-5253.

DIVERSIONS

Navigate the Navasota: Pop your pooch in your canoe and paddle three miles down the Navasota River from Confederate Reunion Grounds State Park to Fort Parker State Park. You can arrange shuttle service through Fort Parker State Park; call (254) 562-5751.

MEXIA

One of the side effects of Texas's strong Hispanic heritage is a number of place names that mystify people because the Spanish pronunciation is used; the other side effect is an even larger number of place names that have been so long pronounced using English rather than Spanish rules that only natives can say them, confusing everybody. An example of the latter is Amarillo, which should be pronounced ahm–ah–REE–yoh but is instead rendered am–uh–RILL–oh. At the opposite end of the spectrum is Mexia, which should be pronounced muh–HAY–uh and, for some inexplicable reason, is. (Stay with me, dogs. We'll work a dog into this story soon somehow, I promise.)

Mexia's mysterious moniker gave rise to a story that dogs the town to this day. (See?) It goes like this. Two travelers new to Texas were approaching the town by car and kept seeing road signs giving the mileage to it. Neither knew how to pronounce the name, and as is so often the case, their joint ignorance led to a lively disagreement with uninformed opinions on both sides. They agreed to stop when they got there and ask someone to tell them how to pronounce the name. So, over a cup of coffee, they posed the question to their waitress: "How do you say the name of this place, anyway?" Drawing herself up to her full five feet and placing her hand on her hip, she looked at the pair as if they were crazy or putting her on. "Why, DAY–ree kween, of course," she twanged and flounced off.

The sad ending to this story is that while there is a Dairy Queen in Mexia, it has no outside seating, so you and your pooch will have to eat elsewhere. But you can tell your dog the joke and laugh as you drive by. Even if he's heard it before.

RESTAURANTS

Kirby's Barbecue: Take your ribs, brisket, or sausage to one of the four tables on the side. 216 Texas 14 North; (254) 562-5076.

Rock'n L Steakhouse: Steak, grilled chicken, sandwiches, and salads are all on the menu at this country restaurant. You and your pooch can eat on the deck at the side of the building. It's about six miles west of Mexia on U.S. 84 at County Road 198; (254) 562-9404.

Sonic Drive-In: If you don't know by now that Sonic is a hamburger place, you haven't been paying attention. Eat at the tables out front. 500 East Milam Street; (254) 562-6955.

McLENNAN COUNTY

WACO

If you want outpourings of sympathy from your friends, tell them you are going to Waco. This Central Texas city once had a reputation as a place where fun was not allowed, it being the home of Baylor University, a college closely identified with a nondrinking, nondancing religious denomination. Well, Toto, you won't know you are in Waco anymore. They're dancing over at the college now, you can imbibe your favorite beverage right out in public in local restaurants, and best of all, Waco is a great place for dogs. It has one of the best—if not the best—city parks for dogs in the state, even though leashes are the law. Most of the local motels accept dogs, and your pooch can dine out at some of the best restaurants in town. So when your friends pat you on the shoulder and mutter condolences in your ear about being sentenced to do time in Waco, just smile and say nothing. Keep it a secret between you and your pooch. You're going to have a good time in Waco.

PARKS, BEACHES, AND RECREATION AREAS

• **Cameron Park** 🐾 🐾 🐾 1/2 See ㉒ on page 298.

At 416 acres, this is not only one of the largest city parks in Texas, it's also one of the best, for people and for leashed dogs. The Brazos River flows through the park and is joined by the Bosque River on the park's west side. Gently sloping banks allow access to the water in many places, and huge pecan trees provide ample venues for naps and leg lifts. Spring-fed pools invite contemplation or a cool drink, while towering bluffs offer spectacular views of the river and countryside. Shaded trails wind through quiet valleys and up rugged hills. Picnic areas and playgrounds make this a family place, although a challenging disc golf course attracts the college crowd, too. Wildflowers riot in the spring, and an occasional road-killed raccoon or opossum can show up at any time. This is a dew-claws up place for dogs.

Sport and I last visited in mid-November, when a golden shower of elm and pecan leaves rained down from the trees that shade almost every square inch of this park. We found a crew waging the Battle of the Leaves at Proctor Springs, a highly landscaped area where water issuing from midway up a limestone bluff has built a travertine hood over the spring itself. The trickling rivulets were just what a thirsty dog was looking for. There's something about wild water that satisfies a dog far better than the namby-pamby chlorinated stuff. Had it been springtime we would have headed straight for Miss Nellie's Pretty Place, a wild-flower garden laced with walking paths. While dogs generally don't care much for flowers, this garden has a bonus: a composting demon-stration area where dogs can sniff decomposing leaves and who-knows-what while you enjoy the blooms. For scenic overlooks, we'd recom-mend Lover's Leap, and not just because we're sentimental. We first visited Emmon's Bluff, where a trail from the west end of the picnic area leads to a spectacular overlook of the Bosque River flowing 10 stories below. However, the footing on the bluff was slippery and there was no guardrail. If you visit here, keep a firm grip on the leash, watch your step, and stay well back from the edge. At Lover's Leap the view is just as fine, and a stone wall assures that your pooch will not go airborne involuntarily.

To get the most enjoyment out of the park, pick up a park map at the Waco Visitor Center at Fort Fisher Park on Interstate 35 at the south end of the Brazos River bridge. One reason you'll need a map is because the park and residential areas interface at several points, and it's easy to think you've reached the end of the park when, in fact, you only have to drive a short distance to reenter it. The map also shows the trails within the park. In general the trails run along the rivers (watch for snakes), but one—designated the "difficult trail" on the map—also winds through gashes in the bluffs and up rugged hills.

To reach the park, follow University Parks Drive west from Interstate 35 about a mile. The park is closed from midnight to until 9 A.M. (254) 750-5980.

• **Flat Rock Area** 🐾🐾½ *See ㉝ on page 298.*

Most of this area is just the way Mother Nature created it, which means it's a great place for dogs. The undeveloped lakefront area has lots of trees but no facilities to intrude upon the weeds and brush. The dead raccoon in the entrance road told us this was a place where a dog could feel good about being a dog. Since the land is managed by the U.S. Army Corps of Engineers, dogs are required to be on leash. However, dogs may be off leash while in the water, and there are numerous places with easy, weed-free access to the edge of the lake. Follow the gravel road to the left just after entering to find the best areas. Watch for snakes.

From the intersection of Flat Rock Road and F.M. 1637 northwest of Waco, go south on Flat Rock Road 2.7 miles to its intersection with Yankie Road and the park entrance on your left. The gate is locked from 9 P.M. to 6 A.M. (254) 756-5359.

• **Koehne Park** 🐾 *See ㉔ on page 298.*

This small park of 10 acres or so gets heavy use by Waco dogs because it's on the city side of Lake Waco and therefore is just minutes away for a dog in dire need of visiting some hills, trees, and grass. There are about 15 picnic sites here, and while landlocked dogs must be leashed, they are free to go off leash in the water.

From Waco, take either North Valley Mills Drive north or Lakeshore Drive west; the park is where they meet. The park is closed from 10 P.M. to 6 A.M. (254) 756-5359.

• Speegleville II Park 🐾½ *See* ⑮ *on page 298.*

There's not much to this park except the Lacy Point Nature Area hike and bike trail, a paved half-mile path—actually an abandoned road— along the lakeshore. There's no water, but there are composting toilets at the parking area. Leashed dogs who fancy themselves bird dogs can get lots of pointing practice among the high weeds bordering the trail.

From Interstate 35, take Highway 6 west about six miles to the exit for North Speegleville Road. Follow that road north 1.2 miles; turn right onto McLaughlin Road. The park entrance is 0.4 miles ahead on your left; from there it's half a mile to the trailhead. The park is closed from 10 P.M. to 6 A.M. (254) 756-5359.

• Speegleville III Park 🐾 🐾 *See* ⑯ *on page 298.*

Listen closely, dogs, because there is going to be a test at the end of this paragraph. At this park you have your choice of two lakeside picnic areas with tables and trees. At one area there is a $1 per person entry fee, and you are banned from the swim beach. At the other area, there is no entry fee, and you can slip off your leash and go into the water. Which one would you rather visit? We thought so.

There is a trick to finding the free day-use area of this park. Just go on past the park entrance 0.6 miles to Overflow Road and turn right. Go 1.4 miles to an unnamed road and turn left, continuing another 0.9 miles to the entrance. Ten huge picnic sites with tables and fire rings, lots of shade, and easy access to the lake arc around an open grassy area. Dogs must be on leash while on land, but they may be off leash in the water.

The fee area of the park has a dozen picnic sites and 10 campsites with water and electricity ($15). The campsites have shade trees and a view of the lake; there is a rest room with showers. There is a $1 per person entrance fee for day use of the picnic area only, which is heavily used in the summer. That's why dogs generally prefer the other, free day-use area. Currently camping is first come, first served, but that may change in the near future; call for up-to-date policies.

From Interstate 35, take Highway 6 west about five miles to the exit for Speegleville III Park. The first right takes you to the fee day-use area and the campground. This part of the park is closed from 10 P.M. to 6 A.M.

The second right, Overflow Road, goes to the free day-use area, which is closed from 9 P.M. to 6 A.M. (254) 756-5359.

RESTAURANTS

Applebee's Neighborhood Grill and Bar: Leashed pooches are welcome at the bench in front of this chain restaurant whose specialty is pork riblets. If your pooch isn't into gnawing bones (not likely), maybe he'd like to share your burger, steak, salad, or sandwich (does a bear live and do other things in the woods?). 614 North Valley Mills Drive; (254) 751-9084.

Diamond Back's Restaurant and Bar: Don't go looking for snakes under the benches outside this trendy new spot; instead, check out the saffron chicken pasta, cowboy T-bone steak, chicken-fried tuna, or pecan redfish. And if your pooch so much as looks thirsty, the friendly manager will bring her a bowl of water. 217 Mary Street (at the corner of Third Street and Franklin Avenue); (254) 757-2871.

El Chico: "Dogs can sit anywhere they want here," the manager said. Don't take him literally; there's a bench out front or a patio out back; take your choice. The menu is Tex-Mex. 2111 South Valley Mills Drive; (254) 662-2750.

Krispy Chicken: Share with your pooch at one of the patio tables on the side. 2307 Franklin Avenue; (254) 757-1230.

Ninfa's: Mama Ninfa is like a goddess to Sport and Samantha. Ninfa invented *tacos al carbon,* and these two *perros* simply worship the flour tortillas stuffed with beef, chicken, or pork tenderloin. When they start making little smacking sounds while sleeping, I'm sure they're dreaming Mama Ninfa is feeding them tacos. Adoring dogs can dine on the benches on the covered sidewalk out front. 215 Mary Avenue (at the corner of Third Street and Franklin Avenue); (254) 757-2050.

Taco Bell: Your *perro* can munch a taco on the patio at 1725 North Valley Mills Drive; (254) 772-5629.

Taco Cabana: Good Mexican food served fast built this national chain with the shocking pink decor. This one reserves a table in the corner of the patio just for leashed dogs. 825 South Sixth Street; (254) 752-4334.

PLACES TO STAY

Best Western—Waco Mall: Mall mutts stay free here; you'll pay $62. 6624 West U.S. 84, Waco, TX 76712; (254) 776-3194 or (800) 346-1581.

Days Inn: Rooms are $56 to $80. Dogs pay $6 each per night. 1504 North Interstate 35, Waco, TX 76705; (254) 799-8585.

Econo Lodge: Pay $48 and tell your pooch to "keep it clean" and you're in. 500 North Interstate 35, Waco, TX 76704; (254) 756-5371.

Fort Fisher Park: Despite its location right on Interstate 35 (or, depending on how you look at it, perhaps because of it) this may be the best campground in Waco. It's right on the Brazos River, close to Cameron Park and local restaurants, and is heavily shaded by large live oak trees. There's plenty of dog-walking room along the river, three free fishing docks, and a waterside picnic area. The 100 campsites with water, electricity, and sewer rent for $12; those with water and electricity only go for $11. An even dozen tent sites are $10. There's good news for the dog who's afraid to sleep outside: Dogs are allowed inside the 15 screened shelters ($12), although all they'll find inside is a picnic table. (Keeping in mind, however, that the mascot of Baylor University is a bear, timid pooches may prefer to sleep under the picnic table just in case that carnivorous dog-eater gets loose in the night.) Rest rooms with showers serve the area. You must keep your pooch on her leash and clean up after her.

Due to budget cutbacks that close the office daily at 4:30, you'll want to make reservations by calling (800) 922-6386. That way, when you arrive you'll find a key to the rest room and/or screened shelters awaiting you. Otherwise, you'll be locked out and will be forced to walk around with your legs tightly crossed until the office opens in the morning (8 A.M. except Sundays, when it opens at 9 A.M.).

Take Exit 335B off Interstate 35; the park entrance is off the frontage road immediately north of South University Parks Drive. P.O. Box 2570, Waco, TX 76702; (254) 750-8630.

Howard Johnson Riverplace Inn: Rates are $40 to $50. Dogs may not be left in rooms alone. 101 North Interstate 35, Waco, TX 76704; (254) 752-8222 or (800) 792-3267.

La Quinta Inn: Rooms are $67 to $74, and your small pooch (25 pounds or under) can lounge in luxury with you. 1110 South Ninth Street, Waco, TX 76706; (254) 752-9741 or (800) NU-ROOMS/687-6667.

Midway Park: Rows of stately pecan trees will enthrall boy dogs here; darting squirrels will entertain girl dogs and boy dogs both. Thirty campsites with water and electricity ($15 except for the pull-throughs, which are $17) and 15 tent sites with water in the area ($13) overlook Lake Waco. There are rest rooms with showers and plenty of shade from live oak and pecan trees. Dogs must be on leash. Currently camping is first come, first served, but that may change in the near future; call for up-to-date policies.

From Interstate 35, take Highway 6 west about four miles to the Midway Park exit; go to the turnaround under the lake bridge and head back east on the frontage road to the entrance. The gate is locked from 10 P.M. to 6 A.M. Route 10, Box 173-G, Waco, TX 76708; (254) 756-5359.

Motel 6: All Motel 6s allow one small pooch per room. There are two locations in Waco. Rooms are $35 at 1509 Hogan Lane, Waco, TX 76705; (254) 799-4957. Rooms are $33 at 3120 South Interstate 35, Waco, TX 76706; (254) 662-4622.

Speegleville I Park: Almost all the 93 campsites here are on the water; all have a picnic table with shade shelter, electricity and water, and barbecue grill. Six rest rooms with showers serve the area. If your pooch likes his comfort when camping and doesn't mind crowds, this is the campground for him. Sites are $15. Currently camping is first come, first served, but that may change in the near future; call the park for up-to-date policies.

From Interstate 35, take Highway 6 west about six miles to the exit for North Speegleville Road; follow that road 2.7 miles to the entrance. The gate is locked from 10 P.M. to 6 A.M. (254) 756-5359.

Speegleville III Park: See Speegleville III Park on page 370 for camping information.

Victorian Inns: Rooms are $44 to $50. There is a $5 fee per night for dogs. 720 Martin Luther King Jr. Boulevard, Waco, TX 76704; (254) 752-3388.

FESTIVALS

Pioneer Heritage Day: Every dog has pioneer ancestors who defended home and hearth from lions and tigers and bears. Well, from bears, anyway. Okay, okay, from marauding raccoons intent on ransacking the supply of dog food on the back porch. Recall those heroic days of yore with your pooch at the Governor Bill and Vara Daniel Historic Village the first Saturday of April. To reach the village, go east of Interstate 35 on University Parks Drive a quarter of a mile and turn left (north) between the Texas Sports Hall of Fame and the sign for the Baylor University Institute of Environmental Studies. For information, call (254) 710-1160.

Summer Saunters: On selected Saturdays and Sundays in June, July, and August, you and your leashed pooch can join in childhood games, sample sarsaparilla, sing spirituals (howling along is encouraged), or just wander around the grounds of the Governor Bill and Vara Daniel Historic Village. It's all about learning about life in a Texas river town of a century ago. If your Huckleberry Hound hasn't slept under the porch of a general store on the main street of town, well, it's about time. To reach the village, go east of Interstate 35 on University Parks Drive a quarter of a mile and turn left (north) between the Texas Sports Hall of Fame and the sign for the Baylor University Institute of Environmental Studies. For information, call (254) 710-1160.

Summer Sounds: Each Thursday night from June through August, you and your leashed hound can attend a free outdoor concert at the amphitheater at Indian Springs Park, at the foot of the historic suspension bridge across the Brazos River on South University Parks Drive, half a mile west of Interstate 35. For information, call (254) 750-5873.

Walk for the Animals: Do your bit for less fortunate pooches the first Sunday in May. Round up some sponsors, snap a leash on your pooch, and take part in this annual one-mile walk that raises money for the Waco animal shelter. Sometimes there are contests for dogs, too, but plans for those were sidetracked down some rabbit trail when we last inquired. They might be reinstated if the public demands them, if you catch my drift. The walk begins at Indian Springs Park, at the foot of the historic suspension bridge across the Brazos River on South University Parks Drive, half a mile west of Interstate 35. For time and information, call (254) 754-1454.

DIVERSIONS

Get suspended: The first bridge across the Brazos River still hangs above the river on 14 cables as big around as your dog's muzzle. Thousands of longhorns crossed this bridge as they went up the Chisholm Trail; no doubt local hounds helped them on their way by barking at them. Now open to foot traffic only, the bridge is a good place from which to see the river. Plus, there's something very satisfying about the click of toenails on wood planking. There's more, too: Take the steps down to the river just east of the toll taker's booth on the south end of the bridge and find Indian Springs, where the Hueco (whence came "Waco") Indians once watered their hounds. Your pooch can sip from the spring and then promenade along a walk beside the river. Park at the foot of the bridge on South University Parks Drive about half a mile west of Interstate 35.

Root around in your roots: Since I have written all or parts of several Texas history textbooks, Sport Dog looks up to me in dumb adoration as her personal expert on all things relating to Texas history. However, I had to admit that I was stumped when it came to identifying Governor Bill Daniel. I was familiar with former governors Price Daniel and W. Lee O'Daniel, but for the life of me I couldn't recall a Bill Daniel having served as governor of Texas. It turns out that Alzheimer's hasn't struck just yet; the gentleman in question served as governor of Guam during the Kennedy administration. (Whether this post was bestowed as a reward or as punishment is open to debate.) The guv and his family donated the collection of historic buildings now known as the Governor Bill and Vara Daniel Historic Village to Baylor University in 1985. The buildings were moved from their original site near Houston to this location, where a small river town of a century ago was re-created. While pooches are banned from most museums and collections of historic structures, they are welcome here as long as they remain leashed. This is a good idea, since on a recent visit there Sport and I met two turkeys and a guinea fowl pecking around on the floor of the cotton gin, one of the buildings in the collection. You and your hound can also wander around in the blacksmith shop, livery stable, saloon, general store, and schoolhouse. Even if your pooch is not interested in history or architecture, she will enjoy being outside on the dirt street or resting under the trees. Admission is $3.

To reach the village, go east of Interstate 35 on University Parks Drive a quarter of a mile and turn left (north) between the Texas Sports Hall of Fame and the sign for the Baylor University Institute of Environmental Studies. The complex is open from 10 A.M. to 4 P.M. Tuesday through Friday and from 1 P.M. to 5 P.M. on Saturday and Sunday. (254) 710-1160.

WEST

Some towns get all confused about why they exist. They think they are supposed to be a trade center, or an educational center, or a government center, or some other kind of center that no other town nearby is. Thank goodness there is no such confusion in West. West exists for only one reason, and the good people of West know what that reason is: kolaches. Early settlers in the area brought their Czechoslovakian heritage and recipes (and maybe a Czech dog or two named Blank, but we have not confirmed this) with them, and this little hamlet on Interstate 35 just north of Waco awakes each morning with just one purpose in mind: to bless the world with some of the best kolaches to be found outside Prague.

For the uninformed among you, a kolache is a sweet yeast roll in the middle of which, before baking, someone with a large thumb made a depression and spooned in a gob of filling, usually fruit such as apple, peach, apricot, strawberry, or the like. Some of the best, however, are poppyseed, prune, and cream cheese. After baking, the cook drizzles the puffy parcels of paradise with icing and stands back while hordes of hungry kolache lovers devour them. Trust me. This happens every day in West, and sales go up significantly whenever I pass through.

But West takes these delightful delicacies to an even higher level. A local meat market makes a particularly delicious sausage, and some inspired baker invented what is known as the sausage kolache, a yeast roll containing a link of sausage. Sausage kolaches are like pigs in blankets, except the sausage is totally hidden inside. Dogs love sausage kolaches, and one of the nicest things about them is they freeze well, so you can carry home a supply. Just don't leave them unprotected in the backseat.

As stated earlier, West is a one-purpose town. It has no parks where dogs can roam. It has no motels where dogs can stay. It has no festivals where dogs can Czech out the goings-on. What it does have is one bakery with one bench out front where you and your pooch are welcome to wrap yourselves around kolaches until you can both spell Czechoslovakia. That's reason enough to go West, young dog.

RESTAURANTS

The Village Bakery: All the warmth emanating from this bakery does not come from the ovens, which when we last visited were turning out rack after rack of kolaches in at least a dozen flavors. The folks here are small-town Texas friendly at its best, and that extends to hounds. There's a bench right outside the front door where you can tie your pooch while you purchase your kolaches, and then you can both get down to the serious business of wolfing down as many as you can hold. The sausage kolaches chased by prune or poppyseed were our favorite. Or was it apricot followed by sausage? Darn. We won't be able to rest until we make it back to West and straighten this out. Research can be such a tough job sometimes. 108 East Oak; (254) 826-5151.

NAVARRO COUNTY

CORSICANA

PARKS, BEACHES, AND RECREATION AREAS

• **Community Park** 🐾 1/2 *See* ⑤⑦ *on page 298.*

As small-town urban parks go, this one is a dandy. Its 46 acres contain just about everything a dog could want—rolling expanses of grass, numerous trees, a paved 0.6-mile walking trail, a creek, legions of squirrels, and a playground for fellow restless travelers of the munchkin variety. Dogs must be leashed here, but they'll have a good time, and judging from the number of dogs we saw roaming nearby front yards and streets when we last visited, they'll meet some interesting new friends as well. We met a three-generation family on the walking trail—grandpa, grandson, and the newest member of the family, a frisky husky puppy.

Sport normally ignores playgrounds—once she was fixed, she lost all interest in swinging—but this one features replicas of a camel and an elephant for kids to climb on, and while Sport normally restricts her hunting activities to raccoons, skunks, and (once) porcupines, she went on red alert when she spotted these lifelike beasts. It took a fair amount of firm leash-gripping, fast talking, and frenzied sniffing to remind her that humans sometimes come up with weird things to put in parks. Fortunately, here the park builders remembered to include rest rooms and water fountains along the walking trail.

From Interstate 45 Business, follow West First Street west to North 13th Street; turn right (north) and go two blocks to the intersection with West Oaklawn Street and the park entrance. The park is closed from midnight until 5 A.M. (903) 654-4840.

RESTAURANTS

Whataburger: The burgers aren't the main attraction here, nor are the tables out front where you can eat. Dogs come for the view of the giant dog and tiger painted on the side of the building across the street. 1709 West Seventh Avenue; (903) 872-6871.

PARKER COUNTY

WEATHERFORD

PARKS, BEACHES, AND RECREATION AREAS

• Cartwright Park 🐾🐾🐾 *See* ❻❽ *on page 298.*

Trees, water, and trails—the magic ingredients for a first-class dog park—all come together in this 145-acre park. Sunshine Lake (45 acres) glows as the centerpiece of a park with ample open areas and lots of oak trees shading picnic tables. The lakeshore is a mowed, gentle slope to the water's edge, where leashed pooches can sip or swim. (Okay, maybe gulp and flounder.) The well-maintained park also has a playground, water, and chemical toilets. Just outside the park entrance is the easternmost access point for the Rails to Trails project, a growing network of hiking trails utilizing abandoned railroad right-of-ways. From here you can hike all the way to Lake Mineral Wells State Park, about 20 miles.

The park is northwest of downtown on F.M. 920. From the intersection with F.M. 51, go 1.9 miles to Cartwright Park Road; turn left; go another 0.3 miles to the park entrance. The park is closed from 10 P.M. to 6 A.M. (817) 598-4241.

• **Lake Mineral Wells State Park** 🐾🐾🐾½ *See* ❻❾ *on page 298.*

Sport and I had a surprise waiting for us when we visited this popular state park. At the entrance gate and other locations in the 3,010-acre park, large red letters warned: "Mountain Lion Advisory." One of the large cats had recently been spotted in the area. If that's not good enough reason to keep your pooch on a leash, remember that six-foot leashes and no unattended pooches are the law at all state parks.

This park was a pleasant surprise in other ways, too. It lies in the Cross Timbers, an area of heavy post oak forest hemmed in by almost treeless prairies to the north, south, and west. In fact, this is one of the most heavily forested state parks we visited, even though most of the trees are relatively small, only a few inches in diameter and 15 or so feet tall. But what they lacked in size, they made up for in number and close spacing. Another surprise was the bluff area overlooking 646-acre Lake Mineral Wells, where rock climbing (bouldering) and rappelling rule. Huge slabs of sandstone sloughed off the cliff face eons ago, forming narrow canyons between three-story rocks the size of houses. This area also contains one of the park's two picnic areas, but it's worth visiting even if you just want to watch the rock climbers do their thing. In fact, for Sport, seeing the climbers in their safety harnesses was a revelation. It was the first time she had ever seen people on leashes. I think she approved, or at least felt there was some justice in the world after all.

Climbers don't have all the fun here, however. The park has 16 miles of trails, of which 10 are multiuse and six are for hiking only. The trails all leave the Cross Timbers Campground and interlace with each other. The main trail is four miles long; there are loop trails off it as short as half a mile. Except for a trail to a primitive backpacking camping area ($6), all the trails are fairly flat and easy walking. The 2.5-mile trail to the primitive camping area is steep and rugged. There is no water along any of the trails.

Remember one thing if you want to go camping here: Make a reservation. This popular park stays full; when Sport and I last visited on an October weekday, there was a waiting list of campers hoping someone with a reservation would not show up. After we checked out the campgrounds, we understood why: They are some of the prettiest you'll find in Texas. The Post Oak Campground has 11 well-spaced, heavily shaded sites with water only ($8). Each site has a picnic table, fire ring, barbecue grill, and lantern post. A rest room without showers serves the area. For more privacy plus a rest room with showers, you might try the Live Oak Campground, which has 47 sites with water and electricity ($11). Some of the sites in this campground sit right on the water, are dubbed premium, and rent for $15. Many of the sites in the Live Oak area are spaced far apart, are heavily shaded, and offer lots of privacy.

The Plateau Campground has 30 sites with water and electricity ($11); a few are the premium $15 sites. This camping area is flatter and more open than Live Oak; consequently, many of the sites are not as private. However, many of the sites are quite large, so if your pooch needs her elbow room, she might like it here. This area is served by a rest room with showers.

The standard state park rules apply to pooches. Keep them on a six-foot leash, pick up after them, keep them off the designated swim beach beside the boat dock and do not leave them unattended. Dogs are also banned from entering any park building, including the 15 screened shelters, which rent for $20.

Reservations for campsites at all state parks must be made by calling the central reservation number, (512) 389-8900, between 9 A.M. and 6 P.M. Monday through Friday. Reservations are strongly recommended, and a deposit is required in order to guarantee a reservation. Specific sites may not be reserved; they are available on a first-come, first-served basis upon arrival.

Lake Mineral Wells State Park is four miles east of Mineral Wells or 14 miles west of Weatherford on U.S. 180. The entry fee is $3 per person. The park is closed except to overnight guests from 10 P.M. to 6 A.M. The park office is normally open from 8 A.M. until 5 P.M., but may stay open until 10 P.M. on Friday and Saturday nights. (940) 328-1171.

RESTAURANTS

Dairy Queen: Sport, Samantha, and resident cat Comet all have a weakness for the Blizzards served up by this chain of burger restaurants. At this one you can eat at the outside tables with your pooch. 815 South Main Street; (817) 594-5216.

Golden Fried Chicken: Gnaw those bones at the outside tables. 1101 North Main Street; (817) 594-4031.

Out to Lunch Tea Room: Be a porch puppy (that's where the tables are) while chowing down on salads, quiches, sandwiches, and homemade desserts. 202 Houston Street; (817) 599-5271.

Pizza Place: You don't have to eat pizza at the tables on the porch; they serve sandwiches and spaghetti as well. 1218 South Main Street; (817) 594-0591.

Yesterdays: There's only one sidewalk table with two chairs, but you'll hardly notice. You'll be too busy looking at the historic architecture all around and attacking your sandwich made on homemade bread, your homemade soup, pasta, garden salad, cookies, brownies, or ice cream soda from the old-time soda fountain. 128-B York Avenue; (817) 599-3903.

PLACES TO STAY

Best Western Santa Fe Inn: Rooms are $49 to $55. Small, well-behaved, housebroken dogs who do not bark are welcome for $3 per night. The inn is off Interstate 20 at Exit 409. 1927 Santa Fe Drive, Weatherford, TX 76086; (817) 594-7401 or (800) 528-1234.

Buxton's Diamond B RV Park: Full-hookup sites rent for $13; tent sites are $10. Your leashed pooch is welcome as long as she does not bark. 4001 Old Brock Road, Weatherford, TX 76087; (817) 594-5817.

Comfort Inn: Rates are $48 to $75. Any housebroken dog is welcome here. 809 Palo Pinto Street, Weatherford, TX 76086; (817) 599-8683 or (800) 221-2222.

Lake Mineral Wells State Park: See Lake Mineral Wells State Park on page 377 for camping information.

Super 8 Motel: Rooms are $43. Dogs pay a $5 fee. Interstate 20 and Highway 171, Weatherford, TX 76086; (817) 594-8702.

Weatherford Campground: RV sites are $18; tent sites are $16. Quiet, leashed, non-barking dogs are welcome but are not allowed in buildings. 2205 Tin Top Road, Weatherford, TX 76087; (817) 594-8801.

FESTIVALS

Parker County Peach Festival: Peaches, pooches (especially pooches named Peaches), and people gather the second Saturday to celebrate this fuzzy fruit with food, arts and crafts, and music. Dogs must be leashed. The festivities take place on the courthouse square at Fort Worth Street and Austin Avenue. For information, call (817) 596-3801.

DIVERSIONS

Get a peachy deal: Local farmers in bib overalls and pickup trucks sell their produce at the Weatherford Public Market, 213 Fort Worth Street. You and your pooch can get your peaches just hours after they're plucked. You might even get to rub noses with a good old farm dog. (817) 594-3801.

Track down Weatherford's past: Anchored by the 1886 Parker County Courthouse, Weatherford's downtown is a storehouse of historic architecture. You and your leashed pooch can follow two historic tours guided by brochures from the Chamber of Commerce, itself located in a historic building, the 1910 Santa Fe Railroad Depot at 401 Fort Worth Street. Or you can just follow your hound's nose. Historic architecture lurks behind every bush. (817) 596-3801.

SOMERVELL COUNTY

GLEN ROSE

PARKS, BEACHES, AND RECREATION AREAS

• **Dinosaur Valley State Park** 🐾 🐾½ *See* ⑦⓪ *on page 298.*

Dinosaur tracks are the main attraction here, but that's not what Sport and Samantha found fascinating—if that's the right word. Just after you pay your entry fee and enter the park, two giants loom above you: a 70-foot apatosaurus and a 45-foot Tyrannosaurus rex. The replicas were built for the Sinclair Oil Company's dinosaur exhibit at the New York World's Fair and were later donated to the park. The unflappable Sport was merely intrigued by what apparently seemed to her to be some of the largest cows she had ever seen. Samantha, on the other hand, the dog who will bark until her head falls off at any cow or horse, cowered in the back of the car and whined as though she was about to be devoured. She had finally met her Top Dog. Too bad it is extinct.

About half this park's 1,274 acres nestle in a bend in the Paluxy River. It's that streambed in which, millions of years ago, several theropods and sauropods slogged along in firm mud that preserved their tracks and eventually changed into limestone. Viewing the tracks will delight your leashed pooch, as the best way to do it is wading in the river, squishing along in the mud and maybe leaving a few tracks of your own for history—sure to be used at some future point to prove that Nike-wearing humans, dogs, and dinosaurs coexisted simultaneously and perhaps repopularizing the joke about the dyslexic agnostic who wondered if there really was a Dog. The park map you obtain when you enter the park will guide you to the three main sites where tracks appear, but you and your leashed pooch are free to wander the river anywhere you like, since there is no designated swimming area from which dogs are barred.

A network of hiking trails, seven miles in all, traverses much of the upland area across the river. The park map details the routes of the trails, which are color coded white, blue, and yellow. The white trail, at 4.5 miles, is the longest. A primitive camping area with seven sites ($8) is about three-quarters of a mile from the trailhead. Mountain bikes are allowed on the trails; be wary of them and of snakes. Also be aware that flash floods on the Paluxy River are not uncommon and may prevent access to the opposite bank or may trap you there for a few hours until the river runs down. Never try to cross the river when it is up. (High water also prevents viewing the dinosaur tracks; if that's the reason for your visit, call ahead to inquire about river conditions.)

A half-mile walk from the parking lot opposite the dinosaur models takes you to the south primitive camping area, which has nine sites ($8). These are some of the finest campsites in the park, since they are located along the river in a grove of large pecan trees.

There is only one campground other than the primitive sites. It has 46 spaces, all with water and electricity and served by a rest room with showers. These sites are $15. They vary widely in appeal. Some are small and close to their neighbors, while others are quite large and somewhat isolated. A number of them have areas making them suitable for use by groups who want to rent adjacent campsites and share a common area for eating and socializing.

Reservations for campsites at all state parks must be made by calling the central reservation number, (512) 389-8900, between 9 A.M. and 6 P.M. Monday through Friday. Reservations are strongly recommended, and a deposit is required in order to guarantee a reservation. Specific sites may not be reserved; they are available on a first-come, first-served basis upon arrival.

As at all state parks, dogs are not allowed in any park buildings, must be on a six-foot leash, and may not be left unattended.

The park is located four miles west of Glen Rose on Park Road 59 (F.M. 205). The entry fee is $5 per person ($3 if you camp). The office is open from 8 A.M. to 5 P.M.; the park closes at 10 P.M. except to overnight guests. (254) 897-4588.

PLACES TO STAY

Cedar Ridge RV Park: RV sites rent for $14 to $16; tent sites are $12. Dogs must be leashed and well behaved. The park is on U.S. 67 about 4.5 miles south of Glen Rose. Route 1, Box 217B, Glen Rose, TX 76043; (254) 897-3410.

Dinosaur Valley State Park: See Dinosaur Valley State Park on page 380 for camping information.

Hideaway Country Log Cabins: These cabins are located on 155 wooded acres where dogs can run off leash, but due to snakes, leashes are recommended. Cabin yards are fenced, shaded, and isolated from each other. Cabins are $75 to $90. There is a onetime $10 per pet charge; no more than two dogs per cabin are accepted. Route 2, Box 148, Bluffdale, TX 76433. Call for directions: (254) 823-6606.

Tres Rios: This multiuse facility has a campground, motel, and cabins as well as an outdoor concert area. Leashed dogs are welcome everywhere except under the stage, where the snack bar is located. RV sites rent for $16, motel rooms for $49, and cabins from $60 to $175; there is a $10 fee for dogs in the motel and cabins. It's located on County Road 312 about a mile east of town, just off U.S. 67. P.O. Box 2112, Glen Rose, TX 76043; (254) 897-4253.

FESTIVALS

Art on the Square: Shop for the work of local artists on the town square Memorial Day weekend. For information, call (254) 897-3838.

Bluegrass Festival: Banjos and fiddles invade Tres Rios (see above) in late April, early September, and late October; your pooch will be toe-tappin' right along with the rest of the crowd. Follow U.S. 67 east of town about a mile and turn south on County Road 312. Call for admission prices: (254) 897-4253.

Celtic Festival: Sounds of the auld country ring out at Tres Rios the second weekend in April. Follow U.S. 67 east of town about a mile and then turn south on County Road 312. Call for admission prices: (254) 897-4253.

DIVERSIONS

Take a dip with the dinosaurs: Dogs love water as much as dinosaurs did, and the Paluxy River was (and is) a playground where splashing is definitely encouraged. You and your pooch can gain access to the river for swimming at a low water crossing about three miles east of town. Turn south off U.S. 67 onto F.M. 200 and you're there almost immediately. Park along the side of the road. The Paluxy is classified as a navigable stream, which means its channel is public property up to the normal high water mark. Just stay on the rocks extending into the water and in the water itself and you'll be legal.

TARRANT COUNTY

ARLINGTON

Arlington is smushed in between Dallas and Fort Worth, and every day thousands of people blaze through on the freeways on their way to one of the big cities, never even considering stopping in little old Arlington. What could a town its size have to offer compared to the giants on either side? The answer is, plenty. In fact, if we had our druthers about where to take our pooch, we'd pick Arlington first. Its parks are large and well suited for dogs, there are plenty of restaurants and motels where dogs are welcome, and one of the best festivals for dogs and people happens here each June when Scottish clans gather for a wee bit o' fun—and bring their dogs along. Your pooch is welcome, too, kilts or no.

PARKS, BEACHES, AND RECREATION AREAS

• **Randol Mill Park** 🐾 🐾 🐾 *See ⑪ on page 299.*

Anyone who has read C. S. Lewis's *The Chronicles of Narnia* knows the significance of the phrase "higher up and deeper in," and those were exactly the words that popped into my mind upon entering this park. While the display of canna lilies at the entrance caught my eye, I knew Sport's level of interest in horticulture borders on zero, unless a tree with a squirrel or raccoon in it is involved. But the farther into this 99-acre park we went, the better it got for dogs. Dogs must remain on leash, and you must pick up after them, but the western half of the park comes near to being as good as it gets for dogs in urban parks. While athletic fields dominate elsewhere, a creek with gently sloping banks gets bigger and bigger as you go deeper into the park, until it finally broadens into a pond decorated with a fountain and a flock of geese. Large post oak trees cast heavy shade on both sides of the creek, and there are almost as many squirrels about as there are picnic tables. It's the kind of place suburban moms bring their kids and their dogs for a morning romp, and while we were there several vans pulled up and disgorged cargoes of energetic two-legged and four-legged children eager to run and play.

The park, at 1901 West Randol Mill Road, is closed from midnight to 5 A.M. (817) 459-5474.

• **River Legacy Park** 🐾 🐾 🐾 ½ *See* **72** *on page 299.*

Sport is a country dog, but she felt right at home in this 450-acre park in the Trinity River bottom. That's because there were huge trees all around, wild animals in the bushes, and even a black cat in a parking lot. It's a good thing dogs must be leashed. We were both taken aback just a bit by the 4.13-mile paved multiuse trail. Walkers, joggers, dogs, bicycle riders, and rollerbladers ambled, puffed, trotted, wheeled, and zipped by, each according to his or her mode. This is a busy trail, which no doubt explains its yellow center stripe and stop signs—yes, stop signs—at intersections. (If you've been considering teaching your dog to read, this is a good place to start.) However, there are dirt side trails where a pooch can give her paws a break from the concrete. A creek winds through the park on its way to join the river, and we watched soft-shelled turtles paddling lazily in the current, waiting for an easy meal to drift to them. Signs along the trail warn visitors to remain calm if a fox or raccoon darts across the trail, but we were not lucky enough to see one. Maybe your pooch will have the thrill.

The park also has a playground, picnic areas, and large expanses of mowed grass. Rest rooms and water are available.

It's located at Northwest Green Oaks Boulevard and North Cooper Street. The park is closed from midnight to 5 A.M. (817) 459-5474.

• **Vandergriff Park** 🐾 🐾 *See* **73** *on page 299.*

If only parks lived up to the promise of the names of the streets they're on, this would be one of the best parks in the world for dogs. The entrance road to the park is named Marrow Bone Spring Street, conjuring up visions of juicy gnawables littering the ground beside a cool, flowing stream. Of course, the leashed dogs who come here won't realize what they're missing, unless they can read. They probably won't find one single bone in this park's 84 acres, even though there are a number of picnic tables to sniff around. There's even a weedy drainage in the southwest corner that might harbor a furry critter or two. But most of the park is taken up by mowed grass, scattered trees, a playground, and athletic fields. Trees provide some shade, and rest rooms and water are available.

The park's address is 2810 Matlock Road, but that's the entrance to a maintenance area. Go south on Matlock Road to the southern end of the park and turn east on Central Park Drive, which intersects with Marrow Bone Spring Street a block later. Take Marrow Bone Spring Street to the parking lot. It's closed from midnight to 5 A.M. (817) 459-5474.

• **Veterans Park** 🐾🐾🐾 *See **74** on page 299*

As soon as Sport and I got out of the car, we were surrounded by 10 preschoolers from a local daycare center who'd come to romp on the playground, stuffed animals tucked into armpits, and snacks clutched tightly in little hands not yet grubby from play. Had Samantha been with us, the snacks would have been poached in short order, but Sport was her usual ladylike self despite being petted and squealed over. There's nothing quite as good for a dog's ego as being reminded she's the center of the universe. Of course, having to be on her leash also reminded Sport that while she might be the Cutest Thing on Earth to a bunch of little kids, she's still just a dog with a little "d" to the Arlington Parks and Recreation Department.

The 103 acres of this park offer much to dogs. There's a small pond with resident geese, and although a sign forbids swimming and wading, it says nothing about sniffing and slurping. In fact, we saw a Jack Russell terrier head straight for the pond after a brief, necessary stop beside a trash can. A 1.44-mile paved walking trail winds through the park, passing through wooded areas and along a dry creek. There's also a disc golf course and rest rooms.

The park is closed from midnight to 5 A.M. 3600 West Arkansas Lane; (817) 459-5474.

RESTAURANTS

J. Gilligan's Bar and Grill: According to the manager, this is THE place for dogs to dine in Arlington. "You won't believe how many dogs you'll see here," he said. Maybe it's the Irish nachos, or it could be the juicy burgers. Either way, you and your pooch can chow down on the patio in back. 400 East Abram Street; (817) 274-8561.

Jim's Hamburgers: A tip from a friend led us to this burger place. Okay, it was more like an enthusiastic endorsement. What the heck. Since we're not using her name, we can tell the truth. She howled about how good the burgers were. And she was right. This is not a place for dogs with dainty appetites. Jim only knows how to make one size burger here: huge, with a half-pound of juicy beef. Your pooch can mooch and you'll still be stuffed. The french fries have the skins on, just the way dogs love potatoes and raccoons. Eat at the covered picnic tables out front. 120 East Division Street; (817) 274-3971.

Lincoln Square Shopping Center: Numerous restaurants dot this sprawling retail center, and many of them have sidewalk tables at which they openly welcome pooches. In addition, there are benches everywhere you look—many of them just steps from the front door of a restaurant—and the shopping center management company welcomes dogs and their owners to eat at those. Just order to go and choose your bench. The center is at 780 Road to Six Flags, near Six Flags Over Texas and The Ballpark in Arlington. Below is a partial list of the restaurants you'll find there.

• **Bubba's Bagel Nosh:** Test your teeth on a concrete doughnut at a sidewalk table. (817) 861-2116.

• **Cafe de France Bakery and Cafe:** *Oui! Oui!* and we don't mean squat or hike. Continental cuisine of the Gallic type is the menu here, served at sidewalk tables. (817) 261-1777.

• **Coffee Haus:** The manager says several dogs regularly drop in for a hot cuppa at the sidewalk tables. (817) 274-0006.

The following restaurants, all in the Lincoln Square Shopping Center, have public benches nearby where you and your pooch may eat, although they do not allow dogs to dine on their premises: **Jason's Deli**, (817) 860-2888; **Lone Star Oyster Bar**, (817) 469-6616; **Portofino Ristorante**, (817) 861-8300; **Rocco's Pasta**, (817) 265-8897; and **Royal Cathay Chinese Cuisine**, (817) 860-2662.

PLACES TO STAY

Arlington Forest Acres: This RV campground is shaded by large trees and accepts small dogs on leash. Campsites are $14. 4800 Kelly Elliott Road, Arlington, TX 76017; (817) 478-5805.

Arlington Kampground: This campground has both RV sites ($15) and tent sites ($10); they ask only that your pooch be kept on her leash. 2715 South Cooper Street, Arlington, TX 76015; (817) 461-0601.

Budgetel Inn—Six Flags: Rooms are $48 to $73. There are no size restrictions or fees, but you must leave a $50 deposit to cover any damages for which your angelic pooch might be blamed. 2401 Diplomacy Drive, Arlington, TX 76011; (817) 633-2400 or (800) 428-3438.

Comfort Inn: All rooms are suites and rent for $85, which includes a deluxe continental breakfast. The $100 deposit for your pooch sounds hefty, but you get it back when you check out if there's been no damage. The hotel offers free trolley service to nearby attractions such as The Ballpark in Arlington, Six Flags Over Texas, and Wet 'n Wild. 1601 East Division Street, Arlington, TX 76011; (817) 261-2300.

Days Inn—Downtown: Rooms range from $35 to $95; dogs are $10 per night per pooch. 910 North Collins Street, Arlington, TX 76011; (817) 261-8444 or (800) 325-2525.

Hawthorn Suites Hotel: You can pay as little as $80 for a traditional room or as much as $170 for a suite with living room and full kitchen. Dogs under 50 pounds are welcome and are $5 extra. There is a nonrefundable deposit of $50 for your pooch. 2401 Brookhollow Plaza Drive, Arlington, TX 76006; (817) 640-1188 or (800) 527-1133.

La Quinta Conference Center: Rooms are $72 to $103. Dogs under 20 pounds are welcome. Each late October this hotel hosts a show of the Staffordshire breed. There's a paved walking path encircling a grassy area out back where you can exercise your pooch or show him off. Highway 360 at Six Flags Drive, Arlington, TX 76011; (817) 640-4142 or (800) NU-ROOMS/687-6667.

Motel 6: Room rates are $38 to $42. All Motel 6s allow one small pooch per room. 2626 East Randol Mill Road, Arlington, TX 76011; (817) 649-0147.

Ramada Inn Arlington: Rooms are $49 to $79. Small dogs under 25 pounds are welcome here. 700 East Lamar Boulevard, Arlington, TX 76011; (817) 265-7711 or (800) 228-2828.

Residence Inn: Room rates are $89 to $110. Dogs pay a fee of $75 to $100 depending on the size of the room. 1050 Brookhollow Plaza Drive, Arlington, TX 76006; (817) 649-7300.

Treetops RV Village: Small dogs could get lost in the large sites in this campground, but big dogs (over 17 inches tall) will have to stay elsewhere. Sites rent for $23. 1901 West Arbrook Boulevard, Arlington, TX 76015; (817) 467-7943 or (800) 747-0787.

FESTIVALS

Raise the Roof 5K Run and Pottery Sale: Leashed dogs and their people are welcome to jog through downtown Arlington and then visit food booths, listen to music, or get a massage. We assume the massages are for two-legged runners only, but you can always ask. The race and festival benefit the building fund for the Arlington Museum of Art; there is a runner entry fee of about $15. The event is held in late April at the Arlington Museum of Art, 201 West Main Street; (817) 468-1112 or (817) 275-4600.

Texas Scottish Festival and Highland Games: Your dog does not have to be of Scottish ancestry to appreciate the goings-on at this early June festival, although it wouldn't hurt to watch a late-night rerun of *Greyfriars Bobbie* before you go. Sometimes the combination of skirling bagpipes and swirling kilts can confuse the non-Scottish dog. It wouldn't hurt to introduce your pooch to Scottish delicacies like shortbread, bridies, and bangers beforehand, either. But for any dog the highlight of this annual meeting of the clans has to be the meeting of the hounds. Virtually every variety of Scottish dog will be represented here—Scotties, Westies, cairns, Skyes, Dandie Dinmonts, collies, shelties, Gordon setters, and golden retrievers. They'll be showing off their hunting and herding skills as well as just generally being lovable and cute. While your pooch is checking out the competition, you can listen to bag piping and drumming contests or Celtic harpists, attend Gaelic language seminars, bare a wee bit o' leg in the bonniest knees contest, taste-test Scotch whisky, or learn the fine points of Scottish country dancing. Admission to the festival is about $10.

Leashed dogs are "Absolutely not a problem," says event coordinator Ray McDonald. "And your dog doesn't have to be a Scottish breed to enter the Wee Beastie contest. Dogs just have to be dressed in some sort of outfit with a Scottish theme. One year a Dachshund in a kilt came in fourth, and we usually have several entries dressed as the Loch Ness Monster."

For details on this year's location and activities, call (817) 654-2293.

DIVERSIONS

Sniff ends endlessly at PetsMart: Dogs shop right alongside their people at PetsMart, at least when they take time out from sniffing each other's rears. The dogs, not the people. There's no telling who you'll meet poring over aisle after aisle of dog food, dog collars, dog leashes, dog beds, dog carriers, dog books, dog greeting cards—you may never come out. 1040 West Arkansas Lane; (817) 860-1780.

AZLE

PLACES TO STAY

West Bay Marina and RV Resort: Sites are $16. Dogs must be leashed at this lakeside campground. 6925 Liberty School Tap Road, Azle, TX 76020; (817) 444-1622.

BENBROOK

PARKS, BEACHES, AND RECREATION AREAS

• **Holiday Park** 🐾 🐾 🐾 ½ *See* 🅖 *on page 298.*

Long, skinny, and crooked as a dog's hind leg, this park takes up most of the western shoreline of Benbrook Lake, and it's land well put to use. Picnic and camping sites dot the well-tended lakefront, with gently sloping grassy banks descending to the water's edge. Dogs must be on leash, unfortunately.

A 7.3-mile horseback and nature trail winds from one end of the park to the other, passing conveniently close to rest rooms and water fountains along the way. You'll see a variety of topography, flora, and fauna along the route. Big bluestem, Indian grass, switchgrass, and love grass sprout amid live oaks, hackberries, elms, pecans, willows, sycamores, and sumacs. When Sport and I last visited it was early October, and the sumac leaves had begun to change, along with those of the Shumard oak. We'd guess that sometime between mid-October and mid-November should be a good time to catch the leaves in their full autumnal glory. The trail ascends a number of low hills that offer great views of the lake and the surrounding country. You may flush a quail or mourning dove in the uplands or a mallard, teal, or pintail along the shore. Most kinds of poisonous snakes found in the United States also live in the area.

Campsites are among the best of the U.S. Army Corps of Engineers parks we've visited. The 105 sites, many of which have no close neighbor, are mostly shaded by large trees and are laid out along several winding loops. Sites with water and electricity are $14; those with water only are $8; primitive sites are also $8. All sites are served by rest rooms with showers. Currently camping is first come, first served, but that may change in the near future; call for up-to-date policies.

From U.S. 377 south of Benbrook, take South Lakeview Drive 1.5 miles to the park entrance. There is no entry fee. The park is closed from 10 P.M. to 6 A.M. (817) 292-2400.

RESTAURANTS

Cafe 1187: Have your sandwich, soup, steak, chicken, pork, or pasta with seafood served up at one of the rocking chairs on the front porch. Then take your pooch for a stroll at Holiday Park right down the road. 8780 F.M. 1187 South; (817) 443-1473.

Riscky's Barbecue: Standard Texas barbecue items such as brisket, ribs, and sausage plus turkey and ham are yours to choose from. Eat at the tables out front. 9000 U.S. 377 South; (817) 249-3320.

Sonic Drive-In: You probably won't find Frankie Avalon here, but you will find the standard menu of burgers and fries, yours for the eating at the tables in front. 6327 Lake Worth Boulevard; (817) 237-5757.

PLACES TO STAY

Holiday Park: See Holiday Park on page 388 for camping information.

COLLEYVILLE

RESTAURANTS

Eduardo's Mexican Restaurant: Two benches out front let you practice balancing your carry-out container of Tex-Mex on your knees while fending off a hungry hound. 240 Grapevine Highway; (817) 485-5942.

Shell's Oyster Bar and Grill: Pasta, seafood, sandwiches, po'boys, and chicken dishes will be served to you and your hungry pooch on the patio out front. 5005 Colleyville Boulevard; (817) 498-2229.

Sonic Drive-In: Corral your canine so she doesn't leave your side and then share a burger and fries with her at the tables out front. 4917 Colleyville Boulevard; (817) 498-4509.

EULESS

RESTAURANTS

Captain's Den: Does your pooch love beer? Here's a place with a grassy beer garden in back where beer only is served, and dogs are welcome to quaff with their people. 316 South Industrial Boulevard; (817) 545-3878.

GRAPEVINE

PARKS, BEACHES, AND RECREATION AREAS

• **Oak Grove Park** 🐾 *See* **76** *on page 299.*

Located at the southern end of Grapevine Lake, this U.S. Army Corps of Engineers park is mostly wild and woolly woods—a pleasant change from the urban congestion all around. Like most Corps of Engineers parks in the area, this one offers few facilities, but there were no fees for day use or camping, either. There is a rest room at the campground, which has about 10 sites with shaded picnic tables.

The park is located one mile north of Highway 114 Business (West Northwest Highway) on Dove Road. The entrance sign is set back off Dove Road, and when we last visited, there was no street sign. It's open 24 hours. (817) 481-4541.

• **Silver Lake Park** 🐾 🐾 *See* **77** *on page 299.*

Wrapped around the southern end of Grapevine Lake, this park is narrow and serpentine, but it offers a number of beautiful lakeside picnic areas, large trees, and mowed grass for the leashed pooch to explore. When we last visited, we saw a collie and her owner doing just that, making slow progress from one good sniffing spot to the next. There is no fee for use of the picnic areas.

The campground has 62 sites, most of them with shade trees and unobstructed views of the lake. Primitive sites with water in the area are $13; sites with water and electricity are $15. There are rest rooms and a playground. The campground is closed from 10 P.M. to 6 A.M.

From Highway 114 Business, take Dooley Road north a mile to the campground entrance. To reach the day-use areas, continue past the campground entrance to a T intersection and turn left onto Park Road 7, which winds through the day-use area. (817) 329-8993.

RESTAURANTS

Willhoites: The Texas buffet includes soup and salad and a dessert bar, or you can have a steak on the covered patio of this recycled old gas station. 432 South Main Street; (817) 481-7511.

PLACES TO STAY

Oak Grove Park: See Oak Grove Park on page 390 for camping information.

Silver Lake Park: See Silver Lake Park on page 390 for camping information.

HURST

PARKS, BEACHES, AND RECREATION AREAS

• Chisholm Park 🐾 🐾 ½ *See* 🕖 *on page 299.*

Things got interesting as soon as Sport and I pulled into this 50-acre park just after sunrise. There's a small lake in the park, and it is populated by a couple of hundred ducks and geese. Sport had recently been grounded for a week (i.e., chained up) because of an unfortunate incident with a neighbor's flock of chickens. ("I guess they are staying over on your property all the time now," the neighbor told us one day. "I never see them anymore." We kept quiet and went home and picked up more chicken feathers out of the yard.)

However, Sport seemed to have absorbed the lesson that what you do at home, you don't do when you are a guest somewhere, and she was a perfect lady.

The park has a large picnic area—tables with barbecue grills—in a grove of post oak trees, a paved jogging trail around the lake, and a playground. There's no rest room, but there is a chemical toilet. Dogs must be leashed.

The park is on Norwood Drive half a mile east of Highway 26, but to find it you have to know that for the first block east of Highway 26, the street is called Hurstview Road. At the end of that block it becomes Norwood Drive. Just go straight ahead; the park will be on your left. It's closed from 10 P.M. to 8 A.M. (817) 788-7320.

RESTAURANTS

Bacon's: You can balance the low-fat pancakes, omelets, and muffins at breakfast with chicken-fried steak, meat loaf, mashed potatoes, or sandwiches at lunch. Dine at one of the sidewalk tables. 737 Grapevine Highway; (817) 281-5911.

Dun-Rite Honey Hams: Sandwiches and soups are the staples here, but the bacon-almond salad is what brings dogs back again and again to eat at one of the patio tables out front. 3809-D Colleyville Boulevard; (817) 656-4267.

MANSFIELD

PARKS, BEACHES, AND RECREATION AREAS

• **James McKnight Park East** 🐾 1/2 *See* ⑲ *on page 298.*

Athletic fields take up most of this park's 27 acres, but amidst all the competitive mayhem there's a trail that crosses Walnut Creek—with all its attendant furry critter possibilities—and connects to James McKnight Park West on the opposite bank. Playgrounds, rest rooms, and picnic tables complete the facilities. Dogs must be leashed.

The park is at 757 U.S. 287 and is open from 6 A.M. to 11 P.M. (817) 473-9371.

• **James McKnight Park West** 🐾 🐾 *See* ⑳ *on page 298*

This 24-acre park lies just across Walnut Creek from its more highly developed sibling; a trail connects the two. We like this one better because it has more space for a leashed dog to roam without getting beaned by a baseball.

The park is at the end of Wisteria Street and is open from 6 A.M. to 11 P.M. (817) 473-9371.

• **Katherine Rose Memorial Park** 🐾 🐾 *See* ㉛ *on page 298.*

This 24-acre park leans heavily toward family recreation with a picnic area, fishing pond, basketball and volleyball courts, a playground, and horseshoe pits. Pooches are family, too, of course, and for them there's a half-mile paved walking trail that you are welcome to share. Just stay on your end of the leash.

The park is at 303 North Walnut Creek Drive. It is open from 6 A.M. to 11 P.M. (817) 473-9371.

• **McClendon Park** 🐾 1/2 *See* ㉜ *on page 298.*

There's a lot crammed into this 16-acre park, including a short nature trail that you and your leashed pooch can hike together. There's also a playground, picnic tables, and rest rooms.

The park is at 740 West Kimball Street. It is open from 6 A.M. to 11 P.M. (817) 473-9371.

PLACES TO STAY

Courtesy Inn: Rooms are $45. Dogs stay for free. 1560 East Broad Street, Mansfield, TX 76063; (817) 473-6118.

NORTH RICHLAND HILLS

RESTAURANTS

Burger Street: Find the beef here and eat at the outside seating area. 6440 Rufe Snow Drive; (817) 577-0329.

Country Steakfingers and Chicken: You may spot a familiar bumper sticker in the parking lot here: "Support Beef. Run Over a Chicken." Have your choice at one of the outside tables. 5752 Davis Boulevard; (817) 581-2298.

Sonic Drive-In: Two locations in North Richland Hills allow you and your pooch to burger down at one of the tables in front: 6724 Davis Boulevard (817-485-1221) and 8875 Grapevine Highway (817-788-5085).

PLACES TO STAY

La Quinta Motor Hotel: Rooms are $67 to $74. Small dogs may stay for no charge. 7920 Bedford Euless Road, North Richland Hills, TX 76180; (817) 485-2750.

Lexington Inn: Rooms are $50 to $85. Dogs pay a $15 fee; small dogs only are allowed. 8709 Airport Freeway, North Richland Hills, TX 76180; (817) 656-8881.

Motel 6: Rooms are $40. Motel 6s allow one small pooch per room. 7804 Bedford Euless Road, North Richland Hills, TX 76180; (817) 485-3000.

VAN ZANDT COUNTY

CANTON

PARKS, BEACHES, AND RECREATION AREAS

• **Purtis Creek State Park** 🐾 🐾 *See ㉞ on page 298.*

As you might expect of a state park named for a creek, this one is not overly large, only 1,566 acres. That makes it perfect for small dogs, but even big dogs like Sport enjoy ample room here outside the day-use area, which has heavily shaded lakeside picnic tables and a swim beach. Leashes are required throughout the park, but even leashed dogs are banned from the water and the beach in the designated swimming area.

A 1.5-mile hiking trail connects the park's two campgrounds, and Sport and I found it a delight on a crisp fall day following a violent thunderstorm the night before. The sandy soil shed the previous night's rainfall but still held little heaps of golden oak leaves blown down by the storm's winds. Clumps of purple berries nodded over the trail as we padded noiselessly along, hoping to scare up a deer or one of the park's numerous raccoons. We found only tracks, but the warmth of the afternoon sun slanting through the trees onto our backs comforted us. There's something about walking through fallen leaves with the sun caressing the back of my neck that conjures images of family gatherings and turkey dinners and the older generations digesting and gabbing while the younger sprint around the yard working up an appetite for more pie. I hope dogs have similar embedded memories, though theirs probably involve heaping plates of table scraps and groaning naps taken where everyone has to walk around them.

Your pooch is not allowed on the park's two fishing piers, but she can fish right alongside you from the beach or your boat. From December to March you can fish for trout in a special pond stocked for the purpose. You'll need a fishing license plus a trout stamp.

The multiuse campground has 59 sites with water and electricity ($11) served by a rest room with showers. The sites are some of the largest we've seen in a state park. Tucked away amid oak, juniper, and an occasional pine tree, the sites offer a high degree of privacy. Each has a picnic table, fire ring, and lantern post. A few front the lake and have a grassy beach—where your leashed pooch is allowed—sloping down to the water. Best of all are the 13 primitive sites ($6) reached by hiking a shaded trail. It's about half a mile to the first site, and most of them are on the water. A faucet is located at the start of the trail, and a composting toilet serves the sites.

Reservations for campsites at all state parks must be made by calling the central reservation number, (512) 389-8900, between 9 A.M. and 6 P.M. Monday through Friday. Reservations are strongly recommended, and a deposit is required in order to guarantee a reservation. Specific sites may not be reserved; they are available on a first-come, first-served basis upon arrival.

As at all state parks, dogs must be kept on a leash no longer than six feet, cannot enter any park building, and may not be left unattended.

From the Dallas/Fort Worth area, travel 65 miles east on U.S. 175 to Eustace, then left (north) on F.M. 316 for 3.5 miles. There is a $2 per person entrance fee. Office hours are 8 A.M. to 5 P.M., and the gate is locked from 10 P.M. until 7 A.M. (903) 425-2332.

RESTAURANTS

The Apple Cart: Don't be upset. Sip a cappuccino while strolling through the 36 acres of shops at the Mountain at Old Mill Marketplace (formerly Wild Willie's II Mountain). It's on U.S. 64 east of the Old Mill Marketplace; (903) 567-5574.

Diamond S Bait and Convenience Store: Located just half a mile east of the entrance to Purtis Creek State Park, this little country store has picnic tables out front where you and your leashed pooch can have a burger, corn dog, deli sandwich, or bowl of chili. How long has it been since you've had a hot, steaming bowl of chili in the parking lot of a bait store while watching people pump gas into their cars? Well, that's too long. 14464 F.M. 316; (903) 425-4337.

Mama's Pioneer Restaurant: Dine on the daily lunch special, steak, or chicken at the tables on the porch. It's on U.S. 64 east at the Mountain at Old Mill Marketplace; (903) 567-6786.

PLACES TO STAY

Best Western: Rooms are $48 to $78. A $10 deposit lets your small pooch share your room. 2251 North Trades Day Boulevard, Canton, TX 75103; (903) 567-6591 or (800) 528-1234.

Days Inn: Rooms are $38 to $99; dogs pay $5. The inn is on Interstate 20 at Exit 527. Route 2, Box 5D, Canton, TX 75103; (903) 567-6588.

Purtis Creek State Park: See Purtis Creek State Park on page 393 for camping information.

DIVERSIONS

Climb every mountain: More than 500 shops selling everything you can imagine (and some you can't) are strewn across the side of a hill, among trees, and down ravines at the Mountain at Old Mill Marketplace (formerly Wild Willie's II Mountain). You and your leashed pooch can wander the 36 acres and window shop, but there are plenty of porches—nearly 500, in fact—where you can tie your dog while you go inside. A cute furry face and a polite request will get you and your hound into many places. It's on U.S. 64 just east of the Old Mill Marketplace. (903) 567-5445.

Trade your dog for a cat: Although there are times you might be tempted to do something so radical—like when you find your best shoes reduced to slobbery shreds of leather—you probably won't want to trade that precious dog for a cat. But if you did, this would be the place you could do it. Each first Monday of the month (and the weekend preceding), more than 6,000 dealers congregate here in one of the biggest antique, arts and crafts, and flea markets anywhere. Another 150 food vendors fuel the frenzied bargain hunters. Leashed dogs are welcome in all outside areas. Admission is free, but parking will cost $3. It's at First Monday Trade Days Park on U.S. 64 in downtown Canton; (903) 567-6556.

WILLS POINT

Wills Point enjoys a distinction shared by no other city in Texas. The state legislature proclaimed it the Bluebird Capital of Texas in 1995. That explains all the birdhouses you see on fence posts along roads. You and your pooch may want to visit during the annual Bluebird Festival—if your bird dog will point bluebirds, that is. (How many birds would a bird dog point if a bird dog would point bluebirds?)

PARKS, BEACHES, AND RECREATION AREAS

• **Lake Tawakoni State Park (not yet rated)** *See* **84** *on page 298.*
One of Texas's newest state parks, this 40-acre park on the shores of Lake Tawakoni was under development when we last visited the area, but it was scheduled to be opened to the public sometime in 1998. The park consists of post oak woodlands, mostly upland regrowth and creek bottom, with some abandoned pastures. For information on its current status and facilities, call the Texas Parks and Wildlife Department at (800) 792-1112.

FESTIVALS

Bluebird Festival: Held the second weekend in April, the Bluebird Festival includes tours of the area bluebird trails (10 in all), arts and crafts, and food. There's even a two-hour outdoor drama ("The Perils of Being a Bluebird," we presume). It all happens downtown on Fourth Street (at its intersection with U.S. 80) except for nature walks held just outside the city limits on F.M. 47 just north of the city limits and on F.M. 751 just north of town; follow the signs. (903) 873-3111 or (800) WP-BLUBIRD.

WISE COUNTY

DECATUR

PARKS, BEACHES, AND RECREATION AREAS

• **Cottonwood–Black Creek Trail** 🐾 🐾 🐾 ½
See **85** *on page 298.*
Part of the LBJ National Grassland, this four-mile trail connects primitive campgrounds at the Black Creek and Cottonwood Recreation Ar-

eas, both located on small lakes. Despite being located on a national grassland, the trail passes through some woodlands, and the terrain is hilly, making for a moderately difficult hike. And while the campsites are primitive, consisting of a picnic table, fire ring, and barbecue pit with no water available, they are shaded and have composting toilets in the area. When Sport and I last visited we saw a number of people fishing in the lakes, so there's the chance you might be able to catch your dinner. The primitive nature of these mini-parks and their relatively isolated locations promise you and your pooch a quiet weekend. Since it takes only half a day to hike the trail, you can start at either campground, hike to the other and spend the night, and return the next day to your starting point, eliminating the need for a shuttle.

Dogs must be on a leash not to exceed six feet in length, but there are no entrance or camping fees; you'll be able to afford to buy a leash or take along a supply of treats so your pooch will always want to be close at hand anyway. Bribery works with dogs, and they love it. In fact, they strongly encourage it.

From Decatur, go north on F.M. 730 eight miles and turn left (west) onto County Road 2360. Proceed 1.8 miles to County Road 2372 and turn right (north); go 0.4 miles to County Road 2461 and turn right again; after one-half mile turn left (west) on Forest Service Road 902 and proceed to the Black Creek Recreation Area. The campground is closed from 10 P.M. until 6 A.M. except to overnight guests. (940) 627-5475.

PLACES TO STAY

Best Western: Rooms are $48 to $54, and there's a $5 pet fee. Your pooch can be no larger than medium size and must be housebroken. 1801 U.S. 81/287 South, Decatur, TX 76234; (940) 627-5982.

Comfort Inn: Small dogs may share your $50 room with you. 1709 U.S. 287 South, Decatur, TX 76234; (940) 627-6919.

Cottonwood–Black Creek Trail: See Cottonwood–Black Creek Trail on page 396 for camping information.

FESTIVALS

Wise County Old Settlers Reunion: Late in July for the last 115-plus years, wise people (and dogs) in Wise County have gathered for a weeklong party that includes a carnival, food booths, and arts and crafts. Leashed dogs may attend. It's held at Joe Wheeler Park on Highway 51 southwest of town. For information, call (940) 627-3107.

WOOD COUNTY

MINEOLA

RESTAURANTS

Fried Green Tomatoes Cafe: Look at the name and the address and you'll think you've stumbled into a mixed-up midnight movie in which a monster is about to jump out and eat you. But as you sit on the bench out front and dig into your hamburger steak, chicken-fried steak, goulash, hamburger, or grilled chicken sandwich, you'll know you've just found a good place to eat. 125 South Pacific Street; (903) 569-5040.

Sonic Drive-In: "People eat here with their dogs all the time," the manager said. "As long as the dog doesn't bother anybody else, there's no problem." How you keep your pooch from mooching french fries or a bite of your burger or foot-long hot dog from you is your problem. Eat on the benches in front. 311 West Broad Street; (903) 569-3187.

QUITMAN

If your dog is a fan of actress Sissy Spacek, bring him here. This is Spacek's hometown. Signs at town entrances proclaim, "We love you Sissy." Dogs probably couldn't care less. The only movie star who impresses a hound is the one with a large, meaty bone in hand, and somehow we just can't see Sissy that way. Unless it's a ham bone.

PARKS, BEACHES, AND RECREATION AREAS

• **Governor Hogg Shrine State Park** 🐾 *See* **86** *on page 298.*

This 27-acre tract is named for James Stephen Hogg, the state's first Texas-born governor. It is the only park in the state with three museums, but dogs will be more interested in the half-mile nature trail with its old iron bridge and the abundant pecan trees with attendant squirrels. There are also picnic tables and rest rooms. There is an admission fee only for the museums.

The day-use only park is on Highway 37 about six blocks south of the Wood County Courthouse. (903) 763-2701.

RESTAURANTS

Sonic Drive-In: It's a good thing dogs never get tired of hamburgers. Otherwise, they might get pretty hungry in small-town Texas. Once again Sonic comes to the ravenous Rover's rescue by allowing doggy dining at the tables in front. 305 East Goode Street; (903) 763-5445.

PLACES TO STAY

Towner Motel: Rooms are $35 to $45. Housebroken dogs are welcome; there is a $5 charge. 210 South Main Street, Quitman, TX 75783; (903) 763-2228.

WINNSBORO

RESTAURANTS

R. H. McCrary Soda Shoppe: "We're all dog lovers around here. We'll bring dogs water and give them some of our homemade bread," the owner said. You and your pampered pooch can sit at one of the picnic tables on the sidewalk out front and have a sandwich on homemade bread, super nachos, fajitas, or a grilled hamburger. And then there are those sodas, malts, and ice cream floats for dessert. 216 North Main Street; (903) 342-5333.

Sonic Drive-In: As long as your pooch puts the bite on the burgers, not other people, he is welcome to eat at the table out front. 815 South Main Street; (903) 342-3216.

FESTIVALS

Down Home Country Fair: Each mid-October brings out jars of home-canned goodies, baked goods, and crafts for judging. There's a pet show for you and your home dog, too. You and your pooch may inspire a whole new category; judging is based on "whatever shows up," according to the event chairperson. And when you're not oohing and aahing over hand-stitched quilts and crispy pickles, you can enjoy the colorful autumn foliage. The leaves are on the trees; the fair is at the city auditorium in City Park, on Highway 11 at the east edge of town. For information, call (903) 342-3666.

DIVERSIONS

Drive your dog crazy: What makes a dog crazier than riding, riding, riding while peering longingly through the car window at the cows, trees, and cats whizzing by just out of reach? It could be riding, riding, riding just to see the colorful autumn leaves. During the entire month of October, Winnsboro's Autumn Trails drive dogs nuts as their owners drive them around and around three loop trails of about two hours each just to look at—leaves. Dogs know leaves are to be sniffed, squatted on, and rolled in. What's the big deal about looking at them? People drive dogs crazy. There's more to do than look at leaves, though. A full schedule of events including sidewalk sales and antique car rallies will help to restore your schnauzer's sanity. (903) 342-3666.

Teach your hound to be Paul Bunyan: Even dogs smaller than 42 ax handles between the eyes will feel as big as Babe the Blue Ox as they help you decorate a Christmas tree you chose and cut yourselves. Don those matching red plaid mackinaws and head for the Christmas tree farms of Wood County from the Friday after Thanksgiving to the last weekend before Christmas to select and cut your own Christmas tree. Winnsboro claims to be the Christmas tree capital of Texas, so even the picky pooch should find a tree she likes. (If you're not into killing trees, you can buy a live tree in a container and plant it after Christmas.) Leashed dogs only are welcome, as these are working farms with animals of their own. Plus, you wouldn't want your hound to be cast in a bleeding role in a remake of *The Texas Chainsaw Massacre*.

The Peddy Christmas Tree Farm is southeast of Winnsboro: Take Highway 11 east about three miles; turn right onto County Road 4430 and go about one mile to County Road 4450; turn left and go about a mile to the farm. Phone (903) 365-2649. The Cypress Springs Tree and Berry Farm is northeast of Winnsboro: Take F.M. 1448 to its intersection with SE 4340 and turn left (north). Follow the signs to the farm. You will also want to visit during April and May, when you can buy fresh strawberries, and during blueberry season in June and July. Call for exact dates to catch the peak of the harvest: (903) 860-2588.

7

EL PASO/ THE GUADALUPE MOUNTAINS

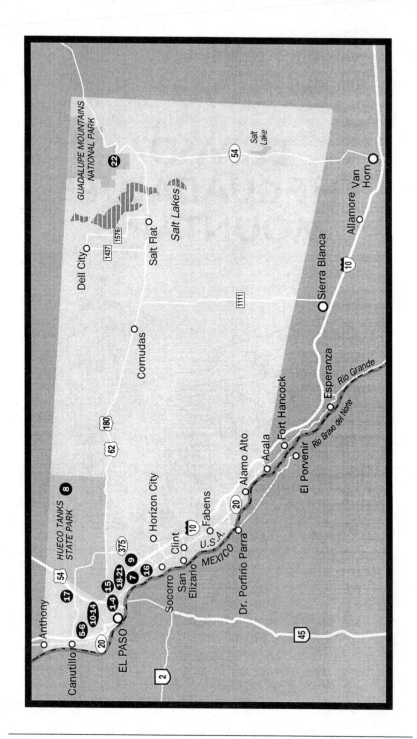

EL PASO/ THE GUADALUPE MOUNTAINS

El Paso calls itself Sun City and brags that the sun shines nearly every day of the year, but your dog doesn't have to be old, retired, and arthritic to enjoy visiting. Dogs have been bringing their people here for more than 400 years. The city's Spanish name—El Paso del Norte—means "pass of the north" and was bestowed by Spanish explorers moving into the area from Mexico. You and your hound can still visit the pass where the first Spanish expedition crossed the Rio Grande in 1585. In fact, dogs splashed across the river with Juan de Oñate and the rest of the explorers. (A later expedition into New Mexico was saved by a dog, says local historian Leon Metz. The Spanish ran out of water and were nearly dead of thirst when a puppy trotted into camp with muddy paws. They followed the dog to water and named the place in his honor.)

The Rio Grande carved El Paso del Norte through the Franklin Mountains, the southernmost peaks in the Rocky Mountain chain. El Paso sits at the mouth of that pass, and the Franklins—looking very much like a dog asleep with her head on her paws in a sort of collapsed Sphinx pose—slice the city in half. Ironically, the mountain forming the dog's head is named Crazycat. Views of the city from the mountains are spectacular, and vice versa.

El Paso has a very strong claim to being the oldest city in Texas, although it's a disputed title—chambers of commerce, instead of keeping busy trying to think up new ways to attract dogs to their towns, sometimes waste time arguing over where dogs have been visiting longest. El Paso's claim to the title is clouded somewhat by the fact that the original settlement from which today's fourth largest city in Texas grew was founded on the south bank of the Rio Grande, in what is today Ciudad Juárez, Chihuahua, Mexico. (Which came first, the state or the dog?)

You're never far from a park in El Paso, even though dogs must be leashed in all of them. Franklin Mountains State Park, which includes almost the entire mountain range of the same name, is the largest urban wilderness park in the United States. Numerous smaller parks are scattered throughout the city. Between visits to parks, dogs can stay in some of the city's finest hotels. Dining opportunities are more limited: the hot desert climate discourages eating outdoors. However, your pooch will be so busy shopping for bargains—of which there are many—she won't even have time to eat many meals at fancy sit-up-and-beg restaurants, anyway.

EL PASO

PARKS, BEACHES, AND RECREATION AREAS

• **Ascarate Park** 🐾1/2 *See ❶ on page 402.*

Some maniacal construction firm must have had a part in planning this 440-acre park; every effort was made to build as much as possible here rather than take advantage of the tremendous view of the Franklin Mountains to the west. There's an amusement park, a golf course, and two artificial lakes with sheer concrete walls preventing access to the water. Picnic areas with trees and grassy spaces are relegated to the rims of the lakes. There is room for a leashed dog to stretch her legs, but more attention to creating a natural rather than an artificial environment in which to do so would have made for a much more pleasant park.

There is a $1 per vehicle entrance fee. The park is located at the intersection of Delta Drive and Manny Martinez Street. From Interstate 10, go east on Trowbridge Drive about two miles to Delta Drive; turn right and go half a mile to the entrance. It is closed from 10:30 P.M. to 6 A.M. (915) 541-4331.

• **Blackie Chesher Park** 🐾🐾1/2 *See ❷ on page 402*

This is the perfect park for traveling dogs entering El Paso from the east. Chances are the last pit stop was many miles ago and was made on a tiny scrap of ground by the side of the road. It's so hard to get into the mood when cars and trucks are whizzing by just feet away. Leashed dogs will leap for joy when you take them exploring the dry wash that runs through the middle of the 34-acre park. While there are few trees in the park, the wash has a thick fur of bushes where most anything could be hiding, making for interesting sniffing. There are athletic fields, a playground, rest rooms, and picnic tables as well. To the west there's a good view of the Franklin Mountains; the mountains to the south are in Mexico. As in all El Paso parks, you are responsible for cleaning up after your pooch.

The park is at the intersection of Interstate 10 and Zaragosa Road, on the southeast corner. It is closed from 10 P.M. to 6 A.M. (915) 541-4331.

• **Chamizal National Memorial** 🐾🐾 🐾 *See ❸ on page 402.*

Give your hound a little lesson in history as you stroll around this 54-acre park. (Dogs must be on a six-foot leash.) A few decades ago, this land was in Mexico, even though it's north of the Rio Grande, the international border. Changes in the river's course due to floods left some land claimed by Mexico on the north side of the river, and some land claimed by the United States on the south side. A treaty signed in 1963 settled the dispute, and to the joy of all dogs who visit El Paso, the land recovered from Mexico became this park, where dogs are welcome even at outdoor events (see Festivals on page 416). The well-tended and land-scaped grounds have a good sprinkling of trees, picnic tables, and gentle slopes to climb. For the person tagging along, there's a free museum of the Chamizal. Dogs are not allowed inside the building, which is open from 8 A.M. to 5 P.M.

The park is located at the intersection of Paisano Drive and San Marcial Street. From Interstate 10, follow Loop 478 (Copia Street) south three-quarters of a mile to Paisano Drive. Go west on Paisano for half a mile, turn left on San Marcial Street, and proceed to the entrance. The grounds, which are lighted at night, are closed from 10 P.M. to 8 A.M. (915) 532-7273.

• **Eastwood Park** 🐾🐾 See ❹ on page 402.

This 47-acre park seems to have something of an identity problem, since it's also known as Album Park. However, your leashed dog will have no trouble deciding why he likes the place: dozens of trees are sprinkled throughout. In arid El Paso, it almost qualifies as a forest. The grassy areas between the athletic fields are spacious. There are rest rooms, picnic tables, and a playground. When Sport and I last visited, snow blanketed the ground and she quickly decided that this strange, cold, white stuff was not to her liking, especially since the snow interfered with the ritual sniffing that precedes squatting. That was fine with me; El Paso requires dog owners to clean up after their pets, and I wasn't eager to stick my hands into the white stuff any more than into the brown stuff.

The park is at the intersection of Parkwood Drive and Album Road, explaining the dual name. From Interstate 10, go north on Yarbrough Drive two miles to Album Road and turn left; the entrance is half a mile up on your right. The park is closed from 10 P.M. to 6 A.M. (915) 541-4331.

• **Franklin Mountains State Park** 🐾🐾🐾 See ❺ on page 402.

Your pooch won't believe she has a whole mountain range to roam, but that's what this park that arrows into the heart of El Paso offers. Its 23,867 acres qualify it to be called the largest urban wilderness park in the nation. Highest elevation within its borders is 7,192 feet.

Dogs will love the fact that the land is almost completely undeveloped. There are few roads in the park and vehicular access is severely limited, although there are 28 miles of hiking trails. The only other facilities are a few picnic sites; water is not available. Dogs must be on a six-foot leash. Entrance to the day-use only park is $2. Dogs pay a $1 trail maintenance fee. Deposit your fees in the lock box at the entrance.

The hiking trails are rugged, steep, and rocky. While walking you may spot mule deer, foxes, and a variety of birds. Rattlesnakes live in the park. Mountain lions are also known to roam here; use caution. When in lion country, make noise as you walk. Sing, recite poems about dogs, or discuss with your pooch the views of the cities and valleys below. Stand erect and make yourself appear as large as possible; lions tend to prey on smaller creatures—like dogs. If you encounter a lion, make noise and stand your ground. Running away might provoke an attack, since that is a typical prey reaction. (In addition, your dog would probably outrun you, making you the prime candidate for lunch.) The park also provides habitat for many Chihuahuan Desert plants and shrubs, including sotol, lechuguilla, ocotillo, cholla, various yuccas, and rare Southwestern barrel cacti.

From Interstate 10 on El Paso's west side, go east on Transmountain Road for 3.3 miles to the entrance. The park's temporary headquarters are in the Magoffin Home State Historical Park, located at 1120 Magoffin Avenue in downtown El Paso. The park is open from 8 A.M. to 5 P.M. (915) 566-6441.

• **Grandview Park** 🐾 *See* ❻ *on page 402.*

It's rare that a park lives up to its name, but this one does. Its 15 acres have a magnificent view of the Franklin Mountains, which loom half a mile to the west and northwest. Your leashed hound may not appreciate the view, but you will. The park has a few trees and a playground, but the view's the thing here. You've looked at far uglier scenes while your dog sniffed for endless minutes looking for that special spot to squat. You are required to clean up after your dog.

From Interstate 10, follow Copia Street north about two miles to McKinley Avenue; turn left and go one block. The park is closed from 10 P.M. to 6 A.M. (915) 541-4331.

• **Hacienda Heights Park** 🐾 *See* ❼ *on page 402.*

The chief thing to recommend this 23-acre park to leashed dogs is its location just a block south of Interstate 10. There's a lot of concrete and asphalt here, but some space sprouts grass, trees, and a few picnic tables. A pool and a baseball field are the principal fixtures. Pick up after your pooch or the law will be after you.

From Interstate 10, go south on Giles Drive (take the McRae Boulevard exit) to the second right, Phoenix Drive. Turn right; the park entrance is in the middle of the block. The park is closed from 10 P.M. to 6 A.M. (915) 541-4331.

• Hueco Tanks State Historical Park 🐾🐾🐾 🐾

See ❽ on page 402.

Rising like an aboriginal cathedral from the desert floor east of El Paso, the jumbled granite boulders of Hueco Tanks State Historical Park hold the largest concentration of painted kachina masks in North America. Counting masks and other subjects, as many as 5,000 pictographs at 44 sites within the 680-acre park spread a visual feast for visitors yearning to know more about First Americans of the Southwest. The park gained its name from the fact that the granite outcrop is honeycombed with thousands of water-catching hollows—*huecos* in Spanish.

Leashed dogs are welcome, and the same rules apply as at all state parks: Leashes can be no longer than six feet. Dogs may not go into any building, and they may not be left unattended.

El Paso's Tigua Indians regard Hueco Tanks as holy ground. Here their ancestors lived, prayed, and left their legacy. Tread this hallowed soil and view these ancient icons, and you begin to appreciate why Tigua tribal sheriff Jesus Padilla says, "To us, this is our church. It is our traditional ceremonial ground. It is sacred."

The Tiguas request that visitors respect the reverence in which they hold this place, and Sport and I think you should, too. Tribal leaders still meet here once a year, young men undergo puberty rites at the park, and individual tribespeople come to pray and nurture their sense of self. "We ask people to come here in peace," Padilla says. "We open up our arms to them, but we ask respect back."

The park has over six miles of hiking trails. Guided tours are offered on Saturdays and Sundays for $2 per person, or you and your pooch can strike out on your own. Rock art lurks in dozens of sites, all inaccessible except by foot. Obtain a map of the park at headquarters; park rangers will describe how to locate some of the more significant sites. Dogs will love walking the trails, many of which wind through vegetated areas and require clambering over boulders. In the unlikely event of recent rains, potholes in the rock may hold water for your pooch, but you should carry an adequate supply for both of you just in case. One of the common plants in the park is ocotillo, a tall, spiny plant nicknamed the devil's walking stick. After rains its orange-red blossoms are spectacular.

Sport and I began one walk at the parking lot beside the Escontrias ranch house, a 19th-century dwelling built by a former owner of the land. Immediately adjacent to the ranch house, the ruins of a Butterfield Overland Mail stage stop weather in the sun. Just at the berm behind the ranch house, a gash in the rock ascends at a sharp angle. Pictographs in red, yellow, orange, and white splash across its ceiling, invisible until you are directly below them.

Follow the well-worn trail south about a quarter mile to the narrow bight between North Mountain on your right and East Mountain on your left. Just inside the narrow passage, on your left, black pictographs drawn by Plains Indians show a hunting scene with deer and a horseman. On one visit, a gray fox darted from a crevice here, giving Sport a thrill and nearly dislocating the shoulder of my leash-holding arm.

A few yards past a bench shaded by large cottonwood trees, the trail forks. The left trail leads to an important Tigua site, Speaking Rock. This trail requires scaling some sheer rock faces dogs can't handle. The right-hand trail is easier walking and takes you to some of the most impressive art in the park. Go right, and at the next fork take a left, ascend the earthen dam, and follow the trail around the base of East Mountain until East and West Mountains begin to pinch in. Then look for a smaller trail to your left. From the roof of a small overhang blazes a mask called the Starry-eyed Man. The use of turquoise paint makes it unique in the park. Other paintings glow red, yellow, white, orange, and black, but only this one uses blue-green.

Across the valley from the Starry-eyed Man shelter, a large juniper tree crowds against the base of West Mountain. Just beyond, a trail—almost invisible and so narrow that Sport was hesitant to enter—leads into a rock shelter with several bedrock mortars in its floor. Above them prances three-foot-tall Horned Dancer. Painted in white and black, the ghostly figure escapes notice at first, but once spotted, it eerily stands out from its background.

Retrace your path to the last fork in the trail and turn right. A short distance past the narrowest gap between East and West Mountains, an oak tree grows horizontally from beneath an overhang. On the roof of that overhang, Tlaloc the Rain God broods. Zig-zag geometric patterns—perhaps representing lightning bolts—make up the round-eyed figure's body.

For a second walk, begin at the parking lot south of park headquarters and follow the paved road (closed to vehicles) to the picnic area. In about a quarter mile, you'll come to some picnic tables on the left, in a small hidden valley. Follow the worn path up the rock face south, until you are about halfway up. Then follow the path to the right to a narrow horizontal slit, Cave Kiva. Inside, eight masks, all on the underside of a huge boulder, comprise the crown jewel of the park. To Sport it must have seemed as if we were entering a giant animal burrow as we scurried on hands and knees through the slit. Once inside the cave, you can stand erect and the interior glows from indirect light. You feel as though you have entered a cathedral, and indeed you have. This site was used for ceremonial purposes.

The masks on the wall of Cave Kiva likely reflect some Tigua religious beliefs, park ranger Alex Mares says. "The masks are believed to be connected to the origin of the kachina. These were benevolent spirits who lived in mountainous areas around springs. If feasts and ceremonies were done properly, the spirits would visit the pueblo and bring blessings of rain, game, or freedom from disease. The faces on kachina dolls of today are very similar to the masks found here. The Indians may have believed these sacred beings lived at Hueco Tanks."

That belief, in fact, is at the heart of Tigua reverence for this arid temple of rock and ancient art. "The masks indicate places used for ceremonies," says Jesus Padilla, "To us, the places where our grandfathers painted the masks are where they left us their message. This is where they tell us never to forget where you are, who you are, what you are. This is not a place for us to play. It is a place to get close to who we are."

The campground has 17 campsites with water and electricity ($11) and three campsites with water only ($8). The campsites back up to the east side of a nearly vertical rock face. Some have shade all day from trees, and all are shaded once the sun gets low in the west. Rest rooms with showers serve the area. No open campfires or solid fuel fires are allowed in the park. Camp stoves using liquid or propane fuel are permitted. It's likely you'll see wildlife visit the campground, perhaps a fox checking around picnic tables for scraps of food or a roadrunner chasing lizards.

There is a $2 daily entrance fee. To reach the park, drive east of El Paso on U.S. 62/180 about 24 miles to F.M. 2775. Go north on F.M. 2775 about eight miles to the park. The park gate is open daily from 8 A.M. to sunset. The office closes an hour and a half before sunset. If you will be arriving after 5 P.M., you must call the park on the day of your arrival to get the combination to the gate. (915) 857-1135.

• **Marty Robbins Park** 🐾½ *See* ❾ *on page 402.*

Out in the West Texas town of El Paso, Sport fell in love with a beautiful park (my apologies to Marty Robbins). Its 31 acres form a bowl, on whose snow-covered, sloping sides kids were sliding down on cardboard when we last visited. For warmer times there's a playground, pool, athletic fields, and a few picnic tables. The scattered trees are small and might benefit from a strategic application of water by visiting dogs. Any other deposits must be cleaned up.

From Interstate 10, go north on George Dieter Road about 2.5 miles to Vista Del Sol Drive. Turn right and take the first right into the park. The park is closed from 10 P.M. to 6 A.M. (915) 541-4331.

• **McKelligon Canyon Park** 🐾🐾½ *See* ❿ *on page 402.*

This is a rugged park for rugged dogs. Its 90 acres in the Franklin Mountains offer steep, rocky trails and hillsides covered with low bushes. It's almost treeless, but in this case that's a plus, as trees would only interfere with the magnificent views of the mountains all around and the city below. Picnic and rest room facilities are primitive, but dogs won't care. Deer and mountain lions roam these mountains, and a dog can get in touch with her wild side here while she's just a pawful of miles from a warm, safe bed and a full food dish. As at all El Paso parks, you are required to clean up after your pooch.

From Interstate 10, go north on Piedras Street about two miles to Fort Street; turn left and go three blocks to Alabama Street; turn north and go about a mile to McKelligon Canyon Road. Turn left and follow the road into the park. A short distance inside the park is a gate, which is open 7 A.M. to 8 P.M. from April 1 to October 31, and 7 A.M. to 5 P.M. from November 1 to March 31. (915) 541-4331.

• **Memorial Park** 🐾🐾 *See* ⓫ *on page 402.*

Sport thought this 43-acre park was neat, even though she had to remain on leash. The park looks like a scrunched-up blanket, and its abundant trees and hillocks reminded Sport of her Hill Country home, I suspect. The park is in the foothills of the Franklin Mountains, with a beautiful view of the mountains to the north and west and the cities of El Paso and Ciudad Juárez spread out in all other directions. The immaculate homes of a historic neighborhood ring the park. As in all El Paso city parks, you are expected to clean up after your pooch. This park is so charming I can't imagine anyone doing otherwise. There are picnic tables and rest rooms, and the south-facing slopes make this an ideal place to catch some rays and Zs.

The park is on both sides of Copia Street in the 1700 block. Follow Copia Street north from Interstate 10 about a mile and a half. The park is closed from 10 P.M. to 6 A.M. (915) 541-4331.

• **Mountain View Park** 🐾 *See* ⓬ *on page 402.*

The view of the Franklin Mountains from this six-acre park helps make up for its small size and lack of amenities. There's some grass, a few trees, a playground—and that view. Dogs must be leashed, and you must clean up after them.

The park is at the intersection of Diana and Tetons Drives. From U.S. 54 North, exit on Hercules Avenue and follow it east about a mile to Diana Drive. Turn left and go one block to the park. It is closed from 10:30 P.M. to 6 A.M. (915) 541-4331.

• **Murchison Park** 🐾 ◀● *See* **13** *on page 402.*

Few parks better illustrate the differences in taste between dogs and their humans. Dogs taste sweet and—no, let's go at this a different way: This one-acre park appeals to humans in a way dogs couldn't care less about. The attraction here is the view of the cities of El Paso and Ciudad Juárez from the foothills of the Franklin Mountains. Night is the best time, when city lights spread out for miles in a blazing tapestry. Highest elevation in the park is 4,222 feet above sea level. Bring your camera and a tripod, and while your pooch naps, take pictures that will amaze your friends. Or, if they don't turn out well, hang them in the doghouse. As I said, dogs couldn't care less about the view anyway. Dogs must be on leash, but you wouldn't want your pooch to fall off the side of the mountain, so it's a good idea.

From Interstate 10 in the downtown area, follow Mesa Street north to Rim Road; turn right and twist and turn about two miles to the park, watching street signs carefully to be sure you don't get sidetracked—Rim Road becomes Scenic Drive along the way. The park is closed from 10 P.M. to 6 A.M. (915) 541-4331.

• **Nations Tobin Park** 🐾½ *See* **14** *on page 402.*

As with several other El Paso parks, the best thing about this one is the view of the Franklin Mountains to the west. By the time Sport and I visited here, views of the mountains no longer excited my jaded pooch. However, she did enjoy nosing about under the picnic tables and exercised her right to do one of her half-squat, half-leg-hikes on one of the few trees. El Paso is Sun City, and you'll get a lot of ol' Sol in this 44-acre park; there's almost no shade. Dogs are required to be leashed, and you must pick up after them.

From U.S. 54 North, exit on Hondo Pass Drive and go east about two miles to Railroad Drive. Turn right and go a quarter mile to the entrance. The park is closed from 10 P.M. to 6 A.M. (915) 541-4331.

• **Ponder Park** 🐾½ *See* **15** *on page 402.*

This 23-acre park is quite handy for dogs traveling Interstate 10 or going to and from the airport. Athletic fields take up most of its southwestern corner, but aside from a children's playground, most of the rest is open space where a leashed dog can roam. A few trees add visual interest and focal points for leg-hiking. Chemical toilets are the only other facilities. While your hound is doing his business, you can enjoy the view of the Franklin Mountains to the west. A city ordinance requires you to pick up after your pooch.

From Interstate 10, go north on Airway Boulevard one block to Viscount Boulevard, turn right, and go two blocks to Catalpa Lane; turn left and go one block to W. H. Burgess Drive, then turn right and proceed to the park entrance in the middle of the block. The park is closed from 10 P.M. to 6 A.M. (915) 541-4331.

• **Shawver Park** 🐾1/2 *See* ⑯ *on page 402.*

Forty-one-acre J. P. Shawver Park lies along the Rio Grande, but that's not why your pooch will like it. She'll appreciate the open spaces, trees, and picnic tables with smellable garbage cans nearby. There's also a pool, a playground, and athletic fields. An El Paso city ordinance requires you to pick up after your pooch.

The park is at the intersection of Yarbrough and Riverside Drives. From Interstate 10, go south on Yarbrough Drive about 3.5 miles to Riverside Drive and the entrance. The park is closed from 10 P.M. to 6 A.M. (915) 541-4331.

• **Veterans Park** 🐾1/2 *See* ⑰ *on page 402.*

By the time Sport and I visited this park, we'd traveled over 20,000 miles and visited several hundred parks. We felt like this one was for us, because we were certainly veterans at this point. So we held a little ceremony in the center of the park's 44 acres. I told Sport what a good dog she was to put up with me all those miles, and she looked up at me with those adoring brown eyes and put her cold, wet nose in my hand and licked it. It was a touching moment. Then I remembered the barbecued ribs I'd eaten for lunch with my fingers.

This park is mostly open space with little shade. There are playgrounds, a pool, an activity center, and athletic fields. And I'll say it one more time: The view of the Franklin Mountains to the west is absolutely gorgeous. Dogs are required to be leashed, and you are required to clean up after them.

From Loop 375 in far north El Paso, turn north onto McCombs Street. Go about 1.25 miles to Salem Drive; turn left and go half a mile to the park. The park is closed from 10 P.M. to 6 A.M. (915) 541-4331.

• **Vista del Sol Park** 🐾1/2 *See* ⑱ *on page 402.*

This 16-acre park has something most others on El Paso's table-flat east side don't: small hills that your leashed pooch can run up and down. There are a few trees, some athletic fields, and a children's playground, but mostly there's just lots of the wide-open spaces West Texas is famous for. Pick up after your pooch, or the poop police will pick you up.

The park is at the intersection of Trawood Drive and Mosswood Street. From Interstate 10, take Yarbrough Drive north about a mile to Trawood Drive; turn right and go a long block to the entrance. The park is closed from 10 P.M. to 6 A.M. (915) 541-4331.

• **Vista del Valle Park** 🐾 *See* **⓳** *on page 402.*

The name of this 23-acre park means "View of the Valley," referring to the Rio Grande Valley to the south, but the name was obviously bestowed before the rampart of buildings blocking the view was built. Still, this park has a special charm. It's in the shape of a dogleg or, if your hound says "G-day, mate" a lot, a boomerang. There are few trees and a small playground, but not much else. Your pooch must be leashed, and you must pick up after her.

From Interstate 10, go north on Hawkins Boulevard about half a mile to the park, at the intersection of Hawkins Boulevard and Gazelle Drive. The park is closed from 10 P.M. to 6 A.M. (915) 541-4331.

• **Washington Park** 🐾 *See* **⓴** *on page 402.*

Most of this 60-acre park is taken up by a zoo. What's left over includes an athletic field and an acre or so of grass with a few trees. Dogs must be leashed, and you must clean up after them. You'll probably welcome the opportunity to have something to do, since there's not much else to keep you busy here.

From Interstate 10, go south on Loop 110 half a mile to Alameda Avenue and turn left; drive three blocks to the intersection of Alameda and Washington Street. The park is closed from 10 P.M. to 6 A.M. (915) 541-4331.

• **Yucca Park** 🐾 *See* **㉑** *on page 402.*

This 17-acre park is pretty much run-of-the-mill for urban parks except for one thing: a private horse stable at its northeast corner, where your leashed dog can stand near the fence and make the acquaintance of some noble steeds or just sniff the barnyard ambience, as she prefers. There are a few trees big enough that a good leg-hiking won't wash them away, some picnic tables, athletic fields, and a playground. You are responsible for picking up after your pooch.

From Interstate 10, go south on Yarbrough Drive about a mile to the park, which is on your left. The park is closed from 10 P.M. to 6 A.M. (915) 541-4331.

RESTAURANTS

Buffalo Soldiers: Heaping barbecue plates and sandwiches are the menu here. Eat at the patio on the side of this restaurant in the Fort Bliss area. 5501 North Dyer Avenue; (915) 566-2300.

Cappetto's: This Italian restaurant welcomes dogs (and their people) at the patio out front. 2716 Montana Avenue; (915) 566-9357.

Cattle Baron: Have your steak, seafood, or chicken on the patio in front, or graze the huge salad bar. Surely your dog will vote for the steak. 1700 Airway Boulevard; (915) 779-6633.

Forti's Mexican Elder: The most famous of El Paso Mexican restaurants welcomes you and your pooch to dine on its side patio. In addition to Mexican food that rises above ordinary Tex-Mex, you can have steak or seafood. 321 Chelsea Street; (915) 772-0066.

Kazi's Bar and Grill: This eatery near the University of Texas at El Paso has a fenced patio out front where your pooch can join you. The menu tends toward burgers and nachos. 2525 North Mesa Street; (915) 544-6667.

Silver Streak: Even slow dogs will be able to catch up with a hamburger, hot dog, or some fried chicken at the patio out front. Locations welcoming dogs are at 1201 Airway Boulevard (915-778-8617) and 1434 North Lee Treviño Drive (915-592-2087).

Sonic Drive-In: The following El Paso locations of this national burger and fries chain have outside tables where your pooch is welcome: 5326 Doniphan Drive, (915) 581-1246; 3925 Dyer Street, (915) 565-0725; 9505 Socorro Road, (915) 858-0890; 6938 Alameda Avenue, (915) 778-5545; 2270 Trawood Drive, (915) 592-1777; and 1865 North Zaragoza Road, (915) 856-1266.

Taco Bell: You don't have to make a run for the border to eat at this location of the chain restaurant; you're already there. Eat on the patio with your pooch. 9505 Viscount Boulevard; (915) 592-3619.

Whataburger: This outlet of the chain hamburger restaurant is friendlier than most to both dogs and people, with a covered patio out front where dogs are welcome and a reading rack inside with newspapers and magazines. Hounds can sip coffee and sniff each other while their humans catch up on the news. 1198 Yarbrough Drive; (915) 590-8866.

PLACES TO STAY

The following explanation may help you track down an El Paso hotel with a minimum amount of time wasted going down the wrong rabbit trails. Within El Paso, Interstate 10 is known as Gateway Boulevard. Addresses listed as Gateway East are on the south (eastbound) side of Interstate 10. Addresses listed as Gateway West are on the north (westbound) side of the freeway. The designations "east" and "west" have nothing to do with location east or west of downtown.

Airport Hilton: This hotel arranged around a series of interior gated courtyards has hosted both dog and cat shows, so you know they like animals—they're just confused about which kind is best. Stay here with your sweet, lovable, well-behaved hound and set them straight. Dogs may stay here with a $25 cash deposit or a credit card imprint and your signature on a pet waiver; your deposit will be refunded if the room passes inspection prior to check-out. Dogs are required to be on leash while on the property; you'll meet other dogs at the designated grassy area in front of the hotel. Rooms are $59 to $189 a night; suites are higher. 2027 Airway Boulevard, El Paso, TX 79925; (915) 778-4241 or (800) 742-7248.

Best Western—Airport: Small dogs may stay for no fee or deposit. Rooms are $56. 7144 Gateway Boulevard East (Interstate 10), El Paso, TX 79915; (915) 779-7700 or (800) 295-7276.

Best Western—Sunland Park: Small dogs are welcome; there is no fee or deposit. Rooms are $60. 1045 Sunland Park Drive, El Paso, TX 79922; (915) 587-4900 or (800) 528-1234.

Camino Real Paso del Norte: Very small dogs—"lapdogs," the clerk said—may stay for no deposit or fee. This historic downtown hotel is famous for its plush interior and stained-glass dome over the bar. Even if your pooch doesn't drink, she'll love people- and dog-watching in the lobby. Rooms are $135 to $150. 101 South El Paso Street, El Paso, TX 79901; (915) 534-3000 or (800) 7-CAMINO/722-6466.

Comfort Inn—Airport: Rooms are $54 to $69. There is a $25 deposit for dogs. 900 North Yarbrough Drive, El Paso, TX 79915; (915) 594-9111 or (800) 221-2222.

Days Inn—Airport: Rates are $45 to $63, which includes a continental breakfast. Dogs up to 20 pounds may stay in smoking rooms; there is no fee or deposit. 9125 Gateway Boulevard West (Interstate 10), El Paso, TX 79925; (915) 593-8600 or (800) 325-2525.

Howard Johnson Lodge: Any size dog is welcome at no charge. Rates are $40 to $70. 8887 Gateway Boulevard West (Interstate 10), El Paso, TX 79925; (915) 591-9471 or (800) 446-4656.

Hueco Tanks State Historical Park: See Hueco Tanks State Historical Park on page 407 for camping information.

La Quinta Inn—Airport: Room rates are $49 to $84, which includes a continental breakfast. Dogs under 25 pounds are welcome; there is no fee or deposit. 6140 Gateway Boulevard East (Interstate 10), El Paso, TX 79905; (915) 778-9321 or (800) NU-ROOMS/687-6667.

La Quinta Inn—Lomaland: Rooms are $51 to $58. A continental breakfast is included. Dogs under 25 pounds may stay for no fee or deposit. 11033 Gateway Boulevard West (Interstate 10), El Paso, TX 79935; (915) 591-2244 or (800) NU-ROOMS/687-6667.

La Quinta Inn—West: Rooms are $51 to $58. A continental breakfast is included. Dogs under 25 pounds may stay for no fee or deposit. 7550 Remcon Circle, El Paso, TX 79912; (915) 833-2522 or (800) NU-ROOMS/687-6667.

Marriott Hotel: Rooms are $64 at this hotel near the airport. Small dogs may stay for no fee or deposit, but you are responsible for damages. 1600 Airway Boulevard, El Paso, TX 79925; (915) 779-3300 or (800) 228-9290.

Motel 6—Central: All Motel 6s allow one small pooch per room. Rooms are $36. 4800 Gateway Boulevard East, El Paso, TX 79905; (915) 533-7521 or (800) 466-8356.

Motel 6—East: All Motel 6s allow one small pooch per room. Rooms are $35. 11049 Gateway Boulevard West, El Paso, TX 79935; (915) 594-8533 or (800) 466-8356.

Motel 6—Lomaland: All Motel 6s allow one small pooch per room. Rooms are $35. 1330 Lomaland Drive, El Paso, TX 79935; (915) 592-6386 or (800) 466-8356.

FESTIVALS

Border Folk Festival: Set your pooch's paws tapping to the sound of music from around the world. Performers present the heritage of diverse homelands on stages on the grounds of the Chamizal National Memorial (see page 404) in mid-September. Leashed dogs are welcome to watch and listen; howling along is not encouraged. For information, phone (915) 532-7273.

The First Thanksgiving: Juan de Oñate led the first major colonization effort into what is now the United States in 1598. He led 400 settlers, 83 ox-drawn wagons, and about 7,000 sheep, goats, cattle, and horses through El Paso on their way into New Mexico. Guarding this procession along with soldiers were an unknown number of fierce dogs. After a four-month ordeal crossing the deserts of Northern Mexico, the expedition reached the Rio Grande near El Paso in late April. After a 10-day rest, Oñate declared a feast and day of thanksgiving. The El Paso Mission Trail Association holds a reenactment the last weekend in April of what they claim to be the first Thanksgiving held in America. Dogs are welcome to attend this event, as they were the first. The festivities are held on the grounds of the Chamizal National Memorial (see page 404), on Paisano Drive at San Marcial Street. For information, call (915) 534-0630.

DIVERSIONS

Blanket your dog with love: No matter from which direction you approach El Paso—unless you parachute in—you'll be entertained for miles and miles (and miles and miles) by billboards advertising the El Paso Saddleblanket Company. After the first dozen or so, you're likely to suspect that anyone who spent that much money on billboards probably had so few funds for construction that the store could hide behind one of the signs. Not so. The huge store is everything promised by the billboards and more. Better yet, owners Dusty and Bonnie Henson love dogs, and their two German shepherds, Cid and Sadie, hang out in the store office. Your pooch can go anywhere in the store except the office, Dusty says. Cid and Sadie get a little excited when they see other dogs, and when dogs their size get excited, anything could happen. Dusty asks that shoppers with dogs not turn left into the office area just after entering the store. His dogs often sit near the sliding glass door, which he would prefer not to have to replace.

You and your dog can shop for a saddle blanket, as the store's name implies, or for a bewildering variety of mostly Mexican imports. The first thing your pooch will spot is the cow skulls by the front door, and the mound of well-used saddle trees is bound to be good for a prolonged sniffing. Meanwhile you'll be examining the wool rugs made in Mexico by Indian weavers, Oriental rugs, jewelry, pottery, tinware, antiques, saddles, hides, and furs. Everything in this store will smell tempting to a dog; come prepared to stay a while. Sport, Samantha, and cat Comet have been sleeping on rugs purchased here for several years and give them four paws up (and a few fleas).

The store at 601 North Oregon, one block south of Interstate 10; (915) 544-1000.

Pamper your perro at PetsMart: After lavishing gifts on yourself at people stores around town, take your pooch to PetsMart and buy something nice for her. Leashed dogs may shop here, but they may not cache Czechs, bones, or chew toys. You'll find everything your dog needs—from food to froufrou—and then some. 655 Sunland Park Drive; (915) 587-7898.

THE GUADALUPE MOUNTAINS

Even near-sighted dogs will notice these mountains about 100 miles east of El Paso. Guadalupe Peak, the highest point in Texas at 8,751 feet, sits just behind El Capitan, which rises to 8,078 feet above sea level. It's an impressive sight, particularly since the mountains rear several thousand feet skyward above salt flats stretching for miles.

The Guadalupe Mountains contain perhaps the least-visited major park in Texas. One reason is the location so far from major cities. There are no accommodations or food service nearby. Another is the wilderness nature of the park: access to the interior is principally by foot. While this park contains some of the most beautiful places in Texas, you can't see most of them with your dog. Dogs are banned from major trails in the park. However, there are a couple of minor trails and some roads your pooch can amble along with you, and Sport and I agree that mountains are best seen from a distance anyway.

PARKS, BEACHES, AND RECREATION AREAS

• **Guadalupe Mountains National Park** 🐾 ◀● *See* ㉒ *on page 402.*

Dogs can only sniff around the edges of this 77,518-acre park, and even then they must be leashed. There is no admission fee, but that's small consolation. Your pooch can stay in the campground with you, so you can cry yourselves to sleep together.

What your pooch will be missing are some of the most interesting geology and nature walks in the state. The Guadalupes are the remains of a limestone reef formed millions of years ago under an ancient sea and later uplifted. Desert surrounds the mountains, which make their own climate, wetter and cooler than the surrounding land. It's also windy here, and the weather can change rapidly, so bring warm clothing and rain gear if you visit, no matter what time of year.

Canyons slash the mountainsides, and a forested basin sits high atop the peaks. McKittrick Canyon, reached by a three-mile-long trail, is the best known because of its spectacular leaf displays in October and November. It is a fairly level, easy walk. In contrast, the 4.5-mile Guadalupe Peak Trail ascends over half a mile to the highest point in Texas. The view—one of the finest in Texas—may tempt you to park your pooch in the campground with a less motivated friend while you make the strenuous walk, which can take up to eight hours round-trip. If you go, wear good hiking boots, carry plenty of food and water, and remember that temperatures and wind speeds at the top may be several magnitudes more miserable than at the bottom. It's not a trip for the faint (or weak) of heart. You may see mule deer or elk, but the other large inhabitants of the high elevations—mountain lions—will probably make themselves scarce. They prefer to hang around the campground, picking off unsuspecting dogs. I'm kidding, of course, but caution is advised. It's better to be careful than poochless.

Although dogs are not allowed on major trails, there are four places you can take your hound for a walk. Two begin at the campground. The Pineries Trail takes you two-thirds of a mile to the ruins of a Butterfield Overland Mail station. A second trail, perhaps half a mile long, leads from the tent camping area to the visitor center.

There are two roads where leashed dogs are allowed on the road surface itself. The Williams Ranch Road is a seven-mile route across the desert. It has great views of the mountains. Four-wheel drive is recommended, but you'll probably be okay with just a high-clearance vehicle. Ask about road conditions at the visitor center, where you'll have to check out a key to the gate blocking the road. The four-mile road to the ranger station at the mouth of McKittrick Canyon is also open to leashed dogs. The road is open from 8 A.M. to 4:30 P.M. except during daylight saving time, when it's open until 6 P.M.

The only camping accessible to dogs in the Texas part of the park (it extends into New Mexico) is at Pine Springs Campground, which is near the visitor center on U.S. 62/180. Sites are well spaced, and many have small trees around; the elevation is nearly 6,000 feet, and enough rain falls to support them. Nights will be brisk, but no campfires are allowed. Bring a warm sleeping bag and a sweater for your cold-natured four-footed companion. (This was one of the campgrounds where I didn't mind sleeping as the filling in a dog sandwich, with Samantha on one side and Sport on the other; they kept me quite snug—and unable to turn over.) The campground has 19 RV sites (no hookups) and 20 tent sites; all rent for $7. Flush toilets and water are nearby. Reservations are not accepted.

The park visitor center is on U.S. 62/180 about 110 miles east of El Paso. It is open from 8 A.M. to 4:30 P.M. (until 6 P.M. from Memorial Day to Labor Day). The park itself closes at 6 P.M. except to overnight guests. For more information contact Guadalupe Mountains National Park, HC 60, Box 400, Salt Flat, TX 79847-9400; (915) 828-3251.

PLACES TO STAY

Guadalupe Mountains National Park: See Guadalupe Mountains National Park on page 418 for camping information.

HOUSTON AREA MAP

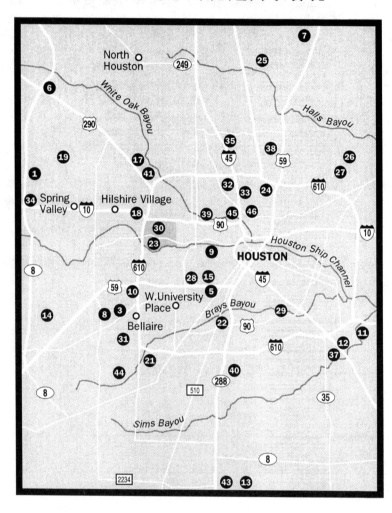

8
HOUSTON/ SOUTHEAST TEXAS

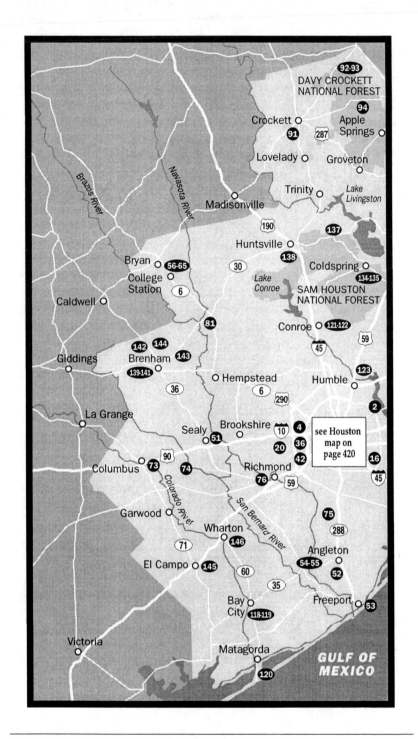

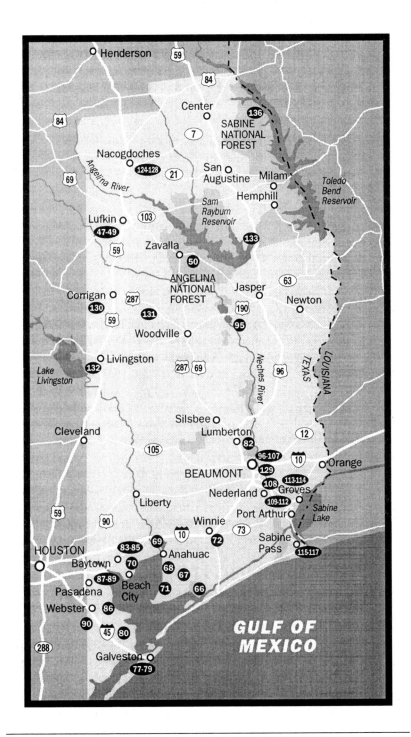

Henderson · 59
84
84
Center
7 · SABINE NATIONAL FOREST
136
Nacogdoches · 124-128 · 21
San Augustine
Milam
Hemphill
69
Angelina River
Sam Rayburn Reservoir
Toledo Bend Reservoir
Lufkin · 103
47-49
59
Zavalla
50 · 133
ANGELINA NATIONAL FOREST
Jasper · 63
Newton
Corrigan · 287
130 · 59 · 131
190
95
Woodville
287 · 69
Livingston · 132
Lake Livingston
Neches River
96
TEXAS
LOUISIANA
Silsbee
Lumberton · 82
Cleveland
12
96-107
105
BEAUMONT · 129 · 10 · Orange
113-114
108 · Groves
Nederland · 109-112
Port Arthur · Sabine Lake
Liberty
59
90
Winnie
73
Sabine Pass
115-117
HOUSTON · 83-85 · 69 · 10 · 72
Baytown · 70 · Anahuac
68
87-89 · 67
Pasadena · Beach City · 71
Webster · 86 · 66
90
45 · 80
288
Galveston
77-79

GULF OF MEXICO

HOUSTON/ SOUTHEAST TEXAS

In a state as large and diverse as Texas, it's hard to choose one area over another as better for dogs. As a friend of mine is fond of saying, "It depends." No matter what standard is used, however, Southeast Texas has to rank near the top. All of Texas's national forests, and therefore the bulk of its public land, are located here. In a state in which about 97 percent of the land is privately owned, that's a doggone big deal. It means that dogs have more room to roam here than anywhere else in the state. Even better, leashes are not required in the national forests outside designated recreation areas. It's a boy dog's dream: millions of trees standing tall and proud, waiting for moisture. Hiking trails within the forests link camping areas, lakes, and highways. There's no better place in Texas to walk a dog.

Some of the best state parks for dogs are also located within a couple hours' drive of Texas's largest city. Village Creek State Park and Lake Houston State Park are both outstanding places to play with your pooch. Within the city itself, the Houston Arboretum and Nature Center is top-ranked. The city also has some of the best jogging trails in the state, and leashed dogs can go on all of them.

One of the favorite activities of Houstonites is getting out of Houston for the weekend, and smaller towns throughout the region offer opportunities to kick back and veg out with your hound. In general, these small towns are very dog-friendly, and many have restaurants where canine customers are welcome. While there are entirely too many people in this part of the state to suit country cousins like Sport, Samantha, and me, visitors and residents alike don't have to go far to escape to woods as deep, dark, mysterious, and marvelous as any in the state.

HOUSTON

People who live in Houston swear by it. They love the small-town nature of many of its neighborhoods; its abundance of cultural, educational, and medical facilities; and its cosmopolitan air. Others swear at it, complaining of traffic, humidity, and overcrowding. Both, of course, have their points. But what do dogs say about Houston? They have mixed feelings, too. The city and surrounding county have great parks, and some of the finest hotels in the world, located in Houston, welcome dogs. But dogs are banned from all restaurants in Houston, so you'll have to do your eating out in the suburbs.

While Memorial Park and Hermann Park are exceptions to the rule, Houston city parks in general suffer by comparison to Harris County parks. I've included numerous city parks along major thoroughfares for the convenience of the traveling dog in dire need of a stop, but if you want to have a really good outdoor experience with your dog while in Houston, try one of the county parks. Almost without exception they are larger, better equipped, better maintained, and have better security.

On the other paw, Houston offers the opportunity to do things with your pooch that you can't do anywhere else in the state. You can visit attractions like the Orange Show, a zany tribute to a fruit that will rekindle the puppy in you. Your hound can bark at the weirdest cars in the world in the Art Car Parade, although hiking legs on tires is considered kitsch. In short, Houston is a world unto itself in Texas dogdom, a place where every dog has his day.

PARKS, BEACHES, AND RECREATION AREAS

• **Agnes Moffett Park** 🐾 **1/2** *See ❶ on page 420.*

This park's 40 acres offer a variety of temptations for leashed dogs, ranging from cars zipping by on a busy street at its northern edge to weedy woods on the south. It's conveniently located next to the Sam Houston Tollway. There's a playground, a swimming pool, a picnic area, lots of trees, a covered basketball court, a Frisbee golf course, and chemical toilets. Just to its east is a heavily wooded area sure to harbor interesting furry creatures that venture forth into the park to lay down fascinating scent trails.

The park is at the intersection of the Sam Houston Tollway and Hammerly Boulevard. Hours are 7 A.M. to 11 P.M. (713) 845-1000.

• **Alexander Deussen Park** 🐾🐾 **1/2** *See ❷ on page 422.*

This park is a good illustration of who has the money to spend—the City of Houston or Harris County. Like other county parks Sport and I visited, this one was large—309 acres—clean, well maintained, and closely patrolled by park rangers. We felt secure here, and on a weekday we had the park nearly to ourselves. However, for at least two miles before we reached the park entrance, we saw signs forbidding parking along the road, so we suspect that weekends and holidays can be quite crowded.

Dogs must be on a five-foot leash here, the first time Sport and I had encountered that restriction, but we soon found it to be the rule in other Harris County parks as well.

The park is basically one huge picnic ground. It's almost completely shaded by pine and oak trees, and areas that have not been cleared are nigh impenetrable. You and your dog will be able to get all the exercise you want on the paved walking trail which takes you by a pen holding several buffalo and winds throughout the park. A picnic area overlooking Lake Houston gives a good view of the lake, although signs abound forbidding swimming, diving, or wading. Not far from the lake, on the one-way road that takes you through the park, we found a small pond with grassy banks sloping gently to the water, where a dog can wet her paws and whistle. Or whistle while she wets her paws.

There is one camping area in the park, restricted to tents only on weekends only, from Friday noon to Monday noon. Reservations are required. Campers are locked in the park at closing and must stay in their campsites during those hours. The campsites are well shaded by pine trees but offer no privacy.

To reach the park, take C. E. King Parkway or North Lake Houston Parkway east from Beltway 8 on Houston's northeast side. It's about three miles to the entrance on Deussen Parkway. Summer hours are 6 A.M. to 9 P.M.; in winter the park closes at 6 P.M. (713) 991-6881.

• **Bayland Park** 🐾 *See* ❸ *on page 420.*
On a city map this park shows up as a big green blob—68 acres' worth. However, by the time streets and athletic fields had been carved out, only a few scraps of space were left for grass and dogs. The few trees on the west end are spindly pines dwarfed by the utility poles made from their deceased big brothers. Even non-baseball playing humans have to take scraps here: There is a playground and rest rooms, but it's not an inviting place to visit unless you have home runs on your mind.

The east end of the park is a little better. Amazingly, the bulldozers spared a small grove of live oak trees, which shade 15 or so picnic tables. A paved jogging path about a quarter of a mile long encircles the picnic area.

The park is at the intersection of Bissonet Street and Hillcroft Avenue. From U.S. 59 West, go east on Bissonet Street about two and a quarter miles. Hours are 7 A.M. to 10 P.M. (281) 496-2177.

• **Bear Creek Park** 🐾 🐾½ *See* ❹ *on page 422.*
Sport and I didn't see any bears here, but we did see more picnic tables and rest rooms than we saw in any other park we visited. Leashed dogs will have more places to look for scraps than they dreamed existed. The park contains 2,200 acres, most of which seem, at first glance, to be given over to picnic tables. There are playgrounds and a golf course, too. Dogs are not allowed on the equestrian trails in the south end of the park. Leashes may not be longer than five feet.

Boy dogs may be intimidated by this park's thousands of oak trees.

There are a few pines around, but the oak trees go on and on. Most areas of the park are shaded all day. Your pooch will appreciate that, as he'll likely work up a tongue-dripping sweat barking at the squirrels. The uncleared underbrush discourages walking outside the picnic areas, but these are so large you and your pooch can roam for hours, going from one tree to the next, looking for the perfect place to squat or hike. If your dog is one of the indecisive types like Samantha, she may well drive you nuts before she settles on the right tree.

To reach the park from Interstate 10 West, go north on Highway 6 about a mile and a quarter to Patterson Road. Turn right and go one-third mile to Bear Creek Drive and turn left. Park hours are 7 A.M. to 10 P.M. (281) 496-2177.

• **Bell Park** 🐾 *See* ❺ *on page 420.*

With its landscaped grounds, numerous trees, graveled paths, and bubbling fountain, this small, acre-and-a-half neighborhood park attracts local dogs for their leashed morning stroll. Two wooden footbridges ring with the sound of clicking toenails during the morning constitutional rush. Several local dogs and their owners—residents of nearby apartments—were busily sniffing their way around the park when Sport and I last visited. One was on leash; the other off. Neither wanted to leave.

The park is at the intersection of Montrose Boulevard and Banks Street, just two blocks south of U.S. 59. Hours are 7 A.M. to 11 P.M. (713) 845-1000.

• **Bill Bane Park** 🐾 *See* ❻ *on page 420.*

This 10-acre park is a good example of making maximum use of space. Athletic fields, playgrounds, a parking lot, picnic tables, rest rooms, and even a small fishing lake are compressed into the least possible amount of space, all divided from each other by a maze of chain-link fences. It's enough to make a dog want to squat and move on.

The park is on Gessner Street just east of where U.S. 290 (Northwest Freeway), the Hempstead Highway, and the Sam Houston Tollway all cross. Exit onto West Little York Road and go east to Gessner Street and the park entrance. The park is open from 8 A.M. to 10 P.M. (281) 353-4196.

• **Bill Crowley Park** 🐾½ *See* ❼ *on page 420.*

Though this county park of 30 acres is highly developed, there are still lots of pine trees for dogs to sniff. Leashes are required attire and can be no longer than six feet.

A paved walking path encircles a picnic ground shaded by those pines. Workers were busy cleaning the grounds when Sport and I last visited, something we found to be quite common in both city and county parks in Houston. They were some of the cleanest parks we visited anywhere in the state. This park also has a playground, athletic fields, a covered basketball court, and rest rooms.

The park is 1.9 miles east of Aldine-Westfield Road on Lauder Road. Winter hours are 8 A.M. to 7 P.M.; summer hours extend to 9 P.M. (281) 591-6951.

• **Bonham Park** 🔥 *See* ❽ *on page 420.*

Most of this approximately eight-acre park is open space with no shade. There are a few small, newly planted trees on the north side and a few scattered pines. Athletic fields are the main feature, and there is a chemical toilet.

The park is at Brae Acres Road and Carew Street. From U.S. 59 West, exit on Beechnut Street. Travel east on Beechnut a quarter of a mile to Brae Acres Road; turn right and go two blocks to the park. It is open from 7 A.M. to 11 P.M. (713) 845-1000.

• **Buffalo Bayou Park** 🐾 ½ *See* ❾ *on page 420.*

This greenbelt park stretches about a mile and a half along Allen Parkway, and leashed dogs love every inch and all 121 acres of it. Steep banks fall off from street level to the bayou, sheltering joggers and walkers from the sights and sounds of the busy streets on either side. A paved jogging path is a popular early morning exercise venue for local residents. Dogs will prefer exploring the brushy banks of the bayou, romping on the expansive grassy areas, and sniffing tree trunks to see who had preceded them.

One access point is at the intersection of Allen Parkway and Montrose Boulevard. Turn west onto Allen Parkway and immediately pull into a small curbed parking area on the right. Or continue west another hundred yards to the Waugh Drive exit and park beside the fountain with the bristly ball spewing water; thirsty dogs are sure to appreciate the chance to get a drink. Hours are 7 A.M. to 11 P.M. (713) 845-1000.

• **Burnett Bayland Park** 🐾 *See* ❿ *on page 420.*

This park of about 10 acres offers dogs on leashes no longer than five feet the chance to sniff a few trees, pad around a paved walking trail, and romp on the grassy areas. There are a number of picnic tables nicely shaded by large trees, and the antics of teenagers shooting baskets at the two covered basketball courts will keep ball-chasing pooches busy a while trying to figure out how to get their mouths around that big ball. There's also a playground and rest rooms.

The park is at the intersection of Chimney Rock Road and Gulfton Drive. From U.S. 59 West, go south on Chimney Rock Road about half a mile. Hours are 7 A.M. to 11 P.M. (713) 845-1000.

• **Charles Milby Park** 🐾 *See* ⓫ *on page 420.*

Pooches will likely enjoy this 66-acre park more than you will, even though they must be on a six-foot leash. It sits on Sims Bayou just downstream of one of Houston's wastewater treatment plants, and the delicious (to a dog) aroma of treated sewage wafted our way as Sport and I walked about under the large oak trees. There are a few picnic tables and swings, but most of the park is open and grassy.

To reach the park, take Highway 3 (Galveston Road) south from Loop 610 East a quarter of a mile to Central Street. Turn left on Central Street and go past the wastewater treatment plant a quarter of a mile to the park entrance. Hours are 7 A.M. to 11 P.M. (713) 845-1000.

• **Charlton Park** 🐾 *See* ⓬ *on page 420.*

Leashed dogs who visit this little park of about nine acres will find something most other Houston parks don't have: hills they can run up and down. The park and its playground and picnic tables are almost totally shaded by large oak trees. The trees, hills, and grass combine to provide a peaceful setting even though the park is within earshot of two major freeways.

From Loop 610 East, follow Interstate 45 south half a mile to Park Place Boulevard. Go east on Park Place Boulevard two blocks to the park. Hours are 7 A.M. to 11 P.M. (713) 845-1000.

• **Christa Adair County Park** 🐾🐾 *See* ⓭ *on page 420.*

This 61-acre park is a smaller version of the Tom Bass Regional Park located just across the road (see page 441). It has no lake or golf course and instead is mainly about picnic grounds, playgrounds, and a nature trail. Leashed dogs (a five-foot leash is required) can enjoy them all with you, and something special as well. As you enter the park, a sign directs you to park attractions, including a mural. Don't pass up the mural, which is located in a pavilion at the east end of the main parking lot. It depicts black family and community life, and a dog—what else—occupies the front and center spot of the mural. It's a good place to practice a little art appreciation with your pooch.

The entrance is on Cullen Boulevard, five and a half miles south of Loop 610, directly across from the entrance to Section III of Tom Bass Regional Park. The park is open from 6 A.M. to 9 P.M. (713) 991-6881.

• **Crain Park** 🐾 *See* ⓮ *on page 420.*

On school days your hound will share the six acres of this park with kids from the adjacent elementary school. There's a playground, covered basketball goals, and a paved jogging path about a quarter mile long. Most of the area, though, is grass dotted with a number of trees large enough to be worthy of the name.

The park is at the intersection of Pella Drive and Triola Lane. From U.S. 59 West, go north on South Gessner Drive about three-quarters of a mile; turn left onto Triola Lane and proceed two blocks. Hours are 7 A.M. to 11 P.M. (713) 845-1000.

• **Dunlavy Park** 🐾 *See* ⑮ *on page 420.*

This three-acre park divides its limited space about half and half between a playground and a softball diamond, but there are many large trees and lots of grass for a dog to make use of.

The park is two blocks south of Richmond Avenue on Dunlavy Street; it joins the north side of U.S. 59. Hours are 7 A.M. to 11 P.M. (713) 845-1000.

• **Evalyn Wilson Park** 🐾🐾½ *See* ⑯ *on page 422.*

Sport and I saw three of the happiest dogs in Houston at this 29-acre park. A boxer, a Border collie, and a black Lab, they were tearing about unleashed (against the rules, of course—a six-foot leash is required). There was a lot to get excited about. A small pond harbors a large population of geese, which the dogs charged and sent waddling into the water. Then their owner pointed out some mourning doves in the grassy picnic area, and the dogs exuberantly sent them flying. They split up for their next adventure, two chasing each other across the soccer fields while the other sniffed along the edge of a wooded area in the southern end of the park. In a few minutes they regrouped and had a drink out of the pond. The park also has tennis courts, playgrounds, and a covered basketball court, but dashing about madly was all these three wanted to do.

The park is on Highway 3 (Galveston Road) about five miles south of Loop 610. Hours are 7 A.M. to 11 P.M. (713) 845-1000.

• **Forest West Park** 🐾 *See* ⑰ *on page 420.*

Forest West Park, which covers about six acres, reflects the character of the surrounding neighborhood, which consists of fairly new homes on small lots on one side, a school on one side, and apartment complexes on the other two sides. That is to say, it's just a bare spot in the midst of suburbia. There's a playground, a few picnic tables, a cluster of pine trees, and chemical toilets.

The park is on the east side of Clifton Middle School. From U.S. 290 West, exit on Pinemont Drive and go east about three-quarters of a mile to Lost Forest Drive. Turn left onto Lost Forest Drive and follow it two blocks to the school. Turn right at the school and park along the street. Hours are 7 A.M. to 11 P.M. (713) 845-1000.

• **Freed Park** 🐾 *See* ⑱ *on page 420.*

Covering about 15 acres, this park presents a pleasing aspect with its many oak trees, but the bare ground bespeaks heavy use by people picnicking and visiting the playground. Leashed dogs will exhaust its possibilities quickly.

The park is conveniently located for traveling dogs passing through on Interstate 10 and badly in need of dewatering. Exit Antoine Drive about a mile west of Loop 610 and go north half a mile to Shadyville Lane. Turn right and proceed two blocks to the park. Hours are 7 A.M. to 11 P.M. (713) 845-1000.

• **Freshmeadow Park** 🐾 *See ⑲ on page 420.*

The name of this park was intriguing. I wanted to see if it lived up to its promise. When Sport and I pulled into the parking lot, we saw cows—on the side of a Ben & Jerry's ice cream truck parked next to a warehouse on the east side of the park. For an instant we toyed with the idea of hijacking a gallon, but we realized that by the time we got to a hiding place where we could eat the purloined goodies, they'd be melted. It's true. Crime does not pay. I consoled Sport with the thought that they probably do not have raccoon-flavored ice cream, anyway.

This park's approximately two acres need something like an ice cream truck to make them interesting. It's flat, featureless, and has only a few small trees. Chemical toilets at each end provide the only scenery worthy of note. Joy. Squat and move on, thrill-seeking canines. Maybe an ice cream truck has turned over just down the road and spilled its contents.

The park is on Campbell Road about a mile south of the Hempstead Highway on the west side of town. It's open from 7 A.M. to 11 P.M. (713) 845-1000.

• **George Bush Park** 🐾 🐾 ½ *See ⑳ on page 422.*

If there were more for a leashed dog to do here, this huge park—7,800 acres—would rate higher. The purpose of the area along Buffalo Bayou is flood control, and most of the land consists of vast grassy fields devoid of trees and anything else of much interest to a person or a dog. The best part for dogs are the small ponds, some of which have picnic tables and young trees around them, that you'll find along Westheimer Parkway, which runs through the southern part of the park. Off this road you'll also find a shooting range, radio-controlled airplane field, equestrian center, and group picnic area with a playground. But in between it's just flat, boring prairie whose table-like surface is marred only by fire ant mounds.

As Sport and I visited the park, we did meet one husky out for a stroll around a small pond, and there appeared to be a beagle-training class going on in one field. Flop-eared dogs with noses pressed to the ground were wandering about tracking what we could only guess. There was a small group of observers watching intently and other dogs who appeared to be waiting their turn.

The park is southwest of Interstate 10 West and Highway 6. Drive south on Highway 6 to its intersection with Westheimer Drive; turn west on Westheimer and go about a quarter of a mile. Turn onto Westheimer Parkway, which runs through the park. It may show up on your map as Cullen-Barker Park; the name has changed. Hours are 7 A.M. to 10 P.M. (281) 496-2177.

• **Godwin Park** 🐾 *See* ㉑ *on page 420.*

Sport was delighted to see this place. We'd visited a number of parks so small that a big dog like Sport had to chase her tail to keep from running out of the borders. This park of about eight acres didn't cramp her style, which included an extensive search for just the right spot to dewater. What it is that trips a dog's valve is a mystery, but Sport and Samantha have taught me that until it's found, you might as well give a dog her leash and let her look, because nothing is going to happen until the magic place appears.

This park has a large playground and several soccer fields, but it's mostly open grassy space with some good-sized live oak trees scattered about. Sport made friends with an elderly couple out for a stroll, each with their tape player and headphones.

The park is at the intersection of Rutherglenn Drive and Balmforth Lane. From South Main Street, drive north on Chimney Rock Road about two miles to Rutherglenn Drive; turn right and go two blocks to the park. Hours are 7 A.M. to 11 P.M. (713) 845-1000.

• **Hermann Park** 🐾 🐾 🐾 *See* ㉒ *on page 420.*

This large urban park—402 acres—doesn't have everything a dog could ask for, but it comes close. Trees, lakes, trails, grass, ducks, squirrels, and other dogs all come together here in a delicious mélange. The only negative I found for this downtown park came in the form of numerous signs along the jogging trail warning people not to use it alone after dark. You'll feel better even in the daytime with your leashed sidekick trotting along at your side. Sport and I haven't made an extensive study of the subject, but we doubt seriously that many people with dogs get panhandled, and we'd bet the ranch that nobody with a dog refusing to fork over cash to a streetperson has been called "tight toes."

Hermann Park is the perfect place for the Renaissance dog, since everything comes together here. Just south of the central business district, where Big Oil and Big Money conduct Big Bidness, the park is an oasis of calm. Around it cluster world-famous art museums and hospitals. Rice University snaps, crackles, and pops just to the west. Ambulances howl into the Texas Medical Center and Ben Taub Hospital at its southwestern corner; a few blocks farther south is the University of Texas Health Science Center, where the famous Doctor Red Duke holds forth. Doctor Duke sometimes includes a dog in his television programs, and if he takes a dog to work with him—as every person in a position to save lives should—this is the closest park to his office. Who knows? You may see a familiar redhead with handlebar mustache dewatering a hound here. Don't embarrass him by asking for an autograph. Even the dog of the most famous doctor in Texas probably does not know how to write his name. (Even if he could, you wouldn't be able to read it any more than you can read a doctor's signature on a prescription.)

Like the rest of Houston, Hermann Park is flat. However, it is far from featureless. Pine trees dominate, and these piquant evergreens piqued Sport's interest. Their fragrance was new to her, and she spent a lot of time sniffing their unusual (to her) fragrance. Suffice it to say that with thousands of pine trees in the park, I tired very quickly of Sport's seeming determination to discover if they all smelled alike.

Dragging Sport along the wide jogging path surfaced with fine gravel and lined with tempting pine trees on both sides, we soon arrived at one of two several-acre lakes in the north end of the park. Recent rains had left the ground muddy and the lakes near to overflowing, and Sport the water dog was in her element. So were the numerous geese and ducks on the lake, who did not take kindly to her intrusion. Raucous honking and quacking drove us a few yards away, where we watched a woman and child throwing crackers into the air to attract pigeons. This was almost too much for Sport, who wanted more than anything to dash into their midst and snack. Whether on the birds or the crackers, I'm not sure.

Hoping to restore tranquillity to the park, I took Sport to the Japanese Garden ($1.50 admission). The garden symbolizes the friendship between the peoples of the United States, Houston, and Japan. Symbolism is lost on Sport. She much prefers real stuff, like the dead raccoon we found on the side of the road on our way into town. Still, she enjoyed the stroll down paths among waterfalls, rocks, azaleas, crape myrtles, Japanese maple, dogwood (always a favorite), and peach trees.

As we exited the Japanese Garden, a shriek in the distance jerked Sport's head around. The miniature park train approached, making noise far out of proportion to its size, and naturally Sport had to respond in kind. We wanted to take a ride, but, alas, dogs are banned from the rails.

The park is just southwest of downtown. It's bounded by Main Street, Almeda Road, Hermann Drive, and Holcombe Boulevard. Hours are 7 A.M. to 11 P.M. (713) 845-1000.

• Houston Arboretum and Nature Center 🐾🐾🐾½
   See ㉓ on page 420.

Your pooch will turn into a whining foot-dragger when you try to get him to leave this 155-acre nature preserve. You won't want to leave, either. Even though they must be leashed here, dogs love this park so much that at least one bereaved owner made a memorial donation in her deceased dog's name. You can persuade your terrier not to tarry by telling her if she doesn't kennel up, you'll get out your checkbook. It's a thought.

The area supports a dense growth of pine, oak, elm, sycamore, hickory, and sweetgum trees. Small ponds and swampy areas mingle with the trees. Over five miles of trails let you explore every part of the wildlife sanctuary. Boardwalks carry you over the wet spots and through the middles of ponds where turtles and water snakes swim. Squirrels dart across paths littered with pine needles and cones. You may encounter such small critters as armadillos, opossums, swamp rabbits, raccoons, frogs, and a variety of birds. Dogs are not allowed in buildings, off trails, or in the water, but they will still find this the best place in Houston proper to take a walk. Sport especially liked the mile-long R. A. Vines Trail. It runs through a hilly (for Houston) area, passes by some small ponds, and crosses a ravine. As do all the other trails, it begins and ends at the visitor center, where you can buy a trail map for a quarter.

The Nature Center is inside Memorial Park at 4501 Woodway Drive. The grounds are open from 8:30 A.M. to 6 P.M.; the visitor center hours are 9 A.M. to 5 P.M. (713) 681-8433.

• Irvington Park 🐾 *See ㉔ on page 420.*

Large pine trees, a playground, a covered basketball court, a baseball field, and a picnic area fill this park of six acres. That sounds more crowded than it is, but the leashed Chihuahua whom Sport and I saw when we last visited seemed to be just the right size for the place.

The park is at the intersection of Cavalcade Street and Cetti Street. From Interstate 45 North before it crosses Loop 610, turn east on Cavalcade; go about three-quarters of a mile to the park. Hours are 7 A.M. to 11 P.M. (713) 845-1000.

• Keith-Weiss Park 🐾🐾 *See ㉕ on page 420.*

If your hound has a thing for elm and pine trees by the thousand, growing so closely together as to block out the sun, she'll love this 499-acre park. Leashed dogs will have so many trees to choose from they may well pass out from dizziness. You, on the other hand, may pass out from being bonked on the head by any tree branches your dog pulls you into.

The park's largely undeveloped character is part of its charm. There are a few picnic tables and a playground on its south end, but for the most part it's just trees, trees, trees, trees, trees—please stop me. Halls Bayou runs across the southwest corner of the park, but the public is barred from its banks because it is a floodway.

The park is on Aldine-Westfield Road about a mile east of the Hardy Toll Road and about four miles south of Houston Intercontinental Airport. Exit the Hardy Toll Road onto Aldine Mail Route Road and drive east about a mile to Aldine-Westfield Road; turn right and go south half a mile to the entrance. Hours are 7 A.M. to 11 P.M. (713) 845-1000.

• **Lake Forest Park** 🐾 *See* ㉖ *on page 420.*

Sport perked up right away when we got to this nine-acre park with a small lake in its center. We'd just come from a park that had the word "lake" in its name but no lake. This park is mostly lake, and there's a place in the northwest corner where a leashed pooch can actually get down to the water and drink. Sport was more than ready. Then she toured the pine trees around the shore, ignored the picnic tables and playground, and pawed in the sandbox as if making a cool place for a nap. Sorry, Sport. We still had miles to go.

The park is just south of the intersection of East Tidwell Road and Mesa Street on Houston's northeast side. From East Tidwell Road, go south on Mesa Street one block to Lake Park Street and turn left. Park along the street near the playground. Hours are 7 A.M. to 11 P.M. (713) 845-1000.

• **Lakewood Park** 🐾 *See* ㉗ *on page 420.*

Sport and I were both getting a little car-weary when we found this nine-acre park right next to a branch of the Houston Public Library. The dozens of tall pine trees, picnic tables, covered basketball court, and playground were no different from many other parks we'd visited. However, the experience turned out to be unique. Sport and I needed a break and a little cheering up after being in the car for several days on end. I tied Sport to a tree, went into the library, and checked the catalog for *Old Yeller.* Sure enough, they had a copy. I leafed through the pages to refresh my memory of the story about saving the corn crop from marauding raccoons and went back outside to collect my raccoon-hunting hound, who is proud to be from the hometown of that book's author, Fred Gipson. As we circled the paved walking path, I told Sport the story of how Old Yeller had saved the corn by sleeping in the field with her human and driving out the rascally raccoons. I don't think she understood a word of it, but we both felt better. Dogs had triumphed again.

The park is in northeast Houston just west of Mesa Drive. From Mesa

Drive, take East Houston Street two blocks west to Feland Drive. Turn right on Feland and go a long block to the park. If you have a Houston library card, check out *Old Yeller* and read your favorite chapter to your pooch. If not, make something up. That's one advantage dogs have over human children. They never notice when you change the story or leave out parts. Hours are 7 A.M. to 11 P.M. (713) 845-1000.

• **Levy Park** 🐾 *See ㉘ on page 420.*

Sport thought this park of five and a half acres rated more than a fireplug, because she was mobbed by a girl's softball team practicing on the diamond that takes up two-thirds of the park. However, on the theory that excessive adulation spoils the hound, I resisted giving a higher rating. However, this park does have some of the largest trees of any Houston city park we visited, even though they stand guard over a disappointingly small patch of grass. However, errant softballs sailing over the fence give retrieving dogs a chance to play hero to an admiring bevy of fit young women—a heady experience. The park has chemical toilets but no other facilities.

The park is half a block south of Richmond Avenue on Eastside Drive. U.S. 59 is just half a block south of the park; exit Kirby Drive and go north two blocks to Richmond Avenue; turn left and proceed three blocks to Eastside Drive and turn left. Hours are 7 A.M. to 11 P.M. (713) 845-1000.

• **MacGregor Park** 🐾½ *See ㉙ on page 420.*

College dogs from the University of Houston just to the north come to this 120-acre park to study. Of course, the number of subjects that can be studied on a six-foot leash is limited, but the abundant pine and oak trees, squirrels, picnic tables, tennis courts, and playgrounds form a fairly full curriculum. For the pooch who wants to further her studies beyond the basics, there's a paved jogging trail. When Sport and I last visited, an overflowing dumpster and a row of chemical toilets provided study materials for extra credit. Sport has possessed a bachelorette degree ever since she got fixed, and she's now working on her master's of mastication, specializing in raccoons.

The park is a good access point for the Levi Vincent Perry Jr. Jogging Trail, which runs miles along Brays Bayou, connecting with Hermann Park two and a half miles to the west (see page 432).

The park is at the intersection of M. L. King Boulevard and Old Spanish Trail. From Loop 610, go north on M. L. King Boulevard a mile and a quarter to the park. Hours are 7 A.M. to 11 P.M. (713) 845-1000.

• **Memorial Park** 🐾🐾½ *See ㉚ on page 420.*

Energetic Houston hounds come to get their exercise and meet with their friends at this 1,431-acre park. Sport and I met at least a dozen dogs during an early morning stroll on the Seymore-Lieberman Exer-Trail, which circles the golf course. While those poor souls so unfortunate as to have to run and sweat without a canine companion wheezed past, Sport and I ambled along on the mowed strip beside the graveled path, enjoying the morning sun, the smell of the tall pine trees, and the bushy-tailed antics of squirrels. Often we'd meet another dog and person similarly engaged, and Sport and her newfound friend would stop sniffing pine needles and home in on each other's private parts. Now and again a show-off dog would whiz by, tongue hanging out and wearing the same agonized expression as her person. Signs warn against jogging the trail alone after dark. Park alongside the trail at numerous points along Memorial Loop Drive.

Between the endpoints of Memorial Loop Drive, on the south side of the street, turn onto Picnic Lane. On weekdays the roads within the picnic area are closed to vehicles except between the hours of 11 A.M. and 3 P.M., making this a good place to take a stroll with the pooch who wants to be alone with you. Picnic tables and rest rooms are everywhere, shaded by tall pines. Sport and I met our first mounted policeman here: I'm not sure if Sport thought she'd met a cruel man riding a very large dog. However, a fragrant pile of horse apples soon convinced her this was not The Big Dog she'd always heard about. On weekends and holidays the picnic area is open to vehicle traffic from 6:30 A.M. to 8:30 P.M.

The park lies southeast of the intersection of Interstate 10 and Interstate 610. Memorial Drive and Woodway Drive cut through the center of the park. Hours are 7 A.M. to 11 P.M. (713) 845-1000.

• Meyerland Park 🐾 See ③ on page 420.

Sport—an exemplary dog—liked this park because it is located next to one of the Houston Independent School District's exemplary schools. However, there's not a lot for a dog to do on the seven acres here. An elaborate playground, tennis courts, and softball fields take up much of the space. Sport did sniff around a few pine trees and quaffed some water from her bowl filled at the water fountain. There being no squirrels in sight, she was then ready to leave.

The park is at the intersection of Jason Street and Pritchett Street. From Loop 610 just south of Bellaire, exit onto North Braeswood Boulevard and go west about half a mile to South Rice Avenue. Turn right and go three blocks to Jason Street; turn left and you'll see the park in the middle of the block. Hours are 7 A.M. to 11 P.M. (713) 845-1000.

• Montie Beach Park 🐾🐾 See ③ on page 420.

There was a lot going on at this park of 23 acres when Sport and I last visited. Despite the leash law, a free-roaming Dalmatian was egging his

---

owner into a game of Frisbee toss. Neighborhood boys were battling on the basketball court, mothers were pushing toddlers in swings on the playground, and a father was teaching two young boys about soccer. In short, the park had a nice, homey feel that the large pine and elm trees only added to.

The park is on Northwood Street about four blocks north of North Main Street north of downtown. Despite its northerly location, the sun was warm the day we visited. Park hours are 7 A.M. to 11 P.M. (713) 845-1000.

• Moody Park 🐾 1/2 *See ㉝ on page 420.*

For me, the visit to this approximately 35-acre park was made worthwhile by the colorful Luis Jiménez sculpture of a vaquero aboard a bucking horse. Public art is scarce in Houston's public parks, and this glassy-looking work was a welcome sight. For Sport, the high point was meeting four dogs, three on the required leash and one not. They were strolling the lighted concrete walking path that winds among the park's pine and oak trees, picnic tables, playground, and athletic fields. There's a nice view of the downtown skyline through the trees.

Sport wanted to take a header down a steep embankment to one of the most trash-laden drainage ditches I've ever seen, but I played wet blanket to her fearless explorer. I pointed out the muddy bank and the new sheepskin seat cover in the car, and she reined in her enthusiasm as I reined her in.

The park is at the intersection of Fulton Street and Irvington Boulevard directly north of downtown. From Interstate 45, exit on Patton Street and head east half a mile to Irvington Boulevard; turn right and go half a mile to the park. Hours are 7 A.M. to 11 P.M. (713) 845-1000.

• Nob Hill Park 🐾 *See ㉞ on page 420.*

This lovely park of about 13 acres is one of the most heavily wooded yet walkable parks Sport and I visited. Large pine trees totally shade the park and its picnic tables and playgrounds, and lay down a carpet of fragrant needles on which to walk. There are a few humps in the park, but nothing to justify it being named after one of San Francisco's most famous landmarks.

The park is at the intersection of Shadowdale Drive and Timberoak Drive. Shadowdale Drive is divided by a deep drainage ditch; you can approach the park only if northbound on Shadowdale. From Interstate 10 West, exit on Gessner Street and head north about a mile to Eddystone Drive; turn left and go four blocks to Shadowdale Drive. Turn right and you'll reach the park in three blocks. Hours are 7 A.M. to 11 P.M. (713) 845-1000.

•**Northline Park** 🔥 *See ㉟ on page 420.*

This neighborhood park of about 14 acres has a pool, tennis courts, baseball fields, a playground, and picnic tables. It is virtually treeless, but there is lots of open grass. The parking lot boasts chemical toilets.

The park is on Nordling Street at its intersection with Twickenham Street. From Interstate 45 North, go east on Parker Road about half a mile to Nordling and turn left to the entrance. Hours are 7 A.M. to 11 P.M. (713) 845-1000.

•**Nottingham Park** 🐾 *See ㊱ on page 422.*

At about 22 acres, this was one of the largest neighborhood parks Sport and I visited. A sea of grass surrounds an island of sizable trees, a magnet for leashed dogs like Sport who dream of a raccoon or squirrel in every tree. However, neither appeared. Sport had to satisfy herself with sniffing a garbage can and two chemical toilets near the softball diamond on the park's west side. Other than some soccer fields, these were the only improvements in the park. There's also a water fountain at the parking lot on the west side.

To reach the park from Interstate 10 West, exit on Kirkwood Drive and go south eight blocks to Kimberly Lane; turn right and continue two blocks to the parking lot on the park's west side. Hours are 7 A.M. to 11 P.M. (713) 845-1000.

•**Reveille Park** 🔥 *See ㊲ on page 420.*

All Texas Aggie dogs know that the team mascot of Texas A&M University is an American collie named Reveille, a fact I related to Sport as we pulled into this park of about 18 acres. She was unimpressed. However, she was slightly more taken with the park, which has a swimming pool, playground, paved jogging trail, picnic tables, and—the good part at last—oak trees that support a population of bushy-tails. Sport loves anything that will run up a tree, and the squirrels obliged. Dogs are required to be on a six-foot leash.

Sims Bayou runs along the southern edge of the park, and while construction had its banks in disorder when we visited, it appears that under normal conditions you can go past the fringe of oak trees and descend to the water.

The park is near the intersection of Loop 610 East and Interstate 45 on Houston's southeast side. From Interstate 45, exit onto Broadway Street and go south two blocks to Dixie Drive. Turn right and continue four blocks to De Leon Street; turn left and go three blocks to the park. Hours are 7 A.M. to 11 P.M. (713) 845-1000.

•**Shady Lane Park** 🔥 *See ㊳ on page 420.*

This park has about 12 acres of mostly open space punctuated by a few pine trees, elm trees, soccer fields, a community center, and a playground. If that sounds like a lot of punctuation, it is. Leashed dogs can stretch their legs here, but that's about all. This park's chief asset is a location convenient to travelers on U.S. 59 North, which at rush hour resembles a parking lot. Long-suffering dogs may need a rest break.

From U.S. 59 North, exit at Parker Road and go west about a quarter of a mile to the park. Hours are 7 A.M. to 11 P.M. (713) 845-1000.

• Stude Park 🐾 *See ❸❾ on page 420.*

This park of about 42 acres right alongside Interstate 10 has gently rolling hills, trees, a playground, and athletic fields. A paved walking path was receiving heavy use by a 90-pound rottweiler the day Sport and I last visited. The rotty was not on the required leash, but we perspicaciously minded our own business. He was a tough-looking customer. The pool and community center were closed when we visited, but a chemical toilet near the baseball fields solved that problem. Walk east on the trail, which connects to White Oak Park (see page 443), for a great view of the downtown skyscrapers. The path runs along White Oak Bayou, a concrete channel totally lacking in charm.

From Interstate 10 just north of downtown, exit on Studemont Street and go north for one block to the park entrance on Stude Street. Hours are 7 A.M. to 11 P.M. (713) 845-1000.

• Sunnyside Park 🐾 *See ❹❶ on page 420.*

Brighter days are surely ahead for this 206-acre park. When Sport and I last visited, improvements were being made as part of a city-wide parks refurbishment program. This heavily wooded park has a great deal of potential, but for now leashed dogs will find little to do here. Most of the park is closed; only about five acres at the north-east corner allow visitors. There you'll find a community center, tennis courts, a playground, a swimming pool, and athletic fields. Most of the trees were cleared, leaving open expanses of grass across which your excluded hound can gaze wistfully at brush- and tree-covered berms and only dream of what delights might be found on the other side.

From Loop 610 East, exit on Highway 288; go a little less than a mile to Bellfort Boulevard and turn east. The park entrance is half a mile ahead on your right. Hours are 7 A.M. to 11 P.M. (713) 845-1000.

• T. C. Jester Park 🐾 🐾 ½ *See ❹❶ on page 420.*

White Oak Bayou is the focal point of this 100-acre park stretching about a mile and a quarter along its banks. We saw several dogs here, none of them obeying the leash law. A rottweiler was retrieving a Frisbee. A Dachshund trotted along behind a group of three women, one of whom was pushing a baby stroller. A few unlucky people were jogging the graveled walking path alone.

This is a park for dogs who love pine trees and open spaces. There's a playground, a pool, and scattered picnic tables, but mostly the park is about room to roam. The trail guides walkers and dogs who need structure, but free spirits have ample opportunity to walk outside the lines. While some parts of the park are totally devoid of underbrush, some of the fringes of the bayou are quite heavily vegetated; there's no telling what an inquisitive hound might turn up there.

To reach the park from Loop 610 on the northwest side of town, exit onto West T. C. Jester Boulevard and go north a little over a mile to a parking area at the intersection with Saxon Drive. Hours are 7 A.M. to 11 P.M. (713) 845-1000.

• **Terry Hershey Park** 🐾 1/2 *See* **42** *on page 422.*

Flood control is a wonderful thing—it provides leashed dogs with parks like this one. Long and narrow, the 500-acre county park runs along Mayd Creek between Interstate 10 West and Memorial Drive. Two loop trails, one two-thirds of a mile and the other a mile and a half, begin at a parking lot on Memorial Drive. The paved trails, playground, and rest rooms all sit safely above the floodplain; only mud dogs would want to brave the thick tangle of brush in the creek bottom, anyway. It's easier to get a drink at the water fountain by the rest rooms. Park rules require you to clean up after your pooch.

This park's playground and picnic area make it a popular one for neighborhood moms to bring their young children for an outing. If your pooch likes to have her ears pulled by kids, she'll like this park.

The park is at 15376 Memorial Drive. To reach it from Interstate 10, exit on Eldridge Road and go south to the first cross street, Memorial Drive. Turn right and go to the park entrance about a quarter of a mile down. The park is open from 7 A.M. to 10 P.M. (281) 496-2177.

• **Tom Bass Regional Park** 🐾🐾🐾 *See* **43** *on page 420.*

Lucky is the dog whose owner knows to take him to this 527-acre park on Houston's south side. Picnic areas and playgrounds are scattered all over the park, making this a great place to take a family dog. A five-foot leash is required, but you and your hound will be able to spend some quality time together here. For starters, there's a lake with a paved walking path about a mile long around it. We saw several dogs taking the morning air with their owners, probably residents of a subdivision across the road. Signs warned against wading, swimming, or eating fish taken from the water, so I suggested to Sport that she not take a drink, either. South of the lake, past a community building and picnic area, a short nature trail winds through thick woods. It's not much as nature trails go, just a quarter mile or so of dirt trail hacked out of the underbrush, but birds flitted through the trees and the vegetation screened us from the noise of traffic on a nearby street. As at some other Houston-area parks, we found the ground dotted with little crayfish mounds, and Sport sniffed for evidence of the residents without success.

Sniffing paid off better at another picnic area nearby, where black cowboys on their way to the Houston Livestock Show were packing up for the day's journey. Horses were standing about, and evidence of yesterday's hay occupied Sport's attention for a few minutes. I gave her a little lecture on black cowboys, pointing out that many of the men who drove longhorns up the Chisholm Trail were black, and that the rodeo sport of bulldogging was invented by a black cowboy. Sport concentrated intently on my every word. At least that's what I tell myself she does when she closes her eyes and goes limp.

Dogs who play cricket or fly radio-controlled airplanes will find designated fields here for those purposes. There's also a Frisbee golf course—dogs sometimes get confused as to why they should not grab a Frisbee just before it sails into a basket, but they have a great time. A regular golf course lies in the center of the park, but dogs are not welcome there. They have the irritating habit of chasing down balls and running off with them, something that drives golfers crazy for some reason.

Signs around the lake warn of the possibility of poisonous snakes. You should also keep a tight grip on the leash in the picnic areas. The park "employs" geese to keep the grassy areas of the park free of weeds, and some dogs think chasing is permitted. It's not.

The park is on Cullen Boulevard (F.M. 865) about five and a half miles south of Loop 610. Hours are 6 A.M. to 9 P.M. (713) 991-6881.

• **Westbury Park** 😺 *See ⓸ on page 420.*

Squirrels, birds, and trees caught my eye as soon as I approached this park of about six acres. There's a swimming pool in one corner and a playground and tennis courts diagonally (I almost said kitty-corner but caught myself) across, but most of this park is grass, with a few mature oak and pine trees. A small picnic area overlooks the playground. Thirsty pooches can water at the fountain on the west end of the grounds. A chemical toilet hides under a tree near the swimming pool. It was a dangerous park for earthworms when I last visited—the first robins of spring were ambushing unwary worms all over the place.

The park is at the corner of Creekbend Drive and Mullins Drive. From West Bellfort Street just east of Hillcroft Avenue, go north on Mullins Drive about half a mile. Hours are 7 A.M. to 11 P.M. (713) 845-1000.

• **White Oak Park** 🐾 *See ⑤ on page 420.*

Dogs who live in the apartments along the street bordering this park are lucky dogs, indeed. They have a great view of the downtown sky-scrapers from their balconies, and just yards away is this 23-acre park with a paved path that connects it to Stude Park to the west. While the bayou contained within the borders has been concreted and channelized, there's still lots of grass and trees for a leashed pooch to savor.

The park is along White Oak Drive between Interstate 45 and Studewood Street just northwest of downtown. Hours are 7 A.M. to 11 P.M. (713) 845-1000.

• **Woodland Park** 🔥 *See ⑥ on page 420.*

Ah, the joy of trees. The relief of trees. Big live oak trees overhang the entire street alongside this park of about 19 acres. Leashed dogs who don't like live oaks will be pleased to see the large pine trees. When Sport and I last visited, there was a lively soccer game taking place on the field at the east end of the park, but she would much rather have joined in the tennis match at the opposite end. Dogs and tennis balls were made for each other, although when a dog does take part in a ten-nis game, a lot of racket usually results. There's also a playground and a community center here.

The park is at the intersection of Houston Avenue and Parkview Street in the triangle where Interstate 10 and Interstate 45 come together just north of downtown. Hours are 7 A.M. to 11 P.M. (713) 845-1000.

RESTAURANTS

City of Houston health regulations forbid taking a dog (other than a service dog) onto the "operational premises" of any establishment serv-ing food. According to a spokesperson for the health department, dogs are not permitted even in restaurant parking lots. Therefore, no restau-rant listings are included for Houston. Sorry, hungry hounds.

PLACES TO STAY

Alexander Deussen Park: See Alexander Deussen Park on page 425 for camping information.

Braeswood Hotel: There's a large grassy area next to the hotel where your pooch can exercise and so on. Dogs pay a $15 fee, and you pay $69 to $89 for a room. 2100 South Braeswood Boulevard, Houston, TX 77030; (713) 797-9000.

Four Seasons Hotel: I hesitate to include this hotel, knowing that if I do, for years I'll be getting letters from readers accusing me of being responsible for the loss of their beloved canine. "My dog ran off to Hous-ton to live in that hotel you wrote about," most of the letters will begin.

"You'll be hearing from my lawyer," most of the letters will end. In between, the writers will list the reasons their pooch abandoned them to take up residence here.

When dogs check in, they receive a welcome gift, and everything that happens after that will help convince them you have been keeping them in a state of enslaved poverty. Your dog will get chew toys, homemade dog biscuits (along with a copy of the recipe to take home to his own chef), and food and water bowls. Then he'll discover the room service menu, with entrées like Barnyard Chase (grilled chicken with fresh corn) and German Shepherd's Pie (ground steak with mashed potatoes). No embarrassing visits from the pizza guy here. Of course there's a choice of desserts: assorted crèmes or sponge cake with whipped cream. Need to go for a post-prandial promenade? Pick up the phone and paw 5-1 for dog walking services, available 24 hours a day. There's a park right across the street.

As if any of these services would fail to meet with your hound's wholehearted approval, the hotel also keeps a record of his preferences for future visits. Advance notice of your arrival with a VIP (Very Important Pet) is requested so that the royal treatment will be ready the instant your impatient Peke walks (or is carried on the royal litter) in the door.

Rates are $290 to $355. 1300 Lamar Street, Houston, TX 77010; (713) 650-1300 or (800) 332-3442.

Hawthorn Suites: Rooms are $109 to $159. Dogs under 35 pounds stay for a $25 fee plus $5 a day for each day after the first. 6910 Southwest Freeway (U.S. 59), Houston, TX 77074; (713) 785-3415.

La Quinta Inn—Astrodome: Rates are $77 to $93. Dogs under 25 pounds are welcome. 9911 Buffalo Speedway, Houston, TX 77054; (713) 668-8082 or (800) NU-ROOMS/687-6667.

La Quinta Inn—Beltway 8: Rooms are $68 to $79. Dogs up to 25 pounds are welcome. 10552 Southwest Freeway (U.S. 59), Houston, TX 77074; (713) 270-9559 or (800) NU-ROOMS/687-6667.

La Quinta Inn—Brookhollow: Rooms are $74 to $81. Dogs must weigh under 25 pounds. 11002 Northwest Freeway (U.S. 290), Houston, TX 77092; (713) 688-2581 or (800) NU-ROOMS/687-6667.

La Quinta Inn—Cypress-Fairbanks: Rates are $66 to $75. Dogs under 25 pounds are welcome. 13290 F.M. 1960 West, Houston, TX 77065; (281) 469-4018 or (800) NU-ROOMS/687-6667.

La Quinta Inn—Greenway Plaza: Rates are $70 to $78. Dogs under 25 pounds are welcome. 4015 Southwest Freeway (U.S. 59), Houston, TX 77027; (713) 623-4750 or (800) NU-ROOMS/687-6667.

La Quinta Inn—Houston Hobby Airport: Rooms are $73 to $80. Dogs under 25 pounds may bunk with you. 9902 Gulf Freeway (Interstate

45), Houston, TX 77034; (713) 941-0900 or (800) NU-ROOMS/687-6667.

La Quinta Inn—Intercontinental Airport: Rooms are $66 to $73. Dogs under 25 pounds can rest their wings here. 6 North Beltway East, Houston, TX 77060; (281) 447-6888 or (800) NU-ROOMS/687-6667.

La Quinta Inn—Loop 1960: Rates are $69 to $80. Dogs must weigh under 25 pounds. 17111 North Freeway (Interstate 45), Houston, TX 77090; (281) 444-7500 or (800) NU-ROOMS/687-6667.

La Quinta Inn—Sharpstown: Rooms are $65 to $72. Dogs must weigh under 25 pounds. 8201 Southwest Freeway (U.S. 59), Houston, TX 77074; (713) 772-3626 or (800) NU-ROOMS/687-6667.

La Quinta Inn—Southwest Freeway: Rooms are $72 to $79. Dogs under 25 pounds are welcome. 10552 Southwest Freeway (U.S. 59), Houston, TX 77074; (713) 270-9559 or (800) NU-ROOMS/687-6667.

La Quinta Inn—Stafford: Rooms are $73 to $81. Dogs must weigh under 25 pounds. 12727 Southwest Freeway (U.S. 59), Houston, TX 77477; (281) 240-2300 or (800) NU-ROOMS/687-6667.

La Quinta Inn—West: Rates are $66 to $73. Dogs under 25 pounds may march right in. 11113 Katy Freeway (Interstate 10), Houston, TX 77079; (713) 932-0808 or (800) NU-ROOMS/687-6667.

La Quinta Inn—Wirt Road: All rooms are $73. All dogs are under 25 pounds—at least if they stay here. 8017 Katy Freeway (Interstate 10), Houston, TX 77024; (713) 688-8941 or (800) NU-ROOMS/687-6667.

La Quinta Inn—The Woodlands: Rooms are $78 to $88. Dogs must weigh under 25 pounds. 28673 Interstate 45 North, Houston, TX 77381; (281) 367-7722 or (800) NU-ROOMS/687-6667.

Motel 6—Astrodome: Rooms are $44. All Motel 6s accept one small pooch per room. 3223 South Loop West (Interstate 610), Houston, TX 77025; (713) 664-6425 or (800) 466-8356.

Motel 6—Hobby: Rooms are $40. All Motel 6s accept one small pooch per room. 8800 Airport Boulevard, Houston, TX 77061; (713) 941-0990 or (800) 466-8356.

Motel 6—Jersey Village: Rooms are $44. All Motel 6s accept one small pooch per room. 16884 Northwest Freeway (U.S. 290), Houston, TX 77040; (713) 937-7056 or (800) 466-8356.

Motel 6—Katy: Rooms are $40. All Motel 6s accept one small pooch per room. 14833 Katy Freeway (Interstate 10), Houston, TX 77094; (281) 497-5000 or (800) 466-8356.

Motel 6—Northwest: Rooms are $44. All Motel 6s accept one small pooch per room. 5555 West 34th Street, Houston, TX 77092; (713) 682-8588 or (800) 466-8356.

Motel 6—Southwest: Rooms are $44. All Motel 6s accept one small pooch per room. 9638 Plainfield Road, Houston, TX 77036; (713) 778-0008 or (800) 466-8356.

Residence Inn by Marriott—Gallería: Rooms at this all-suites hotel are $129 to $205. In addition to the $25 cleaning fee, pets pay $5 extra nightly. 2500 McCue Street, Houston, TX 77056; (713) 840-9757 or (800) 331-3131.

Shoney's Inn and Suites—Gallería: Dogs are welcome if their traveling companions pay a $25 fee. A dog walking area is located next to the hotel. Rooms are $39 to $119, which includes a continental breakfast and 24-hour coffee bar. 6687 Southwest Freeway (U.S. 59), Houston, TX 77074; (713) 776-2633.

Shoney's Inn—Astrodome: Rooms are $39 to $119, which includes a 24-hour coffee bar. Dogs have to pony up a $25 fee. A dog walking area is located next to the hotel. 2364 South Loop West (Interstate 610), Houston, TX 77054; (713) 799-2436.

FESTIVALS

Bayou City Art Festival: Dogs miss much of the art scene in Houston, because most masterpieces molder in stuffy old museums where dogs can't go. Now and again, though, art goes to the dogs and sets up in the streets. Take your hound to this early April festival; she's sure to find just the right piece to hang on her wall. For location and dates, call (713) 521-0133.

Freedom Festival: Dress your dog in her best Statue of Liberty or Uncle Sam costume and celebrate Independence Day with food, music, and fireworks. It all happens July 4 in Sam Houston Park at the corner of Bagby and Lamar Streets in downtown Houston. For information, call (713) 621-8600.

Houston International Festival: The theme of this celebration changes from year to year, but the emphasis is always on fun, food, and entertainment. The festival takes over a 20-block section of downtown from Dallas Street to Rusk Street and Bagby Street to Smith Street, and up to a million people attend during its run the last two weekends in April, so crowd-shy pooches may not like it. However, no dog who's ever even thought of chasing a car should miss the Art Car Parade. She can bark at some 1,500 vehicles from unicycles to hearses, decorated with everything from live grass to pennies. Another favorite with dogs is Dancin' in the Streets, a children's parade. Both parades start on Allen Parkway north of downtown, and the parkland along the street makes a good vantage point for doggy watchers. After you both work up an appetite restraining and being restrained, you can hit the food booths for some serious grazing. For information, call (713) 654-8808.

Japan Festival: Akita alert! Akita alert! Get in touch with your roots at this early April gathering in the Japanese Garden in Hermann Park (see page 432). Blooming cherry trees, azaleas, lilies, and irises provide the background for Japanese dancers, musicians, and martial arts demonstrations. Every dog secretly yearns to know the secrets of Ikeban flower design and origami; he can learn here. Go early and avoid the crowds, as this is a popular event in a fairly small space. The Japanese Garden is at the northwest corner of Hermann Park, near the intersection of Main and Sunset Streets. For information, call (713) 963-0121.

DIVERSIONS

Make a beer run: Visit the Beer Can House and your pooch will never again accuse you of being odd. John Milkovisch retired, had time on his hands (and obviously no dog), and looked for something to do with the 50,000 beer cans he'd worked so hard to empty but had never managed to get rid of. So he decided to make streamers and curtains of them to shade his house. ("I think I can, I think I can, I think I can," he repeated over and over to himself as he did the can-can.) You can't go in, but you can view it from the street and compare your reactions to those of his neighbors. It's at 222 Malone Street, off Memorial Drive just east of Memorial Park (see page 436), making it easy to combine this trip with an outing in the park. Yes, you can. (713) 227-3100.

Orange dogs wonderful?: The Orange Show is the creation of a retired postal worker who wanted to encourage people to "eat oranges, drink oranges, and be highly amused." You and your dog will have to judge for yourselves if he succeeded, but it's impossible to visit and not be awed at what can happen when a weird idea's time comes. Built of concrete, the structure stands out in its neighborhood like a Saint Bernard taking a squat on the 50-yard line during the Super Bowl. Flags wave, whirligigs spin, and brilliant colors assault the eyes. You'll wind through a maze of narrow passageways, some of which lead to observation decks overlooking, for example, a steamboat on wheels sailing on a waterless lake. Signs exhort you to "Love oranges and live." The Orange Show is at 2401 Munger Street, just east of Interstate 45 southeast of downtown. It is open from noon to 5 P.M. weekends and holidays from mid-March through mid-December and from 9 A.M. to 1 P.M. weekdays from Memorial Day through Labor Day. Admission is $1. (713) 926-6368.

Party down with your hound: Every Thursday evening from March through November, music-loving hounds drag their unprotesting owners to Jones Plaza for a free concert. Types of music vary, but not as much as the kinds of dogs who attend. Jones Plaza is downtown, bordered by Smith, Texas, Louisiana, and Capitol Streets. (713) 227-3100.

Shop with your sheltie: Shopping is a major form of entertainment in Houston. Lest your dog feel left out, take him to PetsMart, the department store designed for dogs. He'll feel grand as he prances in the front door on his leash, credit card at the ready. Banish roundworms, hairballs, and fleas (oh, my!) with the wave of a piece of plastic. Stock up on exotic foods (more than 700 kinds). While he's not looking, sneak a copy of an obedience training manual into the shopping cart. The next time you take him shopping, you'll be in charge. Houston-area stores are at 10500 Old Katy Road, (713) 973-7667; 12014 Willowchase Drive, (281) 894-1393; 12533 Westheimer Road, (281) 496-6990; and 5415 West Loop South, (713) 661-5585.

ANGELINA COUNTY

Tree-loving, leg-hiking hounds will think they're in heaven here. Angelina County is the center of the Texas timber industry. Even dogs who never visit the county will likely have hiked a leg on a tree from here: Utility poles made from pine trees grown locally can show up almost anywhere. Are you paper training a puppy on newspaper? The first plant to manufacture newsprint from Southern pine was located in Angelina County, and pulpwood is still a major crop. It's possible the book you are holding right now is printed on paper made from a tree Sport Dog hiked a leg on while we were doing our research. It really is a small world, isn't it?

NATIONAL FORESTS

See the National and State Forests/State Wildlife Management Areas chapter starting on page 621 for important information and safety tips on visiting these areas with your dog.

• **Angelina National Forest** 🐾🐾🐾🐾 🕜 🐕

See page 622 for a description of Angelina National Forest.

LUFKIN

PARKS, BEACHES, AND RECREATION AREAS

• **Jones Park** 🐾 1/2 *See* **⑰** *on page 423.*

A small lake in the center of this park of about 80 acres is a dog's delight, with grassy banks that slope gently to the water. Dogs must be leashed; with ducks, egrets, and cormorants on the lake, that's probably a good thing. Large oak and pine trees shade most of the park, which also has picnic tables, a playground, rest rooms, and tennis courts. You

---

can walk across the dam on the lake's north end to access the part of the park on the opposite shore, which is heavily wooded.

The park is at the intersection of U.S. 69 Business/Highway 103 West and Martin Luther King Jr. Boulevard. It closes at 10 P.M. (409) 633-0250.

• **Kiwanis City Park** 🐾1/2 *See* **48** *on page 423.*

If your dog likes creeks and covered bridges, he'll like this park of about 25 acres. Throw in hundreds of pine trees and a bevy of squirrels, and he may want to homestead. The park is busy with other things, too, but they're all for people—tennis courts, picnic pavilions, a playground, pool, and basketball court. A disc golf course starts in front of the Texas National Guard armory on the east side. In between, though, there's plenty of room for a leashed hound to puzzle over where that squirrel went that was right in front of his nose just seconds ago.

The park is at the intersection of U.S. 59 Business and Loop 266 on the southeast side of town. It closes at 10 P.M. (409) 633-0250.

• **Winston Park** 🐾 *See* **49** *on page 423.*

This park of about 20 acres is heavily developed, with a swimming pool, tennis courts, and athletic fields, but a narrow stand of brush and timber fringes its west side, crossing a small drainage. A rest room is at the north end, and there's a playground for the kiddies. Leashed dogs and their people will find this a pleasant place to stretch their legs and, you know.

The park is on the north side of town, just east of the intersection of U.S. 69 Business West and U.S. 59 Business. Take U.S. 59 Business north from the intersection one block; turn right on Jack Street and go about two blocks to the park. It closes at 10 P.M. (409) 633-0250.

RESTAURANTS

Cafe del Rio: The dog-friendly owner serves Tex-Mex food to dogs and their people at four fenced-in tables on the patio. 1901 South First Street; (409) 639-4471.

PLACES TO STAY

Best Western Expo Inn: Rooms are $54 to $65. Dogs pay a $20 fee. Small dogs are preferred, and the management requests that they be picked up after and kept in a carrier. 4200 North Medford Drive, Lufkin, TX 75901; (409) 632-7300.

Holiday Inn: Rooms are $59. Pooches put down a $10 deposit. 4306 South First Street, Lufkin, TX 75901; (409) 639-3333 or (800) 465-4329.

Motel 6: Rooms are $32. This Motel 6, like others, allows one small pooch per room. 1110 South Timberland Drive, Lufkin, TX 75901; (409) 637-7850 or (800) 466-8356.

FESTIVALS

Downtown Hoe Down: Each late April, ugly dogs in ugly trucks gather in downtown Lufkin for a barbecue cook-off, games, and an ugly truck contest. Your ugly dog could have a pretty good time here. Call for this year's location and dates: (409) 634-6305 or (800) 409-5659.

DIVERSIONS

More bark than bite: Take your dog to the Texas Forestry Museum and let her see how lumberjack dogs cut trees and hauled them to the sawmill, where they became boards used for making doghouses. Dogs are not allowed inside the museum building, but they can visit the outdoor displays, which are more interesting, anyway—at least to a dog. There's a complete early logging train, a forest lookout tower (also good for spotting raccoons), and other antique equipment, all with explanatory signs. If your dog really cares about all this, he'll learn to read. The museum is at 1905 Atkinson Drive; park in the lot out front and walk between the museum and the Texas Forest Service office next door to the displays in back. (409) 632-9535.

ZAVALLA

PARKS, BEACHES, AND RECREATION AREAS

• **Boykin Springs Recreation Area** 🐾½ *See* 🔟 *on page 423.*

This U.S. Forest Service recreation area in the Angelina National Forest contains a nine-acre lake, a hiking trail, a campground, and a picnic area. The 36 campsites each have a picnic table, fire ring, and lantern post; water and rest rooms are nearby. Sites rent for $6. The campground area is quite rugged, with ravines, tall pines, and creeks running through it. Dogs will find much to like, especially if they enjoy fishing.

The recreation area is the northern terminus of the 5.5-mile Sawmill Hiking Trail, which links it to the Bouton Lake Recreation Area. Most of the trail runs through the Neches River bottom. It passes two abandoned sawmill sites and, for part of its length, travels atop the roadbed of an old tramway once used to haul logs to the sawmills. You'll see typical piney woods flora along the route, including longleaf and loblolly pine, bald cypress, dogwood, and magnolia trees. Extremely lucky dogs might spot an endangered red-cockaded woodpecker. There's a swinging bridge across Big Creek, about a mile north of Bouton Lake. If you hike the trail from October through early January, wear highly visible clothing and be alert for deer hunters in the area.

To reach the park, take Highway 63 southeast from Zavalla for 10.6 miles, then turn west onto Forest Service Road 313 and go 2.3 miles to the entrance. There is a $2 per vehicle day-use fee. The park is open from 7 A.M. to 10 P.M. (409) 639-8620.

PLACES TO STAY

Boykin Springs Recreation Area: See Boykin Springs Recreation Area on page 450 for camping information.

Cassells-Boykin County Park: This former state park, now operated by Angelina County, has 27 campsites. No electricity is available, but water is nearby, as are composting toilets. Its main use seems to be as a boat ramp and picnic area. Some of the campsites front the water, and most have views of the lake and are shaded by pines. Camping costs $3 a night. The park is open 24 hours. (409) 632-5531.

Sandy Creek Recreation Area: Thirty campsites overlook Sam Rayburn Reservoir from pine-studded hills. Each site has a picnic table and campfire ring; rest rooms, showers, and a swimming beach are nearby. Campsites rent for $6. The campground is open from March 1 through October 31. From the intersection of Highway 63 and Recreation Road 255 about 15 miles northwest of Jasper, go west 2.8 miles on Highway 63 to Forest Service Road 333A; turn right and go 2.6 miles to the campground. It's open 24 hours. (409) 639-8620.

AUSTIN COUNTY

The nucleus of the Anglo-American settlement of Texas began here along the banks of the Brazos River in 1822. Stephen F. Austin's colony had its headquarters at San Felipe de Austin, which became the political, economic, and social center. The town was still just a jumble of crude log cabins strewn along a muddy road down to the river crossing, but dogs liked it. Steamboats traveled the river down to the coast, bringing in all sorts of interesting people and stuff to smell. Lots of Tom Sawyer and Huckleberry Finn dogs lived here in those days. They had much to entertain them: the community of Cat Spring received its name after an early German settler killed a mountain lion there.

One of the best state parks in Texas for dogs now includes the site of this early Texas settlement, but dogs don't have to put up with a lot of boring historical stuff. Most of the park is forest along the Brazos River, and a network of trails makes it highly accessible to pedestrian pooches.

SAN FELIPE

PARKS, BEACHES, AND RECREATION AREAS

• **Stephen F. Austin State Historical Park** 🐾🐾🐾
  See ⑤ on page 422.
  Ordinarily Sport would growl at me for giving such a high rating to a

historical park—she being a member of the Henry Ford "history is bunk" school of thought—but she heartily agreed in this case. There were two reasons for her agreeability. One was that this was the very last park we visited while doing research for this book, and although Sport loves to travel, she was ready to stay home and lie in the sun in the yard for a while—as was I. The other reason was that only 12 of the park's 667 acres are devoted to history. The centerpiece is a replica of Stephen Austin's dog-run log cabin. Dogs may walk the grounds with you, but they may not go inside the cabin or the small museum on the grounds. Admission is free to this part of the park, and it is open 24 hours a day. The museum is open only on Saturday from 1 P.M. to 3 P.M. and charges $1.

The recreational portion of the park also permits leashed dogs; there they can enjoy one of the finest camping and walking parks in Southeast Texas. There is a $3 per person admission fee.

The park is located on the Brazos River where Stephen Austin established the town of San Felipe de Austin, the seat of government of the Anglo-American colonies in Texas. Austin, the "Father of Texas," brought the first 297 American families to colonize Texas under a contract with the Mexican government. From 1824 to 1836, San Felipe de Austin was the social, economic, and political center of the American colonies in Texas. Many of the seminal events of the movement for Texas independence took place here, and every leading historical figure of the time passed this way. It's enough to make any dog tired of history.

The good news for dogs is that most of the park is a giant cedar elm grove populated not by the ghosts of heroes past but by real live deer, raccoons, opossums, foxes, squirrels, and feral hogs. A network of hiking trails through a densely vegetated area along the Brazos River totals about five miles in all. Sport and I walked the mile-long Cottonwood Trail and saw tracks of raccoons, foxes, deer, and feral hogs. When we last visited there were no trail markers, but local Eagle Scouts were slated to mark the trails in the near future. Sport and I can't wait to go back and hike the Raccoon Bend and Possum Loop Trails.

A nature trail about a quarter of a mile long connects the screened shelter area with the group camping area. Ask for a trail guide at park headquarters. It's keyed to markers along the way and identifies plants common to the area, including poison ivy as well as the ubiquitous cedar elm.

The day-use picnic area is one of the largest and nicest I found in any Texas park. It covers about 50 acres totally shaded by large elm trees, and the squirrel population is substantial. You may have trouble getting your pooch to take time out from squirrel-watching to eat. For a close-up view of the squirrels or the park's abundant deer, buy a bag of corn at park headquarters for a dollar and sprinkle it on the ground nearby. Over enthusiastic dogs may have to be restrained inside a large, self-propelled metal object with transparent wildlife-viewing portals. Unfortunately, these cost between $15,000 and $50,000. Fortunately, you have one already—your car.

The camping area is also totally shaded by large cedar elms. While the sites are spaced fairly far apart, they offer no privacy due to a lack of understory. However, the green canopy overhead stretching out in every direction for hundreds of yards exerts a powerful effect on the senses. There are 40 pull-through RV sites with full hookups that rent for $14. The 40 tent sites with water only rent for $8. Twenty screened shelters rent for $20 each and come with a bonus: a herd of deer that beds down nearby. Sport and I counted 17 deer browsing about on our last early morning visit. All camping areas are served by rest rooms with showers. There are also playgrounds at the campground and at the picnic area.

Reservations for campsites must be made by calling (512) 389-8900 between 9 A.M. and 6 P.M. Monday through Friday. You may reserve a type of campsite, but not a particular site. Dogs are not allowed inside any building, may not be left unattended, and must be on a six-foot leash at all times.

The park is 2.2 miles north of Interstate 10 on F.M. 1458. From December through February, the park office is open from 8 A.M. to 5 P.M. every day except Friday, when it stays open until 8 P.M. From March through November, the office is open from 8 A.M. until 5 P.M. Sunday through Thursday; until 10 P.M. on Friday; and until 8 P.M. on Saturday. The park itself closes each night at 10 P.M. except to campers. (409) 885-3613.

PLACES TO STAY

Stephen F. Austin State Historical Park: See Stephen F. Austin State Historical Park on page 451 for camping information.

BRAZORIA COUNTY

ANGLETON

PARKS, BEACHES, AND RECREATION AREAS

• **Brazos River County Park** 🐾½ *See* 🄼 *on page 422.*

Before you enter this remote park via a twisting maze of roads, paranoid pooches may fear they are being taken to the backside of nowhere to be fitted with concrete shoes prior to visiting the fishes in the river. But all's well that ends well, dogs always say, and once you reach this 75-acre park, all your canine friend's doubts will vanish as he slips into his leash and heads for the nearest giant oak tree. Dryland dogs such as Sport and Samantha are always awed at the size trees can attain when given all the water they need, and this park contains specimens that will thrill any leg-hiker.

The large, shaded picnic ground and playground are the main features of the park for people, but dogs will like the half-mile trail winding along the riverbank. It's on an elevated boardwalk for most of its length, but the thick tangle of spiny berry vines makes this a good thing. At its southern end there's a viewing platform from which a foot trail leads down to the water's edge. It's muddy down there, but tracks showed few dogs had been able to resist a visit. Adventurous hounds will want to take the unpaved nature trails winding through the heavy woods away from the river, where they may meet deer, rabbits, squirrels, or waterfowl. All the trails begin and end at the large picnic pavilion with rest rooms.

To reach the park from F.M. 521 west of Angleton, take County Road 30 west 2.7 miles to County Road 385; turn right and travel 2.2 miles, following the signs, to a T intersection. Turn left and go 50 yards to the park sign; turn right and proceed half a mile to the entrance. The park is open from dawn to dusk. (409) 849-5711 extension 1541.

QUINTANA

PARKS, BEACHES, AND RECREATION AREAS

• **Quintana Beach County Park** 🐾 *See* ㊳ *on page 422.*

A large chunk of this 51-acre beachfront park is devoted to things other than beach. For a clue as to what this park is about, look at the phone number below. There's a large RV campground ($16 to $18 nightly fee), a paved parking lot, a fishing pier, a playground, an interpretive center, and historic homes. City dogs will feel right at home; country dogs will ask, "Where's the beach?" Dogs must be leashed. There is a $2 per vehicle entry fee from May 1 through September 30.

From Highway 36/288, drive south on F.M. 1495 about a mile and a quarter to County Road 723. Turn left and go about two miles to the park. (800) 8-PARK-RV.

PLACES TO STAY

Quintana Beach County Park: See Quintana Beach County Park above for camping information.

WEST COLUMBIA

PARKS, BEACHES, AND RECREATION AREAS

• **Hanson Riverside County Park** 🐾 🐾 1/2 *See* ☎ *on page 422.*

This park's 55 acres have a lot to offer leashed dogs. The San Bernard River runs along the western boundary, and while its steep banks prevent access to the water, it does support the growth of large trees draped with Spanish moss, making the picnic area quite inviting. A deck over the river permits you to fish. On the opposite side of the park, near a large group picnic pavilion, a one-mile nature trail strikes off into the boonies. A boardwalk carries you over swampy areas cut with numerous trails made by critters we could only guess at. The jungle-like growth gives hounds plenty to sniff.

On the open grassy area by the playground, Sport met two forms of life new to her. Small mounds of mud required sniffing, and at one she was met by the occupant, a claw-waving crayfish. Both retreated promptly. Then Sport planted a large paw in the middle of a larger mound of earth and met her first fire ants. She was not favorably impressed, especially when one of the nasty little critters got between two toes and inflicted several painful bites.

The park is on Highway 35 at the east end of the bridge over the San Bernard River. Hours are dawn to dusk. (409) 345-3197.

• **Varner-Hogg Plantation State Park** 🐾 *See* ☎ *on page 422.*

History-buff hounds will be disappointed in this 65-acre park, because in addition to being required to be leashed, they are banned from entering any buildings, and that's what this park is all about. The completely furnished old plantation manor was the home of Governor James S. Hogg.

There is a shaded day-use picnic area and some open grassy space in front of the "Big House" where you can take a picture of your dog striking her best Southern planter dog pose. Admission to the park is $4, which includes a 45-minute guided tour that you can go on while someone keeps your banned pooch company.

From Highway 35, drive 1.4 miles north on F.M. 2852 to the entrance at the end of the road. Hours are 8 A.M. until sunset. (409) 345-4656.

BRAZOS COUNTY

BRYAN–COLLEGE STATION

Bryan and College Station are actually two different towns, but they are almost never thought of separately. The fault, if there is any, lies with the citizens of Bryan, who more than a hundred years ago donated land nearby for the site of a state university. Texas A&M University, the state's oldest public institution of higher education, grew up at the site, which was called College Station. Today the tail wags the dog, so to speak, as the college and its more than 40,000 students dominate their neighboring town.

I hate to make a pooch pout, but I knew Sport would someday find out she is not the most famous dog in Texas, so I felt I should break the news to her. I sat her down and told her about Reveille, the American collie who is the official mascot of Texas A&M and is, without doubt, the best-known dog in Texas. Reveille has an entire company of the university's Corps of Cadets devoted to her care. She lives in the dormitory with them, sleeps in bed with whomever she chooses, and even goes to class. (She's currently working on her doctor of dogmatism.) Best of all, she gets into the football games free. If any dog in Texas has it made in the shade, Reveille is the one.

Texas A&M University occupies a hallowed spot in the heart of all Texas dogs (at least those who don't fear vets), because this is the site of the state's only school of veterinary medicine. If your dog's vet received his or her degree in Texas, this is where it came from. Texas dogs who have a medical condition that their local vet needs help treating can come here for healing at the hands of the experts in the university's small animal clinic. There is a referral fee, plus a fee for treatment, but if anything can be done to treat your pooch, these are the folks who can do it. Your local veterinarian will make the referral; for information, you can call the clinic at (409) 845-2351. Local dogs can visit the vet here without paying a referral fee.

PARKS, BEACHES, AND RECREATION AREAS

• **Bee Creek Park** 🐾1/2 *See* 🏞 *on page* 422.

The best part of this 44-acre park is the Brazos County Arboretum, a wetland area on the park's east side. Leashed dogs will love the natural-surfaced nature trails winding through the brush and along the creek. You're never far from apartment complexes and the sound of city traffic, but this refuge blocks them out, surrounding you with a calming screen of green. Numbered markers keyed to a trail guide available at the parking lot identify many of the trees and other plants for you. There were no guides in the box when Sport and I last visited, but drawing on our vast combined knowledge of the outdoors, we managed to identify many shrubs (the small green things) and trees (the big green things). We were proud.

The park proper has the usual assortment of picnic tables and playground equipment, as well as rest rooms. In addition, there's a pool with a heavy-duty water slide.

From Highway 6 Business, go west on Southwest Parkway one block to Anderson Boulevard and turn left into the parking lot. The entrance to the arboretum area is straight ahead at the end of the parking lot; turn right to get to the picnic and playground area. The park is closed from 1 A.M. to 5 A.M. (409) 764-3773.

• **Brothers Pond Park** 🐾 *See* **57** *on page 422.*

Dogs love secret passageways almost as much as small children do, and this park has one. Its 16 acres run along a small creek surrounded by neighborhood homes, and a narrow splinter connects the west end to the rest of the park via a sidewalk hiding between a privacy fence and thick brush. While most of the park is open grassy space, the creek bottom is heavily wooded, and a half-mile jogging trail parallels it. A playground, picnic tables, and basketball court share the shade. Sport and I hiked down to the creek and found it to be flowing just behind houses across the way. As we emerged from the bushes, a Border collie in the backyard of one house sounded off. Sport answered, and before they could get into a serious discussion of who was top dog of that particular turf, I led her away.

While dogs are supposed to be leashed here, Sport and I saw a yellow Lab running about in what I thought was free play. As we walked toward the creek, I found a yellow bumper on the ground next to some bushes and, thinking someone had lost it, picked it up. I knew Samantha the tennis-ball-chasing dog would love it. A few minutes later, as we returned, a very frustrated yellow Lab was darting about in response to whistled and shouted commands from her person. She was obviously looking for something and couldn't find it. It was then I realized that she was looking for the yellow bumper in my hand. I tossed it into the air for her, and on cue from her handler, she raced to it and joyfully carried it to him. I apologized, bundled Sport into the car, and got out of there.

From the intersection of Highway 6 and Highway 6 Business on the south side of College Station, travel west on Deacon Drive eight blocks to Rio Grande Boulevard. Turn left and go four blocks; park along the street. The park is closed from 11 P.M. to 5 A.M. (409) 764-3773.

• **Camelot Park** 🐾 *See* **58** *on page 422.*

The 16 acres of this park are totally undeveloped, but that's just fine with leashed dogs. They'll appreciate the deep ravines, big trees, brushy thickets, and open grassy areas, as well as the numerous squirrels Sport and I saw dashing about when we lasted visited. The park follows the meanders of a creek and is, to use the appropriate cliché, crookeder than a dog's hind leg. It's in a residential neighborhood just a couple of blocks from the Bryan campus of Blinn College.

To reach the park from Highway 6 Business, go east on Villa Maria Road about two miles. Just past the entrance to Blinn College, turn right onto Rustling Oaks Drive. After one block, turn left onto Camelot Drive and park along the street. The park is closed from 1 A.M. to 5:30 A.M. (409) 361-3656.

• **Central Park** 😺 **1/2** *See* ⑤⑨ *on page 422.*

There's a lot packed into 47 acres here, but the needs of leashed dogs were not overlooked. The north side of the park has two ponds with resident geese, picnic tables and shade trees, and gently sloping banks so a pooch can wade or drink. A one-third-mile jogging trail begins on the south side of the lakes. Athletic fields and a large parking lot are the other main features. Sport was fascinated by something she had not seen in any other park we visited: free-ranging chickens and peacocks. When one of the peacocks gave out that horrible screeching cry that sounds like they're being tortured, Sport tried to hide behind me. She is well acquainted with chickens, having done in one that belonged to a neighbor, but peacocks were too much for her. I guess she's just a chicken dog.

From Highway 6, take the Southwest Parkway exit and travel south on the frontage road to the first street, Krenek Tap Road. Turn right and go one block to the entrance on your left. The park is closed from 1 A.M. to 5 A.M. (409) 764-3773.

• **Hensel Park** 😺 **1/2** *See* ⑥⓪ *on page 422.*

This 30-acre park is just west of a large block of student housing for Texas A&M University, so it's a good place to meet college dogs cutting class, catching up on their studying, or helping their person forget about those upcoming finals. The park has a good mix of open grassy spaces and heavily wooded areas, so there's plenty for a leashed dog to explore. There are picnic tables, playgrounds, and rest rooms, too.

From the intersection of Texas Avenue and University Drive, travel west a long block to Hensel Street and turn left. After about five winding blocks, turn right onto South College Street and go a block to the park entrance and the parking lot. The park is closed from 11 P.M. to 5 A.M. (409) 764-3773.

• **Lake Bryan Park** 😺 😺 *See* ⑥① *on page 422.*

A lake, about nine miles of trails, and 275 acres of rolling hills make for a park dogs will howl about. Dogs must be leashed, and there is a $5 per vehicle entrance fee, but the attitude is laid-back and dogs are definitely welcome.

Dogs can take advantage of the hard work of the Brazos Valley Mountain Bike Association, which has laid out over seven miles of trails, most of which are in the northern part of the park and are accessible only by foot or bike. Pick up a map at the entrance booth, which is also where the trails begin. The trails completely encircle the lake and take you through the heavily wooded areas around it. When bikers are present, walk on the right side of the trail and keep your dog on your right to avoid interference with bikers.

When Sport and I last visited, a nature trail was being built on the island that sits between the twin power plant lakes. You can access the approximately one-mile trail by hiking along the cleared natural gas pipeline right-of-way that runs along the east side of the unimproved camping area; get a park map at the entrance and have the gate attendant point out the area to you. The trail runs through a heavily wooded area.

The oak-shaded day-use picnic area has tables with barbecue grills; it overlooks the lake and the swim beach, where your pooch is banned. Dogs are not allowed in any buildings.

Camping facilities at the park are more limited than the opportunities for camping. Four sites with picnic tables and barbecue grills sit beside the water but have no water or electrical hookups; they rent for $10. Seven sites with water and electricity rent for $15. There are toilets but no showers at both camping areas. All campsites have at least some shade. In addition to the designated campsites, tent camping is permitted nearly everywhere in the park. The limiting factor is parking, which itself is quite limited in some of the areas where you might like to camp. Reservations for campsites should be made by calling (409) 361-3656.

The park is west of Bryan–College Station. From Highway 6/U.S. 190 North, take F.M. 2818 south about four miles to F.M. 1687. Turn right and go 3.3 miles to the park entrance. The park is open from 6 A.M. to 6 P.M. from December 1 to March 1; the rest of the year it remains open until 10 P.M. (409) 361-3781.

• **Lick Creek Park** 🐾 🐾 🐾 *See* ⏀ *on page 422.*

It would be hard to imagine a better park than this for leashed dogs. Its 515 acres, heavily wooded with post oak trees, surround the confluence of Lick Creek and Alum Creek. Grassy meadows mingle with yaupon thickets. Winding through it all are about three miles of dirt roads and trails. Best of all, the trail leaving the parking lot is named Raccoon Run. Sport was a dog who'd found a home.

Sport and I had traveled no more than 50 yards along Raccoon Run's sandy surface when I spotted a grassy meadow cratered with large holes. I immediately knew the cause, and Sport and I left the trail to investigate. Sure enough, the area had not been bombed, but was covered with feral hog tracks, including some of the largest I've ever seen. These huge tracks were at least three inches across and belonged to a hog that could dispatch even a large dog with a single chomp of its jaws. Even if the isolated, undeveloped nature of this park tempts you to slip the leash off, don't. No dog is going to come away a winner in an encounter with one of these beasts.

As Sport and I padded on down the trail, we saw tracks that showed she was not the first dog to travel it, and other tracks that showed the trail is well named. We went down to a creek crossing so Sport could get a drink and returned to the car, comforted by the knowledge that such a peaceful place exists so close to the hubbub of the city. College dogs would do well to forget their studies for a couple of hours and come here to relax.

From Highway 6 South, exit on Greens Prairie Road and travel east 1.8 miles to Rock Prairie Road. Turn right and go 1.4 miles to the entrance on your right. When we last visited, the graveled parking lot was the only facility. The park is closed from 1 A.M. to 5 A.M. (409) 764-3773.

• **Thomas Park** 🐾 *See ⑬ on page 422.*

Sport and I played a little game as we traveled about looking for parks. After 11 months and 25,000 miles, we needed something to add spark to checking out yet another park. So we looked for ones that were unique (or at least greatly different) in some way. If my memory is correct, we found only two parks in all of Texas that were, beyond a shadow of a doubt, shaped like a dog's hind leg. This 16-acre park is one of them. It takes a sharp jog in the middle, right where a dog's leg bends. Mostly open grass to leave room for soccer fields, a playground, and basketball court, it has a border of live oak trees shading a one-third-mile artificially surfaced jogging trail.

The park is four blocks east of Texas A&M University. From Texas Avenue, go four blocks east on Francis Drive to the park. It is closed from 1 A.M. to 5 A.M. (409) 764-3773.

• **Tiffany Park** 🐾 *See ⑭ on page 422.*

This 12-acre park needs a few good, leashed dogs to break it in. Located in a new subdivision beside a new elementary school, the little-used park fairly screams to dogs, "Come roll on my grass!" While the park is heavily people-oriented with tennis courts, playgrounds, soccer fields, and a covered basketball court, there are a few trees, lots of open space, and a fountain. The fountain uses reclaimed wastewater; thirsty pooches may find it has better body and more flavor than the usual insipid stuff from the tap. Yum, yum.

From Highway 6, take University Drive east about two miles to F.M. 158. Turn left and go about one mile to Copperfield Drive; turn left again and proceed a quarter of a mile to the park. Park along Copperfield

Drive. The park is closed from 1 A.M. to 5 A.M. (409) 361-3656.

• **Wolf Pen Creek Park** 🐾 1/2 *See* ⑮ *on page 422.*

This is one of the biggest 19-acre parks Sport and I visited, at least in terms of appeal to leashed dogs. Although dogs are banned from the amphitheater in the center of the park, most of the rest is designed just as a dog would have it. Open grassy spaces surround a pond, and woody areas border the half-mile jogging trail. A black and brown dog of uncertain ancestry was jogging with her owner along the paved trail; both seemed to be sweating—er, glowing—heavily. There are also playgrounds and rest rooms for the non-joggers.

From Highway 6, exit on F.M. 30 and travel south on the frontage road for 0.4 miles to Holleman Drive. Turn right and go 0.6 miles to Dartmouth Street. Turn left and go 0.3 miles to Colgate Drive; turn left again and go a quarter of a mile to the parking lot on your left. The park is closed from 1 A.M. to 5 A.M. (409) 764-3773.

RESTAURANTS

Bruegger's Bagels: Your choosy Chow can agonize over which of 11 kinds of cream cheese to have on her bagel, or she can go straight for the soup and deli sandwiches. Eat at one of the sidewalk tables. 1703 Texas Avenue South, College Station; (409) 694-8990.

Bullwinkle's Grill and Bar: You can have just about anything except moose or squirrel at the open patio out front—chicken-fried steak, chicken strips, sandwiches, grilled chicken, steak, or salads. 1601 Texas Avenue South, College Station; (409) 696-9777.

Dixie Chicken: It's a shame your hunting hound will have to eat his burger at one of the benches on the back porch. This college hangout has more stuffed animal heads on its walls than most museums. It's a carnivore's wonderland of tasty treats. The burgers are priced for the college market—cheap—so you can afford one for each of you. (For an interesting sidelight on the Dixie Chicken, see the diversion "Visit D.C." in the Fort Davis section of chapter 1.) Park in the lot across the alley from the back door. 307 University Drive East, College Station; (409) 846-2332.

Fajita Rita's: Dogs love the tasty little strips of meat that sometimes back out the other end of the tortilla while you're eating fajitas. Here they can sit with you on the patio and watch and wait in quivering anticipation. 4501 Texas Avenue South, Bryan; (409) 846-3696.

Fitz Willy's: College dogs do lunch often here, either at the tables out back or on the front porch. It's basically fast food—burgers, tacos, and salads—but there is a daily lunch special, too. 303 University Drive East, College Station; (409) 846-8806.

Sonic Drive-In: Three locations of this burger-and-fries chain welcome dogs. 914 Texas Avenue South, Bryan, (409) 779-1085; 2900 Texas Avenue South, College Station, (409) 693-0087; and 104 University Drive East, College Station, (409) 696-6427.

Wienerschnitzel: Sit at an outside table and share your hot dog, burger, and fries with your wiener dog at either of two locations. 501 Texas Avenue South, Bryan, (409) 775-1984; 2800 Texas Avenue South, College Station, (409) 764-7361.

Wings 'n More: Finger-lickin' dogs won't care what the "more" in this restaurant's name stands for. Chicken wings are the reason this place exists, and they do them better than any other place Sport, Samantha, and I found. You order your wings regular or garlic, spiced mild, hot, or howl. They're drenched in a spicy sauce and served in a basket with a roll of paper towels. That's where a finger-lickin' dog comes in handy: You can eat with one hand while the other is getting cleaned. Tie your pooch to the railing around the patio and sit next to her. 3230 Texas Avenue South, College Station; (409) 694-8966.

PLACES TO STAY

Comfort Inn: Rooms are $60 to $90. There is a $25 fee for dogs. 104 Texas Avenue South, College Station, TX 77840; (409) 846-7333 or (800) 228-5150.

E-Z Travel: Rooms are $35, and there's a $10 fee for canine guests. Dogs may be no bigger than 10 pounds. 2007 Texas Avenue South, College Station, TX 77840; (409) 693-5822 or (888) 354-2888.

Hilton Hotel—College Station: Lots of dogs with special medical problems who have come to see a specialist at the Texas A&M University veterinary school stay here. Rooms are $70 to $150. Dogs up to 35 pounds are welcome. Pool rooms with outside entrances are available. 801 University Drive East, College Station, TX 77840; (409) 693-7500 or (800) 445-8667.

Holiday Inn: Rooms are $59 to $61. Dogs 18 pounds and under are welcome. 1503 Texas Avenue South, College Station, TX 77840; (409) 693-1736 or (800) 465-4329.

Lake Bryan Park: See Lake Bryan Park on page 458 for camping information.

La Quinta Inn: Rooms are $75 to $85. Company policy limits dogs to 25 pounds, but this inn sometimes makes exceptions. 607 Texas Avenue South, College Station, TX 77840; (409) 696-7777 or (800) NU-ROOMS/ 687-6667.

Manor House: Rooms are $59. Dogs are $7 extra. 2504 Texas Avenue South, College Station, TX 77840; (409) 764-9540.

Motel 6: Rooms are $36. All Motel 6s allow one small pooch per room.

2327 Texas Avenue South, College Station, TX 77840; (409) 696-3379 or (800) 466-8356.

Ramada Inn: Rooms are $53 to $89. Dogs are $10 extra per week. 1502 Texas Avenue South, College Station, TX 77840; (409) 693-9891 or (800) 228-2828.

Relax Inn: Rooms are $35. Dogs must be fully trained and willing to pay a $10 fee. 3604 Highway 21 East, College Station, TX 77848; (409) 778-1881.

FESTIVALS

Bluegrass Festival: Leashed dogs can join in the fun at this annual hoedown the first weekend in June. Headliners such as Ricky Skaggs put on a show that will have your hound's toes a-tappin'. Held at Lake Bryan Park: From Highway 6/U.S. 190 North, take F.M. 2818 south about four miles to F.M. 1687. Turn right and go 3.3 miles to the park entrance. For information, call (409) 361-3656.

Christmas in the Park: Be sure your pooch gets that special gift she wants—have her whisper it as she nuzzles Santa's ear. Meanwhile, you can scarf up free cookies and hot chocolate. It all happens the first three weekends in December in Central Park, 1000 Krenek Tap Road. Dogs must be leashed, and there will be lots of small children about, so excitable dogs should probably just mail their wish list to Santa Dog at the North Pole Doghouse. For information, call (409) 764-3773.

Police Department Easter Egg Hunt: Track down candy eggs instead of raccoons in late March or early April in Central Park, 1000 Krenek Tap Road. Dogs must be leashed. Stealing eggs from other dogs' baskets could be risky: the Easter Egg Police will be watching. For information, call (409) 764-3773.

DIVERSIONS

Burn rubber: Or just gawk at the tricked-out hot rods displayed by members of the Bluebonnet Street Rodders Club. The hopped-up cars (no leg hiking on tires allowed) rev up in mid-August in Central Park, 1000 Krenek Tap Road. Dogs must be leashed. (409) 764-3773.

Burn everything: Each late November before the Texas A&M Aggies play the Texas Longhorns, the Aggies attempt to shore up their sagging spirits by setting fire to enormous amounts of wood. It doesn't always help them beat Texas, but your leashed hound might be able to meet Reveille, the Aggie mascot, an American collie, and if nothing else can toast her tummy in the glow of the biggest fire she'll ever see that does not involve tall buildings. Traditionally, the blaze lights up the corner of Texas Avenue and University Drive. For specific dates, call (409) 260-9898 or (800) 777-8292.

CHAMBERS COUNTY

ANAHUAC

PARKS, BEACHES, AND RECREATION AREAS

• **Anahuac National Wildlife Refuge** 🐾🐾 *See ⑥⑥ on page 423.*

Dogs are welcome on the more than 30,000 acres of this marshland, especially if they are hunting dogs helping to retrieve waterfowl. Dogs may also accompany birders who come to see the many kinds of ducks and geese that winter here. Sport and I saw golden-eyed ducks, American coots, great blue herons, egrets, and a bunch of other birds neither of us could identify. The public viewing area of the refuge has 12 miles of graveled roads you may drive or walk with your dog. As I explained to Sport, walking makes it possible to see a unique bird, because you can "neek" up on it.

Other animals you may see on the refuge include raccoons, opossums, muskrat, nutria, skunks, bobcats, and river otters. One you will want to avoid is the alligator, which is quite common here and quite fond of fresh dog, too. Watch out for snakes and fire ants, and be aware that there is no drinkable water on the refuge. Bring plenty for you and your pooch.

The public viewing area entrance is located about 15 miles south of Anahuac. Follow F.M. 562 south from Highway 61 for eight miles; turn left onto F.M. 1985 and go 4.2 miles to the refuge sign; turn right and follow the graveled road three miles to the information station. The public hunting entrance is another 6.4 miles east on F.M. 1985. Public viewing hours are from dawn to dusk. Public hunting hours are from dawn to noon. There is no hunting on Thanksgiving, Christmas, and New Year's Day. Admission to the refuge is free for birders; hunters pay a $10 fee. (409) 267-3337.

• **Double Bayou Park** 🐾🐾 *See ⑥⑦ on page 423.*

After having been dragged through several parks with strong historical connections in the Anahuac area (see below), Sport was very relieved to find that in this park, in 1832, nothing happened. What was happening when we visited this park of about 20 acres was dog day. A mother dog and two cute puppies met us at the entrance, and farther in the park we met two other dogs, also roaming off leash. They were investigating piles of brush lying all over the park from recent trimming operations on the hundreds of towering pine and oak trees. Your pooch should obey the law and stay on his leash.

Double Bayou meanders along the park's southern boundary, and the banks, while bare and muddy, do slope gently enough to the water to permit easy access. In this part of Texas, though, be wary of alligators as well as poisonous snakes in the water. The park's dirt roads can be muddy when wet, but they make pleasant, shaded walking paths when dry.

Camping is permitted, even though the only facilities provided are rest rooms and two roofed shelters, the larger of which has a water faucet. Camping is free, but you must make a reservation by calling the number below. Camping permits are good for three days.

From Highway 61 east of Anahuac, travel south about seven miles on F.M. 562 to Eagle Ferry Road. Turn right and go 0.3 mile to the park entrance on the left. The park is open 24 hours. (409) 267-8364.

• **Fort Anahuac Park** 🐾 *See* ⓺⓼ *on page 423.*

The first in a series of events leading up to the Texas Revolution took place in this park of about 15 acres. While you wander about reading the half dozen historical markers in the park telling about the Mexican fort that once guarded the mouth of the Trinity River here and the events that led to its abandonment, your leashed hound can enjoy the grass, pine and oak trees, and tidal mudflats. The park also has rest rooms, a playground, athletic fields, and picnic tables. Mostly, though, it's just open space where dogs can run and forget all about history.

In brief, trouble arose over the actions of the commander of the fort, who forced local citizens to help build it without pay. When some refused, including William Barrett Travis, who later commanded the troops at the Battle of the Alamo, the Mexican officer put them in jail. The protests that erupted included the signing of the Turtle Bayou Resolutions. (For more on this, see White Memorial Park, below.)

The park has a few RV hookups; camping is permitted for a maximum of three days. The fee is a bargain-basement $1.50 per day. Call the number below for reservations, which are required.

From Highway 61 in Anahuac, go south on South Main Street about half a mile to the entrance. The park is open 24 hours. (409) 267-8364.

• **White Memorial Park** 🐾 *See* ⓺⓽ *on page 423.*

Sport and I both liked this approximately 20-acre park, but for entirely different reasons which illustrate one of the basic differences between humans and dogs. I liked it because it is near the site where Texan colonists, in 1832, took the first step toward revolution against Mexico by passing the Turtle Bayou Resolutions protesting actions of the government. Sport liked it because work crews had recently trimmed branches from the hundreds of trees in the park and placed them in neat little piles—dozens of them—all over the park. Sap dripping from the ends of the cut branches required sniffing, and the little mounds apparently looked like ideal hiding places for woodland creatures. Therefore, we had to visit one after the

other, sniffing and peering, until I was ready to pass a Turtle Bayou reso-
lution of my own: No more visiting brush piles.

The park has a number of picnic tables scattered among the trees,
and there's a pier on Turtle Bayou. Camping is permitted, even though
there are no facilities provided, but it's free. A reservation is required;
call the number below. Dogs should be leashed.

You'll find the park one block south of Interstate 10 on Highway 61.
The park is open 24 hours. (409) 267-8364.

PLACES TO STAY

Double Bayou Park: See Double Bayou Park on page 464 for camping information.

Fort Anahuac Park: See Fort Anahuac Park on page 465 for camping
information.

White Memorial Park: See White Memorial Park on page 465 for
camping information.

BEACH CITY

PARKS, BEACHES, AND RECREATION AREAS

• **McCollum County Park** 🐾 *See ⑦⓪ on page 423.*

Large live oak and post oak trees and a sweeping view of Trinity Bay
dominate this park of about two acres. Sport was happy to see a squirrel
puzzling over where it had buried that special acorn. However, it took
only a few minutes of sniffing to exhaust the possibilities of this park.
The steep, rough bank prevents safe access to the water, and a leashed
dog can admire only so many trees at a squatting. Four covered picnic
tables overlooking the water and a swing set are the only equipment;
the rest rooms were locked when we visited one February weekend.
Camping is free, but a reservation is required; call the number below.

From Interstate 10, travel south 3.8 miles on F.M. 3180 to its intersection with F.M. 2354; continue another 1.8 miles on F.M. 2354 to McCollum
Park Road, then turn east and go 1.3 miles to the park. The park is open
24 hours. (409) 267-8364.

PLACES TO STAY

McCollum County Park: See McCollum County Park above for camping information.

OAK ISLAND

PARKS, BEACHES, AND RECREATION AREAS

• **Job Beason Park** 🐾 *See ⑦① on page 423.*

Free-roaming dogs barked at Sport and I all over this little community, but none appeared at the approximately five-acre park. Perhaps they were feeling a little crabby. Judging by the number of crab pots stored in yards all over town, crabbing is the main industry here. Besides fishy smells, there's little here to attract a leashed dog, other than the waters of a bayou leading to Trinity Bay just a few yards away. The park has about two dozen widely scattered trees, a rest room, and a swing set. The rest is open grass and gravel roads. Camping for up to three days is permitted by reservation; call the number below for a free permit.

From Highway 61 east of Anahuac, travel south about seven miles on F.M. 562 to Eagle Ferry Road. Turn right and go 3.1 miles to Eagle Road. Turn left and go 1.8 miles to West Bayshore Road. Turn left and follow West Bayshore 0.4 miles to its intersection with Main Street; turn left (you'll still be on West Bayshore Road) and proceed to the park. The park is open 24 hours. (409) 267-8364.

PLACES TO STAY

Job Beason Park: See Job Beason Park above for camping information.

WINNIE

PARKS, BEACHES, AND RECREATION AREAS

• **Winnie-Stowell Park** ♟ *See ⑫ on page 423.*

This park of about 12 acres is devoted mainly to a rodeo arena and open grassy spaces, but the playground area has a thick grove of live oak trees and a few picnic tables, as well as rest rooms.

A few RV campsites with electrical hookups line the street on the west side of the park, but they are not inviting. Still, the price is right—$1.50 per day. Call the number below for a reservation.

The park is on Le Blanc Street one block east of Highway 124, about half a mile south of the intersection of Interstate 10 and Highway 73/124. The park is open 24 hours. (409) 267-8364.

RESTAURANTS

Lercy's Diner: The mud-covered pickups (in Texas at least, generally a sign of good food) and the two tables out front pulled Sport and me off the highway, and we were glad we stopped. We shared the buffet lunch: baked pork chops, mashed potatoes and gravy, corn, fried squash, and a yeast roll. Sport pronounced the pork chop first-rate, and I agreed. While digging in we almost regretted our choice, as a window allowed us to see platter after platter of golden-fried seafood passing by, interspersed now and again with a thick hamburger. Area rice farmers eat here—hence the pickups out front—and the diner caters to hearty appetites. We went away stuffed. 2122 South Highway 124; (409) 296-3299.

PLACES TO STAY

Winnie-Stowell Park: See Winnie-Stowell Park on page 467 for camping information.

COLORADO COUNTY

COLUMBUS

Columbus is a great little town for a weekend stay with a dog. It has a fine park and tree-lined streets just made for walking while you enjoy the historic architecture. Local people welcome dogs, and one restaurant in particular treats dogs as valued customers. Best of all, the quiet, small-town atmosphere is great for soothing jangled big-city nerves, whether human or canine.

PARKS, BEACHES, AND RECREATION AREAS

• **Beason's Park on the Colorado** 🐾 1/2 *See* **73** *on page 422.*

Neither Sport nor I welcomed a five-acre park with more enthusiasm than we hailed this one. Four hours and as many cups of coffee from home, we were cheered by the sight of huge live oak trees and a little rest room building. After we'd checked those out, we nosed around the picnic area and then headed for the Colorado River, which runs along the west side of the park.

Sport did not realize it, but she was walking hallowed ground as she sniffed up and down the riverbank following the tracks of dogs who'd preceded us. While she searched feverishly for a hot raccoon trail, my mind turned back the clock to 1836, when General Sam Houston and the fledgling Texas Army camped here for a week while the Mexican Army under General Santa Anna advanced following their victory at the Alamo in San Antonio.

The land occupied by the park served Houston and his army well, and leashed dogs still find it hospitable. Large live oak and pecan trees shade much of the park, but there's plenty of open grassy space, too, roamed by numerous squirrels. In addition to picnic tables under the oak trees and along the river, there are a covered picnic pavilion and a deck jutting out over the river, reached by a paved walk from the rest room area. The riverbank slopes gently enough that a hound can wet her whistle and paws if she likes. However, you should remember that the Colorado is a conduit for irrigation water for rice farms downstream, and the flow can be swift when water demand is high. Don't wave good-bye to your pooch as she heads off for a new career in agriculture.

The park is on U.S. 90 at the east end of the bridge over the Colorado River, about three blocks east of the courthouse square. It's open from dawn to dusk. (409) 732-2604.

RESTAURANTS

Burger King: Have your burger and fries on the patio in front. 2209 Highway 71; (409) 732-6554.

Chuckwagon Barbecue: Despite the name, this restaurant serves plate lunches on Tuesday through Friday. The owner loves dogs and invites them to sample her meat loaf, fried chicken, chicken-fried steak, chicken tetrazzini, or other daily special. Or they can just duck under one of the covered tables in front and gnaw a bone. 1515 Fannin Street; (409) 732-3744.

. . . Of the Day/A Cafe: Gaze at the courthouse while you eat at one of the sidewalk benches, or take your order across the street and eat in the gazebo on the courthouse lawn. Choose from quiche, roast pork loin, pasta primavera, or hamburgers. 1114 Milam Street; (409) 732-6430.

PLACES TO STAY

Baker Motel: Rooms are $32 to $42. Dogs must be housebroken and may not be left in rooms unattended. 1136 Walnut Street, Columbus, TX 78934; (409) 732-2315.

Columbus Inn: Rooms are $45 to $50. Dogs are $10 extra and are not allowed in deluxe rooms. 2208 Highway 71 South, Columbus, TX 78934; (409) 732-5723.

Country Hearth Inn: Rooms are $58. One very small pet per room is allowed. 2436 Highway 71 South, Columbus, TX 78934; (409) 732-6293.

Happy Oaks RV Park: Dogs must be leashed, but a dog walk is available so they can get some exercise. RV sites are $15. Eastbound travelers on Interstate 10 should take Exit 699 and go half a mile east on the north frontage road. If you're westbound, take Exit 704 and go west on the frontage road three miles. P.O. Box 868, Columbus, TX 78934; (409) 732-5587.

DIVERSIONS

See Texas's toughest water tower: When attempts to demolish this 1883 brick structure with dynamite failed, the United Daughters of the Confederacy acquired it and made it into a museum. Maybe if General Lee had had something like this . . . . The museum is at the southwest corner of the courthouse square and is just one of nearly a dozen historic sites you and your leashed pooch can see along the historical walking tour of downtown. Pick up a free brochure/guide at the visitor center in the 1886 Stafford Opera House at the corner of Spring and Milam Streets. (409) 732-8385.

EAGLE LAKE

PARKS, BEACHES, AND RECREATION AREAS

• **Attwater Prairie Chicken National Wildlife Refuge ½**

See (74) *on page* 422.

Don't count on seeing one of the endangered inhabitants of this refuge. When Sport and I last visited in early 1997, there were an estimated 14 birds living on the nearly 8,000 acres here. All told, the U.S. Fish and Wildlife Service estimated there were only 42 wild birds left as of 1996, and only 89 in captivity. That's a sad remnant of the million or so birds that once lived on six million acres of coastal prairie in Texas and Louisiana. As you might expect, dogs must be leashed here. One hungry dog could do major damage.

Only a tiny portion of the refuge is open to people. Most of it is reserved for the use of the Attwater prairie chicken, which is very sensitive to disturbance. Sport and I walked the Pipit Trail, which circles about a mile around a prairie that had recently undergone a controlled burn to improve the habitat for wildlife. We hadn't gone far from the trailhead when a flock of snow geese overflew us. This was a new experience for Sport: hundreds of clamorous birds just a short distance overhead. She wasn't sure what to do except bound around and bark.

Ditches along the edge of the prairie held water enough to water a pooch who'd made herself thirsty by barking, and soon we found a set of fairly old white-tailed deer tracks in the soft sand. As we neared a creek bottom, we found fresher tracks. In fact, these were as fresh as they get: The deer was still standing in them. A large doe exploded from under a bush and tore across the burned field, black clouds bursting from under her feet. Sport knew what to do now, and before I could think, the leash was ripped from my hands and she was in hot pursuit. Fortunately, Sport and I have been working for some time on the "No" command. We practice it every week when the garbage truck visits our house, and Sport has learned not to chase when I scream "No, Sport!" at the top of my voice. Practically perfect hound that she is, she abandoned pursuit after about the third scream.

An information board located 0.7 miles inside the refuge entrance gate holds general brochures and bird lists. The brochure shows you where to find the auto driving route and two walking trails. Bird-watchers can expect to see a variety of species; 266 kinds of birds have been spotted so far. Among those most likely to be seen year-round are pied-billed grebes, great blue herons, snowy egrets, black vultures, bobwhite quail, American coots, killdeer, red-bellied woodpeckers, blue jays, Carolina chickadees, and loggerhead shrikes.

The refuge is on F.M. 3013 northeast of Eagle Lake. Go six miles from U.S. 90 to the refuge sign; turn left onto an unnamed paved road at the refuge sign and follow it one mile to a T intersection; turn right into the refuge. An information board is 0.7 miles down the gravel road. The refuge is open from sunrise to sunset every day; the visitor center is open from 7:30 A.M. to 4 P.M. Monday through Friday. (409) 234-3021.

RESTAURANTS

Austin's BBQ and Catering: Brisket, chicken, and hot sausage plates with potato salad and beans fly out of this popular spot with five covered tables on the side where you and your pooch can satisfy your carnivorous urges. 507 East Main Street; (409) 234-5250 or (800) 256-0166.

Dairy Delite: You may have trouble deciding whether to have the chili cheeseburger, fish basket, or chicken basket, but just consult your ravenous pooch and you'll find that anything will do. Eat at the tables on the side. 810 East Main Street; (409) 234-7128.

FORT BEND COUNTY

DAMON

PARKS, BEACHES, AND RECREATION AREAS

• **Brazos Bend State Park** 🐾 🐾 🐾 *See ⑦⑤ on page 422.*

The only thing standing between this 4,897-acre parcel and a dog's idea of the perfect place for canines is the park's chief attraction: the American alligator. Alligators have the right-of-way here, so much so that no one, human or canine, is allowed to go into the water. Leashed dogs are welcome, but you should use extreme caution if you want to leave the park accompanied by the same number of feet you brought in.

Despite the dangers to dogs from alligators, Sport and I knew we would have a good time when a ranger cautioned us not to feed the raccoons in the park. Sport loves to chase raccoons (not in parks, of course) almost as much as she likes sleeping on the couch in cold weather, and finding we were in raccoon heaven made us eager to set off on one of the walking trails here. We'd no sooner started down the Creekfield Lake Nature Trail (a paved half-mile trail around an alligator lake) than we spotted raccoon tracks—molded into concrete with deer, bird, and other tracks as ornamentation. Tracking dogs can brush up on their footprint identification skills with the help of a checklist of park animals that includes drawings of animals and their tracks; pick one up for free at the visitor center. Sport and I saw our first alligator on the Creekfield

Lake Trail, sunning itself on a floating mound of vegetation in the lake.

The park has over 21 miles of walking trails ranging in length from one-quarter to 4.1 miles. The park map (available at headquarters) shows the trail locations and trailheads, and an information sheet gives mileages and trail rules. We saw corgies, golden retrievers, Australian blue heelers, and shelties on the trails, in the campgrounds, and in the picnic areas. None appeared bored; apparently the possibility of being eaten by an alligator one minute and bumping into a raccoon or squirrel the next keeps dogs' fun meters approaching the red line. All the trails loop around one of the park's six lakes or skirt the Brazos River, and the marshy ground and thick underbrush host a wide variety of wildlife emitting fascinating scents for hounds to sniff. Dogs will want to walk until you drop.

The park has two day-use picnic areas where you and your pooch can take a break between treks. Both are heavily shaded with large oak and elm trees; if there was one large tree in the park not sporting a thick growth of Spanish moss, I missed it. The ground under the trees in the picnic areas has been cleared, so there's plenty of grass to roam, and sharp-eyed canines can spot a squirrel all the way on the other side. Both picnic areas are near lakes with alligator populations; remember the object is to eat, not be eaten. While it might be tempting (and exciting) to share your lunch with an alligator, feeding them is strictly forbidden. Alligators have no manners or inhibitions, and once they learn to associate people with food, they will help themselves to anything on hand—or foot, or leash.

The park has 77 campsites with water and electricity ($12) in two separate areas, both of which are served by rest rooms with showers. All sites have a 30-amp electrical outlet, picnic table, fire ring, tent pad, lantern post, and barbecue grill. The sites in the Burr Oak Campground are totally shaded, many by the huge trees that give the area its name. The well-spaced sites are surrounded by swampy areas, and a marker in the campground showed that floodwaters had reached a depth of nearly three feet not long before. Here Sport and I met Landys Klyne and her golden retriever Eze of Vancouver, British Columbia, who'd been camping their way across America for the previous three months. Landys said Texas state parks were among the best they'd visited, confirming our suspicions.

Sport and I were more attracted to the Red Buckeye Campground, in which the sites were even more widely spaced and almost as shaded. There were fewer trees here, but they tended to be larger, and there was lots of open grassy areas to roam. Plus, the area is higher and therefore somewhat drier.

The park also has 14 screened shelters that rent for $18. Dogs cannot go inside and cannot be left outside at night, so unless you want to pitch a tent for your dog or have her sleep in the car, you should stay somewhere else. However, the park does have mosquitoes, and the screened shelters may be the answer to your prayers if you don't like having blood-sucking insects feeding on you all night. Other hazards in the park for people and dogs are snakes, feral hogs, and poison ivy.

Reservations for campsites are strongly advised during the spring and on all weekends. You must make reservations by calling (512) 389-8900 between 9 A.M. and 6 P.M. Monday through Friday. You can reserve a type of site, but not a specific site.

To reach the park, drive north from West Columbia on Highway 36 to Damon. Just north of Damon, take F.M. 1462 east for seven miles; turn north on F.M. 762 and go 1.4 miles to Park Road 72. Turn east and go half a mile to the entrance. The entry fee is $3 per person. (409) 553-5101.

PLACES TO STAY

Brazos Bend State Park: See Brazos Bend State Park on page 471 for camping information.

RICHMOND

PARKS, BEACHES, AND RECREATION AREAS

• **T. W. Davis Memorial Park** 🐾 *See ⓰ on page 422.*

Dogs who like sniffing along the well-mowed edges of drainage ditches will like this approximately 20-acre park, which is really more about athletic fields and YMCA than it is dogs. Still, there are a few grassy areas, some trees, and a several benches where a leashed dog and his person can take a break.

The park is at the intersection of F.M. 762 and Loop 762. (281) 341-0791.

RESTAURANTS

Italian Maid Cafe: You'll feel like you're in Italy (if you close your eyes) while you sit at a sidewalk table and dine on cappuccino, veggie sandwiches, pasta, or eggplant parmesan. The owners are dog lovers themselves and can vouch for the fact that even non-Italian dogs love Mediterranean cooking. 209 South Fourth Street; (281) 232-6129.

STAFFORD

RESTAURANTS

Casa Olé: The patio is open only during the warm weather months, but you and your dog are welcome to share your Tex-Mex there. 12203 Murphy Road; (281) 568-9626.

PLACES TO STAY

La Quinta Inn: Rooms are $59 to $70. Dogs under 25 pounds are welcome. 12727 Southwest Freeway (U.S. 59), Stafford, TX 77477; (281) 240-2300 or (800) NU-ROOMS/687-6667.

SUGAR LAND

RESTAURANTS

Carrabba's Italian Grill: Your hound will love this place. The house specialty is veal chops, and there is a dog-friendly patio with three tables to choose from. 2335 Highway 6; (281) 980-4433.

Jason's Deli: Hungry hounds who hanker for deli food will find the cuisine and the patio here to their liking. 15275 Southwest Freeway; (281) 565-3737.

Manhattan Bagel Company: Several local dogs are regular customers here, and the owner says she'd rather have a well-behaved dog than a child as a customer. New York–style bagels baked fresh daily headline the menu; for lunch they're piled high with gourmet deli meats. 15945 Lexington Boulevard; (281) 565-2457.

Outback Steakhouse: Dingoes on a walkabout wind up here on the front porch, where benches and TV trays make it possible for them to enjoy steak, chicken, seafood, or ribs in the company of their favorite aboriginal type human. Call in your order to go or, on weekends, let the cocktail waitress know you'd like to dine with your dog and she'll serve you. Tip well. Dogs don't get treated like this just any old place. 15253 Southwest Freeway; (281) 980-4329.

Skeeter's Grill: Dogs are very welcome on the patio of this family-oriented eatery. (Of course they are—dogs are family members, too.) The menu offers burgers, fajitas, and other Tex-Mex dishes. 15295 Southwest Freeway; (281) 980-0066.

PLACES TO STAY

Shoney's Inn and Suites: Rooms are $62 to $75. Dogs up to 25 pounds stay for no fee or deposit. Just don't leave them unattended in the room (as if you would want to). A vacant field out back is available for walking, and the management is extremely dog-friendly. 14444 Southwest Freeway (U.S. 59), Sugar Land, TX 77478; (281) 565-6655 or (800) 222-2222.

GALVESTON COUNTY

GALVESTON

Water dogs, beach bum dogs, and pampered lapdogs will all love Galveston, because there's something for each of them here. The Gulf of

Mexico provides the perfect playground, beachside restaurants serve up tempting seafood, and one of the premier hotels in Texas treats dogs like the VIPs they are. Take a strong leash when you visit; you may need to drag your dog away.

PARKS, BEACHES, AND RECREATION AREAS

• **Adoue Park** 🐾 *See* **77** *on page 423.*

This block-square park near the historic Strand district is about half playground, half open grass. There are even some trees for leashed dogs to visit, if they consider them worthy.

The park is at the corner of 12th and Winnie Streets. It's open from 6 A.M. until 10 P.M. (409) 766-2138.

• **Galveston Island State Park** 🐾🐾½ *See* **78** *on page 423.*

Sport winced as we entered this beachfront park, and it wasn't just because a cold wind drove rain into her eyes. The park headquarters building and picnic shelters are the dog-ugliest of any we saw. Dogs will be glad they have to be on a six-foot leash here—that way you can pull their head around before they look at an ugly building so long they go blind. You pay your entry fee at the biggest, ugliest structure, the park headquarters.

As I discussed with a ranger, it's a shame the buildings are so intrusive, since this is otherwise a pretty 1,950-acre park. The surrounding area is undeveloped, and the park includes both beachfront on the Gulf of Mexico and salt marshes on the bay side of the island. Four miles of trails wind through the marsh area, and here you can see a multitude of shorebirds. You may also meet poisonous snakes or an alligator, so you should keep a close eye on your pelted pal. Using boardwalks to cross the dunes will help you avoid snakes. The park ranger also issued a warning for owners of small dogs: Watch out for hawks. "Many small dogs are about the size of rabbits, the hawks' natural prey, and they will take them if they get a chance," she said. Jellyfish may also be present on the beach and can inflict nasty stings.

The beach is the main attraction here, and it's relatively unspoiled. Unlike the beaches at parks farther south on the Texas coast, dunes are practically nonexistent here. You'll have a view of the ocean from almost anywhere in the park.

The park has 150 campsites, each with water, electricity, a shaded picnic table, and a barbecue grill. There are no trees in the campground; the only shade is the shelter over the table, and as noted earlier, it's ugly. Rest rooms with showers serve the camping area. Sites nearest the water rent for $15; all the others are $12. The park also has 10 screened shelters, which rent for $18; dogs are not allowed inside these.

Reservations for campsites must be made by calling (512) 389-8900 between 9 A.M. and 6 P.M. Monday through Friday. You may reserve a type of campsite, but not a particular site.

Dogs may not go inside any park building and may not be left unattended. Dogs are also banned from the outdoor theater productions at the Mary Moody Northen Amphitheater in the park.

From Interstate 45, take the 61st Street exit and travel south (right) on 61st Street to Seawall Drive (F.M. 3005); go right (west) on Seawall Drive 10 miles to the park entrance. The park opens at 8 A.M. and closes at 10 P.M. except to overnight guests. Entry costs $3 per person. (409) 737-1222.

• **Seawolf Park** 🔥 ◀● *See ⑦ on page 423.*
Perhaps the best part of this park is the view of the boats moving through the ship channel, but there is room for a leashed dog to wander among the palm trees in the picnic area. The main attraction for people, besides ship-watching, is visiting the two World War II warships on display, a submarine and a destroyer escort. Dogs are not allowed on the ships, so bring along a friend who is not a nautical nut and assign him dog-sitting duties while you take the tour ($2). Parking is $3 per vehicle. Fishing is another $2.

From Broadway Street (Highway 87), turn north onto 51st Street and follow the signs to the park. It is open from dawn to dusk. (409) 744-5738.

RESTAURANTS

Benno's on the Beach: Work up an appetite strolling along the seawall, and then stop in on the patio for seafood, chicken, or burgers. The view of the ocean is as good as the food. Or vice versa. 1200 Seawall Boulevard; (409) 762-4621.

Cafe Michael: The menu ranges from burgers to German food to hot dogs to sandwiches. Choose one of the end tables on the porch and tie your dog to the outside of the railing. 8826 Seawall Boulevard; (409) 740-3639.

PLACES TO STAY

Galveston Island State Park: See Galveston Island State Park on page 475 for camping information.

La Quinta Inn: Rooms are $59 to $135 at this hotel overlooking the beach. Dogs 25 pounds and under stay for free. 1402 Seawall Boulevard, Galveston, TX 77550; (409) 763-1224 or (800) NU-ROOMS/687-6667.

Motel 6: Rooms are $32 to $46. All Motel 6s accept one small pooch per room. 7404 Broadway, Galveston, TX 77554; (409) 740-3794 or (800) 466-8356.

Tremont House Hotel: How many times, when you've checked into a hotel, has your dog received a personalized, handwritten note from the general manager welcoming her to the hotel? Hmmmmm? Not often, we'll bet. But that's exactly what will happen here, and come nighty-night time, there'll be a turndown treat on your doggy's pillow. By now your pooch will probably be expecting to have his own personal valet take him for a walk, and he won't be disappointed. There is one catch: Your dog has to weigh under 20 pounds. This hotel is in the heart of the historic Strand district.

Rooms are $145 to $185. 2300 Ship's Mechanic Row, Galveston, TX 77550; (409) 763-0300 or (800) 874-2300.

FESTIVALS

AIA/Steelcase Sandcastle Competition: Dogs who love to dig in the sand at the beach may be well nigh inconsolable at this affair, because while they can look, they can't put paw to dirt. That activity is reserved for the 65 teams of architects, engineers, and contractors who strive to erect the most imposing edifice of stuff better used for hot dogs to lie in on a summer day. There's also live music. Admission is free. Construction takes place from 11 A.M. until 4 P.M. Judging is completed at 5:30; after that the elements of nature take over to illustrate the folly of building with sand, on sand. The theological implications are lost on dogs and most people. It all happens on Galveston's East Beach (take Seawall Boulevard east to Boddeker Drive) in late May or early June. For info call (713) 622-2081.

LEAGUE CITY

PARKS, BEACHES, AND RECREATION AREAS

• Walter Hall Park 🐾 *See ⑳ on page 423.*

Sport and I gave this 86-acre park a fireplug because it was so torn up by construction when we last visited that we couldn't visualize what it would be like when finished. We could see there will be shaded picnic areas, playgrounds, tennis courts, and softball fields. What we couldn't tell was what there would be for a leashed dog to enjoy other than the obvious. The park fronts on a bayou, so we suspect you ought to be wary of alligators.

The park is on Highway 3 on the north edge of League City. It's open from 7 A.M. until 10 P.M. (409) 766-2411.

GRIMES COUNTY

NAVASOTA

PARKS, BEACHES, AND RECREATION AREAS

• **August Hurst City Park** 🐾 *See* ⑪ *on page 422.*

The five acres or so of this city park have a fine view of the golf course right next to it (where dogs are not allowed), a picnic pavilion, paved jogging trail, playground, and rest rooms. Dogs will appreciate the large oak trees and open grassy spaces between them, but not much else.

The park is on Highway 105 just outside the southwest city limits. Hours are from 8 A.M. until midnight Monday through Thursday and until 1 A.M. on weekends. (409) 825-6450.

RESTAURANTS

Dairy Queen: Sport and Samantha's waistlines give a clue to their favorite food here, the Blizzard. They like the Hawaiian version, with banana, pineapple, and coconut. The chain fast-food eatery also offers burgers, steak fingers, and fries. Not many have tables out front where you can eat with your dog, but this one does. 706 Washington Street; (409) 825-6579.

HARDIN COUNTY

LUMBERTON

PARKS, BEACHES, AND RECREATION AREAS

• **Village Creek State Park** 🐾🐾🐾½ *See* ⑫ *on page 423.*

Your dog can't enter the Big Thicket National Preserve, but she can visit this state park, which is in the Big Thicket and, happily, is also one of the best parks in Texas to take a dog. Dogs must be on a six-foot leash in this 942-acre park and there is an entry fee. Other than that, the news is all good.

Sport and I both felt like wagging our tails when we entered. After days of touring urban parks where the sound of traffic was dulled by trees but never conquered, it was a joy to find still, deep, mysterious woods where wild things live. Deer, squirrels, rabbits, raccoons, and even beavers share these woods with more than 60 kinds of birds. Dogs will also want to watch out for alligators and snapping turtles; they bite.

The creek from which the park takes its name is one of the last free-flowing streams of its size in Texas. Snow-white sandbars gleam at each bend, while birch, beech, sweetgum, ironwood, oak, hickory, and pine trees stand guard over its banks. The serene scenery and gentle current make Village Creek popular with canoeists; a concessionaire within the park can outfit you and your dog for a trip or take you himself.

Other than canoeing, the main mode of transportation within the park is walking. The only road in the park ends a half mile or so inside the front gate. From the parking lot at the end of the road, you and your pooch can hike eight miles of trails within the park. Ask for a free trail guide at park headquarters. Early morning trekkers along the four-mile (round-trip) Water Oak Trail may surprise a beaver at work in the beaver swamp. The mile-long (one way) Village Creek Trail takes you to a swimming beach on the creek. Dogs are barred from the beach and water at the designated swimming area at the end of the trail, but just go upstream or downstream a hundred yards or so and your pooch can swim on leash. Bring along your fishing gear and try for catfish, bass, perch, or crappie—dogs love fresh fish for supper.

As at all state parks, dogs may not go into any park building, nor may they be left unattended. Park superintendent John Parker, himself a dog lover, told me that this is a popular dumping ground for unwanted dogs; if you meet an unsupervised dog, report it to a park ranger. They'll both thank you.

The park has a large, heavily shaded picnic area near a bend in Village Creek. A couple of hundred yards past the picnic area is one of the best camping areas of any state park in Texas. Large, widely spaced sites along the creek are totally shaded all day. Each has a table, fire ring, and lantern post. Water and a composting toilet are nearby. The 17 sites in this walk-in camping area rent for $6 and come with a bonus I found at few other parks in the state: free firewood. The park has so much fallen timber that rangers cut it up and dump it in the campground.

The RV camping area has 25 closely spaced sites, each with full hookups, a table, fire ring, and lantern post. A rest room with showers serves the area. You get free firewood here, too, and the price is only $10. However, these sites afford none of the privacy and feel of being in the woods you get in the walk-in area.

Reservations must be made by calling (512) 389-8900 between 9 A.M. and 6 P.M. Monday through Friday. You can reserve a type of campsite, but not a specific site.

A concessionaire in the park provides rental canoes as well as shuttle service. A canoe and shuttle service for a nine-mile trip is about $30. Renting a canoe for use within the park is about $5 per hour. Take a life preserver for your pooch, and remember those alligators! Call Timber

Ridge Tours at (409) 246-3107 for more information.

From U.S. 96 in Lumberton, go east two miles on F.M. 3513. Turn right onto Alma Drive and continue half a mile to the park entrance on your left. The office is open daily from 8 A.M. to 5 P.M.; the park closes at 10 P.M. except to overnight guests. Entry costs $2 per person. (409) 755-7322.

PLACES TO STAY

Village Creek State Park: See Village Creek State Park on page 478 for camping information.

FESTIVALS

Village Creek Festival: Celebrate the arrival of spring in mid-April with a parade, carnival, and arts and crafts in downtown. For information, call (409) 755-0554.

HARRIS COUNTY

BAYTOWN

PARKS, BEACHES, AND RECREATION AREAS

• **Foote Park** 🐾 *See* ㊳ *on page 423.*

A gloriously muddy ditch runs through the middle of this approximately 12-acre park, and its steep but grassy banks will probably permit your leashed pooch to splash about if she likes. There's a small open, grassy space at the park's west end, some large trees, a few picnic tables, and a playground in those shocking shades of yellow, orange, and blue seen in so many city parks. Sport and I wish we'd been selling those things. We'd never run out of money for T-bone steaks.

The park is at West Main Street and Civic Center Drive. Hours are 6 A.M. to 10 P.M. (281) 420-6597.

• **Roseland Park** 🐾 *See* ㊴ *on page 423.*

This 20-acre park along Cedar Bayou has waterfront picnic tables, a pool, a playground, lots of grass, and a few trees. Leashed dogs can scatter the seagulls along the water, but they'd better watch out for the alligators that live in the bayou.

To reach the park, take Highway 146 Business to East Texas Street; turn right and go about half a mile to Roseland Street and turn right to the park. The park is open from 6 A.M. to 10 P.M. (281) 420-6597.

• **W. L. Jenkins Park** 🐾½ *See* ㊵ *on page 423.*

Local dogs in the know walk their people in this 40-acre park. The western end of the park is developed, with athletic fields, a playground, and a picnic area, but the eastern two-thirds is deep, dark woods with a paved walking trail. Leashed dogs will love sniffing out the scents left by woodland creatures and previous visitors.

The park is on Crosby–Cedar Bayou Road about half a mile north of Highway 146 Business East. Hours are 6 A.M. to 10 P.M. (281) 420-6597.

CLEAR LAKE

PARKS, BEACHES, AND RECREATION AREAS

• **Clear Lake Park** 🐾 *See* 🖤 *on page 423.*

Some dogs like sand and salt water, while others don't like that icky sticky feeling. This 16-acre park has something for both. The park sits at the junction of Mud Lake and Clear Lake, and water dogs can wet their paws, even though they must do so on a five-foot leash. NASA Road 1 cuts through the park, and on the north side of the highway are large open grassy areas where prim pooches can keep their paws pristine. Both parts of the park have trees, picnic tables, and playground facilities.

The park is on NASA Road 1 about five miles east of Interstate 45. Hours are daylight to 11 P.M. (713) 455-8104.

FESTIVALS

Christmas Boat Parade: Amaze your water dog with what can happen when people with boats, money, and time on their hands catch the Christmas spirit. Each second weekend in December, more than 200 elaborately decorated and lighted boats parade around the lake. The prime viewing spot for leashed canines is Clear Lake Park, on NASA Road 1 at the lake. For information, call (281) 488-7676.

DEER PARK

PARKS, BEACHES, AND RECREATION AREAS

• **San Jacinto Battleground State Historical Park** 🐾 🐾½
See 🖤 *on page 423.*

This 1,002-acre park gets half a paw for historical significance. Often there's not much for a leashed dog to enjoy at a historical park, but this one is different. Even if your dog did not have ancestors who were citizens of the Republic of Texas, which won its independence from Mexico here in 1836, she should visit this park. She can watch ships go by, visit a couple of graveyards, and sniff some great trees.

When you enter the park, go first to the parking lot south of the battleship *Texas*. This is where Sam Houston and his army camped the night before one of the most significant battles in history. The Houston Ship

Channel is 50 yards to your west; the 570-foot-tall San Jacinto Monument a quarter of a mile to your east. (The latter is listed in the *Guinness Book of World Records* as the world's tallest stone column memorial.) Huge oceangoing ships ply the waters of the ship channel. Your pooch, like Sport, may meet one of these leviathans proceeding by and find its size and awesome power frightening. Sport decided she'd rather get down from atop the levee alongside the channel and hide behind one of the large live oak trees.

Across the ship channel is one vast network of petrochemical plants that symbolize the modern Texas. Around the San Jacinto Monument the landscape is still pastoral, reflecting the state's origins. Nowhere in the state, perhaps, is the contrast stronger or more vivid between Texas past and Texas present.

Picnic grounds shaded by trees nearly as old as the state overlook the bay east of the monument. There's plenty of room for a dog to roam, but take time to listen, too. There are ghosts here that Texas has yet to put to rest. When the Texas Army charged a Mexican army caught napping that April afternoon, the surprise was so complete that resistance collapsed after only 18 minutes. The killing, however, went on until dark fell hours later. Panicked Mexican troops fled eastward until they reached the water. Texas soldiers shot unresisting Mexicans by the hundreds. When officers tried to stop them, they threatened to kill the officers. The bodies were never recovered from the lake, and the remains of those who died on land were left to rot until farmers complained that their cows were gnawing the bones and spoiling the milk. The Texans felt justified in avenging the deaths of comrades killed in similar fashion at the Alamo and Goliad, but it was a shameful beginning for a proud new nation, and resentment still lingers between some Texans of Anglo and Hispanic descent. One of my dreams is that someday a joint effort between citizens of the United States and Mexico will raise funds for a monument here to the Mexican soldiers who died in the battle. That could signal the beginning of a long-overdue reconciliation. Until we put the past behind us, it will forever color our future.

Dogs are not allowed in the San Jacinto Monument, which houses a museum, nor aboard the battleship. You can also take an elevator to the observation deck inside the monument for a grand view of the countryside. The museum is free; the elevator ride costs $3. Battleship tours are $5.

The park is on Highway 134 two miles north of Highway 225. It is open from 8 A.M. to 7 P.M. (281) 479-2431.

RESTAURANTS

Besaw's Cafe and Saloon: Hot lunches and burgers attract visitors at the nearby San Jacinto Battleground State Historical Park. Pooches hungry from running barefoot in the park can tuck into some grub at one of the tables out front. 3506 Battleground Road; (281) 479-9113.

PASADENA

PARKS, BEACHES, AND RECREATION AREAS

• **Strawberry Park** 🐾 *See* 88 *on page 423.*

This multiuse park of 50 acres has lots of trees and grass for the leashed dog to enjoy, and there's a one-mile paved jogging path for the portly pooch who needs to do penance for too many snacks. You can't escape your fate here: the lights stay on until closing for joggers. Playgrounds, tennis courts, athletic fields, and a swimming pool furnish everyone with something to do—this is a typical urban park designed to serve a multitude of interests.

The park is on Lafferty Street one block north of Spencer Highway. It's open sunrise to 11 P.M. (713) 477-8509.

PLACES TO STAY

Ramada Inn Houston East: Rooms are $49 to $65. Spacious grassy areas for walking your dog are just outside the exterior rooms. 114 South Richey, Pasadena, TX 77506; (713) 477-6871.

SPRING

PLACES TO STAY

Motel 6—North: Rooms at this Houston-area motel are $42. Like all Motel 6s, this one accepts one small pooch per room. 19606 Cypresswood Court, Spring, TX 77388; (281) 350-6400 or (800) 466-8356.

TAYLOR LAKE VILLAGE

PARKS, BEACHES, AND RECREATION AREAS

• **Bay Area Park** 🐾 *See* 89 *on page 423.*

Picnic tables and playgrounds are what this 64-acre park is mainly about, but dogs on the required five-foot leashes will pay more attention to the hundreds of trees, the easily accessible waters of the bayou wrapping around the park, and the flock of geese and ducks who seem to have put themselves in charge of greeting visitors. It was raining cats and dogs when Sport and I last visited, but we could see dogs will find much to like here. The park also has fishing piers, baseball fields, and rest rooms. The ducks and geese hang out around a pool with a fountain spurting in its center. Dogs would surely love to take a dip there as well, but they'd better not, as alligators inhabit the bayou.

The park is on Bay Area Boulevard about five miles east of Interstate 45. Hours are daylight to 11 P.M. (713) 455-8104.

WEBSTER

PARKS, BEACHES, AND RECREATION AREAS

• **Challenger Seven Memorial Park** 🐾🐾½ *See* ⑨⓪ *on page 423.*

Some of the Harris County parks we visited were obviously designed for people, but these 211 acres have a healthy balance between people needs and dog needs. While rules require a six-foot leash, that's the only restriction dogs face here. Even better, most of the park retains its natural vegetation, with cleared areas and trails designed to lead you into the park's wildness rather than subdue it.

The park is dedicated to the memory of the seven astronauts who lost their lives in the explosion of the *Challenger* space shuttle. One of the prettiest places in the park is a small glade with a memorial marker. Several large live oak trees shade porch swings where you and your pooch can sit and reflect on what you mean to each other. To you, your dog means unconditional love and companionship. To your dog, you are a meal ticket, tennis ball tosser, and ogre who seems to regard couches and beds as your own.

To reach the memorial, park in the main parking lot, by the community garden, and take the paved trail leading west behind the rest room. It's about a quarter of a mile to the memorial glade. From there a paved trail leads west to the entrance to a boardwalk, which carries you over wetlands to a bird sanctuary. Three observation towers jut out over the wetlands and make great vantage points for birding or photography. Continue past the boardwalk on the mowed, grassy nature trail; this is the part your dog will love. The trail passes through dense thickets where birds, deer, and all kinds of small critters lurk. Supposedly two miles long, the trail has numerous branches and loops; it might be a good idea to carry along a bag of doggy treats to drop, Hansel and Gretel style, to lead you back out.

The park also has a playground, picnic area, and small lake. Signs warned against eating fish caught in the park; that probably means your pooch shouldn't drink the wild water, either. Water is available at the rest rooms.

To reach the park from Interstate 45, go west half a mile on F.M. 528 to West NASA Boulevard and turn left. Go one mile to the entrance. The park is open from 7 A.M. to 9 P.M. in the summer and from 7 A.M. to 6 P.M. in the winter. (713) 991-6881.

RESTAURANTS

Tortuga Cantina: There's a special table on the covered patio reserved just for dogs. The menu is special, too. The Yucatecan cuisine emphasizes low-fat, healthy foods and includes items such as black beans, spinach tacos, fish tacos, and shrimp tacos. 914 NASA Road 1; (281) 333-3524.

PLACES TO STAY

Motel 6: Rooms are $44. All Motel 6s accept one small pooch per room. 1001 West NASA Road 1, Webster, TX 77598; (281) 332-4581 or (800) 466-8356.

HOUSTON COUNTY

NATIONAL FORESTS

See the National and State Forests/State Wildlife Management Areas chapter starting on page 621 for important information and safety tips on visiting these areas with your dog.

• **Davy Crockett National Forest** 🐾🐾🐾 🐾 ➤
See page 622 for a description of Davy Crockett National Forest.

STATE WILDLIFE MANAGEMENT AREAS

See the National and State Forests/State Wildlife Management Areas chapter starting on page 621 for important information and safety tips on visiting these areas with your dog.

• **Unit 121 Wildlife Management Area** 🐾🐾 ➤
See page 627 for a description of the area.

CROCKETT

PARKS, BEACHES, AND RECREATION AREAS

• **Davy Crockett Memorial Park** 🐾½ *See* ❺ *on page 422.*
This is a big park for a small town. Its approximately 150 acres allow for athletic fields, tennis courts, and a community center with plenty of room left over for leashed dogs to enjoy. Large oak trees dominate the grounds, but a few pines add spice. A fence made of old cross ties along the west side and a log cabin supposedly dating from the 1850s in the center, along with several historical markers, give both you and your pooch something to contemplate as you wander about searching for that perfect place for a squat.

Sport was fascinated when I told her the park was named for Davy Crockett, a hero who died at the Battle of the Alamo in 1836. Actually, she yawned in my face at the news. But when I told her he was famous for wearing caps made of raccoon skins (or at least the actor who portrayed him in a television series was, to the delight of the makers of such headgear), she perked right up. Sport gives half a paw to anything even remotely connected with raccoons. No, Sport, this park is not where Davy Crockett got his raccoons. Yes, Sport, I know raccoons like to hide under old log cabins, but no, we cannot go looking for raccoons under there.

To reach the park from the courthouse square, take South Fifth Street south about half a mile to the entrance on your left, at the intersection with Anson Jones Street. Hours are 6 A.M. to 10:30 P.M. (409) 544-5156.

PLACES TO STAY

Crockett Inn: Rooms are $54. Small, housebroken dogs are welcome. 1600 Loop 304 East, Crockett, TX 75835; (409) 544-5611 or (800) 633-9518.

FESTIVALS

American Heritage Hunt: This is one event Sport does not want to miss: the annual raccoon hunt sponsored by the Texas State Coon Hunters Association and the United Kennel Club. There's a coon hunting dog show during the day and two 250-dog hunts at night. Wow! Talk about making raccoons head for the tall timber! Then there are all those hunting stories around the campfires at night. It's enough to make a raccoon-hunting dog swoon. Head for Crockett in mid-April; call for specific dates and locations of events. (409) 544-2359.

GRAPELAND

PLACES TO STAY

Salmon Lake Park: This is one of those places that's hard to categorize. You can pay $3 per day to picnic here with your leashed dog, who'll pay $2. However, this is more a country-style resort than it is a park. Owner Floyd Salmon is a house mover in addition to being a campground owner, and he has saved old buildings all over East Texas, moved them here, and turned them into rustic accommodations. There are also modern cabins built for the purpose. Rates range from $35 to $100, depending on how many people the cabin sleeps. Dogs under 25 pounds may stay in the cabins for $5 per day. The whole collection of buildings clusters around small fishing ponds and resembles the set for a Western movie. Pine and oak trees shade much of the park's 50 acres.

More than 400 RV hookups, many shaded, rent for $14; tent sites with water and electricity are $5. Rest rooms with showers are available. Oddly, the camping fees are lower during the annual Bluegrass Festival (see below): campsites with hookups are $10 per day, and tent camping is $10 per car for three days. I guess they really want people to come and have a good time without being gouged. Imagine that. Reservations for campsites are normally not required, but for cabins they should be made at least two months in advance.

From downtown Grapeland, take F.M. 227 west 0.2 miles to F.M. 1272. Turn right and go 0.3 miles to Redbud Street; turn left and go half a mile to the entrance. The mailing address is P.O. Box 483, Grapeland, TX 75844; (409) 687-2594.

FESTIVALS

Bluegrass Festival: Leashed dogs pay a $2 entry fee, but they may not be taken into the seating area, so they'll have to stay in the campground or a cabin. Dogs may not go into the water, either, even if they can play *Fire on the Mountain.* You'll enjoy three days of guitar and banjo pickin' and singin' over the Labor Day weekend. Admission is $6 for Friday, $10 Saturday, $6 Sunday, or $20 for all three days. Bands come from Georgia, Missouri, Kentucky, and other states to join in the fun. You'll look out of place without a flop-eared hound dog in tow. The festival is held at Salmon Lake Park; for directions, see the park listing on page 487. For info call (409) 687-2594.

WECHES

PARKS, BEACHES, AND RECREATION AREAS

• **Mission Tejas State Historical Park** 😊 😊 😊 *See* 🐾 *on page 422.*
This park is like Samantha, our dog who eats everything—it's getting bigger. For years it remained at 118 acres, but recently another 245 acres of adjacent land were added, which means leashed dogs will have even more trails to explore.

The huge pine trees, some of which take two people to reach around at the base, will catch your pooch's eye. You'll immediately notice the old log house on the left just after you enter the park. Your dog can't go inside, but you should show her the open passageway between the two parts of the cabin—it's called a dog run or dog trot, because that's where pioneer dogs slept as they guarded the family against Indians, mountain lions, and corn-stealing raccoons.

The other historical building in the park isn't really historical, even though it represents the reason for the park's existence. The log church is a replica of a Spanish mission built in the area in 1690, the first established on what is today Texas soil. To your pooch the little chapel is like the Promised Land: she can stand outside the open doors and look inside, but she can't enter.

The rest of the park is another matter. The pine- and oak-covered hills hide ponds and creeks, and a network of trails connects all the park's significant features: campground, log cabin, mission replica, creek, and pond. Your dog is allowed to go into the creek and pond while on leash, but keep in mind that visitors have reported a five-foot alligator in the pond. The trails in the park range from a quarter of a mile to a mile and a quarter in length; however, at press time additional trails were under construction in the newly purchased acreage. The trails are totally shaded by tall pines and offer great views of tall pines.

A thick litter of pine needles and leaves from other kinds of trees covers the graveled trails, making them delightful for walking. However, Sport the sensitive dog was perplexed by pinecones that occasionally pelted us—perhaps she felt the gods of the trees were out to get us. However, when one bonked her on the head, she gave me an accusing look despite my protestations of innocence.

The park also maintains a bird feeding station with a screening board fence with peepholes, allowing you to watch birds chow down. Dogs will find this extremely boring, since none of the peepholes are at dog height. While you are standing there exclaiming over the pretty birds, your dog will be staring at an unpainted knothole, thinking, no doubt, that people can be really, really dumb sometimes.

Camping facilities in the park are limited but charming. Two campsites with water only are beside the pond; they rent for $6. The other camping area has 10 sites with water and electricity ($9) and five with full hookups ($10). A ravine divides the campground, and sites occupy flat spots on its steep sides. All campsites are totally shaded and have a picnic table, fire ring, and lantern post. Reservations must be made by calling (512) 389-8900 between 9 A.M. and 6 P.M. Monday through Friday. You may reserve a type of site, but not a particular one.

The park is 21 miles northeast of Crockett on Highway 21. There is a $2 per person admission charge. (409) 687-2394.

• **Neches Bluff Overlook Recreation Area** 🐾 🐾 ½
   See ❸ on page 422.

"Now, this is camping," I told Sport as we walked around this primitive recreation area. The site sits on a bluff high above the Neches River, although the tall pines are so thick you can't see the river for them. Heck, the pines are so thick you can't see the forest for the trees, either. Sport loved the trees and the two friendly dogs who bounded up to greet us, unleashed despite the rule requiring dogs to be restrained in national forest recreation areas. Admittedly, there were no signs or fences marking the boundary of this recreation area, and dogs can't read, anyway.

At least most dogs can't, but I swear Samantha can read the words "Purina" or "Alpo" from a mile away.

The campground consists of fire rings scattered among clearings under the trees, and there's a toilet. There's no water and no trash cans—you pack it in, you pack it out. Camping is free, and you're not likely to be disturbed by other campers. It's a great place to camp with a dog. You'll hear birds twittering, the wind moaning in the treetops, and, if the wind is right, the gurgle of the river, but that's it. Dogs and people bond in places like this. They stick by us because they know we brought the food. We stick by them in case there are things in the woods that regard us as food. It works.

One of the trailheads for the 4-C Hiking Trail is on the east side of the road that loops through the campground. Named for the Central Coal and Coke Company, which once logged the area, this 19-mile trail connects to the Ratcliff Lake Recreation Area, where the sawmill was located (see below). The trail follows old logging roads and exposes hikers to a variety of ecosystems ranging from bottomland hardwood to upland pine forests. Along the way you'll pass through both pine and bottomland hardwood forests, through stands of mature pines and young trees. You can camp by ponds along the trail and maybe even catch a fish for supper there. About midway of the trail, the Walnut Creek Campsite has five tent sites and a pit toilet. Near mile 13, the Pond Campsite has two tent sites. Camping is not permitted along the trail from about October 1 through mid-January due to public deer hunting in the national forest. The best times to hike the trail are from mid-January through the end of May; heat, humidity, and bugs make the warm months unpleasant.

To reach the area, take Highway 21 east from Crockett about 25 miles to Forest Service Road 511-3. Turn right and go 0.6 miles to a sign pointing the way to the Neches Bluff Overlook; turn left and follow the road half a mile to the camping area and the 4-C Hiking Trail trailhead information board. (409) 634-7709.

• **Ratcliff Lake Recreation Area** 🐾 🐾 🐾 *See* ❾❹ *on page 422.*

The U.S. Forest Service captured Sport's heart with this swatch of tall pine forest surrounding a small lake. The entrance fee entitles you to picnic, swim, and hike the 1.9-mile Tall Pines Trail. The area is also the southern terminus of the 19-mile 4-C Hiking Trail, which connects to the Neches Bluff Overlook Recreation Area near Weches. (For more information on this trail, see the listing for Neches Bluff, on page 488.)

Dogs will love you forever if you bring them here, even though they must be leashed. At least that's the story Sport and I got from a Jack Russell terrier just completing the Tall Pines Trail with his three favorite teenagers. The sun slanting through the pines and swelling buds on dogwood trees promised spring was on the way, and every member of the group had a wagging tail as they trooped past.

Camping is a delight here. The sites are some of the largest anywhere in Texas—your hound will have his own little private patch of pines, many populated by squirrels. All sites are fully shaded by pines, and most have a view of the lake. Many, in fact, are just feet from the water, and leashed dogs can splash all they want in the campground (keep an eye out for alligators), although they are not allowed at the swim beach near the picnic area and snack bar. You'll have a picnic table, lantern post, fire ring, and, best of all, serenity at your campsite. Rest rooms with showers and water faucets are nearby. Regular sites rent for $7; those with electricity are $10. Pay all fees at the self-service station at the entrance; you're allowed half an hour to stake out a campsite and return to pay.

The campground is on Highway 7 just outside Ratcliff, one mile west of its intersection with F.M. 227. It opens at 7 A.M. and closes at 10 P.M. except to overnight guests. Entry costs $3 per person. (409) 655-2968 or (409) 544-2046.

PLACES TO STAY

Mission Tejas State Historical Park: See Mission Tejas State Historical Park on page 487 for camping information.

Neches Bluff Overlook Recreation Area: See Neches Bluff Overlook Recreation Area on page 488 for camping information.

Ratcliff Lake Recreation Area: See Ratcliff Lake Recreation Area on page 489 for camping information.

JASPER COUNTY

NATIONAL FORESTS

See the National and State Forests/State Wildlife Management Areas chapter starting on page 621 for important information and safety tips on visiting these areas with your dog.

• **Angelina National Forest** 🐾🐾🐾 🐕
See page 622 for a description of Angelina National Forest.

STATE WILDLIFE MANAGEMENT AREAS

See the National and State Forests/State Wildlife Management Areas chapter starting on page 621 for important information and safety tips on visiting these areas with your dog.

- **Angelina Neches/Dam B Wildlife Management Area** 🐾🐾 ½ 🐕
  See page 625 for a description of the area.
- **Unit 125 Wildlife Management Area** 🐾🐾 ½ 🐕
  See page 627 for a description of the area.
- **Unit 129 Wildlife Management Area** 🐾🐾 ½ 🐕
  See page 628 for a description of the area.

JASPER

PARKS, BEACHES, AND RECREATION AREAS

- **Martin Dies Jr. State Park** 🐾🐾 *See* 🅖 *on page 423.*

Water dogs will be in—or at least surrounded by—their element in this 705-acre park located on B. A. Steinhagen Reservoir, a 15,000-acre impoundment on the Neches River. Tree dogs will also be happy here: If there is a square inch of this park not shaded by a towering pine tree, I didn't find it. Dogs must be on a six-foot leash.

While there are two hiking trails here, one about two miles long and the other three-quarters of a mile in length, lakeside camping is this park's forte. Almost every campsite has a view of the lake, and many are just steps from the water. Add fishing to this lake's list of attractions. You don't need a boat—you can fish right from the bank near your campsite or from two fishing piers. There is a designated swimming area at the day-use picnic area in the Hen House Ridge Unit; dogs are prohibited from the water and the adjacent beach. However, they may go in the water on leash anywhere else in the park—but see the warning about alligators and poisonous snakes below.

This park's scenic beauty and its location north of the Houston-Beaumont area make it very popular with summer visitors. As a result, it has high-season and low-season rates for camping. The 115 sites with water and electricity rent for $10 from December 1 through the end of February and for $12 the rest of the year. Off-season rates for the 66 sites with water only are $7; March 1 through November 30 they are $9. The park has 46 screened shelters that are $15 in the off-season and $17 in the high season. Dogs are not allowed inside the shelters. Reservations must be made by calling (512) 389-8900 between 9 A.M. and 6 P.M. Monday through Friday. You can reserve a type of site, but not a particular site.

I didn't find a bad campsite in the park. The sites in the Walnut Ridge Unit north of U.S. 190 are large and are shaded by tall pines. All the underbrush has been cleared, so there's no privacy, but this has a bonus: Your dog can see a squirrel skittering along the ground from a hundred yards away. This campground sits on a promontory jutting into the reservoir, and the view of the lake through the trees from the campsites is enough to put a dog to sleep, but you'll love it.

The Hen House Ridge Unit, south of U.S. 190, has some sites on Gum Slough (sounds yucky and looks it) and some overlooking the lake. You might want to ask to drive around the campground to choose a site on your arrival. Then again, maybe you have a slough-footed dog and prefer the backwater.

Wherever you camp or hike in the park, be aware that there are poisonous snakes and alligators living here. If you see an alligator, don't be misled by their sluggish demeanor and inactivity. They can move very fast when they want to, and one of the times they'll want to is when a dog lowers its head to sniff their snout. One chomp and it's good-bye, Rover.

Birders also like the park; a total of 235 bird species have been observed in the area. The lake is a wintering ground for bald eagles. Ask for a free bird checklist, which includes some suggested birding areas, at park headquarters.

The park is 12 miles west of Jasper on U.S. 190. The office is open from 8 A.M. to 5 P.M. daily. The park closes at 10 P.M. except to campers. Entry costs $2 per person. (409) 384-5231.

PLACES TO STAY

Best Western: Rooms are $49 to $52. Dogs 10 pounds and under may stay here. 205 West Gibson Street, Jasper, TX 75951; (409) 384-7767 or (800) 528-1234.

Days Inn: Rooms are $43 to $46. Small dogs are welcome. 1700 South Wheeler, Jasper, TX 75951; (409) 384-6816 or (800) 325-2525.

Martin Dies Jr. State Park: See Martin Dies Jr. State Park on page 491 for camping information.

Ramada Inn: Rooms are $55 to $58. All dogs are welcome. 239 East Gibson Street, Jasper, TX 75951; (409) 384-9021 or (800) 272-6232.

Traveler's Motel: Rooms are $28 to $31, and your canine companion is $10 extra. Small, housebroken dogs are welcome. 501 Mays Street, Jasper, TX 75951; (409) 384-3428.

Twin Dikes Park: This is one of the better U.S. Army Corps of Engineers parks for dogs around Sam Rayburn Reservoir. The 43 campsites ($13 to $17) have no water or electricity, which means the park is less busy—and crowded with RVs—than other campgrounds. In addition, many of the sites are large—they didn't have to jam them close together to save money on wire and pipe—and completely shaded by tall pines. All have gorgeous views of the lake; many are sited atop little knolls, giving them great visibility. The campground does have a rest room with showers. Dogs must be on a six-foot leash.

At this time, reservations are no longer accepted, but that may change in the future; call the number below for the current policy.

The park is on Recreation Road 255 about four miles west of its intersection with U.S. 96. The park is open from 8 A.M. to 10 P.M. (409) 384-5716.

FESTIVALS

Azalea Trail Arts and Crafts Festival: Beautiful blossoms are wasted on dogs, but pooches do enjoy strolling around the courthouse square downtown pretending to appreciate the photo exhibition, needlework display, and live music. The festival is held in late March. For information, call (409) 384-2762.

JEFFERSON COUNTY

BEAUMONT

Traveling dogs will likely want to light a candle to Saint Radial, the canine patron of tires, after they visit Beaumont. The automobile age began here on January 10, 1901, when a driller struck oil in the greatest quantity found to that date in the world. The Lucas Gusher, also called Spindletop, stimulated the formation of a number of oil companies and ushered in the age of cheap petroleum. Within just a few years the internal combustion engine revolutionized the lives of American dogs. No longer could they follow the wagon or buckboard down the road, hiding in the bushes, until they reached town with the rest of the family. Now people could speed away at the fearsome rate of 20 miles an hour, leaving lonesome hounds behind to wonder what they'd done to deserve such cruel treatment. By the same token, however, lucky dogs could now travel great distances with their humans, learning that dogs' rears everywhere smell the same, even though they keep checking, and checking, and checking.

Beaumont welcomes dogs, even though they must be leashed everywhere. The city has an excellent parks system, and nearby Village Creek State Park (see page 478) is one of the best places in Texas to take a dog, bar none. Some of the best hotels and restaurants in town welcome dogs. It's fun being a dog in Beaumont: You can help your human float an entry in a rubber ducky race or pick your own blueberries, pears, and grapes.

PARKS, BEACHES, AND RECREATION AREAS

• **Alice Keith Park** 🐾 *See* ⑯ *on page 423.*

This park is only nine acres, but it has more large live oak trees than most other parks in Beaumont, with lots of open grassy space in between. The sun popped out as I pulled into the parking lot, and I could visualize Sport wriggling on her back in the grass, one of her favorite "I'm feeling soooo good" bits. The park has picnic tables and something I saw in no other park I visited in the whole state: an above-ground swimming pool. Rest rooms reside regally in the red-brick Georgian-style building on the park's west end. There was a disappointing dearth of squirrels, but the size and number of oak trees makes me think hounds will surely see at least a few scurry for safety when they appear.

The park is at the corner of Lavaca Street and Highland Avenue, just a few blocks west of Lamar State College of Technology. From U.S. 69/96/287 East, take Martin Luther King Jr. Parkway north about a mile to Lavaca Street; turn left and go six blocks to the park. Hours are 8 A.M. to midnight. (409) 838-3613.

• **Athletic Complex** 🐾 *See* **97** *on page 423.*

Many city recreational facilities are called parks but are really athletic complexes; this one is a bit of both. Its 124 acres are mostly devoted to ball fields and parking lots, but there is a heavily wooded area in the northwest corner that leashed dogs will find to their taste. While the woods are so thick as to be impenetrable for the most part, there is a clearing cut through it opposite the entrance to baseball field number 2, and dogs will enjoy sniffing along the edges of these woods. There's also lots of open grassy space on this end of the park, as well as a playground, a few picnic tables, and a jogging trail a mile and a quarter long.

The park is at the intersection of U.S. 90 West and Langham Road, about a mile and a half west of Interstate 10. Hours are 8 A.M. to midnight. (409) 838-3613.

• **Babe D. Zaharias Park** 🐾 *See* **98** *on page 423.*

There's little to break the view at this 27-acre park right beside Interstate 10. Leashed dogs can see all 116 trees, the playground, rest rooms, an F-101 Voodoo jet fighter mounted on a pedestal, and a small building housing a museum depicting the career of the park's namesake, a Beaumont native who was one of the greatest female athletes of all time. Babe Zaharias is one of Sport's heroes, even though she never treed a raccoon. A 1.4-mile graveled jogging trail winds among a forest of soccer field backstops dotting the acres of mowed grass. Water is available at the rest rooms.

From Interstate 10, exit at Gulf Street. The park is on the north side of the freeway. A parking lot beside the museum on the access road is the only one serving the park. It's open from 8 A.M. to midnight. (409) 838-3613.

• **Central Park** 🐾 *See* **99** *on page 423.*

Only 14 acres remain of what was once a much larger park before a medical center and National Guard armory intruded. Still, leashed dogs have a one-third-mile fitness trail to walk, and there's an elaborate playground resembling a medieval castle. Trees are few but large; one shades a picnic table, and other tables are under a pavilion nearby. Hounds who have a person in the hospital next door could meet them here for a mutual dose of caring. It's a known medical fact that a timely application of dog love helps heal all wounds.

The park also has rest rooms, water fountains, and lighted tennis courts. There's a senior citizen center in the northeast corner for dogs who prefer a slower pace.

The park is at the corner of South Fourth Street and Fannin Street, one block north of U.S. 90. Hours are 8 A.M. to midnight. (409) 838-3613.

• **Collier's Ferry Recreation Area** 🐾🐾½ *See* ⑩⓪ *on page 423.*

This 1,232-acre urban park along the bank of the Neches River opened early in 1997, but it's already a favorite with Beaumont dogs. Although leashes are the dress code, dogs love to dip their paws in the river before heading out along the nature trail. Tall pines screen the park from the city, and it's almost possible to forget you are just minutes from downtown. Parts of the park were still closed for construction when I last visited, but a brief glimpse was enough to show that this park will become the centerpiece of Beaumont's park system. For people in the group, there's a playground, picnic tables, rest rooms, and a boat ramp.

From Interstate 10 westbound, exit onto Pine Street and go 2.8 miles to the park entrance. From Interstate 10 eastbound, exit on Gulf Street and go north to Plum Avenue; turn right and go six blocks to Pine Street; turn left and follow it to the park. Hours are 8 A.M. to midnight. (409) 838-3613.

• **Halbouty Park** 🐾½ *See* ⑩① *on page 423.*

This six-acre park is sure to be a hit with water dogs. For one thing, there's a swampy wooded area beside the playground just begging to muddy up those paws. But what's that large, blue, mushroom-shaped thing sitting in the middle of a square of blue rubber? Push the button on the post and it sprays water from a dozen nozzles, misting the whole area with a cooling drench. It's just the thing for a hot dog who's just put in several laps on the 18-station exercise trail around the park's perimeter, and—howlelujah—dogs are allowed to use it. (Just don't teach your pooch to push the button herself, or you'll never get her to leave.) The park also has several picnic tables, a basketball court, a number of large trees, and a brushy, vine-tangled fringe on one side where sharp-nosed hounds may ferret out a furry critter or two. An open grassy area takes up about half the park and would be ideal for a game of toss the

Frisbee, but dogs must remain on leash. If you can do a boomerang throw. . . .

To reach the park from U.S. 69/96/287 North, exit on East Lucas Street. Go east a long block to Concord Road and turn left. Go north about half a mile and turn right on Gober Street; the park is a couple of hundred yards up on your right. Hours are 8 A.M. to midnight. (409) 838-3613.

• Klein Park 🐾 🐾 See ⓸ on page 423.

A small drainage—Walker Branch—runs through this 29-acre park, and leashed dogs will enjoy exploring its banks. A footbridge over the creek leads into a wooded area, and a 1.6-mile graveled exercise trail encircles the long, skinny park. A playground, rest rooms, water fountain, and picnic tables are provided. Benches along the exercise trail are just the thing for the pooch who doesn't want to overdo this exercise thing, which is highly overrated anyway, according to Samantha. A heavily wooded area on the north end of the park is sure to be a hit with dogs, as it is open underneath for the better viewing of squirrels. Tennis courts nearby offer the possibility of finding an errant ball for a game of catch.

The park is on F.M. 364 (Major Drive) half a mile north of its intersection with Highway 105. From U.S. 69/96/287 North, go west on Highway 105 for 1.4 miles to F.M. 364 and turn right. Hours are 8 A.M. to midnight. (409) 838-3613.

• Lefler Park 🐾 🐾 See ⓹ on page 423.

A two-mile paved exercise trail with 18 stations winds through this heavily wooded 42-acre park. Dogs must be leashed, but you wouldn't want them to get loose in the thick tangle of vines and trees off the trail, anyway. As a special reward for walking or jogging the trail with you, give your hound a drenching at the spray station near the playground. It's designed to take the place of wading pools for small children, but grown-ups and dogs are allowed to use it, too. You'll find a drinking fountain and picnic tables at the playground.

From U.S. 69/96/287 North, exit on Dowlen Road and travel east one block to Concord Road. Turn left and go one block to Garner Road; turn right and go one block to Comstock Road. The park is one mile down Comstock Road, which makes two right-angle turns. Hours are 8 A.M. to midnight. (409) 838-3613.

• Magnolia Park 🐾 1/2 See ⓺ on page 423.

Boy dogs will love this 17-acre park. It has 235 trees, most of them large oaks, although there are some pine trees, too. Picnic tables (some with barbecue grills) and a playground share the shade. I didn't see any squirrels when we last visited in early February; perhaps they were waiting for fall showers of acorns. This shady, grassy park requires that dogs be leashed.

From Interstate 10, go north on Magnolia Avenue for 12 blocks. You can park along Weiss Street on the park's south side. Hours are 8 A.M. to midnight. (409) 838-3613.

• **Rogers Park** 🐾 *See ⑩ on page 423.*

Play a game of find-the-trees with your leashed pooch in this park. The city parks and recreation department says there are supposed to be 609 trees here, but while there is a large stand of pine trees at the park's southeast corner, I'd guess there were no more than 209 there. Can your keen-eyed hound find the missing 400 trees? Was there hidden meaning in the large brush piles heaped about the park when I last visited? Dogs all over Beaumont want to know: Is there a maniac with a chain saw loose in Beaumont parks? (Okay dogs, the mystery is solved. An ice storm broke limbs all over town, and the piles of brush were part of the clean-up. There's still the question of those 400 missing trees, however.)

While your dog is puzzling over the problem of the possibly purloined pines, you can relax at a shaded picnic table, watch kids at the playground or wading pool, or raise a racquet at the tennis courts. There's also a covered basketball court.

The park is in west Beaumont at the intersection of Dowlen Road and Gladys Avenue. From U.S. 90, take Dowlen Road north about a mile and a half to the park. Hours are 8 A.M. to midnight. (409) 838-3613.

• **Sprott Park** 🐾 *See ⑩ on page 423.*

Leashed dogs can join you on the half-mile fitness trail around this 10-acre park; it passes along a wooded area on the park's east side and crosses a couple of wooden footbridges. A drainage ditch runs along the park's west side. It's not a wilderness experience, but combined with the picnic tables, rest rooms, playground, and tennis courts, there's plenty to occupy a pooch's attention and perhaps titillate his sniffer. For rainy days, there's a covered basketball court.

The park is at the intersection of Virginia Street and Usan Street. From U.S. 69/96/287 South, go north three blocks on Mercantile Street; turn right and go one block to the park. Hours are 8 A.M. to midnight. (409) 838-3613.

• **Tyrrell Park** 🐾🐾½ *See ⑩ on page 423.*

Just inside the entrance of this 516-acre park is one of the best parts, a 10-acre garden center that is a monument to what work, patience, fertilizer, and the absence of a dog digging up what's just been planted can do. Leashed dogs can tread the pathways with you and admire bed after bed of azaleas, roses, and other shrubs and flowers whose names you will know after you visit, for each is identified by both common and Latin name. Benches and gazebos are strategically placed to afford the best view of each area. At the rear of the garden, you'll be charged by a flock of mallards and one very fat goose, quacking and honking, who obviously live from hand-out to hand-out. Your pooch can get a drink from their pond or from the fountain out front.

A mile and a quarter into the park, past the golf course and opposite the stables, a large picnic area shaded by tall pine trees follows the curve of the one-way road. A disc golf course zigs and zags among the tables, surely leading to some interesting accidents when the Frisbee hits the mustard. Legions of squirrels den in the trees; you may be asked to share your lunch with one. Past experience has shown me they love potato chips. At the picnic area's opposite side you'll find the entrance to Cattail Marsh, a pond about half a mile long by a quarter mile wide. Park at the gravel parking lot and climb the levee to see a variety of ducks and even some large white pelicans. You can walk the graveled road atop the levee all the way around if you like; it's about a mile and a half round-trip. This artificial wetland is how Beaumont purifies its wastewater and creates wildlife habitat at the same time.

The park also has a mile-long nature trail that leaves the park road at the southeast corner of the picnic area; recent rains had left it so muddy as to be unwalkable the last time I visited. Beaumont gets about 60 inches of rain a year; you may find the trail wet as well. If you didn't bring your knee-high waterproof jogging shoes, you can run the paved road in the park; it's a three-mile circuit from the entrance to Cattail Marsh to the garden center and back; distance markers along the way tell you how much longer you have to suffer.

The park has 64 RV campsites ($9), but the campgrounds are simply parking lots with hookups. The sites are not shaded and are laid out on the sardine-can plan. Pay your camping fee at the stable, a quarter mile beyond the point where the road becomes one-way past the golf course.

The park is near the intersection of Interstate 10 West and U.S. 69/96/287 South. From U.S. 69/96/287 South, take Highway 124 south 1.2 miles to Tyrrell Park Road. It's three-quarters of a mile to the park entrance. Hours are 8 A.M. to midnight. (409) 838-3613.

RESTAURANTS

Bando's: This is lite food with a twist: The owners run a catering business that employs real chefs, not short-order grease monkeys (I can see the letters coming in now. . .), and you'll love sitting at the tables outside with your pooch eating quiche baked in Pyrex dishes, chicken salad made using breast meat only, fresh-made soups, pasta, and other to-die-for dishes. 745 North 11th Street; (409) 899-5450.

Broussard's Links Plus Ribs: Sport and Samantha love sausage, and they declared the homemade beef links here definitely worth eating. You can also have brisket or ribs at the tables on the patio. 2930 South 11th Street; (409) 842-1221.

Cafe Arts: Eat at the tables outside the Art Museum of South Texas. See the listing above for Bando's for a description of the food; the restaurants have common ownership. 500 Main Street; (409) 838-2530.

Checkers Drive-In: Fend thy hound from off thy french fries and burgers at the patio on the side; passersby on the street will be greatly amused. 490 North 11th Street; (409) 833-6365.

Sonic Drive-In: Sonic Drive-Ins are the most dog-friendly burger-and-fries chain in Texas. Two Beaumont locations welcome you and your pooch at their tables out front: 8345 College Street (409-866-1800) and 425 North 23rd Street (409-892-3066).

PLACES TO STAY

American RV: This shady park charges $15 for full hookups and provides a special area for walking your dog. 4848 West Cardinal Drive, Beaumont, TX 77705; (409) 842-5060.

Beaumont Hilton: Your pooch can live the high life in this high-rise (for Beaumont), high-rated hotel. Rooms are $79 to $127. Dogs must be small enough to stay in their carrier when left in rooms. 2355 Interstate 10 South, Beaumont, TX 77705; (409) 842-3600 or (800) 445-8667.

Best Western Beaumont Inn: Rooms are $60. Any trained dog is welcome. The continental breakfast is free. 2155 North 11th Street, Beaumont, TX 77703; (409) 898-8150 or (800) 528-1234.

Best Western Jefferson Inn: Rooms are $60. All dogs are welcome. Guests receive a free continental breakfast. 1610 Interstate 10 South, Beaumont, TX 77707; (409) 842-0037 or (800) 528-1234.

Days Inn: Rates are $42. Dogs are $5 extra. 30 Interstate 10 North, Beaumont, TX 77702; (409) 838-0581 or (800) 325-2525.

East Lucas RV Park: Tent sites are $14; RV sites with full hookups are $18. Sites are grassy and shaded, and there's a pet walk for dogs. 2590 East Lucas Drive, Beaumont, TX 77703; (409) 899-9209.

Guest Inn: Rooms are $39. All dogs are welcome for a $10 fee. 2525 North 11th Street, Beaumont, TX 77703; (409) 898-2111.

J & J Motel: Rates are $25 to $33. Dogs pay $5 extra to stay with you. 6675 Eastex Freeway, Beaumont, TX 77708; (409) 892-4241.

La Quinta Inn: Rooms are $75 to $89. Dogs under 25 pounds are welcome. A continental breakfast is included. 220 Interstate 10 North, Beaumont, TX 77702; (409) 838-9991 or (800) NU-ROOMS/687-6667.

Ramada Inn: Rooms are $52, which includes a continental breakfast. Dogs stay free. 1295 North 11th Street, Beaumont, TX 77703; (409) 892-7722.

Ramada Limited: Rooms are $50. There's a $5 fee for dogs. 4085 Interstate 10 South, Beaumont, TX 77705; (409) 842-9341 or (800) 272-6232.

Roadrunner Motor Inn: Rooms are $45 to $50. Dogs must be housebroken and wear their leash when walking down the hallways. 3985 College Avenue, Beaumont, TX 77707; (409) 842-4420.

Travel Inn: Rates range from $30 to $40. Very small dogs are welcome to stay free of charge. 2690 Interstate 10 East, Beaumont, TX 77703; (409) 892-8111.

Tyrrell Park: See Tyrrell Park on page 497 for camping information.

FESTIVALS

Neches River Festival: Retrieve that chewed-up rubber ducky from your doggy's tub and enter it in the Rubber Ducky Derby held each mid-April in Riverfront Park as part of this festival. There's also music, parades, food booths, and boat races. Riverfront Park is at 805 Main Street, behind the City Hall complex. For information, call (409) 838-6568.

DIVERSIONS

Pick pears with pooches: Snap on a leash and take your fruit-loving dog to Griffin's Farm, where you can pick your own mayhaws (in late April), blueberries (in June), or pears and muscadine grapes (in August). Duchess, a Catahoula cow dog, supervises the operation. The farm is open from 7:30 A.M. to 7:30 P.M. Tuesday through Saturday. From U.S. 96/69 North, take Highway 105 west five miles. Turn left at a Mobil station onto Reins Road. After about a mile and a half, at a sharp bend, it becomes Moore Road. Continue another mile to the farm. (409) 753-2247.

NEDERLAND

PARKS, BEACHES, AND RECREATION AREAS

• **Doornbos Park** 🐾½ See **108** on page 423.

For a flat, open, urban park of about 60 acres, this park offers quite a bit for the leashed dog. Trees provide plenty of shade, and there are picnic tables, barbecue grills, playgrounds, athletic fields, and rest rooms. But best of all, a pond with ducks, geese, and a fountain lures dogs to its edges, where some judicious bank-scrambling can result in a drink. When I last visited, a Border collie was intent on deciphering the trail left by some web-footed pond dweller while her person waited in resigned boredom; they live across the street from the park and have been through this routine many, many times.

From U.S. 69/96/287, take Avenue H north about three-quarters of a mile to the park. The park is closed to motor vehicles from 11:30 P.M. to 8 A.M. (409) 724-0039.

PORT ARTHUR

PARKS, BEACHES, AND RECREATION AREAS

• **Adams Park** 😺 *See* 109 *on page 423.*

This park is large—about 200 acres—but it's also largely boring. Acre after acre of open grassy space is broken only by the occasional athletic field. The streets around the park are used as an illegal dumping ground; if your hound has been looking for his very own couch and you aren't particular about where it came from, you may find one here. If you're looking for a pleasant place for a walk with your leashed dog, I suggest you try elsewhere. However, if you don't mind being in the company of a canine who finds other people's castoffs fascinating, this park may be for you.

The park is a quarter of a mile north of U.S. 69/96/287 on Sgt. Lucian Adams Drive. It's open 24 hours. (409) 983-8180.

• **Barbara Jacket Park** 🐾 *See* 110 *on page 423.*

You can run your leashed dog in circles in this park of about 15 acres, for it sits in the center of a traffic circle beneath the town water tower. Large trees, grassy ball fields, a covered basketball court, and a playground are among the offerings. A chemical toilet is on the west side at the ball field; there's a small parking lot here as well.

From Highway 87, turn east on Stillwell Boulevard and go four blocks to the park. It's open 24 hours. (409) 983-8180.

• **Civic Park** 🦮 *See* 111 *on page 423.*

This little park of about two acres is mostly shaded by large oak trees, and there are a few picnic tables and swings. The Intracoastal Waterway is just over the levee to the east; you'll see ships from big to small parading past. You and your leashed pooch can stroll the street atop the levee for a better view.

The park is at the intersection of Lakeshore Drive and Richmond Avenue. It's open 24 hours. (409) 983-8180.

• **Rose Hill Park** 🦮 *See* 112 *on page 423.*

This park of about 10 acres has large live oak trees and a short stretch of Intracoastal Waterway frontage (hidden behind the berm on the east side of the park). There are some picnic tables, a playground, and a chemical toilet. You can climb the levee and look at the canal, perhaps getting a close-up view of a huge oceangoing ship passing at close range, looming over you like a steel cloud. That's guaranteed to give leashed dogs with a guilty conscience nightmares, so if your sweet dog chewed a hole in your best shoes lately, perhaps it's best not to bring him here. On the other hand, he can bark at the ships and chase them away, saving you from the monsters and going from heel to hero.

The park is at U.S. 69/96/287 and Procter Street. All three highways end here, a bit of trivia that may excite your travel-weary dog. On the other hand, it might not. The park is open 24 hours. (409) 983-8180.

PLACES TO STAY

Motel 6—Groves/Port Arthur: Rooms are $30. All Motel 6s allow one small pooch per room. 5201 East Parkway, Groves, TX 77619; (409) 962-6611 or (800) 466-8356.

Ramada Inn: Rooms are $73. Small dogs are welcome. 3801 Highway 73 East, Port Arthur, TX 77642; (409) 962-9858 or (800) 272-6232.

Southwinds Inn: Rooms are $29 to $34. Dogs must put down a $25 deposit. 5101 East Parkway, Port Arthur, TX 77642; (409) 962-3000.

FESTIVALS

Carnival International–Mardi Gras Southeast Texas: Parades, fireworks, games, and food add up to party time for pooches. There's even a special parade just for pets and their people. The date varies according to the Lenten season; call for a schedule of events and locations. (409) 721-8717.

PORT NECHES

PARKS, BEACHES, AND RECREATION AREAS

• **Central Park** 🐾 *See* **113** *on page 423.*

There's lots of open space for a leashed pooch to roam here—about 100 acres. The western side of the park has trees, a playground, and picnic tables, while the eastern side is generally given over to baseball fields. The southern and western parts are mostly just open grass lacking in charm. But then, I'm not a dog, so sniffing acres of grass doesn't excite me.

From the intersection of Highway 366 and Highway 365, go north on Highway 365 a long block to Gulf Avenue and turn right. Proceed two blocks to the park. The park is open from sunrise to sunset. (409) 727-2182.

• **Port Neches Park** 🐾1/2 *See* **114** *on page 423.*

It was hard for Sport and me to decide what we liked best about this park of about 23 acres: the thick cloak of moss-draped oak and pine trees—some with squirrels—or its location on the Neches River, which allowed us to watch tugboats rumbling by. Seagulls swooped overhead, inviting us to toss them a tidbit. We saw a German shepherd and a rottweiler, both unleashed, searching the picnic grounds for scraps and apparently doing quite well. Soon they were playing "King of the Mountain" atop one of the picnic tables. Despite their unfettered fun, dogs are required to be leashed. The park has playgrounds, rest rooms, and a riverfront pavilion with benches where you can hang out and watch the river traffic.

The park is at Merriman Street and Grigsby Street. Take Highway 365 north to Port Neches Avenue and turn right; go two blocks to Llano Street and turn left; go two blocks to Grigsby Street, turn right, and proceed to the park. It's open from sunrise to sunset. (409) 727-2182.

RESTAURANTS

Sonic Drive-In: You probably won't get a look at Frankie Avalon at the tables out front, but you can certainly have a burger and fries. Sport had her first Tater Tots here, and I may never get her to eat french fries again. Yeah, right. 1201 Magnolia Street; (409) 727-7011.

SABINE PASS

PARKS, BEACHES, AND RECREATION AREAS

• **McFaddin Beach** 🐾🐾½ 🐕 *See* **115** *on page 423.*

Officially, this isn't a park, but it's free, and dogs are allowed to run off leash here. When Sport and I last visited, the beach was pretty trashed out despite the county's efforts to keep it clean. However, dogs don't mind trash—to them it's like the croutons in salad. You can drive on the five miles of beach, fish, swim, camp, or just throw sticks into the surf for your retriever. There's no charge.

The beach entrance is on Highway 87 immediately south of Sea Rim State Park, about 22 miles south of Port Arthur. It's open 24 hours. (409) 983-8300.

• **Sabine Pass Battleground State Historical Park** 🔥
See **116** *on page 423.*

Stand at the water's edge on this windswept point and look to your right. Pat the leashed dog at your side. Imagine it is September 8, 1863. (Try to ignore the large drilling platforms blocking your view.) Coming up the river toward you is a fleet of 22 Union warships carrying several thousand troops. They are intent on invading Texas, for this is the Civil War. You, a few troops, and some heroic dogs are all that stand in their way. (I don't know if the Confederates under Dick Dowling had dogs or not, but it sounds good.) When the smoke of battle clears, Union ships are sinking, troops are surrendering by the hundreds (to be guarded by fierce Southern dogs), and Texas is safe from invasion. You can read all about it on the historical markers in the park. With 56 acres and seven historical markers, this park probably has more markers per acre than any other Texas park. And not one of those markers mentions a dog.

Whether your hound likes history or not, he may enjoy camping here at one of the 10 sites with water and electricity ($10) or primitive sites with a covered picnic table ($5). The park has rest rooms, but no showers. There are few trees and little shade; this park is about history and heroism, neither of which care whether you are cool or not. Also in the park are the remains of gun emplacements built during the Spanish-American War; they look like they'd make great doghouses for Great Danes.

From Highway 87 in Sabine Pass, follow Dowling Road a mile and a half to the park. Day-use hours are from 7 A.M. to 10 P.M. (409) 971-2451.

• **Sea Rim State Park** 🐾 🐾 *See* **117** *on page 423.*

Dogs will love this 15,094-acre park, because they are made to feel welcome here. Park personnel like dogs and want them to have a good time. With over five miles of beach to play on, that's a sure thing, even though dogs must remain on leash.

The park is named for its location where tidal marshlands meet the Gulf of Mexico. Most of the park is accessible only by boat, but boardwalks and photography blinds in the marsh let people and pooches view the wildlife up close. (Tell your dog to bring her binoculars and camera.) There's one species you'll want to steer clear of, however: alligators are abundant in the marsh, and they just love tender, juicy puppies, although they'll greedily gobble up any size dog that gets too close. A variety of waterfowl winter in the park, and you may also spot mink, nutria, raccoons, rabbits, opossums, skunks, river otters, and muskrats. All these creatures feed on the plants and fish that the rich wetlands produce.

The park has two day-use picnic and swimming areas on the beach. Dogs are not permitted in designated swimming areas in state parks, but once you walk past the row of poles on each end of the swimming area, your dog can jump right in. She'll want to. The beach here is narrow, but it's hard-packed sand that slopes gently to the water.

The rows of poles also mark the beginning of the primitive beach camping areas ($5). You can pitch your tent anywhere on the beach you like, but there are no facilities. Dogs who require a higher level of comfort can opt for the tent camping area, which has 10 sites with water and sandy tent pads ($7). Nearby is a rest room with showers. If your canine travels in an RV, as many modern dogs do, there's a 20-site paved camping area with water and electricity ($10). No campsite is more than 50 yards from the water.

Reservations must be made by calling (512) 389-8900 between 9 A.M. and 6 P.M. Monday through Friday. You may reserve a type of site but not a particular site. Dogs must be kept on a six-foot leash at all times and may not enter any park building or be left unattended.

The park is 20 miles south of Port Arthur on Highway 87. The office is open from 8 A.M. to 5 P.M. The park closes at 10 P.M. except to campers. The daily entrance fee is $2 per person. (409) 971-2559.

PLACES TO STAY

Sabine Pass Battleground State Historical Park: See Sabine Pass Battleground State Historical Park on page 503 for camping information.

Sea Rim State Park: See Sea Rim State Park on page 504 for camping information.

DIVERSIONS

Blow Bowser's ears back: Load your long-eared hound aboard an airboat for a tour of Sea Rim State Park's marshland. The 50-minute trip will speed you past alligators, raccoons, coyotes, otters, minks, birds, and muskrats at a rate that will make him want to acquire an airboat for personal hunting expeditions. (Just think how many raccoons one dog could catch in a night traveling 50 miles per hour.) Tours are offered hourly Wednesday through Sunday 9 A.M. to 2 P.M. from May through August; on Wednesday, Saturday, and Sunday in September and October; and by reservation only in March and April. Adult tickets are $13.50; when I last checked, there was no charge for dogs, but the park ranger said if their insurance rates go up because of dogs getting caught in the propeller, they may have to start charging. He's a funny guy. The park is 20 miles south of Port Arthur on Highway 87. (409) 971-2559.

MATAGORDA COUNTY

BAY CITY

PARKS, BEACHES, AND RECREATION AREAS

• **Le Tulle Park** 🐾🐾 *See* **118** *on page 422.*

This approximately 30-acre park has one of the prettiest picnic grounds in Texas, due to its location in a dense grove of large live oak trees sculpted into fantastic shapes by the wind and their ceaseless quest for sun. Leashed dogs will love roaming the picnic ground before heading for one of two small lakes whose grassy banks slope gently to the water. A population of resident geese gives even bored dogs something to get excited about.

The park has playgrounds, rest rooms, group picnic pavilions, and lots of open grassy spaces. But it's all those interlocked live oak trees in the central picnic area that really get a boy dog's loins quivering. Hike a leg on one tree and, in effect, you've done it on all of them. It's kind of like an Internet for dewatering. Computer nerd dogs may crash their hard drives here.

The park is on Highway 35 at the west city limits. It closes at dark. (409) 245-9518.

• **Riverside Park** 🐾 🐾 *See* ⑲ *on page 422.*

Only about 20 acres of this 100-acre park are devoted to park pursuits rather than golfing, and the grounds are so inviting one wishes the situation had been reversed. The park occupies a bend in the Colorado River, and heavy woods tempt the leashed dog to explore. Unfortunately, only pockets of woods remain, the rest having been cleared for the golf course. One looks at the few huge live oak trees remaining and wonders what might have been.

The day-use fee entitles you to use the heavily shaded picnic area, the three-quarter-mile jogging trail (which has 10 fitness stations), the playground, and the boat ramp. There's also a swimming beach along the river, but dogs must remain leashed here, too. All in all, there's not a lot for a dog to do. One patch of heavy woods had some gravel roads running through it when Sport and I last visited, and we enjoyed a walk through the brambles. Then I noticed regularly spaced clearings, and I realized this was the site of a future campground. The park attendant confirmed my suspicions. The best part of the park for dogs will be a campground by the time you visit.

Still, the new campground will be a great improvement over the existing one. Sites in the planned section will be spaced well apart, totally shaded by large trees, and screened from each other by underbrush. In contrast, the existing campground by the river was totally cleared before building, so none of the sites are shaded. The sardine approach to campground planning was followed, with spaces being crammed as close together as possible. Campsites have full hookups and rent for $12 whether occupied by an RV or tent. Campers are not charged the daily entrance fee. Reservations are accepted by mail or phone (see contact information below) but cannot be made more than 90 days in advance. Reservations made more than 10 days in advance must be secured by a deposit of one day's fee. There is a 72-hour cancellation policy. Specific campsites cannot be reserved.

To reach the park, follow Highway 60 south from Bay City about a mile to its intersection with F.M. 2668. Go south on F.M. 2668 for 1.6 miles to the park entrance sign. Follow the park road another 1.8 miles, past the golf course and over the railroad tracks, to the headquarters. Hours are 8 A.M. until dark. The day-use entry fee is $3 per person. For more information, contact Route 2, Box 124, Bay City, TX 77414; (405) 245-0340.

RESTAURANTS

Diamond S: Sport and I stopped in for a late breakfast here after a visit to the beach, and it proved to be a wise choice. The picnic tables on the covered deck in front were just the place for six sandy feet. I ordered a dish new to me, breakfast nachos. They came heaped on a platter—tortilla chips mounded with refried beans, scrambled eggs, sausage, jalapeños, cheese, tomatoes, and onions. It was a perfect dish to share with a dog, since nearly every foray into the platter resulted in something falling off the fork or a tortilla chip and hitting the floor. I got plenty to eat, and Sport must have too, since she declined a jalapeño slice and a couple of chunks of tomato. 3608 Avenue F; (409) 245-4846.

PLACES TO STAY

Bay City Inn: Rooms are $42 to $52. All dogs pay a $10 fee. Route 1, Box 129, Highway 35 West, Bay City, TX 77414; (409) 245-0985.

Cattlemen's Motel: Rooms are $41 to $60. Dogs are $4 extra. 905 Avenue F, Bay City, TX 77414; (409) 245-1751 or (800) 551-6056.

Econo Lodge: Dog owners must put down a $10 deposit and are responsible for any damage done by their pooch. Rooms are $46. 3712 Seventh Street, Bay City, TX 77414; (409) 245-5115 or (800) 446-6900.

Riverside Park: See Riverside Park on page 506 for camping information.

MATAGORDA

PARKS, BEACHES, AND RECREATION AREAS

• **Matagorda County Jetty Park** 🐾 🐾 ½ 🐕 *See* **120** *on page 422.*

If the T-shirts are right and life's a beach, this is the place to live it. While there is a small park with sheltered picnic tables, a fishing pier, and chemical toilets right where the highway hits the beach, the chief attraction there for dogs is the collection of fragrant dumpsters. To get to miles of undeveloped beach where your pooch can run off leash as long as she is under voice control, follow her pointing paw and turn left just before the park sign. The dirt road takes you to the beach, which offers miles of relatively unspoiled sand and surf. On weekends and holidays the first mile or so of beach will be crowded, but keep on driving—taking care not to get into the dry, loose sand near the dunes, where you'll get stuck—

and soon you and your pooch will have a long stretch of beach all to yourselves. You can swim, sun, look for shells, explore the dunes, or fish. Surfing is possible when waves are high. Beach camping is also permitted. You'll need to watch out for carcasses of the Portuguese man-of-war, a jellyfish whose tentacles, even buried in the sand, can inflict nasty stings.

Sport and Samantha were fascinated by the story of how Sally and I spent our honeymoon here, spelling out love notes in the sand with seashells and getting stuck in the sand way, way down the beach, but they asked me to spare you the details. They don't like mush unless it's the kind you can eat.

The park is at the mouth of the Colorado River, at the end of F.M. 2031 about six and a half miles south of the town of Matagorda. It's open 24 hours. (409) 863-7861.

PLACES TO STAY

Matagorda County Jetty Park: See Matagorda County Jetty Park on oage 507 for camping information.

DIVERSIONS

Lock up your Lassie: Show your nautical pooch how barge traffic on the Gulf Intracoastal Waterway crosses the Colorado River via a system of locks. Dogs will go Wowza! when they see giant ships raised and lowered as if by magic.

From Highway 60 and F.M. 2031, travel south on F.M. 2031 one block and turn right onto Matagorda Street (there's no sign). Follow the street 4,000 feet (that's what the sign says) to the entrance. (409) 863-7842.

MONTGOMERY COUNTY

NATIONAL FORESTS

See the National and State Forests/State Wildlife Management Areas chapter starting on page 621 for important information and safety tips on visiting these areas with your dog.

• **Sam Houston National Forest** 🐾🐾🐾 🦴 🐕
See page 623 for a description of Sam Houston National Forest.

CONROE

PARKS, BEACHES, AND RECREATION AREAS

• **City VFW Park** 🐾 *See* **121** *on page 422.*
Sport was getting that desperate look on her face as we cruised along Interstate 45 heading north from Houston. This was a dog in dire need of

dewatering. Fortunately, this approximately 15-acre park lies right along-side the freeway. Even better, it's heavily shaded by pine and oak trees and has walking paths and picnic tables. To cap it off, a squirrel darted across the road in front of the car as we pulled in. I almost had to remind Sport what we were here for, but after about three steps in the direction of the tree the squirrel had shot up, nature issued a clarion call that could not be ignored. Came the flood, and the squirrel was better off safely up a tree.

A large children's playground occupies the southwestern part of the park, and there are tennis courts on the southeast corner. Sport gave the park dewclaws up for the large number of squirrels flitting about. I hate parks with squirrels. It's heartbreaking to have to order a big dog who loves hunting more than anything else to get into the car and drive off with her glued to the window whining to get out and chase squirrels.

From Interstate 45, take the Highway 105 exit. Head north on the access road on the east side of the freeway half a mile to Seamands Street. Turn right and go one block to Parkwood Street; turn right into the park. The park closes at dark-thirty. (That's Texas parlance for 30 minutes after dark.) (409) 760-4686.

• **W. Goodrich Jones State Forest** 🐾🐾🐾 *See* **122** *on page 422.*
The part of this forest south of F.M. 1488 has a pond with ducks and geese, a picnic area, and a nature trail. North of the highway is the mile-long Sweetleaf Nature Trail. Pick up a trail guide and a key to the gate at the Texas Forest Service office one mile east of the entrance. If the office is closed, you can park across F.M. 1488 from the trail entrance and walk in.

The trail begins 0.4 miles inside the gate, at a parking area with a picnic table. Walk north along the fence, cross a wooden footbridge, and 50 yards beyond bear right to the beginning of the trail. Waterproof shoes are recommended. Sixty numbered posts along the trail are keyed to the trail guide. You'll learn to identify numerous trees, including winged elm, black gum, and bald cypress, also called the "casket tree" because of the wood's rot-resistant qualities. Sport's favorites were the dogwood and the farkleberry. Yes, there really is such a tree. I think of it as the sacred tree of Samantha, the gas-producing dog. If you don't know how to recognize poison ivy, spend a few extra minutes at number 43. You'll soon have the itch to move on.

For more information, see page 623 in the National and State Forests/State Wildlife Management Areas chapter.

RESTAURANTS

Annie's Country Store: First it was mini-grocery stores inside service stations (or service stations outside mini-grocery stores); now it's all that plus fast food restaurants. Sport and I stopped in for gasoline and also picked up a sliced beef sandwich to share at a table on the deck outside. We could have opted for a hamburger or pizza. Here's a tip: The lady who makes the sandwiches trims all the fat off, and she looks like the type who'd give it to a sad-eyed pooch who could put on a convincing starving act. 2500 North Loop 336 West; (409) 760-2211.

Gene's Hickory Hut: The menu includes more than the usual barbecued brisket, ribs, and sausage. You can also have a hamburger, chicken sandwich, or barbecue-stuffed baked potato. Five picnic tables on the side give you and your dog plenty of seating choices at this place which has a number of regular canine customers. 310 South Frazier Street; (409) 788-2326.

Sonic Drive-In: Share a burger and fries at the picnic tables out front. 9901 Highway 105 West; (409) 588-2100.

PLACES TO STAY

Holiday Inn: Rooms are $75. All dogs are welcome. 1601 Interstate 45 South, Conroe, TX 77301; (409) 756-8941 or (800) 465-4329.

Motel 6: Rooms are $36. All Motel 6s allow one small pooch per room. 820 Interstate 45 South, Conroe, TX 77304; (409) 760-4003 or (800) 466-8356.

DIVERSIONS

Feeling blue or up a tree?: Snap a leash on your dog and take her blueberry picking in June or Christmas tree cutting in December at El Kay Farms. From Interstate 45, take F.M. 2854 west for 12.5 miles and follow the signs into the farm. (409) 597-6107.

MONTGOMERY

PLACES TO STAY

Kelley Pond Recreation Area: This U.S. Forest Service campground in Sam Houston National Forest sits beside a small pond. There are about a dozen primitive campsites with picnic tables, but no other facilities. Camping is first come, first served, and there's no fee.

From F.M. 149 north of Montgomery, travel east 4.4 miles on F.M. 1375 to Forest Service Road 204, then turn and go south for 0.7 miles to Forest Service Road 271; turn right and continue 1.2 miles to the campground. (409) 344-6205.

NEW CANEY

PARKS, BEACHES, AND RECREATION AREAS

• **Lake Houston State Park** 🐾🐾🐾½ *See* **123** *on page 422.*

Do you want your dog to think you are the smartest person on Earth? Then take her to this 4,912-acre park that just could become every Southeast Texas dog's idea of paradise. Dogs must wear a six-foot leash here as in all state parks, though. Even paradise has its drawbacks.

Since all park facilities must be accessed by foot, dogs will soon learn they are superior to humans here—they have twice as many feet. And since dogs get to go barefoot all the time, their toes will be able to breathe free and take full advantage of the soft, sandy soil while human feet will be sweating inside stinky hiking boots.

Located at the junction of Peach and Caney Creeks and the East Fork of the San Jacinto River, the park has 10 miles of hiking and biking trails, and the terrain ranges from flat to hilly and crosses wet areas. The entire park is heavily wooded. Don good footwear and carry plenty of drinking water. Insect repellent and a sharp eye for snakes should also be standard gear.

Sport and I had just spent 10 days pounding the pavement in the Houston area when we first came to this park, and we both thought we reached it just in time. We'd concluded that there were one too many people and one too many dogs in Houston, and they were us. Our first hint that this was a special park came when we reached the headquarters and found that you even have to walk in to pay your entry fee. Wowza! This was a park with potential. We walked past headquarters toward the trailhead area, and before we reached it we heard squirrels and other unidentified critters rustling in the fallen leaves and pine needles on both sides. The tall trees almost completely blocked the sun, and the sounds of crows and other birds rang through the woods. We had found wilderness just in time.

Our first stop was at the sandy beach alongside Peach Creek. Deep white sand edges slow-moving water stained brown by leaves. Picnic tables and barbecue grills stand sentinel above the creek. Sport slogged right through the sand and into the creek, standing belly deep as she drank. She lifted her dripping muzzle and looked at me as if to say that was the best wild water she'd drunk in quite some time. Then we crossed the creek on the footbridge and came to another surprise. The showers at the bathhouse beside the creek are open to the stars. This park was looking more like a first-class nature experience all the time.

Sport wanted to walk the four miles down to the San Jacinto River, but I reminded her that I am older, fatter, and wiser than she is, and we took the one-mile nature trail instead. The trail follows along Peach Creek, dipping and rising as it crosses ravines leading into the creek. Signs identify trees along the way—I never knew there was a tree called the American hornbeam, but there it was. We saw lots of dog tracks in the wet sand, and the mysterious rustlings in the leaves on either side continued. At times the trees and brush closed in so close all around that we walked in a green, leafy tunnel. Sport was in heaven. This was paradise for a dog. Best of all, we saw only one other person the whole time. After a couple of hours, the adrenaline-overdosed Houston scene faded, and we began to feel whole and clean again.

The park also has eight miles of trails reserved for equestrian use. Horseback riders may take their dogs with them on these trails, but the dogs must remain on a six-foot leash, which can be tricky. Only 20 riders per day are permitted; reservations should be made by calling the park office at (281) 354-6881 between 8 A.M. and 4 P.M. Monday through Friday.

Because of the limited facilities available, solitude is likely to be your companion when you visit here. There is a small day-use picnic area at park headquarters, shaded by tall pines. Also at the headquarters are the park's 24 campsites (the number is being expanded). Each has a table, tent pad, and lantern post; pairs of sites share fire rings and water faucets. Access to the sites is by foot only; the sites rent for $6. A cottage that sleeps up to 26 people is available for $150 a day; you must provide your own linens and cooking utensils. Dogs are not allowed inside the cottage or any other park building.

Reservations must be made by calling (512) 389-8900 between 9 A.M. and 6 P.M. Monday through Friday.

To reach the park, take F.M. 1485 south two miles from U.S. 59 in New Caney, then turn right onto Baptist Encampment Road and go 1.7 miles to the entrance on your left. Follow the park road about half a mile to a parking lot at the headquarters. Entry costs $3 per person. (281) 354-6881.

PLACES TO STAY

Lake Houston State Park: See Lake Houston State Park on page 510 for camping information.

NACOGDOCHES COUNTY

NATIONAL FORESTS

See the National and State Forests/State Wildlife Management Areas chapter starting on page 621 for important information and safety tips on visiting these areas with your dog.

• **Angelina National Forest** 🐾 🐾 🐾 ◀● 🐕
See page 622 for a description of Angelina National Forest.

STATE WILDLIFE MANAGEMENT AREAS

See the National and State Forests/State Wildlife Management Areas chapter starting on page 621 for important information and safety tips on visiting these areas with your dog.

• **Alazan Bayou Wildlife Management Area** 🐾🐾½ 🐕
See page 624 for a description of the area.

ETOILE

RESTAURANTS

Oakley Bar-B-Q: Red the half-basset hound guards the picnic tables under the pine trees outside this little cafe, but he's friendly. You can share your chicken or beef barbecue plate with two dogs instead of one. Red's person says he doesn't eat much. There's no street address; it's on Highway 103 in what passes for downtown Etoile; (409) 854-2593.

PLACES TO STAY

Etoile Park: This U.S. Army Corps of Engineers park is small, with only nine campsites, but it has a great view of the sun setting over Sam Rayburn Reservoir, and any dog would be happy to spend the night here under the tall pines, even though she must be on a six-foot leash. The 10 sites are $4 and have a picnic table and fire ring; there is water in the area, and rest rooms by the boat ramp.

The park is on Highway 103 about 13 miles east of Lufkin. It's open from 6 A.M. to 10 P.M. (409) 384-5716.

NACOGDOCHES

PARKS, BEACHES, AND RECREATION AREAS

• **Banita Park North** 🐾 *See* **124** *on page 423.*

If you need to work out a few kinks in your legs from too many miles in the car, bring your leashed pooch to this 10-acre park. It has a half-mile exercise trail that allows you to perform a fitness self-test by seeing how far you can walk and/or jog in 12 minutes. Dogs don't really care how far you can walk, or how fast, as long as you can make it from the pantry to their food bowl before they can bark twice. Large pecan trees shade most of the park, which has a playground, rest rooms, tennis courts, picnic tables, and barbecue grills. (There's nothing like a good, thick, juicy rib eye steak to erase the effects of all that nasty old exercise.) A brushy drainage runs along the west side of the park; unless your dog is vastly different from Sport and Samantha, this will be the place they'll vote as their favorite for taking care of private matters.

The park is one block north of Main Street and one block west of North Street. From North Street, turn west on Baxter Duncan Street and go one block to the park. Hours are 8 A.M. to 10 P.M. (409) 560-2926.

• **Banita Park South** 🐾 *See* **125** *on page 423.*

Your hound will whine as you whiz north past this 10-acre park on

U.S. Business 59, thinking you've missed it—and that there must squirrels under those big pecan trees down there. Tell him to fear not, and turn east on East Pilar Street, go one block, and turn south on South Pecan Street. In another block, you're there. The pecan trees hold down a plush carpet of grass, and there are a few picnic tables, a basketball court, and rest rooms. Hounds with an interest in engineering can inspect the underside of the bridge you just crossed. Hours are 8 A.M. to 10 P.M. (409) 560-2926.

• **Mill Pond Park** 🐾 *See* **126** *on page 423.*

Sport and I didn't find a pond at this 10-acre park, but it may have been hidden by the thick jungle of trees at the park's southern rim. Leashed dogs have a shady hillside to roam, but they have to share it with a basketball court, playground, picnic pavilion, and rest rooms.

To reach the park, take North Street north to Powers Street and turn west. Immediately after crossing the railroad tracks in about a quarter of a mile, turn right and follow F.M. 1638 (there was no sign when I last visited) about a mile to Terry Street; turn left and go down the hill into the park. Hours are 8 A.M. to 10 P.M. (409) 560-2926.

• **Pecan Acres Park** 🐾 **1/2** *See* **127** *on page 423.*

"Dogs must be leashed" was the sign Sport and I saw as we entered the parking lot of this 20-acre park in a pecan grove. It was a good thing the two dogs nearby were law-abiding citizens, because just as we stopped, a brown-and-white rabbit hopped out of the picnic pavilion, closely pursued by a small boy and girl.

This park near Stephen F. Austin State University naturally gets lots of traffic from college students, but we saw a number of young families there using the playground. South of the playground is an access point of the Lanana Creek Trail, a 2.5-mile path that runs from East Austin Street to the north, through the university campus, and on to a soccer complex on East Pilar Street near downtown. As Sport and I headed for the trail we passed through a disc golf course, where an unleashed boxer (technically he was leashed, I suppose, but there was no one holding the end dangling from his collar) was assisting in a game. Just as we got to a footbridge across the creek, we met a black Lab, also with leash dangling (the doggy dress code at SFA, we suppose—it's so cool to show you know the rules but ignore them), dripping from a dip in the creek. The graveled trail is a delight, dipping and winding along through trees and brush. Signs identify trees for the arboreally challenged, which definitely includes both me and Sport. Long-term plans envision a flowing lake, landscaping, and trails on both sides of the creek. For now, though, it's just about perfect for dogs, who prefer their trails like their meat, raw.

When we passed back through the picnic ground on our way to the car, the aforementioned rabbit was hippity-hopping atop a picnic table, sharing his family's supper. I couldn't see clearly what he was eating— Samantha tells me it's not polite to stare, unless you are begging for food—but it certainly looked like he had his head in a bag of potato chips. Junk-food bunnies. What is the world coming to?

The park is on East Starr Avenue about half a mile east of North Street (U.S. Business 59). Hours are 8 A.M. to 10 P.M. (409) 560-2926.

• **Pioneer Park** 🐾 **1/2** *See* **128** *on page 423.*

Strong-legged dogs tired of flat coastal parks will love this 20-acre park, which is divided about in thirds: a flat area along a creek, a gently rolling hilltop area, and the steep climb between the two. The whole park is heavily wooded. Leashed dogs can explore along the creek before trying their mountaineering skills on the slopes up to the picnic area, rest rooms, and playground atop the hills. Besides the usual playground equipment, this park offers two special items: an old fire truck and a World War II tank. Regale your hound with a war story or two about how the dogfaces slogged along beside these tanks in the Great War, round two. These things left tracks even a blind hound could follow in the dark. If raccoons had treads like these, they'd be an endangered species.

To reach the park from the intersection of U.S. 59 South and Loop 224, go north on U.S. 59 Business about half a mile to Len Wood Drive and turn right; it's a long block to the entrance. Hours are 8 A.M. to 10 P.M. (409) 560-2926.

RESTAURANTS

Blank and Company: Sit on the patio and have a salad, steak, seafood, or sandwich with your pooch. 207 1/2 East Main Street; (409) 560-0776.

Butcher's Boy's Meats and Delicatessen: Porch-loving pooches will like sitting at one of the tables on the porch. They'll like it even better if you'll share your hamburger, steak, barbecue plate, or deli sandwich. 603 North Street; (409) 560-1137.

La Hacienda: Large, shady grounds surround the patio here, where you'll be discretely seated in a corner with your hound. Despite the name, it's not just Mexican food: You can have a steak, pot roast, meat loaf, grilled chicken, salad, or the daily special. They're especially proud of their chicken-fried steak. 1411 North Street; (409) 564-6450.

Sonic Drive-In: A visit to a small town in Texas is hardly complete without a burger-and-fries stop at the Sonic. Eat at the picnic tables out front. 2801 North Street; (409) 564-7910.

PLACES TO STAY

Best Western Inn: Rooms are $38 to $51. Small dogs are welcome. 4809 Northwest Stallings Drive, Nacogdoches, TX 75964; (409) 560-1906 or (800) 528-1234.

Continental Inn: Rooms are $36 to $42, but they may be slightly higher during spring graduation at Stephen F. Austin State University. Dogs are $5 extra. 2728 North Street, Nacogdoches, TX 75961; (409) 564-3726.

The Fredonia Hotel: Rooms are $40 to $175 at this downtown hotel. Well-behaved dogs are welcome for a $10 fee. 200 North Fredonia Street, Nacogdoches, TX 75961; (409) 564-1234 or (800) 594-5323.

La Quinta Inn: Rooms are $60 to $72. Well-behaved dogs under 25 pounds are welcome. 3215 South Street, Nacogdoches, TX 75961; (409) 560-5453 or (800) NU-ROOMS/687-6667.

Stag Leap Retreat: "Dogs love this place. We have two creeks, 15 miles of nature trails, and 201 acres of dirt for them to enjoy," the owner told me when describing his family's wooded retreat. Dogs are not allowed inside the guest house, but they have a 24-foot deck where they can sleep. There's also a bunkhouse for kids where dogs can snuggle up to their best buddy. It can be quite a dogfight over who gets to bed down in the top bunk. Meanwhile, you'll be sleeping in a modern cabin with full kitchen and laundry, television, stereo, and a glass wall overlooking the creek bottom below. The second-floor bedroom, with a queen-sized bed and two singles, is 24 feet long and decorated in hunter green, burgundy, pine, and leather. The whole place is very secluded and private. But the part dogs like most, the owner says, is the golf cart furnished for your use on the nature trails. Mann, the resident Boston terrier, thinks golf carts were invented for dogs. The cabin rents for $85 per night, or $60 per night for three nights. Dogs stay free. Route 3, Box 1267, Nacogdoches, TX 75964; (409) 560-0766.

Stratford House Inn: Rooms are $42 to $45. Dogs pay $5 extra. 3612 North Street, Nacogdoches, TX 75961; (409) 560-6038 or (800) 935-0676.

FESTIVALS

Downtown Christmas Festival: If your hound is still looking for that special Christmas gift for her main sniff, take her to this downtown street festival the first weekend of December. Somewhere among the food booths, arts and crafts booths, and strolling carolers, she's sure to find a Yuletide doggy delight. Activities center around East Main Street and Pecan Street. For information, call (409) 569-8700.

Pineywoods Fair: Good old dogs and good old boys come here for the four-wheel-drive mud fling, but there's entertainment for more cerebral dogs as well—commercial exhibits, educational displays, a carnival, and food booths (dogs think better on full stomachs). Dogs must be leashed. Admission is $4. It happens the second week of October at the Exposition Center, 3805 Northwest Stallings Drive. (409) 564-0849.

Texas Blueberry Festival: Fats Domino may not show up here, but lots of dogs do. There's a pet parade, doll parade (Barbie-owning dogs named Ken are sure winners), dancing in the streets, live music, arts and crafts booths, and—oh, yes—sales of fresh blueberries. Some hounds come with blue gums; yours can stain hers here. This oficial festival of the Texas Blueberry Growers Association takes place in mid-June downtown at East Main and Pecan Streets. (409) 564-7351.

NEWTON COUNTY

NATIONAL FORESTS

See the National and State Forests/State Wildlife Management Areas chapter starting on page 621 for important information and safety tips on visiting these areas with your dog.

- **Sabine National Forest** 🐾🐾🐾 ◀● 🐕
See page 622 for a description of Sabine National Forest.

STATE WILDLIFE MANAGEMENT AREAS

See the National and State Forests/State Wildlife Management Areas chapter starting on page 621 for important information and safety tips on visiting these areas with your dog.

- **Unit 122 Wildlife Management Area** 🐾🐾½ 🐕
See page 627 for a description of the area.
- **Unit 125 Wildlife Management Area** 🐾🐾½ 🐕
See page 627 for a description of the area.

ORANGE COUNTY

STATE WILDLIFE MANAGEMENT AREAS

See the National and State Forests/State Wildlife Management Areas chapter starting on page 621 for important information and safety tips on visiting these areas with your dog.

- **Unit 129 Wildlife Management Area** 🐾🐾½ 🐕
See page 628 for a description of the area.

ORANGE

PLACES TO STAY

Best Western: All dogs are welcome, but be forewarned: The manager is a cat lover. Rooms are $59. 2630 Interstate 10 West, Orange, TX 77630; (409) 883-6616 or (800) 528-1234.

Days Inn: Rooms are $50. Dogs must put up a $5 to $10 deposit. 4301 27th Street, Orange TX 77630; (409) 883-9981 or (800) 329-7466.

Holiday Inn Express: Rooms are $65. Dogs pay $10. 2900 Interstate 10, Orange, TX 77632; (409) 988-0110 or (800) 465-4329.

Motel 6: Rooms are $32. All Motel 6s allow one small pooch per room. 4407 27th Street, Orange, TX 77632; (409) 883-4891 or (800) 466-8356.

Oak Leaf Campground: This campground has a fishing lake, pool, and hiking trails on its 60 acres. Dogs must be leashed and must be kept inside at night. RV sites are $17. 6900 Oak Leaf Drive, Orange, TX 77630; (409) 886-4082.

Ramada Inn: Rooms are $66. All dogs are welcome at no charge. 2610 Interstate 10 West, Orange, TX 77632; (409) 883-0231 or (800) 635-5312.

VIDOR

PARKS, BEACHES, AND RECREATION AREAS

• **Claiborne West Park** 🐾🐾½ *See* 🐾 *on page 423.*

This 453-acre park is the only one in the county worth talking about, but it's a dandy. Easy access from Interstate 10, tall pines, hiking trails, and the waters of Cow Bayou combine to make this a park dogs will love. Then when they discover the park has five miles of trails, they'll howl "howlelujah!"

For people, there are playgrounds, a disc golf course, a baseball field, and a primitive campground. Sites are located in a dense stand of pine trees near the baseball field; rest rooms are across the road. Sites rent for $3 and must be reserved by calling (409) 745-2255.

Just after you enter the park, a small office building on your right hides the beginning of the Armadillo Amble, a trail along Cow Bayou. A hundred yards farther on is a fishing pond stocked twice a year with trout; you're allowed to keep five per day if you can catch them. From the pond for the next quarter of a mile, picnic tables sit in the shade of tall pines and other trees, many of which have signs identifying them. If your dog has been wondering whether he's been hiking his leg on a mockernut hickory or a Shumard oak, this is his chance to find out.

Sport and I hiked a portion of the Armadillo Amble, which passes by the southern end of the fishing pond. A rude bridge arches the flood of

Cow Bayou (with apologies to Ralph Waldo Emerson); on the other side, the trail divides. Both trails take you through a swampy bottomland of pines and mixed hardwoods. Sport and I saw tracks and other evidence of dogs, raccoons, and opossums. Then a light mist turned into a serious rain, and we retraced our footsteps past the pond, where die-hard fishers were angling away, hoping to have trout for dinner. Sport prefers catfish herself—fried.

To reach the park, take the F.M. 1442 exit off Interstate 10 and go west on the two-way frontage road on the north side of the highway about two and a half miles to the park entrance. The office is open from 7:30 A.M. to 4 P.M. weekdays year-round. The park opens at 7:30 A.M. every day. It closes at 7 P.M. from November 1 through March 1, at 8 P.M. during March, and at 9 P.M. from April 1 through October 31. (409) 745-2255.

PLACES TO STAY

Claiborne West Park: See Claiborne West Park on page 518 for camping information.

POLK COUNTY

CORRIGAN

PARKS, BEACHES, AND RECREATION AREAS

• **Bull Creek Woodland Trail** 🐾🐾 *See 130 on page 423.*

Leashed dogs traveling U.S. 287 will welcome a rest stop at this 1.5-mile trail through a dense stand of pines and mixed hardwoods. The trail loops from a parking lot alongside the highway and travels both banks of the creek; it's an easy hike. Footbridges cross the creek and swampy areas. Signs identify trees along the way, so by the time your pooch makes the circuit, he'll be ready to qualify as a junior forester. Or perhaps as a champion hiker. Of legs.

The trailhead is on the south side of U.S. 287 where it crosses Bull Creek 8.7 miles west of Corrigan. The trail is open from sunrise to sunset. No phone number is available.

• **Longleaf Pine Woodland Trail** 🐾🐾 *See 131 on page 423.*

Somehow Sport sensed that this trail was special as we entered the parking lot. From her usual position half in the backseat, half perched atop the console between the front seats, she thrust her head forward until her nose touched the windshield, peering intently into the forest. Usually this behavior signifies she's spotted a dog or other four-footed critter that needs investigating. There were none, here, but as soon as I snapped on her leash, she headed straight for a tall longleaf pine tree just inside the entrance to the trailhead. A sign on the tree said it was "born" about 1772. This girl dog who sometimes squats, sometimes hikes, headed straight for it and hiked. Did she know she was dewatering on a tree that began growing while her country was still an English colony? I doubt it. Sport is a sweet dog, but she's always left the historical stuff to me. I suspect that a tree larger than any other, standing somewhat alone, attracts a dog like it does lightning. The only difference is which end gets zapped.

An old road led off through the forest, with signs identifying trees and shrubs I didn't even know existed in Texas, such as cherry. One stump was carved into a shape curiously like the chevron of a sergeant's stripes, and the sign indicated this was where the tree's sap had been gathered to make turpentine.

But the best part of this trail was yet to come. As we penetrated deeper into the woods, the sounds of the infrequent car passing on the highway faded until all we heard was the wind in the tops of the pines 40 feet above. If there is such a thing as a natural symphony for the soul, this is it. A good dog, a soft, sandy trail, and a treetop serenade combined to make this one of my favorite places in East Texas.

From U.S. 59 in Corrigan, go east 8.7 miles on U.S. 287. Turn right onto F.M. 62 and go 0.4 miles to the trailhead parking area on your left. The trail is open from sunrise to sunset. No phone number is available.

LIVINGSTON

PARKS, BEACHES, AND RECREATION AREAS

• **Lake Livingston State Park** 😸 😸 *See* **132** *on page 423.*

With only an hour's drive between them and Houston, this park's 636 acres don't have a chance. Harried Houstonites throng the park spring, summer, and fall, and many bring their leashed dogs with them.

Frankly, Sport and I would rather wander the woods of the national forests nearby, camping where nightfall or the mood catches us, but then we don't require electric fans, air conditioners, satellite television, or all the other things some campers burden themselves with.

The trails in the park were a little disappointing. While there are 4.4 miles of paths, some of them are reserved for equestrian use and others do little more than connect the park's camping areas. And when Sport and I last visited, recent rains had left the trails such a muddy, boggy mess that we turned back after going only a short way. We wanted to visit the duck pond and perhaps spot a deer, raccoon, swamp rabbit, or squirrel along the way, but we didn't think it was worth having to take a bath before we could get back into the car.

Similarly, while swimming is allowed anywhere along the shore of Lake Livingston, it's not as good as it sounds. Concrete retaining walls built to keep the bank from caving make ideal diving platforms, but stumps thrust from the water everywhere. The idea of being impaled at the end of a beautiful belly flop appealed to neither of us. In addition, alligators inhabit the park, making swimming even more of a risk.

There are two day-use picnic areas and a swimming pool, as well as a number of playgrounds. You may rent paddleboats at the park store, and a stable offers guided horseback rides; call (409) 967-5032. Anglers may drown worms all night at the lighted fishing pier at the park store.

Camping, however, remains this park's chief attraction, and according to one park ranger, Houstonites battle to get their favorite site. It's easy to see why—they vary widely in appeal (the campsites, not the Houstonites). Perhaps my least favorite were the sites numbered 98 to 147. While tall pines shade all the sites, they are quite closely spaced and have little or no screening vegetation between them. In addition, the low ground was quite wet when Sport and I last visited, pretty much restricting activity to the parking pad, tent pad, and picnic table. These sites have water and electricity and rent for $11.

Somewhat more appealing were the tent sites, lettered A to P, that sit atop a knoll with a nice view of the lake. These water-only sites rent for $8. The rest of the sites in the park are a mixed bag, with each of three camping loops having some good sites and some not-so-good ones. While some are very large and well screened from other sites, others are so close together as to make one wonder if one would be better off camping in the front yard at home. All these sites except numbers 50 to 71 have water and electricity and rent for $11. The exceptions are dubbed premium sites for two reasons: they have full RV hookups and are on the lakefront, with beautiful views of the water. Here at least you have the option of looking at something besides your neighbor's dog getting into their garbage bag.

Ordinarily Sport and I don't care much for the screened shelters at state parks, partly because dogs are not allowed inside and partly because they lack the aesthetic appeal so important to large hounds. Therefore, we were pleasantly surprised to find the 10 shelters here resembled rustic cabins. Perched on a point jutting into the lake, the cabins have wood walkways connecting them; some have little decks with real brick barbecue pits, not just plate steel grills. And, most importantly, some have a porch area that's just perfect for dogs to curl up on. The shelters rent for $25. They and all campsites in the park are served by rest rooms with showers.

Reservations are essential during the warm weather months. You must call (512) 389-8900 between 9 A.M. and 6 P.M. Monday through Friday. You may reserve a type of campsite, but not a particular site. Dogs must be on a six-foot leash at all times, may not go into any building, and may not be left unattended.

To reach the park from U.S. 59 at the southern edge of Livingston, go west 3.8 miles on F.M. 1988 to F.M. 3126 and turn right. The park entrance is half a mile ahead on the left. The office is open daily from 8 A.M. to 5 P.M.; the park closes at 10 P.M. except to overnight guests. There's a $3 entrance fee for day use; campers pay $2. (409) 365-2201.

PLACES TO STAY

Lake Livingston State Park: See Lake Livingston State Park on page 520 for camping information.

SABINE COUNTY

NATIONAL FORESTS

See the National and State Forests/State Wildlife Management Areas chapter starting on page 621 for important information and safety tips on visiting these areas with your dog.

• **Sabine National Forest** 🐾🐾🐾 ◄● 🐕

See page 622 for a description of Sabine National Forest.

BROOKELAND

PLACES TO STAY

Mill Creek Park: This U.S. Army Corps of Engineers campground has 110 campsites. All have electrical hookups; 57 also have water. There's also a playground, volleyball court, and boat ramp. The campsites perch on two promontories jutting into Sam Rayburn Reservoir, but few sit right beside the water. While many are shaded by pines, others are in full sun. From October 1 through February 28, the sites rent for $10 and $15. Rates the rest of the year are $13 to $15. Camping is first come, first served.

There is no entrance fee to the park unless you are visiting someone at a campsite, in which case you'll pay up to $3 per vehicle. Dogs must be on a six-foot leash. There is no day-use area.

From Highway 96, go west 0.9 miles on Loop 140; turn south on Spur 165 and go 0.6 miles to the entrance. The park is closed from 10 P.M. to 6 A.M. (409) 384-5716.

HEMPHILL

PLACES TO STAY

Lakeview Recreation Area: This campground in Sabine National Forest lives up to its name, offering a good view of Toledo Bend Reservoir. Ten tent sites with water nearby rent for $3. Chemical toilets serve the area. This campground is also a trailhead for the Trail Between the Lakes, a 28-mile hiking trail that runs through the national forest to Sam Rayburn Reservoir near Brookeland. Primitive camping is allowed along the route except during deer hunting season. Also off-limits to camping are areas where colonies of endangered red-cockaded woodpeckers nest. From Hemphill, take Highway 87 south nine miles, go east on F.M. 2928 for five miles, then continue on an unnamed road another five miles to the campground. (409) 787-3870.

Willow Oak Recreation Area: This small U.S. Forest Service campground in Sabine National Forest has 10 tent sites with water and rest rooms nearby ($4). It's on a secluded bay on Toledo Bend Reservoir. From Hemphill, go south 14 miles on Highway 87, then east on Forest Service Road 105 a quarter mile. The campground is open from March 1 through October 31. (409) 787-3870.

MILAM

PLACES TO STAY

Red Hills Lake Recreation Area: This U.S. Forest Service campground in Sabine National Forest has 28 campsites located on a 19-acre lake. The nine sites with electricity and water are $8; the others are $5. Dogs must be leashed within the recreation area but not in the surrounding forest. Facilities include a swim beach, rest rooms with cold-water showers, and a short nature trail. From Milam, go north on Highway 87 about three miles. The campground is open March 1 through October 31. (409) 787-3870.

SAN AUGUSTINE COUNTY

NATIONAL FORESTS

See the National and State Forests/State Wildlife Management Areas chapter starting on page 621 for important information and safety tips on visiting these areas with your dog.

- **Angelina National Forest** 🐾🐾🐾 🐕‍🦺 🐕
  See page 622 for a description of Angelina National Forest.

• **Sabine National Forest** 🐾🐾🐾 🐾 🐕

See page 622 for a description of Sabine National Forest.

BROADDUS

RESTAURANTS

Billie's Restaurant: Two picnic tables on the covered front porch give you a spot where you can eat your to-go order with your dog. Steaks, shrimp, chicken, sandwiches, hamburgers, catfish, and Mexican food are all on the menu. There's no street address; it's on Highway 147, the only real street in town. (409) 872-3929.

PLACES TO STAY

Harvey Creek Recreation Area: This is probably the best $2 campground in Texas. The 40 sites—which are some of the largest we saw in any public campground—sit in a hilly, heavily wooded area overlooking Sam Rayburn Reservoir. Each site has a picnic table, tent pad, fire ring, and lantern post. Rest rooms with showers serve the area. Sites on the western side offer nice views of the lake, and from some you can scramble down the bank to the water. Dogs must be leashed. There's even a boat ramp for the fishing dog.

From Broaddus, take F.M. 83 east 3.1 miles to F.M. 2390. Turn right and go 5.6 miles to the entrance. It's open 24 hours. (409) 639-8620 or (800) 340-0917.

Townsend Recreation Area: Dogs have a way of sending you signals that cannot be ignored, and Sport flashed me a big one as we were driving around this campground. About the third time we spotted two squirrels playing chase-me-around-the-pine-tree, Sport let me know that this was where she wanted to spend the night. This U.S. Forest Service campground has three camping loops, all of which are heavily wooded, but only Loops B and C offer good views of Sam Rayburn Reservoir. (The other loop is, predictably, named A.) When Sport and I last visited, Loops A and B appeared to be undergoing renovation. Most of the picnic table tops and benches were missing, and the rest rooms were locked. However, the fee for camping there was only $2, and leashed hounds will get a lot of privacy. Sites in Loop C have good views of the lake, are quite large, had rest rooms in service, and rented for $4. There was even a campground host in residence. This campground would be a good one to choose if you want to fish the Attoyac Bayou arm of Sam Rayburn Reservoir, you enjoy your privacy, and you don't mind roughing it a bit. The campground opens at 7 A.M. and closes at 10 P.M. except to overnight guests.

From Broaddus, take Highway 147 about a mile and a half north to F.M. 1277, turn left and go 3.6 miles to F.M. 2923, then take another left and go 1.5 miles to the entrance. It's open 24 hours. (409) 639-8620 or (800) 340-0917.

PINELAND

PARKS, BEACHES, AND RECREATION AREAS

• **San Augustine Park** 🐾 🐾 *See* **133** *on page 423.*

There's only one way to describe this park: Water Dog Heaven. While dogs are required to be on a six-foot leash, it's possible for them to be within six feet of the water at all times. The park has 100 campsites, and most of them are just feet from the water's edge at normal lake levels. (Trivia hounds will be fascinated to know that Sam Rayburn Reservoir is the largest lake completely within the borders of the state.) There's also a 1.2-mile nature trail with numbered posts keyed to a free brochure available at the gate. Appropriately, stop number 1 on the trail acquaints you with one of East Texas's most notable and beautiful plants, the dogwood (what else?). This trail is particularly beautiful in spring, when the dogwood is in bloom. The broad, leaf-covered trail loops through a promontory jutting into the lake. Tall pines and hardwoods harbor numerous squirrels; birdcalls ring through the forest.

The campsites have water and electricity, a picnic table, lantern post, and fire ring; all are shaded by pine trees and, except for numbers 89 through 100, are served by a rest room with showers. A composting toilet serves those sites. From October 1 through February 28, the sites rent for $10 and $12. Rates the rest of the year are $12 and $14. Reservations are strongly recommended during the summer months and on major holidays. Call (800) 284-2267. There is a $6.50 service charge, but you can reserve a particular campsite if you choose.

There is no entrance fee to the park for campers or for picnicking outside the camping area, but to visit someone at a campsite the charge is $1 per person up to a maximum of $3.

To reach the park, take F.M. 83 west from U.S. 96 in Pineland. Go 5.3 miles to F.M. 1751, then turn south and go four miles to the entrance. The park is closed from 10 P.M. to 6 A.M. except to overnight guests. (409) 384-5716.

PLACES TO STAY

San Augustine Park: See San Augustine Park above for camping information.

SAN JACINTO COUNTY

NATIONAL FORESTS

See the National and State Forests/State Wildlife Management Areas chapter starting on page 621 for important information and safety tips on visiting these areas with your dog.

• **Sam Houston National Forest** 🐾🐾🐾 🐾 🐕

See page 623 for a description of Sam Houston National Forest.

COLDSPRING

PARKS, BEACHES, AND RECREATION AREAS

• **Big Creek Scenic Area** 🐾🐾🐾 *See* **134** *on page* 422.

This is, paws down, one of the best areas in Texas to take a hiking hound. Located in Sam Houston National Forest, the area is an access point for the 140-mile-long Lone Star Hiking Trail, one of only two such in the state to achieve National Recreation Trail status. Of course, not every dog (or human) is up for 140-mile hikes. Happily, the Big Creek Scenic Area is also the trailhead for four shorter trails looping off the mother of Texas trails. All pass through an area with some of the biggest pine trees Sport and I saw in East Texas—and we looked at a bunch.

An information board at the parking lot and another a hundred yards into the woods, across a small creek, detail the trails. Keep in mind that the distances shown on the information boards are one way. The Magnolia Loop is about a mile long round-trip. The Pine Loop is a mile and a half from parking lot to parking lot. The White Oak Loop will put about two miles on your pedometer, and the Big Creek Loop will rack up just over three miles. The Lone Star Hiking Trail will take you to the Double Lake Recreation Area five miles to the north, a good day hike, especially if you and a friend can bring two vehicles and shuttle back here to pick up your car. Or you can overnight at Double Lake and make a two-day trip. It's a good chance to let your dog learn about backpacking by carrying his own food, water, and nighttime snuggle toy.

Sport and I hiked south on the Lone Star Hiking Trail for a distance, since we had a little time. The trail is built atop an old roadbed for the trains that hauled cut timber from the forest years ago. It's dry, soft sand covered in pine needles. Undergrowth crowds in from both sides, giving the impression of walking in a green tunnel. Sport and I kept hearing things move in the woods, but we couldn't see what they were. According to an information board, it could have been several things besides deer: raccoons, box turtles, beavers, or gray squirrels. Bird life includes pileated woodpeckers (we could hear them beating their brains out on tree trunks, sounding like little feathered machine guns), belted king-fishers, and barred owls. You may, to your surprise, run into a wild tur-key—they are being restocked in the area by the Texas Parks and Wild-life Department.

From Coldspring, take Highway 150 south about four miles to Forest Service Road 217. Turn right and go 1.8 miles to the parking area. (409) 344-6205.

• **Double Lake Recreation Area** 🐾🐾 *See* **135** *on page 422.*

Even though it's more developed than most, this is still one of the best of the U.S. Forest Service campgrounds in Sam Houston National Forest. It's built around Double Lake (really only a single lake—figure that one out), which is stocked with bass, bream, and catfish. Have your pooch bring her fishing pole as well as her leash. The lake has a swim-ming beach where dogs are banned, but elsewhere on the lake—like from your campsite—the water is just feet away and dogs can wade on leash. A two-mile paved walking trail circles the lake; hide in the photo blind on the north end and take candid shots of unsuspecting dogs on the trail. There are also two picnic areas, one near the swim beach (dogs are banned here) and one on the opposite side of the lake at the dam.

The 49 campsites here are some of the best in East Texas. Large, shaded, and private, many of them back up to the water's edge, and the others are just across the road. These back up to the forest; both water- and tree-loving dogs can have it their way here. Campsites with water nearby rent for $7 plus a $2 per day parking fee for vehicles. Water and electric sites are $12 plus the $2 parking fee; full hookups are $15 plus the $2. Only the group campsites can be reserved; call (409) 653-4266.

The 140-mile-long Lone Star Hiking Trail runs through the area and connects to the Big Creek Scenic Area five miles to the south. There is no camping area at the Big Creek Scenic Area; you can leave your vehicle there, hike here to overnight, and return the next day to pick up your car.

From Coldspring, take Highway 150 south about a mile to Forest Ser-vice Road 210. Turn left at the sign and follow the road about half a mile to the self-service fee station. The area opens at 7 A.M. and closes at 10 P.M. except to campers. (409) 344-6205.

RESTAURANTS

Subway: We had to walk over a dog to get in the door of this sand-wich shop, so we were not surprised when the owners told us they love dogs and welcome them to eat on the deck out front. Bowls of water are provided on request, but the resident dog takes care of all little slip-ups that occur in the making of meatball sandwiches. There are no street addresses in Coldspring; the restaurant is at the intersection of Highway 156 and Highway 150. (409) 653-2100.

PLACES TO STAY

Double Lake Recreation Area: See Double Lake Recreation Area on page 527 for camping information.

SHELBY COUNTY

NATIONAL FORESTS

See the National and State Forests/State Wildlife Management Areas chapter starting on page 621 for important information and safety tips on visiting these areas with your dog.

• **Sabine National Forest** 🐾🐾🐾 🔸 🐕
See page 622 for a description of Sabine National Forest.

SHELBYVILLE

PARKS, BEACHES, AND RECREATION AREAS

• **Ragtown Recreation Area** 🐾 1/2 *See* ❿ *on page 423.*

Sabine National Forest surrounds this Forest Service campground on the landward side, and Toledo Bend Reservoir borders it to the east. Tall pines and oaks shade the entire area. There's a boat ramp, fish cleaning house, and rest rooms. The campground has 13 single sites, with one table ($4), and 12 double sites, with two tables ($6). Day use is $2. A one-mile hiking trail circles the campground and follows the lakeshore. Dogs must be leashed while in the recreation area.

From Shelbyville, follow Highway 87 south about five miles to F.M. 139; go about six miles, then go straight on F.M. 3814 another 3.7 miles to Forest Service Road 132; continue 1.5 miles to the self-service pay station. The area is open from March 1 through October 31. (409) 787-3870.

PLACES TO STAY

Ragtown Recreation Area: See Ragtown Recreation Area above for camping information.

DIVERSIONS

Howl your eyes out: The National Hall of Fame Cemetery of Foxhounds is in Sabine National Forest. The area known as Al Boles Field was the scene of many of these dogs' hunts. Established in 1941, the cemetery had 27 graves when Sport and I last visited. The first hound to be buried here was Champion Dawson Stride (July 2, 1933–April 21, 1941). His tombstone reads, in part: "He gave to foxhunting all that he had. He will be remembered and appreciated as long as the chase exists." Other markers are equally laudatory. "Choo Choo. W 10/19/84–D 9/14/94. Truly a great and producing champion." "Singing Sam. W 8/18/1983–D 7/8/1994. Remembered for his outstanding and thrilling voice." "Choctaw Tough Hound. He always gave it all he had." And finally, there was Sport's and my favorite: "Night Jo 44710-I (Henderson Sport X Sunshine). W 9/1/40–D-50. Grandson of Night Rowdy. He was at his best when the going got rough." Your hound won't be the only one sniffing when you leave here.

The cemetery is about six miles east of Shelbyville. From Highway 87, go east on F.M. 417 about a mile to F.M. 2694; turn right and continue to the cemetery on your right. You'll see a National Forest Service marker for Boles Field on your right shortly before the cemetery. It sits at the western end of a campground used by foxhunters (reservation only). (409) 787-3870.

TRINITY COUNTY

NATIONAL FORESTS

See the National and State Forests/State Wildlife Management Areas chapter starting on page 621 for important information and safety tips on visiting these areas with your dog.

• **Davy Crockett National Forest** 🐾 🐾 🐾 🐕
See page 622 for a description of Davy Crockett National Forest.

GROVETON

PARKS, BEACHES, AND RECREATION AREAS

• **Kickapoo Recreation Area** 🚶 *See* **137** *on page 422.*
At about five acres, this is probably one of the smaller U.S. Forest Service recreation areas—it's really just a glorified roadside park. It has picnic tables and barbecue grills, but it has two things most Texas roadside parks don't: rest rooms and several hundred majestic pine trees. Leashed boy dogs will feel like they are hiking their legs in the mother of all roadside parks.

The park is 1.5 miles east of Groveton on U.S. 287. It's open from March 1 through October 31. (409) 634-7709.

WALKER COUNTY

NATIONAL FORESTS

See the National and State Forests/State Wildlife Management Areas chapter starting on page 621 for important information and safety tips on visiting these areas with your dog.

• **Sam Houston National Forest** 🐾🐾🐾 🐕
See page 623 for a description of Sam Houston National Forest.

HUNTSVILLE

PARKS, BEACHES, AND RECREATION AREAS

• **Huntsville State Park** 🐾🐾🐾 *See* **138** *on page 422.*

Pines, ponds, and promenades welcome leashed dogs to this 2,083-acre park. Besides the required six-foot leash, the only other drawback to the park is the fact that the unwary pooch might get gobbled up by an alligator. Under the circumstances, the leash isn't such a bad thing—in fact, you might want to shorten it a couple of feet. And while the 215-acre Lake Raven invites dogs to wade or swim on leash, park rangers warn against doing so. "We don't like to encourage the alligators by feeding them," one said. Yikes!

Located in the tall loblolly and shortleaf pine forest of Sam Houston National Forest, the park has an abundance of wildlife, including white-tailed deer. The park may be closed in early January for a public hunt to remove excess deer; call in advance.

Hiking, biking, camping, and fishing share the outdoor menu. The park has free lighted fishing piers, a boat ramp, and a fish cleaning station. Dogs love nosing around the latter; handouts are sometimes available, and the smell is always wonderful—at least to a dog.

A hiking trail nearly eight miles long takes you completely around the lake. The trail begins at the interpretive center just past park headquarters. Ask for a trail map; it's keyed to numbered markers along the trail to keep you posted on your progress. The trail is an easy walk, but it will take about four hours to complete the circuit. You'll need to take drinking water and a snack. Since part of the trail allows bike riding, walk on the right side of the trail and keep your leashed pooch to your right. Dogs tangled up in bicycle sprockets are so messy to remove. While the best views of the lake are from the dam area in the south end of the park, you're more likely to see wildlife in the north end, park rangers said.

The park has a large, pine-shaded picnic area overlooking an arm of the lake. The clean understory beneath the trees gives every table a clear view of the lake. The gently sloping bank allows easy access to the water, but remember those alligators and, if your dog simply must have a drink, keep a sharp eye for danger.

The park's three campgrounds are similar in character. Each is located on a peninsula with good views of the lake through the trees. Pine and hardwood trees completely shade every site, each of which has a picnic table, fire ring, lantern post, and water nearby. Rest rooms with showers are located in each area, but the Coloneh Camp, unlike the other two, does not have a playground.

The 127 sites in the Coloneh area are designed for tent camping; they have water between each two sites and rent for $9. This area has a lighted fishing pier and fish cleaning station. The Prairie Branch Camp has 38 sites with water and electricity, a playground, lighted fishing pier, and fish cleaning station. Sites here are $12. Sites are also $12 at the Raven Hill Camp, which has 26 pull-through RV sites with water and electricity. The park also has 30 screened shelters ($18); dogs are not permitted inside but may be tethered outside as long as they do not disturb other guests.

Reservations must be made by calling (512) 389-8900 between 9 A.M. and 6 P.M. Monday through Friday. You may reserve a type of site, but not a particular site.

The park is six miles south of Huntsville on Interstate 45. The office is open from 8 A.M. to 5 P.M. Monday through Friday. The park closes at 10 P.M. except to campers. There is a $4 per person entry fee. (409) 295-5644.

RESTAURANTS

Mister Hamburger: Thick malts, homemade onion rings, barbecue, and hamburgers all leap down the throats of hungry hounds and their people on the patio. 710 11th Street; (409) 291-0571.

PLACES TO STAY

Huntsville State Park: See Huntsville State Park on page 530 for camping information.

Motel 6: Rooms are $33. All Motel 6s allow one small pooch per room. 1607 Interstate 45, Huntsville, TX 77340; (409) 291-6927 or (800) 466-8356.

Sam Houston Inn: Rates are $54 to $60. Two small dogs per room are allowed. 3296 Interstate 45 South, Huntsville, TX 77340; (409) 295-9151 or (800) 395-9151.

DIVERSIONS

Visit Sam: Dogs are sentimental creatures, getting all teary-eyed over such piddling things as their last good plateful of biscuits and gravy. I'm sentimental, too, and one of my biggest tear-jerkers is visiting Sam Houston's grave whenever I'm in Huntsville. (I've had some plates of biscuits and gravy that brought tears to my eyes, too, though.) The hero of San Jacinto who went on to become president of the Republic of Texas, governor of the state of Texas, and United States senator from Texas is buried in Huntsville, where he spent his last years. I put Sam Houston in the same class as Abraham Lincoln and Winston Churchill. They did what they believed was right even when it hurt. Houston's grave is in a tree-shaded cemetery chock full of other historical characters, but I never get past Sam's plot. Visiting him is like petting a good dog: It puts things in perspective and reminds you of what is really important in life. From Highway 30/U.S. 190 just east of the Walker County Courthouse in downtown Huntsville, turn north onto Spur 94. Go two blocks to Ninth Street, make a left, and immediately turn right. You'll see the large gray granite monument surrounded by a black cast iron fence and flanked by flags. Park along the street; a gate on the south side of the monument admits you to the cemetery.

Houston's grave evokes emotions in me totally different from those aroused by another tribute to Sam Houston, a 67-foot-tall statue alongside Interstate 45 about five miles south of Huntsville. The 30-ton statue sits on a 10-foot base and is said to be the highest point between Houston and Dallas. Approaching from the south, you can see it from six miles away. Maybe that's what bothers me about it. It's just too much. A quote from Andrew Jackson on Houston's tombstone reads, "The world will take care of Houston's fame." I'd rather the builders of his monument had left it at that. Take your dog by and see if he wants to hike a leg on it. That ought to tell you something.

WASHINGTON COUNTY

BRENHAM

PARKS, BEACHES, AND RECREATION AREAS

• **Henderson Park** 😺 *See* **139** *on page 422.*

At about 20 acres, this is a good-sized park for a small town. Big dogs will have plenty of elbow room. (It takes a lot of room for four elbows.) The trees are scaled for big dogs, too. There's a drainage ditch through the center, but its banks are too steep to allow your pooch to dive in and then jump all over you with muddy paws. Too bad. Picnic tables and a small playground complete the accoutrements.

The park is on Highway 36 Business just south of its intersection with East Horton Street (F.M. 577). Hours are 6 A.M. to 10 P.M. (409) 836-7911.

• **Jackson Street Park** 🐾 *See* ⑭⓪ *on page 422.*

This park of about 30 acres was the nicest and biggest in town when we last visited, although a much larger one was under construction. Railroad buff dogs will appreciate the train tracks that run along the north side; dogs who think diesel locomotives are howling reptiles who love to eat dogs will not. Any leashed dog—between trains, which run frequently—will like the trees, grass, and paved walking path. Hounds have to compete with picnickers, kids at the playground, tennis players, and soccer players, but any dog with soulful eyes and a wagging tail should be able to mooch a petting.

The park is on Jackson Street one block west of its intersection with Tom Green Street (Highway 36 Business). Hours are 6 A.M. to 10 P.M. (409) 836-7911.

• **Linda Anderson Park** 🐾 *See* ⑭① *on page 422.*

Most of this park is smothered in baseball diamonds, but the northern end—about three acres—is a grassy area, much of which is shaded by large trees. There are a few picnic tables and rest rooms, as well as a small playground. Leashed dogs who bring their people here in wet weather may find it a little boggy in some of the low places, but what dog doesn't love to splash through puddles on the way to jumping into the car?

From East Horton Street just west of Highway 105, go north on Independence Road about a quarter of a mile to the park. Hours are 6 A.M. to 10 P.M. (409) 836-7911.

• **Rocky Creek Park** 🐾🐾🐾 *See* ⑭② *on page 422.*

The U.S. Army Corps of Engineers operates four parks on Lake Somerville. This park on the lake's south shore is primarily taken up with campsites. While there is no entry fee as such, the park attendant was quite specific: If you park at a campsite or at a picnic table, you must pay the camping fee. I parked in the shade at an empty campsite to make a few notes and she buzzed up on her scooter to let me know that was not permitted, even though I had already discussed with her why I was in the park. "Well, you're not supposed to park at a site," she said, "but I'll let you go this time." At the time she told me this, all 100 sites in the camping area were empty! This is just not a friendly park. Therefore, your pooch shouldn't be surprised to find that she must remain on a six-foot leash at all times.

You can use the park to access the water for swimming without paying a fee, but you must park in a parking area, not at a campsite, and woe be unto you if you sit at a picnic table! If you do want to use the park just for the day, the best bet is the primitive camping area, reached by taking the first right after you pass the entry booth. About 30 picnic tables with barbecue grills sit beneath large post oak trees. Many of the sites are just yards from the water even when the lake is low. These sites rent for $14 and are served by a rest room with showers. Forty campsites with water and electricity and 100 sites without electricity and with water in the area take up most of a promontory extending into the lake. Both camping areas are well shaded with large post oak trees and have rest rooms with showers. Each site has a barbecue pit and picnic table. Sites with electricity rent for $16 from October through February and $14 from March through September; rates for nonelectric sites are $8 and $10 for the same periods. Sites are available on a first-come, first-served basis.

To reach the park from Brenham, take either Highway 36 north or U.S. 290 west to F.M. 1948 and follow F.M. 1948 to the entrance. The park is open from 6 A.M. until 10 P.M. (409) 596-1622.

• **Washington-on-the-Brazos State Historical Park** 🐾 👣

   See **143** *on page 422.*

The last time Sport and I visited this 240-acre park, it was undergoing major renovations and development. We'll have to return after the bulldozers and concrete trucks leave to see if dogs will approve. Ironically, although the park is the location of the signing of the Texas Declaration of Independence in 1836, dogs are still denied their freedom here and must be leashed. Fittingly, there is no admission charge.

Located on the Brazos River and named for its big sister in the United States, the now-sleepy little burg was the hub of Texas in those stirring times. Dogs hunted raccoons all night and made laws all day, or whatever pioneer dogs did. The town witnessed the writing of the first constitution of the Republic of Texas (which strongly resembled guess whose) and was the capital of the fledgling nation from 1842 to 1845.

Washington-on-the-Brazos State Historical Park, on the outskirts of Washington, is the center each March for the Texas Independence Day celebration. There's a museum, a replica of the building in which the Texas Declaration of Independence was signed, and the home of Anson Jones, the last president of the Republic of Texas. Dogs are banned from all these structures. However, they may visit the extensive and wooded grounds and the picnic area.

The park is located 14 miles northeast of Brenham. Take Highway 105 to F.M. 912, then drive northeast on F.M. 912 for five miles. The park is open from 8 A.M. until sundown; the museum is open from 10 A.M. until 5 P.M. (409) 878-2214.

• **Yegua Creek Park** 🐾🐾🐾 *See* **144** *on page 422.*

Three things distinguish this U.S. Army Corps of Engineers park on Lake Somerville from its close cousin and neighbor, Rocky Creek Park: a campground with outstanding views of the lake, a short nature trail winding through a sandy post oak upland area, and a white sand swim beach. Of course your pooch must remain on a six-foot leash at all times while attempting to enjoy these attributes. The swim beach undulates for half a mile or so around the camping area; no campsite is more than a couple of hundred yards from the water.

Forty campsites, each with water, a picnic table, and a barbecue grill, line the best beach area, but the lack of shade is distressing. There are few trees near the water, and most sites do not even have the benefit of a shade shelter over the picnic table. If your dog is a sun-worshiper, one of these sites may be for you, but you'll broil on summer days. These sites go for $8 from October through February and $10 from March through September. More to my liking were the 41 campsites with water and electricity atop a bluff overlooking the lake. These offered not only great views of the lake but also dense shade, even though the sites were so close together as to invite an attack of claustrophobia. The other drawback to these sites is the lack of easy access to the water because of the steep, though not very high, bluff. These sites rent for $10 during the winter months and $12 during the summer. All campsites are served by rest rooms with showers. They are available on a first-come, first-served basis.

To reach the park from Brenham, take either Highway 36 north or U.S. 290 west to F.M. 1948 and follow F.M. 1948 to the entrance. The park is open from 6 A.M. until 10 P.M. (409) 596-1622.

RESTAURANTS

RCM Short Stop: You and your pooch can share pancakes (Samantha's favorite), burgers, salads, steaks, or seafood at one of the picnic tables on the large covered patio out behind this convenience store with a grill. It's at the intersection of F.M. 1948 and Long Point Road, by the entrance to Rocky Creek Park. (409) 289-4600.

Tex's Barbecue and Catering: "We cook so many different things, it takes a month just to read the menu," the owner joked. She was only kidding a little bit. Besides the usual barbecue brisket and ribs, they serve a delicious pork sausage made in nearby Chappell Hill from an old Polish recipe, chicken, fajitas, catfish, and at least 10 different side orders every day. You can also order meat by the pound or have some slapped between slices of bread and drenched in homemade barbecue sauce. Eat at the picnic tables outside. 4807 Highway 105 East (between Brenham and Washington-on-the-Brazos State Historical Park); (409) 836-5962.

PLACES TO STAY

Coach Light Inn: Housebroken dogs are welcome. (Isn't that a horrible term? Housebroken. Would a dog break if you dropped a house on her? Well, I guess.) Rooms are $38. 2242 South Market Street, Brenham, TX 77833; (409) 836-5657.

Ramada Inn: Rooms are $56 to $70. Dogs pay a $5 fee. 2217 South Market Street, Brenham, TX 77833; (409) 836-1300 or (800) 272-6232.

Rocky Creek Park: See Rocky Creek Park on page 533 for camping information.

Yegua Creek Park: See Yegua Creek Park on page 535 for camping information.

FESTIVALS

Spring Fling: Brenham's courthouse square downtown turns into a sniffing dog's delight each mid-March when it's invaded by food and arts and crafts booths. There's also continuous live entertainment, and I don't mean just dogs sniffing each other's rears. On Main and Alamo Streets in the center of town. (409) 836-7231.

DIVERSIONS

Publish your pooch: Enter an original photograph or painting of your photogenic pound puppy in the annual Washington County postcard contest. All entries must feature a positive image of Washington County life: No dogs sniffing roadkill in bluebonnets, please. The winning entry will be reproduced on a souvenir postcard, making your dog famous and even more conceited than he already is. For contest rules, contact the Washington County Chamber of Commerce, 314 South Austin Street, Brenham, TX 77833; (409) 836-3695.

CHAPPELL HILL

FESTIVALS

Bluebonnet Festival: If your hound is, like Samantha, the flower of the family (i.e., a blooming idiot), she'll fit right in at this mid-April celebration of the Texas state flower. Bluebonnets blanket the Central Texas hills, drawing city dwellers like dead cows draw dogs. (A common misconception is that it's illegal to pick bluebonnets due to their status as the state blossom. It is illegal to damage plants on the right-of-way of public roads, but it's okay to pick the flowers on private property, with the owner's permission.) The little community of Chappell

Hill welcomes visitors with arts and crafts booths, hayride tours, and live entertainment. Chappell Hill is about five miles east of Brenham on U.S. 290. (409) 836-6033.

Fourth of July Parade: Everybody gets into the act at this July 4 strutfest, including dogs. Homemade floats, classic automobiles, and the Marching Kazoo Band are regular features. Anyone else who wants to help celebrate Independence Day and perhaps win a prize is welcome. Held in downtown Chappell Hill, about five miles east of Brenham on U.S. 290. (409) 277-1122.

Scarecrow Festival: The whole town goes bonkers over scarecrows each mid-October, erecting them all over town to separate you from your wits. In between they sneak in arts and crafts booths and a food court to separate you from your money. Your dog will enjoy protecting you from the scarecrows and egging you on to buy more goodies. Held in downtown Chappell Hill, about five miles east of Brenham on U.S. 290. (409) 836-6033.

WHARTON COUNTY

EL CAMPO

PARKS, BEACHES, AND RECREATION AREAS

• **Rotary Park** 🐾 *See* **145** *on page 422.*

This park has about five acres of green, well-tended grass that would be a dog's delight were not most of it a baseball field enclosed behind a six-foot chain-link fence. There are a few trees and picnic tables, rest rooms, a playground, and a walking path about half a mile long with exercise stations along the way.

The park is on East Jackson Street (Loop 525) about a mile east of Highway 71. Hours are 5:30 A.M. to 10 P.M. (409) 541-5000.

RESTAURANTS

Dairy Queen: Dogs like the hamburgers, fries, and ice cream here as much as people do. Eat at the tables out front. 719 North Mechanic Street; (409) 543-6803.

Whataburger: Sport and Samantha choose this chain as their favorite hamburger place, because it started in Corpus Christi, mom Sally's hometown. 909 North Mechanic Street; (409) 543-1455.

PLACES TO STAY

El Campo Inn: Hunting dogs are not welcome here (you probably wouldn't want a muddy Lab fresh from the rice paddies to jump on your beds, either), but other dogs are. Rooms are $47 to $51. 210 West U.S. 59, El Campo, TX 77437; (409) 543-1110.

White Lodge Motel: Trained dogs are welcome. Rooms are $37. 1403 East Jackson Street, El Campo, TX 77437; (409) 543-3358.

DIVERSIONS

Have a rice day: Rice is more than nice in El Campo. It's the main crop hereabouts. Murals on the walls of a number of downtown buildings depict scenes from the "ricent" past. You'll spot them as you drive through town on Highway 71 and on Loop 525. You'll have to look harder to find others, such as the one showing rice farmers; it's a block east of Highway 71 at the corner of East Railroad Street and Washington Street. Some of the paintings show critters your dog may be interested in, such as armadillos, jackrabbits, quail, and—Sport's favorite—a raccoon. For information, contact the chamber of commerce at (409) 543-2713.

WHARTON

PARKS, BEACHES, AND RECREATION AREAS

• **Riverfront Park** 🐾 *See* **146** *on page 422.*

Leashed dogs can trot along the Colorado River on paved paths for half a mile. Most of the 12-acre park is shaded by large pecan trees. Picnic tables with barbecue grills are scattered across the length of the park, and there are rest rooms.

From U.S. 59, turn north into the park at the east end of the Colorado River bridge (beside the big green dinosaur). Double back under the bridge and go south; the park lies along the river. Hours are from dawn to dusk. (409) 532-4811.

RESTAURANTS

Whataburger: Burgers, fries, and breakfast tacos all taste wonderful at the tables out front. 1120 U.S. 59 North; (409) 532-1208.

9
SAN ANTONIO/ SOUTHERN HILL COUNTRY

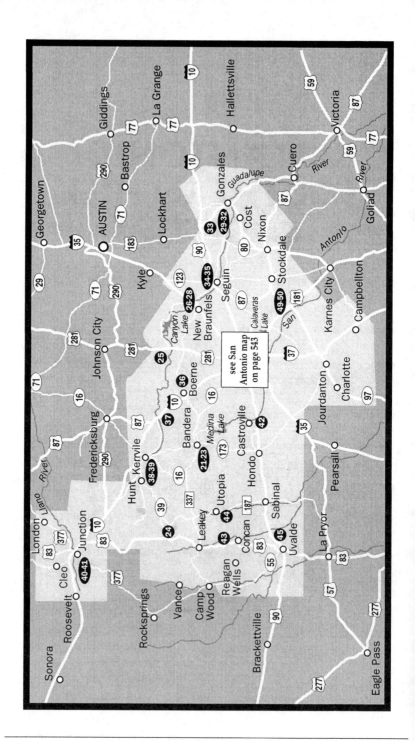

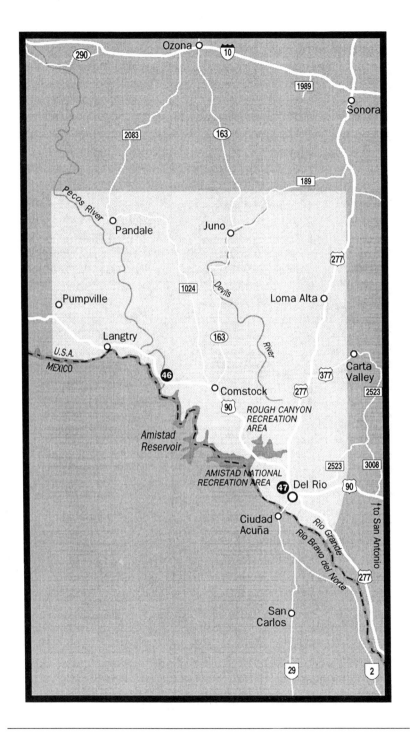

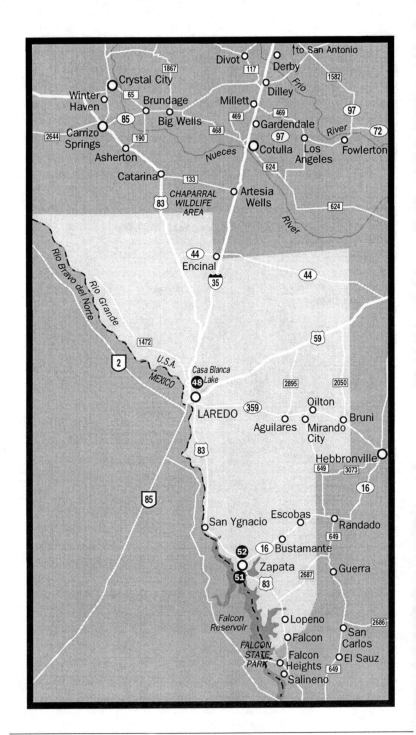

SAN ANTONIO AREA MAP

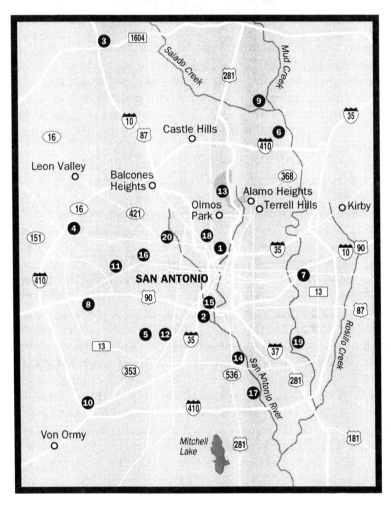

SAN ANTONIO/ SOUTHERN HILL COUNTRY

If most dogs in Texas would just tell the truth, they'd rather live in the Hill Country, where they can enjoy nature but be close enough to a major city for their people to have minor things like income, culture, and cuisine. San Antonio and Austin make it possible for many of us to live this dream. (There are dogs who claim to love living elsewhere in Texas, but they're stretching the rawhide. Texas dogs are known for telling tall tales.)

San Antonio sits at the southern edge of the Hill Country and is bisected by Interstate 10, which itself slashes the Hill Country in twain. Because of its blend of cultures, natural beauty, and history, San Antonio is unique in Texas. That alone should be enough to pique any dog's curiosity (especially if he is a Pekingese). San Antonio is also a city of parks, however, and dogs on leash are welcome at most of them, the notable exception being Bexar County parks.

San Antonio is home to the state's number one tourist attraction, the Alamo, and while your pooch can view it from outside only, she is allowed to visit the grounds of this and four other Spanish missions dating from the 1700s. The San Antonio Missions National Historical Park links the sites and includes parklands along the San Antonio River where your pooch can roam as she imagines how Spanish and First American dogs lived three centuries ago. She can trot proudly along the famed River Walk through downtown and join you at a table at some of the city's finest restaurants. Some of San Antonio's poshest hotels welcome dogs, too.

Best of all for dogs is the fact that San Antonio's downtown is best navigated on foot. Tradition holds that many of the city's streets were laid out to follow trails made by cattle going to and from the river for water, although the crookedness of the trails would suggest the cows were drinking something stronger than water. I'd suggest that perhaps the streets followed paths made by dogs chasing zigzagging rabbits through the underbrush. At any rate, many of the downtown streets are narrow, twisting, and short on parking. While this can be frustrating to drivers, people on foot find the walking delightful, with historic architecture (and pigeons and alley cats) everywhere, shops abounding, and delicious smells wafting from restaurants. It's a doggy wonderland.

San Antonio's rich history and warm welcome for visitors draw people from all over the world. The city began as a Spanish settlement in the early 1700s and became the center of Spain's most successful mission activity in Texas. After Mexico won its independence in 1821, San Antonio was on the frontier between two new nations, Mexico and the United States. Mexico attracted settlers to the vast territory of Texas by giving away large chunks of land virtually free, and settlers flocked in from the United States. Shortly they chafed under Mexican rule and rebelled. One of the most famous battles in history was fought in what is now downtown San Antonio, at the Alamo. All but a few defenders were killed, and the Texas Revolution gained a battle cry, "Remember the Alamo!" Texans remember it still.

After Texas joined the United States, San Antonio became a hub of the military defense system guarding the frontier against Mexico and the Indians, and military bases still contribute mightily to San Antonio's economy. The United States Army's first pilots trained here, and every U.S. Air Force trainee still goes through basic training at San Antonio's Lackland Air Force Base. You'll recognize them by their shaved heads as they walk around town. Let them pet your dog. It's been a long time since they've seen theirs.

But dogs, as we've noted before, care little for history unless it involves old bones. Dogs will be fascinated to know that chili, while it may not have originated in San Antonio, is flavored with chili powder, which did. San Antonio also gave birth to one of Samantha Dog's favorite treats, Fritos corn chips, as well as one of the finest meals any dog ever gobbled, the Frito pie. San Antonio was once famous for its Chili Queens, sidewalk vendors who sold steaming bowls of fiery chili on the public squares. Dogs can only long for the return of those good old days when dogs ran free and begged—or stole—scraps of chili meat all over town.

Note that San Antonio law requires that you keep your dog leashed everywhere in the city. Persons walking their dog must carry a poop container with them and clean up after their pet. Leashes are required in San Antonio and almost everywhere else in the Hill Country. We did find a few small parks where your dog can run free, but for the most part it's leash city, guys.

SAN ANTONIO

PARKS, BEACHES, AND RECREATION AREAS

• **Brackenridge Park** 🐾 🐾 *See ❶ on page 543.*
Somehow this 344-acre park seemed bigger 30 years ago, when I was

chasing three youngsters around it during semiannual trips to the zoo. But even with large portions taken up by the zoo, softball fields, and a golf driving range, there's still plenty of room for the leashed pooch to enjoy a day in what has to be my sentimental favorite among San Antonio parks. Much of the park's charm—for both dogs and people—comes from the San Antonio River, which flows through the park. Its cold, spring-fed waters feel delicious on a hot summer day. Other treats await pooches, too. The Japanese Tea Garden, a maze of pathways, plants, and pools, is set in an old rock quarry. It showcases a variety of plants you and your pooch will both enjoy. Admittedly, your hound may be more interested in the cats hanging about and the squirrels chattering from the trees.

Motorhead hounds—and what traveling dog isn't—can ride the kiddie train with you. Or the two of you can wander the many riding trails amid the trees and brush in the southern part of the park. The zoo, of course, is off-limits to dogs. Sport and Samantha have never been to a zoo, but I'm sure they would think of it as a large open-air cafeteria.

Besides the zoo, picnicking is the main attraction here. On weekends and holidays—especially Easter Sunday—all 167 picnic tables are likely to be filled. Weekdays are a bit more sane, but if your dog is the high-strung type, she may be happier at one of the less-developed parks that attract fewer people. San Antonio law requires that persons walking their dogs carry a poop container and clean up when necessary.

The park entrance is located about half a mile north of the intersection of North St. Mary's Street and Mulberry Avenue. While the park is open 24 hours, you should avoid unlighted areas after dark. (210) 207-3000.

• **Concepción Park** 🐾 🐾 *See* ❷ *on page 543.*

Some parks seem small for their size. This one, in contrast, seems large for its 21 acres. Perhaps that's because the leashed dog can enjoy a number of activities here. Most of the park is open space dotted with trees in which a hound can fantasize treeing a mountain lion. There's a playground where new friends can be made—friends who will fondle a hound's velvety ears and tell her how sweet and pretty she is. The San Antonio River runs along the park's west side, offering the chance to explore its banks. Fishing is permitted; perhaps there will be a rotting fish carcass to be savored. All this is just a hefty dog-biscuit toss from Mission Concepción, where Spanish dogs once attended church or, more likely, kept watch for unfriendly Indians during services. Little is known of those valiant hounds of history, but every dog knows deep in his soul that without dogs, the conquistadores wouldn't have had a chance.

From U.S. 90, go south on Mission Road to East Theo Drive; turn right and go two blocks to the park. The park is open from 8 A.M. to 11 P.M. (210) 207-3000.

• **Dwight D. Eisenhower Park** 🐾 🐾 ½ *See* ❸ *on page 543.*

"This is the perfect park for dogs," gushed Susie Ramsey, mom to Sophie, a springer spaniel. I met them while trekking the Cedar Flats Trail, the most popular path in this 317-acre park. Dogs must be leashed here, but it's a very dog-friendly park, nevertheless. Three main trails—the Cedar Flats, the Yucca, and the Hillview—depart the parking area next to the day-use picnic area. Other trails loop off these main stems, which themselves cross each other, so that it is possible to strike out along any of the well-marked paths and wind up just about anywhere in the park you want to go. For most people, that place is the observation tower atop a 1,278-foot-high hill overlooking the San Antonio skyline to the southeast. The view is spectacular, even though it is often marred by fog, and two electrical transmission lines and a huge gravel pit occupy the foreground. The tower is about a mile and a half from the parking lot; don't believe the sign at the trailhead that says it's just under a mile.

As a regular user of the park, Susie shared her insights. "The Cedar Flats Trail is great for me to run on, because it's paved," she said. "Sophie prefers the natural-surfaced trails, but they are so rocky you have to be very careful to be able to run on them. On weekdays there are few people to distract her from our running, but on weekends we stick more to the natural trails, because fewer people use them."

All the trails wind through a thick forest of mixed juniper and live oak trees, ideal bird habitat. For most of its length the Cedar Flats Trail is level, but about the halfway mark—where you also find a bright red poop container—it begins a gentle climb. The other trails traverse similar terrain, although the Hillview Trail passes across a number of limestone ledges, making walking more of a challenge. At about three miles, it's the longest of the trails.

The Yucca Trail is about a mile and a half long and has six primitive campsites along the way. These must be reserved by calling (210) 821-3120. Campsites are $5 Monday through Thursday and $10 on Friday, Saturday, and Sunday. There is a composting toilet at a junction of the Yucca and Cedar Flats trails near the observation tower, but water is available only at the trailhead, near the children's playground. Also in this area is the picnic area, which has numerous well-shaded picnic tables with barbecue grills scattered among the trees. San Antonio law requires that persons walking their dogs carry a poop container and clean up when necessary. From what we saw—or, rather, didn't see—this law is obeyed religiously. In fact, while walking several miles of the park's trails we did not see one single piece of trash, not so much as a gum wrapper. It's one of the cleanest parks we've ever visited.

From Loop 1604, take F.M. 1535 north about a mile and a half to the entrance. The park is open from 8 A.M. until dark. (210) 207-3000.

• **Gilbert Garza Park** 🐾 *See* ❹ *on page 543.*

This park covers only 21 acres, but Zarzamora Creek has a wonderfully weedy channel as it passes through. Leashed dogs may find almost anything in those weeds, and they'll enjoy looking. There is a paved walking trail that crosses a footbridge across the creek; perhaps there's an ogre or troll under there. The park has little shade.

From Loop 410 West, take Culebra Road east about two miles to Callaghan Road and turn north. The park is half a mile north, at the intersection of Mira Vista Street and Callaghan Road. Hours are 8 A.M. until dark. (210) 207-3000.

• **John F. Kennedy Park** 🐾 *See* ❺ *on page 543.*

This 36-acre park is a good place for dogs to learn about priorities. (It was a good place for Samantha to learn about tamale shucks. She discovered one in the parking lot, wolfed it down, and found it a bit dry. She spent the next five minutes doing that half cough, half gag that means a dog is either going to throw up or die.) But back to priorities. This park sits between a giant air force base to the west, a cemetery to the east, and a high school to the north. It has tennis courts, softball fields, and a swimming pool. You'd think that out of all those hundreds of millions of taxpayer dollars there would have been a little left over for making this park attractive to dogs. Wrong-O. It's flat, it's bare, and the only things for a dog are a few trees, a paved jogging trail, and a soccer field. There are also a few picnic tables, a rest room, and a water fountain. About the only thing of special appeal to dogs are those tamale shucks in the parking lot. . . .

From U.S. 90 West, go south on General McMullen Street about a mile to its intersection with Roselawn Avenue. The park is open from 8 A.M. until midnight. (210) 207-3000.

• **Lady Bird Johnson Park** 🐾½ *See* ❻ *on page 543.*

Most of this park's 78 acres are given over to people pursuits—softball diamonds, soccer fields, picnic grounds, playgrounds, and a children's greenhouse—but if you'll follow Hillpoint Drive all the way into the park past the greenhouse, you'll find an area made just for dogs. A dry creek winds through thick woods around a circular drive with a grassy open area in its center, and just beyond is a limestone hill begging to be climbed. An unpaved trail follows the base of the hill if your pooch left her climbing gear at home. It's the kind of place that would make comedian Tim Allen's dog go "Rhrrrr—rhrrr—rhrrr." Of course, the fact that they must be leashed might also make them go "Grrrr." But this is a very woodsy area in the midst of urban sprawl, and your dog will be glad to find it. San Antonio law requires that persons walking their dogs carry a poop container and clean up when necessary.

From Loop 410 East, go north on Nacogdoches Road about two miles to the park entrance. Hours are 8 A.M. until dark. (210) 207-3000.

• Martin Luther King Park 🐾🐾🐾½ See ❼ on page 543.

Sport and I voted this 161-acre park San Antonio's best for dogs, and Sport was so impressed with it she didn't even try her usual trick of dozing off every time I started singing the park's praises again. (After we'd voted we found the Southside Lions Park; see page 555 .) She was too busy sniffing up every cedar elm and hackberry tree (and there are literally thousands of them) for the raccoon she knew had to be up there somewhere. Salado Creek bisects the park, and except for a clean, well-kept picnic and playground area and a few athletic fields, the rest of the park is woods, woods, and more woods. It's perfect for the pooch who has seen too many tall buildings and parking lots lately. Just a few hours before our last visit, Sport experienced her first multistory parking garage, and after spiraling down four levels with horns honking and tires screeching all around, she was more than ready for the untamed tangles of underbrush and animal tracks along the creek.

From Interstate 10 East, exit on Martin Luther King Drive and go east half a mile to the entrance. Hours are 8 A.M. to 10 P.M. except Sundays, when the park closes at 7 P.M. (210) 207-3000.

• Mateo Camargo Park 🐾 See ❽ on page 543.

Strategically located near Lackland and Kelly Air Force Bases and just across the road from Nelson Wolff Stadium, this park promised to be just the place for a pooch to relax before hitting a home run or joining the Air Force. But it turned out to be a big disappointment. Most of its 45 acres are fenced off and inaccessible, and the rest is taken up by a parking lot and group picnic area. The huge live oak trees shading the picnic area are wonderful, but they are the only thing this park has going for it. San Antonio law requires that persons walking their dogs carry a poop container and clean up when necessary.

From U.S. 90 West, exit at Callaghan Road. Eastbound traffic will reach the park entrance just after exiting. If you are westbound, continue on the access road a few hundred yards to the turnaround and then head back east to the entrance. The park is open from 8 A.M. until dark. (210) 207-3000.

• **McAllister Park** 🐾 🐾 🐾 *See* ❾ *on page 543.*

San Antonio dogs who know about this park either have very smart owners or are very, very lucky. The park was made for dogs. To begin with, it's huge for an urban park—856 acres, about half of which remain in largely a natural state. Two creeks run through the property, which draws much of its character and charm from the wild tangle of vegetation in the creek bottoms. There are wild things in those woods, dogs. Wild things that cross the miles of paved and natural-surface trails, leaving olfactory calling cards (and sometimes scatological ones) for dogs to whiff and wonder over. Wild things that lurk in the bushes, perhaps springing out to arrest the progress (not to mention the heartbeat) of the unwary pooch. This is a place where dogs can win their stripes for bravery for daring to go deep into the bush, while never being out of hearing of busy traffic.

Dogs are required to be leashed, but we saw a chocolate brown chow sunning sans leash near the campground rest room. San Antonio law requires that persons walking their dogs carry a poop container and clean up when necessary.

From the park entrance off Jones-Maltsberger Road, drive past the soccer fields to the picnic area along Mud Creek. Picnic tables with barbecue grills, a playground, and a nature trail share the thick shade of the live oak and cedar elm trees. Farther on, turn right at Bee Tree soccer fields 5, 6, 7, and 8 to the prettiest picnic area in the park. Widely separated picnic sites along Mud Creek sit beneath huge oak trees, surrounded by a thick tangle of vines and underbrush.

A small camping area with eight large, heavily shaded sites would be perfect if the area didn't back up to a busy street. Still, for camping out in the middle of town, it's hard to beat. Each site has a picnic table and barbecue grill. Rest rooms serve the area. A paved nature trail connects the campground with other areas of the park. Reservations are required; call (210) 207-3120 between the hours of 8 A.M. and 4 P.M. Monday through Friday. Campsites are $5 Monday through Thursday and $10 on Friday, Saturday, and Sunday.

From U.S. 281 North, go east on Bitters Road a little over a mile to Jones-Maltsberger Road. Go north on Jones-Maltsberger about a mile to the entrance. The park is open from 6 A.M. until 10 P.M. (210) 207-3000.

• **Miller's Pond Park** 🐾 ½ *See* ❿ *on page 543.*

Most of this park's 42 acres are ideal for dogs. Ducks swim in the pond, which covers an acre or so, and the well-mowed, grassy banks slope gently to the water. When we last visited, clean-up crews were hauling bag after bag of trash out of the woods and water; apparently people love the place a little too much. The park has a community center, a playground, and a paved walking trail (dogs not allowed) with a few picnic tables scattered about. For leashed dogs, though, the main attraction will be the area around and west of the pond, which has some marshy spots, weed patches, and scattered trees. Swimming is not allowed in the lake. San Antonio law requires that persons walking their dogs carry a poop container and clean up when necessary.

From Loop 410 West, exit on Old Pearsall Road and go north a quarter mile to the entrance. Hours are 8 A.M. until dark. (210) 207-3000.

• **Monterrey Park** 🐾 *See* ⓫ *on page 543.*

Were it not for the channelized bed of Zarzamora Creek running through the eastern side of this 51-acre park, it would be pretty boring for dogs. There are scattered trees dotting the open grassy areas between the pool, playground, and athletic fields, but not much else of interest. A creekbed, however, always offers a chance to sample the water and nose about in whatever trash has washed down from upstream. Sport's nose always goes into overdrive whenever she has a creek to explore. This park also has some squirrels and, when we last visited, lots of mourning doves pecking about for seeds.

Dogs must be leashed, although here, as at other San Antonio parks, we saw a number of dogs romping off leash and apparently not in the company of anyone. San Antonio law requires that persons walking their dogs carry a poop container and clean up when necessary.

The park is at 5909 West Commerce Street, about a mile west of General McMullen Road. Hours are from 8 A.M. until dark. (210) 207-3000.

• **Normoyle Park** 🐾 *See* ⓬ *on page 543.*

Is your pooch normoyle? A visit here may give you the answer. The best thing about this 30-acre park is that it is next to the San Antonio Fire Academy, so you can watch firefighter trainees practicing rescues from the training tower while you navigate your pooch around the few grassy areas left over from the parking lot, community center, and athletic fields. Dalmatians will be a big hit here, and you might even meet an eligible firefighter or firefighter dog through the fence. There is a small picnic area on the west side of the park, and rest rooms by the baseball field. San Antonio law requires that persons walking their dogs carry a poop container and clean up when necessary.

From Highway 353, go north on Zarzamora Street to Culberson Avenue; turn left to the entrance in about a quarter mile. The park is open from 8 A.M. until midnight. (210) 207-3000.

• **Olmos Basin** 🐾 🐾½ *See* ⓭ *on page 543.*

This 1,010-acre park sprawled on both sides of U.S. 281 has almost everything a dog could want: grass, trees, a creek, brushy areas, and enough rest rooms, playgrounds, and picnic tables to keep the people in the group happy. By far the best part of this elongated park for pooches is the portion east of U.S. 281. Most of the rest is taken up by athletic fields, a golf course, and a skeet and trap range. The latter led to an interesting time for me and Sport. Sport loves to hunt raccoons, and to her the connection between the report of a shotgun and a raccoon falling from a tree is ironclad. As we were wandering through the trees along the creek, the gun club opened for business, and several groups of skeet shooters began firing at once. Sport immediately began dancing about wildly under the trees, looking up for the rain of raccoons she believed would begin at any moment. How do you explain a shooting range to a dog? If you know, I wish you would let me in on the secret, so that if ever again I find myself in this situation, I can do more than cram Sport into the car and exit the scene as quickly as possible.

The Olmos Basin is part of San Antonio's flood-control system; you may see evidence of recent high water in the form of debris lodged in trees several feet above the ground. During rainy weather, you can expect portions of the park, and the streets running through it, to be closed. But it's precisely those times that make this park so fascinating to dogs. The smells of moldering leaves, bodies of small drowned animals, and rotting urban detritus combine to grab a dog by the nose and lead him from delight to delight—never mind the long-suffering human being dragged along by the leash. This is a park a dog can really get into. Sure, there's the chance to take a long walk among the trees, but what's that compared to finding a fresh set of raccoon tracks in the mud along the creek, or possibly even raccoon tracks with the raccoon still in them?

San Antonio law requires that persons walking their dogs carry a poop container and clean up when necessary.

From downtown, go north on U.S. 281 and exit on Basse Road into the park. Hours are 8 A.M. to midnight. (210) 207-3000.

• **Padre Park** 🐾 🐾 *See* **14** *on page 543.*

Perhaps you're schlepping along the Mission Trail and your pooch is already yawning and rolling his eyes every time you say something about historic architecture. Pull into this 31-acre park just behind Mission San José on the San Antonio River. Behind the baseball field you'll find a delightful tree-shaded picnic area, and behind that, a paved walk along the bank of the San Antonio River. You can stroll along reflecting on what this country was like when the nearby mission was the only outpost of what we conceitedly think of as civilization; your pooch can wonder what's for supper.

From the parking lot for Mission San José, turn left onto San José Drive and then immediately right onto Pyron Street and follow it to the park, about a quarter of a mile. The park is open from 8 A.M. to dark. (210) 207-3000.

• **Roosevelt Park** 🐾 1/2 *See* ⓯ *on page 543.*

This 13-acre park lies along the San Antonio River between downtown and the San Antonio Missions National Historical Park. It's sort of betwixt heaven and hell, as far as dogs are concerned. On the one side is the rush and roar of city traffic; on the other is the serenity of centuries-old churches. Such matters are lost on dogs, of course, who will only be interested in this shady park's large pecan trees, because pecan trees mean squirrels, and in its picnic tables, because picnic tables mean scraps or, at the very least, odoriferous fast-food containers. While there's plenty of grass to roam in the picnic area on the east side of Roosevelt Street, Sport much preferred the crescent of lawn on the west side, abutting the San Antonio River. Recent runoff had deposited a garnish of urban trash at the high water mark, making for fine sniffing. I thought the water was too muddy to drink. Obviously I don't know much about dog water.

From the downtown area, take South St. Mary's Street south to Roosevelt Street; the park entrance will be on your right just after you pass under the railroad bridge. The park is open 24 hours, but the rest rooms are locked from 10 P.M. to 6 A.M. (210) 207-3000.

• **Rosedale Park** 🐾 1/2 *See* ⓰ *on page 543.*

Sport and Samantha adore leftovers, and that's exactly what dogs can expect at this 62-acre park. There's a "mass picnic facility" here, but that's not where the leftovers originate. Large chunks of the park are fenced off for athletic fields and the group picnic area, creating leftover pieces of land outside the fences. While there are few trees in the park, there's lots of grassy spaces where leashed dogs can cavort, and a drainage ditch promises to hold interesting bits of leftovers of another kind from time to time. Dogs will enjoy climbing the many small hillocks in the park while humming "over hill, over dale." (Hill and Dale were chipmunks, right?) San Antonio law requires that persons walking their dogs carry a poop container and clean up when necessary.

This westside park is on North General McMullen Street, but when we last visited, the entrance off that street—which goes to the mass picnic facility—was locked. You can park along West Martin Street at the south end of the park or follow West Martin Street east to North 27th Street and turn left to an alternate entrance. Hours are 8 A.M. until dark. (210) 207-3000.

• **San Antonio Missions National Historical Park** 🐾🐾½ 👅
See ⑰ on page 543.

There isn't another park like this in Texas. It begins at the Alamo in downtown San Antonio and extends nearly 10 miles down the San Antonio River, passing by four other 18th-century Spanish missions. The missions were located along the river so that crops could be irrigated with its waters, and remnants of the irrigation ditches still carry water. Your pooch will practically swoon when she realizes that she's drinking water from ditches that have been flowing for over 250 years. Wild water is one thing, but historic wild water is something else. The National Park Service has built a number of picnic areas along the river as well as a paved walkway. The best part is that leashed pooches are allowed everywhere in the park except inside roofed structures. This means that while dogs cannot enter the Alamo chapel or any of the other churches, they can roam the mission compounds with you. In addition, all the missions have expansive grounds around them where your pooch is welcome.

The San Antonio missions were established to bring Christianity to the South Texas Indians. More than that, however, they were designed to teach the Indians to live as the Europeans did. And since the missions were hundreds of miles from other Spanish settlements, they had to be self-sufficient, raising all their food and making clothing, tools, and other necessary items. Housing the residents and workshops required large buildings and defensive walled compounds. While some of the lesser buildings are represented only by ruins, all the churches survive as active parishes, and visitors may happen onto church services or weddings. Showing respect for such proceedings is just good manners.

The best part of the park for dogs, though, is the parkland along the San Antonio River between Mission San José and Mission Espada. Numerous picnic sites dot the roadside, each with plenty of open grass, trees, and a view of the San Antonio River. The paved walking trail along the river crosses creeks on suspension bridges. While you will of necessity have to drive most of the route, there will be plenty of chances for your pooch to stretch his legs along the way.

The tour route begins at the Alamo, located in downtown San Antonio at the intersection of Alamo and Houston Streets. Signs guide you along the route south on Alamo Street to South St. Mary's Street and Mission Road. The route from Espada Dam south not along public streets is closed from 10 P.M. to 6 A.M. The visitor center (at Mission Concepción, at the intersection of Mission Road and East Theo Avenue) is open daily from 8 A.M. to 5 P.M.; the missions themselves are open daily from 9 A.M.

to 5 P.M. The park is closed on Thanksgiving, Christmas, and New Year's days. You can pick up a park brochure (which includes a map of the park) at the visitor center, or you can request a copy be mailed to you by writing the San Antonio Missions National Historical Park, 2202 Roosevelt Avenue, San Antonio, TX 78210; (210) 534-8833.

• **San Pedro Park** 🐾 *See* ⑱ *on page 543.*

This park of 46 acres is conveniently located just across San Pedro Street from San Antonio College, which is both good and bad. While it's a handy place for dewatering and walking college hounds, its location means that most of its area is taken up with athletic fields and a swimming pool. However, the southwest corner of the park is mostly open space dominated by a curiosity seen in few other parks: huge cypress trees growing not in a stream but in the middle of an open field. Their origin can be traced to the time when San Pedro Springs flowed freely here. Your pooch may appreciate the novelty of being able to hike his leg on a cypress tree without getting his feet wet. San Antonio law requires that persons walking their dogs carry a poop container and clean up when necessary. A playground and picnic tables also occupy space here.

The park is at 1315 San Pedro Avenue about three-quarters of a mile north of Interstate 35. Hours are 8 A.M. until dark. (210) 207-3000.

• **Southside Lions Park** 🐾🐾🐾½ *See* ⑲ *on page 543.*

The city divides this park into two parts, one with 347 acres and the other with 254, but for all practical purposes it's one park, so that's how Sport and I agreed to treat it. We visited this park just after leaving Martin Luther King Park (see page 549), and a squabble immediately broke out. We'd already committed to calling Martin Luther King Park San Antonio's best for dogs, and then along came this park—bigger, with a creek *and* a lake (fishing allowed), with even more trees, and with a hard-surfaced jogging trail. In addition, it has (for people) a pool, playgrounds, great picnic sites along the creek and lake, and lots of shaded open space. We finally agreed to give this park a slight edge over the other one. For one thing, there are cypress trees around the lake, and I have a weakness for cypress trees. (Their knees make me weak?) For another thing, there were ducks and geese on the lake, and Sport has a weakness for those. Which, since dogs must be leashed, she could not indulge. But the main deciding factor was that this park's two parts offer more possibilities and variety. A pooch can visit over and over and not have to sniff the same bush or hike a leg on the same tree twice. Unless he's just checking to see who else has been there since his last visit, of course. San Antonio law requires that persons walking their dogs carry a poop container and clean up when necessary, but the memory—or the smell—lingers on.

The park is on Pecan Valley Drive about half a mile south of its intersection with U.S. 87 Business and is convenient to both Interstate 37 and Interstate 10. It's open from 8 A.M. until dark. (210) 207-3000.

• **Woodlawn Park** 🐾 🐾 ½ *See* ⑳ *on page 543.*

This 62-acre park has the usual assortment of things you'd expect to find in a large urban park—tennis courts, swimming pool, playground, rest rooms, picnic tables, and paved jogging path. It even has a lake of about 15 acres. But something else makes it unique: a lighthouse in the middle of the lake. No, this isn't New England, but there's a barber-pole-striped lighthouse out there. It's the first time I'd seen a lighthouse that looked lost; usually the ships are the ones in trouble.

The lake is actually a flood-control structure, but San Antonians put the lake's waters to good use while they are impounded. There's a boat ramp, so you can launch your canoe and take your pooch for a row. Fishing is also allowed, either from the bank or from a pier. Swimming, alas, is not permitted.

You'll have lots of company on the jogging path. We saw several leashed dogs towing their people around. As at all San Antonio city parks, dogs must be leashed. San Antonio law requires that persons walking their dogs carry a poop container and clean up when necessary.

From Interstate 10 West, go west on Woodlawn Avenue about 1.25 miles to the park. Hours are 8 A.M. to 10 P.M. (210) 207-3000.

RESTAURANTS

The Bayous Riverside: Your pooch can join you at a riverside table at this River Walk restaurant serving oysters, shrimp, fresh Gulf seafood, and Creole cuisine. It's on the River Walk at 517 North Presa Street; (210) 223-6403.

Brackenridge Park Snack Bar: Eat basic snack bar food—burgers, nachos, and candy—at the tables outside. 3910 North St. Mary's Street; (210) 736-9534.

Brenda's Burgers: This little place with tables in front and burgers inside is near Kelly and Lackland Air Force Bases. 5418 Southwest Military Drive; (210) 670-8442.

Burger Boy: Eat at the table out front. 2323 North St. Mary's Street; (210) 735-1955.

Cafe Lite: You'll find sidewalk tables where you and your pooch can sample healthy, low-fat dishes such as chicken chalupas, soups, and sandwiches. 8498 Fredericksburg Road; (210) 614-2600.

Cappy's: Your woods-loving pooch will feel right at home eating on the patio here: Cappy's is located in a renovated lumberyard. Forget that brown stuff on a shingle; the menu runs to seafood, chicken, and steaks. 5011 Broadway; (210) 828-9669.

Casa Rio: Your pooch will be just another River Walk *turista* as you dine on Mexican food at a riverside table. Casa Rio is one of the oldest and best-known restaurants along the River Walk. The people- (and dog-) watching is as good as the food. It's on the River Walk at 430 East Commerce Street; (210) 225-6718.

The County Line: The world's biggest and tenderest beef ribs (Sport, Samantha, and I have researched this extensively, so we know whereof we speak) star on the menu here, where your pooch can join you at a patio table on the River Walk. Order a side of garlic mashed potatoes and brush your pooch's teeth well after he eats. It's on the River Walk at 111 West Crockett Street; (210) 229-1941.

Demo's Greek Foods: How long has it been since your pooch wrapped her lips around a big, steaming plate of moussaka? Well, pardner, that's too long. Head for the patio and order up the sampler plate to introduce your pooch to some new taste treats. 2501 North St. Mary's Street; (210) 732-7777.

Dick's Last Resort: Dogs are allowed at the manager's discretion, and they must be tied to the railing on the outside of the riverside seating area. At least they'll be right next to your table. Dick's is known for its buckets of ribs, shrimp, chicken, catfish, and crab legs and extensive beer list. If your pooch objects to live Dixieland jazz, she may not like it here; there's music seven nights a week. It's on the River Walk at 406 Navarro; (210) 224-0026.

Guadalajara Grill: Surprise! It's Mexican food served on the patio. 301 South Alamo Street; (210) 222-1992.

Hunan River Garden: If your hound refuses to eat one more hamburger, take him out for Chinese food at this River Walk restaurant. Two hours later he'll be ready for another burger. 506 River Walk; (210) 222-0808.

Jack's Cafe and Bar: Naturally dogs are welcome—the place is named after the black Lab whose picture hangs above the bar. It's also fitting that one of the beers served here, brewed by a local microbrewery, wears the label "Bubba Dog." Food runs to the burger and nacho side, with variations from what you'll find at the fast-food joints: a Swiss bacon rye burger and a bean burger (made with refried beans, tortilla chips, and jalapeños) standing out. It's easy to miss this place at a busy intersection, since it's heavily screened by live oak trees and other plants. You'll eat on the deck out front. If it's crowded, the owner asks that you come back later. 2950 Thousand Oaks; (210) 494-2309.

Jazz: Southern Louisiana–style cooking is served in the courtyard. If your pooch has been longing for an étouffée or fresh crawfish, bring him here. 2632 Broadway Avenue; (210) 223-4999.

Jim Cullum's Landing: Southern-style Cajun cooking is served at patio tables on the River Walk. 123 Losoya Street; (210) 223-7266.

Joseph's Storehouse Bakery Restaurant: "Southern comfort" food is how the owner described the menu to Sport and me while we salivated. "Everything is made fresh from scratch—breads, cinnamon rolls, muffins, pies, and cakes," she said. That holds true for the sandwiches, soups, and plate lunches, too. You can eat at the sidewalk tables out front until your tummy is so full your southern half no longer feels comfy. 3420 North St. Mary's Street; (210) 737-3430.

Kangaroo Court: This British-style pub on the River Walk asks that you sit on the edge of the patio so your pooch will be on the public walkway. She won't mind. Her attention will be riveted on your pasta, grilled seafood, steak, or cheesecake. The menu has everything but Mexican food for those who've OD'd on refried beans since arriving in San Antonio. 512 River Walk; (210) 224-6821.

The Laboratory Brewing Company: This microbrewery has a huge patio where you can sample the products of the brewer's art as well as an eclectic menu with items like fish tacos, gorditas, and rattlesnake pasta. Don't worry about it crawling off your plate. It's just a name. 7310 Jones-Maltsberger Road; (210) 824-1997.

La Fonda: All the Mexican food served on the patio here is made from scratch. Your dog understands scratch. It's what you do when you have fleas or when you want the food to be extra good. You'll have to tie your pooch on the outside of the railing around the patio, but you can sit right next to her. 2415 North Main Avenue; (210) 733-0621.

Longhorn Patio Cafe: This Market Square (El Mercado) eatery serves both Mexican and American food at sidewalk tables; there's also an outside bar. 514 West Commerce Street; (210) 229-1072.

Mesteña: Remember all those times you've had to restrain your pooch from chasing down and eating a deer, pheasant, or other wild critter? Your pooch surely does, but he'll forgive you after you've taken him to eat on the covered patio here. Wild game is the specialty of the house. (Chasing down and eating waitpersons is not permitted.) 7959 Broadway Avenue; (210) 822-7733.

Michelino's: Ascend to new heights of culinary delight as you and your pooch dine on the terraced patio overlooking the River Walk. The food is Italian; you'll recognize specialties such as shrimp Alfredo, angel-hair pasta with scallops, chicken parmesan, and spinach lasagna. What you won't recognize is that pooch trying to mooch tortellini from the next table. You know you taught her better than that. 521 River Walk; (210) 223-2939.

Mission Trail Patio: It's a known fact that dogs' appreciation of historic architecture is heightened considerably by frequent food breaks. Stop in while touring the San Antonio Missions National Historical Park, tie your pooch to the railing around the patio, and have some Mexican food or a burger. You'll both enjoy the rest of the tour more. 2906 Mission Road; (210) 977-9726.

Mi Tierra Cafe and Bakery: This San Antonio legend located at Market Square (El Mercado) is open 24 hours. It serves the usual Mexican dishes on the patio, but don't miss the enormous selection of bakery items inside. Have a friend anchor your Akita while you drool over *empanadas, pan dulce,* and other tasty delights. 218 Produce Row; (210) 225-1262.

The Original Mexican Restaurant: This River Walk cafe may claim to be the original, but it serves the same Tex-Mex dishes—enchiladas, *carne guisada,* rice, and beans—as all the rest. Eat at riverside tables. 528 River Walk; (210) 224-9951.

Paesano's River Walk: The menu is Italian, the setting is a patio on the River Walk. All you and your pooch need to fall in love all over again are strolling *mariachis.* 111 West Crockett Street; (210) 227-2782.

Pappasito's Cantina: It's Tex-Mex on the patio at this restaurant where the ambience is as interesting as the food. Big, loud, and busy would be the three adjectives Sport would use to describe this place—along with tasty. 10501 Interstate 10 West; (210) 691-8974.

Presidio: Savor the slow-roasted prime rib or snapper ancho during a special night out at this courtyard restaurant on the River Walk. 245 East Commerce Street, No. 101; (210) 472-2265.

Rally's Hamburgers: Dogs are welcome at the tables in front at this chain hamburger eatery. Store locations and phone numbers are: 925 Bandera Road (210-436-1123), 529 Fair Avenue (210-532-8474), and 211 South Zarzamora Street (210-431-4713).

Rooty's Drive-In: There's a patio here where you can eat hamburgers, salads, pizza, or chicken-fried steak. 847 Northeast Loop 410; (210) 824-5247.

Rosario's: Learn the differences between Tex-Mex and interior Mexican dishes (served here) on the patio at a table next to the fence. If you think all Mexican food revolves around enchiladas and refried beans, the food will be a nice surprise. 1014 South Alamo Street; (210) 223-1806.

TCBY Yogurt: Atone for your culinary sins with frozen yogurt on a balcony overlooking the River Walk. But then, you might fall down those stairs on your way out and die, so you'd better live it up while you can with gourmet cookies, espresso, cappuccino, banana splits, or sundaes. It's on the River Walk at 428 East Commerce Street; (210) 299-1373.

Teka Molino: You and your pooch may never work your way completely through the huge menu of Mexican food here. There's a patio in front. 2403 North St. Mary's Street; (210) 735-5471.

Tycoon Flats: The laid-back ambience of the tree-shaded outdoor patio is almost as important as the food, which runs to burgers, nachos, quesadillas, and taco salads. It's a fun place for dogs and people both, as the name implies. 2926 North St. Mary's Street; (210) 737-1929.

W. D. Deli and Bakery: Tables under the trees provide the perfect setting for enjoying deli sandwiches, salads, dijon chicken, or low-fat pita and veggie sandwiches. 4233 McCullough; (210) 828-2322.

Wendy's Hamburgers: You and your pooch are welcome to eat at the outside tables at any of this chain's stores in San Antonio, but not all locations have outside seating. One that does is at 430 San Pedro Avenue; (210) 222-0009.

Zuni Bar and Grill: This River Walk eatery where your pooch can join you on the patio serves the predictable Southwestern cuisine like fajitas and quesadillas but also branches out into pizza, sandwiches, red snapper, flounder, and rib eyes. 511 River Walk; (210) 227-0864.

PLACES TO STAY

Arbor House at La Villita: Rates at this downtown bed-and-breakfast are $140 to $195. There is a courtyard where you can walk your dog. Small dogs only are welcome with a $25 deposit. 339 South Presa Street, San Antonio, TX 78205; (210) 472-2005.

Best Western Fiesta Inn: Rooms are $79 to $109. Dogs under 15 pounds are welcome at this inn near Fiesta Texas, an amusement park with a country-and-western theme. 13535 Interstate 10 West, San Antonio, TX 78249; (210) 697-9761 or (800) 528-1234.

Best Western Ingram Park Inn: Rooms are $54 to $69. Dogs up to 20 pounds are welcome. 6855 Northwest Loop 410, San Antonio, TX 78238; (210) 520-8080 or (800) 528-1234.

Brackenridge House Bed-and-Breakfast: The carriage house at this fabulous inn in the King William Historic District rents for $125 and is the only room where dogs may stay, but what pooch could object to having her own 1,000-square-foot doghouse? Only small, well-behaved dogs are welcome. There is a fenced yard where your pooch can run. 230 Madison Street, San Antonio, TX 78204; (210) 271-3442.

Clarion Suites Hotel: Room rates are $69 to $99. There is a $25 deposit for dogs. 13101 East Loop 1604 North, San Antonio, TX 78233; (210) 655-9491.

Comfort Inn: Rooms are $49 to $79. Dogs pay a $5 to $10 fee, depending on their size. 4 Piano Place, San Antonio, TX 78228; (210) 684-8606 or (800) 228-5150.

Dwight D. Eisenhower Park: See page 547 for camping information.

Fairmount Hotel: Your pooch will be fascinated to know that this hotel is listed in the *Guinness Book of World Records* as the heaviest building ever to be moved. Yes, this multistory brick hotel really was moved four blocks to its present location and even crossed the San Antonio River on the way! Perhaps that explains the room rates—they're still paying the moving bill. Rooms are $195 to $550. Dogs under 35 pounds are welcome. 401 South Alamo Street, San Antonio, TX 78205; (210) 224-8800 or (800) 642-3363.

Hawthorn Suites Hotel: Rates are $69 to $168. Dogs—pedigreed or not—incur a charge of $50 plus a fee of $5 per day per dog. They may not weigh over 25 pounds. 4041 Bluemel Road, San Antonio, TX 78240; (210) 561-9660 or (800) 527-1133.

Hilton Palacio del Rio: This hotel is right on the famed San Antonio River Walk. Rooms are $160 to $238. Dogs under 20 pounds may stay for a $50 fee. 200 South Alamo Street, San Antonio, TX 78205; (210) 222-1400 or (800) 445-8667.

Holiday Inn Express: Rooms are $69 to $99. Small dogs are welcome. 11939 Interstate 35 North, San Antonio, TX 78233; (210) 599-0999 or (800) 465-4329.

Holiday Inn Market Square: This hotel is just a block from El Mercado. Rooms are $99 to $120. Dogs are welcome as long as they put up a $125 deposit, of which $100 is refundable. 318 West Durango Street, San Antonio, TX 78204; (210) 225-3211.

Holiday Inn Northeast: Rooms are $59 to $85. Dogs may not be left alone in rooms. 3855 Interstate 35 North, San Antonio, TX 78219; (210) 226-4361 or (800) 465-4329.

Holiday Inn River Walk: Dogs under 20 pounds are welcome at this downtown hotel on the River Walk. Rates are $125 to $160. 217 North St. Mary's Street, San Antonio, TX 78204; (210) 224-2500 or (800) 465-4329.

La Mansion del Rio: Dogs under 20 pounds may stay if you sign a waiver accepting responsibility for any damages. Rooms are $230. 112 College Street, San Antonio, TX 78205; (210) 225-2581 or (800) 292-7300.

La Quinta Inn—Airport East: Rooms are $79 to $90. Dogs under 25 pounds are welcome. 333 Northeast Loop 410, San Antonio, TX 78216; (210) 828-0781 or (800) NU-ROOMS/687-6667.

La Quinta Inn—Airport West: Rooms are $79 to $90. Dogs under 25 pounds are welcome. 219 Northeast Loop 410, San Antonio, TX 78216; (210) 342-4291 or (800) NU-ROOMS/687-6667.

La Quinta Inn—Convention Center: Rooms are $99 to $120. Dogs under 25 pounds are welcome. 1001 East Commerce Street, San Antonio, TX 78205; (210) 222-9181 or (800) NU-ROOMS/687-6667.

La Quinta Inn—Ingram Park: Rates are $76 to $95. Dogs under 25 pounds are welcome. 7134 Northwest Loop 410, San Antonio, TX 78238; (210) 680-8883 or (800) NU-ROOMS/687-6667.

La Quinta Inn—Lackland: Rooms are $69 to $90. Dogs under 25 pounds are welcome. 6511 Military Drive West, San Antonio, TX 78227; (210) 674-3200 or (800) NU-ROOMS/687-6667.

La Quinta Inn—Market Square: Rates are $89 to $97. Dogs under 25 pounds are welcome. 900 Dolorosa Street, San Antonio, TX 78208; (210) 271-0001 or (800) NU-ROOMS/687-6667.

La Quinta Inn—South: Rates are $71 to $84. Dogs under 25 pounds are welcome. 7202 South Pan American Expressway, San Antonio, TX 78224; (210) 922-2111 or (800) NU-ROOMS/687-6667.

La Quinta Inn—Toepperwein: Rates are $72 to $88. Dogs under 25 pounds are welcome. 12822 Interstate 35 North, San Antonio, TX 78233; (210) 657-5500 or (800) NU-ROOMS/687-6667.

La Quinta Inn—Vance Jackson: Rooms are $69 to $78. Dogs under 25 pounds are welcome. 5922 Northwest Expressway, San Antonio, TX 78201; (210) 734-7931 or (800) NU-ROOMS/687-6667.

La Quinta Inn—Windsor Park: Rates are $71 to $92. Dogs under 25 pounds are welcome. 6410 Interstate 35 North, San Antonio, TX 78218; (210) 653-6619 or (800) NU-ROOMS/687-6667.

La Quinta Inn—Wurzbach: Rooms are $69 to $75. Dogs under 25 pounds are welcome. 9542 Interstate 10 West, San Antonio, TX 78230; (210) 593-0338 or (800) NU-ROOMS/687-6667.

Marriott River Walk: Rooms are $189 to $205. Dogs under 20 pounds may stay if you agree to accept responsibility for any damages and pay a $25 doggy deposit. 711 East River Walk, San Antonio, TX 78205; (210) 224-4555.

Marriott Rivercenter: Rooms are $209 to $234. Dogs under 20 pounds are welcome. 101 Bowie Street, San Antonio, TX 78205; (210) 223-1000 or (800) 648-4462.

McAllister Park: See page 550 for camping information.

Motel 6—Downtown: Rooms are $46 to $54. All Motel 6s allow one small pooch per room. 211 North Pecos Street, San Antonio, TX 78207; (210) 225-1111 or (800) 466-8356.

Motel 6—East: Rooms are $36 to $40. All Motel 6s allow one small pooch per room. 138 North W. W. White, San Antonio, TX 78219; (210) 333-1850 or (800) 466-8356.

Motel 6—Fiesta Texas: Rooms are $38 to $48. All Motel 6s allow one small pooch per room. 16500 Interstate 10 West, San Antonio, TX 78256; (210) 697-0731 or (800) 466-8356.

Motel 6—Fort Sam Houston: Rooms are $36. All Motel 6s allow one small pooch per room. 5522 North Pan American Expressway, San Antonio, TX 78218; (210) 661-8791 or (800) 466-8356.

Motel 6—North: Rates are $36 to $39. All Motel 6s allow one small pooch per room. 9503 Interstate 35 North, San Antonio, TX 78233; (210) 650-4419 or (800) 466-8356.

Motel 6—Northeast: Rooms are $36 to $39. All Motel 6s allow one small pooch per room. 4621 Rittiman Road, San Antonio, TX 78218; (210) 653-8088 or (800) 466-8356.

Motel 6—Northwest: Rooms are $42 to $48. All Motel 6s allow one small pooch per room. 9400 Wurzbach Road, San Antonio, TX 78229; (210) 593-0013 or (800) 466-8356.

Motel 6—West: Rooms are $38 to $44. All Motel 6s allow one small pooch per room. 2185 Southwest Loop 410, San Antonio, TX 78227; (210) 673-9020 or (800) 466-8356.

Pear Tree Inn by Drury: Rates are $56 to $69. Dogs under 20 pounds are welcome. 143 Northeast Loop 410, San Antonio, TX 78216; (210) 366-9300 or (800) 282-8733.

Quality Inn and Suites: Rooms are $29 to $89. Dogs may stay for a $25 deposit. 3817 North Interstate 35, San Antonio, TX 78219; (210) 224-3030 or (800) 942-8913.

Red Roof Inn: Clean, medium-sized, well-mannered pooches—in a word, yours—may stay here. Rooms are $43 to $68. 333 Wolfe Road, San Antonio, TX 78216; (210) 340-4055 or (800) 843-7663.

Residence Inn by Marriott: Rooms are $90 to $169. Dogs pay $8 to $12 per day depending on size, and "I've seen everything from Chihuahuas to Great Danes," the reservation clerk told me. 1014 Northeast Loop 410, San Antonio, TX 78209; (210) 805-8118 or (800) 331-3131.

Rodeway Inn: There are no restrictions on dog size. Rooms are $50. 900 North Main Street, San Antonio, TX 78212; (210) 223-2951 or (800) 635-4451.

Rodeway Inn Crossroads: Dogs under 20 pounds who like to shop at the nearby Crossroads Mall will want to stay here. Rooms are $56 to $66. 6804 Interstate 10 West, San Antonio, TX 78201; (210) 734-7111 or (800) 228-2000.

FESTIVALS

Fiesta de las Luminarias: Each December the River Walk in the downtown area blazes with lights, but on the first three weekends, more than 2,000 luminarias (candles in paper bags) line the banks starting at sunset. There will also be carolers boating the river. You and your leashed dog can go for a lighted stroll and then eat at one of the restaurants accepting dogs. You'll both go away glowing. For information, call (210) 227-4262.

Fiestas Navideñas: This three-week-long celebration of the yuletide season offers Conjunto music, folk dancing, appearances by Pancho Claus, and a blessing of the animals. Surely your hound couldn't be hurt by a little blessing. And maybe it will remind him that Christmas is coming and he'd better be good if he wants to find more than a used rawhide chew under the tree on Christmas morning. It's held at Market Square (514 West Commerce Street) the first three weeks in December. For information, call (210) 207-8600.

Las Posadas: Dogs will identify strongly with the theme of this traditional Christmastime celebration: Joseph and Mary's search for lodging. (If only they'd had a guidebook …) Costumed players, choirs, and even spectators join in a procession along the River Walk. It'll be dark, so no one will ever notice your leashed, well-behaved pooch. The festival takes place in early December along the River Walk downtown. For information, call (210) 224-6163.

Los Pastores: One of the results of the melding of Catholicism with the First American religions in Mexico was this play depicting the attempts of a band of devils to prevent a group of shepherds from traveling to Bethlehem to worship the baby Jesus. Even dogs will be able to tell the good guys from the bad guys. It's held on the grounds of Mission San José (6539 San José Street) in late December. For information, call (210) 224-6163.

River Walk Holiday Art Fair: Shop for the works of local artists along the downtown River Walk in mid-December. For information, call (210) 227-4262.

Walk for Life: Each first Sunday in November the San Antonio AIDS Foundation sponsors a fund-raising walk from Market Square to HemisFair Plaza and back. Leashed, well-behaved dogs are rewarded at watering stations along the route. For information, call (210) 225-4715.

DIVERSIONS

Pick up a pooper-scooper: Probably the most ignored city ordinance in San Antonio is the one requiring persons walking their dogs to carry a pooper-scooper with them and to use it, but you don't want to risk being caught up in a crackdown on non-scoopers. Take your dog to PetsMart and let her help you pick out that special tool. They have a selection ranging from cardboard disposable models to industrial-strength, Saint Bernard–sized steel dung movers. PetsMart stores in San Antonio are at 12960 Park Central (210-545-6875), 8520 Fourwinds Drive (210-590-0393), and 6055 La Cima (210-523-7995).

Pretend to be a rich dog: San Antonio's elite of a century ago—and their dogs—lived in the King William Historic District just south of downtown. Many of the homes have been restored, and a walk through the neighborhood will make any dog want to move into a plush dog-house with maid service. Maybe taking your dog here is not a good idea. Or maybe you can just click your ruby slippers three times and say, "There's no place like home. There's no place like home." The King William Historic District begins at the corner of King William and South St. Mary's Streets, just south of Durango Boulevard. (210) 227-9160.

Ride a streetcar with desire: Four trolley routes make it easy for you and your lap-size (that's lap-size, not Lab-size) pooch to explore the downtown area. Dogs are permitted on the buses if they sit in your lap. You can visit Market Square, Alamo Plaza, HemisFair Park, La Villita, and the King William Historic District, all for 50 cents a ride. The buses run daily. For route and schedule information, call (210) 227-2020.

Shop for something new at someplace old: The La Villita area was settled in 1731 by immigrants from the Canary Islands, brought to Texas by Spain to tame the wilderness. Using tricks like stretching cowhides across the narrow streets at night to keep the Indians out, they managed to survive. Many San Antonians still proudly trace their ancestry to these "first families" of San Antonio de Bexar. Today the restored homes of these pioneers house a variety of shops offering fine art and handcrafted items. La Villita is a city park; you and your leashed pooch may walk the streets and look at all the wares in the windows; nice doggies may even get to go into stores with the owner's permission. The park is at 418 Villita Street; (210) 207-8610.

Take the Orient Express: Well, it's not really the *Orient Express,* it's the Brackenridge Park *Eagle,* but it does depart from a station just across the street from the Japanese Tea Garden. Close your eyes and you'll swear you're somewhere west of Constantinople. Leashed dogs can take the 15-minute ride through Brackenridge Park for free; people pay $2.25. The train is in Brackenridge Park across from the entrance to the zoo at 3910 North St. Mary's Street; (210) 736-9534.

Texanize your terrier: There's probably a law on the books somewhere forbidding visitors to leave San Antonio without buying at least one souvenir. Accessorize your pooch at We Three, a River Walk shop featuring gourmet salsas and Texas books, cards, and gift items. Leashed dogs are welcome to shop here, but the manager draws the line at leg hiking or squatting on the T-shirts. 518 River Walk; (210) 229-1164.

Walk on water: The San Antonio River Walk (or, if you prefer, the Paseo del Rio) may well be the skinniest, crookedest park in Texas. Its 15 acres hug the river through the entire downtown area, allowing leashed pooches to walk below street level past shops, restaurants, hotels, and other dogs out for a stroll. Many restaurants along the River Walk allow you to have your pooch with you if you sit at a table next to the sidewalk.

After the Alamo, this is probably San Antonio's number one attraction, so if your pooch does not like crowds, it would be well to avoid the River Walk on weekends and holidays. If you visit this park, it is vital that you observe the city ordinance requiring dog owners to carry a poop container and use it when necessary. It's on the San Antonio River between Lexington and South St. Mary's Streets; (210) 207-3000.

ATASCOSA COUNTY

PLEASANTON

This little town located on the fringe of the South Texas brush country prides itself on being "the birthplace of the cowboy." What they neglect to mention is that dogs did most of the work in the early days of ranching, and no cowboy thought of venturing into the brush without his pack of trusty cowdogs. So you might say that Pleasanton was also the birthplace of the cowdog. When the movie of this heroic saga is finally made, the lead role will be played by John Wayne Dog, with supporting roles filled by Clint Eastwood Dog, Slim Pickens Dog, Walter Brennan Dog, and Ward Bond Dog, with a special appearance by Old Yeller.

Given the fact that dogs played such a pivotal role in Pleasanton's history, the fact that they are banned from city parks comes as an unpleasant surprise. It's a doggone shame.

RESTAURANTS

Cactus Garden: Dogs are very welcome to share a table with you on the patio in front. The menu features daily lunch specials, salads, sandwiches, burgers, and steaks barbecued on an outdoor pit, the cowboy/cowdog way. 206 South Main Street; (830) 569-2823.

PLACES TO STAY

Executive Inn: Rooms are $43. 1927 West Oaklawn Street (Highway 97 West), Pleasanton, TX 78064; (830) 569-8747.

BANDERA COUNTY

What do you do when life gives you lemons? You make lemon-flavored dog biscuits. What do you do when the land where you live is so hilly and rocky it's almost useless for farming and ranching livestock? You ranch people and dogs. Bandera County is the dude ranch capital of Texas, a place where people and dogs with Texas in their souls and Houston in their lungs come to kick back and live their own version of *City Slickers*. The county is also home to the apple capital of Texas (apples do grow well here in the high valleys) and a state park famed for its maple trees and their autumn displays of color. Maple trees in Texas? Yep, Shep, they're here, at Lost Maples State Natural Area. While this is a great park for dogs, even better is the Hill Country State Natural Area, where 34 miles of trails, hills, creeks, and valleys all kept as natural as possible beckon the adventurous pooch looking for a wilderness experience. Just remember this is rocky country, pardner, so bring your walking boots.

BANDERA

PARKS, BEACHES, AND RECREATION AREAS

• **Bandera Park** 🐾1/2 *See* ㉑ *on page 540.*

Stretching for three-quarters of a mile along the Medina River, this 77-acre urban park is the answer to a water-loving pooch's prayers. Huge cypress trees, many supporting ropes for the brave (or foolhardy) to swing out over the water on, line the bank. Picnic tables and barbecue pits complete the amenities, for which there is a $5 per car charge on weekends and holidays from June through August. However, for the dog who loves to swim, you will find few places better suited for the purpose. Dogs must remain leashed while on land.

The park is just south of downtown, where Highway 173/16 crosses the Medina River. It's open from dawn to dusk. (830) 796-3765.

• **Hill Country State Natural Area** 🐾 🐾 🐾 *See* ㉒ *on page 540.*

The Hill Country State Natural Area is 5,369 acres of rocky hills, flowing springs, oak groves, grasslands, and canyons that leashed dogs will love to roam. There are 34 miles of trails. The terrain ranges from flat, broad creek bottoms to steep, rocky canyons. Several spring-fed streams and stock tanks in the park provide swimming holes and limited fishing for catfish, perch, and largemouth bass.

The bulk of the site was a donation from the Merrick Bar-O-Ranch with the stipulation that it "be kept far removed and untouched by modern civilization, where everything is preserved intact, yet put to a useful purpose." There is no more useful purpose than taking your dog for an outing, and the area's 22 trails make it possible to do so time and again without ever getting that "been there, done that" feeling that so often plagues jaded traveling dogs. At least until they find the next disgusting thing to sniff.

While the park is primarily for equestrian use, hikers and mountain bikers are welcome, as are their dogs. As at all state parks, dogs must be kept on a six-foot leash and may not enter any buildings. Dogs are permitted to swim in only one area; have a ranger mark the location on your map. Your dog might make a new buddy here: the adjacent Running R Ranch offers horse rentals from two hours to all day; (830) 796-3984. You'll still pay your entry fee when you ride into the park.

The trails have such intriguing names as Ice Cream Hill (before you tackle this one, remember the Texas penchant for dry wit, such as nicknaming 300-pound linebackers "Tiny"), Good Luck, and Cougar Canyon. You'll get a detailed trail map when you enter the park. It shows all the trails with mileages so you can plan your hike according to the energy level you and your pooch have that day. Remember this is steep, rocky country that can be hard on a dog's tender paws. It will also remind you both of those times you should have pushed back from the feed bowl a little sooner.

In keeping with the desire to maintain the park in as natural a state as possible, facilities are limited and spaced far, far apart. (Dogs who are used to parks where they have to sleep nose to rump with neighboring dogs will shout Howlelujah!) There is a composting toilet at the park headquarters and chemical toilets at two primitive camping areas, but that's it. Note that there is no potable water. You should bring or be prepared to chemically treat all the water you will need for drinking, although your dog will probably be more than happy to slurp wild water from the creeks and springs. Using soaps is not permitted in the springs and creeks. You are also required to pack out all garbage. Human and animal wastes must be buried at least 100 feet from water.

The following facilities may be reserved by calling (512) 389-8900 from 9 A.M. to 6 P.M. Monday through Friday. Reservations are strongly recommended. (1) The West Verde Creek area has three primitive campsites. You'll have to walk no more than 50 yards to reach them. (2) The Comanche Bluff area also has three sites no more than 25 yards from parking. (3) The Chaquita Falls area has four sites no more than 75 yards from a road. Sites have fire rings and picnic tables, and adjacent West Verde Creek offers swimming and fishing opportunities. Creekside sites and walk-in sites are $6. Also available by reservation are group campsites designed for equestrian use and a group lodge (where dogs are not allowed).

Four camping areas are available on a first-come, first-served basis only. The primitive backpack camping areas ($6) with fire rings are located 1.5 to 3.5 miles from trailhead parking. Call the park at the number below for availability.

From Bandera, follow Highway 173 south. About a quarter mile past the Medina River, turn right on Ranch Road 1077. Go eight miles to the end of the pavement and continue on the caliche road another two miles, crossing two cattle guards, to the park entrance. The entry fee is $3 per person; if you camp, it's $2. The park is closed on Tuesday and Wednesday from early February through October. Staff hours are 8 A.M. until 5 P.M., and overnight camping is not allowed on Monday nights. From November through early February, the park is open from noon Friday until 10 P.M. Sunday. For more information write Route 1, Box 601, Bandera, TX 78003; (830) 796-4413.

• **Mansfield Park** 🐾 1/2 *See* ㉓ *on page 540.*

Dogs must remain on leash in this park designed mainly to serve the rodeo grounds and athletic fields. However, there is a campground with water, electricity, picnic tables, barbecue pits, and rest rooms with showers in a shady live oak grove beyond the rodeo grounds. Sites for RVs are $8; tent sites are $4.

It's on Highway 16 about a mile north of downtown. (830) 796-3168.

RESTAURANTS

Copper Lantern: Have Mexican food, steak, or catfish on the outdoor patio overlooking Medina Lake. Follow Highway 173 south about two miles; turn left on Wharton's Dock Road and continue about nine miles to the restaurant. (830) 796-4022.

Harvey's Old Bank Steak House: Dogs are welcome on the outdoor patio; choose from steak, chicken, fish, or Mexican food dishes. 309 Main Street; (830) 796-8486.

PLACES TO STAY

Bandera Beverage Barn RV Park Campground: Campsites with water, electricity, and sewer hookups are $10. Dogs must be leashed. Access to the Medina River for swimming, fishing, and tubing is included. The campground is on the northern edge of Bandera on Highway 16. 1503 Main Street, Bandera, TX 78003; (830) 796-8153.

Hill Country State Natural Area: See Hill Country State Natural Area on page 567 for camping information.

Horseshoe Inn Bed-and-Breakfast: Rooms are $45, which includes a full breakfast. There's room for your leashed pooch to roam at this country inn 2.5 miles north of town on Highway 173. Route 3, Box 300, Bandera, TX 78003; (830) 796-3105 or (800) 352-3810.

Mansfield Park: See Mansfield Park on page 569 for camping information.

River Front Motel: The 11 individual cottages rent for $49 to $59. Dogs should remain on leash in the yard, which is not fenced. However, it joins Bandera Park on the Medina River. There are no fees or restrictions on dogs, who are treated as part of the family here. The motel is on Main Street at the Medina River bridge. P.O. Box 875, Bandera, TX 78003; (830) 460-3690.

Skyline Ranch RV Park: Full hookups are $13 at this campground where your leashed pooch has part of 60 acres to roam. Dogs are not allowed in the pasture where the longhorn cattle graze. The campground has access to the Medina River. It's located 1.5 miles north of Bandera on Highway 16. P.O. Box 1990, Bandera, TX 78003; (830) 796-4958.

DIVERSIONS

Forge a bond with your hound: The Bandera Forge, a working blacksmith shop, allows leashed pooches to watch the smithy at work. Go ahead, get that custom hand-forged spiked collar your mastiff has been hounding you for. 803 Main Street; (210) 796-7184.

Furnish the doghouse: Shop for that custom-made cypress lounging bed your pooch has been longing for at Fred Collins' Workshop. If your pooch gets a splinter in her paw, there's a vet right next door. In the summer, you can rent a canoe or inner tubes and float the Medina River with your pooch. It's located one-half mile north of Bandera on Highway 16. Box 1869, Bandera, TX 78003; (830) 796-3553.

MEDINA

A fledgling Texas apple industry budded out around Medina a few years back and still bears fruit regularly. While I didn't find any orchards that welcome dogs to pick their own apples, I did find the next best thing, a bake shop where you and your pooch can sample the fruits of someone else's labors.

RESTAURANTS

Love Creek Orchards Cider Mill and Country Store: Take the apple of your eye to the apple capital of Texas and gobble up fresh apple pastries, apple strudel–flavored coffee, and apple ice cream at the picnic tables outside. Then tie your pooch (he'll forgive you if you buy him some apple pumpkin bread to be washed down with fresh-pressed apple cider) while you search for that special present in the gift shop. They even have a catalog, so you can do your Christmas shopping by mail. 112 Broadway (Highway 16); (830) 589-2588 or (800) 449-0882.

VANDERPOOL

PARKS, BEACHES, AND RECREATION AREAS

• **Lost Maples State Natural Area** 🐾🐾½ 🐾 *See ㉔ on page 540.*

This 2,174-acre park is an outstanding example of Edwards Plateau flora and fauna. Leashed dogs will enjoy the steep, rugged limestone canyons with springs, plateau-top grasslands, wooded slopes, and clear streams. You'll be more interested in the large, isolated stand of Uvalde bigtooth maple trees, whose fall foliage can be spectacular. Generally, the color is best the last two weeks of October and the first two weeks of November. To obtain recorded information about the foliage condition during those two months, call (800) 792-1112 and select 3.

The park is often crowded during the color season, and parking is limited to 250 cars. Schedule trips for weekdays if possible; there's not much else in the vicinity of the park to entertain a bored pooch waiting to get in and see (big deal!) a bunch of trees.

Several rare species of birds, such as the green kingfisher, inhabit the park year-round. The endangered black-capped vireo and golden-cheeked warbler nest and feed in the park in spring and early summer. Wild animals you may meet include gray foxes, white-tailed deer, armadillos, raccoons, and bobcats.

Lost Maples is primarily a hiker's destination. You can drive about a mile into the park to day-use and camping areas, but about 75 percent of the park is accessible only by foot. Obtain a map of the trails when you check in. The shortest—and busiest—of the trails winds along the Sabinal River through the maples. Even when the leaves are just plain old green, this is a beautiful walk of just under a mile round-trip. Or, you can continue along the trail for a total of 4.2 miles, passing three of the park's eight primitive camping areas ($8). Once the trail climbs out of the Sabinal River and Hale Hollow Creek bottoms, it ascends steep limestone hills. This is not a walk for the dog unaccustomed to strenuous exercise, warns park clerk Patsy Greaves. "People take obese dogs on the trails, and it's too hard for them," she said. "We've had to carry several dogs out. Their feet couldn't take the rough trail, and they couldn't walk out by themselves. Use common sense with your dog," she pleaded.

Taking that advice to heart, Sport and I decided to confine our walking to the creek bottoms, where water and shade were always available and the walking was easier. As we headed off from the parking area for the Can Creek and West Trails, a golden retriever was resisting being fitted with his backpack in the parking lot. "He's not crazy about carrying his stuff—but neither am I," said his heavy-laden owner. She and her husband were off for a weekend camping trip at one of the primitive areas in the backcountry.

About a third of a mile up Can Creek the West Trail branches left and plunges into a shaded creek bottom. Sport smelled wilderness experience and strained at the leash, especially when brightly colored lizards streaked across the path. The trail quickly became steep and strewn with loose rocks. Both you and your dog need to be well shod and in good physical condition to take this trail. We were happy to find a spring about a quarter of a mile up the trail, and a short time later we met a dripping-wet golden retriever with a popsicle nose. "He loved the pond," his person exclaimed. Just beyond we found a paradise for water dogs, small spring-fed pools beneath a rock overhang. It was a good place for a break; just beyond the trail began a steep climb up a rocky hill.

After about a mile and a half we reached the first of several primitive camping areas along the trail. Situated in a side canyon, the heavily shaded site had few level places and only a little grass. The site has no water; a quarter mile farther on a composting toilet serves three nearby camping areas. There are no designated campsites as such; pitch your tent anywhere you like in the area. Apparently such do-it-yourself camping appeals to dogs, because we met several on the trail.

The park also has 30 campsites with water and electricity ($12). Each has a shaded picnic table. Many of the sites also have trees, but overall the space is quite open. A rest room with showers serves the area, and the Sabinal River is just steps away. To reserve a campsite, call (512) 389-8900 between 9 A.M. and 6 P.M. Monday through Friday.

Dogs must be on a six-foot leash at all times in state parks. Since there is no designated swimming area here, dogs may go in the water on leash. Dogs may not be left unattended, and they may not enter any building.

The park is located five miles north of Vanderpool on Ranch Road 187. The entrance fee is $4 per person. The park is closed, except to overnight guests, from 10 P.M. to 8 A.M. (830) 966-3413.

RESTAURANTS

Lost Maples Store: This country store just south of Lost Maples State Natural Area really doesn't qualify as a restaurant, but it does have sandwiches year-round and barbecue from about April through December. And hey—it's the only game for miles. Eat at the picnic tables under the live oak trees out front. The store is at the intersection of Highway 337 and Ranch Road 187 north of Vanderpool. (830) 966-3568.

PLACES TO STAY

Campland: Leashed dogs are welcome to hike the trails on the campground's 50 acres. The campground is half a mile south of Lost Maples State Natural Area and may be full during the fall color season; reservations are recommended. The 15 campsites with water and electricity rent for $10; the 35 tent sites go for $8. It's on Ranch Road 187 four miles north of Vanderpool. HC 01, Box 153, Vanderpool, TX 78885; (830) 966-2323.

Foxfire Cabins: Log cabins on six acres with frontage on the Sabinal River rent for $75. Dogs pay $3 each per night. Dogs are allowed to run off leash in the cabin area and have swimming privileges as well. Reservations are accepted with a deposit or credit card number; there's a two-night minimum stay on weekends. The cabins are located on Ranch Road 187 a mile south of Lost Maples State Natural Area. HCR 1, Box 142, Vanderpool, TX 78885; (830) 966-2200.

Lost Maples State Natural Area: See Lost Maples State Natural Area on page 571 for camping information.

BEXAR COUNTY

LEON SPRINGS

RESTAURANTS

Rudy's Country Store and Bar-B-Q: The folks here are kidding when they say they have the worst barbecue in Texas, but they mean it when they say your pooch can join you at one of their outdoor tables. Just tie him outside while you go through the serving line and order up brisket, sausage, ribs, or a great pork chop. It's in Leon Springs at 24152 Interstate 10 West; (210) 698-0418.

COMAL COUNTY

GRUENE

DIVERSIONS

Spend some green in Gruene: The third Saturday and Sunday of each month, noodle around the historic village of Gruene shopping for arts and crafts, antiques, or farm produce while enjoying the pickin' and singin' of local musicians. From Interstate 35, take F.M. 306 west 1.5 miles to Hunter Road; turn left and go half a mile to the town. Get a walking guide from the Greater New Braunfels Chamber of Commerce, P.O. Box 311417, New Braunfels, TX 78131; (830) 625-2385 or (800) 572-2626.

Do something green for Gruene: Each mid-September it's time to clean up after all the people who had fun on the Guadalupe River during the summer. Volunteers meet at the Double Rockin' R Campground on Loop 337 where it crosses the river. From there they spread out up and down the river, trash bags in hand, to be kind to the environment. You and your pooch are welcome to join them and meet other socially responsible pooches and people. (830) 553-5628.

NEW BRAUNFELS

New Braunfels was settled in 1845 by German immigrants, and their influence is still strongly felt here, in language, food, and the industrious character of the people. A traveler's description written in 1854 would still not be far off the mark: "The houses . . . were small, low cottages, of no pretensions to elegance, yet generally looking neat and comfortable. Many were furnished with verandahs and gardens, and the greater part were either stuccoed or painted . . . . As we rode out of town, it was delightful to meet again troops of children, with satchels and knapsacks of books, and little kettles of dinner, all with ruddy, cheerful faces . . . smiling and saluting us—'*guten morgen*'—as we met. Nothing so pleasant as that in Texas before, hardly in the South."

The traveler—Frederick Law Olmsted—also remarked on the clarity and purity of the river we now call the Comal, and it and the nearby Guadalupe River make New Braunfels a cool place to spend a summer day. Leashed dogs are allowed to tube the river with you in city parks but not in Guadalupe River State Park. Wet dogs are some of New Braunfels' biggest fans.

PARKS, BEACHES, AND RECREATION AREAS

• **Guadalupe River State Park** 🐾 🐾 *See* ㉕ *on page 540.*

There are lots of trees in this 1,938-acre park and plenty of grassy areas for leashed dogs to roam, but Sport was profoundly disappointed. Dogs are not allowed to swim in the river, so for her the best part of the park was the row of fragrant garbage cans baking in the sun at the riverside parking area. However, there is some justice: during the drought of 1995 water levels fell so low that people were banned from the river, too, because of high bacterial counts. The Guadalupe River here is emerald green and flows over a gravel bottom bounded on one side by huge cypress trees and on the other by a towering limestone bluff. Okay, so even at normal flows the river is only 60 feet wide and a foot deep. This is Texas.

A graveled walking path parallels the course of the river, shaded by huge cypress trees soaking their knees in the water. Puddles of shade harbor lazy swimmers loafing on tubes, while others roast their hides in the sun, sprawled on mid-river rocks like giant lizards. Your pooch can only look, whine, and bemoan the twist of fate that gave him a fur coat and four feet.

Camping areas are well shaded and offer some privacy for the shy dog (and plenty of chances for visiting for the social dog). The Cedar Sage Camp has 37 tent sites ($12) scattered among thick live oaks and junipers. Each site is screened by vegetation and has a water faucet, tent pad, picnic table, and fire ring. The area has a rest room with showers, but sites do not have electricity. A trail from the playground area near campsite 26 leads to the river a quarter mile below. Sport and I saw a family heading for the river with swim gear and a black Lab. It looked like the perfect way to spend a summer afternoon.

The Turkey Sink Camp caters more to RVers with electrical hookups as well as water at each of the 48 sites. The $15 sites are nicely screened by trees; most are shaded. There is a rest room with showers. A walking trail across from campsite 75 leads to the river about 300 yards away.

The Wagon Ford Camp ($12) is well shaded by pecan trees, which attract large numbers of squirrels, much to the delight and dismay of dogs who cannot chase them. Each of the 20 walk-in sites has a picnic table and a fire ring, but water is available only at scattered faucets. There is a playground and a composting toilet, but no showers. However, you are just a stone's throw from the river here; a river access trail begins at the parking area north of the playground and leads to the water just 100 yards away.

Reservations for campsites must be made by calling (512) 389-8900 between 9 A.M. and 6 P.M. Monday through Friday.

As at all state parks, dogs must be on a six-foot leash and are not allowed to enter any park building. Dogs may not be left unattended.

From the intersection of Highway 46 and U.S. 281, drive west eight miles on Highway 46, then turn north on Park Road 31. Or take Highway 46 east from Boerne 13 miles to Park Road 31. Entry is $4 per person, or $3 if you are camping. The park closes at 10 P.M. except to overnight guests. (830) 438-2656.

• **Hinman Island Park** 🐾 🐾 ½ *See ㉖ on page 540.*

This little park is only a narrow strip along the Comal River, but here leashed dogs are allowed to go into the water. A grassy slope between the street and the water is a good vantage point for watching the action in the water and along the paved walkway beside the river. The picnic tables are free weekdays, but you'll pay $5 for occupying one on weekends and holidays. A playground and a rest room complete the facilities, and a footbridge connects this park with Prince Solms Park across the river.

From Landa Park, take Elizabeth Drive east to Hinman Island Road; turn right and go a quarter mile to a parking area on the right overlooking the river. Hours are 6 A.M. to midnight. (830) 608-2160.

• **Landa Park** 🐾½ *See* ㉗ *on page 540.*

A brochure describes this as a "196-acre natural park." Ha. Nearly every square inch has been paved or "improved" with a golf course, swimming pool, playground, picnic area, tennis court, recreation center, or miniature train track. What's left that's more or less natural are the Comal Springs, the largest in Texas, and the Comal River, billed as America's shortest large river, only four miles long. Dogs are not allowed in the water.

While leashed dogs are welcome, there are just too many people and people things for most dogs' liking. On our last visit we did see a Jack Russell terrier barking his head off at the base of a cedar tree at a squirrel above, doing his best imitation of Bert Lahr's *Wizard of Oz* performance, "I'll rip him to pieces."

For dogs the best part of this park isn't the park proper but the 0.8-mile Panther Canyon Nature Trail. Pick up a map at the park office at 110 Golf Course Drive. Park at the parking area across Landa Park Drive from Comal Springs, number 10 on the map in the park brochure. The graveled trail begins where Comal Springs flows from the base of a cliff and follows a narrow, brushy canyon where you are likely to see whitetailed deer, according to ranger Patricia Grant. Landa Park has 64 kinds of trees. If you want to know what kind your dog is hiking his leg on, pick up a guide ($2) at the park office and zigzag your way from one green trail marker to the next. (See if you can do this without getting hopelessly entangled in the leash.)

From Interstate 35, follow Highway 46 Business west to Landa Street; follow Landa Street to Landa Park Drive and the park entrance. Hours are 6 A.M. to midnight. 110 Golf Course Drive; (830) 608-2160.

• **Prince Solms Park** 🐾🐾½ *See* ㉘ *on page 540.*

Water dogs will love the river side of this approximately 15-acre park, because they can go into the water here as long as they are leashed. There's also plenty of open area to run in, and picnic tables along the bank. Using the tables costs $5 on weekends and holidays. If you want to take your pooch tubing on the river, there's a tube rental across from the park entrance. Park Ranger Patricia Grant suggests renting a tube with a bottom in it for your pooch to sit in. A lot of people take their canine companions tubing here, and the dogs love it.

From Interstate 35, take Seguin Avenue (Highway 46 Business) west to San Antonio Street. Turn right on San Antonio Street and go across the Comal River. Turn left onto North Liberty Avenue; the park will be on your left. Hours are 6 A.M. to midnight. (830) 608-2160.

RESTAURANTS

The Gristmill Restaurant: Your pooch may dismiss this building as just an old barn, but it's really a historic cotton gin where you and he can share an outside table on the banks of the Guadalupe River. Ah, but he'd rather share your chicken-fried steak, rib eye, catfish, hamburger, or chicken. 1287 Gruene Road; (830) 625-0684.

Naegelin's Bakery: Satisfy your sweet tooth at the outside tables, where your pooch can share your doughnut, sweet roll, coffee, or hot tea or chocolate. 129 South Seguin Avenue; (830) 625-5722.

PLACES TO STAY

Budget Inn: Rates are $38. 348 Interstate 35 South, New Braunfels, TX 78130; (830) 625-6266.

Guadalupe River State Park: See Guadalupe River State Park on page 574 for camping information.

Hill Country RV Resort: Lots of Winter Texan dogs stay here because they like the clubhouse, exercise rooms, and cookouts. Especially the cookouts. Rates are $16. Dogs must be leashed and cleaned up after. 131 Ruekle Road, New Braunfels, TX 78130; (830) 625-1919.

Holiday Inn: Rates are $69 to $85. 1051 Interstate 35 East, New Braunfels, TX 78130; (830) 625-8017 or (800) 465-4329.

Landa RV Park and Campground: Whether you park an RV or pitch a tent, you'll pay from $14 to $22 depending on the desirability of the site. Dogs must be leashed and cleaned up after. 565 North Market Street, New Braunfels, TX 78130; (830) 625-1211.

Maricopa Ranch Resort: This rural resort near New Braunfels welcomes small, housebroken dogs. Rates are $65 to $75. Call for directions. P.O. Box 1659, Canyon Lake, TX 78130; (830) 964-3731.

New Braunfels RV Resort: Rates are $18. Dogs must be kept leashed at all times and inside the vehicle after 10 P.M. 420 Business Loop 35 North, New Braunfels, TX 78130; (830) 629-0769.

Rodeway Inn: Room rates are $79 to $106. Dogs must be housebroken. 1209 Interstate 35 East, New Braunfels, TX 78130; (830) 629-6991 or (800) 228-2000.

DIVERSIONS

Tube your troubles away: Stressed-out pooches find that tubing the Comal or Guadalupe Rivers is the ideal way to regain that balanced perspective on life so essential to a pooch's mental well-being. Numerous river outfitters in the area rent tubes, rafts, and inflatable canoes. For a list of outfitters, contact the Greater New Braunfels Chamber of Commerce, P.O. Box 311417, New Braunfels, TX 78131; (830) 625-2385 or (800) 572-2626.

GONZALES COUNTY

COST

DIVERSIONS

Have a blast: Visit the site where the first shot of the Texas Revolution was fired, along the bank of the Guadalupe River. A group of Texans, armed with a rusty old cannon they'd dug up out of a peach orchard where it had been hidden from the Mexicans, met a detachment of the Mexican Army sent to take the cannon. Flying a flag with the slogan "Come and take it," the Texans fired the old cannon—loaded with scrap iron—and sent the Mexican soldiers scampering. It was not a noble beginning for a war that won a new nation its freedom, and nearby Gonzales has long claimed to be the site of the start of the revolution, but history-conscious hounds prefer to visit the actual site. Besides, there's a boat ramp here, and fishers often deposit fish guts and heads in the trash barrel, much to the disgust of visiting people and the delight of their dogs.

From Gonzales, take Highway 97 west five miles to Cost. Read the historical marker where Spur 97 takes off to the north and then follow that road one mile to the battle site. Give a howl for Texas independence.

GONZALES

Gonzales claims to be the "Lexington of Texas," but the first shots of the Texas Revolution were actually fired a few miles away, at the little community of Cost (see above). However, Gonzales is rightfully proud of its history. It sent many of its citizens to fight in the Battle of the Alamo, and it was here that General Sam Houston received word of the Alamo's fall. The winning of the Texas Revolution began here when Houston organized his army and began a strategic retreat that ended with victory at the Battle of San Jacinto. The army was preceded in its retreat by the American settlers, who abandoned their homes and fled for Louisiana with what few belongings they could carry. One of Houston's soldiers later wrote of finding abandoned farmsteads with hungry dogs roaming morosely about.

I believe this is why Texas dogs still do not like to be left behind when their owners travel.

PARKS, BEACHES, AND RECREATION AREAS

• Gonzales Hike and Bike Trail and Historical Walking Tour
🐾½ 🐾 *See ㉙ on page 540.*

I felt violated when I pulled into Gonzales and found myself on a walking trail designed to showcase historic buildings. If you've read many pages in this book, you've probably discovered that I often recommend you convert a driving tour of a town's historic district into a walking tour for you and your pooch. Then I find that Gonzales has gone and stolen my idea. But that's okay. You and your leashed pooch will have a great time walking by the magnificent homes along the route, wondering what it must be like to be a dog who lives in a stately mansion. The tour is even laid out so that if your pooch doesn't care for historic architecture, he doesn't have to look at much of it. The tour begins at the Chamber of Commerce office in the old jail on the town square, where you can pick up a self-guiding brochure. From the chamber office, walk east on St. Lawrence Street if you want to see historic homes. If your pooch would rather observe fleeing squirrels, walk west and follow the trail to the Guadalupe River and then along its banks to Independence Park. The eastern leg is 0.8 miles one way; the western route is 1.6 miles one way. A longer route billed as a driving tour incorporates the eastern part of the walking tour. Get a brochure from the chamber office and really give your pooch a workout.

The Chamber of Commerce is located at 414 St. Lawrence Street. (830) 672-6532.

• Gonzales Lions City Park 🐾 *See ㉚ on page 540.*

Gonzales was settled in 1825 while Texas was still part of Mexico. The town claims to be the only one left in the state retaining the same plan it had when surveyed in 1831. Mexico was far advanced in city planning as compared to the United States, and it required new towns to be laid out in a specified fashion. In the case of Gonzales, the plan called for seven public squares and two strips of land reserved for public use. This park occupies part of one of those strips of land, an area a block wide and three miles long extending east of downtown. Schools occupy part of the strip today, but there's still plenty of room for a leashed dog to wander, and the historic homes on either side give you something to look at while your pooch is investigating every clump of grass.

The open areas of land begin just east of the county courthouse and lie between St. Lawrence and St. Louis Streets. Hours are from 6 A.M. until midnight. (830) 672-2815.

• **Independence Park** 🐾½ *See* **③** *on page 540.*

Most of this 169-acre park is taken up by a golf course and assorted athletic fields, but there is a shaded picnic area along the Guadalupe River, and a two-mile walking path winds through it. Large pecan trees and squirrels dominate. There are rest rooms, a playground, and tennis courts. Dogs must be on a six-foot leash.

The park has 22 RV campsites with water and electricity ($14) and a flexible number of tent sites ($7). The campground abuts the Guadalupe River, but steep banks prevent access to the water. Reservations may be made by calling (830) 672-2815. There is a 48-hour cancellation policy on deposits. Payment for campsites may be made at the golf course headquarters across the street or at the information station in the campground.

The park is on U.S. 183 at the Guadalupe River bridge. Hours are from 6 A.M. until midnight. For information write the City of Gonzales, 820 Joseph Street, Gonzales, TX 78629; (830) 672-2815.

• **Lake Wood Recreation Area** 🐾½ *See* **③** *on page 540.*

This 35-acre park offers access to the Guadalupe River and to 488-acre Lake Wood. Most of the park is shaded by large pecan trees. Picnic areas with tables, barbecue grills, and fire pits line the lakefront and riverbank. Your leashed pooch will have plenty of grassy hillocks to climb in the tent camping and picnicking area, where level ground does not seem to exist. The riverbank is too steep to allow convenient access to the water.

The park campground in the pecan grove has 16 RV sites with full hookups ($15) and 12 tent sites ($12). A rest room with showers serves the area. The campsites are large and widely spaced, but due to a complete lack of ground cover, they offer no privacy. Reservations for campsites may be made up to 90 days in advance.

To reach Lake Wood, follow U.S. 90 Alternate west from Gonzales for five miles, then turn south onto F.M. 2091 and go another five miles to the park entrance. The daily entrance fee is $6 per person. The park office is open from 8 A.M. to 5 P.M. seven days a week. (830) 672-2779.

RESTAURANTS

Sonic Drive-In: Eat burgers and fries at the tables out front. 1803 North Joseph Street; (830) 672-7090.

PLACES TO STAY

Colonial Inn Motel: Any dog may stay for free. You'll pay $38 to $85 for a room. There is no street address; the motel is located on the U.S. 90 Bypass next to the Wal-Mart store, Gonzales, TX 78629; (830) 672-9611.

Gonzales RV Park: The eight pull-through RV sites with full hookups and 50-amp service are $16. The 15 back-in sites with 30-amp service are $14. Dogs must be kept leashed. Barking dogs are not allowed. Dogs may not go into buildings. There is a posted walking area for dogs; owners are expected to wield the pooper-scooper. 2100 North Water Street (U.S. 183), Gonzales, TX 78629; (830) 672-4748 or (800) 695-4748.

Independence Park: See Independence Park on page 580 for camping information.

Lake Wood Recreation Area: See Lake Wood Recreation Area on page 580 for camping information.

DIVERSIONS

Get gassed in Gonzales: The term "service station" is almost an oxymoron these days. It's rare to find a place where someone will pump gas into your car, much less clean the windshield and check the tires and oil. That's why it came as such a shock when I pulled up to the self-service pump at Jud's Chevron in Gonzales and had all the above services performed for free by a friendly young man. "Some ladies in town asked the owner why he didn't do it, so he did," the attendant explained. "I'm here from 11 A.M. to 3 P.M. Monday through Friday just to help customers." Wowza. Your dog will have a ball jumping from seat to seat trying to get at this seldom-seen apparition doing things to the outside of his vehicle. You'll have to wipe the nose smudges and paw prints off the inside of the windows yourself. Jud's is at 1107 St. Joseph Street; (830) 672-2129.

OTTINE

PARKS, BEACHES, AND RECREATION AREAS

• **Palmetto State Park** 😊 🐾 🐾 ½ *See* ㉝ *on page 540.*

Poor Samantha was totally mystified by this park. She tried bobbing for water here—and missed. Then she found water that smelled like boiled eggs, but found no eggs to eat. When this water dog can't find the food and can't gulp running water, she becomes a frustrated dog. That's one reason I rated this 268-acre park so highly. It was a real treat to see boss dog Samantha get her comeuppance. And the price was right, too, a $2 entrance fee.

The San Marcos River flows through the park and contributes much to its character, which runs heavily toward lush undergrowth beneath large pecan, cedar elm, and willow trees. But the basic character of the park derives from the fact that it harbors a relict swamp still maintained by the flow from artesian wells. Three miles of walking trails allow visitors a close-up view of the wide variety of plants nourished by the pond environment, including black willow trees, sycamore trees, red mulberry trees, and the namesake of the park, the dwarf palmetto. This trunkless member of the palm family sports the characteristic fan-shaped fronds common to palm trees but grows low to the ground. You may also meet poison ivy, poison oak, rattlesnakes, water moccasins, copperheads, and coral snakes along the trails.

Samantha had her first frustrating experience as we walked along the one-third-mile Palmetto Trail. We'd just seen two white-tailed deer, which she could not chase, since dogs are required to be on a six-foot leash in all state parks. Then we came to the hydraulic ram pump that supplies water to the swamp. This pump is driven by water pressure from an artesian well, and as part of its normal operation, it releases little spurts of water—a mini geyser—from a ground-level valve along-side the trail. Samantha loves to drink from a hose, fountain, or any source of running water, so she immediately began bobbing for water. However, she could never get the timing right. Water jetted sideways from the valve about once a second, and just as her jaws would snap shut, the water would disappear. Spurt, snap, spurt, snap—so it went for a minute or two until she finally gave up and drank from the pool beneath the valve. But you could tell she thought it would have tasted much better snatched in midair.

Samantha's second frustrating experience of the day came at another artesian well that feeds a pond in the tent camping area. During the 1930s the Civilian Conservation Corps piped the water from the well to a rock-lined pond, letting the water jet into the pond from two pipes beneath an overhanging rock. At last here was water that didn't disappear just as you started to drink. But the sulfurous water smelled just like boiled eggs, and Samantha couldn't figure out why there were no eggs around. Sport was busy investigating the five ducks that charged up, honking raucously and demanding snacks. Samantha almost went berserk when I fed a package of cheese crackers to the ducks and didn't give her any.

Two picnic areas in the park sit on opposite banks of the San Marcos River where it makes a sharp S bend. The picnic tables are well shaded; each has a barbecue grill. Since there is no designated swimming area in the park, dogs are allowed to go into the water. Trails lead from the picnic areas to the river, but the banks are steep and there is really no beach area where it is easy to get into and out of the water. Swimming for people and dogs both is better in the artesian-fed pool and in four-acre Oxbow Lake, both of which are in the first picnic area on your left after you leave park headquarters.

The park has two campgrounds, both with heavily shaded sites with picnic tables, barbecue grills, and lantern posts. The RV area has 19 sites.

One has full hookups and rents for $16; the others have water and electricity and rent for $14. This campground sits on the bank of the river in a dense grove of trees. The 22 large, well-spaced tent sites are also well shaded, but they sit beside Oxbow Lake and the small artesian-fed pool. If it were not for the fact that they sit right beside a highway, they'd be perfect. One particularly large site designed for group use rents for $12; the others are $10.

Reservations for campsites must be made by calling (512) 389-8900 between 9 A.M. and 6 P.M. Monday through Friday. Dogs are not allowed in any park buildings, nor may they be left unattended. Be prepared to show current proof of rabies vaccination upon check-in.

From Interstate 10, follow U.S. 183 south three miles to Park Road 11. Park headquarters are two miles west of U.S. 183. There's a $2 entrance fee. The park closes at 10 P.M. except to overnight guests. (830) 672-3266.

RESTAURANTS

S and T: This little country store serves up hamburgers, sloppy joes, chili, and what they claim to be the best hot dogs in Texas. You can eat at the picnic tables scattered around under the trees. They also have basic picnic supplies. The store is on Park Road 11 just before the entrance to Palmetto State Park; there's no phone.

PLACES TO STAY

Palmetto State Park: See Palmetto State Park on page 581 for camping information.

S and T RV Park: Campers who find the nearby Palmetto State Park full often wind up in this small, shaded RV park where sites with full hookups are $14. Dogs must be leashed. Route 5, Box 214, Gonzales, TX 78629; there's no phone.

DIVERSIONS

Sell your dog down the river: Well, sometimes it's a nice thought, especially when you come home and find the contents of your kitchen trash can strewn and chewed upon the living room rug. Most times, though, you'd rather run the river with your dog. Use your own canoe or rent one at Spencer Canoes in Martindale, (512) 357-6113. Put in at Luling City Park and travel 14 miles to Palmetto State Park, portaging around one dam along the way; or put in at Palmetto State Park and take out at Slayden Bridge, 7.5 miles downriver. For a two-day trip, put in at Luling City Park and take out at Slayden Bridge, overnighting in Palmetto State Park along the way. Boaters wishing to overnight in the state park should reserve a campsite by calling (512) 389-8900. Take-in and takeout points are limited, since the river is mostly bordered by private land. There are no rapids, but there is almost always a steady current, so little rowing is required. A little dog paddle will do nicely.

GUADALUPE COUNTY

SEGUIN

PARKS, BEACHES, AND RECREATION AREAS

• **Central Park** 🐾 *See* ❸❹ *on page 540.*

This little downtown park is only half a city block, but it has beautiful trees, benches, and a fountain in the center. It's just south of the courthouse; you and your pooch can promenade around to the north side of the courthouse and see the world's largest pecan, a 1,000-pound statue that looks like a chunk of dry dog food on steroids. Sport was not impressed. She thought it needed the world's largest squirrel to make it interesting.

The park is at the intersection of Highway 123 (Austin Street) and Nolte Street. (830) 401-2480.

• **Max Starcke Park** 🐾🐾 *See* ❸❺ *on page 540.*

Forget the section of this park west of Highway 123. Its 75 or so acres are highly developed, with a golf course, playground, horseshoe pits, and hydroelectric plant. Leashed dogs can use only a narrow strip between the Guadalupe River and the golf course. Large pecan trees shade picnic tables here and make for a beautiful setting, but the riverbank is too steep to allow access to the water, and there isn't much room even for a leashed dog.

However, follow River Drive east under the highway bridge and enter a whole different park. Except for a couple of baseball fields and a large playground, this approximately 50-acre section of the park appears to have been built by and for dogs. Row after row of large pecan trees— each of which seems to have its own squirrel—march along the river. Beneath the canopy, neatly mowed grass bears scarcely an interruption from picnic tables or other human-oriented intrusions. When Sport and I last visited, we watched a crow chase an owl through the trees as squirrels darted about burying pecans for the coming winter. Your pooch's feet will be glad to know that glass containers are banned from this park.

The park lies along both sides of Highway 123 on the north side of the Guadalupe River. It is closed from 11 P.M. to 7 A.M. (830) 401-2480.

RESTAURANTS

Kirby's Korner: This restaurant with a large covered patio on the side claims to have the best hamburgers in Texas, made from fresh-ground chuck. Your pooch will be glad to research this while you sample the grilled chicken salad or stuffed baked potatoes. Don't expect a definitive answer, though, until your hound has wolfed down every hamburger in the state. 606 North Highway 123 Bypass; (830) 379-6031.

PJ's Restaurant: It's burger wars in Seguin: this place on the courthouse square is famous among locals for its huge hamburgers, although it has Mexican food as well. Order to go and eat at one of the shaded picnic benches in Central Park, half a block south. 110 East Court Street; (830) 379-4000.

Schlotzsky's Deli: The sandwiches at this chain eatery have a well-founded reputation for being delicious. They start with a fresh-baked sourdough bun, and then several kinds of meats, cheeses, and veggies are layered on. Share one with your pooch at one of the outside tables. 330 North Highway 123 Bypass; (830) 372-3663.

Walnut Creek Diner: Sit on the patio and sample menu offerings ranging from cheeseburgers to chicken-fried chicken. 339 West Court Street; (830) 379-3300.

PLACES TO STAY

Econo Lodge: Rooms are $40. There's a $5 fee plus a $10 deposit for dogs. 3013 North Highway 123 Bypass, Seguin, TX 78155; (830) 372-3990.

KENDALL COUNTY

BERGHEIM

RESTAURANTS

Bergheim Barbecue: Just a few miles west of Guadalupe River State Park, this roadside eatery is an oasis for stressed-out water dogs not allowed to swim in the park. There's nothing like a smoky bone to take away the pain of rejection. The welcome mat is out here; dine with your dog at a dozen picnic tables scattered about in a live oak grove. Enjoy barbecue, breakfast tacos, burgers, and even live music sometimes. It's on Highway 46 in Bergheim; (830) 336-2992.

BOERNE

PARKS, BEACHES, AND RECREATION AREAS

• **City Park and Cibolo Wilderness Trail** 🐾🐾🐾 *See* **36** *on page 540.*
The northern end of this park is an uninviting (to dogs) jumble of athletic fields and multiuse buildings. But the 75-acre southern part is a

rare treasure: a relatively undisturbed Hill Country environment still in its natural state. Leashed dogs may explore it with you.

The Cibolo Wilderness Trail actually encompasses six separate trails totaling about four miles. The Prairie Trail winds through a native Texas prairie with six-foot-tall grass. The Creek Trail borders Cibolo Creek, a clear, clean stream lined with huge cypress trees. A playground and picnic area greet you at the creek. You can also see western soapberry, black walnut, pecan, honey mesquite, black cherry, and Texas sophora trees, among many others. Birders like the Woodland Trail; pick up a bird checklist at the Nature Center at the trailhead.

While at the Nature Center you may run into Kate, a German shepherd who does volunteer work there with her human, Jennings Carlisle. The 14-pound brindle tomcat strolling in the door to leap into a basket in the office for a nap is Tonka (he's built like a truck), who sleeps in the woods by night, eats at the Nature Center by day, and is willing to be petted by anyone, anytime, anywhere.

The park is on Highway 46 East just outside town. Follow the paved park road past the athletic fields to the Nature Center and trailhead; signs point the way. The park is closed from 10 P.M. to 8 A.M. (830) 249-4616.

RESTAURANTS

Subway: The sandwiches at this chain run heavy on the veggies and light on the meat, so you know they're good for you. Sport prefers hers without bell or jalapeño peppers. Share with your pooch at one of the tables in front. 1101 South Main Street; (830) 249-4832.

PLACES TO STAY

Best Western: Rooms range from $50 to $68. Dogs pay a $10 fee. 35150 Interstate 10 West, Boerne, TX 78006; (830) 249-9791 or (800) 299-9791.

Key to the Hills Motel: Rooms are $54. Well-behaved dogs are welcome, but they may not be left in rooms unattended. 1228 South Main Street, Boerne, TX 78006; (830) 249-3562 or (800) 690-5763.

COMFORT

PARKS, BEACHES, AND RECREATION AREAS

• **Comfort City Park** 🐾 *See* ③ *on page 540.*

This park is small, just one square city block, but it has shade trees, a playground, and gazebo. It may be just what the traveling pooch with floating back teeth is looking for.

The park is at the intersection of Highway 27 west and Main Street; there is no phone.

RESTAURANTS

Buzzie's Barbecue: There's only one picnic table on the porch out front, but "A lot of people eat out there with their dogs," says co-owner Brenda Hughes. You may request a bowl of water for your pooch, too. 415 Highway 27; (830) 995-2915.

KERR COUNTY

Sport believed me when I told her the name of this county was an upscale spelling of the name applied to dogs of high pedigree but mixed breeding. She's so gullible. But then, what dog wouldn't rather be referred to as a "kerr" instead of a cur? It has a certain panache.

This is ranch country, where most dogs work for a living and stay in the back of pickup trucks when they are not herding sheep, goats, or cattle. Still, I did find a few places where a dog can go for a good time on his day off.

CENTER POINT

PLACES TO STAY

Marianne's Bed-and-Breakfast: "I take any size dog," says Marianne, "and I have a large fenced yard they can run around in." There is no fee for dogs. Rooms with private bath are $70 to $75; a cottage is $85. German-style breakfast, a hot tub, and wildlife viewing on the 18-acre ranch are included. It's located nine miles east of Kerrville on Highway 27. Route 1, Box 527, Center Point, TX 78010; (830) 634-7489.

HUNT

RESTAURANTS

Gallops on the River: You and your pooch will have to choose between two patios right on the Guadalupe River as well as decide whether you want hamburgers, steaks, or seafood. It's located in the River Inn Resort, seven miles west of Hunt on Highway 39; (830) 238-4233.

KERRVILLE

Kerrville is a popular town with tourist dogs. It has a number of excellent parks along the Guadalupe River. Although the state park has an attitude about dogs, they are more welcome—on leash—at city parks. While we found few places where you can eat with a dog, many area motels and bed-and-breakfasts will be pawsitively tickled to host your hound.

PARKS, BEACHES, AND RECREATION AREAS

• **Kerrville-Schreiner State Park** 🐾🐾 *See ❸❽ on page 540.*

This is a fairly large park—517 acres—with a lot of potential for dogs, but unfortunately, it's just not dog-friendly. Sport and I know that dogs must be kept on leash at all state parks, so that didn't bother us. We were disappointed to find that dogs are not allowed in the Guadalupe River running through the park, nor are they allowed in the beach area. That pretty much confines the leashed pooch to the camping areas and to the several trails that loop out from and return to the camping areas located in the part of the park lying west of Highway 173.

The 7.7 miles of park trails are the kind the explorer dog would love getting lost on, and that's exactly the problem. When Sport and I last visited, it was a hot July day, but we decided to hike one of the trails shown on the park map. These trails are designated Blue, Yellow, and Orange and are rated for difficulty, with the Yellow Trail being easy walking, the Blue Trail long but of moderate difficulty, and the Orange Trail, which loops off the Blue Trail and climbs a steep hill overlooking the area, being rated very difficult. Sport and I decided to tackle the Blue Trail, but we quickly ran into trouble. The trail was poorly maintained and poorly marked. Numerous forks in the trail invited us down them, but there were no markers to let us know where the actual trail was. Rather than become lost in 100-degree heat, we decided to abandon our hike. We checked out another trail and found it to be just as confusing. This was quite disappointing, as the trails wind through heavily vegetated areas with lots of deer and other critters to see and leave enticing scent trails. If you decide to hike one of these trails, we suggest you take along plenty of water and a snack for you and your dog and notify a park ranger or a traveling companion where you intend to go. It might be some time before you find your way back. In cool weather that might be a joy; in summer heat it could be dangerous.

The dog owner would probably do well to simply write off the camping areas along the river, since your pooch will be tormented by the sound of people playing in rushing water he cannot even go near. Four improved camping areas and one primitive camping area are on the west side of Highway 173. Again, Sport and I suggest you forget the primitive camping area, as it appeared to consist of an unmowed strip of grass along the side of the park road. We couldn't see paying $9 for that. The Deer Field and Mountain View Loop Camps are designed for RVs. All sites are pull-through and have water and electricity. Those with sewage hookups rent for $14; those with water and electricity only go for $12 unless they have 50-amp service, in which case they are $13.

There are lots of pecan and oak trees and grassy areas, but the spaces are notably lacking in spaciousness. Sport and I much preferred the looks of the Fawn Hide-a-Way and Fox Run Loop tent camps, where sites have water and rest rooms with showers nearby; the charge is $9. These sites are spaced well apart and have plenty of shade, although the lack of understory brush lets you see from one end of the campground to the other. If your shy dog likes her privacy, she will not find it here.

Dogs are only tolerated in this park, not welcomed. "Pick up after your dog," the park clerk growled. The message was clear; we weren't really wanted. As at all state parks, dogs must remain on a six-foot leash, may not enter any building, and may not be left unattended, but at least at some parks a cute dog gets smiled at.

Reservations for campsites must be made by calling the central reservation number, (512) 389-8900, between 9 A.M. and 6 P.M. Monday through Friday. A deposit is required in order to guarantee a reservation. Sites are available on a first-come, first-served basis upon arrival. Reservations are strongly recommended during the summer and on weekends.

The park is located on Highway 173 at its intersection with Loop 534. From Interstate 10, take Highway 16 south to Loop 534. Turn left (south) on Loop 534 and follow it to Highway 173. Turn east on Highway 173 and go half a mile to the park entrance. The entrance fee is $3 per person. The park closes at 10 P.M. except to overnight guests. (830) 257-5392.

• **Louise Hays Park** 🐾🐾 ½ *See* ㉟ *on page 540.*

As urban parks go, this one ranks high on Sport's list of favorites. In addition to the usual picnic tables, barbecue pits, and playgrounds, the park has the Guadalupe River running through it. Rivers mean brushy areas populated with furry four-footed critters like squirrels, opossums, and raccoons—the makers of scent trails that smell like the nectar of the gods to this pooch with a passion for pursuit. After you enter the park, drive east and pass under the highway bridge. Follow the park road to a parking area at the far eastern end of the park. Below a dam at that point the river is ideal for wading. As we parked at an entrance to the three-quarter-mile river trail that runs through the park, Sport was immediately impaled on the horns of a dilemma of the sort that delights dogs. On one side was a dumpster fragrant with the odors of the recent Fourth of July celebration. On the other was a squirrel poised provocatively on a rock. Sport may not be the world's brightest dog, but even she was able to deduce in a fraction of a second that squirrels disappear, while dumpsters stay put and just get better (that is to say, more fragrant) with age. Just as I snapped the required leash in place, we launched in pursuit of the squirrel. As usual the chase was in vain, but it soon brought us to the river, where Sport discovered an even greater delight. Small footbridges cross the river at several points, but the shallow water when we visited invited walking across in the water. Sport splashed to midstream, where she found a narrow channel in the limestone about a foot deep, into which she promptly wedged her body and happily sat for five minutes letting the water course over her. Then we were off to explore the rest of the trail, which leads beneath large cypress and pecan trees.

The day-use only park is in Kerrville just off Highway 16 where it crosses the Guadalupe River. Turn west onto Spur 98 and follow it to the entrance. The park is open from 7:30 A.M. until 11 P.M. (830) 257-8000.

RESTAURANTS

Bill's Bar-B-Que: Chow down on Texas cuisine—that is, meat, beans, and tater salad—at one of the picnic tables. Thirsty dogs may request a bowl of water. 1909 Junction Highway; (830) 895-5733.

Taco To Go: Sport and Samantha make this place serving a variety of tacos a regular stop on their travels. There's a table on a grassy strip between the street and the restaurant where dogs can join you. In addition to tacos, you can get a plate lunch (featuring Mexican food, of course) or a bowl of *menudo,* a savory soup whose main ingredients are beef tripe and hominy. It's said to be a cure for hangovers. Neither my dogs nor I can testify to that, but it is tasty, and there always seem to be more chunks of tripe than I have room for, so my canine clean-up crew never goes away empty. 428 Sidney Baker Street; (830) 896-8226.

PLACES TO STAY

Best Western Sunday House Inn: Located at the intersection of Interstate 10 and Highway 16, this hillside motel with lots of trees and 10 acres of pooch-walking territory just outside its door welcomes you and your traveling pooch. Dogs pay $10 per night; people have to cough up $60 to $70. 2124 Sidney Baker Boulevard, Kerrville, TX 78028; (830) 896-1313 or (800) 677-9477.

Flagstaff Inn: Small dogs may stay for free. Rooms are $30 to $50. 906 Junction Highway, Kerrville, TX 78028; (830) 792-4449.

Guadalupe River RV Resort: The cottages here are off-limits to your dog, but you may park your RV for the night for $21 to $23. You are required to pick up after your pooch. The bonus is that leashed pooches may go for a dip in the adjacent Guadalupe River. 2605 Junction Highway, Kerrville, TX 78028; (830) 367-5676 or (800) 582-1916.

Hillcrest Inn: This tree-shaded motel has a courtyard with benches and tables that you and your pooch may use if you clean up after her. Any size dog is welcome for a $5 fee. Rooms are $38 to $75. 1508 Sidney Baker Boulevard, Kerrville, TX 78028; (830) 896-7400 or (800) 221-0251.

Inn of the Hills River Resort: Dogs under 20 pounds may share a smoking room with you for no fee. There is a walking track where you may exercise your pooch. Rates are $55 to $85. 1001 Junction Highway, Kerrville, TX 78028; (830) 895-5000 or (800) 292-5690.

Kerrville-Schreiner State Park: See Kerrville-Schreiner State Park on page 588 for camping information.

Save Inn: Small, quiet, well-behaved dogs are welcome, but they may not be left in rooms alone. Rates are $36 to $50, plus $10 per pooch. 1804 Sidney Baker Boulevard, Kerrville, TX 78028; (830) 896-8200 or (800) 219-8158.

Wittlinger's Turtle Creek Lodge: Your pooch will have to sleep in the kennel here, but supervised dogs can run free on the over three acres of grounds and go for a swim in the creek. Owner Anne Wittlinger Kelley says her Labrador retriever, Princess, thinks the lodge is the best place to visit in the whole world. Princess is only sorry she doesn't get to live there; when you and your pooch visit, you'll have the whole place to yourselves. There is no fee for dogs, but every group must put up a $250 security deposit, since the Kelleys do not live on the site. The lodge rents for $125 for up to four people. There's a floating dock on Turtle Creek, a fireplace, covered deck, kitchen, and equipment for croquet and horseshoes. 1520 Upper Turtle Creek Road, Kerrville, TX 78028; (210) 828-0377.

FESTIVALS

Kerr County Fair: Your leashed dog can go anywhere here except the rabbit show. We wonder why. There are so many things going on she'll never miss the bunnies, however. All events take place inside a huge show barn with concrete floor, and dogs can tag along to the arts and crafts booths, food booths, ballet and dance demonstrations, and Doggy Dog Show (open to Kerr County dog owners in kindergarten through 12th grade). There's even a beauty pageant (for people) with talent and evening gown competitions, but dogs are not allowed to vote for their favorites. Tail-wagging is encouraged, of course. The fair takes place the second weekend in October at the Hill Country Youth Exhibition Center, five miles east of the Kerrville courthouse square on Highway 27. For information, call (830) 257-6833.

DIVERSIONS

Piddle around at Peddlers Square: Putting an antique mall in an old lumberyard and using the racks formerly used to store 2 x 4s and 1 x 12s to display merchandise may not be a unique idea, but it works for Peddlers Square. You and your leashed pooch are welcome to browse and even buy something; Sport and I came away with a liquor tin at a price so cheap we howled about it for miles. 425 Clay Street; (830) 257-8505.

Hang out with cool cats: In the 1850s camels owned by the U.S. Army lived nearby. The predecessor of the present-day Camp Verde General Store served intoxicants to the soldiers; the camels had to fend for themselves. Today cats rule here. Sport and I were stopped dead in our tracks by a sign on the door: "Cats can come in and go out until 5." And indeed Rooney, Stonewall, and Miss Garfield, who was sprawled atop the counter when we went in, pretty much have the run of the place. However, dogs are welcome as long as they do not chase the cats. "We used to have a dog, too," the clerk told us. "Precious would stay in the store unless some people stopped at the roadside park over by the creek. Then she would go over and greet them." Precious, unfortunately, made the trip one too many times and met her end in the road.

The name general store still fits well. You can shop for chain saw sculptures or bandannas with watermelons on them (Sport is looking for one with raccoons) or candy or even a pair of hand-carved wooden doors from a cathedral in Spain ($35,000). Sport and I settled on trying to decide which was better: IBC root beer or Sioux City Sarsaparilla, Moon Pies or the homemade fried peach pies. While Samantha gobbles everything with a haste that makes any rating she gives suspect, Sport always takes treats gently, chews them carefully, and wags her tail a number of times proportionate to the quality of the food. The homemade fried peach pie washed down with some IBC root beer was a clear winner; her tail wagged until I thought it would drop off.

The best part of the Camp Verde General Store lies across the street. A Texas Department of Transportation roadside picnic area sits beside cypress-shaded Verde Creek, and your pooch can go for a dip and a sip. Sport and I thought about poor Precious getting run over in the road and decided leashes can sometimes be a good thing, so we used ours. The store is 11 miles south of Kerrville on Highway 173; (830) 634-7722.

KIMBLE COUNTY

Like much of the rest of the Texas Hill Country, Kimble County is goat country. Your pooch will love watching herds of these four-legged eating machines. One of Samantha's favorite car games is "cows," a canine version of "beaver." (If you are not familiar with this game, you obviously have not traveled much with bored children whining "Are we there yet?" for mile after agonizing mile. A "beaver" is anything you want it to be: a red car or an out-of-state license plate are two common ones. The object of the game is to be the first to spot the beaver. Don't bother keeping score, as this just leads to more whiny fights.) With Samantha, a beaver is anything with four legs out in a pasture. Just say, "Cows, Sammy!" and she goes crazy barking at them. She does not seem to distinguish among cows, goats, horses, or deer. Samantha is, to put it as kindly as possible, not the world's smartest dog.

Sport, our intellectual dog, wanted to know why there are so many goats in the Texas Hill Country. The main reason the Hill Country has so many goats is that in the 1840s, the Sultan of Turkey wanted his people to learn how to grow cotton. You read right: The sultan of Turkey wanted his people to learn how to grow cotton. For centuries the sultans of Turkey jealously guarded the Angora goat, a breed that originated among the cold, rocky peaks of the Himalayas and spread to Turkey. The hair of the Angora is highly prized, as it can be woven into mohair, one of the lightest and warmest fibers known. Not until 1849 did the sultan, in gratitude for work done by an American in teaching Turkish farmers to grow cotton, allow seven Angoras to be brought to the United States. Crossbred with Spanish goats, which are also today common in the Hill Country, Angoras multiplied to the point that some 80 percent of the goats in the entire United States live within 100 miles of Kimble County.

However, your pooch will be much more interested in the fact that Kimble County prides itself on having an abundance of clear, flowing streams. You and your leashed pooch will be able to play in the water at both state and city parks within the county.

JUNCTION

PARKS, BEACHES, AND RECREATION AREAS

• **Schreiner Park** 🐾 *See* **40** *on page 540.*

Dogs must remain on leash in this park of about 15 acres along the South Llano River. The pecan trees shading picnic tables and barbecue pits make this a pleasant stop for a stretch if you're just passing through on Interstate 10. You can water your pooch from one of the red-painted faucets scattered about or let her wet her whistle at the dam located about midway in the park. Steep banks restrict access to the water in most places. Sport and I checked out the rest rooms and decided you'd be better off visiting a service station or convenience store.

Take the exit for Business Loop 481 from Interstate 10 and follow the loop to the Llano River Bridge; the park lies on the north side of the bridge. It is open 24 hours. (915) 446-2622.

• **South Llano River State Park** 🐾🐾🐾½ *See* **41** *on page 540.*

Your water-loving pooch will find much to like about South Llano River State Park, which adjoins the Walter Buck Wildlife Management

Area south of Junction. Dogs must remain on leash in the 2,640-acre park, but they are allowed to swim with you in the river as long as they do not bother any other swimmers. The park superintendent was very emphatic on this point: "If I see a dog pawing a kid or bothering anyone, I will tell its owner to remove it from the water," he said. Park personnel are not intent on keeping you and your pooch from having a good time, however: they rent tubes ($3 a day) so you can float the river like Cleopatra, barging along towed by a paddling pooch.

Texas state parks forbid the use of a leash longer than six feet, and dogs may not be left unattended (which includes being tied outside) or taken into any park building.

Water, trees, and wildlife dominate this beautiful park. The park has two miles of river frontage and a 500-acre wooded bottom where huge pecan trees grow. In winter hundreds of wild turkeys roost in the trees, and the bottom is closed to visitors from October through March in order not to disturb them. Observation blinds are provided where you and your pooch can hide to watch turkeys moving to and from the roost. Judging from the number of turkeys Sport and I saw while visiting the campground, however, you probably won't need to use the blinds. Your pooch may also spot wood ducks, white-tailed deer, squirrels, jackrabbits, javelinas, foxes, beavers, bobcats, cottontails, and armadillos. Several exotic species such as axis deer, black buck antelope, and fallow deer are often spotted in the park. Feral hogs and javelinas can pose a threat to your dog, so give them plenty of room if you see some.

Nearly seven miles of trails give the energetic pooch ample room to roam. For a short, tree-shaded hike, take the Buck Lake Trail, which branches off the access road to the day-use area by the river. This trail loops around some small ponds that attract a variety of birds, which can include green kingfishers, great blue herons, mallards, red-headed woodpeckers, or about 200 other species. To access a maze of trails in the wildlife management area, drive to the east end of the campground and turn down the narrow gravel road at the sign for the walk-in camping area. Park on the left and walk on down the gravel road to a paved road; turn left and in a few yards turn left off the paved road onto a dirt road. In about 100 yards a trail will branch to the left and take you up a steep hill to a scenic overlook from which you can see the entire river bottom. Retrace your steps to the dirt road and turn left to access the rest of the roads in the wildlife management area (a map is available at park headquarters). Steep hills and rocky roads will challenge you and your pooch; be sure to carry plenty of water.

Throughout the wildlife management area you will see small wooden boxes sitting on the ground. These are blinds used by deer hunters during fall public hunts, when the park is closed to visitors. You and your pooch are free to use them for wildlife observation and photography.

A developed campground with water, electricity, and rest rooms with showers ($10) caters to the RV crowd. The campsites are spacious and well separated. Most are shaded by large trees with plenty of grassy areas in between for the conducting of important canine concerns. Sport and I much preferred the walk-in camping area ($6) with its tent pads, picnic tables, composting toilet, fire rings, and lantern poles scattered among juniper and oak thickets. We surprised a doe and her fawn on our way in. No site was more than 150 yards from the farthest end of the parking lot.

Reservations for campsites must be made by calling the central reservation number, (512) 389-8900, between 9 A.M. and 6 P.M. Monday through Friday. A deposit is required in order to guarantee a reservation. Sites are available on a first-come, first-served basis upon arrival. Reservations are strongly recommended during the summer and on weekends.

To reach the park, travel Interstate 10 to Junction, then go south on U.S. 377 five miles to Park Road 73. The entry fee to this park is $2 per person. The park office is open 8 A.M. to 5 P.M. except Fridays in summer, when it remains open until 10 P.M. (915) 446-3994.

RESTAURANTS

Come 'n Git It: You can tie your dog to the railing around the patio out back while you chow down on steaks, burgers, or chicken before her begging eyes. 2341 North Main Street; (915) 446-4357.

Lum's: Scarf down some barbecue or a deli sandwich at one of the tree-shaded patio tables. The manager requests that dogs be well behaved; large dogs are, unfortunately, unwelcome. 2031 North Main Street; (915) 446-3541.

PLACES TO STAY

Carousel Inn: "I'd rather have a dog than a grump," the owner says. Rooms are $28 to $45. 1908 Main Street, Junction, TX 76849; (915) 446-3301 or (800) 876-9171 (reservations only).

Days Inn: Pooches are charged $4 per visit, and no big dogs are accepted. Rooms are $54. The motel is located on Interstate 10 at Exit 457. 111 Martinez Street, Junction, TX 76849; (915) 446-3730 or (800) 325-2525.

Fox Hollow Cabins: You and your small pooch who normally lives indoors may share a cabin beside the South Llano River. Call before bringing your dog. Completely furnished cabins have kitchens. Rates are $45 to $55, and a two-day minimum is required. Drive nine miles south of Junction on U.S. 377 and turn left at the sign "Cabin Rentals." HC 15, Box 236, Junction, TX 76849; (915) 446-3055.

Hills Motel: This small motel prefers small, housebroken dogs, who must remain leashed at all times while on the property. All rooms are $40. 1520 North Main Street, Junction, TX 76849; (915) 446-2567.

KOA Junction: "If we didn't accept dogs, we'd lose 80 percent of our business," says manager Bob Taylor. "Just keep your dog on a leash and clean up after her." This campground on the North Llano River alongside Interstate 10 charges $20 for a site with hookups, $15 without. Cabins (no linens furnished) rent for $27.50. 2145 North Main Street, Junction, TX 76849; (915) 446-3138.

Lakeview Lazy Dazy: Dogs of any size stay free at this campground on the South Llano River just a skip and a jump from downtown Junction. Dogs must be leashed at all times. Sites for RVs are $12; tent sites are $10. From Interstate 10, take Exit 457 and follow F.M. 2169 west for one mile to its intersection with Business Loop 481, then cross 481 into the campground. 502 Cedar Creek Road, Junction, TX 76849; (915) 446-2355.

Lazy T Motel: Housebroken dogs of any size are welcome at this motel as long as they are not left alone in rooms. "We are dog lovers," the owner says. "We have several of our own, all spoiled rotten." Rooms are $30. 2043 North Main Street, Junction, TX 76849; (915) 446-2565.

Pecan Valley RV Park: Your leashed pooch can enjoy swimming in the North Llano River and viewing wildlife at this private campground seven miles west of Junction, but he can stay no longer than a week. Sites with hookups are $16; tent sites are $12.50. "If people don't start cleaning up after their dogs, we will have to start charging a fee," the owner warned. Eastbound on Interstate 10, take Exit 445 to F.M. 1674. Westbound on Interstate 10, take Exit 451 to F.M. 1674. In either case, follow signs to the campground. HC 87, Box 22B, Junction, TX 76849; (915) 446-3065 or (800) 426-3065.

South Llano River State Park: See South Llano River State Park on page 593 for camping information.

FESTIVALS

Kimble Kounty Kow Kick: This annual arts and crafts festival is held in early September in Schreiner Park in Junction. Your pooch will probably take more of an interest in the food booths than in the knickknacks. Take the exit for Business Loop 481 from Interstate 10 and follow the loop to the Llano River Bridge; the park lies on the north side of the bridge. For information, call the Kimble County Chamber of Commerce at (915) 446-3190 or (800) KIMBLE 4.

MEDINA COUNTY

CASTROVILLE

Is nothing sacred? Everyone has heard that nothing is certain except death and taxes. But a tax on dogs? Yes, four-footed friends, Castroville levies an annual tax of $1 on all dogs kept within the city limits. Dogs of Texas, unite! Next they'll be taxing the air you breathe, or the bones or smoked pigs' ears you chew. You've got to stop this madness before it gets out of paw.

On a happier note, Castroville was settled by people from a region on the border between France and Germany called Alsace-Lorraine, and the old part of town still resembles a 19th-century European village. One of the steep-roofed old homes now houses a restaurant where you and your pooch can devour Alsatian-inspired cooking. There's not a lot for a dog to do here except eat, but that has never been grounds for complaint with my two canines.

PARKS, BEACHES, AND RECREATION AREAS

• **Castroville Regional Park** 🐾½ *See* ㊷ *on page 540.*

Sport and I know where the grinch who stole Christmas lives—right here in this 126-acre park on the banks of the Medina River, where we visited in December. Imagine a beautiful park with large pecan trees and grassy areas sloping down to the bank of a crystal stream shaded by towering cypress trees draped with Spanish moss. Picture a hot dog on a summer day just dying to dive into the water. Then confront the reality: sign after sign along the bank warning "No swimming. No diving. No wading." Only a grinch could put up signs like that in a place like this. It's enough to break a water dog's heart.

The park does have rest rooms and playgrounds and acres and acres of grass where a leashed dog can roam. The pecan trees promise plenty of squirrels, but we saw none on our visit. Perhaps they read the park rule against gathering pecans and moved out.

The north end of the park has a swimming pool and, nearby, a 35-site RV park. The sites are very closely spaced, with just enough room between sites for a shade tree. All the sites have full hookups and rent for $10. Dogs are required to be on leash in the campground, and you must clean up after them. Reservations are not accepted.

To reach the park from U.S. 90 west, turn south onto Athens Street and go 0.4 miles to Lisbon Street. Turn right and go another 0.2 miles to the entrance. The park is open 24 hours. For information, write the City of Castroville, 1209 Fiorella Street, Castroville, TX 78009 or call (830) 538-2224 from 8 A.M. to 5 P.M. Monday through Friday.

RESTAURANTS

Alsatian Restaurant: Housed in a historic home, this restaurant serving Alsatian foods (and others) welcomes you and your pooch on the patio out back. Enter from Madrid Street just to the south of the restaurant, behind the Castroville Emporium. Alsatian dried sausage stars in several recipes, but you can also have a Reuben sandwich, chicken crepes, Strasbourg chicken, pecan chicken, schnitzel, or grilled salmon. 403 Angelo Street; (830) 931-3260.

Sonic Drive-In: You may not know what to expect when dining at an Alsatian restaurant, but there's no mystery here. It's burgers and fries, folks. 955 U.S. 90 East; (830) 538-9424.

Vue d'Alsace: Dine on the covered porch in back, but please watch out for the resident cats. The menu reflects the ethnic heritage of the early settlers, but you can get a burger or chicken-fried steak, too. The restaurant is at the Alsatian Inn, 1650 U.S. 90 West; (830) 931-3220.

PLACES TO STAY

Best Western Alsatian Inn: Rooms are $70; dogs pay $5 a night. 1650 U.S. 90 West, Castroville, TX 78009; (830) 538-2262.

Castroville Regional Park: See Castroville Regional Park on page 597 for camping information.

FESTIVALS

Market Trail Days: Shop for crafts the second Saturday of each month (except January and February) on Houston Square, in front of the historic St. Louis Church. Leashed dogs are welcome. From U.S. 90, take Angelo Street north to the square. For information, call (830) 931-2331.

Old-Fashioned Christmas: Take care of that last-minute Christmas shopping for all the pooches on your list the first Saturday in December at Houston Square, in the center of town. Leashed dogs may shop with you; remind them to bring their list. From U.S. 90, take Angelo Street north to the square. For information, call (830) 538-3142.

HONDO

This little town is known for a sign along U.S. 90, which runs through the middle of town: "This is God's country. Please don't drive through it like Hell." If God does claim this country, He must not like dogs. There's not much here for a dog to fall in love with.

RESTAURANTS

Billy Bob's Hamburgers: If possible, there are probably more Billy Bobs in Texas than there are drive-in hamburger joints. But you won't find many places where the two come together, especially when there are picnic tables out back under pecan trees. 1905 19th Street (U.S. 90); (830) 426-5345 or, if you're calling from San Antonio, (830) 741-8355.

McDonald's: If you need a description of the menu here, you've been dead for the last half-century and don't need to eat, anyway. Have your burgers and fries at the picnic tables out front. 409 19th Street (U.S. 90); (830) 426-5300.

Sonic Drive-In: Burgers, fries, tables in front. Been there, done that. 705 19th Street (U.S. 90); (830) 426-4635.

REAL COUNTY

Anyone who's seen a commercial for a certain brand of beer brewed in San Antonio is familiar with the slogan "brewed with water from the country of 1,100 springs." However, many people don't have any more idea where this country is than a dog knows that dog food comes from any place but a grocery store. Well, listen up, dogs. The country of 1,100 springs begins in Real County, and dog food comes from—you don't want to know.

The Frio ("cold" in Spanish) River rises in northern Real County and is fed by numerous springs and creeks. This rugged country of limestone hills covered with pecan, live oak, sycamore, and cypress trees is some of Texas's most scenic. However, almost every square inch is privately owned, so opportunities to enjoy it any way other than through a car window would be rare if not for the fact that the hospitable folks here enjoy sharing it with others. Guest cabins and campgrounds line the Frio River, and many of them welcome dogs who want to swim in the clear, clean, cold waters and take long walks through the hills.

LEAKEY

PLACES TO STAY

Cedar Hollow Springs: You'll want to join your pooch on the porch of this cabin on 155 acres, because a deer and bird feeder will attract all kinds of critters for you to watch. Chasing is not permitted, of course. Your pooch will need to save that energy for exploring the hills and valleys and caves, oh my. The cabin is $60. Reservations require a two-night minimum, with a three- or four-night minimum for major holidays. Credit cards are not accepted, and checks are accepted for deposits only. Balances must be paid in cash or traveler's checks. P.O. Box 913, Leakey, TX 78879; (830) 232-6753.

Crider's Frio River Camp: The RV sites rent for $24. Dogs must be leashed, but they may swim off leash in the river. It's located seven miles south of Leakey on U.S. 83. P.O. Box 265, Leakey, TX 78873; (830) 232-5584.

Frio Pecan Farm RV Park: Located amid a pecan grove on the bank of the Frio River, this campground is bossed by Harry and Trudy Florence, who are in turn bossed by Whiskey, a Border collie/kelpie cross who may well be one of the smartest dogs we've ever met. The first time I met Whiskey, Harry was busy talking to some other people and Whiskey wanted to play. He knew Harry was busy, so he politely picked up a small limb from a pecan tree and laid it at my feet, wagging his tail like crazy and indicating as only a dog can with body language that my job was to throw the stick so he could fetch it. Being a fast learner, I complied. Whiskey is a dog not to be denied.

As befits his status as head honcho of this farm and its 983 pecan trees—all available for leg-hiking—Whiskey has free run of the place. Lesser pooches—yours included—must remain leashed and are not allowed to go into the river. (Whiskey swims in the river, but only when Harry tells him to.) The five RV sites with full hookups rent for $20. Each has a picnic table, barbecue grill, and unobstructed view of the pecan grove on one side and the Frio River on the other. That golden blur in the background is Whiskey, directing Harry's work in the grove.

Reservations made before April 1 for June, July, and August must be for a minimum of five nights. After April 1, reservations for shorter time periods are accepted, but never for less than two nights. A 50 percent deposit is required and will be forfeited if you cancel fewer than 14 days prior to arrival.

The RV park is located one mile east of Leakey on Ranch Road 337. P.O. Box 425, Leakey, TX 78873; (830) 232-5294.

Jack's Place: Calling all dogs named Jack, or even John Fitzgerald. The Frio River is just outside the front door, beyond the huge oak trees and deck with porch swing. This is a good place to bring your friends; rates begin at $100 for up to four people. Dogs pay $10 each per night and must put up a $100 deposit. Reservations require a two-night minimum, with a three- or four-night minimum for major holidays. Credit cards are not accepted, and checks are accepted for deposits only. Balances must be paid in cash or traveler's checks. Rio Frio Bed'n Breakfast and Lodging, P.O. Box 155, Rio Frio, TX 78879; (830) 232-6633.

Rio Frio Bed n' Breakfast and Lodging: The office for this reservation service cuddles up to one of Texas's national wonders, the national champion Texas live oak tree. (If we can have a National Beer of Texas, as is advertised, we can have national wonders, too.) This huge tree will inspire awe in any boy dog's loins. When we last checked, the home housing the office was slated to become a bed-and-breakfast itself, so your pooch may someday be able to admire this tree from the comfort of the porch. For now, there are five other properties—none offering breakfast—where dogs are welcome. They are listed individually. Note that reservations require a two-night minimum, with a three- or four-night minimum for major holidays. Credit cards are not accepted, and checks are accepted for deposits only. Balances must be paid in cash or traveler's checks. Rio Frio Bed n' Breakfast and Lodging, P.O. Box 155, Rio Frio, TX 78879; (830) 232-6633.

Rio Lindo: Enjoy the view from the cabin atop the hill, then follow the trail to the Frio River for a swim. With a fireplace inside and a patio outside, there's not much more a pooch could wish for, except water for people to drink. Due to concern about the water quality in the well supplying the cabin, you must bring your own drinking water. The cabin rents for $90. Dogs pay $10 each per night and must put up a $100 deposit. Reservations require a two-night minimum, with a three- or four-night minimum for major holidays. Credit cards are not accepted, and checks are accepted for deposits only. Balances must be paid in cash or traveler's checks. Rio Frio Bed'n Breakfast and Lodging, P.O. Box 155, Rio Frio, TX 78879; (830) 232-6633.

River Hideaway: Peace in the valley can be yours here, but there's also the Frio River for swimming, a volleyball net, hammock, and porch swing. Or you can catch up on your laundry using the washer and dryer. Yeah, right. Rates begin at $130 for up to four people; you can all wash your clothes. Dogs pay $10 each per night and must put up a $100 deposit. Reservations require a two-night minimum, with a three- or four-night minimum for major holidays. Credit cards are not accepted, and checks are accepted for deposits only. Balances must be paid in cash or traveler's checks. Rio Frio Bed'n Breakfast and Lodging, P.O. Box 155, Rio Frio, TX 78879; (830) 232-6633.

Welcome Inn: Rooms range from $45 to $75 at this in-town, full-service motel. The higher rate gets you a kitchenette. Dogs pay $5 each per visit. At Seventh Street and U.S. 83. P.O. Box 729, Leakey, TX 78873; (830) 232-5246.

Whiskey Mountain Inn: The six cabins on 18 acres rent for $40 to $50; housebroken pooches not only stay for free but also get to roam off leash. However, the owner cautions that the property joins U.S. 83, so dogs with car-chasing tendencies should be restrained. The resident dog is

Oscar Mayer, a dachshund. Located south of Leakey. HCR 1, Box 555, Leakey, TX 78873; (830) 232-6797.

DIVERSIONS

Go nutty in Leakey: Buy your pecans in the shade of the 983 trees on which they grew, under the watchful eye of Whiskey, the boss dog of the Frio Pecan Farm. Pecans are generally available beginning about October 15. This farm's pecans have won more than 350 awards. Whiskey doesn't have to compete. He knows he's the best. As proof, his person, Harry Florence, bought Whiskey a brand-new pickup truck with one of those third doors made just for dogs.

The farm is located on Ranch Road 337 one mile east of Leakey. (830) 232-5294.

UVALDE COUNTY

While the best outdoor fun for dogs is to be had on public land elsewhere in Texas, here the reverse is true. There are few parks, and the only big one in the lot, Garner State Park, merely tolerates dogs. There is one leash-free park, in the appropriately named town of Utopia, but it's tiny. The best places to have fun with your pooch are on private land. Cabins and private campgrounds throng the banks of the Frio, Sabinal, and Nueces Rivers, and many of them welcome dogs. Even better, many of the private accommodations are on ranches with acreage where dogs are free to roam, roam, roam and swim, swim, swim.

CONCAN

PARKS, BEACHES, AND RECREATION AREAS

• **Garner State Park** 🐾🐾½ *See* ㊸ *on page 540.*

The clear, cold waters of the Frio River attract half a million people a year to this 1,419-acre park, more than any other Texas state park, and that's a problem for dogs. While leashed dogs are allowed, they are not permitted in the water or areas adjacent to the river. They can hike and run until the thing they want most in the world is a refreshing dip, but they can't have it.

Besides swimming, camping is the main activity in the summer. You can expect to find all 500-plus campsites, cabins, and screened shelters booked months in advance. When we last visited, it was December, and there was a public deer hunt going on, so much of the park was closed. However, the Pecan Grove and Oakmont Camps we saw are representative of what you can expect: tightly packed campsites well shaded by pecan and oak trees with the river just yards away. Dogs are not allowed on grounds adjacent to a swimming area, so they may not go into the picnic area next to the river. It's a cruel world when you're a dog.

Campsites with water only rent for $10 except premium sites near the water, which go for $12 from Labor Day to Memorial Day and $15 during the summer. Regular sites with water and electricity are $15; premium sites are $17 in the off-season and $18 from Memorial Day through Labor Day. Screened shelters—from which dogs are banned—are $20 to $22 during the off-season; premium shelters are $25 during the summer months. Cabins (no dogs allowed in cabins or the cabin area) are $55 and $65 during the winter and $70 during the summer. Competition for reservations is dog-eat-dog; the earlier you call, the better chance you have of success. Reservations are accepted up to 11 months in advance. Call (512) 389-8900 between 9 A.M. and 6 P.M. Monday through Friday.

The entrance is on F.M. 1050 half a mile east of U.S. 83. Entry costs $5 per day unless you camp, in which case you pay $3. The park closes at 10 P.M. except to overnight guests. (830) 232-6132.

RESTAURANTS

Smoke Shack: Dogs just love to eat stuff they find on the side of the road, and this little spot lets you join them without losing your appetite. No roadkill appears on the menu here. Instead, you can sit at the picnic tables in the shade of the oak trees and have a hot dog, burger, fajita, taco, chicken or steak finger basket, smoked turkey sandwich, or barbecue plate. There's no address; it's at the intersection of U.S. 83 and Highway 127. (830) 232-6605.

PLACES TO STAY

Bee's Camp: Despite the name, this one's for dogs, too. Tent sites on the bank of the Frio River rent for $20; RV sites are $25; screened shelters go for $40. Dogs must be leashed. P.O. Box 215, Concan, TX 78838; (830) 232-5717.

Cold River Junction: This is more a resort than a campground, with 50 acres of land and access to the Frio River for swimming and tubing, a country store and gift shop, tasty barbecue, summer dances, and the Red Dog game room. Dogs must be leashed. Tent sites are $15; RV sites are $18; screened shelters are $30 to $40 depending on the season. Box 162, Concan, TX 78838; (830) 232-5444.

Frio Country: Leashed dogs can choose from a cabin in the hills or right on the Frio River. Rates are $80 to $150. RV sites are $20. Reservations are required and are accepted up to one year in advance. Since not all cabins allow dogs, be sure to specify your needs when you call. P.O. Box 188, Concan, TX 78838; (830) 232-6625.

Garner State Park: See Garner State Park on page 602 for camping information.

Seven Bluff Cabins and RV Park: The seven cabins on the Frio River rent for $60 to $110. One dog per cabin is allowed, and there is a $5 per day fee. Campsites with full hookups rent for $15 to $18. Dogs must be leashed while on the 19 acres surrounding the cabins, but they are allowed off leash in the river. This place is located four miles south of Garner State Park on County Road 348. P.O. Box 184, Concan, TX 78838; (830) 232-5260.

Yeargan's River Bend Resort: Dogs are allowed to stay only in the campground, but they are free to wander the entire 33 acres along the Frio River on leash. Swimming, of course, is allowed. Tent and RV sites rent for $20, and screened shelters for $25. HCR 70, Box 616, Concan, TX 78838; (830) 232-6616.

REAGAN WELLS

DIVERSIONS

Hum a happy tune: This little settlement on the bank of the Dry Frio River is home to a small group of woodworkers who call themselves The Hummers. They believe that the wood they craft into boxes, kitchen utensils, vases, and other objects hums a cosmic tune whose name is truth. Whether dogs appreciate such philosophical matters is questionable. What is certain is that people from all over the United States come to this modest workshop whose yard is strewn with piles of native Texas woods—all salvaged from dead trees, never trees cut for the purpose. Dogs can sniff among the piles of mesquite, juniper, walnut, cherry, ebony, and other woods while you watch craftspeople saw, sand, and polish, or browse the showroom. Leashes are recommended; when I last visited I counted 15 cats—eight sunning on the roof—and one dog in residence. An unleashed dog who forgot his manners for just a minute or two could cause more havoc in Reagan Wells than this tiny community has seen in years. You wouldn't want your pooch to be that pooch.

One other caution is in order. Ranch Road 1051 runs in the canyon of the Dry Frio River, which lives up to its name most of the time. However, when we last visited, flood debris trapped in trees and fences showed that several miles of the road had recently been under water. Highway crews were working to replace several concrete slab low-water crossings that had been washed away. Unless your pooch is the kind of dog who would enjoy getting marooned with 15 cats, check road conditions before traveling in wet weather.

Reagan Wells is at the end of Ranch Road 1051 eight miles west of U.S. 83. (830) 232-6167.

UTOPIA

PARKS, BEACHES, AND RECREATION AREAS

• **Utopia Community Park** 🐾 🐕 *See ㊹ on page 540.*

Sport and I knew we had found a dog-friendly park when we pulled up to the park office and were greeted by Bear, a golden retriever, and Willie, whom park manager Jill Jebbia described as "part German shepherd and part handsome stranger." They were quickly joined by Runner, a white goat who also has free run of the park. Utopia is an unincorporated town and has no city government; therefore, there is no leash law, even for goats. (This is one town that lives up to its name.) There is no entrance fee if you just want to dewater your hound and stretch your legs, but picnickers or all-day users pay $2.

This park of about five acres is heavily shaded by large live oaks, and the Sabinal River along its edge soaks the knees of huge cypress trees. Swimming and fishing are allowed in the river; a dam backs up a small lake where swans paddle elegantly about. Picnic tables and rest rooms complete the amenities. The large concrete slab in the middle of the park is for dances; if you don't want your weekend camping trip set to the boot-scootin' music of a gang of amplified cowboys, call ahead to be sure no dance is scheduled. On the other hand, if you've been trying to teach your terrier the two-step, this just might be the place.

Tent camping without electricity is $6; electricity is another $1. The four screened shelters rent for $8. This is not a big-city park with a maintenance budget; it's pretty rustic. Given the condition of the screens when we visited, taking along a can of insect repellent would be prudent.

The park is on Ranch Road 1050 just west of its intersection with Ranch Road 187. For information, write P.O. Box 6, Utopia, TX 78884; (830) 966-3321.

PLACES TO STAY

Bear Creek Cabins: Cabins with fenced yards are $75 on this working ranch on F.M. 1050 about four miles east of Garner State Park. Dogs should be leashed outside the yard. Reservations are required. P.O. Box 453, Utopia, TX 78884; (830) 966-2177.

Utopia Community Park: See Utopia Community Park above for camping information.

UVALDE

PARKS, BEACHES, AND RECREATION AREAS

• **Uvalde Memorial Park** 🐾1/2 *See ㊺ on page 540.*

One of Uvalde's chief claims to fame is that it is located at the intersection of the two longest highways in the United States—U.S. 83 and U.S. 90. That fact alone should capture the attention of traveling dogs, to whom all highways seem to go on forever, often without a convenient spot for watering or dewatering. This approximately five-acre park provides a place for leashed dogs to do both and to stretch their legs as well.

The park lies on both sides of the Leona River, and if that seems a bit ambitious for a park this tiny, remember that this is South Texas, where rivers tend to run short of water most of the time. The Leona, whose name means "lion," is more of a pussycat, and a baby one at that. Still, when we last visited there was enough water in the river for a thirsty pooch to drink her fill without draining it dry, and a half-mile paved walking path looping under the U.S. 90 bridge was just the ticket for relieving the cramps in Sport's legs. Mine, too. Large live oak trees shade the grassy, well-tended picnic area, and there are rest rooms and a playground. All things considered, this is a gem of a small-town park.

The park is located at 337 East Main Avenue (U.S. 90) about a quarter mile east of its intersection with U.S. 83. Open 24 hours. (830) 278-6155.

RESTAURANTS

Jorge's Tacos: Sport and I sampled several kinds of tacos at the picnic tables out front. Sport declared the *mollejas* (sweetbreads) her favorite, while I opted for the *chorizo con huevos* (spicy sausage and eggs). You can choose from about 20 different kinds. 308 West Main Avenue; (830) 278-4721.

PLACES TO STAY

Best Western Continental Inn: Rates are $35 to $45. Dogs are not allowed in nonsmoking rooms. 701 East Main Street, Uvalde, TX 78801; (830) 278-5671.

Holiday Inn: Rates are $57 to $60. 920 East Main Street, Uvalde, TX 78801; (830) 278-4511.

Park Chalk Bluff: This campground is named for the large white bluff on the Nueces River, which runs through camp. Dogs must be leashed, but that's the only restriction. Cabins rent for $35 to $65. Campsites with water and electricity are $15; tent sites with water nearby in the large pecan bottom are $10. There is also a daily entrance fee of $3 per person. You and your pooch can rent a paddleboat ($5 per hour or $10 half-day) or splash across the river for free and go hiking on the other side. The campground is on Highway 55 about 18 miles northwest of Uvalde. HCR 33, Box 566, Uvalde, TX 78801; (830) 278-5515.

Wes Cooksy Park: Leashed dogs are welcome at this lakeside campground with a swimming beach. Huge live oak trees shade the waterfront area. There are 42 campsites. Those with full hookups rent for $15;

sites with water and electricity rent for $10; tent sites with water and electricity nearby are also $10. Rest rooms with showers serve the campground. Reservations are not accepted. The park is three miles south of Camp Wood on Highway 55. Box 313, Camp Wood, TX 78833; (830) 597-3223.

DIVERSIONS

Be hysterical: Sport and Samantha's mom, Sally Victor, has taught them to be hysterical historians like her. Your pooch may not dig historic houses, but she is sure to enjoy keeping you company as you walk through Uvalde's historic neighborhoods. Pick up a brochure at the Convention and Visitors Bureau, 300 East Main Avenue; (830) 278-4115 or (800) 588-2533.

VAL VERDE COUNTY

COMSTOCK

PARKS, BEACHES, AND RECREATION AREAS

• **Seminole Canyon State Historical Park** 🐾🐾 🐾
See ㊻ on page 541.

Leashed dogs are welcome everywhere in this 2,173-acre park except the place where you would most like to go, the world-famous rock art sites. (Of course, as at all state parks, dogs are banned from all buildings.) However, two guided tours daily allow you and a companion to take turns dog-sitting and both see the art. It's well worth the trouble.

The Pecos River style of art—large, multicolored, and abstract—occurs nowhere else in North America. Painted beginning some 4,000 years ago, the art is a window into the hearts and souls of hardy peoples who lived in huge caverns carved into the limestone walls of streams where the Rio Grande and the Devils and Pecos Rivers join.

The paintings so much a part of everyday life three millennia ago, whose meanings read like the daily newspaper of the time, are largely a mystery to us today. Archaeologist and National Park Service Ranger Joe Labadie explains why. "These paintings were done in a cultural island about 50 miles square," he says. "Although it is clear that these are religious, sacred paintings in the truest sense, we will never know the real stories they tell, because no culture survives to tell us. The people had no form of writing, so they passed knowledge on by oral tradition. Some people think the paintings were mnemonic devices for the stories of the culture. But by the time the first Spanish explorers arrived in the area, the people who painted this art were gone." With them disappeared the rich stories only hinted at today by brightly colored animals, birds, human figures, and supernatural-looking shamans looming from cavern walls.

There's plenty for dogs to do in this park as well. Eight miles of hiking trails wind across the desert and down into rugged limestone canyons. Sport and I hiked from the campground to the mouth of Seminole Canyon, which overlooks the Rio Grande and the most famous of the rock art sites, Panther Cave. When the sun is low in the west, you can see into the cave with binoculars. The level trail is about six miles round-trip, and the view of the canyon and river, especially early or late in the day, is well worth the walk. There's also the chance you'll bump into one of the park's white-tailed deer or javelinas. If your pooch is not a desert dog, she may not be familiar with the adage that everything in the desert—including plants—either sticks, stings, or bites. Keep a firm grip on the leash when around thorny plants; the best insurance is not to wander off the trail.

The Windmill Nature Trail is less than a mile round-trip, but a brochure keyed to numbered sites along its length teaches you about native plants of the Chihuahuan Desert and even has a pronunciation key in the back to help you with the Spanish names. Even dogs with Chihuahua blood sometimes need a little help with words like *guayacan, guajillo, tasajillo,* and *cenizo.*

The campground sits on level ground well back from the canyon edge. Eight tent sites with water nearby rent for $8. Twenty-three other sites with water and electricity rent for $11. All sites have a tent pad, picnic table, and barbecue grill, and rest rooms with showers are nearby. This is desert country, so the only shade is from small shrubs.

Dogs must be kept on a six-foot leash and may not be left unattended in the campground or elsewhere. For camping reservations, call (512) 389-8900 between 9 A.M. and 6 P.M. Monday through Friday.

From Comstock, drive west on U.S. 90 nine miles to the park entrance. The entrance fee is $2 per person, or $1 if you're camping. (915) 292-4464.

PLACES TO STAY

Seminole Canyon State Historical Park: See Seminole Canyon State Historical Park on page 607 for camping information.

DIVERSIONS

Go with the flow: The rugged canyon walls of the Rio Grande, Devils, and Pecos Rivers make huge Lake Amistad one of the most scenic in Texas. You can hire a guide and seek striped bass, largemouth bass, or catfish. Or you and your pooch can enjoy the scenery from the ideal vantage point, a boat, using the services of a local tour company. Manuel and Inez Hardwick operate High Bridge Adventures, named for one of the spectacular sights on their tours, the railroad bridge across the Pecos River just upstream from the Rio Grande. They often host dogs on their tours of the lake. Low water levels may prevent access to the Pecos River and several rock art sites, so if that's your objective, call before going. In fact, the owners suggest you call or write regarding lake conditions and areas accessible for tours in any case. P.O. Box 816, Comstock, TX 78837; (915) 292-4495.

DEL RIO

Del Rio sits on the Rio Grande just a few miles from giant Lake Amistad and even closer to Mexico, which makes it a top tourist destination. Unfortunately, dogs are welcome almost everywhere in Del Rio except the one place you'd least expect: the parks. Dogs are totally banned from all city parks. However, just outside town is the Amistad National Recreation Area, where leashed dogs are welcome. Even better is the fact that you will pay no user fees for camping, picnicking, swimming, hunting, or fishing on public land around the lake.

PARKS, BEACHES, AND RECREATION AREAS

• **Amistad National Recreation Area** 🐾 🐾 ½ *See* ㊼ *on page 541.*

This sounds like a big park at 57,292 acres, but 44,000 of those acres are water, and most of the 540 miles of shoreline are accessible only by boat. However, that can be part of the charm for the leashed dog with a spirit of adventure. When your pooch really wants to get away from it all, consider a camping trip up the Devils River arm of Lake Amistad. The farther upriver you go the better the scenery becomes and the fewer people you'll meet. Camping is allowed within the recreation area anywhere up to elevation 1,144, so your choice of campsites is limitless as well as free. The fishing is fine up the river, too, so you and your pooch will eat well and heart-healthy.

Desert surrounds Lake Amistad, and its South Texas location means the climate is warm year-round. To be honest, it's comfortably warm six months out of the year, unbearably hot five months out of the year, and alternately cool and warm the rest of the time. There is no such season as winter in Del Rio, and spring and fall make fleeting appearances for only a day or two at a time. The arid climate means vegetation is generally of the thorny desert type, and there is little natural shade. Your pooch will be glad to go swimming several times an hour.

Eight picnic areas cluster around canyons on the lake's American side. All are accessible either from U.S. 277/377 or U.S. 90 and are clearly signed. However, you'll benefit by dropping by park headquarters at 4121 U.S. 90 west in Del Rio for a map and other literature. The most heavily used areas are the San Pedro, Black Brush Point, and Air Force Marina picnic areas on U.S. 90.

Give your hound a special treat and take him on a wilderness outing off the beaten path. About half a mile north of the U.S. 277/377 bridge across the San Pedro Canyon arm of the lake, park at a pedestrian entry gate on the west side of the highway. This gate is an access point to about 600 acres surrounding a small side canyon. Sport and I found lots of deer and javelina tracks and jumped up a covey of scaled quail. The terrain is rugged, and the walking is strenuous, but you'll probably have the whole area to yourselves unless it's deer hunting season. Avoid this and other public hunting areas around the lake from October until early January; you and your pooch will not be welcomed by any hunters who happen to be there.

The national recreation area extends about 85 miles up the Rio Grande and about 26 miles up the Devils River. At the time of writing, access to the Pecos River had been blocked for several years by a large sandbar. Keep in mind while on the Rio Grande that the middle of the channel is the border with Mexico, and if you fish in Mexican waters, you are required to have a Mexican fishing license, which is available at sporting goods stores and motels in Del Rio. Boating hounds can get a free brochure, "Pecos River District Self-Guided Tour," from the National Park Service headquarters. It details how to find Panther and Parida Cave, two of the premier rock art sites, and other attractions.

The National Park Service maintains four primitive campgrounds around the lake: 277 North, San Pedro, Governor's Landing, and Spur 406. Reservations are not accepted. The primitive campgrounds have no water, but they do have chemical toilets; camping is free. As you might expect, the campgrounds offer little other than a place to pitch your tent or park your RV. At normal water levels the shore is just a few feet away from each of the 50 sites. The 277 North campground is on U.S. 277/377 six miles north of Del Rio. San Pedro is on U.S. 90 about 2.5 miles west of its intersection with U.S. 277/377. Governor's Landing is adjacent to U.S. 90 about 10 miles west of Del Rio. To reach the Spur 406 campground, take U.S. 90 west of Del Rio about 15 miles and then follow Spur 406 four miles to the camp.

The recreation area begins about five miles north of Del Rio on U.S. 277/377 and about five miles west of Del Rio on U.S. 90. There is no entrance fee. For more information contact HCR 3, Box 5J, Del Rio, TX 78840; (830) 775-7491.

RESTAURANTS

Don Marcelino's: This longtime Del Rio Tex-Mex restaurant has two locations, both of which welcome leashed dogs. Eat at the table out front at 1110 Avenue F; (830) 775-6242. You and your dog are also welcome on the patio at 507 East Gibbs Street; (830) 775-5428.

Flamingo 50s: Hamburgers and french fries are the menu at this drive-in restaurant with a period theme. You and your hound can eat at covered outdoor tables. 1750 Avenue F; (830) 775-4001.

Meme's Kleen Kitchens: These two drive-in burger restaurants are some of Del Rio's oldest eateries. You can dine at the outdoor tables at 401 East Gibbs Street (830-775-5389) and 210 Canal Street (830-775-3696).

Sonic Drive-In: Burgers, fries, tables out front—you know the drill. 1109 Avenue F; (830) 774-1261.

PLACES TO STAY

American Campground: The 83 RV sites rent for $16; tent camping costs $12. Water, rest rooms, and showers are nearby. For the nontenting pooch who does not own a large home on wheels (there are a few), 12 log cabins (no plumbing or kitchen) go for $15. There's lots of room to walk your dog, too. It's on U.S. 90 six miles west of the city limits. HCR 3, Box 44, Del Rio, TX 78840; (830) 775-6484 or (800) 525-3386.

Amistad National Recreation Area: See Amistad National Recreation Area on page 609 for camping information.

Amistad RV Park: RV sites are $15, and tent sites are $10. Dogs must be leashed. The park is on U.S. 90 West. HCR 3, Box 50, Del Rio, TX 78840; (830) 774-6578.

Best Western Inn of Del Rio: Rooms are $59 to $86. There is a fee of $5 per dog per night. 810 Avenue F, Del Rio, TX 78840; (830) 775-7511.

Best Western La Siesta: Rooms are $59 to $77. Dogs pay $5. 2000 Avenue F, Del Rio, TX 78840; (830) 775-6323 or (800) 336-3537.

Days Inn: Rooms are $43 to $51. The pet fee depends on the size of the dog. 3808 U.S. 90 West, Del Rio, TX 78840; (830) 775-0585 or (800) 329-7466.

Del Rio Motor Lodge: Rooms are $23 to $40. Pooches must plunk down a $50 deposit, which is refundable after the room is inspected for doggy damage. 1300 Avenue F, Del Rio, TX 78840; (830) 775-2486 or (800) 882-9826.

Desert Hills Motel: Rooms are $35. Dogs pay a $5 fee. 1912 Avenue F, Del Rio, TX 78840; (830) 775-3548.

Economy Inn: Rooms are $46. Dogs stay free. 3811 U.S. 90 West, Del Rio, TX 78840; (830) 775-7414.

Holiday Trav-L-Park: RV sites are $18. Tent sites are $18. Dogs must be leashed and cleaned up after. On U.S. 90, about 9.5 miles west of Del

Rio. HCR 3, Box 40, Del Rio, TX 78840; (830) 775-7275 or (800) 545-2364.

Lakeview Inn: Rooms are $27 to $45. Any size dog is welcome, if housebroken, at this inn on U.S. 90 West. HCR 3, Box 38, Del Rio, TX 78840; (830) 775-9521 or (800) 344-0109.

La Quinta Inn: Rooms are $63 to $70. Dogs must be under 25 pounds. 2005 Avenue F, Del Rio, TX 78840; (830) 775-7591 or (800) NU-ROOMS/ 687-6667.

Motel 6: Rooms are $30. All Motel 6s allow one small pooch per room. 2115 Avenue F, Del Rio, TX 78840; (830) 774-2115 or (800) 466-8356.

Rough Canyon Inn: Rooms are $28 to $55. All dogs are welcome. Take U.S. 277/377 north from Del Rio 17 miles; turn west on Recreation Road 1 and go seven miles to the inn. HCR 1, Box 30, Del Rio, TX 78840; (830) 774-6266.

RV Barn Campground: All campsites—RV or tent—are $15. Dogs must be kept inside at night and leashed otherwise. There is a designated dog walk; you are expected to handle the clean-up chores. 4411 U.S. 90 West, Del Rio, TX 78840; (830) 774-5151.

Western Motel: Rooms are $26 to $34. Dogs stay free. 1203 Avenue F, Del Rio, TX 78840; (830) 774-4661.

FESTIVALS

Fiesta de Amistad: Amistad means "friendship" in Spanish, and anyone who has a friend knows that to have one, you have to be one. Except where dogs are concerned, of course. They're so perfect they take us for our own rotten selves. Del Rio and its sister city across the Rio Grande, Ciudad Acuña, work at being friends. People from Ciudad Acuña own businesses in Del Rio, and vice versa. From middle to late October each year the two towns celebrate their friendship and interdependence with a series of events ranging from battles of the bands to international footraces to ceremonies involving the mayors of the two towns meeting on the international bridge for a big hug. It's enough to give you a case of the warm fuzzies. Dogs will be welcome at (and probably more interested in) the international parade that winds through both cities; they can watch from curbside. If your hound has never had the chance to bark at a low-rider car bounding down the street, she has not lived a full life. For information on specific dates, events, and parade routes, contact the Del Rio Chamber of Commerce at (830) 775-3551 or (800) 889-8149.

DIVERSIONS

Get the picture: Some of the oldest and best art in North America adorns the walls of rock shelters in the Del Rio area. You and your pooch can visit some of these sites by boat, accompanied by a guide who can help interpret what you see. Arrangements are flexible. Take your own boat and hire a guide ($50 and up), or rent a boat locally ($75 and up). Large groups can tour for as little as $10 each but never as cheaply as a dog, who rides free. For information or reservations write Lake Amistad Tours, HCR 3, Box 44, Del Rio, TX 78840 or call (830) 775-6484 or (800) 525-3386. Do-it-yourselfers can get a self-guided tour brochure from the National Park Service headquarters on U.S. 90 West on the north side of Del Rio. The mailing address is HCR 3, Box 5J, Del Rio, TX 78840; (830) 775-7491.

Visit the lair of the body snatchers: The grave of Judge Roy Bean is just one of the interesting things you and your pooch can visit at the Whitehead Memorial Museum, and your pooch will be fascinated to know the judge was dug up and moved here from his original burial site. Museum director Lee Lincoln welcomes dogs with but one reservation: "If the dog makes a deposit, the owner has to make a withdrawal." Digging (or depositing) at the judge's gravesite would be considered in bad taste. Bad dog for even thinking about it.

Roy Bean was one of the most colorful characters in Texas history. While living in San Antonio he ran a dairy but was forced out of business by customers who complained of minnows in the milk and by creditors who wanted to be paid. He moved west following the construction of the railroad in the 1880s, running a tent saloon. No doubt water in the whiskey was harder to detect and the customers were not as particular. He settled just west of the Pecos River in Langtry and started a saloon he named the Jersey Lilly after his favorite actress, Lillie Langtry. He was appointed justice of the peace despite his lack of legal training and became famous for such stunts as fining a corpse $40—the amount of cash found on the body—for carrying a pistol. There's a replica of Bean's saloon just a few steps from his grave; pooches can stretch out on the porch and dream of getting their law degree, something Bean never even considered. Dogs may also visit the other buildings on the two-acre grounds; exhibits deal primarily with local history. There's even an irrigation ditch on the back side of the property where a thirsty pooch can get a drink.

The museum is open Tuesday through Saturday from 9 A.M. until 4:30 P.M. and on Sunday from 1 P.M. to 5 P.M. Admission is $3. 1308 South Main Street; (830) 774-7568.

WEBB COUNTY

LAREDO

Texas did not invent the concept of the friendly border where cultures blend into something not quite like either parent, but the Texas-

Mexico border certainly carries the concept to new heights. Dogs are not exempt from the process. In fact, a Chihuahua from Texas can visit the Mexican state with the same name. A visit to this region turns your ideas about what is Texas—and Mexico—upside down. I've met black-haired, brown-eyed people with Hispanic surnames who spoke better English than I, but no Spanish. I've met red-haired, green-eyed people with European surnames who spoke perfect Spanish, but no English. Everywhere the spoken language along the border exemplifies that there are not two separate cultures along the border, there is one— different from either parent. One border resident told me, "I regard the United States as my father and Mexico as my mother." That pretty well sums up the prevailing sentiment. The last time Sport and I visited Laredo, we overheard a conversation in rapid-fire Spanish that would periodically shift into English when those phrases were more convenient. From what we could tell, there is no easy Spanish equivalent of "fluid drive" and "hydraulic clutch."

The experiences Sport and I had in Laredo made me realize that what dogs hear when we talk to them must be very similar to our listening to a conversation in a foreign language of which we know a few words. Like us, dogs pick out a few familiar syllables from a stream of unknown ones: Jabberty jabberty jabberty jabberty good dog jabberty jabberty jabberty let's go jabberty jabberty kennel up jabberty jabberty (expletive) I slammed the door on my finger.

Dogs are welcome in Laredo, even though the city does have a leash law. A state park just outside town is one of the friendliest toward dogs of any I found. Most hotels and several restaurants accept dogs, and, with the proper papers, you can even take your *perro* across the border.

PARKS, BEACHES, AND RECREATION AREAS

• **Lake Casa Blanca State Park** 🐾1/2 *See* 48 *on page 542.*

The 371 acres of this park are perhaps the most highly developed of any state park I visited. This park is the main recreational facility for the city of Laredo, which has very limited city parks, and much of its surface is taken up by volleyball, basketball, and tennis courts, along with a swimming pool and a baseball field. Group picnic areas gobble another large hunk of the park.

Despite all the development, there's still adequate room for a leashed dog to have a good time, as long as she doesn't mind doing so in the company of a lot of people. This is not a park for the shy dog.

The park sits at one end of an 1,100-acre lake, and dogs as well as people will appreciate the fact that many of the picnic sites and tent campsites sit right at water's edge. There's little natural shade, but most of the picnic tables have shade shelters. Most sites also have a view of the lake, although there are some in shallow draws and on a flat on the east side of the park that have limited views. No matter where you are in the park, though, the most common view you will have will be other people viewing you. Voyeur dogs love it here.

Whether dogs can go into the water depends on where in the park they are. There are designated swimming areas at all the day-use picnic areas, and state park regulations prohibit dogs from such spots and the adjacent beach. To be safe, curve to the right after you pass park head-quarters and follow the paved road all the way around the lake to the opposite side. Continue past the RV campground to the picnic area and fishing pier on your left. From that point on to the park boundary, your pooch can swim as long as he remains on leash. This part of the park is also the least developed, and there's plenty of open space with dirt trails for you to hike your hound.

The park has 12 RV campsites with water and electricity that rent for $9. Tent camping is allowed almost anywhere in the park for $6. Most sites have a picnic table with shade shelter and a barbecue pit. Others have just a picnic table with no shade. A rest room with showers is located at the RV campground on the east side of the lake; other rest rooms in the park lack showers. You may reserve a campsite by calling (512) 389-8900 from 9 A.M. until 6 P.M. Monday through Friday. Dogs are not allowed in any buildings. They must be kept on a six-foot leash and may not be left unattended. You may be asked to show current proof of rabies vaccination.

To reach the park, follow U.S. 59 east one mile from Laredo and turn north on Loop 20. The park entrance will be on your right in about a quarter mile. There is a $2 entry fee. (956) 725-3826.

RESTAURANTS

Charlie's Corona of Laredo: Tex-Mex food is famous in Texas; Charlie's Corona is famous in Laredo. Park in the lot in back and enter through the double doors to the covered patio. Steak, seafood, and Tex-Mex share the menu. Sport and I shared a fittingly named dish, *Los Dos Amigos,* a chicken enchilada covered in sour cream and a cheese enchilada doused with chili con carne. We both voted for the chicken enchilada as our favorite, which means neither of us got as much of it as we wanted. The tostadas were excellent—made from flour tortillas, not greasy, and very crispy. They crunched almost as loud as a raccoon's ribs when a big hound bites down on them, a sound Sport has treated me to on more than one occasion. The patio may appear mothballed during the winter, but the friendly waitpersons will set up a table for you and your pooch on request. 3902 San Bernardo Avenue; (956) 725-8227.

Las Asadas: Chow down on Tex-Mex on the patio at this busy, noisy restaurant. Interstate 35 North at Del Mar Boulevard; (956) 726-1822.

PLACES TO STAY

Best Western Fiesta Inn: Comfort-loving pooches won't howl over the fact that the kennels that used to be out back are no more. Now they can sleep with you in your room. Wowza! This is progress of the kind traveling hounds howl about. But it gets even better: the approximately half-acre space where the kennels used to be is now a tree-shaded, grassy mini-park complete with picnic tables where your pooch can, you know, do what dogs do. (Don't be jealous—there's a courtyard with swimming pool and free continental breakfast for you.) Rooms are $55 to $65. Small and medium-size dogs are welcome with a credit card imprint or a $20 cash deposit. You are expected to clean up after your dog. 5240 San Bernardo Avenue, Laredo, TX 78041; (956) 723-3603.

Family Gardens Inn: Rooms are $53. Dogs put down a $25 deposit. 5830 San Bernardo Avenue, Laredo, TX 78041; (956) 723-5300.

Family Gardens Inn: Rooms are $35. 9006 Mines Road, Laredo, TX 78045; (956) 726-9811.

Gateway Inn: Rooms are $35. 4910 San Bernardo Avenue, Laredo, TX 78041; (956) 722-5272.

Holiday Inn Civic Center: Rooms are $69 to $90. Any well-trained dog is welcome. 800 Garden Street, Laredo, TX 78040; (956) 727-5800.

Holiday Inn on the Rio Grande: You can't get much closer to Mexico without going there; this hotel is right on the river. Rooms are $88 to $128. Dogs require a $20 deposit. 1 South Main Street, Laredo, TX 78040; (956) 722-2411.

Lake Casa Blanca State Park: See Lake Casa Blanca State Park on page 614 for camping information.

La Quinta Inn: Rooms are $76 to $86. Well-trained dogs under 25 pounds are welcome. 3610 Santa Ursula Avenue, Laredo, TX 78041; (956) 722-0511 or (800) NU-ROOMS/687-6667.

Motel 6: Rooms are $42. All Motel 6s allow one small pooch per room. 5310 San Bernardo Avenue, Laredo, TX 78041; (956) 725-8187 or (800) 466-8356.

Motel 6—North: Rooms are $44. All Motel 6s allow one small pooch per room. 5920 San Bernardo Avenue, Laredo, TX 78041; (956) 722-8133 or (800) 466-8356.

Red Roof Inn: Rooms are $50 to $56. If you leave your dog in the room alone, notify the front desk so that maids can be warned. 1006 West Calton Road, Laredo, TX 78041; (956) 727-5032 or (800) 843-7663.

DIVERSIONS

Jump the border with your hound: Everybody knows the best shopping is across the border in Nuevo Laredo. What most people don't know is that all you need to legally take your hound across the border (and back!) with you is a health certificate (about $15) proving that your pooch is up to date on all her shots. You'll breeze through the border checkpoints faster than a greyhound can run down a rabbit. And with that rottweiler at your side, the customs agents will show you a level of respect you thought was reserved only for the Pope. The Laredo Animal Clinic specializes in this service; they're at 6001 McPherson Road; (956) 725-PETS or (956) 727-5031.

WILSON COUNTY

FLORESVILLE

PARKS, BEACHES, AND RECREATION AREAS

• **Pecan Park** 🐾 *See ㊾ on page 540.*

This park's six acres are a good place to dewater your dog and stretch your legs on the paved walking path. Young pecan trees cover the park but, when we last visited, had not yet achieved the majesty of which the species is capable. When they do, this park will be wonderful. In the meantime, the playground, picnic tables, and rest room overwhelm the rest of the grounds. But when was the last time your hound complained of a lack of scenery?

The park is at the intersection of Highway 97 West and Third Street. It's open 24 hours. (830) 393-3105.

• **River Park** 🐾 *See ㊿ on page 540.*

Normally a 35-acre park would offer a lot for a dog, but this one doesn't. It's almost totally taken up by people stuff—athletic fields, for the most part. There are rest rooms and a small picnic area under pecan trees along the San Antonio River, but the steep, weedy banks prevent access to the water, and it won't be much fun walking your dog unless you like to stumble around bumping into baseball diamonds and chain-link fences.

The park is on Highway 97 West about two miles west of its intersection with U.S. 181 in Floresville. It's open from 8 A.M. until 10 P.M. (830) 393-3105.

RESTAURANTS

Sonic Drive-In: Enjoy your hamburger, Tater Tots, and cherry limeade at one of the tables out front. 1108 10th Street; (830) 393-0070.

PLACES TO STAY

Roadside Inn: There are no fees, deposits, or size limits for dogs, but noisy dogs are not welcome. Rooms are $36. U.S. 181, Floresville, TX 78114; (830) 393-3244.

ZAPATA COUNTY

There's good news and bad news for dogs here. The good news is that neither the county nor the major town in it have a leash law. The bad news is that there is practically no public land in the county where you can take your pooch.

ZAPATA

PARKS, BEACHES, AND RECREATION AREAS

• **City Park** 🐾🐾½ 🐕 *See* **51** *on page 542.*

The name "city park" is a misnomer, since there is no incorporated city here, but that's what it's called for lack of a better name. The five acres or so are mostly open grass with a few trees, but the star attraction for some dogs will be the pond at the southern end of the park where they can joyfully belly-flop in and swim; the whole park is leash-free. There are a few picnic tables under trees at the edge of the pond, where you can sit and wonder at your pooch's silly antics. The rest rooms were nonfunctioning (as in no doors, no water) when we last visited. Dogs don't mind those little details.

The park is at the end of Sixth Avenue three blocks west of U.S. 83. There is no phone.

• **Romeo T. Flores Memorial Park** 🐾½ 🐕 *See* **52** *on page 542.*

This county park of about 20 acres is in an unincorporated town, which means there are no local ordinances, including one requiring leashes on dogs. Your pooch is free to roam the park's mostly open area off leash, celebrating the joys of anarchy. Rebel dogs especially will love the place.

There are a few picnic tables and a rest room—locked when I lasted visited—but not much else.

From U.S. 83, go north five blocks on Third Avenue. There is no phone.

RESTAURANTS

4 Milpas: Take your Tex-Mex to the picnic table behind the restaurant. There is no street address; the restaurant is on U.S. 83 South. (956) 765-4847.

PLACES TO STAY

Executive Inn: Small dogs only may stay here. Rooms are $44 to $49. There is no street address; the hotel is on U.S. 83 South. P.O. Box 686, Zapata, TX 78076; (956) 765-6982.

Redwood Lodge: Rooms are $39 to $44. There are no size limits, fees, or deposits for dogs, but the room will be inspected after the first night's stay, and if there's a problem, you're gone. There is no street address; the hotel is located on U.S. 83 South. P.O. Box 31, Zapata, TX 78076; (956) 765-4371.

TEXAS MAP · SEE PAGE 10

NATIONAL AND STATE FORESTS/STATE WILDLIFE MANAGEMENT AREAS

Despite its mighty size, Texas is mighty short on public lands. Roughly 97 percent of the land in Texas is privately owned—as it should be, staunch supporters of private property rights will be quick to point out. Native Texans find nothing remarkable about this situation, having grown up with it. Newcomers to the state, however, sometimes have difficulty adjusting to the fact that almost everywhere you go, you are trespassing if you leave the right-of-way of whatever road you happen to be on.

Still, Texas dogs do not suffer overmuch from this lack of public places in which to cavort. While the total amount of public acreage is comparatively small, it's still a lot of land to a dog who has to power four feet to cover it, and it's broken into so many pieces scattered all over the state that at least a squidge of public land is never far away. And, happily, most large tracts of public land are concentrated in the eastern half of the state, where the majority of dogs live.

Public parks account for most of the acreage in government hands, but two other categories of public lands offer significant recreational opportunities for adventurous pooches. The four national forests in Texas contain 637,541 acres. The five state forests, with a total of just over 7,600 acres, are tiny in comparison, but they offer some great recreational opportunities for dogs. In addition, the Texas Parks and Wildlife Department owns about 700,000 acres and manages another 400,000 acres primarily for wildlife and public hunting, but limited recreational use may be made of these areas as well.

Texas national forests offer about 25 developed recreational areas with fee campgrounds. However, unless an area is closed for hunting or another reason, you are free to camp anywhere in the national forests for no fee. When using primitive campsites, you should bury all human and animal wastes and pack out all trash. Fires should be put "dead out," and all evidence of your campsite should be removed. The national forests also contain several hiking trails, two of which have achieved National Recreation Trail status.

And now for the really good news. While dogs are required to be kept on a leash no longer than six feet at all times while in U.S. Forest Service recreation areas, they may roam off leash in general forest and wilderness areas. However, every rose has a thorn, and there's a big one to consider in this case. As Sport and I visited national forests, we saw a distressing number of "lost dog" signs posted on trees. Every one of those signs began with an eagerly anticipated trip to an area where a happy hound could run free. But forests are big places where there are no familiar landmarks, and city dogs, especially, may not be able to find their way back to you should they dash off in pursuit of a deer or other animal. If your dog is not very obedient to voice commands or has a tendency to wander, you'd be well advised to keep her on a leash while in the national forests. Otherwise, you may be putting up one of those tear-stained signs yourself.

NATIONAL FORESTS

ANGELINA NATIONAL FOREST

The 153,174 acres of this forest wrap around one of Texas's largest lakes, massive Sam Rayburn Reservoir. Seven developed recreation areas and two wilderness areas nestle among the pines. A 5.5-mile hiking trail connects the Bouton Lake and Boykin Springs recreation areas. Obtain a trail map at the district ranger office in Lufkin. Dogs are required to be on leash in developed recreation areas, but they may roam free in the general forest area.

For more information, contact Angelina National Forest, Angelina Ranger District, 1907 Atkinson Drive, Lufkin, TX 75901; (409) 639-8620.

DAVY CROCKETT NATIONAL FOREST

This forest is a checkerboard affair of 162,012 acres stretching from Weches in the north to Groveton in the south. It has but one developed camping area. Its centerpiece is the 20-mile Four C Hiking Trail, a National Recreation Trail that follows abandoned logging railroad roadbeds through the forest, crossing part of the Big Slough Wilderness and offering panoramic views of pine-forested bottomlands. Dogs must be leashed only in the Ratcliff Lake Recreation Area.

For more information, contact Davy Crockett National Forest, Neches Ranger District, 1240 East Loop 304, Crockett, TX 75835; (409) 544-2046, or Trinity Ranger District, P.O. Box 130, Apple Springs, TX 75926; (409) 831-2246.

SABINE NATIONAL FOREST

Highly fragmented into dozens of individual tracts, this forest's 160,608 acres fleck the Texas side of gigantic Toledo Bend Reservoir, the second largest lake in Texas, which we share with our neighbor to the east, Louisiana. There are six developed camping areas along the lakeshore. Within the forest, dogs may be off leash, but leashes are required neckwear within the developed recreation areas.

For more information, contact Sabine National Forest, Tenaha Ranger District, 101 South Bolivar Street, San Augustine, TX 75972; (409) 275-2632, or Yellowpine Ranger District, 201 South Palm Street, Hemphill, TX 75948; (409) 787-3870.

SAM HOUSTON NATIONAL FOREST

This 161,657-acre forest named for one of Texas's greatest heroes now serves as a playground for residents of the city by the same name located just 30 miles to its south. Four recreation areas and the 140-mile-long Lone Star Hiking Trail furnish ample opportunity for the visiting pooch to stretch her legs. Twenty-seven miles of this trail are designated a National Recreation Trail. Dogs must be leashed in the recreation areas but not in the general forest.

For more information, contact Sam Houston National Forest, Raven Ranger District, P.O. Drawer 1000, New Waverly, TX 77358; (409) 344-6205.

STATE FORESTS

Most of the state forests are used primarily for demonstration and research and offer little or nothing in the way of public facilities. However, one, the W. Goodrich Jones State Forest, contains two recreation areas and a nature trail where you and your pooch can learn about what it takes to grow these substitute fireplugs for dogs.

W. GOODRICH JONES STATE FOREST

Named in honor of the founder of the Texas Forestry Association, this 1,725-acre forest is small in size but big on fun and research. From its inception, it has been designated a demonstration forest where management techniques, genetic studies, and product utilization studies are carried out. The forest is primarily loblolly pine; the oldest trees date from about a century ago, when the area was first logged.

The Sweetleaf Nature Trail of Interpretive Forestry is located in the northwest corner of the forest along Rice Branch. Two recreation areas are located on the south side of F.M. 1488.

The forest is a mile west of Interstate 45 on F.M. 1488. The Texas Forest Service office a mile east of the entrance to the recreation areas and the Sweetleaf Nature Trail is open Monday through Friday from 8 A.M. to 5 P.M. For more information, contact the Texas Forest Service, Route 7, Box 151, Conroe, TX 77384; (409) 273-2261.

STATE WILDLIFE
MANAGEMENT AREAS

Your pooch just may be one of the hunting variety who will enjoy stalking birds, squirrels, or rabbits with you. The benefit of being a hunting dog is that your pooch may be off leash while hunting and may roam the entire area with you, while non-hunting dogs must be leashed and are allowed only in camping areas. Dogs are allowed to hunt only squirrels, rabbits, hares, and game birds in season, but some counties have no closed season on squirrels, rabbits, or hares. Therefore, you and your dog may hunt those species any time the season is open and the area is not closed for a special hunt by permit only. Not all wildlife management areas are places you'd want to go to have fun with your pooch; in this book we list and describe only those where you're sure to have a good time.

Hunting on wildlife management areas requires that you purchase not only a hunting license ($19) but also an Annual Public Hunting Permit ($40). If you do not wish to hunt or fish, you may purchase a Limited Public Use Permit for $10. This permit allows you to use wildlife management areas for camping, hiking, photography, and nature study. However, if you are not hunting squirrels, rabbits, hares, or game birds as noted above, your dog must remain in the campground. Only if your dog is hunting with you can she go anywhere in the area. Therefore, if your purpose is to be with your dog—as it should be— buy the hunting license and annual permit. The small investment will provide many more hours of enjoyment for you and your pooch. As long as you carry a gun or bow and arrow with you, and the season is open for hunting rabbits, hares, squirrels, or game birds, you are considered to be hunting and are therefore entitled to use the area, whether your actual objective is to kill anything or not. This ploy, if you want to call it that, will gain you and your pooch access to public lands that, during most of the year, you will have almost to yourselves. In addition, the fees you pay go directly to support the operation of the wildlife management areas and keep them open, since these places are wholly supported by user fees. Shortly after you purchase your Annual Public Hunting Permit, you will receive a map booklet giving the locations of all wildlife management areas and detailing the times when each area will be open for hunting.

ALAZAN BAYOU WILDLIFE MANAGEMENT AREA

Busy highway U.S. 59 zips by just a mile to the east of this 1,973-acre tract between the Angelina River and Black Bayou. You and your traveling dog en route between Houston and Texarkana can stop in for a road break, or you can spend hours aggravating wildlife such as mourning doves, quail, squirrels, waterfowl, rabbits, and hares most days from September to March. For more information, contact the district office at 11942 F.M. 848, Tyler, TX 75707; (903) 566-1626.

ANGELINA NECHES/DAM B WILDLIFE MANAGEMENT AREA

If chasing coyotes over 13,445 acres, much of which is swamp, sounds like something your pooch would like to do, this venue is for you. Coyotes may be hunted with dogs from September through March, and there is no closed season on rabbits and hares, so your hound will always have quarry to harry. Staying out of the area during the deer season from October through early January would probably be wise, however. For more information, contact the district office at 11942 F.M. 848, Tyler, TX 75707; (903) 566-1626.

AQUILLA WILDLIFE MANAGEMENT AREA

This 9,700-acre Central Texas unit surrounds Aquilla Lake southwest of Hillsboro and extends almost to the city limits of that town. You and your pooch may hunt doves, quail, waterfowl, squirrels, rabbits, and hares during season. Access is via a network of farm and county roads off Highway 22. For more information, contact the district office at 1601 East Crest Street, Waco, TX 76705; (817) 799-2564.

BLACK GAP WILDLIFE MANAGEMENT AREA

Remote, rugged, and attractive in an arid sort of way, this 106,915-acre parcel of mountains and desert along the Rio Grande adjacent to Big Bend National Park is one of Sport's favorite places in the whole world. You can roam for days without ever seeing another person, fish in the Rio Grande, and camp in some of the most splendidly isolated spots left in Texas. Our favorite time to visit is from November through February, when the blue quail season is open, rabbits and hares are fair game, and the weather is pleasant. Be aware that this is rattlesnake, javelina, and cactus country. Dog boots are an excellent idea because of the abrasive volcanic rock that covers much of the area. Carry plenty of water for you and your pooch when walking, as the dark rock retains heat and can be as much as 40 degrees hotter than the air temperature. The area will be closed from time to time for public hunts; consult the public hunting lands map booklet for details. The area is located in Brewster County, 50 miles south of Marathon via U.S. 385 and Ranch Road 2627. For more information, contact the regional office at 3407 South Chadbourne Street, San Angelo, TX 76904; (915) 651-4748.

GRANGER WILDLIFE MANAGEMENT AREA

A thickly forested river bottom surrounded by agricultural fields makes for ideal wildlife habitat, with food, cover, and water in close proximity. The area's 11,043 acres are divided between Lake Granger's 4,400 acres and 6,643 land acres. The wildlife management area consists of four separate tracts of land around the lake, interspersed among U.S. Army Corps of Engineers parks. Be aware that this area is heavily infested with feral hogs; keep a close eye on your dog. The area is in Williamson County, five miles north of Taylor on Highway 95 or eight miles east of Granger on F.M. 971. For more information, contact the district office at 1601 East Crest Street, Waco, TX 76705; (817) 799-2564.

JAMES E. DAUGHTREY WILDLIFE MANAGEMENT AREA

Take 4,000 acres of brush and rolling hills and plunk them down beside a lake, and you've created dog heaven, otherwise known as the James E. Daughtrey Wildlife Management Area. From Tilden, take Highway 16 north three miles to F.M. 3445; go east 5.5 miles to the headquarters. Deer, quail, and rabbits abound here. Primitive dirt roads lacing the area make great paths for perambulating pooches. Camping is available at nearby Choke Canyon State Park. For more information, contact the district office at 1607 Second Street, Pleasanton, TX 78064; (830) 569-8700.

LAS PALOMAS WILDLIFE MANAGEMENT AREA—OCOTILLO UNIT

This desert area of 2,082 acres borders the Rio Grande, with vegetation ranging from dense cane thickets along the river to barren creosote bush flats atop the hills. The chief attraction for you and your *perro* is magnificent isolation with a paved road cutting through the middle of it; you can leave civilization behind without needing four-wheel drive. The times we've camped here, as much as two days have gone by without a single vehicle traveling the highway through the area. There are some fantastic rock formations, the products of erosion, at the heads of the canyons on the east side of the highway. This area is open for hunting only during the mourning dove season. It's about 37 miles northwest of Presidio on Ranch Road 170. For more information, contact the regional office at 3407 South Chadbourne Street, San Angelo, TX 76904; (915) 651-4748.

SOMERVILLE WILDLIFE MANAGEMENT AREA

Deep sand and post oak trees cover the 3,180 acres of this area around Lake Somerville. The best news for you and your pooch is that the season on squirrels, rabbits, and hares never closes here; the only time you may not go on the unit is during brief special-permit deer hunts. Otherwise, the place is yours to enjoy year-round. The area is about 20 miles northeast of Giddings off F.M. 180. For more information, contact the district office at 715 South Highway 35, Rockport, TX 78382; (512) 790-0306.

UNIT 121 WILDLIFE MANAGEMENT AREA

Why some wildlife management areas are deserving of glamorous and descriptive names while others are toe-tagged with numbers we do not know. However, this 6,414-acre unit shares the East Texas pine forest with its neighbor Davy Crockett National Forest and has seasons for waterfowl, quail, doves, squirrels, rabbits, and hares, so you and your pooch can enjoy its wildness most months of the year. You would do well to avoid visiting from October through early January, when deer hunters may be present. The area is about five miles northwest of Crockett. For more information, contact the district office at 11942 F.M. 848, Tyler, TX 75707; (903) 566-1626.

UNIT 122 WILDLIFE MANAGEMENT AREA

About 50 miles north of Beaumont, 38,313 acres of Newton County between Newton and Burkeville give you and your pooch an opportunity to seek out waterfowl, doves, quail, squirrels, rabbits, and hares in season, taking time out from October through early January for deer season. Creeks and dirt roads lace the land; your dog can indulge her secret desire to wander country roads while humming John Denver tunes. For more information, contact the district office at 11942 F.M. 848, Tyler, TX 75707; (903) 566-1626.

UNIT 125 WILDLIFE MANAGEMENT AREA

Surely 24,698 acres of forest where you and your hunting hound can roam most of the year deserve a name, but for now it's just Unit 125. Seasons on waterfowl, quail, doves, squirrels, rabbits, and hares mean you and your pooch can hang out here most of the year except during the October through early January deer season. The boundaries are highly irregular and extend discontinuously in an arc from about six miles northwest of Kirbyville to about 15 miles to the northeast of town. For more information, contact the district office at 11942 F.M. 848, Tyler, TX 75707; (903) 566-1626.

UNIT 129 WILDLIFE MANAGEMENT AREA

The Big Thicket National Preserve—where your pooch cannot set paw—is a near neighbor to this 16,606-acre holding split into three tracts about 15 miles north of Vidor. Pine forest covers the hills. You and your pooch can hunt waterfowl, doves, quail, rabbits, and hares except during the deer season from October through early January. For more information, contact the district office at 11942 F.M. 848, Tyler, TX 75707; (903) 566-1626.

INDEX

ACKNOWLEDGMENTS

I'm not going to say this book could not have been done without the help and encouragement of the people listed below, but I do know their contributions made it better. Thank you all.

My biggest debt of gratitude is to Deborah Douglas, who first alerted Foghorn Press to the fact that there was a hungry, dog-owning writer from Mason, Texas, who needed a project.

Thanks to Judith Pynn for her assistance and continued friendship.

Many people provided information and arranged accommodations during my year of travel and research. To each of the following, a big Arf! and a wish that your nose may always be cold: Penny Reeh, Pattie Sears, Ernie Loeffler, Autumn Thurman, Jan Hardin, Judy Stone, Kathi Weathington, Molly Alexander, Elizabeth Taylor, Cynthia DuBois, Kim Dillon, Judy Ramos, Peggy Boone, Regina Rowe, Jim Glendinning, Bill Ivey, Charlotte Allen, Stacey Krauszer, Sherri Greenlee, Page Colby Michel, June Calcotte, Sudie Johnson, Yutta Matalka, Paula Mason, Susan Cottle Leonard, Terri Bortness, John and Judy Jurek, Tyler and Elizabeth Hodge, Tomari Hodge, H.G. and Gail Hodge.

Special recognition and thanks go to my wife, Sally Victor, who not only brought dogs back into my life after an absence of some years but also relinquished the telephone, put up with my absence for weeks at a time, and endured having to keep quiet when I was home and writing. All for an occasional pat on the head.

And finally, thanks to Comet the cat, who shares his bed, his food bowl, and his people with Sport and Samantha.

CREDITS

Editor in Chief	Kyle Morgan
Editors	Karin Mullen
	Jean Linsteadt
	Donna Leverenz
Production Assistants	Jan Shade
	Jean-Vi Lenthe
	Mark Aver
Acquisitions Editor	Judith Pynn
Cover and Interior Illustrations	Phil Frank

ABOUT THE AUTHOR

Sport Dog and **Samantha Dog** visited every corner of Texas—and most of the rounded-off places—during the course of researching this book. They tramped through parks, romped in the water at beaches, dined at every kind of restaurant (their favorite was steak), and bedded down in motels, campgrounds, and fancy hotels. They endured pampering, petting, and the adulation of envious dogs and dog owners who thought being a traveling dog was the greatest job in the world.

Sport and Samantha logged some 25,000 miles in a sport utility vehicle (Sport thinks it was awfully nice of Detroit to name so many cars after her) driven by their friend and slave, **Larry D. Hodge**. When he is not working for his canine companions, Larry writes travel articles for *Texas Highways* magazine and serves as a contributing editor for *Texas Parks and Wildlife* magazine. "That guy really knows how to bring home the dog food," Samantha says gratefully.

Sport and Samantha live with Larry and his wife, Sally Victor, in a 125-year-old home in Mason, surrounded by centuries-old live oak trees inhabited by squirrels, raccoons, and the occasional skunk. Reluctantly sharing his home with the dogs is Comet the cat. Life is never dull there.

Larry and friends Sport, center,
and Samantha, right.

FOGHORN ✠ OUTDOORS

Founded in 1985, Foghorn Press has quickly become one of the country's premier publishers of outdoor recreation guidebooks. Through its unique Books Building Community program, Foghorn Press supports community environmental issues, such as park, trail, and water ecosystem preservation. Foghorn Press books are available throughout the United States in bookstores and some outdoor retailers. If you cannot find the title you are looking for, visit Foghorn's Web site at www.foghorn.com or call 1-800-FOGHORN.

The Dog Lover's Series

- *The California Dog Lover's Companion* (800 pp) $20.95—New 3rd edition
- *The Florida Dog Lover's Companion* (586 pp) $20.95—New 2nd edition
- *The Seattle Dog Lover's Companion* (256 pp) $17.95
- *The Boston Dog Lover's Companion* (416 pp) $17.95
- *The Atlanta Dog Lover's Companion* (288 pp) $17.95
- *The Washington D.C. Dog Lover's Companion* (288 pp) $17.95—New!

The Complete Guide Series

- *California Camping* (768 pp) $20.95—New 10th anniversary edition
- *California Hiking* (688 pp) $20.95
- *California Waterfalls* (408 pp) $17.95
- *California Fishing* (768 pp) $20.95
- *California Golf* (1056 pp) $24.95—New 7th edition
- *California Beaches* (640 pp) $19.95
- *California Boating and Water Sports* (608 pp) $19.95
- *Pacific Northwest Camping* (656 pp) $20.95—New 6th edition
- *Pacific Northwest Hiking* (648 pp) $20.95
- *Washington Fishing* (480 pp) $20.95—New 2nd edition
- *Tahoe* (678 pp) $20.95—New 2nd edition
- *New England Hiking* (416 pp) $18.95
- *New England Camping* (520 pp) $19.95
- *Southwest Camping* (544 pp) $17.95
- *Utah and Nevada Camping* (384 pp) $18.95
- *Baja Camping* (288 pp) $14.95—New 2nd edition
- *Florida Camping* (672 pp) $20.95—New!

A book's page length and availability are subject to change.

For more information, call 1-800-FOGHORN,
e-mail: foghorn@well.com, or write to:
Foghorn Press
340 Bodega Avenue
Petaluma, CA 94952

TEXAS CHAPTER REFERENCE MAP

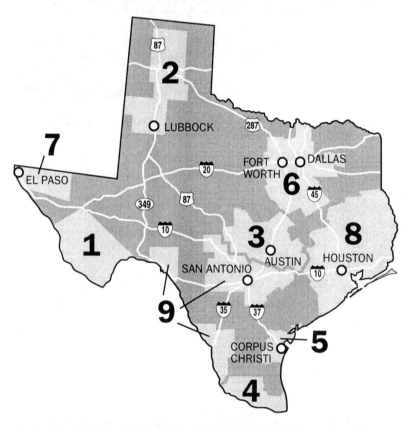